Insights into Advancements in Intelligent Information Technologies:

Discoveries

Vijayan Sugumaran
Oakland University, USA & Sogang University, South Korea

Information Science
REFERENCE

Managing Director:	Lindsay Johnston
Senior Editorial Director:	Heather A. Probst
Book Production Manager:	Sean Woznicki
Development Manager:	Joel Gamon
Acquisitions Editor:	Erika Gallagher
Cover Design:	Nick Newcomer, Lisandro Gonzalez

Published in the United States of America by
Information Science Reference (an imprint of IGI Global)
701 E. Chocolate Avenue
Hershey PA 17033
Tel: 717-533-8845
Fax: 717-533-8661
E-mail: cust@igi-global.com
Web site: http://www.igi-global.com

Library of Congress Cataloging-in-Publication Data

Insights into advancements in intelligent information technologies: discoveries / Vijayan Sugumaran, editor.
    p. cm.
  Includes bibliographical references and index.
  Summary: "This book offers the latest the field has to offer in research, methodologies, frameworks, and advances in the field of intelligent information technologies"--Provided by publisher.
  ISBN 978-1-4666-0158-1 (hardcover) -- ISBN 978-1-4666-0159-8 (ebook) -- ISBN 978-1-4666-0160-4 (print & perpetual access) 1. Information technology--Technological innovations. 2. Artificial intelligence--Industrial applications. I. Sugumaran, Vijayan, 1960-
  T58.5.I5648 2012
  658.4'038011--dc23
                                    2011051814

British Cataloguing in Publication Data
A Cataloguing in Publication record for this book is available from the British Library.

All work contributed to this book is new, previously-unpublished material. The views expressed in this book are those of the authors, but not necessarily of the publisher.

Table of Contents

Detailed Table of Contents

This paper investigates software engineering techniques for designing and reengineering knowledge-based system generators, focusing on inference engines and domain specific languages. Indeed, software development of knowledge-based systems is a difficult task. We choose a software engineering approach to favor code reuse, evolution, and maintenance. We propose a software platform named LAMA to design the different elements necessary to produce a knowledge-based system. This platform offers software toolkits (mainly component frameworks) to build interfaces, inference engines, and expert languages. We have used the platform to build several KBS generators for various tasks (planning, classification, model calibration) in different domains. The approach appears well fitted to knowledge-based system generators; it allows developers a significant gain in time, as well as it improves software readability and safeness.

This paper provides a model based on the Multi Agent System (MAS) paradigm that acts as a methodological basis for evaluating the dynamics in a collaborative environment. The model dynamics is strictly driven by the competence concept. In the provided MAS, the agents represent the actors operating on a given area. In particular, the proposed agents are composed of three distinct typologies: (i) the territorial agent, (ii) the enterprise agent, and (iii) the public agent. Each agent has its local information and goals, and interacts with others by using an interaction protocol. The decision-making processes and the competencies characterize in a specific way each one of the different agent typologies working in the system.

Chapter 3

Our paper studies a logic UIA$_{LTL}$, which is a combination of the linear temporal logic LTL, a multi-agent logic with operation for passing knowledge via agents' interaction, and a suggested logic based on operation of logical uncertainty. The logical operations of UIA$_{LTL}$ also include (together with operations from LTL) operations of strong and weak until, agents' knowledge operations, operation of knowledge via interaction, operation of logical uncertainty, the operations for environmental and global knowledge. UIA$_{LTL}$ is defined as a set of all formulas valid at all Kripke-Hintikka like models N$_C$. Any frame N$_C$ represents possible unbounded (in time) computation with multi-processors (parallel computational units) and agents' channels for connections between computational units. The main aim of our paper is to determine possible ways for computation logical laws of UIA$_{LTL}$. Principal problems we are dealing with are decidability and the satisfiability problems for UIA$_{LTL}$. We find an algorithm which recognizes theorems of UIA$_{LTL}$ (so we show that UIA$_{LTL}$ is decidable) and solves satisfiability problem for UIA$_{LTL}$. As an instrument we use reduction of formulas to rules in the reduced normal form and a technique to contract models N$_C$ to special non-UIA$_{LTL}$-models, and, then, verification of validity these rules in models of bounded size. The paper uses standard results from non-classical logics based on Kripke-Hintikka models.

Chapter 4

Intelligent tutoring systems (ITS) aim at development of two main interconnected modules: pedagogical module and student module .The pedagogical module concerns with the design of a teaching strategy which combines the interest of the student, tutor's capability and characteristics of subject. Very few effective models have been developed which combine the cognitive, psychological and behavioral components of tutor, student and the characteristics of a subject in ITS. We have developed a tutor-subject-student (TSS) paradigm for the selection of a tutor for a particular subject. A selection index of a tutor is calculated based upon his performance profile, preference, desire, intention, capability and trust. An aptitude of a student is determined based upon his answering to the seven types of subject topic categories such as Analytical, Reasoning, Descriptive, Analytical Reasoning, Analytical Descriptive, Reasoning Descriptive and Analytical Reasoning Descriptive. The selection of a tutor is performed for a particular type of topic in the subject on the basis of a student's aptitude.

Chapter 5

Studies show that supply chain structure is a key factor affecting information sharing. Business-to-business (B2B) e-hubs have fundamentally changed many companies' supply chain structure, from a one-to-many to a many-to-many configuration. Traditional supply chains typically center around one company, which interacts with multiple suppliers or customers, forming a one-to-many structure. B2B e-hubs, on the contrary, usually connect many buyers and sellers together, without being dominated by a single company, thus forming a many-to-many configuration. Information sharing in traditional supply chains has been studied extensively, but little attention has been paid to the same in B2B e-hubs. In this study, the authors identified and examined five information sharing strategies in B2B e-hubs. Agent performances under different information sharing strategies were measured and analyzed using an agent-based e-hub model and practical implications were discussed.

Chapter 6

Sam Kin Meng, University of Macau, China
C. R. Chatwin, University of Sussex, UK

Before Internet consumers make buying decisions, several psychological factors come into effect and reflect individual preferences on products. In this paper, the authors investigate four integrated streams: 1) recognizing the psychological factors that affect Internet consumers, 2) understanding the relationship between businesses' e-marketing mix and Internet consumers' psychological factors, 3) designing an ontology mapping businesses' e-marketing mix with Internet consumers' decision-making styles, and 4) developing a shopping agent based on the ontology. The relationship between businesses' e-marketing mix and Internet consumers' psychological factors is important because it can identify situations where both businesses and Internet consumers benefit. The authors' ontology can be used to share Internet consumers' psychological factors, the e-marketing mix of online business and their relationships with different computer applications.

Chapter 7

S. Kuppuswami, Kongu Engineering College, India
T. Chithralekha, Pondicherry University, India

In this paper, the authors describe a new architecture for the language faculty of an agent that fulfills the interaction requirements of task delegation. The architecture of the language faculty is based on a conceptualization of the language faculty of an agent and a definition of its internal state paradigm. The new architecture is behavior-management based and possesses self-management properties. This architecture is compared with existing abstract self-management architectures, which examines how the new architecture solves unresolved issues of older models. The architecture description is followed by a case study - **Mul**tilingual Natural Language **A**gent **I**nterface for Mail Service, which illustrates its application.

Chapter 8

Hung W. Chu, Manhattan College, USA
Minh Q. Huynh, Southeastern Louisiana University, USA

In this study, the authors examine the effects of information systems/technologies (IS/T) on the performance of firms engaged in growth strategies based on mergers and acquisitions (M&A). A model derived from a resource-based theory of the firm is developed to predict the influence of IS/T on performance of firms. Data on the financial performance of 133 firms are used to gauge the impact of IS/T on various M&A objectives. The results suggest that IS/Ts implement M&A objectives that seek to increase overall efficiency better than those that seek to introduce new products or efforts to increase sales. Future studies to examine the process of introducing new products from resource-based theory are suggested.

Incremental load is an important factor for successful data warehousing. Lack of standardized incremental refresh methodologies can lead to poor analytical results, which can be unacceptable to an organization's analytical community. Successful data warehouse implementation depends on consistent metadata as well as incremental data load techniques. If consistent load timestamps are maintained and efficient transformation algorithms are used, it is possible to refresh databases with complete accuracy and with little or no manual checking. This paper proposes an Extract-Transform-Load (ETL) metadata model that archives load observation timestamps and other useful load parameters. The author also recommends algorithms and techniques for incremental refreshes that enable table loading while ensuring data consistency, integrity, and improving load performance. In addition to significantly improving quality in incremental load techniques, these methods will save a substantial amount of data warehouse systems resources.

Chapter 10

Yield forecasting is critical to a semiconductor manufacturing factory. To further enhance the effectiveness of semiconductor yield forecasting, a fuzzy-neural approach with collaboration mechanisms is proposed in this study. The proposed methodology is modified from Chen and Lin's approach by incorporating two collaboration mechanisms: favoring mechanism and disfavoring mechanism. The former helps to achieve the consensus among multiple experts to avoid the missing of actual yield, while the latter shrinks the search region to increase the probability of finding out actual yield. To evaluate the effectiveness of the proposed methodology, it was applied to some real cases. According to experimental results, the proposed methodology improved both precision and accuracy of semiconductor yield forecasting by 58% and 35%, respectively.

Chapter 11

Research efforts toward effective e-Government infrastructures have gained momentum, motivated mainly by increasing demands to improve citizen participation in public processes, promote social e-Inclusion, and reduce bureaucracy. One of the biggest challenges is providing effective techniques to handle the inherent heterogeneity of the systems and processes involved, making them interoperable. This paper presents a semantically enriched middleware for citizen-oriented e-Government services (CoGPlat), which facilitates the development and operation of new e-Government applications with higher levels of dynamism. It introduces the use of composition techniques based on semantic descriptions and ontologies. Requirements like autonomy, privacy and traceability are handled by applying policies that govern the interactions among services.

Credit scoring is an important topic for businesses and socio-economic establishments collecting huge amounts of data, with the intention of making the wrong decision obsolete. In this paper, the authors propose four approaches that combine four well-known classifiers, such as K-Nearest Neighbor (KNN), Support Vector Machine (SVM), Back-Propagation Network (BPN) and Extreme Learning Machine (ELM). These classifiers are used to find a suitable hybrid classifier combination featuring selection that retains sufficient information for classification purposes. In this regard, different credit scoring combinations are constructed by selecting features with four approaches and classifiers than would otherwise be chosen. Two credit data sets from the University of California, Irvine (UCI), are chosen to evaluate the accuracy of the various hybrid features selection models. In this paper, the procedures that are part of the proposed approaches are described and then evaluated for their performances.

This article examines the improvements provided when multimedia information in traditional SCADAS are included in electric facility management and maintenance. Telecontrol use in the electric sector, with the fundamental objective of providing increased and improved service to the operators who manage these systems, is also described. One of the most important contributions is the use of an agent network that is distributed around the electric facility. Through the use of multi-agent technology and its placement in embedded systems, to the authors design a system with a degree of intelligence and independence to optimize data collection and provide reaction proposals for the operator. The proposed agent-based architecture is also reviewed in this article, as are the design of an example agent and the results obtained in a pilot experience using the proposed hardware platform.

With the development of Web 2.0 technologies, the sharing of photographs has increased. In this paper, the authors evaluate the art of photography, analyze how to develop intelligent photograph sharing system, and explain the requirements of such systems. The authors present an architecture of an intelligent Web 2.0 based system and in future hope to add more modules for retention of users on the system. The system focuses on Web 2.0 usage, web mining for personalization service, and brings a different approach to collaborative filtering.

Chapter 15

T. Purusothaman, Government College of Technology, India

M. Rajalakshmi, Coimbatore Institute of Technology, India

S. Pratheeba, Indian Institute of Science, India

Distributed association rule mining is an integral part of data mining that extracts useful information hidden in distributed data sources. As local frequent itemsets are globalized from data sources, sensitive information about individual data sources needs high protection. Different privacy preserving data mining approaches for distributed environment have been proposed but in the existing approaches, collusion among the participating sites reveal sensitive information about the other sites. In this paper, the authors propose a collusion-free algorithm for mining global frequent itemsets in a distributed environment with minimal communication among sites. This algorithm uses the techniques of splitting and sanitizing the itemsets and communicates to random sites in two different phases, thus making it difficult for the colluders to retrieve sensitive information. Results show that the consequence of collusion is reduced to a greater extent without affecting mining performance and confirms optimal communication among sites.

Chapter 16

Bireshwar Dass Mazumdar, Institute of Technology, Banaras Hindu University, India

R. B. Mishra, Institute of Technology, Banaras Hindu University, India

The Multi agent system (MAS) model has been extensively used in the different tasks of e-commerce like customer relation management (CRM), negotiation and brokering. For the success of CRM, it is important to target the most profitable customers of a company. This paper presents a multi-attribute negotiation approach for negotiation between buyer and seller agents. The communication model and the algorithms for various actions involved in the negotiation process is described. The paper also proposes a multi-attribute based utility model, based on price, response-time, and quality. In support of this approach, a prototype system providing negotiation between buyer agents and seller agents is presented.

Preface

INTRODUCTION

Multi-agent systems and semantic technologies have been recognized as one of the important Information Technologies to minimize the cognitive load on decision makers and help promote interoperability between various systems to gain access to necessary data/information in collaborative problem solving. Significant progress has been made over the last few years in the development of multi-agent systems and Semantic Web applications in a variety of fields such as electronic commerce, supply chain management, resource allocation, intelligent manufacturing, mass customization, simulation, and healthcare. While research on various aspects of multi-agent systems and semantic technologies is progressing at a fast pace, there are still a number of issues that have to be explored in terms of the design and implementation of multi-agent systems for decision support. For example, formal approaches for agent-oriented modeling and simulation for decision making, ontology based Information System, ontology engineering, semantics for data integration, agent based decision support systems, multi-agent systems for business intelligence, and semantic technologies for knowledge management are some of the areas in need of further research.

Intelligent agent and multi-agent systems are increasingly being employed in various web applications, particularly in searching for information on the Web. Semantic Web, the next generation Web technology, is supposed to improve this information retrieval process as well as help execute various tasks using intelligent agents. For example, a software agent would gather all the necessary information from a multitude of sources in order to support the user in a problem solving task. A fundamental problem in the current Internet search mechanisms is the vagueness of user's information needs. Search queries on the Internet are rarely longer than 2-3 terms, and a search session tends to consist of 6-7 queries. The more advanced search options are only used by a small fraction of users. The search applications have very little information about the documents the users are looking for. Even in those cases where longer queries are posted, current search applications cannot uncover and address the user's real information needs. The terms are only understood as key words that are matched against term frequencies in documents, and there is no attempt at understanding their meanings or how they are related to each other.

The idea of semantic search is to use precisely defined domain vocabularies – ontologies – to interpret user queries and retrieve documents based on content rather than term matching. It is however unclear how this can be best done in a large-scale search environment. Building semantic indices seems unfeasible due to space and time requirements, and it is not reasonable to ask users to post semantically defined queries. This would require the users to browse through potentially thousands of concepts that he or she might not even understand and select the appropriate ones. Most systems today use ontologies to expand or reformulate the queries without much involvement from the user. Thus, these systems do not take into account the intent and the information needs of the user.

From the users' point of view, the standard query reformulation approach is adverse for several reasons. First, since the ontology is used as a standardized vocabulary for all users, we cannot be sure that they reflect the exact terminology used by any individual user. If the queries are altered without user's knowledge, the user has no opportunity to correct the system's understanding of his or her information needs. Second, users are often vague because they are not entirely sure about what they are searching for. The ontology provides a conceptual summary of the domain and could help understand his or her needs, but it is often too large and too complex to be presented directly to the user. What is needed is a more interactive way of semantically exploring the user's information needs, where the user and the system collaborate to uncover the desired information.

Novel approaches to Web searching are being developed where the search framework supports semantic query interpretation and expansion and allows users to interactively drill down the result set for the information they need. Central to this approach is the definition of ontological profiles. An ontological profile is an enriched ontology, in which each class, instance and relationship is given a weight that characterizes its prominence with respect to the documents or logs at hand. For example, the profile may reveal that a certain user group uses Thinkpad and Vaio synonymously with the concept of laptops, but with different probabilities and different links to other concepts. Moreover, we may use the weights to rank the user group's references to instances of laptop, thereby generating a list of their most popular laptop models. Constructed with reference to the result set from a search machine, the profile provides a semantically ranked summary of all the retrieved documents. Similarly, an ontological profile based on query logs gives us a semantic understanding of the language used by users.

These approaches, for example, take an existing OWL ontology for a domain and build ontological profiles that reflect the users' language and the content of a representative set of Web documents from the domain. Techniques from ontology learning will be evaluated and adapted for this purpose. During query processing, the user queries are first mapped onto ontological concepts using the profile and thereafter expanded with the terms referring to the concepts in the standard document index. This results in a semantic query expansion approach that also takes into account the fact that the user may utilize different terminology compared to the authors of the documents. Thus, the outcome of this stream of research is an integrated search environment that makes use of existing ontologies and an existing search engine. This environment includes text mining components for generating ontological profiles, a query interpretation module for query expansion, and an interactive visualization module for presenting semantic maps and allowing the user to browse the map and produce more refined semantic queries.

ORGANIZATION OF THE BOOK

In Chapter 1, "Generating Knowledge-Based System Generators: A Software Engineering Approach" by Sabine Moisan, investigates software engineering techniques for designing and reengineering knowledge-based system generators, focusing on inference engines and domain specific languages. Indeed, software development of knowledge-based systems is a difficult task. The author chose a software engineering approach to favor code reuse, evolution, and maintenance. Moisan proposes a software platform named LAMA to design the different elements necessary to produce a knowledge-based system. This platform offers software toolkits (mainly component frameworks) to build interfaces, inference engines, and expert languages. The author has used the platform to build several KBS generators for various tasks (planning, classification, model calibration) in different domains. The approach appears well fitted to knowledge-based system generators; it allows developers a significant gain in time, as well as it improves software readability and safeness.

Authors Ilaria Baffo, Giuseppe Confessore, and Graziano Galiano, in Chapter 2, "A Model to Increase the Efficiency of a Competence-Based Collaborative Network," provide a model based on the Multi Agent System (MAS) paradigm that acts as a methodological basis for evaluating the dynamics in a collaborative environment. The model dynamics is strictly driven by the competence concept. In the provided MAS, the agents represent the actors operating on a given area. In particular, the proposed agents are composed of three distinct typologies: (i) the territorial agent, (ii) the enterprise agent, and (iii) the public agent. Each agent has its local information and goals, and interacts with others by using an interaction protocol. The decision-making processes and the competencies characterize in a specific way each one of the different agent typologies working in the system.

Chapter 3, "Algorithm for Decision Procedure in Temporal Logic Treating Uncertainty, Plausibility, Knowledge and Interacting Agents," studies a logic UIALTL, which is a combination of the linear temporal logic LTL, a multi-agent logic with operation for passing knowledge via agents' interaction, and a suggested logic based on operation of logical uncertainty. Author V. Rybakov describes that the logical operations of UIALTL also include (together with operations from LTL) operations of strong and weak until, agents' knowledge operations, operation of knowledge via interaction, operation of logical uncertainty, and the operations for environmental and global knowledge. UIALTL is defined as a set of all formulas valid at all Kripke-Hintikka like models NC. Any frame NC represents possible unbounded (in time) computation with multi-processors (parallel computational units) and agents' channels for connections between computational units. The main aim of the chapter is to determine possible ways for computation logical laws of UIA LTL. Principal problems that are being dealt with are decidability and the satisfiability problems for UIA LTL. The authors find an algorithm which recognizes theorems of UIA LTL (so they show that UIALTL is decidable) and solves satisfiability problem for UIALTL. As an instrument, the authors use reduction of formulas to rules in the reduced normal form and a technique to contract models NC to special non-UIALTL -models, and then, verification of validity these rules in models of bounded size. The chapter uses standard results from non-classical logics based on Kripke-Hintikka models.

Authors Kiran Mishra and R.B. Mishra take to Chapter 4 to discuss intelligent tutoring systems (ITS) in their work "Multiagent Based Selection of Tutor-Subject-Student Paradigm in an Intelligent Tutoring System." More specifically, they investigate the ITS' aim at development of two main interconnected modules: pedagogical module and student module .The pedagogical module concerns the design of a teaching strategy that combines the interest of the student, tutor's capability, and characteristics of subject. Very few effective models have been developed which combine the cognitive, psychological, and behavioral components of tutor, student, and the characteristics of a subject in ITS. Mishra and Mishra have developed a tutor-subject-student (TSS) paradigm for the selection of a tutor for a particular subject. A selection index of a tutor is calculated based upon his performance profile, preference, desire, intention, capability, and trust. An aptitude of a student is determined based upon his answering to the seven types of subject topic categories: analytical, reasoning, descriptive, analytical reasoning, analytical descriptive, reasoning descriptive, and analytical reasoning descriptive. The selection of a tutor is performed for a particular type of topic in the subject on the basis of a student's aptitude.

Chapter 5 discusses how studies show that supply chain structure is a key factor affecting information sharing. Yifeng Zhang and Siddhartha Bhattacharyya discuss in their chapter, "Information Sharing Strategies in Business-to-Business E-Hubs: An Agent-Based Study," how Business-to-Business (B2B) e-hubs have fundamentally changed many companies' supply chain structure, from a one-to-many to a many-to-many configuration. Traditional supply chains typically center around one company, which interacts with multiple suppliers or customers, forming a one-to-many structure. B2B e-hubs, on the contrary, usually connect many buyers and sellers together, without being dominated by a single company, thus forming a many-to-many configuration. Information sharing in traditional supply chains has been studied extensively, but little attention has been paid to the same in B2B e-hubs. In this study, the authors identified and examined five information sharing strategies in B2B e-hubs. Agent performances under different information sharing strategies were measured and analyzed using an agent-based e-hub model, and practical implications were discussed.

Sam Kin Meng and C. R. Chatwin authored Chapter 6, "Ontology-Based Shopping Agent for E-Marketing." Meng and Chatwin note that before Internet consumers make buying decisions, several psychological factors come into effect and reflect individual preferences on products. In this chapter, the authors investigate four integrated streams: 1) recognizing the psychological factors that affect Internet consumers, 2) understanding the relationship between businesses' e-marketing mix and Internet consumers' psychological factors, 3) designing an ontology mapping businesses' e-marketing mix with Internet consumers' decision-making styles, and 4) developing a shopping agent based on the ontology. The relationship between businesses' e-marketing mix and Internet consumers' psychological factors is important, because it can identify situations where both businesses and Internet consumers benefit. The authors' ontology can be used to share Internet consumers' psychological factors, the e-marketing mix of online business, and their relationships with different computer applications.

Chapter 7 continues on with "A New Behavior Management Architecture for Language Faculty of an Agent for Task Delegation" by S. Kuppuswami and T. Chithralekha. In this chapter, the authors describe a new architecture for the language faculty of an agent that fulfills the interaction requirements of task delegation. The architecture of the language faculty is based on a conceptualization of the language faculty of an agent and a definition of its internal state paradigm. The new architecture is behavior-management based and possesses self-management properties. This architecture is compared with existing abstract self-management architectures, which examines how the new architecture solves unresolved issues of older models. The architecture description is followed by a case study - Multilingual Natural Language Agent Interface for Mail Service, which illustrates its application.

In the next chapter, authors Hung W. Chu and Minh Q. Huynh examine the effects of Information Systems/Technologies (IS/T) on the performance of firms engaged in growth strategies based on mergers and acquisitions (M&A). Chapter 8, "Effective Use of Information Systems/Technologies in the Mergers and Acquisitions Environment: A Resource-Based Theory Perspective," discusses the model, derived from a resource-based theory of the firm, developed to predict the influence of IS/T on performance of firms. Data on the financial performance of 133 firms are used to gauge the impact of IS/T on various M&A objectives. The results suggested that IS/Ts implementation of M&A objectives that seek to increase overall efficiency is better than those that seek to introduce new products or efforts to increase sales. Future studies to examine the process of introducing new products from resource-based theory are suggested.

Chapter 9, "Incremental Load in a Data Warehousing Environment," by Nayem Rahman, discusses that incremental load is an important factor for successful data warehousing. Lack of standardized incremental refresh methodologies can lead to poor analytical results, which can be unacceptable to an organization's analytical community. Successful data warehouse implementation depends on consistent metadata as well as incremental data load techniques. If consistent load timestamps are maintained and efficient transformation algorithms are used, it is possible to refresh databases with complete accuracy and with little or no manual checking. This chapter proposes an Extract-Transform-Load (ETL) metadata model that archives load observation timestamps and other useful load parameters. Rahman also recommends algorithms and techniques for incremental refreshes that enable table loading while ensuring data consistency, integrity, and improving load performance. In addition to significantly improving quality in incremental load techniques, these methods will save a substantial amount of data warehouse systems resources.

In Chapter 10, Toly Chen talks about how yield forecasting is critical to a semiconductor manufacturing factory in the chapter, "A Fuzzy-Neural Approach with Collaboration Mechanisms for Semiconductor Yield Forecasting." To further enhance the effectiveness of semiconductor yield forecasting, a fuzzy-neural approach with collaboration mechanisms is proposed in this study. The proposed methodology is modified from Chen and Lin's approach by incorporating two collaboration mechanisms: favoring mechanism and disfavoring mechanism. The former helps to achieve the consensus among multiple experts to avoid the missing of actual yield, while the latter shrinks the search region to increase the probability of finding out actual yield. To evaluate the effectiveness of the proposed methodology, it was applied to some real cases. According to experimental results, the proposed methodology improved both precision and accuracy of semiconductor yield forecasting by 58% and 35%, respectively.

Ivo José Garcia dos Santos and Edmundo Roberto Mauro Madeira wrote "A Semantic-Enabled Middleware for Citizen-Centric E-Government Services." This chapter highlights that research efforts toward effective e-government infrastructures have gained momentum, motivated mainly by increasing demands to improve citizen participation in public processes, promote social e-inclusion, and reduce bureaucracy. One of the biggest challenges is providing effective techniques to handle the inherent heterogeneity of the systems and processes involved, making them interoperable. This chapter presents a semantically enriched middleware for citizen-oriented e-government services (CoGPlat), which facilitates the development and operation of new e-government applications with higher levels of dynamism. It introduces the use of composition techniques based on semantic descriptions and ontologies. Requirements like autonomy, privacy, and traceability are handled by applying policies that govern the interactions among services.

Chapter 12, "Comparison of the Hybrid Credit Scoring Models Based on Various Classifiers" by Fei-Long Chen and Feng-Chia, speaks to why credit scoring is an important topic for businesses and socio-economic establishments collecting huge amounts of data, with the intention of making the wrong decision obsolete. In this chapter, the authors propose four approaches that combine four well-known classifiers: K-Nearest Neighbor (KNN), Support Vector Machine (SVM), Back-Propagation Network (BPN), and Extreme Learning Machine (ELM). These classifiers are used to find a suitable hybrid classifier combination featuring selection that retains sufficient information for classification purposes. In this regard, different credit scoring combinations are constructed by selecting features with four approaches and classifiers than would otherwise be chosen. Two credit data sets from the University of California, Irvine (UCI), are chosen to evaluate the accuracy of the various hybrid features selection models. Chen and Feng-Chia describe then evaluate the performances of the procedures that are part of the proposed approaches

Chapter 13, "Facilitating Decision Making and Maintenance for Power Systems Operators through the Use of Agents and Distributed Embedded Systems," examines the improvements provided when multimedia information in traditional SCADAS are included in electric facility management and maintenance. Authors A. Carrasco, M. C. Romero-Ternero, F. Sivianes, M. D. Hernández, D. I. Oviedo, and J. Escudero also discuss telecontrol use in the electric sector, with the fundamental objective of providing increased and improved service to the operators who manage these systems. One of the most important contributions is the use of an agent network that is distributed around the electric facility. Through the use of multi-agent technology and its placement in embedded systems, the authors design a system with a degree of intelligence and independence to optimize data collection and provide reaction proposals for the operator. The proposed agent-based architecture is also reviewed in this chapter, as are the design of an example agent and the results obtained in a pilot experience using the proposed hardware platform

Authors Arzu Baloglu, Mudasser F. Wyne, Yilmaz Bahcetepe penned "Web 2.0 Based Intelligent Software Architecture for Photograph Sharing." They highlight that with the development of Web 2.0 technologies, the sharing of photographs has increased. In this chapter, the authors evaluate the art of photography, analyze how to develop intelligent photograph sharing system, and explain the requirements of such systems. The authors present architecture of an intelligent Web 2.0 based system and in future hope to add more modules for retention of users on the system. The system focuses on Web 2.0 usage, Web mining for personalization service, and brings a different approach to collaborative filtering.

In Chapter 15, "Collusion-Free Privacy Preserving Data Mining," authors M. Rajalakshmi, T. Purusothaman, and S. Pratheeba discuss how distributed association rule mining is an integral part of data mining that extracts useful information hidden in distributed data sources. As local frequent itemsets are globalized from data sources, sensitive information about individual data sources needs high protection. Different privacy preserving data mining approaches for distributed environment have been proposed but in the existing approaches, collusion among the participating sites reveal sensitive information about the other sites. This chapter proposes a collusion-free algorithm for mining global frequent itemsets in a distributed environment with minimal communication among sites. This algorithm uses the techniques of splitting and sanitizing the itemsets and communicates to random sites in two different phases, thus making it difficult for the colluders to retrieve sensitive information. Results show that the consequence of collusion is reduced to a greater extent without affecting mining performance and confirms optimal communication among sites

This book concludes with Chapter 16, "Multi-Agent Negotiation in B2C E-Commerce Based on Data Mining Methods" by Bireshwar Dass Mazumdar and R. B. Mishra. The chapter discusses the multi agent system (MAS) model, which has been extensively used in the different tasks of e-commerce like customer relation management (CRM), negotiation, and brokering. For the success of CRM, it is important to target the most profitable customers of a company. This chapter presents a multi-attribute negotiation approach for negotiation between buyer and seller agents. The communication model and the algorithms for various actions involved in the negotiation process re described. The chapter also proposes a multi-attribute based utility model, based on price, response time, and quality. In support of this approach, a prototype system providing negotiation between buyer agents and seller agents is presented.

Vijayan Sugumaran
Oakland University, USA & Sogang University, South Korea

Acknowledgment

Dr. Sugumaran's research has been partly supported by Sogang Business School's World Class University Program (R31-20002) funded by Korea Research Foundation.

Chapter 1
Generating Knowledge–
Based System Generators:
A Software Engineering Approach

Sabine Moisan
INRIA, France

ABSTRACT

This paper investigates software engineering techniques for designing and reengineering knowledge-based system generators, focusing on inference engines and domain specific languages. Indeed, software development of knowledge-based systems is a difficult task. We choose a software engineering approach to favor code reuse, evolution, and maintenance. We propose a software platform named LAMA to design the different elements necessary to produce a knowledge-based system. This platform offers software toolkits (mainly component frameworks) to build interfaces, inference engines, and expert languages. We have used the platform to build several KBS generators for various tasks (planning, classification, model calibration) in different domains. The approach appears well fitted to knowledge-based system generators; it allows developers a significant gain in time, as well as it improves software readability and safeness.

DOI: 10.4018/978-1-4666-0158-1.ch001

SOFTWARE ENGINEERING AND ARTIFICIAL INTELLIGENCE DEVELOPMENT

Among the different types of cooperation between artificial intelligence (AI) and software engineering, many deal with applying AI techniques for better software development. By contrast, we propose to use software engineering techniques to improve AI software development, in particular knowledge-based system design.

Knowledge-Based Systems (KBS) are programs that rely on explicit knowledge to automatically perform various tasks usually devoted to human beings. A task here means an application-independent problem-solving activity, such as classification, diagnosis, design, or planning. Indeed, creating a new KBS relies on a model of the task to perform. Such a model includes two major categories of knowledge. First, a reasoning strategy, often named problem solving method, mirrors the reasoning process of an expert performing the task. Second, concepts make explicit the important features involved in the task and in the application domain; they are usually modeled by means of ontologies.

Knowledge-based systems are mainly composed of three parts: a knowledge base storing expertise in a particular domain, a fact base containing facts about an end-user problem in this domain, and an engine, written by a software designer. Relying on the expert's knowledge, the engine performs inferences to solve the end-user problem. All actors (designer, expert, and end-user) should have tools that correspond to their needs. A lot of work have been devoted in the knowledge engineering community aim to help experts manage knowledge base development and maintenance, through customized high level tools and methods. However, when developing knowledge-based systems, there is another major source of difficulties: (re)designing the various software tools that will be used by experts or end-users to interact with the system, such as inference engine, knowledge acquisition tools, knowledge editors/verifiers, etc. Each element by itself represents a great amount of code. Moreover, all elements must work together, although every one may evolve independently. It is the designer's job to develop, maintain, and customize these tools. This corresponds to a software engineering activity which implies to convert a *cognitive model*, as expressed by experts, into a *software model* and eventually an *operational system* implemented in a regular programming language.

At the present time designers seldom receive adapted support. The tools they have to cope with are usually not at the right abstraction level. Knowledge engineering tools do not offer development, integration and testing facilities. For instance, modifying (part of) the behavior of an engine is difficult and prone to errors since the semantics is often hidden inside the engine code and mixed with programming idiosyncrasies, that lie at a much lower level of abstraction. In the realm of Software Engineering many works have been done on software reuse, maintenance, evolution, and safety. We expect that customizing such approaches to fit KBS needs may lead to dramatic improvement in their development and adaptation.

A META GENERATOR APPROACH

Knowledge-based systems were first developed using *ad hoc* customized approaches. Then, based on similarities among activities and across application domains, the notion of KBS *generators* emerged in the late 80s. KBS generators take advantage of the cross-domain similarities by abstracting the common artificial intelligence concepts and by pooling representation techniques in the same environment. Such development environments provide a panel of reasoning mechanisms and knowledge representations that can be shared and adapted to different domains. They usually propose knowledge acquisition, learning, and verification tools, various editors, and an inference engine. Some of these elements are used only during the KBS elaboration (such as knowledge verification tools), whereas other can be active even during operational use of the final system (engine or learning tools). However, all of them are necessary to conveniently design KBSs. Except for general rule-based shells (such as Jess; Friedman-Hill, 2002), most generators are more or less dedicated to a given range of applications or to a given task (e.g., classification) through their inference mechanisms. They are yet domain-independent, hence their KBS instances may apply to various domains (e.g., classification of cardiologic diseases, of astronomic objects, of biological organisms). Such specialized generators are closer to expert ways of reasoning and often lead to more efficient KBSs.

Generators have proved useful to improve the KBS development cycle by sharing common elements. They properly meet experts' or end-users' modification needs at the cognitive level, since they support modification and maintenance of knowledge base contents and, in some respect, minor modifications in reasoning strategies. At the software level however, when new functionalities are required in one of the elements provided by a generator, modifications are difficult. But, over their life-time, reconfigurations of generator elements are unavoidable. Major modifications of elements are usually impossible in commercial generators. Even in open source or home-made generators, modifications are complex since important features are often hidden inside and scattered over various pieces of code. It is thus tedious to find out *where* the parts of code that correspond to one functionality are located, and a change at one place may have hazardous effects. To cope with modifications and evolution, each generator element should offer versatile, reusable, and maintainable functionalities.

To this end, we propose to go one step further and to enable the *reuse and extension* of each element provided by a generator, for example,

inference engines, interfaces, knowledge base description languages, or knowledge verification tools. We have analyzed these elements to extract sharable and thus reusable primitive building blocks. Our approach was to identify these common blocks and to base the design of generators themselves on the reusable structures they constitute. The final objective of this "meta" approach is to generate *operational* knowledge-based system code, not only models or simulators. It is implemented in a software platform, named LAMA.

THE LAMA PLATFORM

LAMA is an object-oriented software platform to produce KBS generators from reusable customizable elements. The platform gathers several extensible toolkits to design, test, and modify KBS software elements. Each toolkit is devoted to one element and offers generic components (or "building blocks") suitable for this element. The components can be adapted to different tasks (like planning or classification) or to different applications.

LAMA focuses on three main types of tools that must be provided to experts and/or end-users: graphical interfaces (especially editors), knowledge base development tools, and inference engines. Thus LAMA provides toolkits for these three concerns. These toolkits are adapted to the abstraction level of designers: they stand at a conceptual level, allowing designers to manipulate concepts or functionalities, before diving into programming language details. In LAMA toolkits, the code that implements a concept or functionality is encapsulated in one or several well identified components. This code implements general structures or strategies, but with extension points to plug possible variants. This setup allows designers to reuse the common parts of code in the components and to adapt only the parts that must be tuned.

Figure 1. LAMA architecture and toolkits

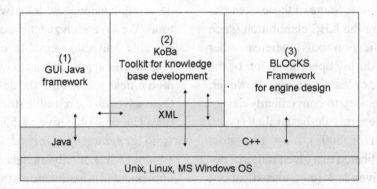

The toolkits are rooted in our long experience of the design of various KBS generators for computer aided design, classification, or planning, and in domains as different as civil engineering, astronomy, medicine, or biology. The proper generality level of the components was an important issue during our domain analysis. Too much generality is not suitable for efficiency, while too specific components, though easily applicable, are hardly reusable. Our solution was to restrict the range of target systems: we focus on knowledge-based systems and we do not try to cover all artificial intelligence systems. We also choose a limited range of tasks, such as planning or classification.

The architecture of LAMA is shown in Figure 1. We use software engineering practices especially to enforce reuse and specialization and to avoid redundant coding efforts. We mainly rely on *component frameworks* to provide high level tested software architectures and implementations for each element.

Below is a description of the three toolkits for graphical interfaces, knowledge base development, and engine design. The latter two are the most original and will be the focus of this paper.

Graphical Interfaces

Interfaces are an important part of a knowledge-based system both during its development and test by experts and during its final use. LAMA proposes a Java framework (1) that supports the development of dedicated editors to create and browse knowledge bases (see an example of a graph editor for planning operator hierarchies on Figure 2). The same framework is also used to develop tools to display run-time information. It is a rather classical graphic framework, relying on a common layer of graphic elements which may be extended for particular purposes. The common layer includes windows, buttons, menus etc. but also graphs (trees or dags with various connectors). It allows designers to customize interfaces so that experts may design and edit knowledge bases as well as run and debug them. Thanks to Java, a distributed architecture can also be developed for remote usage. Furthermore, XML translation facilities are provided for knowledge base storage.

Knowledge Bases

Experts roughly describe their knowledge in a knowledge base, in terms of domain concepts, hierarchies of concepts, and know-how rules. To this end, they use a language that may be graphical or textual. LAMA proposes a toolkit, KOBA (item (2) on Figure 1), to design textual knowledge description languages (the graphical versions are the matter of the previous GUI toolkit) and their associated compilers/verifiers. Such languages

Figure 2. Example of an interface window built with LAMA for the planning task

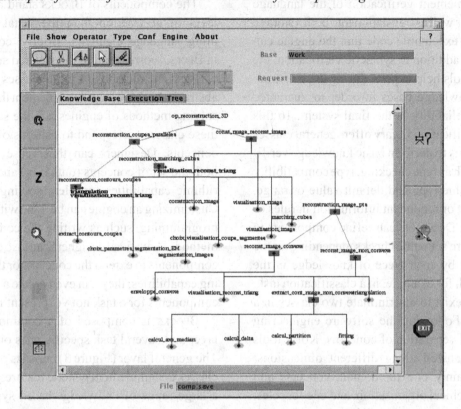

provide human readable formats for writing, documenting, and consulting knowledge bases. The toolkit provides usual knowledge representation schemes, used in many KBSs: structured objects (frames), hierarchical organizations (graphs), and inference rules. Different extensions of these basic representations are also available for the existing tasks: for instance, rules with variables that are useful during complex planning, or fuzzy rules that are necessary during classification.

The toolkit aims at customizing expert-oriented languages, independently of any programming language. Such expert languages belong to the category of Domain Specific Languages, a current trend in software engineering. They offer a syntax and semantics to describe all knowledge pieces relevant to a task, for example, operators in a planning task or hierarchies of classes in a classification task. Experts use a suitable DSL

to develop a knowledge base for a particular application. In addition to the language, a generator must provide other tools to verify the correctness of the knowledge in a base, to generate executable code from the expert language, or to store knowledge in an interoperable format. Thus the KOBA toolkit offers a generator of parsers, a component framework for knowledge representation schemes, and three libraries of reusable and extensible components for knowledge verification, code generation, and XML storage, respectively. Library components can be either directly reused or specialized by the designer who provided that they respect their APIs.

A designer who wants to customize a new DSL needs first to define the syntax of the language to generate a new parser. Then he/she uses the libraries to enrich the concrete syntax with actions that will be executed during parsing. These actions implement verification of the language semantics as well as translation into both a storage format and executable code that the engine can manage. In addition to syntactic verification, the resulting tools help experts during the construction of knowledge bases in order to guarantee sufficient reliability in the final system. To this end, the verification library offers general classes and functions to perform basic knowledge verifications, such as type checking, type compatibility between value type and default value or range, inconsistent or redundant information in rules or hierarchies. Designers can refine components to provide more semantic checks, depending on the role played by each piece of knowledge in the task at hand, for example, in a classification task, rules must exist to discriminate two classes in a taxonomy. Following the software engineering principle of separation of concerns, KoBa tools are all organized along different dimensions/ models, mainly one for domain concepts and their hierarchical organization, and one for rules. KoBa proposes general models and templates for common features shared by different languages. Once a DSL definition is completed, a knowledge base written with this DSL can be parsed and eventually translated, according to the parser actions. Parsing yields code to be processed by an inference engine, intermediate formats to be visualized by a graphical tool, run by a simulator, or stored as XML.

Inference Engines

The BLOCKS component framework (item (3) on Figure 1) is the core of the LAMA platform. It helps designers create new engines and reuse or modify existing ones. It is an object-oriented framework, in the sense of (Johnson, 1997). Written in C++, it offers reusable and adaptable components for designing knowledge-based system engines without extensive code rewriting.

The components of BLOCKS stand at a higher level of abstraction than the usual programming language elements. Briefly, components in BLOCKS correspond to interrelated sub trees of classes. The methods of these classes constitute abstract reasoning steps to implement the problem solving methods of engines and the structure of these classes correspond to patterns of ontology concepts. Designers can thus reuse or extend both the set of concepts (ontology) and the algorithmic capabilities (problem solving method). Customizing an engine can be done with minimal programming, such as writing the code of some methods. Advanced designers can also create new components to extend the concepts or the reasoning capabilities; they can even create a new set of components for a task not yet present in BLOCKS.

BLOCKS is composed of a common general layer and several task specific ones on top of it. The general layer (Figure 3) consists of about 75 classes that implement generic features useful for a large range of knowledge-based systems: for instance, inference rules, structured frames, or history management. By specializing (abstract or concrete) classes in the general layer, a designer may define customized sub-layers adapted to different task models. These layers contain only concrete classes (the instances of which will populate the knowledge bases) and methods or functions that will constitute reasoning steps in an engine strategy.

BLOCKS is not reduced to unsubstantial (abstract) classes and generic functions, on the contrary it offers structured classes with rich behavior and relationships that reflect the usual interactions between concepts in KBS engines. Class interfaces are complete enough to cover most designer needs without modifications, but we have made provision for extension points, in particular in methods. Specialization, composition, and extension points allow designers to fine tune engine behavior. Designers must respect the global organization of the classes, their relation-

Figure 3. Sketchy UML conceptual model of Blocks general layer, showing its main packages

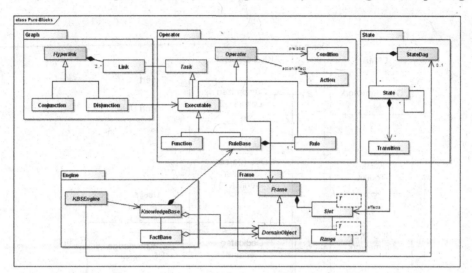

ships, and functions. Complying with the "protocol of use" of components is difficult but necessary. It is an important issue, which is outside the scope of this paper: we have proposed an automatic verification tool based on model-checking techniques, as well as practical design rules to ensure sound component adaptation (Moisan, Ressouche, & Rigault, 2001, 2003, 2004).

Using Lama

Figure 4 illustrates the way Lama toolkits are used. The designer first defines a new DSL (b), choosing consensual terms in the literature, from existing ontologies, or through interviews with experts. This leads to a concrete syntax and concepts extensions. The KoBa toolkit allows the designer to implement a parser, a code generator, and a verifier by extending the common features provided. In parallel, the designer also uses the GUI toolkit to develop all suitable graphical interfaces (a). Then Blocks provides classes, methods and functions to compose a new engine program that corresponds to the chosen strategy (c). It is the responsibility of the designer to decide upon the strategy of the engine, that is to implement the control of the engine reasoning steps.

At this point, the designer obtains a KBS *generator* with its main elements, which can be used by experts to produce several KBS instances. For example, a classification generator can apply to various domains, like classification of cardiologic diseases, of astronomic objects, of biological organisms.

An expert in a particular domain can feed the engine with knowledge about his/her domain, guided by the language and the corresponding editors provided by the designer (d). Experts do not modify the language nor the engine behavior. The knowledge consists of descriptions of domain classes, objects and know-how. For instance, it could be a taxonomy of galaxies, or of animals with the know-how rules to discriminate individuals in these taxonomies. This constitutes a knowledge base, which complements the engine, providing an executable *knowledge-based system*.

Finally, end-users can solve particular problems involving the given expertise and reasoning strategy. They only provide facts describing their problems (e) and run the knowledge-based system against these facts. The given results ensue from

Figure 4. Generation of a KBS using LAMA

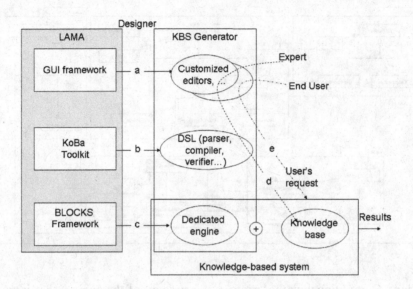

the domain expertise and engine behavior. For instance, if the task is classification, the end-user problem is an object to classify and the result a list of candidate classes with attached likelihoods.

USE CASES AND EXPERIMENTS

Over the past decades LAMA has been used to design or modify different generators. First, we re-wrote existing planning systems that were initially developed from scratch. This intensive code (re)writing activity was the motivation of the platform development and allowed us to identify LAMA basic elements. These first successful experiments encouraged us to systematically use the platform to develop new engines, tools, and languages. After, planning, we addressed a completely different task, classification, resulting in two generators. In parallel, we investigated a model calibration task as an extension of our work in planning. These three tasks have been implemented in LAMA and are briefly presented below. For instance, Figure 5 shows the specific

layers in BLOCKS, and the different engines that have been derived.

Planning Task

We have first developed several KBSs for a task called *program supervision* which consists in automating the use and correct composition of existing programs. This task mainly relies on planning techniques. It introduces the notions of *supervision operators*—corresponding in our case to programs or compositions of programs—that manipulate *data* (arguments of programs). Operators are combined into a plan to achieve a processing goal. We have developed a layer for this task and three variants of generators.

Each generator led to one engine and one knowledge description language. Yet, since representation needs are very similar the three languages are in fact variants of one extensible language, named YAKL. The program supervision model involves generic concepts, such as data, programs, sequences of programs, data flows and attached knowledge as diverse as algorith-

Figure 5. Overview of inference engines developed with BLOCKS. Some typical applications are indicated in the package body of each generator

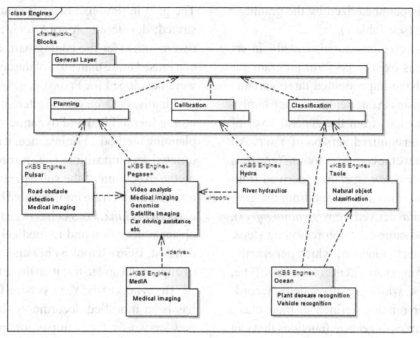

mic purpose, scientific foundations, conditions of applicability, know-how of everyday users. The YAKL language offers a concrete syntax to describe the concepts of this abstract model. We have, in parallel, defined a formal semantics for the language (Moisan, 2003).

An example of the textual form of YAKL is shown below. It describes an image thresholding operator (we suppose that a type *Image* has been previously defined, with a *noise* attribute and a type *UserRequirement* with a *detail level* attribute). This example describes the achieved functionality (thresholding), input and output arguments, a precondition on image noise, and the calling syntax, here a shell command that has to be launched at execution time with the actual values of arguments. We use both frame-based and rule-oriented descriptions. Frames are used for operators and arguments, whereas inference rules are used for decision criteria at execution time. The example shows an initialization rule to be executed just before operator execution. A

Table 1.

Primitive { name thresh-1
Functionality thresholding
Input Data
Image **name** in_image **comment** "original image"
Input Parameters
Float **name** threshold
default 25
Output Data
name out_image **comment** "thresholded image"
...
Preconditions in_image.noise == Gaussian **Initializations** **Rule { name** init-high **comment** " if many details required, threshold must be low" **Let** requirement a UserRequirement **If** requirements.detail_level == "many" **Then** threshold := 20 }
...
Call
language shell
syntax cd in_imag1.path ";" thresh -s threshold out_image }

knowledge base editor that supports YAKL and its variants has been developed using the GUI framework. It is parameterized by the grammar of the language (see Table 1).

Several—more or less sophisticated—inference mechanisms exist to perform program supervision. We have implemented three variants of such mechanisms in three engines, each implying model extensions from the general layer of figure 3 and a customized version of YAKL. All these engines share the common notions (and thus classes) of *Supervision Operator* (derived from both classes *Operator* and *Frame* from the general layer) or *Data* (derived from *DomainObject*). They all use the same common reasoning steps, such as the "select" function, which generically picks an item from a set of items of the same type, or the "sort" one, which organizes items according to an order relation defined in their class. These are examples of generic functions that can be widely applied during engine reasoning, e.g. to select a rule to execute as well as a planning operator to fire.

However each engine requires specific extensions from the general classes. First, the PEGASE+ engine performs pure hierarchical planning which consists in recursively refining a hierarchy of operators. This engine introduces, among others, a notion of "Optional Operator" that may be applied or not, and an associated type of rule to decide on the applicability of such operators. This has been done by specializing the following classes: *Supervision Operator*, *Rule* and *Link* between operators. PEGASE+ has been successfully applied to domains such as galaxy identification in astronomical imaging (Thonnat, Clément, & Ossola, 1995) or vehicle detection in satellite imaging (Shekhar, Burlina, & Moisan, 1997).

The second engine, MEDIA (Crubézy, Aubry, Moisan, Chameroy, Thonnat, & di Paola, 1997), integrates dynamic planning steps. It extends the planning layer with new components, such as a *Weak Condition* class, derived from *Condition* that

is a non-mandatory condition that can be relaxed. MEDIA is a typical example of successful reuse. The gain in time had been dramatically demonstrated: developing MEDIA took a PhD student two months (for the coding part, after analysis) and reused more than 90% of the components that were developed for PEGASE+.

Finally, PULSAR, was an attempt towards combining hierarchical and dynamic operator-based planning methods. For instance, it introduces unordered decompositions (i.e., no order is imposed on the execution of the sub-operators of a given operator), which are implemented by specializing class *HyperLink*. PULSAR has been applied to road obstacle detection and to medical imaging (van den Elst, 1996). It took a PhD student four months to implement and to test it on these two examples.

The syntax of the YAKL version for each engine has been modified accordingly, by introducing new keywords, for example, for optionality rules in PEGASE+, or for weak preconditions in MEDIA. YAKL exhibits general knowledge modeling features, in a way similar to several general purpose languages for knowledge or ontology definition and exchange (e.g., KIF; Genesereth & Fikes, 1992), or more recently, OIL (for Web applications, see Fensel, Horrocks, van Harmelen, Decker, Erdmann, & Klein, 2000). Its major contribution lies in a natural description of strategic and semantic knowledge about software components (programs in our case), in a domain-independent way. YAKL is in the same line as recent work, for example, on UPML (Fensel et al., 2003), on describing problem-solving methods and on facilitating their reuse in an Internet-based environment.

Classification Task

Our first classification engine, named TACLE, was a C++ implementation of a previous Lisp engine. TACLE classifies an object in a predefined taxonomy (hierarchical description of all the possible classes of objects for a given domain). This

Figure 6. Some specializations for classification task. Above are BLOCKS general layer classes (from Figure 3).

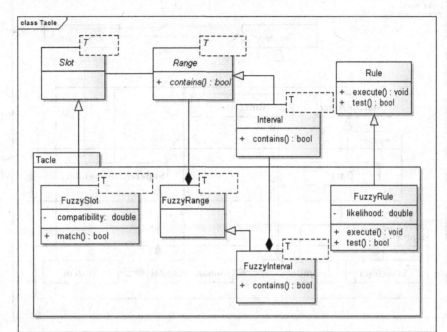

attempt to tackle a completely new task, very far from the planning one, was our first experiment in adding a new layer to BLOCKS. This classification layer primarily introduces an implementation of the fuzzy theory to take into account uncertainty on object attribute values and on rules. Figure 6 shows a few classes using this theory that have been derived from the BLOCKS general layer.

It took us three months to implement TACLE which used (directly or by specialization, see Figure6) more than 85% of the general layer. It introduces 20 classes (half of them being very simple), among which 14 derive from BLOCKS components. This experience permitted us to fine tune the boundary between the general layer and specialized ones.

More recently, in collaboration with INRA, an engineer designed a new engine (OCEAN) to perform semantic image interpretation, that is, to assign a meaning to data automatically extracted from images.

Model Calibration Task

Numerical models can be used to simulate physical processes in order to understand past phenomena or forecast future behavior. Model *calibration* is an essential step to tune numerical models. It involves adapting numerical parameters of equations with respect to real measures, so that the simulation results of the numerical model fit the ground truth. This task shares concepts and reasoning steps with program supervision, such as the notion of parameters to tune and the steps of numerical code execution, of result evaluation, and of parameter adaptation. So it has been easy to move to a new layer, a new language (OVAL), and a new engine (HYDRA) by specializing general layer and planning items (see Figure7). OVAL offers a specific vocabulary: for instance, it allows experts to describe a *numerical model* that simulates the behavior of a system in the real world. A numerical model is defined as a composition of *data, parameters* (reused from program supervi-

Figure 7. Major HYDRA *class extensions*

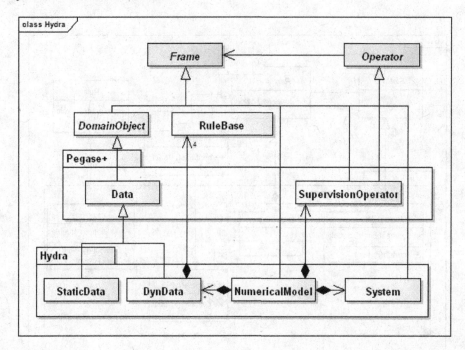

sion), and a simulation program. OVAL completely reuses the YAKL syntax for the execution of the simulation code, its result evaluation, and its parameter tuning.

The OVAL vocabulary also corresponds to HYDRA class extensions; for example, two classes have been derived from program supervision class *Data*: static and dynamic ones. We also defined a new class *NumericalModel* as a composition of *Data, Parameter* and *Supervision Operator* (the simulation code). In total, this engine introduces 13 classes and 9 major method definitions, one for each new/modified reasoning step, plus a few utilities.

Using OVAL we have designed a knowledge-based system called CaRMA (Calibration of River Model Assistant) that allows us to capitalize expertise about good calibration practice in hydraulics but also to provide reusable techniques to domains other than hydraulics. It has been partly developed at Cemagref Lyon and tested in hydraulic model calibration, on quite different cases of French rivers (Vidal, Moisan, Faure, & Dartus, 2005). The whole

system includes both numeric and symbolic tools to cover all the calibration steps. In particular, it makes use of a program called Mage developed at Cemagref to perform the simulations.

BENEFITS OF THE APPROACH

Reuse, Adaptation, and Interoperability

LAMA relies on software engineering techniques, primarily to avoid redundant coding efforts. It places designers at a level of abstraction higher than that supported by programming languages, because the building blocks correspond to (parts of) generator functionalities that can be manipulated at a conceptual level. The platform allows designers to share common parts when it is possible or to adapt their behavior to specific needs by extensions of common structures and methods. Reuse and specialization are better software engineering practices than rewriting similar codes

Table 2. Comparison of development efforts for three engines

Engine	Pegase+	Tacle	Hydra
Derived classes	16	15	11
New classes	2	5	2
Lines of (real C++) code	3,000	2,000	1,500
Lines of the reasoning part (engine control)	850	150	250

from scratch or patching existing ones. Thus LAMA reduces the designers' effort and favors rapid code development and evolution to follow strategic changes. It also ensures better programming safety, because libraries and components can be tested and verified only once and less code has to be written from scratch. Moreover, changes in the behavior of an element do not affect the common LAMA environment. Designers can test, compare or modify different elements in a unified framework.

Another objective of the platform was to be able to couple knowledge based systems performing different tasks in a unified environment. Indeed, from an architectural point of view, common structures and tools facilitates communication and cooperation between different systems built on the platform. It also facilitates tests and comparisons among all the final knowledge-base systems written on top of LAMA toolkits. Several engines can be applied on the same knowledge base, as well as several knowledge bases in different applications may be tested with the same engine, without changing the environment.

Moreover, since we rely on software standards for programming (C++) or for knowledge warehousing (XML-family), the resulting KBSs can interface with many other tools on the market place, for instance, with existing Web tools for ontology descriptions, or with "classical" software, such as numerical computation software. We have already mentioned the connection of HYDRA with the Mage FORTRAN simulation program; it also connects with GNUPLOT for curve display. Along the same line, PEGASE+ also interfaces with Matlab.

Reduced Coding Efforts

Table 2 summarizes some figures about three engines, one for each task, just to give a rough idea about the coding effort necessary to build a new engine. BLOCKS itself is about 75 classes and 5,000 lines of C++ code (not including comments and support classes, such as lists or strings).

This table raises some points, First, PEGASE+ has been the most used of our engines, and it is the only one with a sophisticated history backtracking mechanism, hence its higher number of code lines. On the other hand, HYDRA, which reuses a lot from PEGASE+, requires less extra code. Second, the number of classes that are to be developed (completely new classes or derived from existing classes) is rather similar among engines. Third, an engine reasoning part, that is the algorithm of its problem solving method, is on the order of a few hundreds of lines, which is a tractable size when it comes to modifications.

RELATED WORK

Both software engineering and artificial intelligence have proposed solutions to facilitate reuse and customization, but these solutions differ by the nature of what is reused or customized and by the techniques used.

Reuse in Software Engineering

In the software engineering community, reuse targets not only analysis and design models, but also software architectures and code to facilitate the design of operational systems. Initial work started on general purpose frameworks, especially for graphical interfaces (similar to the GUI framework of LAMA), concurrent systems, compilation, or general parsers like yacc. Then concerns evolved toward the application level, such as J2E Java components for e-commerce on the Web (Bodoff, Armstrong, Ball, & Carson, 2004). Such recent trends are at the same semantic level as LAMA. A lot of tools now exist, ranging from libraries like Boost (www.boost.org), component frameworks (Johnson, 1997), or more complex environments. In the domain of graphical interfaces, we can cite the Qt graphics view framework (Molkentin, 2007) or Java graphic frameworks (e.g., Swing or Java3D). For graph representation and management, GRAPHVIZ (www.graphviz.org) is a popular framework. Concerning parsing, environments like SPIRIT (parser framework, part of Boost libraries) or ANTLR (www.antlr.org) are the modern successors of the earliest parser generators. Rapid development of domain specific languages is also a current line of research: for instance, MetaCase (Kelly & Tolvanen 2008) or Eclipse Modeling Project (Gronback, 2009) address the same aspects as KoBa, but they also support a graphical form.

All researches are too numerous to be cited here, since a complete presentation is not the purpose of this paper. However they were a source of inspiration for LAMA.

Modeling Concerns in Artificial Intelligence

Most artificial intelligence work in this area focus on reusing knowledge itself (especially ontologies) or parts of reasoning strategies (problem solving methods). In the knowledge acquisition community, reusability often targets ontology management and task modeling, as in (Oussalah, 2003), PROTÉGÉ (Gennari et al., 2003), or Par-KAP (de Nunes Barros, Hendler, & Benjamins, 1997). They propose knowledge *modeling* or knowledge

acquisition tools, while we target KBS generator *implementation*. Most systems focus on *formal* abstract models of ontologies and methods, for example, the libraries of COMMONKADS (Breuker, 1995) or KADS (Schreiber, Wielinga, & Breuker, 1999), whereas we propose reusable *operational* components. Technically, customization can be made possible through abstract component reuse, open-source approaches, as in Jess shell, or plugins, as in PROTÉGÉ. We rather rely on concrete components to be composed or derived and on code generation for efficiency.

Tools have been proposed that intend to cover all steps of a KBS design (from cognitive model to implementation or simulation). We can cite DSTM (Trichet & Tchounikine, 1999), UPML (Fensel et al., 2003) or TASK (Talon & Pierret-Golbreich, 1996). Although also dedicated to KBS design, they are more expert-oriented than LAMA. In our approach, like in DSTM or in TASK, we take into account not only the task modeling but also the effective and efficient execution of the resulting KBSs. DSTM aims at prototyping a cognitive model before implementing it. TASK proposes different languages for the different steps of KBS design, and in particular a formal specification language for dynamic engine behavior. UPML objective is to describe problem-solving methods and to facilitate their reuse in an Internet-based environment; it is in the same line as the program supervision layer of LAMA. Such tools provide the means to specify a KBS and some tools even propose code implementation, by automatic translation of formal models. However, they do not offer real software development tools to designers of KBSs. In this sense they stand upstream from LAMA which promotes software level design of KBS elements from reusable operational components.

Implementation Concerns in Artificial Intelligence

Some frameworks and libraries relying on component engineering are more concerned with implementation issues of AI systems, but they do not target knowledge-based systems; for instance, frameworks have been developed for agent platforms (Briot, Charpentier, Marin, & Sens, 2002) or for learning tools, for example, MLC++ (Kohavi, John, Long, Manley, & Pfleger, 1994) or WEKA (Witten, Frank, Trigg, Hall, Holmes, & Cunningham, 1999).

Other systems address parts of the LAMA platform or more task-specific concerns. In the first category we can cite AROM (Page et al., 2001) for knowledge base edition, which is close to the knowledge base KOBA toolkit of LAMA. In the second category, we can find several works which aim at introducing some flexibility in AI tools for a particular task. For instance, the NASA's inference engine SHINE (James, 2001) provides a "toolbox" of AI facilities for KBSs (reasoning processes, memory-data structures…). It also translates its knowledge into C/C++, but since it targets critical missions, it mainly focuses on real-time performance. In the same line, faced to an expanding problem domain, the MSTAR search engine (Wissinger, Ristroph, Diemunsch, Severson, & Freudenthal, 1999) can be customized to implement different search methods, through a search operator toolkit. This idea is even more developed in the SearchToolKit (Chew, Henz, & Ng, 2000), which proposes to tailor inference search engines by plugging reusable modules to implement various search methods. The idea of constructing a KBS from reusable components is also the objective of a software toolkit for distributed KBSs (Soshnikov, 2000). It mainly targets network integration and heterogeneous environments. Like LAMA, this toolkit relies on frames, rules, and hierarchies and on (Java) class libraries. It uses CORBA interfaces for information exchange, while we have rather experimented an agent-based approach when it comes to distribution (Lejouad-Chaari, Moisan, Sevestre-Ghalila, & Rigault, 2007).

All these systems can be compared to specific layers in our approach; for instance, searching is not currently addressed by LAMA, but like planning or classification it may correspond to a layer extension. LAMA adds the notion of a general layer common to several tasks. This general layer is important and can be viewed as an implementation of a meta-model of KBSs, based on well-established concepts to serve as the basis for KBS development. It can be compared to the UML Profile proposed in (Abdullah, Paige, Kimble, & Benest, 2007) or to the JavaDON architecture (Tomic, Jovanovic, & Devedzic, 2006). Both stand at the same meta level of KBS representation as LAMA and also have a clear software engineering perspective. A main difference is that both rely uniquely on rules as inference mechanism, whereas we propose to mix a rule engine with other engines (e.g., planning or classification engines). There are also some differences in goals (stress on Web applications for JavaDON), methods (UML profiling or open-source), or achievements (no code generation from the UML Profile yet).

CONCLUSION

In this paper we proposed a software engineering approach to generate knowledge-based systems and their generators. The LAMA platform complements usual knowledge management tools. It gathers generic libraries and component frameworks for high-level design and implementation of elements of KBS. It is based on reuse, composition, and refinement. Yet, genericity is not at the expense of efficiency: for instance, in a video understanding application, a planning system generated with PEGASE+ provides high versatility but accounts for less that 4% of the overall execution time, which is close to the cost of the code that would have been written anyway to control the application. Our objective is operational code reuse, not only (formal) model reuse. This approach has proved appropriate and led to a significant gain in development time and in code readability. It proves that a generic approach to KBS development is effective across application domains, that is, it reduces development time, facilitates modifications, and improves software quality.

The LAMA project started in the 90s and since that time new software engineering methods have emerged that could benefit to its implementation. For instance, recent work on DSL frameworks, such as MetaCase or the Eclipse Modeling Project, could improve language generation in the KOBA toolkit. We are also planning to introduce Model Driven Engineering approaches into LAMA as a means to make the model of generators more explicit, to be able to manage and modify it directly, and to automatically produce component glue code. This will provide designers with an effective tool at a more global level than component assembly, thus raising the abstraction level. Such evolution in implementation paradigms will facilitate the interaction with designers but they will not affect the underlying philosophy of LAMA that is based on reuse, genericity, separation of concerns, and code generation.

REFERENCES

Abdullah, M. S., Paige, R., Kimble, C., & Benest, I. (2007, August). A UML profile for knowledge-based systems modelling. In *Proceedings of the 5th ACIS International Conference on Software Engineering Research, Management & Applications (Sera'07)*, Busan, Korea (pp. 871-878). Washington DC: IEEE Computer Society.

Bodoff, S., Armstrong, E., Ball, J., & Carson, D. B. (2004). *The J2E tutorial* (2nd ed.). Boston: Addison-Wesley Longman.

Breuker, J. (1995, November). Problems, tasks and problem solving methods: Constructing the common KADS. In *Proceedings of First International Workshop on Knowledge-Based Systems for the (Re) Use of Program Libraries (KBUP'95)*, Sophia Antipolis, France. INRIA.

Briot, J.-P., Charpentier, S., Marin, O., & Sens, P. (2002, July). A fault-tolerant multi-agent framework. In *International Joint Conference on Autonomous Agents and Multiagent Systems*, Bologna, Italy (pp. 672-673). ACM Publishing.

Chew, T. Y., Henz, M., & Ng, K. B. (2000). A toolkit for constraint-based inference engines. In E. Pontelli & V. S. Costa (Eds.), *Practical aspects of declarative languages, Second International Workshop PADL'00* (pp. 185-199). Springer-Verlag.

Crubézy, M., Aubry, F., Moisan, S., Chameroy, V., Thonnat, M., & di Paola, R. (1997). *Managing complex processing of medical image sequences by program supervision techniques*. Paper presented at SPIE International Symposiuon Medical Imaging, Newport Beach, CA.

de Nunes Barros, L., Hendler, J., & Benjamins, V. (1997, August). Par-KAP: A knowledge acquisition tool for building practical planning systems. In M. E. Pollack (Ed.), *15th International Joint Conference on Artificial Intelligence (IJCAI'97)*, Nagoya, Japan (p. 1246-1251).

Fensel, D., Horrocks, I., van Harmelen, F., Decker, S., Erdmann, M., & Klein, M. (2000, October). OIL in a nutshell. In R. Dieng & O. Corby (Ed.), *12th International Conference on Knowledge Engineering and Knowledge Management (EKAW'2000)*, Juan les Pins, France. Springer-Verlag.

Fensel, D., Motta, E., van Harmelen, F., Benjamins, R., Crubezy, M., & Decker, S. (2003). The unified problem-solving method development language UPML. *Knowledge and Information Systems*, 5(1), 83–131. doi:10.1007/s10115-002-0074-5

Fridman-Hill, E. (2002). *Jess in action: Java rule-based systems (In Action series)*. Greenwich, CT: Manning Publications.

Genesereth, M., & Fikes, R. (1992). *Knowledge interchange format version 3.0 reference manual* (Tech. Rep. No. 94305). Palo Alto, CA: Computer Science Department, Stanford University.

Gennari, J., Musen, M., Fergerson, R., Grosso, W., Crubezy, M., & Eriksson, H. (2003). The evolution of Protégé: An environment for knowledge-based systems development. *International Journal of Human-Computer Studies*, *58*, 89–123. doi:10.1016/S1071-5819(02)00127-1

Gronback, R. C. (2009). *Eclipse modeling project: A domain-specific language (DSL) toolkit.* Reading, MA: Addison-Wesley.

James, M. L. (2001, March). An autonomous diagnostic and prognostic monitoring system for NASA's deep space network. In *Proceedings of the IEEE Aerospace Conference,* Big Sky, MT (pp. 403-414). Washington DC: IEEE Computer Society.

Johnson, R. E. (1997). Frameworks = (Components + Patterns). *CACM*, *10*(40), 39–42.

Kohavi, R., John, G., Long, R., Manley, D., & Pfleger, K. (1994). *MLC++: A machine learning library in C++.* In *Proceedings of the 6th International Conference on Tools with Artificial Intelligence,* New Orleans, LA (pp. 740-743). Washington DC: IEEE Computer Society.

Lejouad-Chaari, W., Moisan, S., Sevestre-Ghalila, S., & Rigault, J.-P. (2007, August). Distributed intelligent medical assistant for osteoporosis detection. In Proceedings of the *29th International Conference of the IEEE Engineering in Medicine and Biology Society,* Lyon, France (pp. 4347-4350). Washington DC: IEEE Computer Society.

Moisan, S. (2003). *Program supervision: Yakl and Pegase+ reference manual* (Tech. Rep. No. 5066). Sophia Antipolis, France: INRIA.

Moisan, S., Ressouche, A., & Rigault, J.-P. (2001). Blocks, a component framework with checking facilities for knowledge-based Systems. *Informatica, Special Issue on Component Based Software Development*, *25*(4), 501–507.

Moisan, S., Ressouche, A., & Rigault, J.-P. (2003, September). Behavioral substitutability in component frameworks: A formal approach. In *Proceedings of the Specification and Verification of Component-Based Systems (SAVCBS'2003) Workshop at ESEC/FSE 2003,* Helsinki, Finland (pp. 22-28).

Moisan, S., Ressouche, A., & Rigault, J.-P. (2004). Towards formalizing behavorial dubstitutability in component frameworks. In *Proceedings of the 2nd International Conference on Software Engineering and Formal Methods* Beijing, China (p. 122-131). Washington, DC: IEEE Computer Society Press.

Molkentin, D. (2007). *The book of Qt 4: The art of building Qt applications.* Munich, Germany: Open Source Press.

Oussalah, M. (2003). Reuse in KBS: A component approach. *Expert Systems with Applications*, *24*(2), 173–181. doi:10.1016/S0957-4174(02)00140-9

Page, M., Gensel, J., Capponi, C., Bruley, C., Genoud, P., Ziebelin, D., et al. (2001). A new approach in object-based knowledge representation: the AROM System. Paper presented at IEA/AIE'2001, Budapest, Hungary.

Schreiber, G., Wielinga, B., & Breuker, J. (1999). *KADS: A principled approach to knowledge-based system development.* London: Academic Press.

Shekhar, C., Burlina, P., & Moisan, S. (1997). Design of self-tuning IU systems. In *Proceedings of the DARPA Image Understanding Workshop,* New Orleans, LA (Vol. 1, pp. 529-536).

Soshnikov, D. (2000). Software toolkit for building embedded and distributed knowledge-based systems. In *Proceedings of the 2nd International Workshop on Computer Science and Information Technologies* (pp. 103-111).

Talon, X., & Pierret-Golbreich, C. (1996). *TASK: From the specification to the implementation.* Paper presented at the 8th International Conference on Tools with Artificial Intelligence (ICTAI).

Thonnat, M., Clément, V., & Ossola, J. C. (1995). Automatic galaxy description. *Astrophysical Letters and Communication, 31*(1-6), 65-72.

Tomic, B., Jovanovic, J., & Devedzic, V. (2006). JavaDON: An open-source expert system shell. *International Journal of Expert Systems with Applications, 31*(3), 595–606. doi:10.1016/j.eswa.2005.09.085

Trichet, F., & Tchounikine, P. (1999). DSTM: A framework to operationalize and refine a problem-solving method modeled in terms of tasks and methods. *International Journal of Expert Systems with Applications, 16*(2), 105–120. doi:10.1016/S0957-4174(98)00065-7

van den Elst, J. (1996). *Modélisation de connaissances pour le pilotage de programmes de traitement d'images.* Unpublished doctoral dissertation, Université de Nice.

Vidal, J.-P., Moisan, S., Faure, J.-B., & Dartus, D. (2005). Towards a reasoned 1-D river model calibration. *Journal of Hydroinformatics, 7*(2), 79–90.

Wissinger, J., Ristroph, R., Diemunsch, J., Severson, W., & Freudenthal, E. (1999). MSTAR extensible search engine and model-based inference toolkit. *SPIE, 372,* 554–570. doi:10.1117/12.357671

Witten, I., Frank, E., Trigg, L., Hall, M., Holmes, G., & Cunningham, S. (1999). Weka: Practical machine learning tools and techniques with Java implementations. In *Proceedings of the ICONIP/ANZIIS/ANNES'99 International Workshop: Emerging Knowledge Engineering and Connectionist-Based Info. Systems* (pp. 192-196).

This work was previously published in International Journal of Intelligent Information Technologies, Volume 6, Issue 1, edited by Vijayan Sugumaran, pp. 1-17, copyright 2010 by IGI Publishing (an imprint of IGI Global).

Chapter 2
A Model to Increase the Efficiency of a Competence-Based Collaborative Network

Ilaria Baffo
Institute of Industrial Technologies and Automation, National Research Council; University of Rome "Tor Vergata" Italy

Giuseppe Confessore
Institute of Industrial Technologies and Automation, National Research Council, Italy

Graziano Galiano
Institute of Industrial Technologies and Automation, National Research Council, Italy

ABSTRACT

This paper provides a model based on the Multi Agent System (MAS) paradigm that acts as a methodological basis for evaluating the dynamics in a collaborative environment. The model dynamics is strictly driven by the competence concept. In the provided MAS, the agents represent the actors operating on a given area. In particular, the proposed agents are composed of three distinct typologies: (i) the territorial agent, (ii) the enterprise agent, and (iii) the public agent. Each agent has its local information and goals, and interacts with others by using an interaction protocol. The decision-making processes and the competencies characterize in a specific way each one of the different agent typologies working in the system.

INTRODUCTION

The rapid evolution in customer requirements is forcing major changes in the overall industrial system. One possible strategy for facing these changes is based on the adoption of a collaborative way of working where different abilities and

DOI: 10.4018/978-1-4666-0158-1.ch002

competencies are brought together with the goal of exploiting benefits and sharing the risks. This idea is supported by the increasing relevance of the collaboration as new multi disciplinary research field (Camarinha-Matos & Afsarmanesh, 2004).

This paper aims at providing a model for understanding the dynamics of a network composed of heterogeneous actors, and suggests a competence-based collaborative way of working, where the competence is defined as the ability to perform activities by using a combination of knowledge, skill and attitude. As Camarinha-Matos and Afsarmanesh (2006) argue in their work, the definition of a model certainly represents one of the main topics concerning the collaborative network organization research field.

The model represents actors working on a given geographical area, where the area boundaries are both physical, and due to the existence of consolidated business connections among the actors. A typical example for explaining the model environment is an industrial district defined as a socio-territorial entity where there is a community of people, firms, public entities and agencies for local development (Molina-Morales, 2001).

The model is based on the concepts of *competence measure* and *competence map* used in Confessore, Liotta, and Rismondo (2006) to solve the problem of assigning to collaborative enterprises the activities required for carrying out an emerging business process. In particular, the competence measure of an enterprise is defined as the distance between the competencies required for executing a given activity and the capability of the enterprise to perform the activity.

We provide a Multi Agent System -MAS- (see Jennings & Wooldridge, 1995) model consisting of a set of agents that encapsulate the behavior of different entities within the real system (Tah, 2005).

This model represents a territorial system in which the actors share information about their degree of competence in doing the activities without revealing private data. In fact, the competence represents an aggregate data based on a local evaluation, and all the actors measure themselves with respect to the same set of competencies given by the competence map (see also Hammami, Burlat, & Champagne, 2003). On the basis of the previous MAS, the new model considers new agent typologies and new features for the decision-making processes in order to allow the evaluation of the impact of new configurations of the network

with respect to key performance indicators. The new configurations of the network are generated whenever emerging business processes and possible public funding (e.g., as calls for National and European research project) arise, and it is required to define the roles and responsibilities through the actors. Our approach is to consider the execution of business process as distributed problem solving carried out by co-operating agents (Kuhlmann, Lamping, & Massow, 1998). In particular, the paper shows that decisions making processes are always less dependent on a single subject but are the outcome of different decisions of several agents acting in the same system. Specifically in this model, as suggested by Vanderhaeghen and Loos (2007), two decisional levels (global and local) are considered.

The rest of the paper is organized as follows: the next section describes the scenario of model application; the third section introduces the static model based on multi agent theory and in the fourth the dynamics of this model is described. Finally, the last sections are committed to model validation and conclusion.

THE SCENARIO

The paper provides a model for the understanding of the dynamics of a collaborative network. The network is represented by a coordinator and private/public actors. The coordinator makes decisions for increasing the territorial attractive capacity with respect to new investments and new projects. Its main tasks are:

1. The monitoring of new business opportunities by doing intensive market analysis. The outputs are: the proposal of activities to the agents in order to meet the business opportunities; the identification of new possible attractive industrial sectors that could be exploited with the actual territorial resources;

2. The monitoring of call for National and International research projects. The output is to suggest possible combinations of actors in order to create the suitable composition of partners meeting the call requirements;

3. Providing to the actors the competence map in order to meet both the business and funding opportunities while using a competence-based criterion as a way for comparing the actors' capabilities.

Due to the competence-based criterion, each private actor has the main goal of increasing its competencies. In fact, this condition allows it to obtain an increasing number of activities of an emerging business process or it allows becoming an eligible actor for a research project as a partner. A greater number of activities and participation in research projects, generate greater revenue for the private actor that could be invested again for increasing the competencies by generating a positive feedback. From the public actors' side, the competence-based criterion stimulates the collaboration and the growth of the territorial innovation capability. In fact, the systematic participation in research projects in collaboration with other actors allows to manage new funds useful for undertaking innovative research programs on behalf of the overall territorial system and for supporting the knowledge transfer to enterprises, through the collaboration.

Summarizing, the competence-based criterion driving either the business process activities assignment or the public funding exploitation, generates a process of continuous development of the territorial competencies, furthers the collaboration between public and private actors, and increases the knowledge and technology transfer from public actors to private ones. Moreover, the growth of investments pulls new research projects and business processes by attracting new enterprises and new public actors that are motivated to join the collaboration or to work in the profitable territory.

For measuring the benefits given by the competence-based collaborative network, the following Social Wellness indicators are suggested:

- Number of new research projects/business processes approved and finished. These indicators represent a measure of the territory attraction with respect to research project and business processes, respectively.

- Number of new competencies characterizing the territory. The set of competencies is not static since new competencies can be required, and others can be no longer useful to realize a research project or a business process. This indicator is useful for understanding how the network evolves with respect to the competencies.

- Number of actors operating on the territory divided into public and private ones. It indicates the development of the collaborative network with respect to actors' composition.

MULTI AGENT SYSTEM

The MAS is composed of classes of interacting agents each one having its local information and goals. In this setting, the decision-making processes and the competencies characterize in a specific way each one of the different agents working in the system. In particular, it is assumed that the agents are being represented by three distinct typologies: (*i*) the Territorial Agent (TA), (*ii*) the Enterprise Agent (EA), and (*iii*) the Public Agent (PA). TA represents the coordinator, while each EA (e.g., representing a private company), and each PA (e.g., representing a public institutions as research centers, laboratories etc.) interacts with the other agents in order to pursue its goals. The following notations are used throughout the paper:

- Let $E = \{e_1, e_2, ..., e_z\}$ and $P = \{p_1, p_2, ..., p_r\}$ be the sets of z EAs, and r PAs, respectively. Let $M = E \cup P$ be the set of $z + r$ agents.

- Let $A = \{a_1, a_2, ..., a_k\}$ be the set of k activities in which a business process or a research project can be decomposed.
- Let $C = \{c_1, c_2, ..., c_w\}$ be the competence map, that is a set of w competencies globally accepted by all the agents.
- Let $C_1, ..., C_k$ be the k sub-sets representing the competencies required for the execution of each activity (i.e., for all $a_i \in A$ a sub-set $C_i \subseteq C$ is given).
- Let $\tilde{C}_j \subseteq C$ be the z sub-sets representing the competencies of each EA and PA.

Next, the decisional processes are explained.

Territorial Agent

According to the described scenario, TA acts as a coordinator and has to solve two main decisional problems, as follows:

- The Assignment Problem (AP) in order to assign each activity to exactly one of the EA.
- The Agent Composition Problem (ACP), that is, the problem of defining the best composition of agents with respect to a call for research project, namely the one having the maximum probability with respect to the funding requirements. The ACP can be modeled as a special case of the AP.

The Assignment Problem

The linear Assignment Problem (AP) is one of the basic and fundamental models in operation research, computer science and discrete mathematics. In its most familiar interpretation, it answers the question of finding an assignment of n workers to n jobs that has the lowest cost, if the cost of assigning worker i to task j equals

c_{ij} (Krokhmal & Pardalos, 2009). Hereby we assimilate the workers to EAs and the task to a set of k activities, minimizing the value ω_{ij}.

By solving the Assignment Problem, TA obtains the efficient allocation of the activities of a business process to the EAs. The values ω_{ij} representing the capability of $e_j \in E$ with respect to the execution of the activity $a_i \in A$ are given. These values are provided by each EA and are computed as described in the next section *Competence Evaluation*.

Given the binary decision variable x_{ij} equal to 1 if the activity a_i is assigned to the enterprise agent e_j, and 0 otherwise, for all $e_j \in E$, $a_i \in A$, the goal is to minimize the value of

$$z = \sum_{i \in A} \sum_{j \in E} \omega_{ij} x_{ij} \qquad (1)$$

subject to the constraint that each activity can be assigned to exactly one enterprise and all activities have to be assigned:

$$\sum_{j \in M \cap E} x_{ij} = 1, \text{ for all } a_i \in A \qquad (2)$$

In this, the specific problem of the second traditional constraint of the PA is not present because each EA can accept and execute more than one activity.

The Agents Composition Problem

By solving the Agent Composition Problem, TA obtains the efficient allocation of the activities of a research project to the EAs and PAs. The ACP can be referred to an AP considering further constraints modeling the quality of the agent's composition. In this setting, the PAs have to provide the value ω_{ij} representing their capability with respect to the execution of the activity $a_i \in A$ as well as the EAs.

TA has to minimize the value of

$$z = \sum_{i \in A} \sum_{j \in M} \omega_{ij} x_{ij} \qquad (3)$$

subject to the constraint that each activity can be assigned to exactly one agent and all activities have to be assigned:

$$\sum_{j \in M} x_{ij} = 1 \text{ for all } a_i \in A \quad (4)$$

Given the solution of the decisional problem and due to the fact that the probability of the project proposal acceptance increases with respect to the compositions of the agent in terms of typology, for all $a_i \in A$, TA has to evaluate the composition quality (Q) by computing the following values:

$$S_E = \sum_{j \in E} x_{ij} \quad (5)$$

$$S_P = \sum_{j \in P} x_{ij} \quad (6)$$

$$S = S_E + S_P \quad (7)$$

$$Q = 1 - [\, |S_E/S - EA_{\%}| + |S_P/S - PA_{\%}| \,] \quad (8)$$

where, S_E and S_P represent the number of agents belonging to the solution for each typology (i.e., $S_E \leq z, S_P \leq r$), $EA_{\%}$ and $PA_{\%}$ represent the percentage of the agent's typologies respecting the call for project. The quality value Q is in [0, 1], and the maximum value correspond to the solution in which the composition of agents exactly respects the call for project requirement. Although these constraints represent a model simplification, they aim at give a preliminary description of the MAS behavior with respect to the research project opportunities. Considering this aspect, the TA can decide, with respect to single funding call, to impose a specific composition of the team detriment of global competence level, or maximize the global competence rendering more flexible the partnership arrangement.

Enterprise Agent

Each EA has to: (*i*) be able to define its degree of competence with respect to the competencies required by the activities of a business process; (*ii*) solve the decisional problem of choosing which typology of investment to select in order to increase its competence, that can be referable to a special case of the Capital Budgeting Problem (Sassano, 2004); (*iii*) decide if a coordinator proposal can be profitable or not.

Competence Evaluation

Each EA has to evaluate its degree of competence with respect to each activity, thus it has to define the value ω_{ij}. Let $C = \{c_1, c_2, ..., c_w\}$ be the competence map, that is a set of w competencies globally accepted by the agents.

The following parameters can be introduced as shown in Confessore et al. (2006):

- Each sub-set C_i can be represented by a binary vector $u(a_i)$ composed of w elements, where the h-th element (i.e., $u_h(a_i)$) is equal to 1 if activity a_i requires the competence c_h for being executed, and 0 otherwise.

- Each sub-set $\tilde{C}_j$ is modeled as a vector $v(e_j)$ composed of w elements, where the h-th element (i.e., $v_h(e_j)$) is equal to 0 if the agent e_j does not have the competence c_h, and is equal to a positive value ε_{jh} otherwise. In particular, ε_{jh} represents the degree of competence of e_j w.r.t. competence h. The maximum value of ε_{jh} is 1.

The definition of the two vectors $u(a_i)$, and $v(e_j)$ allows to synthesize two relevant information: (*i*) which agent has the competencies for carrying out one activity; (*ii*) which level of performance each enterprise could deploy in executing a specific activity. The vector $g(a_i, e_j) = \min\{u_h(a_i), v_h(e_j)\}$, extracts from vector $v(e_j)$ exactly those elements that match the corresponding elements of $u(a_i)$ having positive values. In other words, we catch the competencies of e_j with respect to the ones required by a given activity a_i. The value of ω_{ij}

is obtained by computing the Euclidean distance between $g(a_i, e_j)$, and $u(a_i)$:

$$\omega_{ij} = euc(g(a_i, e_j), u(a_i)) \tag{9}$$

that represents the capability of e_j with respect to the execution of the activity a_i; clearly, being the values of $g(a_i, e_j)$ and of $u(a_i)$ ranging from 0 and 1 then $\omega_{i,j} \in [0, 1]$.

Capital Budgeting Problem

The Capital Budgeting (CB) is the planning process used to determine a firm's long term investments through mathematical programming techniques. The CB deals with the question of the best investment to undertake, the amount to spend and the sources of financing the investments (Kalu, 1999). The basic assumption is that the sum of the benefits of individual projects maximizes the total welfare of the organization. The problem faced in this context is to select the investments maximizing the total return in term of competence while respecting the budget constraints (Baffo, Confessore, & Rismondo, 2007). The best solution is the one producing the maximum competence increment. The following parameters are introduced:

- Let L be the set of possible investments.
- Let $Q(e_j)_{[h,i]}$ be a matrix of parameters where the generic element $q_{hi}(e_j)$ represents the return of competence $c_h \in C$ for $e_j \in E$, with respect to the investment $i \in L$.
- Let ε_{jh} be a positive value in $[0, 1]$ representing the degree of competence of the enterprise e_j with respect to a specific $c_h \in C$.
- A budget $B(e_j)$ representing a monetary value, for all $e_j \in E$.
- Cost of investment $b_i(e_j)$, for all $i \in L$, and $e_j \in E$.

The methodology proposed for generating the matrix's data is inspired by the logic of Analytic

Table 1. Reference Scale for Competence's Increments

Local Weights	Competence's Variance
0-0.2	0%
0.2-0.25	10%
0.25-0.3	15%
0.3-0.5	30%
0.5-0.7	50%
0.7-0.85	70%
0.85-1	90%
1	100%

Hierarchy Process (AHP) (Saaty, 1980). It is a structured technique for helping people deal with complex decisions. Firstly, it decomposes the decision problem into a hierarchy of more easily comprehended sub-problems, each of which can be analyzed independently. Once the hierarchy is built, the decision makers systematically evaluate its various elements, comparing them to one another in pairs. The AHP converts these evaluations into numerical values that can be processed and compared over the entire range of the problem. A numerical weight or priority is derived for each element of the hierarchy, allowing diverse and often incommensurable elements to be compared to one another in a rational and consistent way (Saaty, 2008). The aim of applying this methodology in this context is to obtain an estimate of possible competence's increase against the activation of one or more investments. Then, the values found as a result of comparison to one another in the sub-form of normalized vectors, have been compared with a reference scale that quantify competence's increment with respect to the weight caused by AHP application.

In the Table 1 an exemplar of the reference scale is provided.

These data are the input to the Capital Budget Problem that can be modeled.

Given the binary decision variable x_i equal to 1 if the investment i is selected, and 0 otherwise, the goal is to maximize the value

$$\sum_{h \in C} \sum_{i \in L} q_{hi} x_i \qquad (10)$$

while respecting the constraints as follows:

$$\sum_{i \in L} b_i x_i \leq B(e_j), \text{ for all } e_j \in E \qquad (11)$$

$$\sum_{i \in L} (\varepsilon_{jh} + q_{hi}(e_j)) \leq 1 \text{ for all } e_j \in E, c_h \in C \qquad (12)$$

The constraint (12) models the idea that for each competence there exists a threshold value equal to 1. This value acts as the maximum value for doing one best activity given the common scale of benchmark values.

Once the decisional problem is solved, the EAs update their competencies, that is $\varepsilon_{jh}' = \varepsilon_{jh} + q_{hi}(e_j)$ if x_i equal to 1, thus the investment $i \in L$ is selected, for all $e_j \in E$ and $c_h \in C$. It is worth noting that the system dynamics is based on the hypothesis that if the actors do not invest in a competence for long time, the value ε_{jh} decreases.

Projects Participation Evaluation

Each EA decides to participate in a business process or a research project based on the following data:

- Capacity availability.
- Profitability with respect to the increment of the degree of competencies.
- Profitability with respect to the collaboration. For instance the collaboration with other actors could remain also when the project ends.
- Project relevance at scientific and research levels.

Public Agent

Each PA has the task of declaring to the coordinator TA its competence values with respect to the competence map provided by TA.

Competence Evaluation

The PAs measure their competencies with respect to the ones required for the activities execution similar to the enterprise agents.

Project Participation Evaluation

The PAs have to evaluate their competencies in order to decide if it is profitable or not to participate in a research project with respect to the following data:

- Capacity availability.
- Return on specific competencies.
- Profitability with respect to the collaboration. For instance, the collaboration with other actors could remain also when the project ends.
- Project relevance at scientific and research levels.
- Return on knowledge transfer with other PAs or EAs.

THE MULTI AGENT SYSTEM DYNAMICS

This section summarizes the main features of the interaction protocol exploited by the agents, then defines the dynamics of the MAS. It is supposed that the agents react in response to two possible events, namely, an emerging business or a funding opportunity arises. The result of each decisional problem contributes to the definition of a new system configuration (see Figure 1).

Figure 1. Protocol of communication

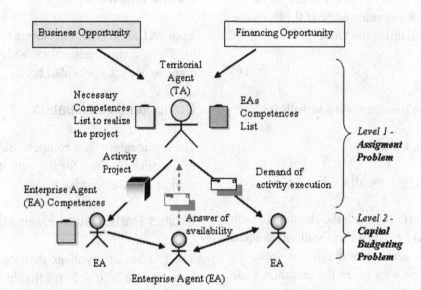

Whenever a business opportunity occurs, two levels of interaction between the agents can be defined.

First level: The information flow is from TA to the EAs and PAs and vice versa.

Information Domain: TA manages a list of codified competencies (i.e. the competence map, globally accepted by the agents), and a list of agents operating in the system. TA decomposes the business process into a set of activities, and defines the subset of competencies required for each activity.

Goal: TA has to allocate each activity of the business process according to competence-based criterion, thus maximizing the total degree of competencies for realizing the project (see section "*The Assignment Problem*").

Communication Protocol: TA communicates to the EAs the set of activities and the related set of competencies required for performing them. Each EA then communicates to TA an aggregate data describing its level of competencies (see section *Competence Evaluation*).

Second level: It corresponds to the EA's actions in response to the business opportunities.

Since at the first level a TA decides by using the competence-based criterion, each EA has to improve its degree of competence by selecting possible investment.

Information Domain: Each EA knows the competence map.

Goal: Each EA solves the problem of selecting from a set of profitable investment the sub-set of them maximizing the return of competence while satisfying its budget (see section "*Capital Budgeting Problem*").

Communication Protocol: Each EA communicates its availability in executing the activities, or its degree of competencies in order to stimulate new collaborations.

Funding Opportunities

Also in this scenario, whenever a funding opportunity occurs, two levels of interaction between the agents can be defined. In this paper, the funding opportunities arise when the TA observes a call for research project.

First level: The information flow is from TA to the EAs and PAs. It is important to note that for

Table 2. u(a)

	c_1	c_2	c_3	c_4	c_5	c_6	c_7
a_1	1	1	1	1	0	0	0
a_2	0	0	1	0	0	0	0
a_3	1	0	1	0	0	0	1
a_4	0	1	0	1	1	1	1
a_5	1	1	0	1	1	0	0
a_6	0	1	0	1	0	0	0
a_7	0	1	1	1	0	0	0
a_8	0	1	0	0	1	1	1
a_9	0	0	1	0	0	1	0
a_{10}	0	0	1	0	1	0	0

the EAs the participation in a research project can be viewed as an alternative profitable investment, while for each PA it represents certainly the best way for increasing and enlarging its competencies and attracting new scientific and industrial collaborations.

Information Domain: TA manages a list of codified competencies, a list of agents acting on the system. Furthermore, TA knows the competencies that best suite a call for project, and codifies the composition of agent typologies that have the greater probability of obtaining the financial fund approval.

Goal: TA has to decide the best composition of agents.

Communication Protocol: TA contacts the agents for proposing the project participation, and solves the decisional problem in section "*The Agents Composition Problem*".

Second level: it corresponds to the EA and PA actions in response to the funding opportunities.

Information Domain: each agent knows its degree of competencies.

Goal: Both EAs and PAs aim at carrying out the activities of the research project by collaborating.

Communication Protocol: The EAs and PAs response to the TA request by communicating their availability to execute the project activities. If they decide to participate then communicate to TA their competencies. The probability of obtaining the public funding will be a function of the agent's composition and on the total degree of competencies. The agents collaborate during the project duration and they have a return of competencies due to the research project collaboration.

MODEL VALIDATION

In the preliminary test, the new business process, new research project opportunities, and the map of codified competencies are generated at random. This condition does not represent a limitation since the next step will be the customization of the presented MAS with respect to a real scenario. The assignment problem has a trivial resolution applying the formula (1). The CBP is solved by a genetic algorithm implementation (Goldberg, 1989).

In the following tables (Tables 2 and 3), what happens in 3 different time slots for 3 enterprises that act in a hypothetical territory with 7 competencies is shown.

1. t=0, TA assigns the activities to EAs based on the data reported in Table 2 and Table 3.

Table 3. $v_h(e_j)$

	e_1	e_2	e_3
budget	407	225	725
c_1	0.1495	0.5840	0.000
c_2	0.7747	0.0000	0.0000
c_3	0.2419	0.0000	0.0000
c_4	0.6431	0.4161	0.6967
c_5	0.7330	0.6644	0.0461
c_6	0.0000	0.0000	0.5583
c_7	0.0000	0.0000	0.0000

Table 4. $Q(e_1)_{hi}$

$Q(e_1)_{hi}$	0	1	2	3	4
1	0.015	0.000	0.000	0.022	0.015
2	0.000	0.000	0.000	0.116	0.116
3	0.024	0.000	0.024	0.036	0.000
4	0.193	0.000	0.000	0.000	0.000
5	0.000	0.110	0.073	0.000	0.000
6	0.000	0.000	0.000	0.000	0.000
7	0.000	0.000	0.000	0.000	0.000

Table 5. $Q(e_2)_{hi}$

$Q(e_2)_{hi}$	0	1	2	3	4
1	0.000	0.058	0.175	0.000	0.000
2	0.000	0.000	0.000	0.000	0.000
3	0.000	0.000	0.000	0.000	0.000
4	0.000	0.000	0.000	0.062	0.062
5	0.066	0.000	0.066	0.100	0.000
6	0.000	0.000	0.000	0.000	0.000
7	0.000	0.000	0.000	0.000	0.000

The result of the first assignment is the following:

- the activities a_{11} and a_{12} are assigned to e_1;
- all other activities are assigned to e_3;
- no activity is assigned to e_2.

2. t=1, the enterprises solve the CBP, selecting the investment most profitable with respect to their own competence level.

In Tables 4, 5 and 6, the increments of competence for each enterprise and for every investment are shown.

Table 6. $Q(e_3)_{hi}$

$Q(e_3)_{hi}$	0	1	2	3	4
1	0.000	0.000	0.000	0.000	0.000
2	0.000	0.000	0.000	0.000	0.000
3	0.000	0.000	0.000	0.000	0.000
4	0.104	0.000	0.000	0.070	0.070
5	0.000	0.007	0.050	0.000	0.000
6	0.056	0.056	0.056	0.000	0.000
7	0.000	0.000	0.000	0.000	0.000

Table 7. $v_h(e)$ updated

	e_1	e_2	e_3
c_1	0.1860	0.8170	0.0000
c_2	0.8900	0.0000	0.0000
c_3	0.3260	0.0000	0.0000
c_4	0.8360	0.5400	0.9400
c_5	0.9160	0.8960	0.0575
c_6	0.0000	0.0000	0.7250
c_7	0.0000	0.0000	0,0000

Solving the CBP, the solution for which investment has to be selected by each enterprise is the following:

- e_1 will invest in the projects i_0, i_1, i_2, i_3;
- e_2 will invest in all projects;
- e_3 will invest in all projects.

The updated competencies for each enterprise are shown in Table 7.

3. t=3, TA re-assigns new activities to enterprises having updated competencies. The solution of the AP at this time is the following:
   ○ the activities a_9 and a_{11} are assigned to e_1;
   ○ the activity a_6 is assigned to e_2;
   ○ the activities a_4, a_5, a_7, a_8, a_{10}, a_{12} and a_{13} are assigned to e_3.

The assignment is changed based on the new competencies, that is based on the decisions taken by other agents.

This simple example, though doesn't represent the dynamics of the whole agent system, is useful to validate the functioning of the model with respect to a local system development.

CONCLUSION

This paper analyzes a competence-based collaborative network, identifying roles, decisions making processes and the interaction protocol between the actors. The model is based on the Multi Agent System paradigm and it is driven by the competence concept.

Even if the model does not capture all the aspects of the collaboration, it represents a further step toward the representation of the collaborative networks, and the understanding of what and how a network of actors has benefits from the collaboration. Actually, both the dynamics and the decisional problems are faced by the implementation of ad hoc algorithms. In the future, our plan is to add new features to the MAS in order to suggest the model as a valid way for studying the complex connections between collaborative actors. It will be implemented using a real case-study as initially carried out in Baffo, Dedonno, Confessore, and Rismondo (2006).

REFERENCES

Baffo, I., Confessore, G., & Rismondo, S. (2007). *Uno strumento di modellazione e simulazione della dinamica di una rete di attori operanti in un territorio*. Paper presented at the XXVIII Italian Conference of Regional Science.

Baffo, I., Dedonno, L., Confessore, G., & Rismondo, S. (2006). *Descrizione ex-post di una rete relazionale territoriale e realizzazione di uno strumento per la simulazione dinamica ex-ante*. Paper presented at the XXVII Italian Conference of Regional Science.

Camarinha-Matos, L. M., & Afsarmanesh, H. (2004). Towards next business models. In L. Camarinha-Matos & L. M. Afsarmanesh (Eds.), *Collaborative networked organizations: A research agenda for emerging business models* (pp. 3-6). Boston: Springer.

Camarinha-Matos, L. M., & Afsarmanesh, H. (2006). A modelling framework for collaborative networked organizations. In L. Camarinha-Matos, L. M. Afsarmanesh, & H. M. Ollus (Eds.), *Network-centric collaboration and supporting frameworks* (Vol. 224, pp. 3-14). Boston: Springer.

Confessore, G., Liotta, G., & Rismondo, S. (2006). A new model for achieving value added goals in a collaborative industrial scenario. In L. Camarinha-Matos, L. M. Afsarmanesh, & H. M. Ollus (Eds.), *Network-centric collaboration and supporting frameworks* (Vol. 224, pp. 121-128). Boston: Springer.

Goldberg, D. (1989). *Genetic algorithms in search, optimization, and machine learning*. Reading, MA: Addison-Wesley.

Hammami, A., Burlat, P., & Champagne, J. P. (2003). Evaluating orders allocation within networks of firms. *International Journal of Production Economics*, *86*, 233–249. doi:10.1016/S0925-5273(03)00066-5

Jennings, N. R., & Wooldridge, M. (1995). Applying agent technology. *Applied Artificial Intelligence*, *9*, 357–369. doi:10.1080/08839519508945480

Kalu, T. C. U. (1999). Capital budgeting under uncertainty. *International Journal of Production Economics*, *58*, 235–251. doi:10.1016/S0925-5273(98)00121-2

Krokhmal, P. A., & Pardalos, P. M. (2009). Random assignment problems. *European Journal of Operational Research*, *194*, 1–17. doi:10.1016/j.ejor.2007.11.062

Kuhlmann, T., Lamping, R., & Massow, C. (1998). Intelligent decision support. *Journal of Materials Processing Technology*, *76*, 257–20. doi:10.1016/S0924-0136(97)00357-9

Molina-Morales, F. X. (2001). European industrial district: Influence of geographic concentration on performance of the firm. *Journal of International Management*, *7*, 277–294. doi:10.1016/S1075-4253(01)00048-5

Saaty, T. L. (1980). *The analytic hierarchy process: planning, priority setting, resource allocation*. New York: McGraw Hill.

Saaty, T. L. (2008). Relative measurement and its generalization in decision making: Why pairwise comparisons are central in mathematics for the measurement of intangible factors - the analytic hierarchy/network process. *RACSAM (Review of the Royal Spanish Academy of Sciences, Series A, Mathematics), 102*(2), 251-318.

Sassano, A. (2004), *Modelli e algoritmi della ricerca operativa.* Venice, Italy: Franco Angeli.

Tah, J. H. M. (2005). Towards an agent-based construction supply network modelling and simulation platform. *Automation in Construction, 14*, 353–359. doi:10.1016/j.autcon.2004.08.003

Venderhaeghen, D., & Loos, P. (2007). Distributed model management platform for cross-enterprise business process management in virtual enterprise networks. *Journal of Intelligent Manufacturing, 18*, 553–559. doi:10.1007/s10845-007-0060-6

This work was previously published in International Journal of Intelligent Information Technologies, Volume 6, Issue 1, edited by Vijayan Sugumaran, pp. 18-30, copyright 2010 by IGI Publishing (an imprint of IGI Global).

Chapter 3
Algorithm for Decision Procedure in Temporal Logic Treating Uncertainty, Plausibility, Knowledge and Interacting Agents

V. Rybakov
Manchester Metropolitan University, UK

ABSTRACT

Our paper studies a logic UIA_{LTL}, which is a combination of the linear temporal logic LTL, a multi-agent logic with operation for passing knowledge via agents' interaction, and a suggested logic based on operation of logical uncertainty. The logical operations of UIA_{LTL} also include (together with operations from LTL) operations of strong and weak until, agents' knowledge operations, operation of knowledge via interaction, operation of logical uncertainty, the operations for environmental and global knowledge. UIA_{LTL} is defined as a set of all formulas valid at all Kripke-Hintikka like models N_C. Any frame N_C represents possible unbounded (in time) computation with multi-processors (parallel computational units) and agents' channels for connections between computational units. The main aim of our paper is to determine possible ways for computation logical laws of UIA_{LTL}. Principal problems we are dealing with are decidability and the satisfiability problems for UIA_{LTL}. We find an algorithm which recognizes theorems of UIA_{LTL} (so we show that UIA_{LTL} is decidable) and solves satisfiability problem for UIA_{LTL}. As an instrument we use reduction of formulas to rules in the reduced normal form and a technique to contract models N_C to special non-UIA_{LTL}-models, and, then, verification of validity these rules in models of bounded size. The paper uses standard results from non-classical logics based on Kripke-Hintikka models.

DOI: 10.4018/978-1-4666-0158-1.ch003

INTRODUCTION, INITIAL DISCUSSION, AIMS

Temporal, modal and multi-agents' logics motivated in AI and CS are popular areas nowadays. They are intended to describe reasoning about knowledge, properties of computational processes and basic formal laws inherent to the domain areas. Various formalizations of *uncertainty* in logical framework are reasonably well considered in recent publications (Crestani & Lalmas, 2001; Elvang-Goransson, Krausel, & Fox, 2006; Kaelbling, Cassandra, & Kurien, 1996; Lang, 2000; Mundici, 2000; van Rijsbergen, 2000) attempts to undertake formalizations in logical framework for *plausibility* are also known (Babenyshev & Rybakov, 2008). Multi-agent logics are especially broadly represented in contemporary research in AI and CS (Bordini, Fisher, Visser, & Woolridge, 2004; Dix, Fisher, Levesque, & Sterling, 2004; Fisher, 2005; Hendler, 2001; Kacprzak, 2003; van der Hoek & Woolridge, 2003). Traditionally, multi-agent system is a system composed of multiple interacting intelligent agents (though sometimes agents are considered as autonomous); multi-agent systems can be used to solve problems which are difficult or impossible for an individual agent or monolithic system to solve. Examples of problems which are appropriate to multi-agent systems research include online trading, disaster response, and modelling social structures.

Often multi-agent logics use technique from multi-modal logics (Fagin, Halpern, Moses, & Vardi, 1995; Fagin, Geanakoplos, Halpern, & Vardi, 1999; Halpern & Shore, 2004), applying modal-like operations K_i responsible for knowledge of individual agents. Any operation K_i usually behaves as S5-modality, and, therefore, technique based on Kripke multi-models may be broadly used. The exact nature of the agents is a matter of some controversy. They are sometimes claimed to be autonomous, though, in fact, autonomy is seldom desired; instead interdependent systems are needed. In particular, therefore, we intend to consider agents which may interact and pass knowledge to each other.

Another related area in logical research from AI and CS is temporal logics. One of important applications such logics in CS is specification formalism for reactive systems. Temporal logics were suggested for distinguishing properties of programs in late 1970s (Pnueli, 1977; Pnueli & Kesten, 2002). The temporal framework most used is linear-time propositional temporal logic LTL, which has been studied from various viewpoints of its application (Clark, Grumberg, & Hamaguchi, 1994; Manna & Pnueli, 1992, 1995). Temporal logic has numerous applications to safety, liveness and fairness, to various problems arising in computing (Barringer, Fisher, Gabbay & Gough, 1999). Model checking for LTL formed a direction in logic in computer science, which uses, in particular, applications of automata theory (Vardi, 1994, 1998). Temporal logics themselves can be considered as a special case of hybrid logics, e.g., as a bimodal logic with some laws imposed on interaction of modalities to imitate the flow of time. Mathematical theory devoted to study of various aspects of interaction for temporal operations (e.g., axiomatizations of temporal logics) and to construction of effective semantic theory based on Kripke/Hintikka-like models and temporal Boolean algebras, formed a highly technical branch in non-classical logics (Gabbay & Hodkinson, 1990; Goldblatt, 1992, 2003; Hodkinson, 2000; van Benthem 1983, 1991; van Benthem & Bergstra, 1994). Computational and relative problems in non-classical logics themselves formed a highly technical branch in contemporary research (Maksimova, 2003, 2006).

In our paper we would like to consider a logic called UIA_{LTL}, which is a hybrid of LTL, multi-agent logic with interacting agents, and logic with *uncertainty* and *plausibility* operations. Such logic has all expressive powers of background logics and, therefore, may model all inherent properties, and besides describe possible interaction of combined logical operations. Actually, it is an open question which basic logic can be put in the background to develop multi-agent systems. There are many approaches, but, if the logic used as the basis is very expressive - the undecidability phenomenon can happen (cf. Kacprzak, 2003, with reduction the decidability to the domino problem). For some combinations of the linear temporal logic LTL with multi-agents' systems results on undecidability are also known (cf. for instance, van der Meyden & Shilov, 1999). If we are especially interested in decidability then, still, the background logic must me expressive enough to handle properties interesting for AI and CS community. Thus, we would like to keep a proper balance of desirable properties (such as expressiveness and decidability).

The logic UIA_{LTL} we suggest, is a combination of the linear temporal logic LTL, a multi-agent logic with an operation for passing knowledge via agents' interaction, and a suggested logic based on operations of logical *uncertainty and plausibility*. The language of UIA_{LTL} includes, together with logical operations form LTL, operations of strong and weak *Until*, agents' knowledge operations, operations of knowledge via interaction, the operations for environmental and global knowledge, and *logical uncertainty* and *plausibility* operations. UIA_{LTL} is defined as a set of all formulas valid at all Kripke-Hintikka like models N_C. Any frame N_C represents possible unbounded (in time) computation with multi-possessors (parallel computational units) and agents' channels for connections between computational units. Main problems we are dealing with are the decidability and the satisfiability problems for UIA_{LTL} So, the aim of our paper is to suggest an algorithm which can compute true and satisfiable statements in a UIA_{LTL}. By developed in the paper technique, we find an algorithm which recognizes theorems of UIA_{LTL} (so we show that UIA_{LTL} is decidable), and solves satisfiability problem for UIA_{LTL}. As an instrument we use (i) reduction of formulas to rules in the reduced normal form, (ii) a technique to contract models N_C to special non-UIA_{LTL}-models, and,

(iii) verification of validity these rules in models of bounded size. We also note that some definitions for environmental knowledge and global knowledge (in this framework) are expressible via time operations of kind Until, and discuss possible variations of the implemented logical language.

This paper actually is based on (and extends) our previous research published in (Rybakov, 2007b, 2008); it primarily uses and extends technique from the paper (Rybakov, 2008) and inherits general structure of proofs from (Rybakov, 2008). The main distinction here is we include in the logical language operations of logical uncertainty and plausibility (to model human reasoning in changing environment) and study their interconnections in chosen framework. Though the prime aim is as before to find algorithms solving satisfiability— we feel it is a leading direction in logic for AI and CS (to find deciding algorithms). Though our results are only theoretical value, we do not implement our algorithms via prepared software.

The paper uses standard results from non-classical logics based upon Kripke-Hintikka like models. Some familiarity with this technique is desirable for readers, though we give below all necessary definitions and notation to follow the presentation of the results, and the paper, in this respect, is self contained.

Preliminaries, Notation, Logical Language

We first recall necessary definitions, facts and notation. We need to describe mathematical semantic models for our logic. These models are Kripke/Hintikka-like frames

$$N_C := \langle \cup_{i \in N} C(i), R, R_1, ..., R_m, Next \rangle,$$

which are tuples, where N is the set of natural numbers, $C(i)$ are some disjoint nonempty sets $(C(i) \cap C(j) = \varnothing$ if $i \neq j)$, $R, R_1,...,R_m$ are binary accessibility relations on $\cup_{i \in N} C(i)$. The relation

R represents linear flow of time: for all elements a and b from the set $\cup_{i \in N} C(i)$,

$$\forall a, b \in \cup_{i \in N} C(i)[aRb \Leftrightarrow [a \in C(i) \, and \, b \in C(j) \, and \, i \leq j]].$$

Relations R_j represent agents' accessibility relations in time clusters $C(i)$: any R_j is a reflexive, transitive and symmetric relation, and

$$\forall a, b \in \cup_{i \in N} C(i)[aR_j b \rightarrow [a, b \in C(i) \, for some \, i)]].$$

The binary relation *Next* distinguishes worlds of neighbouring time clusters:

$$\forall a, b \in \cup_{i \in N} C(i), [a \, Next \, b \Leftrightarrow [\exists i \, ((a \in C(i)) \, and \, (b \in C(i+1))]],$$

i.e., *a Next b* says that *b* is situated in time cluster next to the time cluster containing *a*.

An informal meaning of the frame N_C is: it represents possible unbounded (in time) computation with multi-processors, that is, any $i \in N$ (any natural number i) simulated time tick i, any $C(i)$ consists of processors (computational units) evolved in computation at tick time i. Any R_j is an accessibility relation for the agent j between these computational units. R is the accessibility relation in N_C in time from now to future (as it is specified above, it is a linear relation). Within any $C(i)$ (which means in the same time moment) all computational units ($u \in C(i)$) are mutually accessible by time (but not by agents accessibility relations).

Properties of computation are modelled (rather just encoded) by sets of propositions (propositional letters) P, any $p \in P$ simply names a property (like p = the computational thread t(p) is faulty terminated, etc.). For any N_C and a set of propositions P, a model based on N_C and a valuation V *for letters from P* is the tuple

$$M := \langle \cup_{i \in N} C(i), R, R_1, ..., R_m, Next, V \rangle,$$

where V is a mapping of P in the set of all subsets of $\cup_{i \in N} C(i)$, i.e. $\forall p \in P, V(p) \subseteq \cup_{i \in N} C(i)$. We aim to model a logic of reasoning about properties for computations in chosen mathematical models. As always, we have to consider Boolean combinations of properties and implement temporal operations.

In addendum, we would like to include in our language operations for agents' knowledge and operations for determination of logical uncertainty. As we know, standard truth functional binary logic usually only makes use of two state symbols, true or false, to represent the degree of truth of a meaning. Yet even Aristotle realized that any binary logic that divided meanings into either true or false had its limitations. And, to addendum to multi-valued logics (which consider intermediate truth values between true and false), logics where truth values may be not always computable, but sometimes just to be *uncertain* are plausible approach to represent truth values of statements. So, it is relevant to consider how we could express uncertainty of statements in models, which are proposed by us above.

To built a propositional logical language to express reasoning, we use a (potentially infinite) set of propositional letters P and following symbols for logical operations: Boolean operations $\wedge, \vee, \rightarrow, \neg$, temporal binary operations: U (until), U_w (weak until) and U_s (strong until), and the unary operation *Next*. Also it includes (unary) operations K_j $1 \leq j \leq m$ for agents' knowledge, and additional unary operations CK_L (local knowledge), CK_G (global knowledge), **IntK** (interactive knowledge), and **Pl** (plausible), **N** (next time). To handle uncertainty we add the (unary) operation **Unc**. Formation rules for formulas are as usual: any propositional letter p is a formula, if φ and ψ are formulas then

$$\varphi \wedge \psi, \varphi \vee \psi, \varphi \rightarrow \psi, \neg \varphi;$$

$$\varphi U \psi, \varphi \, U_s \, \psi, \varphi \, U_w \, \psi, N \varphi;$$

$CK_L\varphi$, $CK_G\varphi$, $\mathbf{K_j}\,\varphi$, $\mathbf{IntK}\,\varphi$,

$\mathbf{Unc}\,\varphi$ and $\mathbf{Pl}\,\varphi$

are also formulas. Informal (intended) meaning of the operations is as follows.

$\mathbf{Unc}\,\varphi$ means that the statement φ is *uncertain* in the current state of the current time cluster.

$\mathbf{Pl}\,\varphi$ says that the statement φ is *plausible* in the current state of the current time cluster.

$K_j\varphi$ means the agent *j knows* φ in the current state of a time cluster.

$CK_L\varphi$ means that φ is a *local common knowledge* in the current state of a time cluster, that all agents knows φ.

$CK_G\varphi$ means φ is a *global common knowledge* in the current state of a time cluster (i.e. that since now all agents will know it always).

$\mathbf{IntK}\,\varphi$ means that in the current state φ *may be known by interaction between agents*.

$\mathbf{N}\varphi$ has meaning φ holds in the *next time cluster* of states (state);

$\varphi\mathbf{U}\psi$ can be read: φ holds until ψ will hold;

$\varphi\mathbf{U_w}\,\psi$ has meaning φ weakly holds until ψ will hold;

$\varphi\mathbf{U_s}\,\psi$ has meaning φ strongly holds until ψ will hold;

For a given frame $N_C := \langle \cup_{i\in N} C(i), R, R_1, ..., R_m, \text{Next} \rangle$ and a model $M := \langle \cup_{i\in N} C(i), R, R_1, ..., R_m, \text{Next}, V \rangle$ with a valuation V, truth values of formulas at elements (worlds) of M may be computed by the following rules (below we denote $(M, a) \Vdash_V \varphi$ to say that the formula φ is true at a in the frame N_C with respect to the valuation V).

$\forall p \in P\ (M, a) \Vdash_V p \Leftrightarrow a \in V(p)$;

$(M,a) \Vdash_V \varphi \vee \Psi \Leftrightarrow (M,a) \Vdash_V \varphi (M,a) \Vdash_V \Psi$;

$(M,a) \Vdash_V \varphi \wedge \Psi \Leftrightarrow \cdot (M,a) \Vdash_V \varphi \wedge (M,a) \Vdash_V \Psi$;

$(M, a) \Vdash_V \varphi \rightarrow \psi \Leftrightarrow \{ \neg[(M,a) \Vdash_V \varphi]$ or $[(M,a) \Vdash_V \psi] \}$;

$(M,a) \Vdash_V \neg\varphi \cdot \Leftrightarrow \cdot not[(M,a) \Vdash_V \varphi]$;

$(M, a) \Vdash_V \mathbf{Unc}\,\varphi \Leftrightarrow (a \in C(i)\ \&\ \exists\, b \in C(i)\ (M, b) \Vdash_V \varphi\ \&$

$\exists\, c \in C(i)\ (M, c) \Vdash_V \neg\varphi)$.

That is, we say φ is *uncertain* if there are two states in time cluster $C(i)$, i.e. in time *i*, where φ is true at one of these states and is false at the another one. This looks as quite plausible way to express uncertainty of the statement φ (though, clearly, only one of possible ones, it could be many various ideas on how to express uncertainty in logical framework).

The next step is for explanation how to compute that the truth of a formula φ is *plausible* at current state. We suggest:

$(M, a) \Vdash_V \mathbf{Pl}\,\varphi \Leftrightarrow \exists i\ (a \in C(i)\ \&$

$\|\{ b\ |\ b \in C(i)\ (M, b) \Vdash_V \varphi \}\| > \|\{ b\ |\ b \in C(i)\ not[\,(M, b) \Vdash_V \varphi]\|\|)$,

where, for any set X, $\|X\|$ is the cardinality of X. For finite X, recall, $\|X\|$ is the number of elements in X. Therefore the rule above says that the truth of φ in a state of time moment *i* is *plausible* if there more states in the current time *i* where φ true then the ones where φ is false (so to say more witnesses for true than witnesses for false, so we use voting principle here). Next rule,

$(M,a) \Vdash_V K_j\varphi \Leftrightarrow \forall b[(a \cdot R_j \cdot b) \rightarrow (M, b) \Vdash_V \varphi]$.

Thus, we see $K_j\varphi$ says that the agent *j* knows φ if the formula φ holds in all states available for the agent *j* from the current state. Next rule,

$$\left(M,a \right) \Vdash_{V} \mathrm{IntK}\varphi \cdot \Leftrightarrow \exists a_{i1}, a_{i2}, ..., a_{ik} \in M$$

$$[aR_{i1}a_{1}R_{i2}a_{i2}...R_{ik}a_{k} \cdot \& \cdot \left(M, a_{k} \right) \Vdash_{V} \varphi].$$

The intended meaning of **IntK**φ was to say that that φ is known via interaction of agents. As we see, the rule above says us that φ may be known by interaction between the agents if there is a path of transitions by agents accessibility relations which leads to a state where φ holds. So, it looks as passing by agents information that φ holds via their information channels (so it, as seems, makes the term *interaction* relevant in this framework).

(M, a) $\Vdash_{V}$ **CK**$_{E}$ $\varphi \Leftrightarrow \forall j \forall b$ [a R b $\Rightarrow$ (M, b) $\Vdash_{V}$ φ].

So, φ is of *environmental knowledge* if it holds in all states which are accessible in the *current time point* for any agent.

(M, a) $\Vdash_{V}$ **CK**$_{G}$ $\varphi \Leftrightarrow \forall b$ [a R b $\Rightarrow$ (M, b) $\Vdash_{V}$ φ].

Thus, φ is of *global common knowledge* if it holds in all states in all future (and current) time clusters. This definition differs from standard meaning of just common knowledge (it does not refer to agents) but is seemed to be meaningful and plausibly justified. Rules for temporal operations are below:

*(M, a) $\Vdash$-**N**$\varphi \Leftrightarrow \forall b$ [(a Next b) $\Rightarrow$ (M, b) $\Vdash$- φ];*

(M, a) $\Vdash_{V}$ φ **U**$\psi \Leftrightarrow \exists$ b [(a R b) & ((M, b) $\Vdash_{V}$ ψ) &

$\forall c$ [(a R c R b) & not(b R c) $\Rightarrow$ (M, c) $\Vdash_{V}$ φ]];

(M, a) $\Vdash_{V}$ φ **U**$_{w}\psi \Leftrightarrow \exists$ b [(a R b) & ((M, b) $\Vdash_{V}$ ψ) &

$\forall c$ [(a R c R b)&$\neg$(b R c)&(c $\in$ C(i)) $\Rightarrow$ $\exists$ d $\in$ C(i) (M, d) $\Vdash_{V}$ φ]];

(M, a) $\Vdash_{V}$ φ **U**$_{s}\psi \Leftrightarrow \exists$ b [(a R b) & b $\in$ C(i)&

$\forall c \in$ C(i) ((M, c) $\Vdash_{V}$ ψ) & $\forall c$ [(a R c R b)&$\neg$(b R c)&) $\Rightarrow$

(M, c) $\Vdash_{V}$ φ]].

We comment below the amendments made in the rules for computation of truth values for temporal operations. The rules for computation truth values of temporal operations above unavoidably differ from the ones for LTL itself. The matter is, in our semantic frames, we have time clusters of states for each tick i of time but not merely one state as for LTL itself. It is easy to observe that the computation of the time binary operation **U** is only slightly different from the standard one—it is sufficient for ψ to be true as minimum at one state of the achieved in future time cluster. We immediately see that this assumption comes from the structure, as we have time clusters $C(i)$ but not time points i, as for LTL.

The time operation **U**$_{w}$ more significantly differs from the standard operation **U**—it is sufficient for the formula φ to be true only in one state of all possible time clusters before the statement ψ will true inside some state. The temporal operation strong until – φ**U**$_{s}$ ψ – expresses the property that there is a time point i, where the formula ψ is true inside $C(i)$ at totally all states and the formula φ holds in any state of all time clusters $C(j)$ with time points j proceeding i.

Definition of Logic UIA$_{LTL}$, Initial Observations

Here we are going to define our logic UIA$_{LTL}$ for description of interdependencies of operations uncertainty, plausibility, temporal and agents' operations. Recall that, for any given Kripke structure M:= $\langle$ N$_{C}$,V $\rangle$ and any given a formula φ, we use the following definitions. The formula φ is said to be satisfiable in M (denotation – $M \Vdash_{Sat} \varphi$) if there exists some state b in the model M ($b \in N_C$), at which φ is true: $(M, b) \Vdash_V \varphi$. The formula φ is called valid at M (denotation – $M \vdash \varphi$) if, for all b from M ($b \in N_c$), φ is true at b (i.e. $(M, b) \Vdash_V \varphi$). Given a frame N_c and a formula φ, we define

1. the formula φ is satisfiable in N_c (denotation $N_c \Vdash_{Sat} \varphi$) if there is some valuation V in N_c such that the following holds:

$\langle N_C, V \rangle \Vdash_{Sat} \varphi$.

2. the formula φ is valid in N_c (notation: $N_C \Vdash \varphi$) if not ($N_C \Vdash_{Sat} \neg \varphi$).

Now we define our logic UIA_{LTL} semantically, as the set of all logical laws which are true in all our models, more formally –

Definition 1. *The logic UIA_{LTL} is the set of all formulas which are valid in all frames N_C.*

Definitions above say us that a formula φ is called satisfiable if and only if there exists some valuation V in a Kripke frame N_C which makes φ satisfiable: $N_c \Vdash_{Sat} \varphi$. It is immediate to observe, that a formula φ is satisfiable if and only if $\neg\varphi$ is not a theorem of UIA_{LTL}, that is *not*($\neg\varphi \in UIA_{LTL}$). Conversely, a formula φ is a theorem of UIA_{LTL} iff the formula obtained by negation to φ - $\neg\varphi$ - is not satisfiable. Applying temporal operations U and N we are able to express all usual temporal and modal operations. For example, it is easy to verify, that all modal operations may be expressed as follows:

Proposition 2. *For any formula φ,*

1. $\Diamond\varphi \equiv \text{true } U \varphi \in UIA_{LTL}$;
2. $\Box\varphi \equiv \neg (\text{true } U \neg\varphi) \in UIA_{LTL}$.

Furthermore, for example, the temporal operation $F\varphi$ (φ *holds eventually, in terms of modal logic, φ is possible (denotation $\Diamond\varphi$)*) to be determined in

our logic as true $U\varphi$; in own turn, the operation G ($G\varphi$ *meansφ holds henceforth*) is expressed *as* $\neg F \neg\varphi$. In accepted formalization of uncertainty operation, the following interconnections with possibility and necessity can be easily derived:

Proposition 3. *The following holds:*

(i) $\text{Unc } \varphi \rightarrow \Diamond\varphi \wedge \Diamond\neg\varphi \in UIA_{LTL}$;
(ii) $\Diamond\varphi \wedge \Diamond\neg\varphi \rightarrow \text{Unc } \varphi \notin UIA_{LTL}$;
(iii) $\Box \varphi \rightarrow \neg \text{Unc } \varphi \in UIA_{LTL}$;
(iv) $\neg \text{Unc } \varphi \rightarrow \Box \varphi \notin UIA_{LTL}$.

For an illustration, we put below proofs, which are very simple. For the case (i), let $\langle N_C, V \rangle$ be a model, $a \in C(i) \subseteq N_C$, and $(N_C, a) \Vdash_V \text{Unc } \varphi$. Then for some $b,c \in C(i)$, $(N_C, b) \Vdash_V \varphi$ and $(N_C, b) \Vdash_V \neg\varphi$. Consequently, $(N_C, a) \Vdash_V \Diamond\varphi \wedge \Diamond\neg\varphi$, thus $\text{Unc } \varphi \rightarrow \Diamond\varphi \wedge \Diamond\neg\varphi \in UIA_{LTL}$.

To show (ii) it is sufficient to take a model based at N_C with $C(1) = \{a\}$, $C(2) = \{b,c\}$, and $V(p) = \{c\}$. Then, $(N_C, a) \Vdash_V \Diamond\varphi \wedge \Diamond\neg\varphi$ and $(N_C, a) \Vdash_V \neg \text{Unc } \varphi$.

So, $\Diamond\varphi \wedge \Diamond\neg\varphi \rightarrow \text{Unc } \varphi \notin UIA_{LTL}$.

To do with (iii), if for a model $\langle N_C, V \rangle$ and $a \in N_C$, $(N_C, a) \Vdash_V \Box\varphi$, then for any b, where $a R b$, $(N_C, b) \Vdash_V \varphi$, in particular, we have that $(N_C, a) \Vdash_V \neg \text{Unc } \varphi$. Consequently, $\Box \varphi \rightarrow \neg \text{Unc } \varphi \in UIA_{LTL}$.

For, (iv), it is sufficient to take the model based at N_C with $C(1) := \{a\}$, $C(2) := \{b,c\}$, and $V(p) := \{c\}$ from the proof (ii) above. Then, $(N_C, a) \Vdash_V \neg \text{Unc } \varphi$ and $(N_C, a) \Vdash_V \neg\Box\varphi$.

So, $\neg \text{Unc } \varphi \rightarrow \Box \varphi \notin UIA_{LTL}$, which concludes the proof.

Also, the following simple laws holds for uncertainty:

Proposition 4. *The following holds:*

(i) $\text{Unc } \varphi \rightarrow \text{Unc } \neg\varphi \in UIA_{LTL}$;
(ii) $\text{Unc } (\varphi \wedge \psi) \rightarrow \text{Unc } \varphi \vee \text{Unc } \psi \in UIA_{LTL}$;
(iii) $\text{Unc } (\varphi \vee \psi) \rightarrow \text{Unc } \varphi \vee \text{Unc } \psi \in UIA_{LTL}$.

Proof. (i) Let $\langle N_C, V \rangle$ be a model, $a \in C(i) \subseteq N_C$, and $(N_C, a) \Vdash_V$ **Unc** φ. By definition of the truth value, then, there are $b, c \in C(i)$, such that $(N_C, b) \Vdash_V \varphi$ and $(N_C, c) \Vdash_V \neg\varphi$. Consequently, $(N_C, a) \Vdash_V$ **Unc** $\neg\varphi$.

So, **Unc** $\varphi \to$ **Unc** $\neg\varphi \in UIA_{LTL}$.

(ii). Let $(N_C, a) \Vdash_V$ **Unc** $(\varphi \wedge \psi)$, $a \in C(i)$. Then there are $b, c \in C(i)$, such that $(N_C, b) \Vdash_V (\varphi \wedge \psi)$ and $(N_C, c) \Vdash_V \neg(\varphi \wedge \psi)$. Therefore we have either $(N_C, c) \Vdash_V \neg\varphi$ or $(N_C, c) \Vdash_V \neg\psi$. Consequently, either $(N_C, a) \Vdash_V$ **Unc** φ, or $(N_C, a) \Vdash_V$ **Unc** ψ, Hence, **Unc** $(\varphi \wedge \psi) \to$ **Unc** $\varphi \vee$ **Unc** $\psi \in UIA_{LTL}$.

For (iii), assume $(N_C, a) \Vdash_V$ **Unc** $(\varphi \vee \psi)$, $a \in C(i)$. Then there is some $b \in C(i)$, where $(N_C, b) \Vdash_V \neg(\varphi \vee \psi)$, i.e., $(N_C, b) \Vdash_V \neg\varphi$ and $(N_C, b) \Vdash \neg \psi$. Besides, there is an $c \in C(i)$, where $(N_C, c) \Vdash_V (\varphi \vee \psi)$, so, either $(N_C, c) \Vdash_V \varphi$ or $(N_C, c) \Vdash_V \psi$.

Consequently, $(N_C, a) \Vdash_V$ **Unc** $\varphi \vee$ **Unc** ψ. Hence, **Unc** $(\varphi \vee \psi) \to$ **Unc** $\varphi \vee$ **Unc** $\psi \in UIA_{LTL}$. Proof is complete.

Regarding logical operation *plausibility*, the following properties may be easily derived:

Proposition 5. *The following holds:*

(i) $\neg(\mathbf{Pl}\,\varphi \wedge \mathbf{Pl}\,\neg\,\varphi) \in UIA_{LTL}$;

(ii) $\mathbf{Pl}\,(\varphi \wedge \psi) \to \mathbf{Pl}\,\varphi \wedge \mathbf{Pl}\,\psi \in UIA_{LTL}$;

(iii) $\mathbf{Pl}\,(\varphi \vee \psi) \to \mathbf{Pl}\,\varphi \vee \mathbf{Pl}\,\psi \notin UIA_{LTL}$;

(iv) $\mathbf{Pl}\,\varphi \wedge \neg\,\varphi \to \mathbf{Unc}\,\varphi \in UIA_{LTL}$;

(v) $\mathbf{Pl}\,\varphi \to \mathbf{Pl}\,\mathbf{Pl}\,\varphi \in UIA_{LTL}$;

(vi) $\mathbf{Pl}\,\varphi \to \varphi \notin UIA_{LTL}$.

Proof. (i): Let $\langle N_C, V \rangle$ be a model, $a \in C(i) \subseteq N_C$, and $(N_C, a) \Vdash_V \mathbf{Pl}\,\varphi$.

Then there are more worlds in $C(i)$, where is true, therefore the following holds: $(N_C, a) \Vdash_V \neg \mathbf{Pl}\,\neg\varphi$. If $(N_C, a) \Vdash_V \mathbf{Pl}\,\neg\varphi$ we reason similarly, so (i) holds. For (ii), let $\langle N_C, V \rangle$ be a model, $a \in C(i) \subseteq N_C$, and $(N_C, a) \Vdash_V \mathbf{Pl}\,(\varphi \wedge \psi)$. Then the cardinality of the set of worlds form $C(i)$, were $\varphi \wedge \psi$ is true is bigger cardinality of the set of worlds where this formula is false, and then the similar holds for each formula φ and ψ separately. Consequently,

$(N_C, a) \Vdash_V \mathbf{Pl}\,\varphi \wedge \mathbf{Pl}\,\psi$. Thus, $\mathbf{Pl}\,(\varphi \wedge \psi) \to \mathbf{Pl}\,\varphi \wedge \mathbf{Pl}\,\psi \in UIA_{LTL}$.

For (iii) take a model based at N_C with $C(1) :=$ $\{a, b, c\}$, where $V(\varphi) = \{a\}$, $V(\psi) = \{b\}$. Then,

$(N_C, a) \Vdash_V \mathbf{Pl}\,\varphi \vee \mathbf{Pl}\,\psi\,(N_C, a) \Vdash_V \neg(\mathbf{Pl}\,\varphi \vee \mathbf{Pl}\,\psi)$.

So, $\mathbf{Pl}\,(\varphi \vee \psi) \to \mathbf{Pl}\,\varphi \vee \mathbf{Pl}\,\psi \notin UIA_{LTL}$.

(iv). If $\langle N_C, V \rangle$ is a model, $a \in C(i) \subseteq N_C$, and $(N_C, a) \Vdash_V \mathbf{Pl}\,\varphi \wedge \neg\varphi$, then, for some $b \in C(i)$, $(N_C, b) \Vdash_V \varphi$, which in sum gives $(N_C, a) \Vdash_V \mathbf{Unc}\,\varphi$. Hence, $\mathbf{Pl}\,\varphi \wedge \neg\,\varphi \to \mathbf{Unc}\,\varphi \in UIA_{LTL}$.

For (v), let $\langle N_C, V \rangle$ be a model, $a \in C(i) \subseteq N_C$, and $(N_C, a) \Vdash_V \mathbf{Pl}\,\varphi$. Then for all $b \in C(i)$, $(N_C, b) \Vdash_V \mathbf{Pl}\,\varphi$, in particular, then we have $(N_C, a) \Vdash_V \mathbf{Pl}\,\mathbf{Pl}\,\varphi$. So, $\mathbf{Pl}\,\varphi \to \mathbf{Pl}\,\mathbf{Pl}\,\varphi \in UIA_{LTL}$. (vi) is still more evident.

Notice also that based at logical operations derived above we can very simply express some knowledge operations postulated for our language.

Proposition 6. *For any formula* φ,

(i) $\mathbf{CK}_G\varphi \equiv \square\,\varphi \in UIA_{LTL}$;

(ii) $\mathbf{CK}_E\varphi \equiv \wedge_{1 \leq i \leq n} (\mathbf{K}_i\varphi) \in UIA_{LTL}$.

This implies that the initially specified language for UIA_{LTL} is a bit *superfluous*. Now we can omit operations for environmental and global common knowledge (since they are expressible via others). They were initially postulated to describe directly expressive properties of the language.

Usage of our combined language with standard and modified temporal operations together with our various knowledge operations, and logical uncertainty/plausibility operations gives an impressive power to the formulas. Say, the formula $\mathbf{Unc}\,\varphi \to \mathbf{Unc}\,\psi$ says that uncertainty φ implies uncertainty ψ, which may encode implicit dependence ψ from φ. For instance, the formula $\square\neg\mathbf{K}_1\neg\,\varphi$ tells us that, for any possible future time cluster $C(i)$ and for any state situated inside this cluster $C(i)$, the knowledge φ is *discoverable* for the agent 1, it has access to a state x where the statement φ holds. By involvement the new (strong and weak) temporal operations $\mathbf{U}_s$ and $\mathbf{U}_w$, we can model (represent) unique features of distribution truth values of formulas inside models.

For example, the formula $\Box_w \varphi := \neg \,(\text{True } \mathbf{U}_s \neg \varphi)$ codes the *weak necessity*, it says that in any time cluster $C(i)$ there is a state where φ is true. The formula $\neg(\varphi \mathbf{U}_w \Box \varphi) \wedge \Diamond \Box \varphi$ says that, there is an earliest future time cluster $C(i)$, since which φ will be true in all states of all time clusters, but, before $C(i)$ φ fails in a state of any time cluster. These and similar properties just impossible to describe in standard language of LTL, and just in standard multi-agents' logic, simply no logical operations which could handle such subtle properties.

The logic UIA_{LTL} in spite of its high expressive properties, would be not much useful, if we would be not a position to evaluate, which logical laws work for this logic. This could be done either via construction of an axiomatic system for UIA_{LTL} with a collection of axioms and inference rules or by an attempt to find an algorithm, which can recognize logical laws for UIA_{LTL} (i.e. to compute its true and satisfiable formulas). From computational viewpoint the second option is more preferable because this case we are immediately dealing with algorithm determining true theorems of UIA_{LTL}. Therefore in next section we are focused on finding an algorithm solving decidability problem for UIA_{LTL}.

Key Results, Decidability Algorithm

As one of useful tools, we will implicitly model the universal modality, which will be useful instrument (we do not wish to directly put the universal modality in the language to avoid over-complicated language, which definitely may bring problems to show decidability). This approach is an effective one for facilitation constructions of proofs, and for impressive their contractions. This is a consequence of the possibility (i) to avoid any reasoning by induction on the length of formulas, and (more important) (ii) the possibility

to read of in considerations formulas with nested operations. Such approach is based on our previous techniques to handle inference rules (Rybakov, 1984, 1992, 1995, 1997, 2001, 2005a, 2005b, 2007a, 2008; Rybakov, Kiyatkin, & Oner, 1999). Actually here we extend our previous research of logic for discovery presented in Rybakov (2007b) and a logic with multi-agent approach and interacting agents based on LTL (Rybakov, 2008). The initial idea is to describe formulas by inference rules and, next, to transform resulting rules in a special normal reduced forms. To remind basic concepts, a (sequential) (inference) rule is an expression $\mathbf{r} := \varphi_1(x_1, ..., x_n), ..., \varphi_m(x_1, ..., x_n) / \psi(x_1, ..., x_n)$, where $\varphi_1(x_1, ..., x_n), ..., \varphi_m(x_1, ..., x_n)$ and $\psi(x_1, ..., x_n)$ are some formulas (in our case -- formulas in the language of UIA_{LTL}) built on letters $x_1, ..., x_n$. These letters $x_1, ..., x_n$ are called variables of $\mathbf{r}$ (in notation, $x_i \in Var(\mathbf{r})$).

Definition 7. *A rule* **r** *is said to be* **valid** *in a model* $\langle N_C, V \rangle$ *with the valuation V (we will use notation* $N_C \Vdash_V \mathbf{r}$ *) if*

$$[\forall a\,((N_C, a) \Vdash_V \wedge_{1 \le i \le m} \varphi_i)] \Rightarrow \forall a\,((N_C, a) \Vdash_V \psi).$$

If this fails, the rule **r** *is said to be* **refuted** *in* N_C, *or* **refuted** *in* N_C **by the valuation V.** *A rule* **r** *is said to be* **valid** *in a frame* N_C *(denotation:* $N_C \Vdash \mathbf{r}$ *) if, for each valuation V of letters Var(**r**),* $N_C \Vdash_V \mathbf{r}$.

To apply representation of formulas by rules, for any given formula φ we can transfer φ in the rule $x \to x / \varphi$ (where $x \to x$ (which is the tautology) is the premise of this rule and φ is the rule conclusion), and, then, employ the technique of reduced normal forms for inference rules as follows. It is immediate to see that φ and $x \to x / \varphi$ are equivalent w.r.t. truth:

Lemma 8. *A formula φ is a theorem of UIA_{LTL} iff the rule $x \to x / \varphi$ is valid in any frame N_c.*

Given a rule R, we say R has the *reduced normal form* if $R = \alpha / x_1$, where

$$\alpha := \bigvee_{1 \leq j \leq m} [\bigwedge_{1 \leq i, k \leq n, i \neq k} [x_i^{t(j,i,0)} \wedge (\mathbf{Unc}\ x_i)^{t(j,i,1)} \wedge (\mathbf{N}\ x_i)^{t(j,i,2)} \wedge$$

$$(x_i \mathbf{U}\ x_k)^{t(j,i,k,0)} \wedge (x_i \mathbf{U_w}\ x_k)^{t(j,i,k,1)} \wedge (x_i \mathbf{U_s}\ x_k)^{t(j,i,k,2)} \wedge$$

$$\bigwedge_{1 \leq s \leq m}(\neg\ K_s \neg x_i)^{t(i,j,m,3)} \wedge (\mathbf{IntK}\ x_i)^{t(j,i,3)} \wedge (\mathbf{Pl}\ x_i)^{t(j,i,4)}]),$$

and all x_s are certain letters (variables), $t(j,i,z)$, $t(j,i,k,z) \in \{0,1\}$ and, for any formula α above, $\alpha^0 := \alpha$, $\alpha^1 := \neg\alpha$.

Definition 9. *For any rule R_nf in the reduced normal form, and any given rule R, R_nf is said to be a normal reduced form for R if and only if, for any frame N_C. $N_C\ ||$- $R \Leftrightarrow N_C\ ||$- R_nf.*

Following closely to arguments of Lemma 3.1.3 and Theorem 3.1.111 from Rybakov (1997), we can prove

Theorem 10. *There is an algorithm running in (single) exponential time, which, for any given rule R, constructs its normal reduced form R_nf.*

For illustration the technique, we put below a draft for proof of this theorem. Assume we are given with a rule $R := \varphi_1(x_1, ..., x_n), ..., \varphi_m(x_1, ..., x_n) / \psi(x_1, ..., x_n)$. It is evident that R is equivalent to the rule $\varphi_1(x_1, ..., x_n \wedge ... \wedge \varphi_m(x_1, ..., x_n) \wedge (x\_c \equiv \psi(x_1, ..., x_n)) / x\_c$, where x_c is a new variable. Therefore we can restrict the case by consideration only rules in the form φ / x_c.

If $\varphi = \alpha o \beta$, where o is a binary logical operation and both formulas α and β are not simply variables or unary logical operations applied to variables (which both we call final formulas), take two new variables x_α and x_β and the rule

$$R\_1 := (x\_\alpha \wedge x\_\beta) \wedge x\_\alpha \equiv \alpha \wedge x\_\beta \equiv \beta / x\_c.$$

If one of formulas α or β is final and the other one is not, we apply this transformation to only non-final formula. It is clear that R and R_1 are equivalent w.r.t. validity in frames.

If $\varphi = *\alpha$, where * is a unary logical operation and α is not a variable, take a new variable x_α and the rule

$$R\_1 := (*x\_\alpha) \wedge x\_\alpha \equiv \alpha / x\_c.$$

Again rules R and R_1 are equivalent. We continue this (similar) transformation over the resulting rules

$$\bigwedge_{j \in J} \delta\_j \wedge \bigwedge_{i \in I} (x\_(\alpha\_j) \equiv \alpha\_j) / x\_c$$

until all formulas δ_j and α_j in the premise of the resulting rules will be either atomic formulas, - logical operations applied to variables -, or variables. As result, we obtain a rule R_2. Evidently this transformation is *linear* in terms of the length of R, and the rule R_2 has size linear in R. Next, we transform the premise of R_2 to the disjunctive normal form and, next, transform the resulting premise to perfect disjunctive normal form (which has the disjunctive members of uniform length each of which contains all the components required in the definition of reduced normal forms) and obtain as the result an equivalent rule R_3. This transformation, as well as all known ones for reduction Boolean formulas to disjunctive normal forms, is *exponential*. As the result, the final rule R_3 will have the required form. This concludes the proof.

Bearing in mind Lemma 8, in order to prove decidability of UIA_{LTL} it is sufficient to find an algorithm, which would determine rules in reduced normal form which are valid in all frames N_C. For this a crucial role plays the following lemma. Proof of this lemma is not based on standard filtration technique or dropping points (this is a consequence the fact that we have interaction of agents – potentially unbounded paths of combinations of agents' accessibility relations), however we can find a proof via a refinement and combinations of known techniques.

Lemma 11. *For any rule R_nf in the reduced normal form, R_nf may be refuted in a frame N_C*

if and only if R_nf can be refuted in a some frame of sort N_C, where time clusters C(i) are of size at most square polynomial in size of R_nf.

Now we need a modification of our frames N_C, which actually gives us frames with looping time, but anyway such models are necessary to describe theorems of UIA_{LTL} (these are the following *bent finite models*). For any given frame N_C and any given numbers k,m, where $m>k>1$, the new frame $N_C(k,m)$ is defined as follows:

$$N_C(k,m):= \langle \cup_{1 \le i \le m} C(i), R, R_1, \ldots, R_n, \text{Next} \rangle.$$

Here R is the accessibility relation from the frame N_C which is extended by pairs (x,y), where $x \in C(i), y \in C(j)$ and $i,j \in [k,m]$.

In the frame $N_C(k,m)$, each relation R_j is simply transferred from the frame N_C. The relation *Next* in $N_C(k,m)$ is the relation from N_C extended by $\forall a \in C(m) \forall b \in C(k)(a \text{ Next } b = true)$. For arbitrary valuation V of all letters from a formula φ in the frame $N_C(k,m)$, the truth values of φ may be computed at elements of the frame $N_C(k,m)$ by the modified rules to the ones for frames N_C above (actually just in accordance with standard meaning of truth values for time operations and knowledge modalities).

For agents' knowledge operations and operation of knowledge via agents' interactions, operations of uncertainty and plausibility rules are exactly the same as for the case of frames N_C before. Therefore we only explicitly define below the rules for time operations. We need the notation: for any time cluster $C(i)$, $NxtC(i)$ is the next (by the operation *Next* for worlds) for $C(i)$ cluster $C(j)$. The operation *Nxt* is evidently a function. Let $a \in C(i) \subseteq N_c(k,m)$.

$$\forall a \cdot (N_c(k,m),a) \Vdash_V \varphi U \psi \cdot \Leftrightarrow$$

$$\exists t \in N(t \ge 0) \,\&\, \exists b \in Nxt^t C(i)[(N_c(k,m),b) \Vdash_V \psi$$

$$\&\forall t_1((t_1 \in [0,t-1] \to \forall c \in Nxt^{t_1}C(i)((N_c(k,m),c) \Vdash_V \psi)].$$

$$(\forall a \cdot N_c(k,m),a) \Vdash_V \psi U_w \psi \cdot \Leftrightarrow$$

$$\exists t \in N(t \ge 0) \,\&\, \exists b \in Nxt^t C(i)$$

$$[(N_c(k,m),b) \Vdash_V \psi \,\&\, \forall t_1((t_1 \in [0,t-1] \to$$

$$\exists c \in Nxt^{t_1}C(i)((N_c(k,m),c) \Vdash_V \varphi)].$$

$$\forall a(N_C(k,m),a) \Vdash_V \varphi U_s \psi \Leftrightarrow$$

$$\exists t \in N(t \ge 0) \,\&\, \forall b \in Nxt^t C(i)$$

$$[(N_c(k,m),b) \Vdash_V \psi \,\&\, \forall t_1((t_1 \in [0,t-1] \to$$

$$\forall c \in Nxt^{t_1}C(i)((N_c(k,m),c) \Vdash_V \varphi)].$$

The following lemma (which includes Lemma 11 as base for the proof) is main result which allows us to get deciding algorithm.

Lemma 12. *For any rule R_nf in the reduced normal form, R_nf may be refuted in some frame N_C if and only if R_nf is refuted in a certain bent frame $N_C(k,m)$ by a valuation V (with some special properties), where the size of the bent frame $N_C(k, m)$ is bounded as exponential from a polynomial in size of the rule R_nf.*

Using our technical results (Theorem 10, Lemmas 8 and 12), we obtain

Main Theorem. *The logic UIA_{LTL} is decidable. The algorithm determining whether a formula φ is a theorem of UIA_{LTL} (if $\varphi \in UIA_{LTL}$) is based on verification of validity the rule $(x \to x/\varphi)\_nf$ in the reduced normal form at frames $N_C(k,m)$ (w.r.t. special valuations) of size exponential from a polynomial on size of $(x \to x/\varphi)\_nf$.*

We would like to conclude the section with some observations concerning possible modifications of proposed language. For instance, uncertainty operation **Unc** may be defined via the current time cluster $C(i)$ and the next time cluster $C(i+1)$, motivating uncertainty as possible different truth values in the current and the next time cluster $C(i+1)$, i.e.

$$\forall a \cdot (N_c, a) \parallel_V \mathrm{Unc}\varphi \cdot \Leftrightarrow \cdot$$

$$\$b, c\hat{I}C(i)\grave{E}C(i+1)[((N_c, b) \parallel_V \mathrm{Unc}\varphi) \,\&\, ((N_c, c) \parallel_V \mathrm{Unc}\neg\varphi)]$$

Or, else, we could go further in this direction and consider possible other different truth values in a bounded future time. With plausibility operation **Pl**, some other definitions for its truth value may be considered as well. For example, we may treat a statement φ as (weakly) plausible if φ holds at least one state of the current time cluster. Also, various operations allowing to model U_s and U_w may be suggested. For example, we could consider the following new relation R_s on frames $N_c : \forall i \in N, \forall a,b \in C(i)(aR_s b)$.

The relation R_s plays especial role: it represents local universal modality (we may interpret it as accessibility relation of a supervise agent (or an omniscient agent) who knows the state of information at any state of the current time cluster $C(i)$). To use this special role of R_s denote $\square_s := K_s$, $\lozenge_s := \neg K_s \neg$. Below the notation $\equiv_{sem}$ is meant to say that the truth values of formulas in frames N_c coincide. It is easy to see that

$$(i) \cdot \varphi U_w \psi \equiv_{sem} \lozenge_s \varphi U \lozenge_s \psi; \cdots (ii) \cdot \varphi U_s \psi \equiv_{sem} \square_s U \square_s \psi.$$

Therefore if we possess the operation $\lozenge_s$, it is possible to define the weak and strong *Until*. If we proceed this way, the resulting logic UIA_{LTL}^S in the language with K_s and without U_s and U_w obeys the technique presented in this paper for UIA_{LTL}. We may conjecture that following this our

paper we can obtain the decidability for the new logic with a similar estimation of complexity.

CONCLUSION, FINAL DISCUSSION, FUTURE WORK

Obtained results: Our article suggests a technique based at Kripke/Hintikka models to show decidability of the logic UIA_{LTL} and a number of similar logics. We find an algorithm which recognizes theorems of UIA_{LTL} (so we show that UIA_{LTL} is decidable) and solves satisfiability problem for UIA_{LTL}. This is based on suggested reductions of formulas to rules, then, rules to rules in the reduced normal form, and, then, at a technique to contract models N_C into some special non-UIA_{LTL}-models, and, then, at verification of validity of these rules in models of bounded size. Instruments which we offer are seemed to be reasonably flexible and may work for other various logics with from AI and CS.

Possible applications: Implementations to any AI framework involving proposed above logical operations (including standard and new temporal operations, operations for agents' knowledge, knowledge via agents' interaction, local and global knowledge, uncertainly, plausibility) might be useful (provided this framework uses (needs to know) logical laws, true statements, formulas). Implementations must be based on software for checking validity of rules in proposed models, and such software is not available by now (to best my knowledge). But, even in present stage, the results of the paper can already work as shows lemmas of this paper (showing interdependencies of proposed logical operations). Such simple laws can be easy computed by hands – without computer. For statements with deeply nested logical operations the help of computer is, of course, crucial.

Future work: There are a number of interesting open questions concerning logic UIA_{LTL}, and the paper framework in general. For example, axiomatizations of the logic UIA_{LTL} and its suggested variants are open questions. The clarification of complexity for decision algorithms is interesting open question also. Possible refinements and improving performance of suggested algorithms are important also.

Logics obtained from UIA_{LTL} by refining via introduction operations *Since* and *Previous* based on $C(i)$ with $i \in Z$, by considering indexing time based on integers (but not only natural numbers as above) are actual and interesting. And it seems these questions may be approached by evolving suggested technique.

Another not touched yet area is study and determination of admissible rules for UIA_{LTL} and similar logics. Algorithms determining admissible rules would be of especial interest.

ACKNOWLEDGMENT

This research is supported by Engineering and Physical Sciences Research Council (EPSRC), UK, grant EP/F014406/1

REFERENCES

Babenyshev, S., & Rybakov, V. (2008). Logic of plausibility for discovery in multi-agent environment—deciding algorithms. In *Knowledge-based intelligent information and engineering system* (LNAI 5179, pp. 210-217).

Barringer, H., Fisher, M., Gabbay, D., & Gough, G. (1999). *Advances in temporal logic*. Dordrecht, The Netherlands: Kluwer Academic Publishers.

Blackburn, P., & Marx, M. (2003). Constructive interpolation in hybrid logic. *Journal of Symbolic Logic, 68*(2), 463–480. doi:10.2178/jsl/1052669059

Bordini, R. H., Fisher, M., Visser, W., & Wooldridge, M. (2004). Model checking rational agents. *IEEE Intelligent Systems, 19*(5), 46–52. doi:10.1109/MIS.2004.47

Clarke, E., Grumberg, O., & Hamaguchi, K. P. (1997). Another look at LTL model checking. *Formal Methods in System Design, 10*(1), 47–71. doi:10.1023/A:1008615614281

Crestani, F., & Lalmas, M. (2001). Logic and uncertainty in information retrieval. In *Lectures on information retrieval* (LNCS 1980, pp. 179-206).

Daniele, M., Giunchiglia, F., & Vardi, M. (1999). *Improved automata generation for linear temporal logic*. Paper presented at CAV'99: International Conference on Computer-Aided Verification, Trento, Italy.

Dix, J., Fisher, M., Levesque, H., & Sterling, L. (2004). Special issue on logic-based agent implementation. Editorial. *Annals of Mathematics and Artificial Intelligence, 41*(2-4): 131- -133.

Elvang-Goransson, M., Krausel, P., & Fox, J. (2006). Acceptability of arguments as 'logical uncertainty'. In *Proceedings of the European Conference on Symbolic and Quantitative Approaches to Reasoning and Uncertainty* (LNCS 747, pp. 85-90).

Fagin, R., Geanakoplos, P., Halpern, J., & Vardi, M. (1999). The hierarchical approach to modelling knowledge and common knowledge. *International Journal of Game Theory, 28*(3), 331–365. doi:10.1007/s001820050114

Fagin, R., Halpern, J., Moses, Y., & Vardi, M. (1995). *Reasoning about knowledge*. Boston: MIT Press.

Fisher, M. (2005). Temporal development methods for agent-based systems. *Journal of Autonomous Agents and Multi-Agent Systems, 10*(1), 41–66. doi:10.1007/s10458-004-3140-4

Gabbay, D., & Hodkinson, I. (1990). An axiomatisation of the temporal logic with until and since over the real numbers. *Journal of Logic and Computation, 1*, 229–260. doi:10.1093/logcom/1.2.229

Goldblatt, R. (1992). *Logics of time and computation* (CSLI lecture notes, No. 7). Palo Alto, CA: Stanford.

Goldblatt, R. (2003). Mathematical modal logic: A view of its Evolution. *Journal of Applied Logic*, *1*(5-6), 309–392. doi:10.1016/S1570-8683(03)00008-9

Halpern, J., & Shore, R. (2004). Reasoning about common knowledge with infinitely many agents. *Information and Computation*, *191*(1), 1–40. doi:10.1016/j.ic.2004.01.003

Hendler, J. (2001). Agents and the semantic web. *IEEE Intelligent Systems*, *16*(2), 30–37. doi:10.1109/5254.920597

Hodkinson, I. (2000). Temporal logic and automata. In Gabbay, D. M., Reynolds, M. A., & Finger, M. (Eds.), *Temporal logic: mathematical foundations and computational aspects* (*Vol. 2*, pp. 30–72). Oxford, UK: Clarendon Press.

Kacprzak, M. (2003). Undecidability of a multi-agent logic. *Fundamenta Informaticae*, *45*(2-3), 213–220.

Kaelbling, L. P., Cassandra, A. R., & Kurien, J. A. (1996). Acting under uncertainty: Discrete Bayesian models for mobile-robot navigation, In *IEEE/RSJ International Conference on Intelligent Robots and Systems (IROS'96)* (pp. 963-972). Washington, DC: IEEE Computer Society.

Lang, J. (2000). Possibilistic logic: complexity and algorithms. In *Handbook of defeasible reasoning and uncertainty management systems* (pp. 179–220). New York: Springer.

Maksimova, L. (2003). Complexity of some problems in positive and related calculi. *Theoretical Computer Science*, *1*(303), 171–185. doi:10.1016/S0304-3975(02)00450-4

Maksimova, L. (2006). Definability and interpolation in non-classical logics. *Studia Logica*, *82*(2), 271–291. doi:10.1007/s11225-006-7203-1

Manna, Z., & Pnueli, A. (1992). *The temporal logic of reactive and concurrent systems: Specification*. Berlin, Germany: Springer-Verlag. doi:10.1007/978-1-4612-0931-7

Manna, Z., & Pnueli, A. (1995). *Temporal verification of reactive systems: Safety*. Berlin, Germany: Springer-Verlag. doi:10.1007/978-1-4612-4222-2

Mundici, D. (2000). Foreword: Logics of uncertainty. *Journal of Logic Language and Information*, *9*, 1–3. doi:10.1023/A:1008374211520

Pnueli, A. (1977). The temporal logic of programs. In *Proceedings of the 18th Annual Symposium on Foundations of Computer Science* (pp. 46-57).

Pnueli, A., & Kesten, Y. (2002). A deductive proof system for CTL*. In *Proceedings of the 13th Conference on Concurrency Theory* (LNCS 2421, pp. 24-40).

Rybakov, V. V. (1984). A criterion for admissibility of rules in the modal system *S*4 and the intuitionistic logic. *Algebra and Logic*, *23*(5), 369–384. doi:10.1007/BF01982031

Rybakov, V. V. (1992). Rules of inference with parameters for intuitionistic logic. *Journal of Symbolic Logic*, *57*(3), 912–923. doi:10.2307/2275439

Rybakov, V. V. (1995). Hereditarily structurally complete modal logics. *Journal of Symbolic Logic*, *60*(1), 266–288. doi:10.2307/2275521

Rybakov, V. V. (1997). Admissible logical inference rules. In *Studies in logic and the foundations of mathematics*. New York: Elsevier.

Rybakov, V. V. (2001). Construction of an explicit basis for rules admissible in modal system S4. *Mathematical Logic Quarterly*, *47*(4), 441–451. doi:10.1002/1521-3870(200111)47:4<441::AID-MALQ441>3.0.CO;2-J

Rybakov, V. V. (2005a). Logical consecutions in intransitive temporal linear logic of finite intervals. *Journal of Logic Computation, (Oxford Press)*, *15*(5), 633- -657.

Rybakov, V. V. (2005b). Logical consecutions in discrete linear temporal logic. *Journal of Symbolic Logic*, *70*(4), 1137–1149. doi:10.2178/jsl/1129642119

Rybakov, V. V. (2006). Linear temporal logic with until and before on integer numbers, deciding algorithms. In D. Grigoriev, J. Harrison, E. A. Hirsch (Eds.), *Computer science – theory and applications* (LNCS 3967, pp. 322-334).

Rybakov, V. V. (2007a). Until-since temporal logic based on parallel time with common past. In S. N. Artemov & A. Nerode (Eds.) *Logical Foundations of Computer Science* (LNCS 4514, pp. 486-497).

Rybakov, V. V. (2007b). Logic of discovery in uncertain situations – deciding algorithms. In *Proceedings of Knowledge Based Intelligent Systems: KES 2007,* Verti sul Mare, (LNAI 4693, pp. 950-958).

Rybakov, V. V. (2008). Logic with interacting agents based at linear temporal logic, deciding algorithms. In *Artificial Intelligence and Soft Computing – ICAISC 2008* (LNAI 5097, pp. 1243-1253).

Rybakov, V. V., Kiyatkin, V. R., & Oner, T. (1999). On finite model property for admissible rules. *Mathematical Logic Quarterly*, *45*(4), 505–520. doi:10.1002/malq.19990450409

Thomason, S. K. (1972). Semantic snalysis of tense logic. *Journal of Symbolic Logic*, *37*(1).

van Benthem, J. (1983). *The logic of time*. Dordrecht, The Netherlands: Synthese Library.

van Benthem, J. (1991). *The logic of time*. Dordrecht, The Netherlands: Kluwer.

van Benthem, J., & Bergstra, J. A. (1994). Logic of transition systems. *Journal of Logic Language and Information*, *3*(4), 247–283. doi:10.1007/BF01160018

van der Hoek, W., & Wooldridge, M. (2003). Towards a logic of rational agency. *Logic Journal of the IGPL*, *11*(2), 133–157. doi:10.1093/jigpal/11.2.133

van der Meyden, R., & Shilov, N. V. (1999). Model checking knowledge and time in systems with perfect recall. In *Proceedings of the 19th Conference on Foundations of Software Technology and Theoretical Computer Science* (LNCS 1738, pp. 432-445).

van Rijsbergen, C. J. (2000). Another look at the logical uncertainty principle. *Information Retrieval*, *2*(1), 17–26. doi:10.1023/A:1009969229281

Vardi, M. (1994). *An automata-theoretic approach to linear temporal logic*. Paper presented at the Banff Workshop on Knowledge Acquisition (Banff'94).

Vardi, M. (1998). Reasoning about the past with two-way automata. In *Automata, Languages and Programming* (LNCS 1443, pp. 628-641).

This work was previously published in International Journal of Intelligent Information Technologies, Volume 6, Issue 1, edited by Vijayan Sugumaran, pp. 31-45, copyright 2010 by IGI Publishing (an imprint of IGI Global).

Chapter 4
Multiagent Based Selection of Tutor–Subject–Student Paradigm in an Intelligent Tutoring System

Kiran Mishra
IT BHU, India

R. B. Mishra
IT BHU, India

ABSTRACT

Intelligent tutoring systems (ITS) aim at development of two main interconnected modules: pedagogical module and student module. The pedagogical module concerns with the design of a teaching strategy which combines the interest of the student, tutor's capability and characteristics of subject. Very few effective models have been developed which combine the cognitive, psychological and behavioral components of tutor, student and the characteristics of a subject in ITS. We have developed a tutor-subject-student (TSS) paradigm for the selection of a tutor for a particular subject. A selection index of a tutor is calculated based upon his performance profile, preference, desire, intention, capability and trust. An aptitude of a student is determined based upon his answering to the seven types of subject topic categories such as Analytical, Reasoning, Descriptive, Analytical Reasoning, Analytical Descriptive, Reasoning Descriptive and Analytical Reasoning Descriptive. The selection of a tutor is performed for a particular type of topic in the subject on the basis of a student's aptitude.

DOI: 10.4018/978-1-4666-0158-1.ch004

INTRODUCTION

ITS (Intelligent Tutoring System) concerns with the design and development of a computer program to teach or educate a candidate (student) based upon his requirement and capability. Among the many issues in this regard such as: design of a student model, subject (domain) model, tutor/ pedagogical model and interaction (communication) of the various models; one of the key issues is the proposal of appropriate tutor-subject-student paradigm or a strategy which selects the subject according to the student requirement and capability and then a tutor corresponding to the subject for the aptitude of student. Selection of a tutor for a particular subject topic is a major problem because the characteristic of tutor differ for each topic of subject. The characteristics of tutor such as desire, intention, capability, commitment, trust and preferences vary from one tutor to another. In the same way matching of difficulty level of a subject topic and aptitude level of student is important. One can study a subject topic according to his or her aptitude level. The model or paradigm for the selection of tutor-subject-student (TSS) calls for the adequate and suitable knowledge of the cognitive, mental and behavioral characteristics of the student and the tutor as well. The characteristics and nature of the subject is also of prime importance. Various models of ITS have been developed which address the different issues of student, subject domain, expert/tutor domain, and their communication or interaction protocol. Very few pedagogical modules have been developed which clearly address the selection of tutor-subject-student paradigm taking into consideration the cognitive, psychological and behavioral components of student, tutor and also the characteristics of subject.

The prime objective of our work is to develop and test a mixed model which contains the cognitive (learning), psychological parameters of the tutor and the students; the difficulty level and characteristics of the subject domain. The model is deployed for the selection of a tutor for a student to learn a particular subject topic. We have calculated the trust level of a tutor based upon his capability, commitment, desire, intention and performance profile. The subject domain problem is divided into seven types (A- Analytical, R-Reasoning, D-Descriptive, AR-Analytical Reasoning, AD-Analytical Descriptive, RD-Reasoning Descriptive and ARD-Analytical Reasoning Descriptive). Software engineering is taken as a subject domain and various questions with different levels are prepared. The student aptitude for a particular type of subject category is enumerated based upon his answers to the particular subject topic category. Selection index of a tutor for a particular subject category is determined and aptitude of student for the particular subject category is also determined. A matching algorithm is deployed between the student aptitude level for a particular subject topic and the selection index of tutor for the particular subject topic. Thus a selection paradigm of tutor-subject-student is established. The comparison of various methods has been performed on the basis of performance index calculated by a heuristic method comprised of weighted sum of various parameters in different modules.

The rest of the contents of the paper are divided into the following sections. Section 2 presents background. Section 3 presents problem description and section 4 describes our proposed models and computation of parameters and characteristics of tutor, subject and student i.e. an agent based cognitive model and experimentation. Section 5 discusses the implementation, communication and selection procedure. Section 6 contains the results and discussion. Comparison and evaluation is provided in section 7 and conclusion is presented in section 8.

BACKGROUND

In this section we provide an overview on the existing work on intelligent tutoring system.

Researchers addressed different modules of intelligent tutoring system in their study. In his study Lee analyzed WBI learners' adaptation styles and characteristics related with the styles by retrospectively assessing the perceptions of various aspects of WBI (Web Based Instruction)(Lee, 2001). Papanikolaou, Grigoriadou, Magoulasb, and Kornilakisa (2002) used learner's knowledge level and individual traits as valuable information to represent learner's current state and personalize the educational system accordingly, in order to facilitate learners to achieve their personal learning goals and objectives. They identified three levels of learner's performance and developed multiple educational material modules for each of these levels (Papanikolaou et al., 2002). Tang et al. proposed a system that finds relevant content on the web, and personalize and adapt this content based on the system's observation of its learners and the accumulated ratings given by the learners (Tang & Mccalla, 2003). To determine an appropriate level of difficulty parameter for the course materials, Chen, Lee, and Chen proposed a collaborative voting approach for adjusting course material difficulty (2005). Chen, Liu, and Chang, presented a prototype of personalized Web-based instruction system (PWIS) based on the proposed modified Item Response Theory (IRT) to perform personalized curriculum sequencing through simultaneously considering courseware difficulty level, learner's ability and the concept continuity of learning pathways during learning (2006). Baker Ryan developed a profile of the attitudes and motivations associated with off task behavior, and compared this profile to the attitudes and motivations associated with other behaviors in intelligent tutoring systems (2007). Chen proposed genetic based personalized e-learning system that based on the results of pre-test can conduct personalized curriculum sequencing through simultaneously considering courseware difficulty level and the concept continuity of learning paths to support web based learning (2008). Leung & Li proposed a model of personalized learning

environment through 1) learning object design based on elaboration theory and e-learning standards; 2) applying item response theory (IRT) in student ability test; 3) managing course materials by a dynamic conceptual network (DCN); and 4) adopting a user profile to understand students' behaviors (Leung & Li, 2007). Schiaffino, Garcia, and Amandi presented eTeacher, an intelligent agent that provides personalized assistance to e-learning students. eTeacher observed a student's behavior while he/she was taking online courses and automatically built the student's profile. This profile comprised the student's learning style and information about the student's performance, such as exercises done, topics studied, exam results. In their approach student's learning style was automatically detected from the student's actions in an e-learning system using Bayesian networks (Schiaffino et al., 2008).

None of the authors have described the complete model of ITS containing the three modules and their parameters. This paper describes TSS-ITS—a system for selection of tutor-subject-student paradigm in intelligent tutoring system. Student's aptitude has been calculated and based on aptitude level subject topic has been assigned to the student. Various tutor's characteristics have been also considered and based on these characteristics the best tutor has been assigned to the student by coordinator. A heuristic method has been developed to determine the performance index of each of the method for their comparison.

PROBLEM DESCRIPTION

In intelligent tutoring system selection of a subject topic according to the student's aptitude level and then selection of a tutor for that subject topic is an important issue. The model, in this paper addresses these issues: subject topic selection and tutor selection. These two selections are related with two main problems. First one is that aptitude level of student should match with subject topic dif-

Figure 1. Basic model

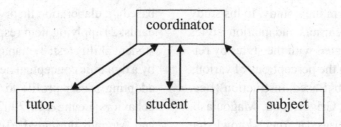

ficulty level and second is that tutor's performance, preference, capability, desire, intention, commitment varies for subject topic category. We take five tutor agents and calculate their performance based on subject topic completed by tutor agent, subject topic not completed in time by tutor agent and subject topic returned by tutor agents. Based on this performance, capability of tutor agent is calculated. Desire, choice, preference, intention, commitment, trust and index of performance tutor agent are calculated. Coordinator calculates aptitude level of five students for A, R, D, AR, AD, RD and ARD subject topic category. Difficulty level (H, L, M) of subject topic category for analytical, reasoning, descriptive, analytical-reasoning, analytical-descriptive, reasoning descriptive and analytical-reasoning-descriptive is decided. Aptitude of student is calculated based on the number of correct solution, incorrect solution and number of not solved questions by student. Student communicates with coordinator for assigning tutor. Coordinator calculates student's aptitude for the subject topic. Then coordinator asks to the tutor agents for their profiles. Tutor agents send their profile to the coordinator. Coordinator matches subject topic category with tutor agent's profile. A tutor with the best selection index is selected.

PROPOSED COMPUTING MODEL

There are four components or modules in our model, i.e., coordinator, student, tutor and subject. Coordinator module is central in the model. It interacts with rest of the modules. Student communicates with coordinator and says for assigning tutor. Tutor's performance, capability, intention, commitment, desire and trust are calculated in the tutor module of the basic model. Student tells to the coordinator for assigning tutor for a subject topic. Coordinator checks student's aptitude for the subject topic and then for that subject topic selects a tutor based on multiplication of his or her performance with difficulty weight and index of performance value. After selection of tutor, coordinator assigns tutor to the student for the subject topic. Figure 1 represents our proposed model. Cognitive computations for our model has described in the following section.

Cognitive Computations

Cognitive computations models have been developed by many researchers, taking into account the mental states, psychological parameter and cognitive constituents to display human behavior in general and specific tasks in particular. BDI (Belief, Desire, and Intention) theory has been developed to model the mental states in cognitive task i.e. learning and adaptation. Agent based models have been developed in this context which define an agent to be "an entity whose state is viewed as consisting of mental components such as beliefs, capabilities, choices, and commitments. What makes any hardware or software component an agent is precisely the fact that one has chosen to analyze and control it in these mental terms" (Shoham, 1993). A generic classification of an agent's attitudes is defined as follows: informational attitudes i.e. knowledge and beliefs, motivational attitudes, i.e., desires and intentions, commitments. A mental states approach, specifically the belief-desire-intention (BDI) model (Georgeff, Pell, Pollack, Tambe, & Wooldridge, 1999) to identify and model student's emotion has been described (Jaques & Vicari, 2007). The mental states approach describes an agent as an intentional system that have certain mental attitudes that are attributed to human beings, like "believe", "need", "desire", etc.

Tutor's Characteristics

The attitudes of a tutor agent are described with the cognitive parameters such as: desire, intention, capability, commitment, trust, preferences, and index of performance. The mental state parameters are the same as developed by (Kumar & Mishra, 2008; Mazumdar & Mishra, 2009) used for Hybrid model in semantic web and MAS model for negotiation in B2C E-commerce respectively. But our data set for the parameters and some formulas are different from them. The characteristics of a tutor agent are computed with the following parameters. The equations are based upon the empirical relation between different quantities in the right hand side (RHS) to the quantity on the left hand side (LHS).

a. Performance is the measure of goodness of functionality of an entity. Performance can also be defined as the success in meeting pre-defined objectives, targets and goals (IPD, n.d.) In e-commerce when evaluating the performance of different sellers the key factor considered the business efficiency. A total score is then calculated for each seller is based on the weight score of business efficiency constituent components (He, Jennings, & Leung, 2003). In the same way, we can define performance of a tutor. Subject topic completed by tutor agent, subject topic

not completed by tutor agent and subject topic returned by tutor agent multiplied by corresponding weights are respectively called complete, incomplete and return weighted task. Performance is defined as the ratio of the difference between the sum of complete and incomplete weighed task and return weighed task to the sum of weights.

$$P_i^j = \frac{T_i^{j,c} * w_c + T_i^{j,nct} * w_{nct} - T_i^{j,r} * w_r}{w_c + w_{nct} + w_r}$$

In our problem we assume that $w_c = 0.8$, $w_{nct} = 0.3$ and $w_r = 0.9$. The higher value of w_r gives negative impact through formula.

The performance computed by the above formula has not any type of indication about the difficulty of subject topic.

Here P_i^j is the performance of ith tutor for j[th] subject topic.

$T_i^{j,c}$ is the jth type subject topic completed by i[th] tutor agent.

$T_i^{j,nct}$ is the jth type subject topic not completed in time by i[th] tutor agent.

$T_i^{j,r}$ is the jth type subject topic return by i[th] tutor agent.

w_c is weight assign for the completed each subject topic.

w_{nct} is weight assign for the not completed each subject topic in time.

w_r is the weight assign for the each return subject topic.

b. The second type of performance i.e. performance with difficulty weight is calculated on the basis of difficulty weight. The difficulty weight w_d is related with level of difficulty of subject topic.

$$p_{iw}^{j} = P_{i}^{j} * w_{d}$$

Here p_{iw}^{j} is the performance of ith tutor for j^{th} subject topic with difficulty weight.

c. Capability seems to focus on the positive abilities of the tutors and what they are capable of achieving. The term capability can be defined as that knowledge, skills, and judgments that enable a tutor to perform his/her role (Reid & Newhouse, 2004). The capability is computed on the basis of performance with difficulty weight and total number of subject topic type. It is the ratio of summation of performance with difficulty weight as to the multiplication of total number of subject topic type with summation of difficulty weights.

$$(Capability)_{i} = \frac{\sum_{j} p_{iw}^{j}}{Total\ no\ of\ subject\ topic\ type * \sum w_{d}}$$

The capability shows the how much subject topic can be handled by a particular tutor agent.

Here $(Capability)_{i}$ is the capability of the ith tutor agent.

w_{d} is the difficulty weight assign according to the subject topic difficulty.

d. $$X_{i}^{s} = \frac{T_{i}^{s,c} * w_{s,c} + T_{i}^{s,nct} * w_{s,nct} - T_{i}^{s,r} * w_{s,r}}{w_{s,c} + w_{s,nct} + w_{s,r}}$$

In our problem we assume that $w_{s,c}$ =0.8, $w_{s,nct}$ =0.3 and $w_{s,r}$ =0.9. The higher value of $w_{s,r}$ gives negative impact through formula.

Here X_{i}^{s} is a parameter for calculating the desire.

$T_{i}^{s,c}$ is the number of completed selected subject topic type s by i^{th} tutor agent.

$T_{i}^{s,nct}$ is the number of selected subject topic type s not completed in time by i^{th} tutor agent.

$T_{i}^{s,r}$ is the number of selected subject topic type s return by i^{th} tutor agent.

$w_{s,c}$ is weight assign for each completed selected subject topic type s.

$w_{s,nct}$ is weight assign for each selected subject topic type s which not completed in time.

$w_{s,r}$ is the weight assign for each return subject topic type s.

e. Desires can refer to a (desired) state of affairs in the world (and the other agents), but also to (desired) actions to be performed (Castelfranchi, & Falcone, 1998). An agent's desires are conceived of as the states of the world that the agent wishes to bring about (Bell, 1995; Kraus, Sycara, Evenchil, 1998). The desires are the motivational state of the system. They have information about the objectives to be accomplished, i.e., what priorities or payoffs are associated with the various current objectives. The fact that the agent has a desire does not mean that the agent will do it. The agent carries out a deliberative process in which it confronts its desires and beliefs and chooses a set of desires that can be satisfied (Jaques & Vicari, 2007).

Desire denotes that tutor agent wish to teach the subject topic which is based upon the total factor X and difficulty weight. Desire is the ratio of summation of total factor X multiplied with difficulty weight as to the total number of subject topic type multiplied by the summation of difficulty weights.

$$(Choice)_{i} = (Desire)_{i} = \frac{\sum_{s} X_{i}^{s} * w_{d}}{Total\ no\ of\ subject\ topic\ type * \sum_{s} w_{d}}$$

f. An agent's preference plays an active role in social practical reasoning, where an action is to be selected in order for given intention to be fulfilled (Panzarasa, Jennings, & Norman, 2002).

Multiplication of number of completed selected subject topic type s, not completed selected subject topic type s and returned selected subject topic type s with corresponding preferential weights are respectively called weighted completed, not completed and returned preference task. Ratio of the difference between the sum of weighted completed and not completed preference task and returned preference task as to the sum of preferential weights is called selected task index. Preference is defined as the ratio of sum of selected task index multiplied by difficulty weight as to the total number of subject topic type.

$$(\Pr eference)_i = \frac{\sum w_d * \left(\frac{\left(T_i^{s,c} * w_{p,c} + T_i^{s,nct} * w_{p,nct} - T_i^{s,r} * w_{p,r} \right)}{w_{p,c} + w_{p,nct} + w_{p,r}} \right)}{Total\ no\ of\ subject\ topic\ type}$$

In our problem we assume that $w_{p,c}$ =0.8, $w_{p,nct}$ =0.5 and $w_{p,r}$ =0.7. The higher value of $w_{p,r}$ gives negative impact through formula.

Here $w_{p,c}$ is preferential weight assign for each complete selected subject topic type s.

$w_{p,nct}$ is the preferential weight assign for each selected subject topic type s which not completed in time.

$w_{p,r}$ is the preferential weight assign for each return subject topic type s.

g. Intention is actually the goal that an agent wants to achieve; an agent's intention will give a guideline of what to do (Wu, Ekaette, & Far, 2003). Intention is a fundamental characteristic that agents involve a special kind of "self commitment" to acting (Bratman,

1990; Von, 1980). An agent's individual intention towards a state of affairs entails the agent's commitment to acting towards the achievement of that state. Intentions are viewed as that subject topic that a tutor agent has committed to teach. The intention computed on the basis of choice (desire) and preference (Panzarasa et al., 2002). It is the multiplication of choice and preference.

$$(Intention)_i = (Choice)_i * (\Pr eference)_i$$

h. Tutors must have commitment to tutoring. Commitment ignites action. To commit is to pledge you to a certain purpose or line of conduct (Prism, Ltd., n.d.). Commitment means the act of binding yourself (intellectually or emotionally) to a course of action (Farlex, n.d.). Commitment is computed on the basis of intention and capability (Panzarasa et al., 2002). Commitment is the multiplication of intention and capability.

$$(Commitment)_i = (Intention)_i * (Capability)_i$$

i. Trust is a subjective expectation an agent has about another's future behavior based on the history of their encounters (Mui, Mohtashemi, & Halberstadt, 2002). Trust is the firm belief in the competence of an entity to act dependably, securely, and reliably within a specified context (Grandison & Sloman, 2000). Trust of a party A to a party B for a service X is the measurable belief of A in that B behaves dependably for a specified period within a specified context (in relation to service X) (Olmedilla, Rana, Matthews, & Nejd, 2005). Trust is the firm belief in the competence of an entity to act as expected such that this firm belief is not a fixed value associated with the entity but rather subject to the entities' behavior and

Table 1. Subject-topics profile of different tutor agents

Subject topic Type	Total subject topic	Total No Of subject topic Completed In Time					Total No Of subject topic not Completed In Time					Returned task(not completed)				
		Tut1	Tut2	Tut3	Tut4	Tut5	Tut1	Tut2	Tut3	Tut4	Tut5	Tut1	Tut2	Tut3	Tut4	Tut5
Analytical	10	6	8	5	7	4	2	1	3	2	4	2	1	2	1	2
Reasoning	10	8	6	4	5	7	1	3	4	3	2	1	1	2	2	1
descriptive	10	7	5	4	8	6	0	3	4	1	4	3	2	2	1	0
AR	10	4	5	7	6	8	4	3	3	3	1	2	2	0	1	1
AD	10	6	3	7	6	8	2	5	1	2	1	2	2	2	2	1
RD	10	5	4	6	8	7	3	4	3	1	2	2	2	1	1	1
ARD	10	4	5	6	7	5	4	4	2	2	4	2	1	2	1	1

applies only within the context at a given time (Azzedin & Maheswaran, 2002).

From the above definitions it is clear that trust depends upon history of work done in a context, his performance of work that one can believe. All these factors amount to the proficiency, capability and strong intention, i.e., one's commitment to the work. Thus, the trust is computed on the basis of commitment and capability of a tutor agent. It is the multiplication of commitment and capability (Castelfranchi & Falcone, 1998).

$$(Trust)_i = (Commitment)_i * (Capability)_i$$

j. The index of performance helps to select a tutor agent for a particular subject topic. α is a factor and $0 < \alpha < 1$. It is computed on the basis of trust and reputation of a tutor agent. Reputation is based on tutor agent's performance.

$$IN_i = \alpha(Trust)_i + (1 - \alpha)(Re\,putation)_i$$

Where

IN_i is the index of performance.

Weights are taken by heuristic and experience of the authors.

For selecting a tutor agent first coordinator agent finds out what type of subject topic taught by the ith tutor with best quality, and then if selection index i.e. multiplication of performance with difficulty weight of ith tutor and index of performance for i[th] tutor agent is maximum then i[th] tutor agent's proposal is invited for selection.

From the above mathematical model of the social and cognitive function we calculate the important parameters related to social state and cognitive state of different tutor agents.

Table 1 shows the subject-topic profile of different tutor agents. There are five main columns in this table. Column 1 represents the different subject-topic type, i.e., analytical, reasoning, descriptive, AR-Analytical-Reasoning, AD-Analytical-Descriptive, RD-Reasoning–Descriptive, ARD-Analytical-Reasoning-Descriptive. Column 2 represents total number of subject-topic type; each subject topic type is 10. Column 3 represents total number of subject-topic type completed in time by different tutor agents. Column 4 represents total number of subject-topic type not completed in time by different tutor agents. Column 5 represents subject-topic type returned by different tutor agents. Column 3, 4 and 5 has five sub columns that represent five tutor agents as Tut1, Tut2, Tut3, Tut4, and Tut5.

Table 2 shows tutor agent's subject topic preference. Column1 shows preferences of tutor agents. Column 2 shows topic type completed in time by tutor agent. Column 3 shows topic type

Table 2. Subject topic preference of tutor agents

For tutor Tut1			
Preferences	Completed In Time	Not Completed In Time	Return
Reasoning	3	3	4
Descriptive	6	2	2
Analytical	5	3	2
For tutor Tut2			
Preferences	Completed In Time	Not Completed In Time	Return
Analytical	5	3	2
AR	6	2	2
Descriptive	4	4	2
For tutor Tut3			
Preferences	Completed In Time	Not Completed In Time	Return
Analytical	6	2	2
Reasoning	8	1	1
AD	4	3	3
AR	5	3	2
For tutor Tut4			
Preferences	Completed In Time	Not Completed In Time	Return
Analytical	3	6	1
Descriptive	8	1	1
Reasoning	2	3	5
AR	1	5	4
For tutor Tut5			
Preferences	Completed In Time	Not Completed In Time	Return
Analytical	6	4	0
Reasoning	3	5	2
Descriptive	2	5	3
AR	3	4	3
AD	2	7	1

not completed in time and Column 4 shows subject topic type returned.

From the calculation obtained from cognitive computation model (Figure 2), Table 3 has been prepared.

In Figure 2 set {PA1a,…PA1g} represents tutor agent1's performance with difficulty weight for A, R, D, AR, AD, RD and ARD respectively. Set {PA2a,…PA2g} represents tutor agent2's performance with difficulty weight for A, R, D, AR, AD, RD and ARD respectively. Set {PA3a,… PA3g} represents tutor agent3's performance with difficulty weight for A, R, D, AR, AD, RD and ARD respectively. Set {PA4a,…PA4g} represents tutor agent4's performance with difficulty weight for A, R, D, AR, AD, RD and ARD respectively. Set {PA5a,…PA5g} represents tutor agent5's performance with difficulty weight for A, R, AR, AD, RD and ARD respectively. Set {capof-

Figure 2. Performance with difficulty weight and capability of tutor agents

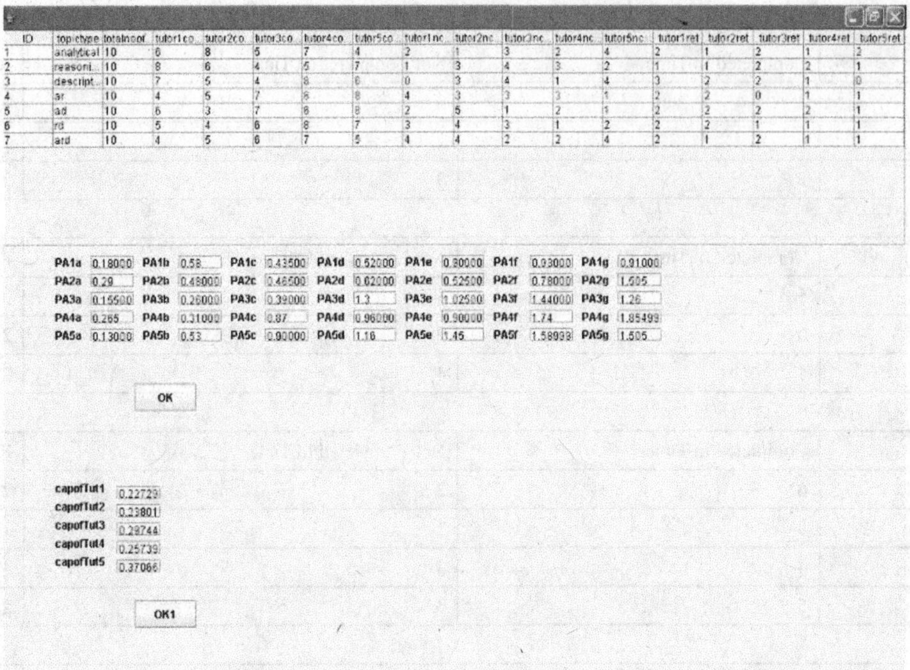

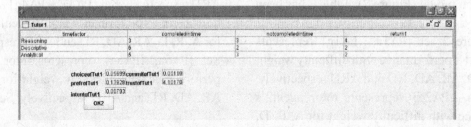

Table 3. Performance with difficulty weight of tutors

Tutor	Analytical	Reasoning	Descriptive	AR	AD	RD	ARD
Tutor1	.18	.58	.435	.52	.90	.93	.91
Tutor2	.29	.48	.465	.62	.52	.78	1.505
Tutor3	.155	.26	.39	1.3	1.02	1.44	1.26
Tutor4	.265	.31	.87	.96	.90	1.74	1.854
Tutor5	.13	.53	.90	1.16	1.45	1.58	1.505

Figure 3. Choice, preference, intention, commitment and trust of tutor agent1

Figure 4. Index of performance of tutor agents

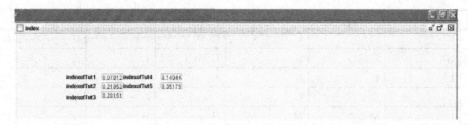

Table 4. Capability, choice, preference, intention, commitment, trust and index of performance of tutors

Tutor	capability	choice	preference	intention	commitment	Trust	Index of performance
Tutor1	0.227	0.056	0.139	0.0079	0.001	.0004	.07
Tutor2	0.238	0.144	0.236	0.034	.007	.001	.21
Tutor3	0.297	0.29	0.33	0.097	.022	.005	.28
Tutor4	0.257	0.122	0.232	0.028	.006	.001	.14
Tutor5	0.370	0.31	0.36	0.113	.025	.005	.35

Table 5. Selection index, i.e., performance with difficulty weight*index of performance

Tutor	analytical	reasoning	descriptive	AR	AD	RD	ARD
Tutor1	.0126	.0406	.03045	.0364	.063	.0651	.0637
Tutor2	.5	.1008	.09765	.1302	.1092	.1638	.31605
Tutor3	.0434	.0728	:1092	.364	.2856	.4032	.3528
Tutor4	.0371	.0434	.1218	.1344	.126	.2436	.259
Tutor5	.0182	.1855	.315	.406	.5075	.553	.5267

Tut1,…capofTut5} represents capability of tutor agents. Five tutor agents have considered.

Figure 3 shows choice, preference, intention, commitment and trust of tutor1. Figure 4 shows index of performance of the tutors. These values have also been calculated for tutor2, tutor3, tutor4 and tutor5. From these values, Table 4 has prepared.

Columns of Table 4 represent capability, choice, preference, intention, commitment, trust and index of performance of tutors.

Table 5 represents selection index; multiplication of performance with difficulty weight and index of performance.

For these values three levels have been assigned H-High, M-Medium and L-Low. If value falls between 0-3 then assign it L if value falls between 3-7 assign it M and if value falls between 7-10 assign it H. Here because values are between .0126 and .553 scaling has performed and for assigning levels following rules have used:

Rule 1: IF value between .0126 and .174, assign L
Rule 2: IF value between .175 and .390, assign M
Rule 3: IF value between .391 and .553, assign H

Table 6 represents labels of selection index of tutors for analytical, reasoning, descriptive,

Table 6. Labels of selection index

Tutor	Analytical	Reasoning	Descriptive	AR	AD	RD	ARD
Tutor1	L	L	L	L	L	L	L
Tutor2	H	L	L	L	L	L	M
Tutor3	L	L	L	M	M	H	M
Tutor4	L	L	L	L	L	M	M
Tutor5	L	M	M	H	H	H	H

AR-Analytical-Reasoning, AD-Analytical-Descriptive, RD-Reasoning-Descriptive, and ARD-Analytical-Reasoning-Descriptive.

Subject Model

For subject model we have taken software engineering. Other subjects can be taken as subject model. Generally questions are formulated to test the reasoning process, analytical capability, and descriptive power of the candidate. We have taken a logical correlation of these parameters (Analytical, Reasoning, and Descriptive) such as AR-Analytical Reasoning, AD-Analytical Descriptive, RD-Reasoning Descriptive and ARD-Analytical Reasoning Descriptive. We have identified that each subject topic is from which category and up to which level, i.e., High, Medium or Low. We have prepared Table 7 with domain experts i.e. people involved in the teaching of software engineering.

Student Model

Student model calculates aptitude of students for analytical, reasoning, descriptive, AR-Analytical Reasoning, AD-Analytical Descriptive, RD-Reasoning Descriptive and ARD-Analytical Reasoning Descriptive.

Aptitude for Student

One's aptitude is his inherent capacity, talent or ability to do something. Having a high aptitude for something means he is good at doing that some-

thing (About.com, n.d.). Aptitude tests measure a student's performance. Student's knowledge level is approached through a qualitative model of the level of performance that learners exhibit with respect to the concepts they study and is used to adapt the lesson contents (Papanikolaou et al., 2002).Questions of five difficulty level has been given to the students and based on response (i.e., correct, incorrect, not solved), aptitude of student has been calculated using formula given below.

The aptitude for analytical has been calculated as follows:

$$AA = \frac{W_A * \sum_1^3 XiWi + W_B * \sum_1^3 XiWi + W_C * \sum_1^3 XiWi + W_D * \sum_1^3 XiWi + W_E * \sum_1^3 XiWi}{AQ_1 + BQ_2 + CQ_3 + DQ_4 + EQ_5}$$

Where AA is aptitude for analytical and W_A, W_B, W_C, W_D, W_E are weights corresponding to difficulty level. $W_A=5$, $W_B=4$, $W_C=3$, $W_D=2$ and $W_E=1$. These values have chosen based on the difficulty of the subject topic. Most difficult topic has 5 weights and least difficult (easy) topic has 1 weight.

$AQ_1=3$, $BQ_2=3$, $CQ_3=4$, $DQ_4=4$ and $EQ_5=6$ are number of questions with difficulty levels a, b, c, d, and e respectively.

$Xi_{(i=1,2,3)}$ is number of correct solutions, incorrect solutions and number of not solved questions.

$w_{i\,(i=1,2,3)}$ is weight corresponding to correct solution, incorrect solution and not solved. $w_1=3$, $w_2=-1$ and $w_3=0$.

Table 7. Levels of subject topic

Subject topic	Analytical	Reasoning	Descriptive	AR	AD	RD	ARD
Software process	L	L	H	L	M	M	M
Desired char of software process	L	L	H	L	M	M	M
Software development process models	L	L	H	L	M	M	M
Software requirements	L	L	H	L	M	M	M
Problem analysis	L	L	H	L	M	M	M
Requirement specification	L	L	H	L	M	M	M
Validation	M	M	M	M	M	M	M
metrics	H	L	M	M	H	M	M
Architecture views	L	L	H	L	M	M	M
Architecture style of C &C view	L	L	H	L	M	M	M
Evaluating architecture	H	M	M	H	H	M	H
Effort estimation	H	M	M	H	H	H	H
Project scheduling and staffing	H	M	M	H	H	H	H
Software configuration mgmt plan	L	M	H	M	M	H	M
Quality plan	L	M	H	M	M	H	M
Risk mgmt	H	L	M	M	H	M	M
Project monitoring plan	M	L	H	M	H	M	M
Function oriented design	M	M	H	M	H	M	H
Object O design	M	M	H	M	H	M	H
Detailed Design	L	H	H	M	M	H	H
Programming principles and guidelines	L	H	H	M	M	H	H
Coding process	L	H	H	M	M	H	H
refactoring	L	H	H	M	M	H	H
Verification	H	H	H	H	H	H	H
Metrics	H	L	M	M	M	M	M
Testing fundamentals	M	L	H	M	H	M	M
Black Box Testing	M	M	H	M	H	H	H
White Box Testing	M	M	H	M	H	H	H
Testing process	M	L	H	M	H	M	M
Defect analysis and prevention	H	L	H	M	H	M	H
Metrics	H	L	M	M	M	M	M

Figure 5. Aptitude values of student5

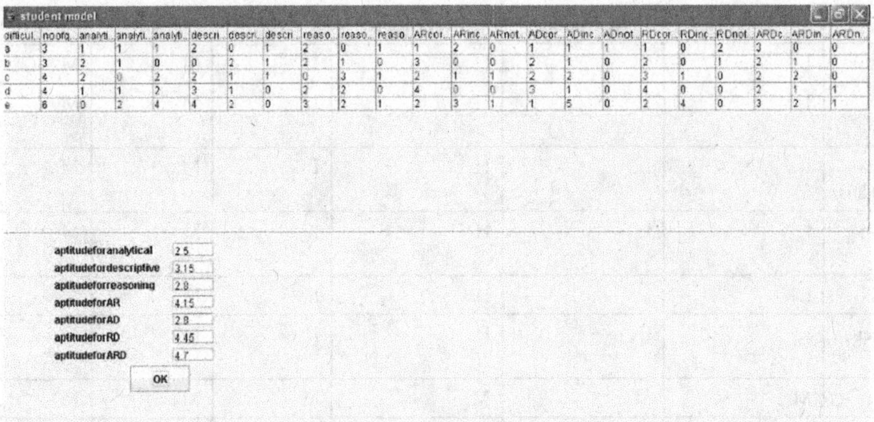

By using the same formula, aptitude of student for reasoning, descriptive, AR, AD, RD and ARD has been calculated (Figure 5).

Experimentation

In the experimentation we have taken the students of BTech. part III and BTech. part IV of our department. Questionnaire of subject topic category i.e. analytical, reasoning, descriptive, AR, AD, RD and ARD was given to the student. There were objective type questions in analytical and reasoning categories while rest of the categories contained subjective type questions. Questions of five difficulty level were taken in each category. 3 questions of difficulty level a, 3 questions of difficulty level b, 4 questions of difficulty level c, 4 questions of difficulty level d and 6 questions of difficulty level e were taken. Thus there were total 20 questions. Exam data of students have been shown in Table 8. Columns of Table 8 represents difficulty levels, number of questions, correct, incorrect and not solved questions in A, R, D, AR, AD, RD and ARD category. Time for the test was one hour. Performance of the students was first calculated and then aptitude was determined .The calculation is based on formula for aptitude shown in section 4.3.1.Labels have been assigned

to the aptitude values of students. Then selection procedure (section 5.2) has been performed.

With different data sets, aptitudes for different students have been calculated.

From the result obtained from computation model, Table 9 has been prepared. In this table aptitude for analytical, reasoning, descriptive, AR, AD, RD, ARD for different students is represented. For these values three different levels, i.e., L-Low, M-Medium and H-High have assigned and Table10 has prepared. If value falls between 0-3 then assign it L if value falls between 3-7 assign it M and if value falls between 7-10 assign it H. Here because values are between 1.7 and 4.7 scaling has performed and for assigning levels following rules have used:

Rule 1: IF value between 1.7 and 2.6 assign L.
Rule 2: IF value between 2.7 and 3.8 assign M
Rule 3: IF value between 3.9 and 4.7 assign H

IMPLEMENTATION

We have used java language for the implementation of the system. We have used JADE for representing interaction between modules.

Table 8. Exam data of students

Student	Difficulty level	No. of questions	A correct	A incorrect	A Not solved	D correct	D incorrect	D Not solved	R correct	R incorrect	R not solved	AR correct	AR incorrect	AR not solved	AD correct	AD incorrect	AD not solved	RD correct	RD incorrect	RD not solved	ARD correct	ARD incorrect	ARD not solved
Student1	a	3	2	1	0	1	2	0	2	1	0	1	1	1	1	2	0	1	2	0	1	2	0
	b	3	1	1	1	2	1	0	1	1	1	2	1	0	1	2	0	2	1	0	2	1	0
	c	4	2	2	0	2	1	1	2	2	0	1	2	1	2	2	0	2	1	1	2	2	0
	d	4	2	1	1	1	2	1	1	2	1	2	2	0	2	1	1	1	2	1	2	1	1
	e	6	3	2	1	3	2	1	3	3	0	3	2	1	2	3	1	3	3	0	5	1	0
Student2	a	3	1	1	1	2	1	0	1	2	0	2	0	1	2	1	0	1	1	1	3	0	0
	b	3	1	2	0	1	1	1	2	1	0	1	2	0	2	1	0	2	1	0	1	2	0
	c	4	3	1	0	1	3	0	3	1	0	1	3	0	3	0	1	3	1	0	3	1	0
	d	4	1	3	0	2	2	0	2	2	0	3	1	0	2	1	1	4	0	0	2	1	1
	e	6	2	2	2	2	4	0	3	2	1	4	2	0	4	2	0	3	3	0	3	2	1
Student3	a	3	1	1	1	2	1	0	1	1	1	1	2	0	1	1	1	1	1	1	1	2	0
	b	3	2	1	0	2	0	1	2	1	0	2	1	0	2	1	0	1	2	0	1	1	1
	c	4	2	1	1	2	2	0	2	2	0	3	1	0	2	1	1	3	1	0	2	1	1
	d	4	2	0	2	3	1	0	1	2	1	2	1	1	2	0	2	1	2	1	2	0	2
	e	6	3	3	0	2	3	1	3	2	1	2	2	2	3	2	1	2	4	0	4	1	1
Student4	a	3	1	2	0	1	1	1	1	2	0	1	1	1	2	1	0	1	1	1	1	2	0
	b	3	2	1	0	0	2	0	2	1	0	1	2	0	2	0	0	1	1	0	2	1	0
	c	4	2	2	0	3	1	1	3	1	0	3	1	0	2	0	2	3	1	1	2	1	1
	d	4	2	1	1	2	1	0	1	2	1	2	2	0	0	2	2	1	3	0	2	2	0
	e	6	2	0	4	3	3	1	3	3	0	2	2	2	5	1	0	2	4	0	5	1	0
Student5	a	3	1	1	1	2	0	1	2	0	1	1	2	0	1	1	1	1	0	2	3	0	0
	b	3	2	1	0	0	2	1	2	1	0	3	0	0	2	1	0	2	0	1	2	1	0
	c	4	2	0	2	2	1	1	0	3	1	2	1	1	2	2	0	3	1	0	2	2	0
	d	4	1	1	2	3	1	0	2	2	0	4	0	0	3	1	0	4	0	0	2	1	1
	e	6	0	2	4	4	2	0	3	2	1	2	3	1	1	5	0	2	4	0	3	2	1

Table 9. Aptitude values of students

Student	Analytical	Reasoning	Descriptive	AR	AD	RD	ARD
Student1	3.1	2.65	2.65	2.4	1.7	2.4	3.05
Student2	2.1	3.2	2.15	3.0	4.6	4.2	4.5
Student3	3.15	2.55	4.0	3.15	3.2	2.1	2.55
Student4	2.65	2.85	2.1	2.5	3.65	2.2	3.1
Student5	2.5	2.8	3.15	4.15	2.8	4.45	4.7

Table 10. Aptitude levels of students

Student	Analytical	Reasoning	Descriptive	AR	AD	RD	ARD
Student1	M	M	M	L	L	L	M
Student2	L	M	L	M	H	H	H
Student3	M	L	H	M	M	L	L
Student4	M	M	L	L	M	L	M
Student5	L	M	M	H	M	H	H

Figure 6. Class diagram of the system

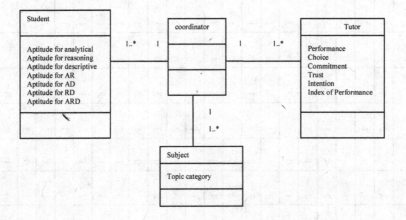

UML Diagram

Class diagram for our system is shown in Figure 6. There are one to many associations between coordinator and student, one to many associations between coordinator and tutor and one to many associations between coordinator and subject. Figure 7 represents interaction diagram. It represents how coordinator, tutors and student communicate. In interaction diagram rq is request for tutor by student to coordinator, que is set of question for testing the student aptitude, a is answer provided by student, sb is subject information, p is profile of a tutor asked by coordinator, pr is response about profile asked by coordinator and at is assigned tutor by coordinator to student.

Figure 8 shows the communication between coordinator, tutors and student in JADE.

In our system agent communication is implemented using FIFA ACL messages. We have used

Figure 7. Interaction diagram

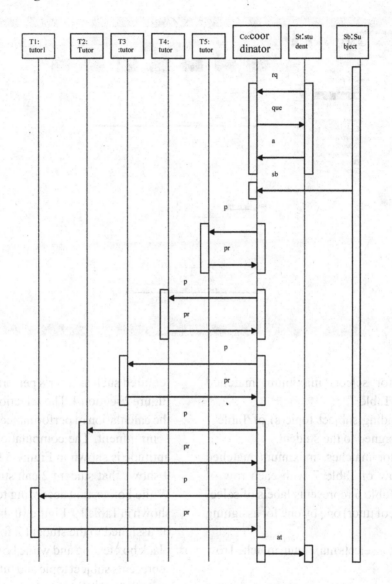

the REQUEST, SUBSCRIBE and INFORM messages. Student uses REQUEST message for request to the coordinator for tutor assignment. Coordinator uses REQUEST messages for requesting to the tutors to provide their profiles. Tutors use INFORM messages to send their profiles to the coordinator. Coordinator sends SUBSCRIBE message to the student to inform that tutor has been assigned.

Selection Procedure:

The coordinator has been used following steps in the selection procedure of subject and tutor for a student:

1. First coordinator takes Table 10 which represents aptitude level of students. Then matches one by one each row of Table 10 with each row of Table 7 (Table 7 represents levels of subject topic).

Figure 8. Snap-shot of communication among student, coordinator, tutor1, tutor2, tutor3, tutor4 and tutor5

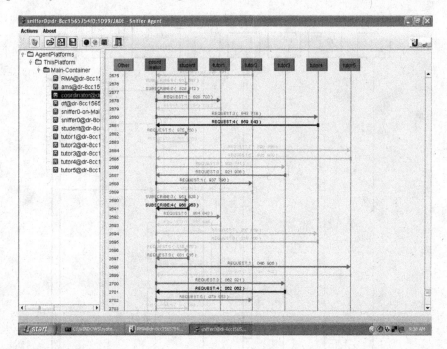

2. Coordinator selects maximum matched row(s) of Table 7.
3. Corresponding subject topic(s) of Table 7 can be assigned to the student.
4. Coordinator matches, maximum matched subject row of Table 7 with each row of Table 6 (Table 6 represents labels of selection index of tutor) one by one for assigning tutor.
5. Coordinator selects maximum matched row of Table 6.
6. Coordinator assigns corresponding tutor (maximum matched row of Table 6) to the student.

RESULT

The overall result of our work concerns with the selection of the subject according to the aptitude level of the student and tutor corresponding to that subject. Other intermediate results have been shown in the previous sections as and when

required such as tutor's performance as shown in Figure 2 section 4. The selection index is based on the calculation of performance, capability, desire, commitment. The computation result of student aptitude is shown in Figure 5 section 4.3. Figure 9 shows that student 2 can study Black box and White box testing according to his aptitude level shown in Table 10. Figure 10 shows that tutor 5 can be assigned to the student 2 for this subject topic black box testing and white box testing. Figure 11 represents subject topic and tutors selected by our system for all five students. Student1 can study validation and tutor 5 can be assigned. Student 2 can study black box testing and white box testing and tutor 5 can be assigned. Student 3 can study project monitoring plan, testing fundamentals, and testing process and tutor 4 can be assigned. Student 4 can study validation and tutor 5 can be assigned. Student 5 can study effort estimation, project scheduling and staffing and tutor 5 can be assigned.

Figure 9. Student2 can study Black Box testing and White Box testing

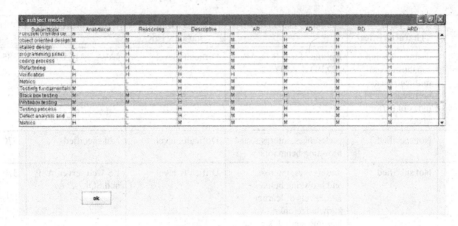

Figure 10. Tutor5 has selected for student2

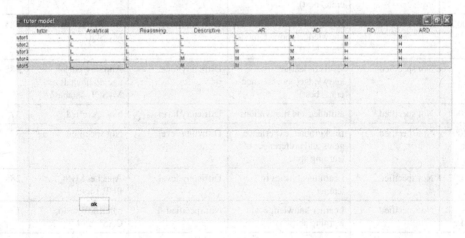

Figure 11. Subjects and tutors for students

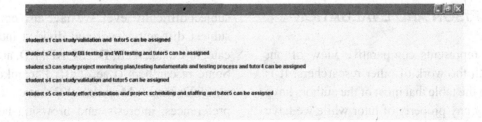

Table 11. Comparative view with other models

Author	Tutor characteristics	Student's characteristics	Subject/Domain characteristics	Implementation	Performance Index
Our Proposed model	desire, intention, capability, commitment, trust, preferences, and index of performance	Aptitude for A,R,D, AR, AD,RD & ARD	Difficulty level	JAVA, JADE	.385
Lee, 2001	Not specified	preferences, interests, and browsing behaviors	Difficulty level	Not specified	.370
Papanikolaou et al., 2002	Not specified	preferences, interests, and browsing behaviors, levels of learner knowledge(unknown, learning started, learned, well-learned)	Difficulty level	IIS web server. ASP, and SQL-server	.370
Tang & Mccalla, 2003	Not specified	preferences, interests, and browsing behaviors	Not specified	Not specified	.17
Chen et al., 2005	Not specified	levels of learner knowledge(poorest, moderate, best)	Difficulty level	IIS Web server, PHP, My SQL	.285
Chen et al., 2006	Not specified	levels of learner knowledge(poorest, moderate, best)	Difficulty level	IIS Web server, PHP, My SQL	.285
Chen, 2008	Not specified	levels of learner knowledge(poorest, moderate, best)	Difficulty level	AppServ package, PHP analyzer, MySQL database	.285
Baker Ryan, 2007	Not specified	attitudes and motivations	Difficulty level	Not specified	.37
Zhang et al., 2001	Not specified	Background, experience, goals and preferences of learning style.	Difficulty level	Not specified	.37
Leung & Li, 2007	Not specified	Learning abilities of learner	Difficulty level	Apache, MySQL, PHP, Linux	.285
Suraweera & Mitrovic, 2004	Not specified	Learner knowledge and learning abilities	Not specified	Microsoft visio, CASE tool	.17
Schiaffino et al., 2008	Not specified	Learning style, performance	Not specified	Not specified	.17
Jeremic & Devedži, 2004	Not specified	Performance,	Not specified	HTML, JSP	.136

COMPARISON AND EVALUATION

Table 11 represents comparative view of our model with the work of other researchers. It is clear from the table that most of the authors have not specify any property of tutor while we have calculated tutor's desire, intention, capability, commitment, trust, preferences, and index of performance. Most of the researchers have considered subject difficulty level. We have also considered subject difficulty level and divided into seven categories, i.e., A, R, D, AR, AD, RD, and ARD. Some researchers (Lee, 2001; Papanikolaou et al., 2002; Tang & Mccalla, 2003) have considered preferences, interests, and browsing behaviors in student's characteristics while some (Chen et al., 2005; Chen et al., 2006; Chen, 2008) have considered levels of learner knowledge. In our system we have calculated student's aptitude and considered it as student characteristics.

Performance of each method has been evaluated. Most of the authors have taken preference, interest and learning background (knowledge) of the students in general and browsing behavior for web based system in particular. In the evaluation process we have considered different importance values and weights to the three modules (student, tutor and subject) and various parameters for each of the modules respectively. For example the student module, tutor module and subject module have been assigned the importance values as Ist=0.5, Itu=0.3,and Isb=0.2 respectively. Again each of these importance value is equally divided in to sub values depending on number of parameters assigned to the particular module i.e. X=Ist/n, Y=Itu/m and Z=Isb/p where X, Y, Z are the importance value of the modules as stated above and n, m, and p are the number of parameters in the respective modules. For example if an author has taken three parameters preference, interest and browsing behavior in student model then weight given to student module is 0.5 and is divided into three parts 0.5/3=0.17 .0.17 is importance value given to student parameters. Weightage to each parameter to a module is also given heuristically on the basis of their effectiveness in learning process. For example weight for interest is .5, weight for preference is .3 and weight for browsing behavior is .2.In the same way weight in tutor module is .5 for capability, .3 for commitment and .2 for desire. Value for tutor characteristic is Itu/m=0.3/3=0.1 where .3 is importance value given to tutor model. Since difficulty (single parameter) has been considered by most of the researchers in subject model, value for difficulty is Isb/p=0.2/1= 0.2. Here .2 is importance value given to subject module. Thus the general formula to calculate performance index (PI) is as follows:

$$PI=X*(Ist_1+Ist_2+...Ist_n)+Y(Itu_1+Itu_2+...Itu_m)+Z(Isb_1+Isb_2+....Isb_p)$$

For authors who have considered single or two modules and few parameters which are not exactly the same as our proposed parameters we take the equivalent or some of equivalent their parameters to our module parameters.

Performance Index of Models

Our Model

In calculating performance index of our model we have been taken capability, commitment and desire parameter of tutor module. Aptitude of student has been taken equivalent to interest and preference. Performance index of our model=0.1*[0.5+0.3+0.2]+.17*[.5+.3]+.2=.385.

Lee model (Lee, 2001) In calculating performance index of Lee model three parameters interest, preference and browsing behavior have been considered. Performance Index of Lee model=[0]+[.17*.5+.17*.3+.17*.2]+[.2]=.370.

Papanikolaou et al. model (Papanikolaou et al. 2002) Performance index of Papanikolaou et al. model=[0]+[.17*.5+.17*.3+.17*.2]+[.2]=.370.

Tang et al. model (Tang & Mccalla, 2003) Performance index of Tang et al. model=[0]+.17*[.5+.3+.2]+[0]=.17.

Chen model and Chen et al. model (Chen et al., 2005; Chen et al., 2006; Chen, 2008) Performance index of Chen model and Chen et al. model= [0]+.17*[.5]+.2=.285. Here level of learner knowledge has been taken equivalent to interest.

Baker model (Baker Ryan, 2007) In calculating performance index of Baker model attitude is equivalent to interest and motivation is equivalent to preference and browsing behaviour. Performance index of Baker model=[0]+.17*[.5+.3+.2]+0.2=.37.

Zhang et al. model (Zhang et al., 2001) In calculating performance index of Zhang et al. model experience and goals and preferences have been taken. Performance index of Zhang et al. model=[0]+.17*[.5+.3+.2]+.2=.37.

Multiagent Based Selection of Tutor-Subject-Student Paradigm in an Intelligent Tutoring System

Table 12. Computing assessment of models

Author	Student				Subject				Tutor			
	Ma	He	Ag	Mc	Ma	He	Ag	Mc	Ma	He	Ag	Mc
Our Proposed model	H	M	L	M	L	H	L	M	H	M	L	M
Lee, 2001	L	L	L	L	L	H	L	M	-	-	-	-
Papanikolaou et al., 2002	H	L	L	M	L	H	L	H	-	-	-	-
Tang & Mccalla, 2003	L	H	L	M	-	-	-	-	-	-	-	-
Chen et al., 2005	H	M	L	M	H	M	L	M	-	-	-	-
Chen et al., 2006	H	M	L	M	H	M	L	M	-	-	-	-
Chen, 2008	L	H	L	M	H	M	L	M	-	-	-	-
Baker Ryan, 2007	H	L	L	M	L	L	L	L	-	-	-	-
Zhang et al., 2001	L	M	L	M	M	H	L	M	-	-	-	-
Leung & Li, 2007	H	M	L	M	-	-	-	-	-	-	-	-
Suraweera & Mitrovic, (2004)	L	M	L	M	-	-	-	-	-	-	-	-
Schiaffino et al., 2008	L	M	L	M	-	-	-	-	-	-	-	-

Leung et al. model (Leung & Li, 2007) In calculating performance index of Leung et al. model learning abilities of learner has been taken equivalent to interest and preference. Performance index of Leung et al. model=[0]+.17*[.5+.3]+.2=.285.

Suraweera and Mitrovic model (Suraweera & Mitrovic, 2004) In calculating performance index of Suraweera and Mitrovic (2004) model, learner knowledge is equivalent to interest and reference and learning abilities is equivalent to browsing behaviour. Performance index of Suraweera and Mitrovic model=[0]+.17*[.5+.3+.2]+[0]=.17.

Schiaffino et al. model (Schiaffino et al., 2008) In calculating performance index of Schiaffino et al. model learning style is equivalent to browsing behaviour and performance is equivalent to interest and preference. Performance index of Schiaffino et al. model=[0]+.17*[.5+.3+.2]+[0]=.17.

Jeremic and Devedži model (Jeremic & Devedži, 2004) In calculating performance of Jeremic model value of parameter, i.e., performance has been considered .17 and importance value has been considered by both interest and preference because performance is equivalent to interest and preference. Performance index of Jeremic and Devedži model=[0]+.17*[.5+.3]+[0]=.136

Rule of combination for logical correlation:

Rule 1: Same level: LÅL =>L; HÅH=>H; MÅM=>M.

Rule 2: Different level with difference of one level: LÅM =>M; MÅH=>H.

Rule 3: Different level with difference of two levels: LÅH =>M.

Here Ma: mathematical, He: heuristic, Ag: algorithmic Mc= MaÅHeÅAg.

From Table 12, we are able to know the nature of computational load on each of the method. It depends upon the number of computing modules and the parameters in each of the module. Only our computing method considers three modules where as seven methods consider two modules and four methods considered only one module.

Most of the methods considered two or three parameters in the module concerned. Considering increased number of modules and parameters although increases the computing overhead but gives proportionally increase in the performance index which is obvious from the Table 11.Our method is more effective in the sense that it covers three component of ITS uniformly.

CONCLUSION

In this paper, we have made an attempt to tackle an important issue in the pedagogical model of ITS for the selection of tutor-subject-student paradigm. The computation and correlation of psychological, cognitive and mental parameters of the student and tutor are important aspects of our TSS model. The nature and characteristics of a particular subject depicted on the problems of analytical (A), reasoning(R), descriptive (D), and their combination as such AR, AD, RD and ARD contribute significantly in the selection procedure of TSS. Basically this paper brings out a computational methodology based on heuristic for the selection of TSS combination. Adding a question-answer set for a particular subject provides an experimental set-up in this context. We have made the comparison of the various methods on the basis of calculating the performance index of each method. It is found that our proposed method covers a wide range of parameters in the modules and thus yields a highest value of performance index. The comparative view of the use of different degree (High/Medium/Low) of use of mathematical (Ma) heuristic (He) and algorithmic (Ag) approach in each of the method and their logical combination produces a qualitative assessment of the computational overhead. Higher computational overhead reflects more detail computation leading to better accuracy of the result. In future, we would like to develop a modal logic to formulate the problem and also a wide range of experimentation. We have taken

only the most dominant parameter, i.e., aptitude of student, the other parameter such as interest of psychological nature and stress, comfort, boredom etc. pertaining to ergonomics are to be incorporated in future work.

REFERENCES

About.com. (n.d.). Retrieved February 12, 2009, from http://www.about.com

Azzedin, F., & Maheswaran, M. (2002). Towards trust-aware resource management in grid computing systems. In *Proceedings of the International Symposium on Cluster Computing and the Grid (CCGRID-2002),* Berlin, Germany (pp. 452).

Baker Ryan, S. J. D. (2007, April 28-May 3). Modeling and understanding students' off-task behavior in intelligent tutoring systems. In *Proceedings of CHI 2007: Learning & Education,* San Jose, CA (pp. 1059-1068). ACM Publishing.

Bell, J. (1995). Changing attitudes in intelligent agents. In M. Wooldridge & N. R. Jennings (Eds.), *Proceedings of the ECAI-94 Workshop on Agent Theories, Architecture and languages* (pp. 40-50). Berlin: Springer.

Bratman, M. E. (1990). What is intention? In P. R. Cohen & M. J. Pollack (Eds.), *Intentions in communication* (pp. 15-31). Cambridge, MA: MIT Press.

Castelfranchi, C., & Falcone, R. (1998). Principles of trust for MAS: Cognitive anatomy, social importance and quantification. In *Proceedings of the International Conference on Multi-Agent Systems (ICMAS'98),* Paris, France (pp. 72-79).

Chen, C. (2008). Intelligent web-based learning system with personalized learning path guidance. *Computers & Education, 51,* 787–814. doi:10.1016/j.compedu.2007.08.004

Chen, C. M., Lee, H. M., & Chen, Y. H. (2005). Personalized e-learning system using item response theory. *Computers & Education, 44*(3), 237–255. doi:10.1016/j.compedu.2004.01.006

Chen, C. M., Liu, C. Y., & Chang, M. H. (2006). Personalized curriculum sequencing using modified item response theory for web-based instruction. *Expert Systems with Applications, 30*(2), 378–396. doi:10.1016/j.eswa.2005.07.029

Farlex. (n.d.). *Commitment.* Retrieved September 5, 2008, from http://www.thefreedictionary.com/commitment

Georgeff, M., Pell, B., Pollack, M., Tambe, M., & Wooldridge, M. (1999). The belief-desire-intention model of agency. In *Proceedings of the International Workshop on Intelligent Agents V: Agent Theories, Architectures, and Languages,* Paris (Vol 5, pp. 1-10). Springer Verlag.

Grandison, T., & Sloman, M. (2000). A survey of trust in internet applications. *IEEE Communications Surveys and Tutorials, 4*(4), 2–16.

He, M., Jennings, N. R., & Leung, H. (2003). On agent-mediated electronic commerce. *IEEE Transactions on Knowledge and Data Engineering, 15*(4), 985–1003. doi:10.1109/TKDE.2003.1209014

IPD. (n.d.). *What is performance.* Retrieved September 5, 2008, from http://www.ipdoccupiers.com/Advisors/Whatisperformance/tabid/1384/Default.aspx

Jaques, P. A., & Vicari, R. M. (2007). A BDI approach to infer student's emotions in an intelligent learning environment. *Computers & Education, 49,* 360–384. doi:10.1016/j.compedu.2005.09.002

Jeremic, Z., & Devedži, V. (2004). *Design pattern ITS: Student model implementation.* Paper presented at the IEEE International Conference on Advanced Learning Technologies (ICALT'04).

Kraus, S., Sycara, K., & Evenchil, A. (1998). Reaching agreements through argumentation: A logical model and implementation. *Artificial Intelligence, 104,* 1–69. doi:10.1016/S0004-3702(98)00078-2

Kumar, S., & Mishra, R. B. (2008). A hybrid model for service selection in semantic web service composition. *International Journal of Intelligent Information Technologies, 4*(4), 55–69.

Lee, M. G. (2001). Profiling students' adaptation styles in web-based learning. *Computers & Education, 36,* 121–132. doi:10.1016/S0360-1315(00)00046-4

Leung, E. W. C., & Li, Q. (2007). An experimental study of a personalized learning environment through open-source software tools. *IEEE Transactions on Education, 50*(4). doi:10.1109/TE.2007.904571

Mazumdar, B. D., & Mishra, R. B. (2009). Multiagent paradigm for the agent slection and negotiation in a B2C process. *International Journal of Intelligent Information Technologies, 5*(1), 61–83.

Mui, L., Mohtashemi, M., & Halberstadt, A. (2002). A computational model of trust and reputation. In *Proceedings of the 35th International Conference on System Science* (pp. 280-287).

Olmedilla, D., Rana, O., Matthews, B., & Nejdl, W. (2005). Security and trust issues in semantic grids. In *Proceedings of the Dagsthul Seminar, Semantic Grid: The Convergence of Technologies* (Vol. 05271).

Panzarasa, P., Jennings, N. R., & Norman, T. J. (2002)... *Formalizing Collaborative Decision-making and Practical Reasoning in Multi-agent System, 12*(1), 55–117.

Papanikolaou, K. A., Grigoriadou, M., Magoulasb, G. D., & Kornilakisa, H. (2002). Towards new forms of knowledge communication: The adaptive dimension of a web based learning environment. *Computers & Education, 39*, 333–360. doi:10.1016/S0360-1315(02)00067-2

Prism, Ltd. (n.d.). *Commitment.* Retrieved September 5, 2008, from http://www.prismltd.com/commit.htm

Reid, D., & Newhouse, C. P. (2004, December 5-8). But that didn't happen last semester: Explanations of the mediated environmental factors that affect online tutor capabilities. In R. Atkinson, C. McBeath, D. Jonas-Dwyer, & R. Phillips (Eds.), *Beyond the comfort zone: Proceedings of the 21st ASCILITE Conference,* Perth (pp. 791-797). Retrieved from http://www.ascilite.org.au/conferences/perth04/procs/reid.html

Schiaffino, S., Garcia, P., & Amandi, A. (2008). eTeacher: Providing personalized assistance to e-learning students. *Computers & Education, 51,* 1744–1754. doi:10.1016/j.compedu.2008.05.008

Shoham, Y. (1993). Agent oriented programming. *Artificial Intelligence, 60*(1), 51–92. doi:10.1016/0004-3702(93)90034-9

Suraweera, P., & Mitrovic, A. (2004). An intelligent tutoring system for entity relationship modeling. *International Journal of Artificial Intelligence in Education, 14*(3-4), 375-417. ISSN:1560-4292

Tang, T. Y., & Mccalla, G. (2003, July 20-24). Smart recommendation for evolving e-learning system. In *Proceedings of the 11th International Conference on Artificial Intelligence in Education, Workshop on Technologies for Electronic Documents for Supporting Learning,* Sydney, Australia (pp. 699-710).

Von, W. G. H. (1980). *Freedom and determination.* Amsterdam, The Netherlands: North Holland Publishing.

Wu, W., Ekaette, E., & Far, B. H. (2003). Uncertainty management framework for multi-agent system. In *Proceedings of ATS* (pp. 122-131).

This work was previously published in International Journal of Intelligent Information Technologies, Volume 6, Issue 1, edited by Vijayan Sugumaran, pp. 46-70, copyright 2010 by IGI Publishing (an imprint of IGI Global).

Chapter 5
Information Sharing Strategies in Business-to-Business E-Hubs:
An Agent-Based Study

Yifeng Zhang
University of Illinois at Springfield, USA

Siddhartha Bhattacharyya
University of Illinois at Chicago, USA

ABSTRACT

Studies show that supply chain structure is a key factor affecting information sharing. Business-to-business (B2B) e-hubs have fundamentally changed many companies' supply chain structure, from a one-to-many to a many-to-many configuration. Traditional supply chains typically center around one company, which interacts with multiple suppliers or customers, forming a one-to-many structure. B2B e-hubs, on the contrary, usually connect many buyers and sellers together, without being dominated by a single company, thus forming a many-to-many configuration. Information sharing in traditional supply chains has been studied extensively, but little attention has been paid to the same in B2B e-hubs. In this study, the authors identified and examined five information sharing strategies in B2B e-hubs. Agent performances under different information sharing strategies were measured and analyzed using an agent-based e-hub model and practical implications were discussed.

DOI: 10.4018/978-1-4666-0158-1.ch005

1. INTRODUCTION

Information sharing plays an important role in modern supply chain management. Pioneered by industry leaders such as Wal-Mart and Proctor & Gamble, information sharing is now routinely practiced by many companies (Li & Lin, 2006; Zhou & Benton Jr, 2007). For example, through sharing information, Thomson Consumer Electronics reduced its lead times and planning cycles from four weeks to one week, and Boeing was able to cut its cycle times in half and reduce parts defect rate by 56% (Li et al., 2006). With better visibility into operations of the whole supply chain, firms can make better decisions on many aspects of supply chain management, such as inventory replenishment, shipping, pricing, and capacity allocation etc.

One challenge in implementing information sharing is to employ an appropriate information sharing strategy and select the right information to share. A wide range of information can be shared in supply chains, but the effects of sharing different types of information can vary greatly (Li et al., 2006). Information commonly shared in supply chains include demand information (Hosoda et al., 2008), supply information (Swaminathan, 1997), inventory information (Gavirneni, 2006), cost information (Karabati & Sayin, 2008; Mukhopadhyay et al., in Press), and shipping information (Zhang et al., 2006). Selecting the appropriate level of sharing is also a key aspect of information sharing strategy (Samaddar et al., 2006). Information sharing can be classified as transactional, operational, or strategic, in an ascending order of level of sharing. On the one hand, if the level of sharing is too low, the information shared might not be useful. On the other hand, if the level of sharing is too high, the information might be used against the sharing party in a competitive environment.

One key factor that needs to be considered when deciding on an information sharing strategy is the supply chain structure (Li et al., 2006).

First appeared in the late 90s and can be found in almost all industries today, business-to-business (B2B) e-hubs have fundamentally changed many companies' supply chain structure in the past two decades. B2B e-hubs are Internet-based platforms where multiple trading partners can conduct transactions and collaborate and exchange information with each other (Kaplan & Sawhney, 2000).

B2B e-hubs are fundamentally different from traditional supply chains in structure. Traditional supply chains are usually dominated by one company; while B2B e-hubs typically connect a large number of firms together. In other words, traditional supply chains have a one-to-many structure, where one dominant company interacts with many of its suppliers or customers. E-hubs, on the contrary, have a many-to-many structure where many buyers interact with many sellers. It is not uncommon for an e-hub to have thousands or even tens of thousands of participants. B2B e-hubs create both new opportunities and new challenges for information sharing. On the opportunity side, e-hubs make it much easier for companies to obtain industry-wide information because e-hubs typically connect a large number of companies in the same industry. Facilitating industry-wide information sharing is considered a critical success factor for e-hubs (Powell, 2001). On the challenge side, companies might be unwilling to share information on e-hubs because of increased transparency and competition (Lu & Antony, 2003; Owan & Nickerson, 2002).

Information sharing in traditional supply chains has been studied extensively (Aviv, 2001; Cheung & Lee, 2002; Gavirneni, 2002; Li, 2002; Xu et al., 2001). However, little attention has been paid to information sharing strategies in B2B e-hubs (Shevchenko & Shevchenko, 2005). Many questions remain to be answered. For example, which information should companies share in B2B e-hubs? Are certain types of information more valuable than others? What effects does information sharing have on different aspects of operation? These are the questions that this paper aims to address. Specifically, we examined five information sharing strategies that are formed on the basis of various types of aggregate demand and inventory information in e-hubs. An agent-based e-hub model was constructed and used to simulate agents' operations under different information sharing strategies. Agent performances were measured and compared between different information sharing strategies.

The rest of the paper is organized as follows: Sections 2 and 3 review related literature, Section 4 describes information sharing strategies examined in this study, Section 5 explains the agent-based e-hub model, Sections 6 and 7 describe and discuss results, and Section 8 discusses limitations and future research.

2. INFORMATION SHARING STRATEGIES IN TRADITIONAL SUPPLY CHAINS

Li et al. (2006) conducted a systematic study of information sharing strategies in traditional supply chains. They examined five information sharing strategies in a linear supply chain: a) sharing order information between adjacent stages of the supply chain, b) sharing end demand with all stages, c) sharing inventory information with the adjacent upstream stage (suppliers), d) sharing outbound shipment information with the adjacent upstream stage, and e) sharing both end demand and inventory information, i.e., a combination of strategy b) and c). The authors measured the supply chain performance in terms of inventory cost and fill rate and found that the impact of information sharing depends on demand patterns and the supply chain structure. The study shows that various information sharing strategies consistently improve supply chain performance under relatively stable demand. But when the variance of end demand is high, the effect of information sharing strategies varies; and no strategy is uniformly superior. The hybrid strategy, i.e., strategy e), was found to be

a powerful concept for managing product mix uncertainty.

Samaddar et al. (2006) proposed a framework that classifies information sharing strategies in supply chains along two dimensions: volume (how much information is shared) and strategic consequences (what kind of information is shared). The volume of the information shared can be none, partial, or complete. With no information sharing, the retailer shares no information with the supplier other than what is needed for the transaction. With partial information sharing, the retailer shares with the supplier its demand distribution and inventory policy. With complete information sharing, the retailer shares with the supplier its demand in real time. On the strategic consequence dimension, the information shared can be transactional, operational, strategic, or strategic and competitive. For example, sharing inventory position with a supplier is considered at the operational level; while sharing point-of-sales information is considered at the strategic level. Along these two dimensions, Samaddar et al. (2006) classified information sharing strategies in supply chains into four categories: low volume operational information, high volume operational information, low volume strategic information, and high volume strategic information.

Among the different types of information communicated in supply chains, demand and inventory information are probably the most commonly shared and extensively studied. Sharing of both types of information has been shown to be valuable. For example, HoSoda's (2008) study shows that a supplier can benefit from the point of sales data that her retailer shares with her. Using the shared information, the supplier can increase its demand forecast accuracy by 8% to 19%. Yue and Liu's (2006) study shows that the manufacturer can benefit from the demand forecast information that the retailer shares with her. In the context of a two-stage linear supply chain that comprises of one supplier and one retailer, Xe et al. (2001) showed that the supplier can make more accurate demand forecasting if the retailer shares its demand information with her. Chu and Lee (2006) studied two factors: cost of information sharing and volume of the market demand (high or low), on a retailer's decision of whether to share demand information with its supplier or not. Li (2002) studied the condition under which retailers are willing to share demand information with their supplier in a supply chain that comprises of one supplier and many retailers. Wikner (1991) proposed a method for downstream supply chain players to share demand information with upstream players that divides orders into two parts: the actual demand and the demand forecast.

The value of sharing inventory has also been extensively studied (Cachon & Fisher, 2000). Gavirneni (2006) showed that having access to her customer's day-to-day inventory position is more beneficial to a supplier than only knowing parameters of the customer's inventory policy. Information on retailers' inventory position can also be used by a supplier to improve its decision on inventory replenishing and shipment allocation among multiple retailers (Cheung & Lee, 2002; Gavirneni, 2001, 2002). In the context of a two-stage linear supply chain that comprises of one retailer and one supplier, Gavirneni (2002) showed that the total supply chain cost is lower when the retailer shares its inventory position with the supplier. Sharing of inventory position has also been shown to be valuable in divergent supply chains that comprise of one supplier and multiple retailers. Moinzadeh (2002) proposed a new ordering policy for the supplier to take advantage of such information. Cheung and Lee (2002) showed that the supplier can make better shipping arrangements when it has access to her multiple retailers' inventory positions.

3. BUSINESS-TO-BUSINESS E-HUBS

B2B e-hubs first appeared in late 90s; and, like many other e-commerce technologies, went through a dramatic boom-and-bust cycle over the past two decades (Day *et al.*, 2003). Today, hundreds of e-hubs exist in many industries. For example, SupplyOn is a successful European e-hub in the automotive industry. It became profitable in 2003 and has that more than 75% of the world's top 100 automotive suppliers as its customers (White *et al.*, 2007). Exostar is a well-established e-hub in the aerospace industry that connects more than 40,000 companies. Elemica is a leading e-hub in the chemical industry. Its trading volume increased from $10 billion to $50 billion from 2004 to 2007 (see Forbes's B2B directory for more examples of B2B e-hubs: http://www.forbes.com/bow/b2b/main.jhtml).

B2B e-hubs play an increasingly important role in many companies' procurement and distribution operations. They represent a shift from the hierarchical to market-like inter-organizational relationships (Malone et al., 1987). They enable companies to conduct transactions and manage their supply chain processes more efficiently on a global scale (Eng, 2004). Participants of e-hubs benefit from lower procurement cost, lower product cost, and better capacity utilization (Kathawala et al., 2002). Many companies use B2B e-hubs as a spot procurement channel that supplements long-term contract-based procurement (Kleindorfer & Wu, 2003; Lee et al., 2006). Yadav and Varadarajan (2005) argued that to fully participate in an e-hub, a company needs to go through four types of product migration: information migration, transaction migration, fulfillment migration, and post-purchase support activities migration.

The increased adoption of B2B e-hubs has profound implications for information sharing. B2B e-hubs are at a unique position for collecting and disseminating industry-wide information, which are very important for many supply chain/network decisions, such as inventory and risk management (Grey et al., 2005; Ketzenberg et al., 2007). The value of sharing aggregate information was demonstrated by Guo et al. (2006). In the study, the authors assumed a supply chain

Table 1. Information sharing strategies

Information Sharing Strategy	Information Shared
ISS-1	None
ISS-2	Aggregate Hub Demand (AHD)
ISS-3	Aggregate End Demand (AED)
ISS-4	Aggregate Buyer Inventory Position (ABI)
ISS-5	AED and ABI

that includes multiple retailers who order a homogeneous product from a manufacturer. Each retailer's demand risk includes a systematic part that affects all retailers and an idiosyncratic part that affects an individual retailer only. The authors proposed a method for eliciting and aggregating information on the demand risk from individual retailers; and showed that the information can be used to achieve accurate demand forecast and useful for hedging against aggregate market risks. As a result, information sharing is believed to be important for supply network collaboration on e-hubs (Zhu, 2002).

There are also obstacles to implementing information sharing in B2B e-hubs, such as short-term customer-supplier relationships and lack of trust between business partners. However, various studies show that these obstacles can be overcome. For example, Lancastre and Lages's (2006) study showed that it is possible to connect a large number of buyers and suppliers through B2B e-hubs and developed meaningful business relationships. Through case studies, White et al. (2005) showed that new information technologies, such as e-hubs, enable companies to maintain a highly integrated and also very flexible relationship with their business partners.

Despite of the fundamental structural differences between B2B e-hubs and traditional supply chains and profound implications of B2B e-hubs for information sharing, we are unaware of any research on information sharing in B2B e-hubs. In this study, we constructed an agent-based e-hub model that includes multiple buyer and seller

agents and examined effects of various information sharing strategies on the agents.

4. INFORMATION SHARING STRATEGIES IN B2B E-HUBS

Earlier discussions show that demand information and inventory information are two general types of information that are commonly shared between supply chain partners. In this study, we identified three specific types of demand and inventory information that can be easily collected by an e-hub: aggregate end demand (AED), aggregate hub demand (AHD), and aggregate buyer inventory position (ABI). Considering an e-hub that has multiple buyers and multiple sellers, AED is the total demand received by all buyers, i.e., the total end demand. AHD is the total demand received by all sellers. And ABI is the aggregate inventory position of all buyers.

In this study, we define an Information Sharing Strategy (IIS) as the combination of information that buyer agents share with seller agents. Apparently, many ISS can be formed based on the three types of information identified above. In this study, we focused on five such strategies (see Table 1). ISS-1 is the baseline scenario where buyers share no information with sellers and each seller only knows its own demand. Under ISS-2, AHD is made available to all sellers. Under ISS-3, AED is shared with all sellers. Under ISS-4, ABI is shared with sellers. Under ISS-5, both AED and ABI are shared with sellers. Please note that

ISS-3 represents a higher level of sharing than ISS-2 because AED is more accurate and sensitive information than AHD; and ISS-5 is a hybrid strategy that combines ISS-3 and ISS-4.

The five ISS were selected to facilitate examination of the effects of sharing different types of information. Specifically, agent performances under the five ISS were compared in the following fashion to allow us to examine particular effects:

ISS-1 vs. ISS-2: To examine the effect of sharing AHD

ISS-2 vs. ISS-3: To examine whether AED is more beneficial than AHD

ISS-1 vs. ISS-4: To examine the effect of sharing ABI

ISS-3 vs. ISS-4: To examine potential differences between sharing AED and sharing ABI

ISS-3 vs. ISS-5: To examine marginal effect of sharing ABI on top of sharing AED

ISS-4 vs. ISS-5: To examine marginal effect of sharing AED on top of sharing ABI.

5. METHODOLOGY

5.1 Agent-Based Modeling and Supply Chain Management

The methodology for this study is Agent-Based Modeling (ABM). ABM undertakes a bottom-up approach to the modeling of individual agents and the way they act and interact; the overall dynamics emerges from the collective interaction of heterogeneous agents. ABM is noted to be useful for problems that cannot be mathematically modeled, or where analytical solutions are not readily obtainable (Axtell, 2000). Complex adaptive systems like supply networks fall into this category, and thus constitute a natural application area of ABM (Langdon, 2005; Langdon & Sikora, 2006; Lin et al., 1999; Sikora & Shaw, 1998; Surana et al., 2005).

Even though a relatively new methodology, ABM has received considerable attention from supply chain management researchers (Akkermans, 2001; Hong et al., 2007; Ram & Liu, 2005; Sadeh et al., 2003; Schlueter-Langdon et al., 2000). Agent-based supply network frameworks have been proposed in a number of studies (Allwood & Lee, 2005; Ito & Abadi, 2002; Sadeh et al., 2001). The importance of appropriately calibrating agent attributes and capabilities was highlighted in Caridi et al. (2005) and Gjerdrum et al. (2001).

ABM has been used to study a wide range of supply chain/network problems, such as the Bullwhip effect - amplification of order variances (Parunak et al., 1999), order fulfillment (Lin *et al.*, 2000), impacts of electronic brokers on the value of manufacturing process postponement Robinson and Elofson (2001), trust between supply chain partners (Macal & North, 2003a, 2003b), horizontal competition among retailers Xie and Chen (2004), and supplier selection Lin et al. (2005).

One of the advantages of ABM is its ability to explicitly model the high level of complexity inherent in many supply chain management issues. This has been demonstrated by its successful application in many real-world supply chain management situations, ranging from a single retail store Signorile (2002), to automotive supply networks (Wilke, 2002), electromechanical distribution systems Cavalieri et al. (2003), to the paper tissue production/distribution system Datta et al. (2007).

5.2 An Agent-Based E-Hub Model

An agent-based e-hub model was built using the Swarm[1] toolkit. Swarm is an object-oriented toolkit that provides various facilities for developing agent-based models. It provides the underlying simulation facilities, including random number generation and various distributions, and also the means for graphically observing results and for experimentation. Specific models can be developed

Figure 1. Class diagram of the E-Hub model

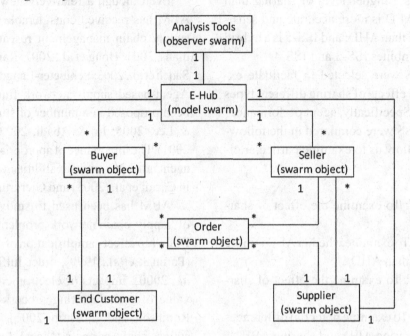

by deriving from the provided Swarm classes and implementing model and agent specific behaviors.

Figure 1 shows the class diagram of the e-hub model. Class names are given in the boxes, with names in brackets indicating the Swarm classes from which they are derived. The Analysis Tools class contains various visual analysis and data collection tools, and manages multiple runs of the model. The E-Hub class defines structure of the e-hub and the relationships between agents. The E-Hub class is a swarm class and contains four types of agents: End Customer, Buyer, Seller, and Supplier. The agents interact with each other through orders. Figure 2 provides a business view of the e-hub model. It shows that the model includes one end customer agent, three buyer agents, three seller agents, and one supplier agent.

Agents in the model operate in discreet time steps or periods. At the beginning of each period, the end customer agent generates a random demand in the range of [20, 40]. The demand is divided into three pieces of equal size and passed to the buyer agents in the form of orders. Buyer agents then try to fulfill the orders. If they have enough

inventories on hand, they fulfill all orders and ship them to the end customer. Otherwise, they backlog unfilled orders for future fulfillment. Orders are fulfilled on a first-come-first-served basis. After incoming orders are processed, buyers determine whether they need to replenish inventories. If the answer is yes, they decide how many units and from which seller to order. Buyers determine the order size using an economic order quantity policy (explained in details next) and select the seller who offers the earliest shipping time to order from. After buyer agents finish their operations, it is the seller agents' turn. Seller agents' operations are identical to buyer agents', except for the ordering policy, which are discussed in details next. In the last phase of a period, the supplier agent fulfills orders placed by the seller agents. The supplier agent is assumed to have infinite amount of inventories; thus always fulfill sellers' orders on time. Transmission of purchase orders from a downstream agent, such as a buyer, to an upstream agent, such as a seller, is assumed to be instantaneous; while shipping

Figure 2. Agents and relationships in the E-Hub model

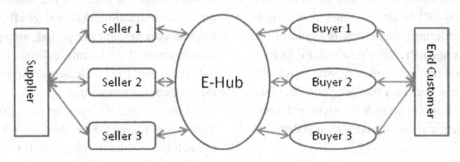

of fulfilled orders is subject to a delay of two to three periods.

Buyer agents and seller agents use an economic order quantity policy to replenish their inventories (Chen, 1998; Chen *et al.*, 2000; Chen & Zheng, 1994; De Bodt & Graves, 1985). The policy specifies that when the inventory position *IP* is below a reorder point *R*, an order of size *Q* will be created. Inventory position *IP* is the sum of on-hand inventory and outstanding orders *G*, minus back orders *B* (see Equation 1). Reorder point *R* is determined by demand forecast, lead-time, and a reorder point coefficient (see Equation 2). Order quantity *Q* is determined by demand forecast, setup ordering cost, and unit holding cost (see Equation 3). Demand forecast is calculated using the moving average of historical demands (see Equation 4).

Equation 1

$$IP_t = I_t + G_t - B_t$$

Equation 2

$$R_t = (L + \alpha)\hat{\theta}_t$$

Equation 3

$$Q_t = \begin{cases} \sqrt{(2C_o\hat{\theta}_t / C_h)} & if \quad IP_t < R_t \\ 0 & otherwise \end{cases}$$

Equation 4

$$\hat{\theta}_t = \sum_{t-W+1}^{t} d_t / W$$

where:

$\hat{\theta}$: demand forecast,
α: reorder point coefficient,
B: back order,
C_o: setup ordering cost,
C_h: holding cost per unit per period,
d: demand received,
G: outstanding order,
I: inventory on hand,
IP: inventory position,
L: lead-time,
R: reorder point,
t: time step/period,
Q: order size,
W: demand forecast window.

Buyer agents always use the order policy described above, but seller agents only use it under ISS-1 when no information is shared. Modified versions of the policy are used by seller agents under other ISS to incorporate the information shared (Ketzenberg et al., 2007). When AHD or AED is shared, the calculation of demand forecast is modified. Specifically, moving averages of AHD or AED, depending on which one is shared, instead of an agent's own demand, is used to calculate the demand forecast (see Equation 5 and 6). When ABI is shared, a new condition is added for reordering (Glasserman & Tayur, 1994). Now a seller agent creates a new order if its own inventory position is below a reorder point (R), and ABI is also below a reorder point (R') (see Equation 7). Reorder point R' is calculated based on a coefficient and the estimated market demand.

Equation 5

$$\hat{\theta}_t = \sum_{t-W+1}^{t} \frac{(AHD)_t}{N_s} / W$$

Equation 6

$$\hat{\theta}_t = \sum_{t-W+1}^{t} \frac{(AED)_t}{N_s} / W$$

Equation 7

$$Q_t = \begin{cases} \sqrt{(2C_o\hat{\theta}_t / C_h)} & if \quad (IP_t < R_t) and (ABI_t < R_t') \\ 0 & otherwise \end{cases}$$

where N_s is the number of sellers on the e-hub, which is three in this case.

Agent performance is determined by various types of costs that they incur. Both buyer and seller agents incur three major costs: inventory holding cost, stock-out penalty cost, and setup ordering cost. Inventory holding cost is the cost of storing and maintaining inventories. It is one of the most important performance indicators in supply chain management. Stock-out penalty cost is the opportunity cost of not being able to fill a customer's order on time. It also represents a loss of goodwill with the customer. Stock-out penalty cost is often associated with service level, which measures the percentage of orders that are filled on time. Setup ordering cost is the fixed cost for placing an order regardless of the size of the order. Both inventory holding and stock-out

penalty costs are linear to the number of units under consideration. All cost coefficients, e.g. holding cost per unit per period, are specified in accordance with the literature (Chen, 1999; Zheng & Federgruen, 1991). Please see the appendix for the cost coefficient values.

Multiple runs of simulation are performed for each model setting (ISS in this case). The process of each run can be divided into three phases: 1) creating and configuring swarms and agents, 2) executing agent behaviors, and 3) destroying agents and swarms and preparing for the next run if necessary. In the first phase, swarms and agents are created and configured in a hierarchical manner; with the top level swarms created first and the lower level swarms and agents created by the corresponding higher level swarms. Part of the process of configuring agents is to schedule their behaviors using a global scheduler. In phase two of the simulation, the behavior schedule is started and agent behaviors are executed. The schedule will continue executing until the termination condition is met, upon which agents and swarms are destroyed to release memory spaces. Use of random number generators needs special consideration to ensure comparability between different model settings. Two generators are used for demand implementation – one for generating end demands and the other for allocating the demands among buyer agents, and a third generator is used for all other purposes.

6. RESULTS

Thirty runs of simulation, each with a different set of random seeds, were executed for each ISS. Each run lasts for 1000 periods, of which the first 300 periods were considered warm-up periods and excluded from the calculation of agent performances. Agent performances were calculated based on the costs that they incur for their operations. Costs were first averaged across periods in each run of simulation for each agent

Table 2. Seller Costs under Different ISS

	ISS-1	ISS-2	ISS-3	ISS-4	ISS-5
Total Cost	144.67 (4.32*)	140.25 (3.90)	134.94 (2.30)	114.42 (25.06)	128.75 (17.07)
Holding Cost	96.77 (3.96)	86.36 (3.78)	78.28 (1.98)	76.87 (10.59)	57.9 (3.58)
Penalty Cost	0.39 (0.18)	0.33 (0.17)	1.61 (1.92)	3.06 (13.06)	15.8 (26.00)
Setup Ordering Cost	47.51 (0.78)	53.56 (0.11)	55.05 (0.12)	34.49 (0.49)	55.0 (0.14)

*: variance

and then averaged across agents of a same type, i.e., sellers or buyers.

In the following discussions, we primarily focus on seller agents because they are the agents who actively utilize the information shared by the buyer agents. We also present results for the buyer agents. Sections 6.1 to 6.3 describe results for seller agents, and section 6.4 describes results for buyer agents.

6.1 Effects of Sharing Demand Information on Sellers (ISS-1 vs. ISS-2, ISS-2 vs. ISS-3)

Seller performances under ISS-1 and ISS-2 were first compared to examine if sellers can benefit from aggregate hub demand (AHD). Seller performances under ISS-2 and ISS-3 were then compared to examine if AED is more beneficial than AHD. Table 2 shows the average holding cost, stock-out penalty cost, setup ordering cost, and the total cost, which is the sum of the previous three costs that seller agents incur under different ISS.

First, we examine total cost incurred by sellers under the three ISS. It can be seen from Figure 3 and Table 2 that sellers' total cost under ISS-3 is lower than that under ISS-2, which is in turn lower than that under ISS-1. Sellers' total cost under ISS-3, ISS-2, and ISS-1 are 134.9, 140.3, and 144.7 respectively. T-test shows that the difference in total cost between ISS-2 and ISS-1 is statistically significant at 0.05 level (see Table 3). This suggests that sellers can benefit from shared AHD. T-test shows that the difference in total cost

between ISS-3 and ISS-2 is also statistically significant at 0.05 level (see Table 3). This suggests that sellers benefit more from shared AED than from shared AHD.

Next, we examine the cost components, i.e., inventory holding cost, stock-out penalty cost, and setup ordering cost. There are substantial differences in inventory holding cost among the three ISS (see Figure 3). Holding cost under ISS-1 is higher than that under ISS-2, which in turn is higher than that under ISS-3. T-tests show that both the difference between ISS-1 and ISS-2 and the difference between ISS-2 and ISS-3 are statistically significant at 0.05 level (see Table 3). Since holding cost is linear to the inventory level on hand, this result suggests that sellers keep fewest inventories on hand when they have access to the more accurate demand information, i.e., AED, and keep most inventories on hand when they do not have access to any aggregate demand information.

Differences in stock-out penalty cost among the three ISS are minimal (see Figure 3). Penalty cost is very low under all three ISS. This suggests that sellers maintained a high service level, i.e., fulfilling most of the buyer's orders promptly, under all three ISS.

Differences in setup ordering cost among the three ISS are significant but demonstrate an opposite pattern as the inventory holding cost (see Figure 3). Setup ordering cost under ISS-1 is lower than that under ISS-2, which in turn is lower than that under ISS-3. T-tests show that both the difference between ISS-1 and ISS-2

Figure 3. Seller costs under ISS-1, ISS-2, and ISS-3

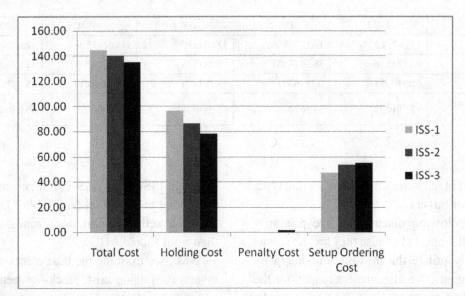

Table 3. Seller Costs T-Tests

	Sharing Demand Information		**Sharing Inventory Information**		**Sharing Demand and Inventory Information**	
	p-value (ISS-1 vs. ISS-2)	p-value (ISS-2 vs. ISS-3)	p-value (ISS-1 vs. ISS-4)	p-value (ISS-3 vs. ISS-4)	p-value (ISS-3 vs. ISS-5)	p-value (ISS-4 vs. ISS-5)
Total Cost	0.00	0.00	0.00	0.00	0.00	0.00
Holding Cost	0.00	0.00	0.00	0.04	0.00	0.00
Penalty Cost	0.61	0.00	0.00	0.05	0.00	0.00
Setup Ordering Cost	0.00	0.00	0.00	0.00	0.92	0.00

and the difference between ISS-2 and ISS-3 are statistically significant at 0.05 level (see Table 3). Since setup ordering cost is linear to the number of orders (not the size of orders) placed, this result suggests that sellers placed most orders or ordered most frequently under ISS-3 and ordered least frequently under ISS-1.

Overall, we can see that: 1) Sellers benefit from shared aggregate hub demand because of lower inventory levels; 2) Sellers gain additional benefit from shared aggregate end demand also because of lower inventory levels; 3) Shared demand information enables sellers to lower inventory levels

significantly while maintaining a high service level; and 4) Sellers order more frequently when they have access to shared demand information.

6.2 Effects of Sharing Inventory Information on Sellers (ISS-1 vs. ISS-4, ISS-3 vs. ISS-4)

Seller performance under ISS-4 was first compared to those under ISS-1 to examine if sellers can benefit from shared ABI. Seller performance under ISS-4 was then compared to those under

Figure 4. Seller costs under ISS-1 and ISS-4

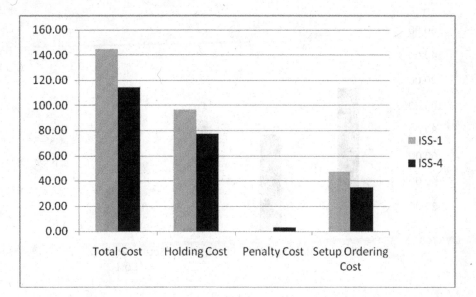

ISS-3 to examine potential differences between sharing ABI and sharing AED.

It can be seen from Table 2 and Figure 4 that sellers inventory holding cost and setup ordering cost under ISS-4 are lower than their counterparts under ISS-1, while the change in stock-out penalty cost is in the opposite direction. The total cost under ISS-4 is also substantially lower than that under ISS-1. T-tests show that the differences in all costs, including the total cost, between the two ISS are statistically significant at 0.05 level (see Table 3). It can be seen from Figure 4 that the decrease in holding cost and setup ordering cost are much larger than the increase in penalty cost. That is the reason for the significant net decrease in total cost. These cost changes suggest that, when having access to ABI, sellers are able to order less frequently, keep fewer inventories on hand, and still maintain a high service level.

This is a very interesting result. One would think that in order to lower inventory levels and maintain a similar service level, the sellers need to order more frequently, in smaller quantities, as they did under ISS-2 and ISS-3. However, sellers

under ISS-4 did the opposite, i.e., ordering less frequently, in larger quantities. To achieve this, the sellers must have changed the timing of their order placing so that the orders arrive just in time, neither too early nor too late. They are able to do this because they have access to buyers' inventory position information. They use not only their own inventory position, but also the shared ABI to decide when to place new orders.

Next, costs that sellers incur under ISS-4 and ISS-3 were compared to examine possible differences in sharing ABI and AED. It can be seen from Figure 5 that there are minimal differences in inventory holding cost and stock-out penalty cost between the two ISS; but setup ordering cost under ISS-4 is substantially lower than that under ISS-3. As a result, total cost under ISS-4 is substantially lower under ISS-4 than under ISS-3. T-tests show that differences in all costs are statistically significant at 0.05 level (see Table 3). These results suggest that sellers benefit more from shared ABI than shared AED because they can order less frequently while maintaining a similar inventory and customer service level under ISS-4.

Figure 5. Seller costs under ISS-3 and ISS-4

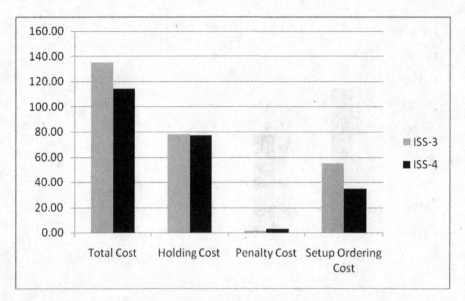

6.3 Marginal Effects of Sharing Demand or Inventory Information on Sellers (ISS-3 vs. ISS-5 and ISS-4 vs. ISS-5)

Seller performance under ISS-5 was first compared to that under ISS-3 to examine the marginal effect of sharing ABI on top of AED. Seller performance under ISS-5 was then compared to that under ISS-4 to examine the marginal effect of sharing AED on top of ABI.

It can be seen from Figure 6 and Table 2 that, compared to those under ISS-3, seller inventory holding cost under ISS-5 decreases substantially; stock-out penalty cost increases substantially; setup ordering cost changes minimally; and total cost decreases. T-tests show that differences in all but the setup ordering cost costs are statistically significant at 0.05 level (see Table 3). These results suggest that sellers who already have access to AED can gain additional benefits from ABI.

These results show that the marginal effect of sharing ABI on top of AED on sellers is positive. What is more interesting is that sellers incur higher stock-out penalty cost under ISS-5 than under ISS-3. This contrasts with what we found

in the comparison between ISS-4 and ISS-1 where sellers only incur minimally higher stock-out penalty cost under ISS-4 than under ISS-1 (see Figure 4). This suggests that the additional benefits that sellers obtain from ABI when they already have access to AED is less significant than the benefit that they obtain from the same information when they do not have access to AED.

Next, seller costs under ISS-5 are compared to those under ISS-4 to examine marginal effects of sharing AED on top of ABI. It can be seen from Figure 7 that sellers incur lower inventory holding cost, higher penalty cost, and higher setup ordering cost under ISS-5 than those under ISS-4. The total cost under ISS-5 is higher than that under ISS-4. The differences in all costs, including total cost, between the two ISS are statistically significant at 0.05 level (see Table 3).

These results show that the marginal effect of sharing AED on top of ABI on sellers is negative, meaning that seller performance in the scenario where both AED and ABI are shared is lower than in the scenario where only ABI is shared. This contrasts with the positive effect of sharing AED when sellers have no access to ABI, as discussed in section 6.1. The contrast suggests that there is

Figure 6. Seller costs under ISS-3 and ISS-5

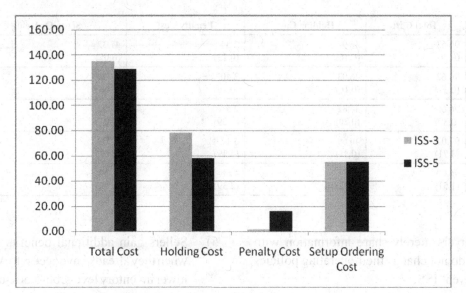

Figure 7. Seller costs under ISS-4 and ISS-5

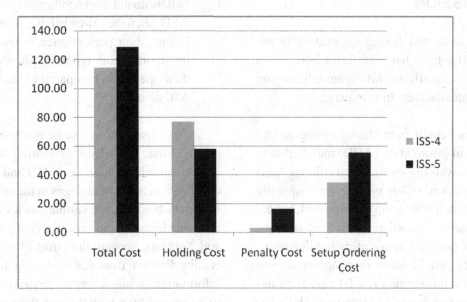

certain negative interactions between AED and ABI. It shows that the value of a type of information depends on the contexts in which it is shared and used. In other words, the information that is beneficial in one context might become harmful when shared and utilized in a different context.

6.4 Effects of Information Sharing on Buyers

The costs that buyers incur under all five ISS are very similar (see Table 5). This is true for all three cost components, i.e., inventory holding cost, stock-out penalty cost, and setup ordering cost, as well as for the total cost. This is understandable

Table 5. Buyer costs under different ISS

	Total Cost	Holding Cost	Penalty Cost	Setup Ordering Cost
ISS-1	96.63 (0.26)	46.97 (0.16)	2.34 (0.13)	47.32 (0.05)
ISS-2	96.62 (0.37)	46.93 (0.16)	2.40 (0.16)	47.29 (0.06)
ISS-3	96.66 (0.39)	46.82 (0.20)	2.57 (0.29)	47.27 (0.07)
ISS-4	97.07 (3.71)	46.60 (0.31)	3.17 (4.49)	47.30 (0.07)
ISS-5	96.90 (1.51)	44.78 (0.42)	4.86 (2.39)	47.27 (0.07)

because buyers merely share information with sellers but do not change their operating policies under different ISS.

7. DISCUSSION

Our results show that sharing aggregate information in B2B e-hubs has significant impacts on seller agents and effects of different information sharing strategies vary. In summary:

1) Sellers benefit from shared aggregate hub demand information (AHD) mainly due to lower inventory levels. When utilizing AHD information, sellers order more frequently and incur higher setup ordering cost, but the increase in setup ordering cost is out-weighed by the decrease in inventory holding cost.

2) Sellers benefit more from aggregate end demand information (AED) than from aggregate hub demand information (AHD) due to the same reasons that they gain benefit from AHD (compared to no information sharing).

3) Sellers benefit from shared aggregate buyer inventory position (ABI) due to lower inventory holding cost and lower setup ordering cost.

4) Sellers benefit more from ABI than from AED due to lower setup ordering cost.

5) Sellers gain additional benefits from ABI when they already have access to AED due to lower inventory levels, but stock-out penalty cost increases when sellers incorporate both types of information into their operations.

6) Sellers do not gain additional benefits from AED when they already have access to ABI. In fact, their performance is lower if they incorporate both types of information into their operations compared to incorporating ABI alone.

A few observations can be made from these results. First, the effects of sharing both types of demand information, i.e., AHD and AED, are consistent in terms of changes in the costs: lower inventory holding cost, similar stock-out penalty cost, and higher setup ordering cost (see point 1 and 2 above). Second, the effect of sharing ABI is quite different from that of sharing the demand information. While lower inventory levels seem to be caused by a higher order frequency when demand information is shared and utilized, the same benefit, i.e. lower inventory levels, is achieved with a lower order frequency when ABI is shared and utilized. This suggests that aggregate inventory information is more valuable than aggregate demand information. Third, a higher level of sharing might not always be more beneficial. While the marginal effect of sharing ABI on top of AED is positive, the marginal effect of sharing and utilizing AED on top of ABI is negative. This is especially interesting because the simple effect of sharing and utilizing AED (when no other information is shared) is positive. A similar effect was reported in Li et al. (2006), which found that effects of information sharing strategies depend on the end demand pattern.

Our findings in this study have several implications for B2B e-hub practitioners. First, it demonstrates the value of information sharing, especially sharing of aggregate information, on e-hubs. Despite fundamental structural differences between traditional supply chains and e-hubs (Li et al., 2006), our study shows that sharing demand and inventory information on e-hubs are beneficial, just like sharing information in traditional supply chains (Gavirneni, 2002; Gavirneni, 2006; Hosoda et al., 2008; Yue & Liu, 2006). Because of increased competition and transparency in e-hubs, firms are less willing to share information in e-hubs than in traditional supply chains (Lu & Antony, 2003). Our study shows that it is not necessary to share information about individual firms; aggregate information is also valuable. Firms can use shared aggregate information to improve operation efficiency and lower costs. Second, different types of information are of different value. Our study suggests that aggregate buyer inventory position is more valuable than aggregate end demand information, which in turn is more valuable than aggregate hub demand. Third, more might be less when it comes to information sharing on e-hubs. Sharing and utilizing multiple types of information, such as aggregate buyer inventory position and aggregate end demand information, might be less valuable than sharing and utilizing just one type, such as aggregate buyer inventory position.

8. LIMITATIONS AND FUTURE RESEARCH

One limitation of this study is that our e-hub model includes a small number of buyers and sellers, while real-world e-hubs often have a large number of participants. It will be interesting to see how the number of agents influences the effect of information sharing, even though we do not expect the influences to be significant. The buyer agents in our model assume a passive role as mere information providers. They are assumed to share information with sellers without any condition. In reality, buyers may want to charge a fee for sharing information, however. Also, we did not consider competitions among agents. These are important issues that can be examined in future studies.

REFERENCES

Akkermans, H. (2001). Emergent supply networks: System dynamics simulation of adaptive supply agents. In *Proceedings of the 34th Hawaii International Conference on System Sciences*.

Allwood, J., & Lee, J. (2005). The design of an agent for modelling supply chain network dynamics. *International Journal of Production Research*, *43*(22), 4875–4898. doi:10.1080/00207540500168295

Aviv, Y. (2001). The effect of collaborative forecasting on supply chain performance. *Management Science*, *47*(10), 1326–1343. doi:10.1287/mnsc.47.10.1326.10260

Axtell, R. (2000). *Why agents? On the varied motivations for agent computating in the social sciences*. Retrieved from http://docs.google.com/viewer?a=v&q=cache:o0vtAsiH7S8J:citeseerx.ist.psu.edu/viewdoc/download%3Fdoi%3D10.1.1.90.9253%26rep%3Drep1%26type%3Dpdf+Axtell,+R.+(2000).+Why+agents%3F+On+the+varied+motivations+for+agent+computating+in+the+social+sciences.&hl=en&gl=us&pid=b-l&srcid=ADGEESgml7tFbcHv4zCeHuD4BBbDtXOBfJLX2uL9ffMgyiA15V8wyXZY0SvhRrFcdjKzJ27uy3qEg920fa0TF5DSeGUnPgZ-9KyU3k0T4LVY_2rhVXiSD9eQW7sGjfgdrkoSSmAO70uiK&sig=AHIEtbQx5cug6U2FKBNOGHB9HxxvwndWVQ

Cachon, G. P., & Fisher, M. (2000). Supply chain inventory management and the value of shared information. *Management Science, 46*(8), 1032–1048. doi:10.1287/mnsc.46.8.1032.12029

Caridi, M., Cigolini, R., & Marco, D. (2005). Improving supply-chain collaboration by linking intelligent agents to cpfr. *International Journal of Production Research, 43*(20), 4191–4218. doi:10.1080/00207540500142134

Cavalieri, S., Cesarotti, V., & Introna, V. (2003). A multiagent model for coordinated distribution chain planning. *Journal of Organizational Computing and Electronic Commerce, 13*(3/4), 267–287. doi:10.1207/S15327744JOCE133&4_07

Chen, F. (1998). Echelon reorder points, installation reorder points, and the value of centralized demand information. *Management Science, 44*(12), 221–234. doi:10.1287/mnsc.44.12.S221

Chen, F. (1999). Decentralized supply chains subject to information delays. *Management Science, 45*(8), 1076–1090. doi:10.1287/mnsc.45.8.1076

Chen, F., Ryan, J. K., & Simchi-Levi, D. (2000). The impact of exponential smoothing forecasts on the bullwhip effect. *Naval Research Logistics, 47*, 269–286. doi:10.1002/(SICI)1520-6750(200006)47:4<269::AID-NAV1>3.0.CO;2-Q

Chen, F., & Zheng, Y. (1994). Evaluating echelon stock (r, nq) policies in serial production/inventory systems with stochastic demand. *Management Science, 40*, 1426–1443. doi:10.1287/mnsc.40.11.1426

Cheung, K., & Lee, H. (2002). The inventory benefit of shipment coordination and stock rebalancing in a supply chain. *Management Science, 48*(2), 300–306. doi:10.1287/mnsc.48.2.300.251

Chu, W. H. J., & Lee, C. C. (2006). Strategic information sharing in a supply chain. *European Journal of Operational Research, 174*(3), 1567–1579. doi:10.1016/j.ejor.2005.02.053

Datta, P., Christopher, M., & Allen, P. (2007). Agent-based modelling of complex production/distribution systems to improve resilience. *International Journal of Logistics: Research and Applications, 10*(3), 187–203. doi:10.1080/13675560701467144

Day, G. S., Fein, A. J., & Ruppersberger, G. (2003). Shakeouts in digital markets: Lessons from b2b exchanges. *California Management Review, 45*(2), 131–150.

De Bodt, M., & Graves, S. (1985). Continous review policies for a multi-echelon inventory problem with stochastic demand. *Management Science, 31*, 1286–1295. doi:10.1287/mnsc.31.10.1286

Eng, T. (2004). The role of e-marketplaces in supply chain management. *Industrial Marketing Management, 33*, 97–105. doi:10.1016/S0019-8501(03)00032-4

Gavirneni, S. (2001). Benefits of co-operation in a production distribution environment. *European Journal of Operational Research, 130*, 612–622. doi:10.1016/S0377-2217(99)00423-3

Gavirneni, S. (2002). Information flows in capacitated supply chains with fixed ordering costs. *Management Science, 48*(5), 644–651. doi:10.1287/mnsc.48.5.644.7806

Gavirneni, S. (2006). Price fluctuations, information sharing, and supply chain performance. *European Journal of Operational Research, 174*(3), 1651. doi:10.1016/j.ejor.2005.04.037

Gjerdrum, J., Shah, N., & Parageorgiou, L. (2001). A combined optimization and agent-based approach to supply chain modelling and performance assessment. *Production Planning and Control, 12*(1), 81–88. doi:10.1080/09537280150204013

Glasserman, P., & Tayur, S. (1994). The stability of a capacitated, multi-echelon production-inventory system under a base-stock policy. *Operations Research, 42*(5), 913–925. doi:10.1287/opre.42.5.913

Grey, W., Olavson, T., & Shi, D. (2005). The role of e-marketplaces in relationship-based supply chains: A survey. *IBM Systems Journal, 44*(1).

Guo, Z., Fang, F., & Whinston, A. B. (2006). Supply chain information sharing in a macro prediction market. *Decision Support Systems, 42*(3), 1944–1958. doi:10.1016/j.dss.2006.05.003

Hong, S., Nag, B. N., & Yao, D.-Q. (2007). Modeling agent auctions in a supply chain environment. *International Journal of Intelligent Information Technologies, 3*(1), 14–36.

Hosoda, T., Naim, M. M., Disney, S. M., & Potter, A. (2008). Is there a benefit to sharing market sales information? Linking theory and practice. *Computers & Industrial Engineering, 54*(2), 315. doi:10.1016/j.cie.2007.07.014

Ito, T., & Abadi, S. M. (2002). Agent-based material handling and inventory planning in warehouse. *Journal of Intelligent Manufacturing, 13*, 201–210. doi:10.1023/A:1015786822825

Kaplan, S., & Sawhney, M. (2000). E-hubs: The new b2b marketplaces. *Harvard Business Review*, (May-June): 97–103.

Karabati, S., & Sayin, S. (2008). Single-supplier/multiple-buyer supply chain coordination: Incorporating buyers' expectations under vertical information sharing. *European Journal of Operational Research, 187*(3), 746–764. doi:10.1016/j.ejor.2006.05.046

Kathawala, Y., Abdou, K., & Franck, C. (2002). Supply chain/electronic hubs: A comparative analysis. *Benchmarking: An International Journal, 9*(5), 450–470. doi:10.1108/14635770210451460

Ketzenberg, M. E., Rosenzweig, E. D., Marucheck, A. E., & Metters, R. D. (2007). A framework for the value of information in inventory replenishment. *European Journal of Operational Research, 182*(3), 1230. doi:10.1016/j.ejor.2006.09.044

Kleindorfer, P. R., & Wu, D. J. (2003). Integrating long- and short-term contracting via business-to-business exchanges for capital-intensive industries. *Management Science, 49*(11), 1597–1615. doi:10.1287/mnsc.49.11.1597.20583

Lancastre, A., & Lages, L. F. (2006). The relationship between buyer and a b2b e-marketplace: Cooperation determinants in an electronic market context. *Industrial Marketing Management, 35*, 774–789. doi:10.1016/j.indmarman.2005.03.011

Langdon, C. S. (2005). Agent-based modeling for simulation of complex business systems: Research design and validation strategies. *International Journal of Intelligent Information Technologies, 1*(3), 1–13.

Langdon, C. S., & Sikora, R. T. (2006). Conceptualizing co-ordination and competition in supply chains as complex adaptive system. *Information Systems and E-Business Management, 4*, 71–81. doi:10.1007/s10257-005-0005-6

Lee, L. H., Lee, C., & Bao, J. (2006). Inventory control in the presense of an electronic marketplace. *European Journal of Operational Research, 174*, 797–815. doi:10.1016/j.ejor.2005.03.018

Li, J., Sikora, R., Shaw, M. J., & Woo Tan, G. (2006). A strategic analysis of inter organizational information sharing. *Decision Support Systems, 42*(1), 251. doi:10.1016/j.dss.2004.12.003

Li, L. (2002). Information sharing in a supply chain with horizontal competition. *Management Science*, *48*(9), 1196–1212. doi:10.1287/mnsc.48.9.1196.177

Li, S., & Lin, B. (2006). Accessing information sharing and information quality in supply chain management. *Decision Support Systems*, *42*(3), 1641–1656. doi:10.1016/j.dss.2006.02.011

Lin, F., Strader, T., & Shaw, M. (2000). Using swarm for simulating the order fulfillment process in divergent assembly supply chains . In Luna, F., & Stefansson, B. (Eds.), *Economic simulations in swarm: Agent-based modeling and object oriented programming* (pp. 225–249). Boston: Kluwer Academic Publishers.

Lin, F., Sung, Y., & Lo, Y. (2005). Effects of trust mechanisms on supply-chain performance: A multi-agent simulation study. *International Journal of Electronic Commerce*, *9*(4), 91–112.

Lin, F., Tan, G., & Shaw, M. (1999). Multiagent enterprise modeling. *Journal of Organizational Computing and Electronic Commerce*, *9*(1), 7–32. doi:10.1207/s15327744joce0901_2

Lu, D., & Antony, F. (2003). Implications of b2b marketplace to supply chain development. *The TQM Magazine*, *15*(3), 173–179. doi:10.1108/09544780310469271

Malone, T., Yates, J., & Benjamin, R. (1987). Electronic markets and electronic hierarchies: Effects of information technology on market structure and corporate strategies. *Communications of the ACM*, *30*(6), 484–497. doi:10.1145/214762.214766

Moinzadeh, K. (2002). A multi-echelon inventory system with information exchange. *Management Science*, *48*(3), 414–426. doi:10.1287/mnsc.48.3.414.7730

Mukhopadhyay, S. K., Yao, D.-Q., & Yue, X. (in press). Information sharing of value-adding retailer in a mixed channel hi-tech supply chain. *Journal of Business Research*.

Owan, H., & Nickerson, J. A. (2002). *A theory of B2B exchange formation*. Retrieved from http://ssrn.com/abstract=315121

Parunak, H. V. D., Savit, R., Riolo, R. L., & Clark, S. J. (1999). *Dasch: Dynamic analysis of supply chains*. Ann Arbor, MI: Center for Electronic Commerce, ERIM, Inc.

Powell, A. (2001). *The role of b2b exchanges and implications for the future*. New York: The Conference Board, Inc.

Ram, S., & Liu, J. (2005). An agent-based approach for sourcing business rules in supply chain management. *International Journal of Intelligent Information Technologies*, *1*(1), 1–16.

Robinson, W., & Elofson, G. (2001). Electronic broker impacts on the value of postponement in a global supply chain. *Journal of Global Information Management*, *9*(4), 29–43.

Sadeh, N. M., Hildum, D. W., & Kjenstad, D. (2003). Agent-based e-supply chain decision support. *Journal of Organizational Computing and Electronic Commerce*, *13*(3/4), 225–241. doi:10.1207/S15327744JOCE133&4_05

Sadeh, N. M., Hildum, D. W., Kjenstad, D., & Tseng, A. (2001). Mascot: An agent-based architecture for dynamic supply chain creation and coordination in the internet economy. *Production Planning and Control*, *12*(3), 212–223. doi:10.1080/095372801300107680

Samaddar, S., Nargundkar, S., & Daley, M. (2006). Inter-organizational information sharing: The role of supply network configuration and partner goal congruence. *European Journal of Operational Research, 174*(2), 744. doi:10.1016/j.ejor.2005.01.059

Schlueter-Langdon, C., Bruhn, P., & Shaw, M. J. (2000). Online supply chain modeling and simulation . In Luna, F., & Stefansson, B. (Eds.), *Economic simulations in swarm: Agent-based modeling and object oriented programming* (pp. 251–272). Boston: Kluwer Academic Publishers.

Shevchenko, A. A., & Shevchenko, O. O. (2005). B2b e-hubs in emerging landscape of knowledge based economy. *Electronic Commerce Research and Applications, 4*(2), 113. doi:10.1016/j.elerap.2004.10.001

Signorile, R. (2002). Simulation of a multiagent system for retail inventory control: A case study. *Simulation, 78*(5), 304–311. doi:10.1177/0037549702078005552

Sikora, R., & Shaw, M. J. (1998). A multi-agent framework for the coordination and integration of information systems. *Management Science, 44*(11), 65–78. doi:10.1287/mnsc.44.11.S65

Surana, A., Kumara, S., Greaves, M., & Raghavan, U. N. (2005). Supply-chain networks: A complex adaptive systems perspective. *International Journal of Production Research, 43*(20), 4235–4265. doi:10.1080/00207540500142274

Swaminathan, J. M. (1997). *Effect of sharing supplier capacity information*. Retrieved from http://citeseerx.ist.psu.edu/viewdoc/summary?doi=10.1.1.46.3933

White, A., Daniel, E., Ward, J., & Wilson, H. (2007). The adoption of consortium b2b e-marketplaces: An exploratory study. *The Journal of Strategic Information Systems, 16*, 71–103. doi:10.1016/j.jsis.2007.01.004

White, A., Daniel, E. M., & Mohdzain, M. (2005). The role of emergent information technologies and systems in enabling supply chain agility. *International Journal of Information Management, 25*, 396–410. doi:10.1016/j.ijinfomgt.2005.06.009

Wikner, J., Towill, D. R., & Naim, M. (1991). Smoothing supply chain dynamics. *International Journal of Production Economics, 22*, 231–248. doi:10.1016/0925-5273(91)90099-F

Xie, M., & Chen, J. (2004). Studies on horizontal competition among homogenous retailers through agent-based simulation. *Journal of Systems Science and Systems Engineering, 13*(4), 490–505. doi:10.1007/s11518-006-0178-7

Xu, K., Dong, Y., & Evers, P. (2001). Towards better coordination of the supply chain. *Transportation Research Part E, Logistics and Transportation Review, 37*, 35–54. doi:10.1016/S1366-5545(00)00010-7

Yadav, M., & Varadarajan, R. R. (2005). Understanding product migration to the electronic marketplace: A conceptual framework. *Journal of Retailing, 81*(2), 125–140. doi:10.1016/j.jretai.2005.03.006

Yue, X., & Liu, J. (2006). Demand forecast sharing in a dual-channel supply chain. *European Journal of Operational Research, 174*, 646–667. doi:10.1016/j.ejor.2004.12.020

Zhang, C., Tan, G.-W., Robb, D. J., & Zheng, X. (2006). Sharing shipment quantity information in the supply chain. *Omega, 34*, 427–438. doi:10.1016/j.omega.2004.12.005

Zheng, Y.-S., & Federgruen, A. (1991). Finding optimal (s, s) policies is about as simple as evaluating a single policy. *Operations Research, 39*(4), 654–665. doi:10.1287/opre.39.4.654

Zhou, H., & Benton, W. C. Jr. (2007). Supply chain practice and information sharing. *Journal of Operations Management, 25*(6), 1348–1365. doi:10.1016/j.jom.2007.01.009

Zhu, K. (2002). Information transparency in electronic marketplaces: Why data transparency may hinder the adoption of b2b exchanges. *Electronic Markets, 12*(2), 92–99. doi:10.1080/10196780252844535

ENDNOTE

[1]   http://www.swarm.org/index.php/Main_Page

APPENDIX

Buyer setup ordering cost: 300

Buyer holding cost per unit per period: 1.5

Buyer stock-out penalty cost per unit per period: 15

Buyer shipping delay: 2

Seller setup ordering cost: 600

Seller holding cost per unit per period: 1

Seller stock-out penalty cost per unit per period: 10

Seller shipping delay: 2

Supplier shipping delay: 3

This work was previously published in International Journal of Intelligent Information Technologies, Volume 6, Issue 2, edited by Vijayan Sugumaran, pp. 1-20, copyright 2010 by IGI Publishing (an imprint of IGI Global).

Chapter 6
Ontology–Based Shopping Agent for E–Marketing

Sam Kin Meng
University of Macau, China

C. R. Chatwin
University of Sussex, UK

ABSTRACT

Before Internet consumers make buying decisions, several psychological factors come into effect and reflect individual preferences on products. In this paper, the authors investigate four integrated streams: 1) recognizing the psychological factors that affect Internet consumers, 2) understanding the relationship between businesses' e-marketing mix and Internet consumers' psychological factors, 3) designing an ontology mapping businesses' e-marketing mix with Internet consumers' decision-making styles, and 4) developing a shopping agent based on the ontology. The relationship between businesses' e-marketing mix and Internet consumers' psychological factors is important because it can identify situations where both businesses and Internet consumers benefit. The authors' ontology can be used to share Internet consumers' psychological factors, the e-marketing mix of online business and their relationships with different computer applications.

INTRODUCTION

During the last 15 years, the popularity of the Internet has been growing exponentially (Hou & Cesar, 2002). One result of the online information explosion is the growing popularity of computer-based intelligent shopping agents that are mainly used to assist consumers to find and compare suitable product items they are looking for. However, most of the currently available intelligent shopping agents only request consumers to define various criteria for the product in terms of price limitation and required product features. Then consumers search the suitable product items offered by different online stores. In order to

DOI: 10.4018/978-1-4666-0158-1.ch006

satisfy customer needs, intelligent agents should also consider additional factors.

From the customer viewpoint, before consumers make buying decisions, they are influenced by several psychological factors when looking for their favorite business web site to buy a suitable product. From the business viewpoint, the tools of e-marketing mix are provided by the business company web sites to look for target customers. An intelligent shopping agent, which can understand the relationship between the consumers' psychological factors and businesses' e-marketing mix, can increase business revenues and at the same time can save online consumers a lot of searching time.

PSYCHOLOGICAL FACTORS

Consumers' decision-making style is defined as a mental orientation characterizing a consumer's approach to making choices (Sproles & Kendall, 1986). In this research field, the consumer-characteristics approach, focusing on cognitive and affective orientations related to consumer decision-making (Sproles, 1985; Westbrook & Black, 1985), is one of the most promising approaches as it deals with the mental orientation of consumers in making decisions. In a consumer market, consumers may approach the market by using some basic decision-making styles, e.g. high-quality consciousness. The consumer personality, similar to the concept of personality in psychology, is what must be characterized. Identifying the basic characteristics of decision-making styles can be used to:

1. educate consumers about their specific decision-making characteristics,
2. profile an individual's consumer style,
3. counsel families on financial management.

ELECTRONIC - CONSUMER STYLE INVENTORY (E-CSI)

The origin of the consumer characteristics driven approach is the exploratory study by Sproles (1985) that identified 50 items related to his or her mental orientation. Sproles and Kendall (1986) reworked this inventory (50 items) to reduce them to 40 items under the title, Consumer Style Inventory (CSI).

Bruskin/Goldberg Research reports that 75% of Internet shoppers consider credit-card security a primary concern (Hou & Cesar, 2002). In addition, Hoffman, Novak and Peralta (1999) state that consumers' online information privacy is the primary barrier to online shopping.

Self-service technologies on the web can lead to factors that can cause positive or negative reactions to the Internet shopping service. Meuter et al. (2000) find that subjects are most satisfied with technologies that can save time (30%), work reliably (21%), be easy to use (16%), meet a salient need (11%), and offer greater control and access (8%). The facilities offered by e-businesses are so important that they can affect consumers when shopping on-line.

To sum up, in order to deal with the emergence of e-commerce activities, it is necessary to consider the psychological factors that can affect the willingness of consumers to purchase products on the web. Therefore, additional item(s) should be added to the psychological factors reported by Sproles and Kendall (1986) in order to fit the E-commerce environment. Based on survey data and using the factor analysis technique, the eight factor items of the E-CSI model (Sam & Chatwin, 2005a) for four different types of products; namely Apparel, IT item, Jewelry and Car, are created as shown in Table 1.

According to the loading information of factor items shown in Table 1, an eight-factor consumer style model can be applied to all four types of products. However, there is no particular pro-

Table 1. E-Consumer style characteristics: The loadings of eight factor model

Loadings:	Apparel	IT item	Jewelry	Car
Factor 1 – High-Quality, become buying habit Conscious Consumer				
Getting very good quality is very important to me.	.35	.81	.58	.81
Once I find a product or brand I like, I stick with it.	.75	.35	.40	.59
Factor 2 – Brand Conscious Consumer				
The well-known national brands are best for me.	.78	.62	.77	.67
The higher the price, the better its quality.	.84	.78	.46	.63
I prefer buying the best-selling brands.	.77	.82	.73	.84
Factor 3 – Novelty-Fashion Conscious Consumer				
I usually have one or more products of the very newest style.	.82	.80	.74	.85
Fashionable, attractive styling is very important to me.	.73	.87	.59	.79
Factor 4 – Price Conscious Consumer				
I buy as much as possible at sale price.	.81	.80	.71	.61
The lower price products are usually my choice.	.76	.56	.87	.81
I look carefully to find the best value for the money.	.40	.70	.45	.57
Factor 5 – Product Portability Conscious Consumer				
When buying products, portability is very important to me.	.85	.86	.80	.83
The smaller the product size, the more I prefer.	.83	.57	.78	.82
Factor 6 – Web Site Content Conscious Consumer				
When I go shopping online, security is very important.	.38	.50	.32	.52
It is very important for the web sites to offer communication channels to me for enquiry.	.75	.82	.82	.83
It is very important for the web sites to offer product searching service to me.	.90	.87	.92	.83
It is perfect if the web sites can offer me richness information about products.	.86	.84	.85	.79
Factor 7 – Web Site Animation Conscious Consumer				
It will be annoying to get a lot of animated effect on the business web sites.	.74	.85	.78	.82
Factor 8 – Web Site Interface Conscious Consumer				
Design layout of business web site is one of the important factors to make buying decisions.	.89	.86	.96	.90

file of consumer style that is suitable for all the product types.

A PROFILE OF CONSUMER STYLE

A profile of Consumer Style is now developed for each of the product types, as shown in Table 2(a) – (d), based on the highest loading item for each characteristic. The group mean was calculated by averaging the raw scores on the highest loading item for each factor. This result yields scores of 1 to 5 for each product on each characteristic.

E-MARKETING MIX

Although many web businesses terminated operations or ceased to exist from April 2000 to December 2001, those e-retailers that developed and introduced new internet-based marketing techniques (e-marketing), which have been widely considered in the formation of current marketing strategy; managed to increase their business activity.

The emergence of the Internet has caused consumer markets to evolve into the highly interactive and global shop fronts of today. The marketers have shifted their focus towards satisfying personalized needs rather than aggregate needs. According to Hoffman and Novak (1997), marketers should focus on developing new paradigms for electronic commerce on the Web.

There are several e-marketing models such as 4Cs model (Lauterborn, 1990), 4Ss model (Constantinides, 2002) and $4Ps+P^2C^2S^3$ model (Kalyanam & McIntyre, 2002). However, most of the models cannot fully focus on the World Wide Web environment. Some elements of these models are focused on operational controls inside the organization, except for the $4Ps+P^2C^2S^3$ (reference) model. As a result, $4Ps+P^2C^2S^3$ model is adopted for this research.

There are different e-marketing strategies adopted by different business web sites among different industries or in a particular industry. Why are there different e-marketing strategies for different business web sites? It is due to the fact that their target customers are different. There are different requirements for online customers compared to traditional business customers:

- Online customers look for a suitable business web site to buy suitable products
- Online businesses look for target customers

E-MARKETING MIX MODEL REPRESENTED IN AN ONTOLOGY

The characteristics of companies, products, and promotional products are captured in an ontology (Figure 1). All instances of the class Company, Comp, have a slot called E_Marketing_Mix, which is an instance of the class Prodtype_eMark. The E_Marketing_Mix class has three slots, namely, Prom, Prod, and Cust_Serv. These are instances of the class Prom_Str, Prod_Str, Cust_Serv_Str, respectively, as shown in Figure 1.

Figure 2 shows the slots of the Comp (Company) class represented in the ontology tool Protege 2000. Each business web site has a unique URL and offers different product categories. In addition, each business web site offers different e-marketing tools for different product categories, indicated by multiple instances (E_Marketing_Mix) of the Prodtype_eMark class. Figure 3 shows the slots of the class Prodtype_eMark and their cardinalities and types.

For the eMark class, since the eleven elements of the e-marketing mix model are very important for the development of the intelligent agent, these elements are created as sub-classes of the eMark class (Noy & McGuinness, 2001) instead of being created as slots in the eMark class, as shown in Figure 4.

Table 2. A profile of E-Commerce consumer style: (a) Apparel; (b) IT item; (c) Jewelry; (d) Car

(a) Apparel			
Your Name: _____			
Style Characteristics	**Your Score**	**Group Mean**	**Verbal Interpretation of your Consumer Style**
High-Quality, buying habit conscious	3.2	2.6	You are average in demanding and buying the same high-quality products.
Brand Conscious	2.8	3.3	You are average to above average in brand name consciousness.
Novelty-Fashion Conscious	2.1	3.3	You are high in novelty and fashion consciousness.
Price Conscious	3.8	2.6	You are low in price consciousness – price matters little to you
Portability Conscious	1.2	3.0	You are very high in portability consciousness, demanding a great deal of product flexibility.
Web Site Content Conscious	2.6	1.7	You are below average in web site content consciousness, not considering any facilities inside the web sites very much
Web Site Animation Conscious	2.6	2.4	You are average in web site animation consciousness, animation effect does not affect your buying decisions very much
Web Site Interface Conscious	4.5	2.9	You are very low in web site interface consciousness, there is no effect of web site interface on your buying decisions

(b) IT-item			
Your Name: _____			
Style Characteristics	**Your Score**	**Group Mean**	**Verbal Interpretation of your Consumer Style**
High-Quality, buying habit conscious	3.2	1.7	You are below average to low in demanding and buying the same high-quality products.
Brand Conscious	2.8	2.7	You are average in brand name consciousness.
Novelty-Fashion Conscious	2.1	3.1	You are high in novelty and fashion consciousness.
Price Conscious	3.8	2.8	You are below average to low in price consciousness – price matters little to you
Portability Conscious	1.2	2.4	You are very high in portability consciousness, demanding a great deal of product flexibility.
Web Site Content Conscious	2.6	1.6	You are below average in web site content consciousness, not considering any facilities inside the web sites very much
Web Site Animation Conscious	2.6	2.4	You are average in web site animation consciousness, animation effect does not affect your buying decisions very much
Web Site Interface Conscious	4.5	3.0	You are very low in web site interface consciousness, there is no effect of web site interface on your buying decisions

(c) Jewelry			
Your Name: _____			
Style Characteristics	**Your Score**	**Group Mean**	**Verbal Interpretation of your Consumer Style**
High-Quality, buying habit conscious	3.2	2.3	You are below average in demanding and buying the same high-quality products.
Brand Conscious	2.8	3.4	You are below average in brand name consciousness.

continued on following page

Table 2. Continued

Novelty-Fashion Conscious	2.1	3.9	You are high in novelty and fashion consciousness.
Price Conscious	3.8	3.3	You are below average in price consciousness – price matters little to you
Portability Conscious	1.2	3.0	You are very high in portability consciousness, demanding a great deal of product flexibility.
Web Site Content Conscious	2.6	1.8	You are below average in web site content consciousness, not considering any facilities inside the web sites very much
Web Site Animation Conscious	2.6	2.5	You are average in web site animation consciousness, animation effect does not affect your buying decisions very much
Web Site Interface Conscious	4.5	2.9	You are very low in web site interface consciousness, there is no effect of web site interface on your buying decisions

(d) Car			
Your Name: _____			
Style Characteristics	**Your Score**	**Group Mean**	**Verbal Interpretation of your Consumer Style**
High-Quality, buying habit conscious	3.2	1.7	You are below average to low in demanding and buying the same high-quality products.
Brand Conscious	2.8	2.7	You are average in brand name consciousness.
Novelty-Fashion Conscious	2.1	3.9	You are high in novelty and fashion consciousness.
Price Conscious	3.8	3.2	You are below average to low in price consciousness – price matters little to you
Portability Conscious	1.2	2.7	You are very high in portability consciousness, demanding a great deal of product flexibility.
Web Site Content Conscious	2.6	1.7	You are below average in web site content consciousness, not considering any facilities inside the web sites very much
Web Site Animation Conscious	2.6	2.5	You are average in web site animation consciousness, animation effect does not affect your buying decisions very much
Web Site Interface Conscious	4.5	3.0	You are very low in web site interface consciousness, there is no effect of web site interface on your buying decisions

Each e-marketing mix element contains several e-marketing tools. In order to know whether the e-business web site adopts an e-marketing mix element, it is very important to identify the keyword(s) associated with each e-marketing tool of an e-marketing mix element.

Identification of Keywords

The keywords associated with each supporting e-marketing tool can be identified based on the analysis of around 100 randomly selected business web sites selling different categories of products. The analysis is performed by a web crawler program (Shkapenyuk & Suel, 2002) and the results

are shown in Table 3. Some keywords appear in business web sites as links, some appear as text. Some of the business web sites adopt the same keywords for a particular e-marketing tool. All those keywords used for a particular e-marketing tool are grouped as a keyword list which acts as a checklist to determine whether the corresponding e-marketing tool is adopted. For instance, most of the business web sites state clearly that they adopt "SSL" technology (keyword: SSL) so that the business transactions are secure. Thus, "SSL" is the appropriate keyword for security marketing tool. On the other hand, some business web sites use another keyword, namely, "encrypt" without mentioning SSL technology. These

Figure 1. Some classes, instances and relationships between e-business web site and E-Marketing Mix in the business domain. Black box: class and dotted box: instance. Arrow represents slot or instance of (io). Dotted line: instances about other E-Marketing Mix elements not mentioned in this figure.

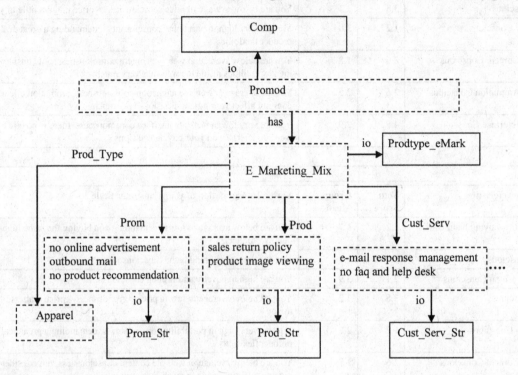

Figure 2. Screenshot from the slots of the class Comp

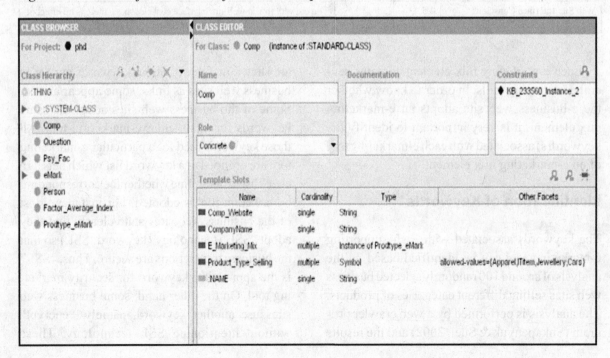

Figure 3. Different elements of E-Marketing Mix indicated by slots in Prodtype_eMark class

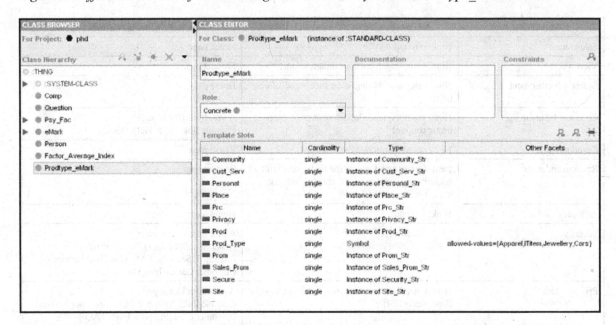

two keywords are grouped to form a keyword list stored in the ontology. If at least one of the keywords is mentioned in business web sites, those business web sites are said to provide the associated e-marketing tool. Assuming that the weights of all supporting tools for that particular strategy are equal, a marketing strategy is said to be executed by the business company if there are at least half of the e-marketing tools provided for the marketing strategy.

Based on the analysis, it was also found that all product pages of the same product types under the same business web sites offer the same e-marketing tools to the customers.

Determination of Pricing Strategy

In online shopping, pricing is an important factor and it is critical that companies adopt appropriate pricing strategies to be successful and to maintain a competitive edge. In our intelligent agent, the pricing strategy is analyzed based on whether the online stores provide low price products. The prices of the same product item from different

Figure 4. eMark class and its sub-classes

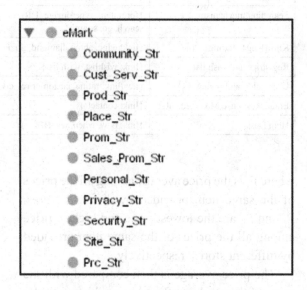

stores may be different. To get a quick idea about the acceptable price for a particular product, the price average can be calculated by the following formula:

$$P_A = \frac{\left(P_L + P_H\right)}{2}$$

Table 3. Keywords for e-marketing tools identified in business web sites

E-Marketing Tool	Keywords used in business web sites	Web page where keywords appear
Sales return	{link: return policy}	Home page
Viewing	{link: view, larger, enlarge, image, zoom}	Product page
Online advertisement	{link: sale, save, saving, clearance, new collection}	Home page
Code and Coupon	{link: promotional code, discount code, electronic coupon}	A link from Home page Possible link: Help, Help Desk,
Outbound mail	{text: newsletter, subscribe, sign-up}	Home page
Recommendation	{text: Recommend, create the look, wear with, related items, similar items, choices, suggest, may also like, might}	Product page
Affiliates	{link: affiliate}	Home page
Security	{text: ssl, encrypt}	A link from Home page Possible link: Security Policy, Privacy Statement, Privacy & Security, FAQ, Customer Service, Customer Care, About Us
Privacy_item	{text: not sell, not provide, not share, not disclose, never sell}	A link from Home page Possible link: Privacy Policy, Customer Service, Customer Care, Support, Help, FAQ
Cookies	{text: cookie}	A link from Home page Possible link: Same as above
Order Tracking	{link: track order, order status, order tracking}	Home page
Searching mechanism	{form item: type=image, URL of button image: search, go, submit}	Home page
Knowledge sharing	{link: educ, about diamond, guide, basics}	Home page
Registries and wish list	{link: wishlist, wish list}	Home page/Product page
User rating and review	{text/link: rating, customer review, review}	Product page
Email Response Management	{link: contact us}	Home Page
Help Desk	{link: how, when, what}	Home Page

where P_A is the price average among all the prices of the same item provided by different stores. P_L and P_H are the lowest price and highest price among all the prices of the same item provided by different stores, respectively.

The price average is then compared with the price of the product offered by each store to determine if the price is low.

The pricing strategy of a particular online business store can be determined if there are more than half of the low-price suitable products offered by that online store. However, for the apparel industry, most of the items found through different popular intelligent shopping agents such as MySimon

and Nextag were available at only one business store. As a result, the pricing strategy could not be determined for the apparel industry in EMMSA.

CONSUMERS' DECISION-MAKING STYLES REPRESENTED IN AN ONTOLOGY

All instances of the person class have different psychological factors, such as price factor, etc. The instances of the Price Conscious factor class incorporates slots such as Price_Q1, Price_Q2, Price_Q3 (corresponding to three questions in

Figure 5. Relationship among classes in consumers' psychological factors domain

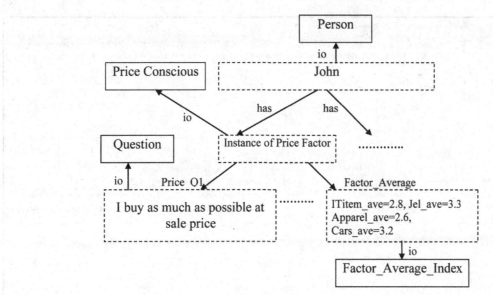

Figure 6. Hierarchical structure of psychological factor class

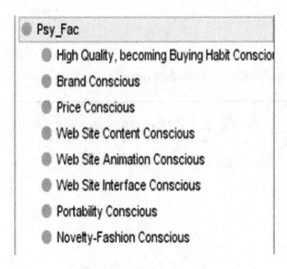

In Figure 6, there is a class for each psychological factor, which is important in describing the concepts of this model so that it is easier to access each psychological factor. Inside the class of each psychological factor, the elements of each psychological factor and its factor average values for different type of products obtained from Table 2(a)–(d) are included as slots, as shown in Figure 7.

Factor_Average, which is a slot in each psychological factor, is an instance of the class Factor_Average_Index, shown in Figure 8. It contains the average index for different product types as slots – Apparel, IT Item, Cars and Jewelry. Figure 9 shows the Person class which describes a person with his/her own decision-making styles.

RELATIONSHIP BETWEEN E-MARKETING MIX MODEL & INTERNET CONSUMERS' PSYCHOLOGICAL FACTORS

In order to determine the relationship between the E-Marketing Mix model and the Internet consumers' psychological factors, a survey was

price conscious factor), and Factor Average (average score of the corresponding factor), as shown in Figure 5. The solid rectangles in Figure 5 represent classes and the dotted rectangles indicate instances. Arrows represent slots and instance of (io). Dotted lines indicate instances of other psychological factors and their corresponding questions, not shown in this figure.

Figure 7. Slots in high quality, becoming buying habit consciousness class

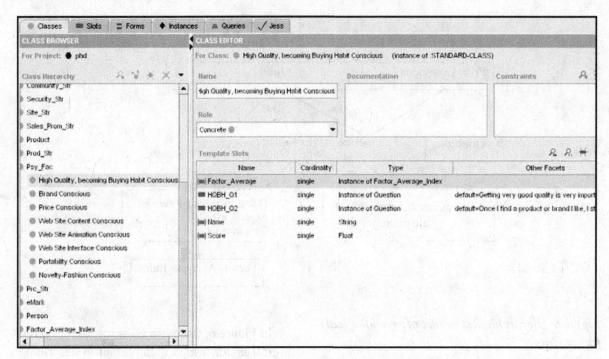

Figure 8. Attributes for factor average class: average index for each product type

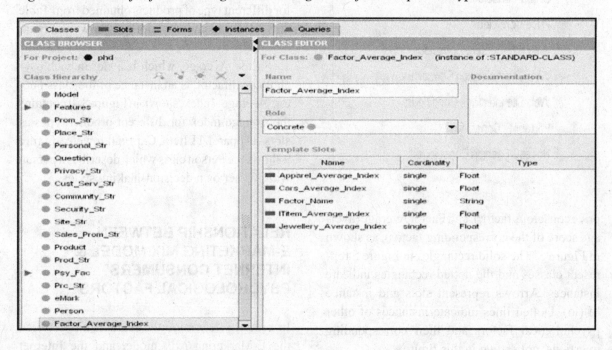

Figure 9. A Person class: Each consumer has its own decision-making styles

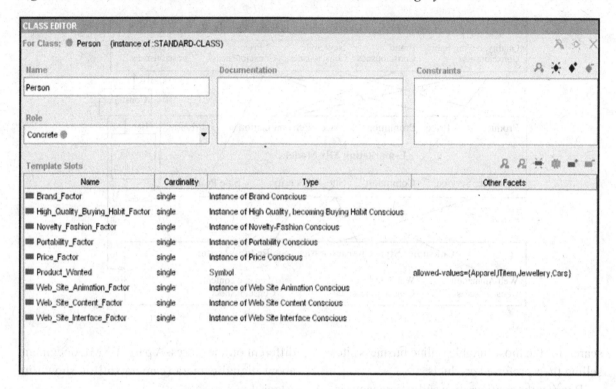

administered. The questionnaire was based on the items related to the E-Marketing model (Kalyanam & McIntyre, 2002) and the E-CSI model (Sam & Chatwin, 2005a). The items were measured on a scale from one to five, starting from "strongly disagree" to "strongly agree". The survey data were obtained from 359 people, some of whom were students and some were in industry. The sample data had a mean age of 36.5 years and was evenly divided between the sexes. The result of the analysis showed that there are several strong relationships between various factors (Sam & Chatwin, 2005b), as indicated in Figure 10.

Based on the relationships that were identified, several related ontology rules are developed, as shown in Figure 11. They are applied to the fact base which contains the web site addresses of all those businesses offering suitable products to consumers.

Confidence Level

Within the rules, confidence level refers to how relevant a business web site is to an online consumer. The confidence level can be further reduced as more psychological factors of online consumers are not matched with the e-marketing mix elements of business web sites. After all the rules are fired against a business web site, the confidence level of that business web site can be determined.

ONTOLOGY-BASED E-MARKETING MIX SHOPPING AGENT (EMMSA)

Nowadays, a sizeable and still-growing fraction of all software is deployed on intranets or the Internet (Joshua, 2003). Rule-based systems are commonly used in web-based applications (Berstel & Bonnard, 2007). EMMSA is a rule-based software tool provided to online consumers to

Figure 10. Relationship between E-marketing mix Model and Internet consumers' decision-making styles

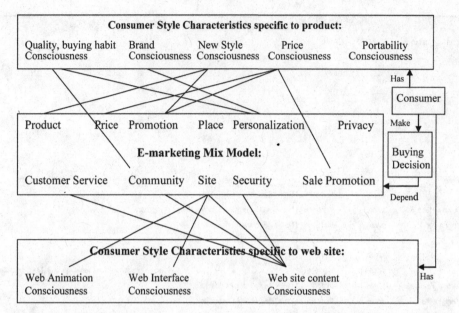

search for the most suitable online business sites selling their preferred products.

Because the configuration and maintenance issues are much simpler than fat-client architectures (The Unitime Version 8 Smart Client Advantage, 2006), thin-client architectures are usually the preferred way to deploy an application on the Web. EMMISA has been developed with a combination of Java Servlets and JavaServer Pages. Figure 12 illustrates the homepage of EMMSA where the consumers select product type, product criteria and answer psychological questions about their shopping style.

Architecture of Intelligent Agent

Figure 13 illustrates the overall architecture of EMMSA, which consists of the following modules:

Module 1: Search Suitable Products

The ontology maintains a set of XML documents, each of which contains information of all items related to a specific type of products offered by different online stores. A part of XML document about digital camera (camera.xml) is shown in Algorithm 1.

Based on the product criteria and product type (a) selected by the consumer, the suitable product items (g) for the consumer can be found out by searching the corresponding XML product information document (b) using XQuery, an XML query language that can be integrated in Java through XQuery API for Java (XQJ). For instance, the XQuery path expression of searching camera. xml for any Canon items with price less than $2000 is shown below. It will return the product model, seller and product web page address of all suitable items.

```
doc("camera.xml")//
digitalcamera[price < 2000 and brand
= 'Canon'] / (model | seller | ad-
dress)
```

Figure 11. Rules relating E-Marketing Mix Model and consumers' psychological factors

```
Rule_1:

Confidence_Level = 10
If  (Person.High_QLY_Buy_BHT.Above_Average)
     If (Comp.E_Marketing_Mix.Personal.Strategy_Executed &
     Comp.E_Marketing_Mix.Community.Strategy_Executed)
          Go to Rule_2
     Else
          Confidence_Level = Confidence_Level - 1
          Go to Rule_2
Else
  Go to Rule_2
```

```
Rule_2:

If (Person.Brand_Factor.Above_Average)
     If (Comp.E_Marketing_Mix.Personal.Strategy_Executed)
          Go to Rule_3
     Else
          Confidence_Level = Confidence_Level - 1
          Go to Rule_3
Else
     Go to Rule_3
```

```
Rule_3:

If (New_Style.Above_Average)
     If (Comp.E_Marketing_Mix.Prod.Strategy_Executed &
Comp.E_Marketing_Mix.Prom.Strategy_Executed)
          Go to Rule_4
     Else
          Confidence_Level = Confidence_Level - 1
          Go to Rule_4
Else
     Go to Rule_4
```

```
Rule_4:

If (Price.Above_Average)
     If (Comp.E_Marketing_Mix.Prc.Strategy_Executed &
Comp.E_Marketing_Mix.Prom.Strategy_Executed &
Comp.E_Marketing_Mix.Sales_Prom.Strategy_Executed)
          Go to Rule_5
     Else
          Confidence_Level = Confidence_Level - 1
          Go to Rule_5
Else
     Go to Rule_5
```

```
Rule_5:

If (Web_Site_Content.Above_Average = False)
     Go to Rule_6
Else
     If (Comp.E_Marketing_Mix.Cust_Serv.Strategy_Executed &
     Comp.E_Marketing_Mix.Community.Strategy_Executed &
          Comp.E_Marketing_Mix.Site.Strategy_Executed &
          Comp.E_Marketing_Mix.Security.Strategy_Executed)
          Skip
     Else
          Confidence_Level = Confidence_Level - 1
          Go to Rule_6
```

```
Rule_6:

If (Web_Animation.Above_Average or Web_Interface.Above_Average)
     If (Not Comp.E_Marketing_Mix.Site.Strategy_Executed)
          Confidence_Level = Confidence_Level - 1
```

Figure 12. Screenshot – Digital camera with price range "$120 – $210", brand name "Sony" and resolution "7 – 8MP" selected

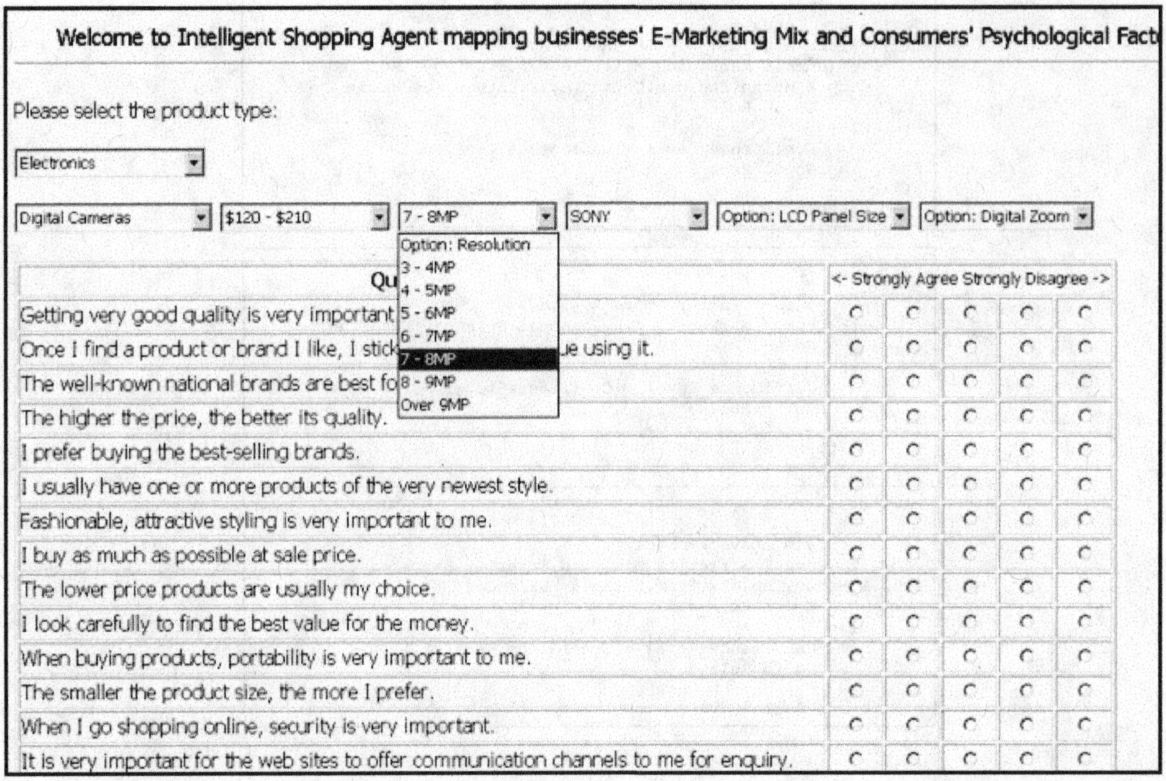

Module 2: Calculate Scores

The scores of the psychological questions (c) will be used to evaluate the score for consumers' psychological factors (d). Based on Table 1, the score of each psychological factor for each consumer can be determined by the following formula:

$$Weight_i = \frac{Loading_i}{\sum_{j=1}^{n} Loading_j}$$

where $Weight_i$ is the weight of the ith psychological question with respect to a particular factor and $Loading_i$ is the loading of the ith psychological question with respect to a particular factor. The overall score for the psychological factors is computed as follows:

$$Score_{pf} = \sum_{i=1}^{n} (Score_i * Weight_i)$$

where $Score_{pf}$ is the score of each psychological factor for each consumer and $Score_i$ is the score of the ith psychological question with respect to a particular factor.

Module 3: Analyze Consumers' Psychological Factors

Based on the selected product type from the consumer, the score of a particular psychological factor (d) is compared with the corresponding average index (e). The score can be interpreted to be average or not (h), as shown in the following rule:

If (Person.Price_Factor.Score <

Figure 13. Architecture of EMMSA

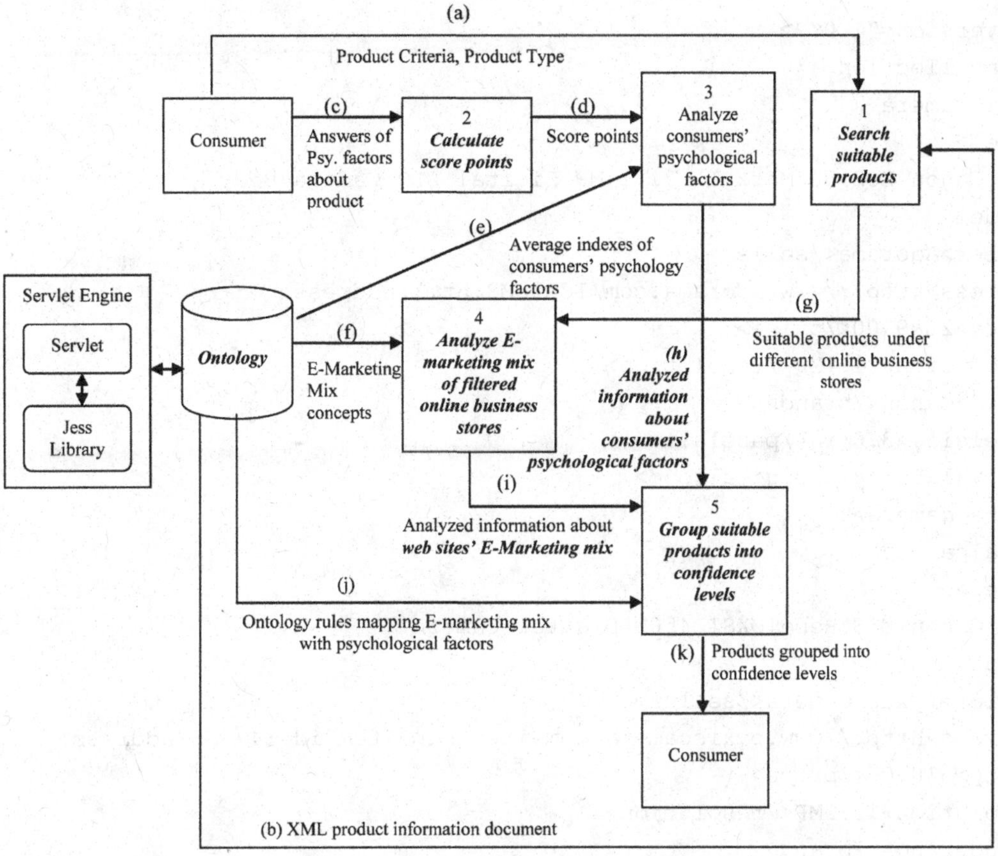

Person.Price_Factor.Factor_Average.ITitem_Average_Index)

then the score is above average

In this module, the Jess library (Eriksson, 2004; Friedman-Hill, 2006), a rule-base engine, can be used to link to the ontology in order to access the average indexes of each psychological factor for a particular product type.

Jess Library

The core of the Jess library is the jess.Rete class (Friedman-Hill, 2006). Every jess.Rete object has its own independent working memory, its own list of rules, and its own set of functions. It provides a convenient central access point although there are many other classes in the library. EMMSA will use the Jess library embedded in the servlet engine in order to access the ontology rules as well as the knowledge base.

There is a default constructor used to create Rete object as follows:

```
import jess.*;
...
Rete engine = new Rete();
```

Once a new object is created, one of the powerful ways to manipulate Jess from Java Servlets is to use the executeCommand method which accepts a String argument and returns a jess.Value. The String is interpreted as an expression in the Jess language, and the return value is the result of evaluating the expression.

Algorithm 1.

```xml
<?xml version="1.0"?>
<cameracollection>
<digitalcamera>
  <model>
        Canon EOS 5D Mark II 21.1 MP Digital SLR Camera Body
  </model>
  <seller>Adorama</seller>
  <address>http://www.adorama.com/ICA5DM2.html/address>
  <price>2699.00</price>
  <resolution>21.1MP</resolution>
  <brand>Canon</brand>
  <panelsize>3.0 in</panelsize>
  <digitalzoom>8x</digitalzoom>
</digitalcamera>
<digitalcamera>
  <model>
        Canon EOS Rebel XSI 450D Digital Camera
  </model>
  <seller>Pyxis Camera</seller>
  <address>http://www.pyxiscamera.com/item.php?item_id=147336/address>
  <price>618.00</price>
  <resolution>12.2MP</resolution>
  <brand>Canon</brand>
  <panelsize>3.0 in</panelsize>
  <digitalzoom>6x</digitalzoom>
</digitalcamera>
......
</cameracollection>
```

In order to add a fact to Jess's working memory and get access to the jess.Fact object, you might do the following:

```
import jess.*;
...
Rete engine = new Rete();
Value v = engine.
executeCommand("(assert (fact1))");
Fact f = v.factValue(engine.getGlobalContext());
```

In order to resolve a jess.Value, you need a jess.Context object. The method getGlobalContext in jess.Rete is a convenient way to obtain one. Commands executed via executeCommand may refer to Jess variables; they are interpreted in this same global context.

Using executeCommand to interact with Jess has one other advantage: It is thread-safe. Only a single call to executeCommand can be simultaneously executing on a given instance of jess.Rete. The lock object is internal to the Rete instance, so

Figure 14. Four storage areas holding different suitable product pages

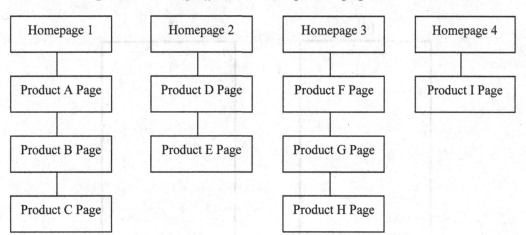

executeCommand is synchronized independently of any other concurrency controls.

JessTab

JessTab is a Protege plug-in that provides an interface to run Jess under Protege. Because Protege and Jess are implemented in Java, they can run together in a single Java virtual machine. JessTab permits Jess to run as an interactive tool and provides a set of additional Jess functions for manipulating Protege ontologies and knowledge bases

Accessing the Average Indexes of Each Psychological Factor

Based on the product type selected by the online consumers, the average index of each psychological factor can be accessed by using the Jess library to connect to the ontology. The following Java code segment uses JessTab to interact Protege ontology and uses Jess library to access to the apparel average index of price conscious factor and store the Double value in App_Index .

```
try{
  Rete engine = new Rete();
  engine.executeCommand("(load-pack-
age JessTab.JessTabFunctions)");
```

```
  engine.executeCommand("(load-proj-
ect EMMSA.pprj)");
  Value Apparel_Index = engine.
executeCommand("(slot-get price " + "
  Apparel_Average_Index)");
  App_Index = Apparel_Index.
DoubleValue(engine.getGlobalCon-
text());
}
catch (JessException je) {
  System.err.println(je);}
```

Module 4: Analyze E-Marketing Mix of Online Business Stores

The online business stores obtained from (g) are analyzed based on the terms of e-marketing mix (f) to find out the e-marketing tools supported by their web sites (i). The filtered suitable product pages are grouped in a storage area as shown in Figure 14. Since all product pages under the same web site offer the same e-marketing tools to customers, it is not necessary to scan all the filtered product pages. Instead, only one filtered suitable product page is scanned under the same business web site. For instance, in Figure 14, there are three suitable products offered by Homepage 1, but only one product page is scanned from its source code to check for any e-marketing tools offered to cus-

Figure 15. (a) Lowest psychological scores (b) Average psychological scores

(a) *(b)*

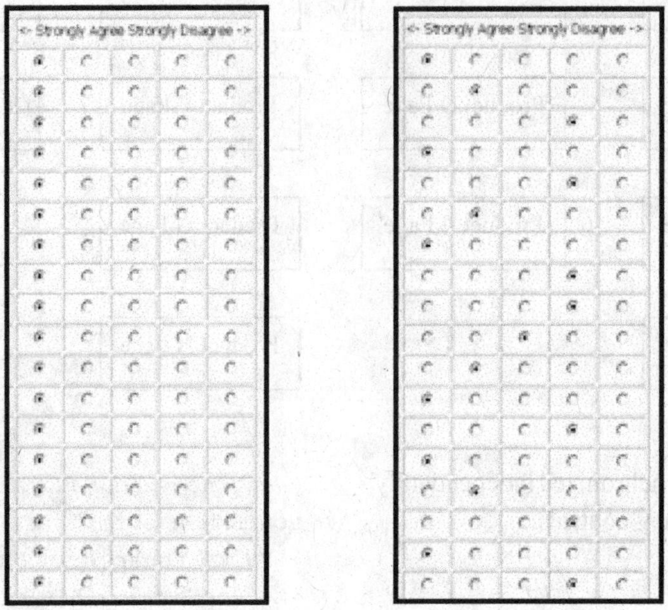

tomers. Since some of the e-marketing tools can only be found on the home page of the business web site based on Table 3, the home page is also scanned in addition to scanning the product page.

Module 5: Search Suitable Web Sites

The confidence level of each suitable product item sold by an online business store can be determined by applying the analyzed information about consumer's psychological factors (g) and the e-marketing tools supported by the online business store (i) on the ontology rules (j) defined on Figure 11. All suitable product items are then grouped (k) according to their corresponding confidence levels. As a result, consumers can browse the product pages of suitable product items based on different confidence levels.

SAMPLE RUN OF INTELLIGENT SHOPPING AGENT (EMMSA)

In the sample run of EMMSA, a product from each of the four categories of products is searched one hundred times (each time running with a particular set of search criteria and two sets of answers for psychological questions as below):

1. lowest scores (highest psychological demand) shown in Figure 15(a).
2. average scores shown in Figure 15(b)

For instance, the product "Pants" is chosen with material "Denim" and price between $80 and $150 as shown in Figure 16 with lowest score points chosen. After the submit button is pressed, the list box is displayed as shown in Figure 17. The outputs of the sample run are shown in Figures 18, 19 and 20.

Figure 16. Pants chosen with material "Denim" (lowest score points selected)

Questions	<- Strongly Agree Strongly Disagree ->				
Getting very good quality is very important to me.	⊙	○	○	○	○
Once I find a product or brand I like, I stick with it and continue using it.	⊙	○	○	○	○
The well-known national brands are best for me.	⊙	○	○	○	○
The higher the price, the better its quality.	⊙	○	○	○	○
I prefer buying the best-selling brands.	⊙	○	○	○	○
I usually have one or more products of the very newest style.	⊙	○	○	○	○
Fashionable, attractive styling is very important to me.	⊙	○	○	○	○
I buy as much as possible at sale price.	⊙	○	○	○	○
The lower price products are usually my choice.	⊙	○	○	○	○
I look carefully to find the best value for the money.	⊙	○	○	○	○
When buying products, portability is very important to me.	⊙	○	○	○	○
The smaller the product size, the more I prefer.	⊙	○	○	○	○
When I go shopping online, security is very important.	⊙	○	○	○	○
It is very important for the web sites to offer communication channels to me for enquiry.	⊙	○	○	○	○
It is very important for the web sites to offer product searching service to me.	⊙	○	○	○	○
It is perfect if the web sites can offer me richness information about products.	⊙	○	○	○	○
It will be annoying to get a lot of animated effect on the business web sites.	⊙	○	○	○	○
Design layout of business web site is one of the important factors to make buying decisions.	⊙	○	○	○	○

Figure 17. List box available for choosing suitable products with different confidence levels

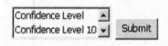

ANALYSIS OF RESULTS

Based on the above sample run, the confidence level can be analyzed as shown in Table 4(a) – (b) and Table 5. The analysis shows the following facts:

1. When the lowest psychological scores are selected, confidence level 9 contains the maximum number of product items and there are only few or no suitable product items categorized in confidence level 10 as shown in Table 4(a). When average psychological scores are selected, confidence level 10 contains the maximum number of product items while the number of product items dramatically decreases in confidence level 9 as shown in Table 4(b).

2. When the lowest psychological scores are selected, there are some product items categorized in confidence level 6 and 7 as shown in Table 4(a). However, when average psychological scores are selected, there are no product items categorized in confidence level 6 and 7 as shown in Table 4(b).

3. The product items are categorized into fewer categories of confidence level when average psychological scores are selected.

4. Based on Table 5, Apparel and Jewelry have a much higher standard deviation than I.T. items and car items no matter whether the lowest or average psychological scores are selected.

Figure 18. Outputs displayed for confidence level 9 (442 suitable products)

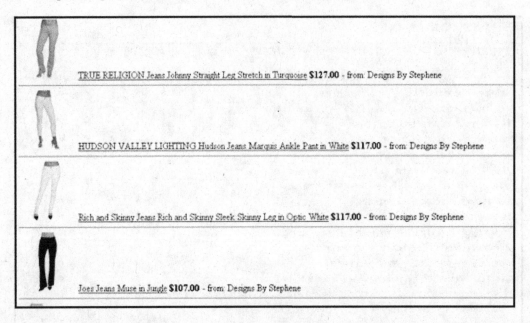

Figure 19. Outputs displayed for confidence level 8 (58 suitable products)

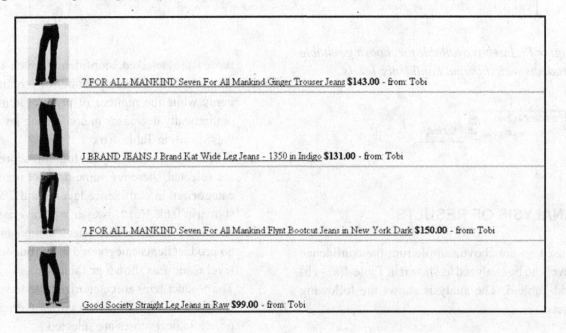

5. Based on Table 4(a), there are on average around 40% of all product items from all product types filtered into the category of lower confidence levels by using EMMSA with lowest psychological scoring points selected by online consumers. However, I.T. items themselves can filter 94%, a rate much higher than the mean. If I.T. items are ignored, the average filtered rate will be around 21%.

6. Based on Table 4(b), there are around 16% of all product items filtered into the category

Figure 20. Outputs displayed for confidence level 6 (103 suitable products)

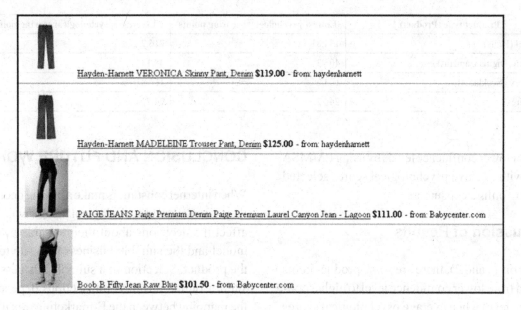

Table 4(a). Suitable product items for different confidence levels: (a) Lowest psychological scores; (b) Average psychological scores

(a) Lowest psychological scores					
	Confidence Level				
Product type (Product)	Level 10	Level 9	Level 8	Level 7	Level 6
Apparel (Pants)	0	73%	10%	0	17%
I.T. item (Digital Cameras)	6%	77%	5%	5%	7%
Jewellery (Necklaces)	0	79%	7%	2%	12%
Car (Tires)	0	84%	0	0	16%
(b) Average psychological scores					
	Confidence Level				
Product type (Product)	Level 10	Level 9	Level 8	Level 7	Level 6
Apparel (Pants)	83%	0	17%	0	0
I.T. item (Digital Cameras)	82%	16%	2%	0	0
Jewellery (Necklaces)	86%	14%	0	0	0
Car (Tires)	84%	16%	0	0	0

Table 5. Standard deviation of product items from confidence level 6 to 10 among different product types

Product type (Product)	Lowest psychological scoring points	Average psychological scoring points
Apparel (Pants)	184.81	216.73
I.T. item (Digital Cameras)	40.93	45.13
Jewellery (Necklaces)	103.2	114.82
Car (Tires)	24.72	24.72

of lower confidence levels by using EMMSA with average psychological scores selected by online consumers.

Discussion of Results

Based on 1) and 2), there are some product items shifted from lower confidence level to higher confidence level when average psychological scores are selected. It means that the consumers can get more suitable product items if they are not too demanding about what they think about products. In addition, the e-marketing mix of most online business stores can satisfy the needs of consumers as a result of a few or even no product items categorized into a low confidence level.

In addition, based on 1), there are only a few online business stores which can fully satisfy consumers with the lowest psychological scores.

Furthermore, based on 4), I.T. and car product items are more evenly distributed across confidence level 6 to 9. Meanwhile, with the lowest psychological scoring points selected, only I.T. product items are included in all confidence levels from 6 to 10, but car product items are only included in confidence levels 6 and 9. In addition, based on 5), the filtering rate of I.T. items is 94%. As a result, EMMSA is more effective for I.T. items.

Finally, based on 5) and 6), EMMSA is more effective when lower psychological scoring points are selected.

CONCLUSION AND FUTURE WORK

When internet consumers make a buying decision, they have several psychological factors which can affect the decisions about their suitable product model and the suitable business web site to buy the product. Selection of a suitable business web site for online business transactions depends on the mapping between the E-marketing mix model provided by individual business web sites and the psychological factors of internet consumers. Our ontology is designed in such a way that this mapping is made visible to the online businesses. This tool will be a significant asset to online businesses wanting to increase their market share.

In our ongoing research, we are investigating techniques to classify the levels of the e-marketing tools supported by a business store so that the confidence level of a suitable item provided by a business can be more accurate.

REFERENCES

Berstel, B., & Bonnard, P. (2007). Reactive Rules on the Web. In *Proceedings of Summer School Reasoning Web 2007* (LNCS 4636, pp.183-239).

Constantinides, E. (2002). The 4S Web-Marketing Mix Model. *Electronic Commerce Research and Applications*, *1*(1), 57–76. doi:10.1016/S1567-4223(02)00006-6

Eriksson, H. (2004). *JessTab Manual: Integration of Protégé and Jess*. Linkoping, Sweden: Linkoping University.

Friedman-Hill, E. J. (2006). *Jess - The Rule Engine for the Java Platform*. Albuquerque, NM: Sandia National Laboratories.

Hoffman, D. L., & Novak, T. P. (1997). A New Marketing Paradigm for Electronic Commerce. *The Information Society . Special Issue for Electronic Commerce, 13*(1), 43–54.

Hoffman, D. L., Novak, T. P., & Peralta, M. A. (1999). Information Privacy in the Marketspace: Implications for the Commercial Uses of Anonymity on the Web. *The Information Society, 15*, 129–139. doi:10.1080/019722499128583

Hou, J. W., & Cesar, R. (2002). *Internet Marketing: An Overview*. Oxford, MS: University of Mississippi, School of Business Administration.

Joshua, D. (2003). *Rich Internet Applications, sponsored by Macromedia and Intel*. Framingham, MA: IDC.

Kalyanam, K., & McIntyre, S. (2002). The Marketing Mix: A Contribution of the E-Tailing Wars. *Journal of the Academy of Marketing Science, 30*(4), 483–495. doi:10.1177/009207002236924

Lauterborn, B. (1990). New Marketing Litany: Four P's Passe: C-Words Take Over. *Advertising Age, 61*(41).

Meuter, M. L., Amy, L. O., Robert, I. R., & Mary, J. B. (2000). Self-Service Technologies: Understanding Customer Satisfaction With Technology – Based Service Encounters. *Journal of Marketing, 64*(3), 50–64. doi:10.1509/jmkg.64.3.50.18024

Noy, N. F., & McGuinness, D. L. (2001). *Ontology Development 101: A Guide to Creating Your First Ontology*. Palo Alto, CA: Stanford University.

Sam, K. M., & Chatwin, C. R. (2005a). Multiproduct Generalizability of a Scale for Profiling International Internet Consumers' Decision Making styles in E-Commerce. In *Proceedings Conference on Information Management in Modern Enterprise* (pp. 132-138).

Sam, K. M., & Chatwin, C. R. (2005b). The Mapping Between Business E-Marketing Mix and Internet Consumers' Decision-Making Styles in E-Commerce. In *Proceedings of the Fifth International Conference on Electronic Business (ICEB 2005)*.

Shkapenyuk, V., & Suel, T. (2002). Design and implementation of a high-performance distributed web crawler. In *Proceedings of the IEEE International Conference on Data Engineering (ICDE)* (pp. 357-368).

Sproles, G. B. (1985). *From Perfectionism to Fadism: Measuring Consumers' Decision-Making Styles* (pp. 79–85). Proceedings, American Council on Consumer Interests.

Sproles, G. B., & Kendall, E. L. (1986). A Methodology for Profiling Consumers' Decision-Making Styles. *The Journal of Consumer Affairs, 20*(4), 267–279.

Unitime Systems Literature. (2006). *The Unitime Version 8 Smart Client Advantage*. Boulder, CO: Unitime Systems.

Westbrook, R. A., & Black, W. C. (1985). A Motivation-Based Shopper Typology. *Journal of Retailing, 61*(1), 78–103.

This work was previously published in International Journal of Intelligent Information Technologies, Volume 6, Issue 2, edited by Vijayan Sugumaran, pp. 21-43, copyright 2010 by IGI Publishing (an imprint of IGI Global).

Chapter 7
A New Behavior Management Architecture for Language Faculty of an Agent for Task Delegation

S. Kuppuswami
Kongu Engineering College, India

T. Chithralekha
Pondicherry University, India

ABSTRACT

*In this paper, the authors describe a new architecture for the language faculty of an agent that fulfills the interaction requirements of task delegation. The architecture of the language faculty is based on a conceptualization of the language faculty of an agent and a definition of its internal state paradigm. The new architecture is behavior-management based and possesses self-management properties. This architecture is compared with existing abstract self-management architectures, which examines how the new architecture solves unresolved issues of older models. The architecture description is followed by a case study - **Mul**tilingual Natural Language **A**gent **I**nterface for Mail Service, which illustrates its application.*

DOI: 10.4018/978-1-4666-0158-1.ch007

1. INTRODUCTION

Software Agents differ from other software by their ability to work on delegation. The interaction requirements of task delegation necessitate that an agent is able to work on abstract task specifications given by users and ask for and receive advice in human terms during task execution (Bradshaw, 1997). Hence, from an interaction perspective of delegation, an agent is required to support natural language interaction. The natural language interaction should also be collaborative in order that an agent is able to suggest alternatives or ask for advice during task execution.

To cater to the language requirements of global users, the collaborative natural language interaction should be supported in at least a subset of languages available. The agent should be able to dynamically configure its language of interaction according to the user's choice or preference. Only then, an agent's service could be made available across language barriers.

Therefore, collaborative natural language interaction (CNLI) with dynamic multilingualism (DM) have been identified as the two functions required to be attributed to an agent for fulfilling the interaction aspects of task delegation. Also, these two functions should be able to exhibit the required agent properties. In the existing agents with natural language capabilities, a comprehensive architecture for the language ability of an agent that accommodates both CNLI and DM along with the required agent properties have not received the required focus.

The objective of this paper is to define the architecture of the language ability of an agent. This language ability component interacts with the functional component of the agent in order to accomplish the goal of the agent. The newly defined architecture derives its base from earlier works (Chithralekha & Kuppuswami, 2008) which are:

- Conceptualization of Language Faculty
- Definition of New Internal State Paradigm for Language Faculty

The need for a new architecture for the language faculty was necessitated because of the paradigm shift brought about in the fundamental conceptualization of an agent described in the above two works. The shift is that the language autonomy of agent is diversified into the management and behavior dimensions, in contrast to the existing agents which possess only a single dimension of autonomy.

The definition of the architecture is described in the abstract, macro and micro levels of abstractions. In the micro level, the architecture for realizing the management dimension of autonomy has been focused in detail. This is performed by considering the properties required for an agent to self-manage it and attributing them in the architecture. For the behavior dimension, the existing behavior-based architectures (Brooks, 1986; Rao & Georgeff, 1991; Muller et al., 1995; Wooldridge, 1999) could be used. Hence, this behavior dimension has not been explored into.

After the architecture has been designed, it is compared with the existing generic self management architecture (Kramer & Magee, 2007) to explicate how certain unresolved issues in it have been addressed in the newly defined architecture. The added advantage of the architecture is that it is not only suitable for the language ability of an agent but also generic in nature. Hence, it is suitable for realizing a functional ability of an agent also if self-management properties are to be attributed in it.

The case study illustrates the use of this architecture in developing a **Mul**tilingual natural language **A**gent **I**nterface (MULLAI) for mail server.

The remainder of this paper is organized as follows. Section 2 provides an overview of the background of this work and emphasizes the need for the new architecture by explaining how the existing behavior-based architecture falls short in contributing for architecture of the language faculty. Section 3, 4 and 5 describe the architecture of the language faculty at the abstract, macro and micro levels correspondingly. Comparison of the defined architecture with the existing generic self-management architecture is given in Section 6. Section 7 describes the application of the architecture using a case study. The conclusion is given in Section 8.

2. BACKGROUND

This section describes about the two research works which form the basis of the newly defined architecture. In addition, it also proceeds to discuss the need for the new architecture which is triggered because of these two research works.

The definition of architecture is a continuation of our research work which focuses on attributing language ability to an agent for fulfilling the interaction requirements of task delegation. The following are the two significant milestones that were reached before the definition of the architecture:

- Conceptualization of Language Faculty of an Agent
- Definition of New Internal State paradigm for Language Faculty

These milestones contribute for the background of the defined architecture. Hence, an overview of the same is given below.

2.1 Conceptualization of Language Faculty of an Agent

The ultimate objective of this research work was to attribute language abilities inherent of an agent to fulfill the interaction requirements of task delegation. Hence, the interaction aspects of task delegation were studied and the following two language abilities were identified to be very essential to fulfill the interaction requirements of delegation.

- **Collaborative Natural Language Interaction (CNLI):** Proactive / Reactive

interaction with the user in natural language either to explicate the delegated task request, or to convey the result of execution or suggest alternate ways of carrying out a particular task.

- **Dynamic Multilingualism (DM):** Supporting natural language interaction in multiple languages and altering the language of interaction dynamically to the language required or preferred by the user.

The characteristic agent properties that were required to he fulfilled in these two language abilities were derived. This was carried out by considering the typical agent properties and interpreting their semantics from a language perspective.

A survey of the language ability of existing agents was carried out to determine whether the two identified language abilities were fulfilled in them together with the characteristic agent properties that were identified as essential for these abilities. The result of the study revealed that CNLI and DM were not attributed together in a single agent. The agent properties required for CNLI were found to be fulfilled in them. But DM, together with its properties was not found to be attributed in any agent.

Hence, an attempt to attribute the two required language abilities with their characteristic properties was taken up as the aim of this research work. In the first step towards achieving this aim, the language autonomy of the agent that enables for natural language interaction had to be diversified into two dimensions viz. the management and behavior dimensions as follows:

- **Language Ability Management Autonomy:** Enables the agent to manage its language abilities pertaining to the languages supported
- **Language Behavior Autonomy:** Enables the agent to carry out CNLI in each of the languages supported

The language ability management autonomy is the new form of autonomy that was introduced in this research work. It was hypothesized to be composed of four sub-autonomies viz.

- **Language competence management autonomy:** Enables the agent to manage the language competencies in the languages supported
- **Language knowledge Management Autonomy:** Enables the agent to manage the language knowledge in the languages supported
- **Language Configuration Management Autonomy:** Enables the agent to configure its competence and knowledge to the required language
- **New Language Acquisition Management Autonomy:** Enables the agent to acquire new languages to extend the degree of multilingualism

The language ability of an agent that possesses both the two management and behavior dimensions of autonomy was termed in this research work as a Language Faculty to be synonymous to the language faculty of humans.

2.2 Definition of New Internal State Paradigm for Language Faculty of an Agent

Since the language faculty is realized as a combination of two dimensions of autonomies, its internal state and its dynamism cannot be captured by the existing internal state definitions of agents (Brooks 1986; Muller & Pischel, 1994; Muller, Pischel, & Thiel 1995; Rao & Georgeff, 1991; Wooldridge, 2000, 1999) as their focus is only towards action/behavior and does not encompass the management aspect. The definition of the internal state should help to accommodate both the management context and the behavior contexts. In addition, it should enable the agent

to be internally aware that it supports multiple languages so that dynamic multilingualism and knowledge discovery across languages is possible. This has also not been taken care of in the existing approaches of achieving multilingualism in agents (Connell, 2000; Huang, Haft, & Hsu, 2000; Pazienza et al., 2005; Ritter et al., 1999; Ren & Shi, 2000; Turunen & Hakulinen, 2000; http://www.microsoft.com/msagent/downloads/user.asp). Hence, a new paradigm consisting of the following three abstractions were defined:

- **Belief (B):** Beliefs that the language faculty holds about language
- **Task Context (T):** Corresponds to each of the four management level autonomy functions
- **Behavior Context (B):** Corresponds to the behaviors which are controlled by the task Context

The dynamism of the (BTB) abstraction was defined to explicate how an agent's reasoning mechanism alternates between the three abstractions. That is, the language percept received by the agent makes true some of the beliefs of the language faculty. According to the beliefs which become true, the task context(s) corresponding to any of the four management level autonomy functions are activated. After this, a particular behavior context under the activated task context becomes true and the corresponding language behavior is performed.

A complete description of the above two works is given in Chithralekha and Kuppuswami (2008).

2.3 Need for a New Architecture of Language Faculty

The need for a new architecture of language faculty could be realized by considering the existing agent architectures. The existing architectures of agents could be classified into four types as follows:

- Logic-Based Architectures (Wooldridge, 1999)
- Reactive Architecture (Brooks, 1986)
- BDI Architecture (Rao & Georgeff, 1991) and
- Hybrid Architecture (Muller et al., 1995; Wooldridge, 1999)

A detailed description of these architectures could be found in (Wooldridge, 1999).

These existing architectures are only behavior-based architectures and help to accommodate only a single behavior dimension of autonomy. Since, the language faculty has to accommodate two-dimensions of autonomy pertaining to the management and behavior dimensions, the existing architectures fall short in fulfilling the requirement. Hence, a new architecture for the language faculty of an agent has to be designed. This is explained in the subsequent section.

3. ABSTRACT ARCHITECTURE OF THE LANGUAGE FACULTY

In order to explicate the architecture of the language faculty comprehensively, it is elaborated in the following levels of abstraction, viz.

- Abstract Architecture
- Macro Architecture
- Micro Architecture

This section describes about the abstract architecture. The macro and micro levels are described in the subsequent sections.

The architecture of the language faculty should help to accommodate the conceptualization of the language faculty and its internal state counterpart namely the BTB paradigm. Hence, the core architectural components and their interactions which fulfill these have to be identified first. This would contribute for the abstract architecture.

The language faculty is to be realized as a combination of language ability management autonomy and language behavior autonomy. The management autonomy is constituted by four different autonomies. These autonomies correspond to the various management tasks that the language faculty has to perform, to manage the language behaviors it supports in the various languages. These tasks could be generically visualized as language behavior management tasks. Hence, the architecture should help to lay emphasis on behavior management with modular distribution of the management functions and organize the language behaviors under these management functions in such a way that the language behaviors are best managed by these management tasks. This would shift the focus of the agent architecture from the conventional behavior based architectures to that of a behavior management based architecture where the required behavior management task takes the control first, followed by the behavior.

Thus, behavior management and behavior contribute for the two major components. Additionally, an interface component is required to interface with the environment. In order to facilitate the control flow as required by the BTB paradigm, the three components are to be arranged in a three layered organization as shown in Figure 1. The resulting abstract architecture would consist of three layers namely, the interface layer, behavior management layer and the behavior layer.

These layers communicate with each other by using messages. Whereas the existing agents are composed of only the interface and behavior layers, the behavior management layer is the new layer which is introduced in this work.

4. MACRO ARCHITECTURE OF THE LANGUAGE FACULTY

The description of the macro architecture is expressed in terms of the following:

Figure 1. Abstract architecture of the language faculty

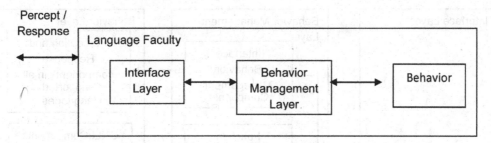

- Identification of the Components
- Organization of the Components
- Interaction of the Components.

4.1 Identification of the Components

This section describes about the components that make up the behavior management layer and the behavior layer. The Interface layer is the usual interface to the agent. Hence, it is not explored into.

For the Behavior Management layer, the four tasks of the behavior management layer are considered and the components that are required to accomplish these tasks are given in Table 1. Table 1 shows that the competence management task is realized by two components namely the interface behavior management and function behavior management components. The interface management helps to manage the 'perceive' and 'response' competences in every language supported. The function management helps to manage the CNLI rendering behaviors of every language. The Knowledge Behavior Management task is

accomplished using the Knowledge Behavior Management Component. This component helps to manage the language knowledge servicing behaviors corresponding to every language which is supported by the agent. The new behavior acquisition task is to be performed by the new behavior acquisition management component. The configuration behavior management task is proposed to be accommodated in the above identified management components themselves and not realized as a separate component. This will be described in the subsequent micro level architecture description.

Using the identified components, the component level architecture of the language faculty is given in Figure 2.

4.2 Organization of the Components

The overall organization of the language faculty is a vertically layered organization with two pass control as shown in Figure 3. The two pass control signifies that the information flows up

Table 1. Components of the behavior management layer

Task	Components Identified
Competence Behavior Management	Interface Behavior Management Component
	Function Behavior Management Component
Knowledge Behavior Management	Knowledge Behavior Management Component
Configuration Behavior Management	Task functionality to be attributed within the other identified management components.
New Behavior Acquisition Management	New Behavior Acquisition Management Component

Figure 2. Architecture of the language faculty of an agent

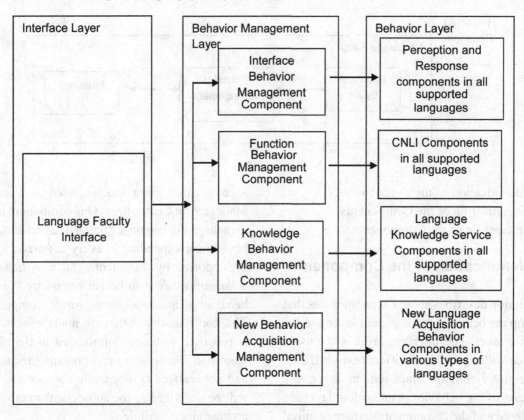

the architecture in the first pass and the control flows down in the second pass. That is, the user's natural language request flows up to the functional ability layer through the lower language faculty layer and the action or result is conveyed again through this language faculty layer.

Integrating the three layered organization proposed for language faculty and the vertical organization of an agent with language ability, the overall organization is as given in Figure 4.

4.3 Interaction between the Components

At the highest level of abstraction, the interaction happens between the interface layer, behavior management layer and the behavior layer. But, the overall functionality of the language faculty is achieved through the interactions between the

components of the behavior management layer. This is because the components of the various behavior layers do not communicate directly. All their interactions happen only through the behavior management layer. Hence, the interactions that happen between the behavior management layer components alone are explained.

The interactions between the components and the purpose of their interactions with respect to the language faculty are described in Table 2.

5. MICRO ARCHITECTURE

The micro level architecture explores into the internal details of the individual components of the three layers. The first layer interface component has a trivial function, and hence its architecture is not explored into at the micro level. With respect

Figure 3. Vertical organization of an agent with language ability

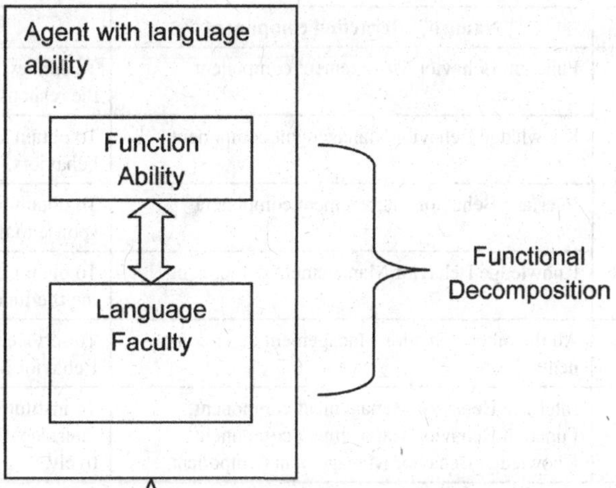

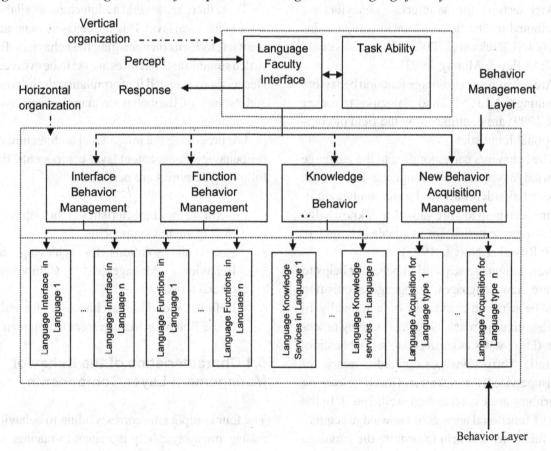

Figure 4. Overall organization of components in an agent with language faculty

Table 2. Components of the behavior management layer and their interactions

Component	Name of interacting component	Purpose of interaction
Interface Behavior Management Component	Function Behavior Management component	To convey the percept received and receive the response of the function behaviors.
	Knowledge Behavior Management component	To obtain knowledge resources for interface behaviors.
Function Behavior Management component	Interface Behavior Management component	To obtain percept from and convey response to the environment.
	Knowledge Behavior Management component	To obtain knowledge required for performing the function.
Knowledge Behavior Management Component	All the other Behavior Management layer components	To service the knowledge requests of the Behavior Management layer components
New behavior acquisition management component	Interface Behavior Management component, Function Behavior Management component Knowledge Behavior Management component	To institute the newly acquired language interface, functions and knowledge respectively.

to the third layer namely the behavior layer, the internal architecture of the identified components are already available and reported in the literature as described below.

Architectures for the interface behaviors are contributed by the field of human computer interaction (Clerckx et al., 2006; Stephanidis et al., 1997; Hefley & Murray, 1993).

Architectures for language function behaviors pertaining to NLP, NLG and dialoguing (Crocker et al, 1999) are contributed by the field of computational linguistics.

The behaviors corresponding to the language knowledge services are language knowledge representation dependent and corresponding architectures that help to store and retrieve knowledge in this representation are available (Harmelen, 2007; Russel & Norvig, 1995).

New Language acquisition behavior helps to acquire new languages. Language acquisition could be achieved cognitively or functionally. In the cognitive approach, language learning procedures (http://www.cs.utexas.edu/~ml/publication/nl.html), (http://www.cs.cmu.edu/~acarlson/semisupervised) that make use of machine learning algorithms are used (Hu & Atwell, 2005). In the case of functional approach, knowledge acquisition functions that help to acquire the language

knowledge automatically or semi-automatically from a knowledge engineer (Lavrac & Mozetic, 1989). Architectures for both of these language acquisition behaviors are available.

Thus, there are several architectures available at the behavioral level. But, the behavior management has to focus on managing the behaviors, for which suitable architectures are yet to be evolved. Hence, there is a need for formulating the internal architecture of the behavior management layer components.

For proposing the micro level architecture of the behavior management layer components, the following activities are performed:

- Defining the characteristics of the Behavior Management Components
- Issues and solutions for achieving the Behavior Management Component Characteristics
- Defining individual architectures for each of the Behavior Management Components

5.1 Characteristics of the Behavior Management Layer Components

The four components corresponding to behavior management layer help the agent to manage its interface, function and knowledge in all the languages supported and also acquire knowledge pertaining to all the above three in a new language. These management tasks actually help the agent to self-manage it. Usually, a self-management system is expected to exhibit the following properties:

- Self-organization – self organizing systems must adapt dynamically to environmental changes by re-organizing themselves.
- Self-adaptation – self adaptive software is one which modifies its behavior in response to changes in its operating environment. A system is open adaptive if new behaviors could be introduced during run time.
- Self-configuration – can dynamically adapt to changes in the environment, where the changes could include the deployment of new components, or removal of existing ones.
- Self-healing – can discover, diagnose and react to disruptions automatically. They can detect system malfunctions and initiate corrective actions.
- Self-optimization – can monitor and tune resources automatically to meet end-user or business needs.
- Self-protecting – can anticipate, detect, identify and protect against threats. They can take corrective actions to make themselves less vulnerable.

The above properties have been borrowed from the two contexts that discuss about self-management namely, software architecture (Kramer & Magee, 2007) and autonomic computing (Serugendo et al., 2006; http://www-3.ibm.com/autonomic/pdfs/). The latter three properties, though are relevant with respect to the self-management, are beyond the scope of this work. Hence, the former three properties are considered and worked upon to formulate the micro level architecture.

Since the behavior management components should help to provide for self-management, the design issues for each of the self-management properties – self-organization, self-adaptation and self-configuration are considered individually and suitable solutions are proposed. Using these proposed solutions, the micro-level architecture is built progressively for each of the four behavior management components. These are explained below.

5.2 Issues and Solutions for Achieving the Behavior Management Component Characteristics

In this section, the various design issues that arise for achieving self-organization, self-adaptation and self-configuration properties in the behavior management layer are considered. The corresponding proposed solutions for achieving the said properties are described subsequently. These solutions form the basis for the individual architectures of the behavior management layer components.

5.2.1 Self-Organization Issues and Solutions

Self-organization relates to the capacity of the system to spontaneously produce a new organization in case of environmental changes. That is, components should be able to dynamically bind together under user requests or for pursuing their own goals. This requires that a component listens to events or percepts in the environment and carries out the dynamic binding with an appropriate component. The various design alternatives in incorporating the listener and carrying out the dynamic binding are as follows:

Alternative 1

Listeners could be put in each of the behavior components and the behavior component that recognizes its event or percept gets activated.

Figure 5. Behavior management component and its manager and behavior roles

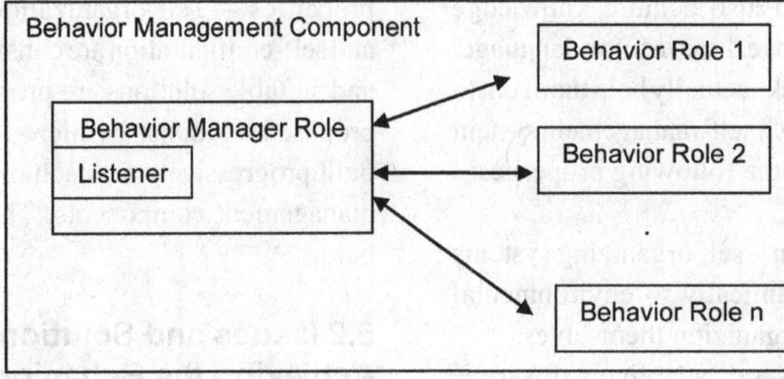

Limitations

- Every behavior component should have its own listeners.
- The percept should be broadcast to all behaviors resulting in communication overhead.
- Communication failure would result in the required behavior not being activated.
- Not compatible with the macro architecture described above as there is no role for behavior management in behavior initiation which should have been the case.

Alternative 2

The second alternative is to have a listener in the behavior management component instead of the behavior components. Based on the percept that is received, the behavior management component decides which of the behavior component to activate thereby self-organizing itself for providing the corresponding behavior.

Limitations

- Though it is compatible with the above described behavior management architecture, yet resources for the two components (two processes) are required –the behavior

management and the behavior. This is an overhead on the system.

Alternative 3

This alternative is closely aligned with that of the second alternative, with the listener incorporated with behavior management. The difference is that the behavior management is conceived to be composed of manager and behaviors roles. The behavior manager role is active by default and the listener waits for the relevant percept that any of the behaviors under its control could accomplish. When it receives the relevant percept it relinquishes its behavior manager role and takes on the required behavior role. That is, the dynamic binding that is very much required of self-organization is accomplished in the most effective manner. After completion of the behavior role, it resumes the behavior management role. This is depicted in Figure 5.

Among the three alternatives, the third alternative is the one chosen for achieving self-organization. The architecture of the management components is proposed using this alternative only. This helps to achieve the behavior configuration management in every component by the dynamic binding to the required language behavior role.

5.2.2 Self-Adaptation Issues and Solution

The functional behavior of the agent should adapt to the user so as to provide the preferred behavior. In order to provide for this, both the functional behavior as well as the knowledge required to perform the functional behavior should be configured accordingly. There are two ways of achieving this adaptation as follows:

- Every behavior component has individual observers to observe the user interactions and deduce the behavior preferred by the user.
- A separate component tries to observe the user and deduces the adaptation parameters for the behavior. It intimates these parameters of adaptation to the other components so that they can adapt themselves accordingly.

In the former approach, which is proposed in Kramer and Magee (2007), the limitation is that there is an overhead of observers in every behavior component. Also, it does not comply with the above proposed macro architecture. There is also possibility that there is inconsistency between the deduced values of the adaptation parameters between the various observers. In the latter approach, which is suggested in this paper, there is a single observing component, which deduces the parameters of adaptation and intimates the other components that require it. This approach helps to overcome the above limitations.

Since, the user has to be observed so as to deduce his behavior preferences, it requires that this observing component is part of the interface. Hence, adaptation is realized as part of Interface Behavior Management component. These adaptation values are conveyed to the knowledge and competence management components which adopts the corresponding language behavior role

in order to provide service to the user in the corresponding language.

5.2.3 Self-Configuration Issues and Solution

A self-configuration architecture will be able to acquire new services and make them available for use in a seamless manner. The two alternative ways of achieving this are as follows:

- Every behavior management component acquires the required competence and knowledge and deploys it.
- A separate behavior acquisition management component acquires the required competence and knowledge for all the three behavior management components which is deployed by them individually.

Both of the alternatives could be supported by the proposed micro level architecture. But, the latter alternative is more appropriate as it follows from the macro level architecture given in Figure 6. Another compelling reason for deciding this alternative is because the new behavior acquisition function requires a combined view of both the functional domain ontology and language ontology. Since, these ontologies are separated between function behavior management and knowledge behavior management respectively, the overall view of domain ontology and functional domain ontology is not possible, if the new behavior acquisition function is shared between the three management components, which is the case in the first alternative. Hence, the latter approach is found to be appropriate in all aspects. Thereby, the behavior acquisition management helps to acquire the interface behavior, function behavior and knowledge for the newly acquired language behavior.

Since the self-management properties are to be achieved by all the behavior management layer components, all of them share a common

Figure 6. Internal architecture of the function and knowledge behavior management component

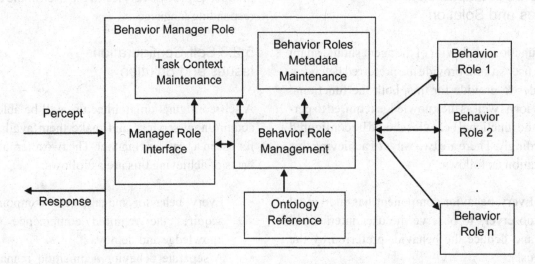

architecture. However, for the purpose of self-adaptation, the interface behavior management accommodates an additional component. Similar is the case for the new behavior acquisition management component. These additional components follow from the description discussed above.

5.3 Individual Architecture for the Behavior Management Layer Components

This section describes the individual architectures of each of the behavior management layer components. These architectures are derived from the solutions described above.

5.3.1 Function Behavior and Knowledge Behavior Management Components

The basic architecture of a behavior manager component is given in Figure 6. This architecture is suitable for supporting function behavior and knowledge behavior management components.

The incoming percept is received by the manager role interface. This component corresponds to the listener component given in Figure 5. This percept is used to update the management task context. The task context maintenance component is responsible for maintaining the task context regarding the corresponding management task. Metadata about every behavior role helps the role management to keep track of the various behavior roles it maintains, under what conditions they should be activated, the procedures for their activation etc. Both these maintenance functions include typical functions of adding and updating the corresponding data which it maintains. The behavior roles management component determines which of the behavior roles to assume based on the current task context and activates the required behavior role.

The functions which the behavior role management should support are as follows:

- Dynamic Role binding
- Role inclusion
- Role deletion
- Role Management level inference.

Dynamic role binding helps the manager role to bind to the required behavior role. This helps to enforce the self-organization whereby, the manager configures to the appropriate behavior

Figure 7. Architecture of the interface behavior management component

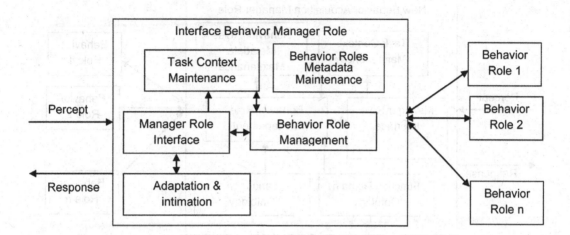

role when required. Role inclusion is required to include a new role in the set of roles being supported. This is achieved by updating the role metadata and the task context. Role management level inference helps to perform a management level inference of the behavior roles like that of which of the behavior roles is very reliable, dependable, or secure etc. This function is required when the other aspects of self-management like that of self-healing, self-protection etc. have to be supported. The ontology reference corresponds to function domain ontology in the case of function behavior management and language ontology in the case of knowledge behavior management.

Now, using the solutions proposed for self-adaptation and self-configuration, the required changes are incorporated in the above basic architecture to result in the architecture of the interface behavior management and new behavior acquisition management components.

5.3.2 Architecture of the Interface Behavior Management Component

The architecture of this component is similar to that given in Figure 6 except that the behavior role management has an additional adaptation and intimation component as given in Figure 7.

This new sub-component helps to observe the user and model his preferences and convey the same to other components in order to provide for an adaptive behavior. Since this component requires controlling only the interface behavior roles, it does not require any ontology reference as in the case of the function behavior and knowledge behavior management components. Hence, this is not given in the architecture.

5.3.3 Architecture of the New Behavior Acquisition Management Component

The same architecture given in Figure 6 is used with the only difference that the ontology reference has both the function domain ontology and generic language ontology. Both of them are required for acquiring a new language behavior. The acquired behavior is deployed in the interface, function and knowledge management components using their role inclusion function. The architecture is given in Figure 8.

Thus, the architecture of the behavior management layer at two levels of abstraction has been described. Table 3 summarizes how the three self-management properties are fulfilled in the architecture.

Figure 8. Internal architecture of the new behavior acquisition management component

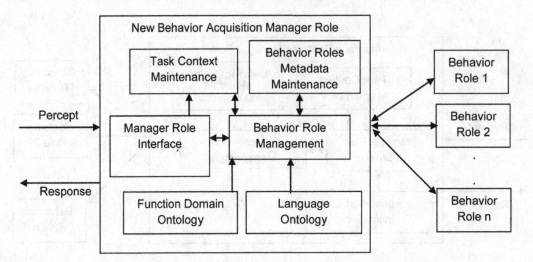

Table 3. Properties of self-management and their fulfillment by the language faculty

Property	Fulfillment of property
Self-Organization	the manager roles of interface, function and knowledge management components are dynamically bound with the required language behavior roles in order to provide the interaction in the required or preferred language.
Self-Adaptation	Language preferences of the user are deduced by the adaptation sub component in the interface behavior management component by observing the user's language use and the working environment in the corresponding language is provided automatically. The adaptation is also open adaptive as new language behaviors could be automatically introduced without user support by the new behavior acquisition component.
Self-Configuration	New Behavior acquisition component acquires new language behaviors. It deploys these behaviors in the language faculty without user involvement.

6. PROPOSED BEHAVIOR MANAGEMENT ARCHITECTURE VS EXISTING SELF-MANAGEMENT ARCHITECTURE

The described behavior management architecture provides for self-management architecture of agents. In the existing literature, there is an abstract and generic three layered self-management architecture proposed by Kramer and Magee (Kramer & Magee, 2007). They have identified certain issues that should be addressed by each of the three layers for which solutions are yet to be found. Since the newly described behavior management architecture provides for solutions for these issues, this architecture is compared

with the existing abstract architecture to evince the advantages.

Figure 9 contrasts the proposed behavior management architecture for agents with that of the existing self-management architecture proposed by Kramer and Magee (2007). The behavior layer corresponds to the component control layer. The behavior layer consists of the behaviors corresponding to each of the management functions. The behavior management layer corresponds to the change management layer. The behavior management layer has all the management components clearly identified. The internal architecture of these components are also described above. The distribution of the management functions follow from the various aspects of an agent functionality

Figure 9. Comparison of abstract self-management architecture with the proposed behavior management architecture for language faculty of an agent

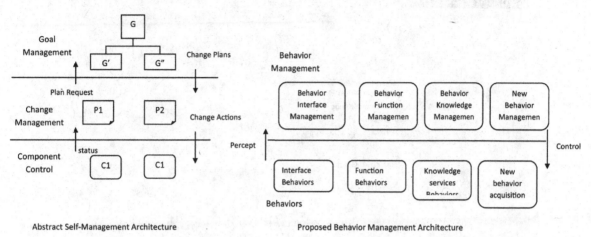

Abstract Self-Management Architecture   Proposed Behavior Management Architecture

Table 4. Issues in the layers of self-management architecture and corresponding solutions in proposed behavior management architecture

Name of Layer in Self-Management Architecture	Issues in existing Self-Management Architecture	Solution in defined Behavior Management Architecture for Language Faculty
Component control	Preserving safe application operation during change.	Until the components are self-organized appropriately, the language faculty is in the passive state.
Change management	Distribution and decentralization of change management functions.	Change management functions are distributed in terms of changes in interface, function and knowledge corresponding to the management components.
Goal Management	Precise specification of application goals and system goals concerned with self-management.	The language faculty is able to acquire new languages and provide its services in that language. This is taken care of by the new behavior acquisition management component.

management namely the interface, competence, knowledge, and augmentation of the three aspects using acquisition.

Table 4 enlists the issues that are specified to be addressed in the abstract self-management architecture and the solutions provided in the behavior management architecture.

Thus, the described behavior management architecture provides the solutions for the various issues identified in the abstract self-management architecture. This results in a complete and comprehensive self-management architecture for the language faculty of an agent.

7. CASE STUDY: MULLAI – MULTILINGUAL NATURAL LANGUAGE AGENT INTERFACE FOR MAIL SERVICE

MULLAI has been developed by utilizing the solutions proposed for the conceptualization of the Language Faculty, the internal state BTB paradigm and the currently defined Behavior Management Architecture which derives its base from the former two. Thereby, it contributes as a test bed for analyzing the appropriateness of the proposed solutions. The natural language interface has been provided for mail service operations like

Figure 10. Interface behavior management dynamically binds with Tamil language Behavior

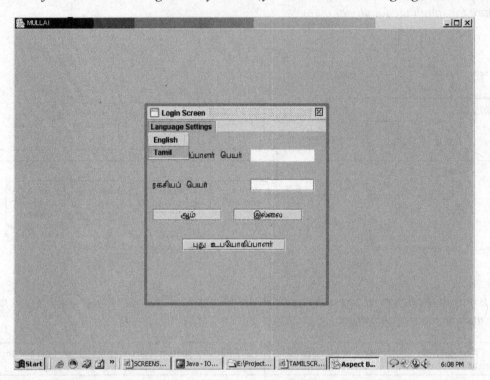

- List
- Read
- Delete
- Compose
- Reply
- Save

Multilingualism has been realized using two languages–English and Tamil. Of these languages, the system was initially built with support for English language only. The Tamil language has been acquired and implemented in the system. The Surgemail has been used as the back end mail server.

The screen shots in Figures 10 and 11 indicate the dynamic binding of interface and competence management functions to the required language. Screen shot 12 (Figure 12) shows the interface screen for performing knowledge management operations. Figures 13 through 16 indicate few of the screen shots used for new language acquisition.

8. CONCLUSION

The language ability of an agent plays a crucial role while considering the user interaction aspect of task delegation. This paper describes about an architecture that has been defined for the language ability of an agent for task delegation. The language ability of an agent has been conceptualized as a language faculty with its corresponding internal state paradigm, in the previous works of this architecture. The defined architecture has been built on these research contributions.

The architecture has been described in abstract, macro and micro detail levels of abstraction. The resulting architecture is a generic behavior management based architecture which fulfills certain self-management properties. A comparison of the defined architecture with the existing self-management architecture has been given to evince how the defined architecture provides solutions for certain issues that were unresolved in the existing

Figure 11. Function behavior management dynamically binds with Tamil language

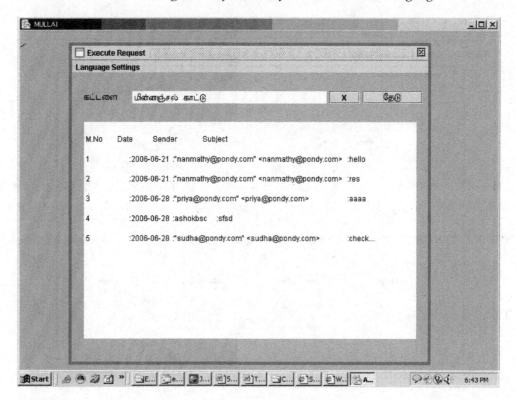

Figure 12. Interface for update of language knowledge

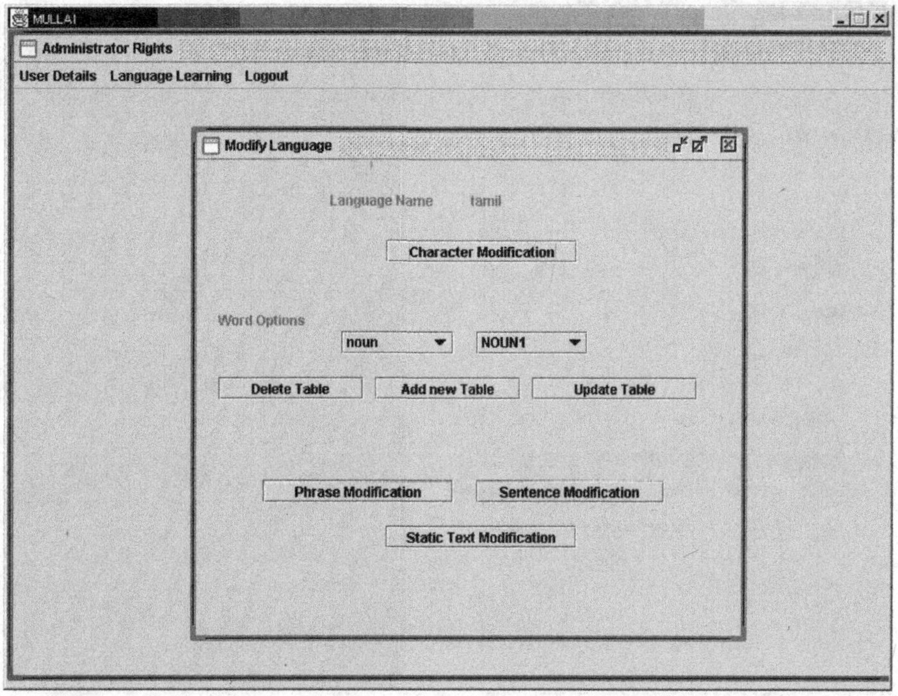

Figure 13. Interface for creating tables for storing language knowledge

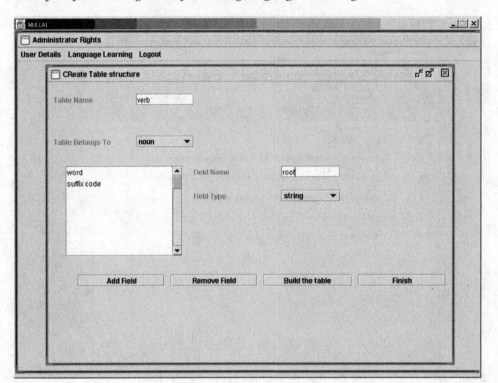

Figure 14. Acquiring basic language details

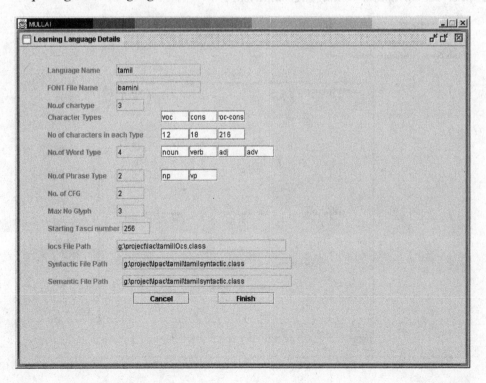

Figure 15. Character coding details acquisition

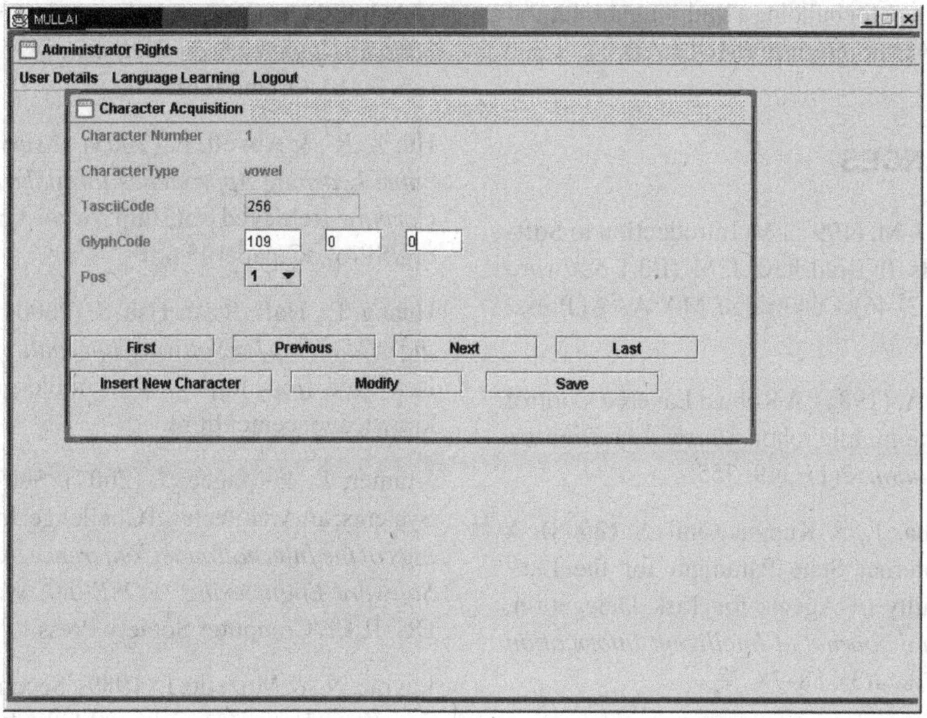

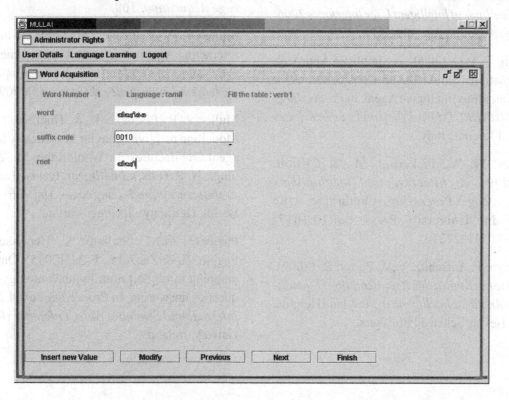

Figure 16. Word details acquisition

one. The case study illustrates the application of the architecture for building a Multilingual Natural Language Agent interface (MULLAI).

REFERENCES

Bradshaw, J. M. (1997). An Introduction to Software Agents. In Bradshaw, J. M. (Ed.), *Software Agents* (pp. 3–46). Cambridge, MA: AAAI Press/ MIT Press.

Brooks, R. A. (1986). A Robust Layered Control System for a mobile robot. *Journal of Robotics and Automation, 2*(1), 349–355.

Chithralekha, T., & Kuppuswami, S. (2008). A Generic Internal State Paradigm for the Language Faculty of Agents for Task Delegation. *International Journal of Intelligent Information Technologies, 4*(3), 58–78.

Clerckx, T., Vandervelpen, C., Luyten, K., & Coninx, K. (2006). A Task-Driven User Interface Architecture for Ambient Intelligent Environments. In *Proceedings of Intelligent User Interfaces 2006*, Sydney, Australia (pp. 309-311).

Connell, T. A. O. (2000). A Simplistic Approach to Internationalization: Design Considerations for an Autonomous Intelligent Agent. In *Proceedings of the Sixth ERCIM Workshop on User Interfaces for All*, Florence, Italy.

Crocker, M. W., Pickering, M., & Clifton, C. (1999). *Architecture and Mechanisms for Language Processing*. Cambridge, UK: Cambridge University Press. doi:10.1017/ CBO9780511527210

Harmelen, F., Lifschitz, V., & Porter, B. (2007). *Handbook of Knowledge Representation (Foundations of Artificial Intelligence)*. Maryland Heights, MO: Elsevier Science Publishers.

Hefley, W. E., & Murray, D. (1993). Intelligent User Interfaces. In *Proceedings of the First International Conference on Intelligent User Interfaces* (pp. 3-10). Orlando, FL.

Hu, X. R., & Atwell, E. (2005). *A survey of Machine Learning Approaches to Analysis of large Corpora*. Retrieved from http://www.bultreebank. org/SProLaC/paper05.pdf

Huang, E., Haft, R., & Hsu, J. (2000). *Developing a Roadmap for Software Internationalization*. Retrieved from http://www.symbio-group.com/ knowledge_center.html

Kramer, J., & Magee, J. (2007). Self-Managed Systems: an Architectural Challenge. In *Proceedings of the International Conference on Future of Software Engineering (FOSE'07)*. Washington, DC: IEEE Computer Society Press.

Lavrac, N., & Mozetic, I. (1989). Second Generation Knowledge Acquisition Methods and their refinement. *Second Generation Expert System, ACM SIGART Bulletin, Special Issue on Knowledge Acquisition, 108.*

Muller, J. P., & Pischel, M. (1994). Modeling Interacting Agents in Dynamic environments. In *Proceedings of the Eleventh European Conference on Artificial Intelligence (ECAI94)* (pp. 709-713).

Muller, J. P., Pischel, M., & Thiel, M. (1995). Modelling reactive behavior in vertically layered agent architectures. In Wooldridge, M., & Jennings, N. R. (Eds.), *Intelligent Agents: Theories, Architectures, and Languages* (pp. 261–276). Berlin, Germany: Springer Verlag.

Pazienza, M. T., Stellato, A., Henriksen, L., Paggio, P., & Zanzotto, F. M. (2005). Ontology mapping to support multilingual ontology-based question answering. In *Proceedings of the Fourth International Semantic Web Conference (ISWC)*, Galway, Ireland.

Rao, A. S., & Georgeff, M. P. (1991). Modeling rational agents within a BDI architecture. In Fikes, R., & Sandewall, E. (Eds.), *Proceedings of Knowledge Representation and Reasoning (KR&R)*. San Mateo, CA: Morgan Kaufmann Publishers.

Ren, F., & Shi, H. (2000). A General Ontology Based Multilingual Multi-Function Multi-Media Intelligent System. In *Proceedings of the IEEE International Conference on Systems, Cybernetics*, Nashville, TN (pp. 2362-2368).

Ritter, M., Meier, U., Yang, J., & Waibel, A. (1999). A Multimodal Translation Agent. In *Proceedings of Auditory Visual Speech Processing*. Face Translation.

Russel, S., & Norvig, P. (1995). *Artificial Intelligence: A Modern Approach*. New York: Prentice Hall.

Serugendo, G. D. M., Fitzgerald, J., Romanovsky, A., & Guelfi, N. (2006). *Dependable Self-Organizing Software Architectures – An approach for Self-Managing Systems* (Tech. Rep. No. BBKCS-06-05). London, UK: Birkbeck College, School of Computer Science and Information Systems.

Stephanidis, C., Karagiannidis, C., & Koumpis, A. (1997). Decision Making in Intelligent User Interfaces. In *Proceedings of the Second International Conference on Intelligent User Interfaces* (pp. 195-202).

Turunen, M., & Hakulinen, J. (2000). *Jaspis – A Framework for Multilingual Adaptive Speech Applications*. Paper presented at the Sixth International Conference of Spoken Language Processing, Beijing, China.

Wooldridge, M. (2000). *Reasoning about rational agents*. Cambridge, MA: MIT Press.

Wooldridge, M. J. (1999). Intelligent Agents. In Weiss, G. (Ed.), *Multiagent systems – A modern approach to Distributed Artificial Intelligence* (pp. 27–78). Cambridge, MA: MIT Press.

This work was previously published in International Journal of Intelligent Information Technologies, Volume 6, Issue 2, edited by Vijayan Sugumaran, pp. 44-64, copyright 2010 by IGI Publishing (an imprint of IGI Global).

Chapter 8
Effective Use of Information Systems/Technologies in the Mergers and Acquisitions Environment:
A Resource–Based Theory Perspective

Hung W. Chu
Manhattan College, USA

Minh Q. Huynh
Southeastern Louisiana University, USA

ABSTRACT

In this study, the authors examine the effects of information systems/technologies (IS/T) on the performance of firms engaged in growth strategies based on mergers and acquisitions (M&A). A model derived from a resource-based theory of the firm is developed to predict the influence of IS/T on performance of firms. Data on the financial performance of 133 firms are used to gauge the impact of IS/T on various M&A objectives. The results suggest that IS/Ts implement M&A objectives that seek to increase overall efficiency better than those that seek to introduce new products or efforts to increase sales. Future studies to examine the process of introducing new products from resource-based theory are suggested.

DOI: 10.4018/978-1-4666-0158-1.ch008

I INTRODUCTION

Mergers and acquisitions (M&A) are commonly used by large and small companies to enhance their competitive positions. Since the 1980s, the number of high profile M&A has increased—as expected—as the economy grew. Even during economic contractions, M&A announcements still capture the public's attention. For instance, Bear Sterns and Washington Mutual were acquired by JPMorgan Chase in 2008, Merrill Lynch was acquired by Bank of America in 2009, and on June 10, 2009, Fiat has completed the acquisition of Chrysler.

Nevertheless, with a few notable exceptions (JPMorgan Chase, Cisco, ExxonMobil, and GE), most companies engaged in M&A transactions fail to reap their expected benefits. The high profile merger of America Online and Time Warner in 1999 is perhaps the most notorious example in recent years. In addition, Alcatel's acquisition of Lucent Technologies in 2006 did not improve its financial position. Further, six months after Bank of America's acquisition of Merrill Lynch in 2009, the CEO of Bank of America conceded that acquiring Merrill Lynch might have been a mistake. Others, such as News Corp.'s acquisition of Dow Jones in 2007, have had mixed reviews.

From a strategic perspective, M&A are supposed to deliver a distinct competitive advantage. The acquiring party will gain talent, technologies and techniques from the acquired firm, possibly leading to the development of new products, better services, or more efficient operating systems. Successful M&A require firms to integrate their operations, personnel, cultures, and information systems to gain strategic capabilities. Thus, integration is the source of value creation in M&A (Chu & Hartman, 2009; Giacomazzi, Panella, Pernici, & Sansoni, 1997; Haspeslagh & Jemison, 1991). Because information systems/technologies (IS/T) play an important role in the operation of business, an M&A often fails when these enterprise systems are not integrated appropriately and create potential counter-synergies (Alaranta, 2005).

The resource-based theory (RBT) is a frequently used theoretical lens in strategic management and it is well suited to apply in this analysis. The RBT suggests that a company is made up of a collection of resources that the company will use to generate value. If a company is engaged in an M&A activity, the company will obtain new resources, such as IS/T, and if the combined firm improves its use of its new collection of resources, the RBT would indicate that the merger makes sense.

Whereas the track records of M&A have been much investigated in academic journals, only a few studies have examined the influence of IS/T on those track records. In strategic management literature, IS/T is often examined as a resource that needs to be aligned with other functional activities or goals. The results have suggested that IS/T be deployed in ways that allow it to interact with other resources in order for companies to obtain competitive advantage (Mata, Fuerst, & Barney, 1995). Thus, RBT is used as a conceptual framework to examine the relationship between IS/T and M&A performance. Specifically, this study focuses on the following key questions: Does the use of IS/T resources in the process of implementing M&A objectives yield a competitive advantage? If so, what is the relationship between IS/T performance and M&A performance?

This study is important in several respects: First, the understanding of IS/T factors in relation to M&A can provide critical information for the planning of the transition and integration of IS/T resources between the target and acquirer. Second, identifying and recognizing the importance of alignment between IS/T usage-contribution and strategic objectives can improve IS/T's effectiveness and efficiency. Finally, an insight into the assessment of how IS/T is used as a resource to develop competitive advantage in an M&A deal is a valuable tool for the corporate planner. The results from this study can be used not only dur-

Figure 1. Resource-Based theory of a firm

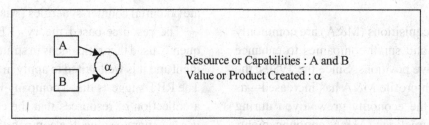

Resource or Capabilities : A and B
Value or Product Created : α

ing the integration stage of the M&A or during the planning and negotiating stages of the M&A process but also in the implementation of strategic change resulting from changes in company strategy.

Section II of this paper addresses RBT as the conceptual foundation for this study. Section III describes the framework that guides the research and hypotheses to be tested. Section IV discusses the research design, and includes a description of participants, measures, and instruments used. Section V presents data analysis and interprets the findings. Conclusions are drawn and implications for future research are presented in Section VI.

II CONCEPTUAL BACKGROUND

A Resource-Based Theory and Mergers and Acquisitions

Resource-based theory (RBT) is a theoretical perspective that describes how firms can build their businesses and develop their competitive advantages from the resources and capabilities that they currently possess or are planning to acquire (Dollinger, 1999). RBT focuses on the firm's internal environment, its internal capabilities, and on the need for a fit between the external market context in which a company operates. Within this theoretical perspective, a firm is composed of a set of resources, and the firm uses these resources to create value by producing its products or services. RBT suggests that a firm's unique resources and

capabilities provide the basis for a strategic plan. The strategy chosen should allow the firm to optimally exploit its core competencies relative to opportunities in the external environment.

This paper investigates the use of resources and capabilities during the integration phase of an M&A based on the RBT perspective of the firm (Barney, 1991; Dierickx & Cool, 1989). As Haspeslagh and Jemison (1991) argued, a resource-based (or capabilities-based) perspective aids in the understanding of the integration process, its interdependence with the specific resources of acquirer and target, and the value creation process. The research focus of this paper, then, is on the dynamics of post-M&A management. Thus, this study departs from the dominant agency-based theoretical framework generally employed by economists to analyze M&A.

The RBT of the firm posits that firms can be conceptualized as a collection of resources and capabilities that create value in society (see Figure 1). The value of the firm is determined based on an estimate of the future earnings that the firm can generate from its value creation process.

The RBT further posits that firms compete on the basis of "unique" corporate resources that may be valuable, rare, difficult to imitate, and/or non-substitutable with other resources (Barney, 1991; Conner, 1991; Schulze, 1994). Additionally, the RBT posits that the resources needed to conceive, develop, and implement strategies are heterogeneously distributed across firms and that these differences among firms remain stable over time (Barney, 1991).

Applying the RBT, many scholars have conceptualized various types of resources or capabilities. Grant (1991) provided a classification of resources into tangible, intangible, and personnel-based resources. Tangible resources include the financial capital and the physical assets of the firm, such as plant, equipment, and stocks of raw materials. Intangible resources encompass such assets as reputation, brand image, and patents. Intangible personnel-based resources include technical know-how and other knowledge assets, including aspects such as organizational culture, employee training, and loyalty.

Resources can be viewed as the basic units of analyses, as firms strive to create competitive advantage by assembling resources that collectively create organizational capabilities (Grant, 1991). *Capabilities* refers to an organization's ability to assemble, integrate, and deploy valued resources in combination (Amit & Schoemaker, 1993; Russo & Fouts, 1997; Schendel, 1994). The term *capabilities* subsumes the notion of organizational competencies (Prahalad & Hamel, 1990) and is rooted in processes and business routines. Grant (1995) described a hierarchy of organizational capabilities, in which specialized capabilities are integrated into broader functional capabilities such as marketing, manufacturing, and IS/T capabilities. Functional capabilities, in turn, integrate to form such organizational capabilities as new product development, customer support, and so on. For example, a firm's customer support capability may derive from the cross-functional integration of its marketing, IS/T, and operations capabilities.

B RBT and M&A Objectives

RBT offers three basic scenarios in which M&A would make sense. In the first scenario, the union of the two firms allows the new firm to create the same set of products that were produced prior to the union but with fewer resources; that is, one set of resources will be disposed of by the combined firm. Such resources may be physical assets that can be reduced via sale of the assets or, in the case of employees, via head-count reduction. In this scenario, the M&A makes sense because the remaining resources are used more efficiently. In the second scenario, the union of the two firms allows the new firm to create some new products or services that the firm was not able to offer prior to the merger, thereby creating a new stream of revenue and more revenue for the combined firm. In this scenario, existing resources are not expected to be eliminated from the newly integrated firm; the merger would make sense because the existing resources are more efficiently used. The third scenario is similar to the second scenario in that there is no reduction in the available resources; however, the new company does not create new products or services. In this scenario, the merger will allow the firm to generate more sales of the existing products and services. This merger would make sense if available resources would be more productive after the M&A. The acquirer is not limited to just one of the above scenarios to justify the M&A but often applies some combination of these three scenarios during the announcement of the M&A.

C IS/T Research in M&A

The review of scholarly literature reveals a consistent lack of research studies on M&A using IS/T as a reference point. Of the 14 articles with IS/T as a topic of examination in an M&A setting, the focus is often on the performance of IS/T itself, not the performance of the M&A effort. Except for four articles (Main & Short, 1989; Sumi & Tsuruoka, 2002; Weber & Pliskin, 1996; Wilcox, Chang, & Grover, 2001), the IS/T literature focused on how IS/T is affected in an M&A setting. Moreover, although the M&A analyzed by Main and Short (1989) was acknowledged as a success, Main and Short (1989) did not specify how the performance of the M&A was measured. Weber and Pliskin (1996) used managerial self-assessment to judge the performance of M&A, but they were not able to find significant contributions from IS/T. Sumi and Tsuruoka (2002) used cost and speed of integration to determine the success of a single case.

Many of the remaining studies are case analyses in which fewer than five mergers were analyzed (Alaranta, 2005; Chin, Brown, & Hu, 2004; Couturier & Kumbat, 2000; Main & Short, 1989; Mehta & Hirschheim, 2007; Shin & Dick, 2005; Stylianou, Jeffries, & Robbins, 1996; Sumi & Tsuruoka, 2002). The few cases analyzed may be problematic in terms of generalizing the lessons learned to other cases because every M&A is different from every other M&A. Except through individual case analysis and theoretical frameworks (Buck-Lew, Wardle, & Pliskin, 1992; Main & Short, 1989; Sumi & Tsuruoka, 2002), the opportunities for IS/T to add value in an M&A have not been fully explored. While McKiernan and Merali (1995) used a survey, they did not offer theoretical implications for their results. This study hopes to provide some empirical evidence to improve the understanding of the relationship between IS/T and M&A.

III FRAMEWORK AND HYPOTHESES

A Conceptual Framework

While the existing knowledge about the relationship between IS/T and M&A is limited, some understanding can be derived from the way that RBT is applied in the IS/T discipline. IS/T resources and capabilities can include hardware, software, communications, IS/T applications, and IS/T personnel. These IS/T resources, however, are hardly unique. Over the past few decades, IS/T has become widely available to most firms. While many companies still use some proprietary systems, open systems have gained wider acceptance due to the lower cost of use. Strategic use of IS/T applications can provide distinct benefits to firms like American Airlines and Federal Express.

However, since IS/T applications are prone to imitation, competitors, given enough time, can develop similar systems to erode the competitive advantage created from the original IS/T applications. A firm gaining competitive advantage through IS/T can quickly lose this advantage if a competitor chooses to reverse engineer the resource, hire any of the individuals involved in the creation of the IS/T's competitive advantage of that firm, or duplicate it through various other means (Mata et al., 1995). Hence, IS/T resources, such as hardware, software, applications, and personnel, are neither unique nor inimitable.

Mata *et al.* (1995) listed five attributes of IS/T resources: (a) customer switching costs, (b) access to capital, (c) proprietary technology, (d) technical IS/T skills, and (e) managerial IS/T skills. The authors argued that "managerial IS/T skills" are the only attribute that could provide any sustainable advantage from IS/T. They further argued that IS/T management skills, which are often distributed heterogeneously across firms, could serve as a source of distinct advantage. This proposition was reinforced by Baharadwaj's (2000) findings that firms with high IS/T capability in customer orientation, IS/T skills, and abilities to create synergy using IS/T, tended to outperform other firms on a variety of profit and cost-based performance measures.

Baharadwaj (2000), however, focused on organizations that were not specifically involved in M&A. Thus, the three scenarios of synergy posited by RBT have not been explored, and it is still not clear how IS/T helps to create synergy in a successful M&A performance. The conceptual framework of this study specifies the IS/T antecedents of M&A performance that may contribute to the positive synergy in an M&A process. The proposed research framework is presented in Figure 2. This simple framework aims at showing the relationship among key factors in this study: M&A performance, IS/T performance, strategic objectives, and IS/T contribution.

B Dependent Variable: M&A Performance

For this study, the only dependent variable is the performance of the M&A. There are at least three ways to measure such performance: senior executives' opinions of M&A performance collected via survey instruments, changes in stock price collected via Center for Research in Securities Pricing (CRSP), or changes in financial performance collected via COMPUSTAT. However, the opinions of the senior executives tend to be biased towards better performance (Cook & Spitzer, 2001). Furthermore, measuring changes in the stock prices due to the progress of M&A integration may be contaminated by other corporate activities such as announcement of strategic partnerships or changes in senior executive teams. Hence, this study uses the changes in financial performance as the best possibility of determining the performance of the M&A.

There are various financial ratios that measure corporate profitability and/or performance: return on asset (ROA), return on equity (ROE), and return on invested capital (ROIC). Among these measures, ROIC is best suited for M&A studies, according to Selden and Colvin (2003), primarily because ROIC is the best indicator of how well a firm would do with additional capital. On the other hand, while ROE measures how effectively a company's management uses investors' money, it is not appropriate for measuring M&A performance. For instance, in a case in which the total equity is the same for two firms, the ROE measure may be different because the two companies may have different levels of long-term debt. Using ROA to measure M&A performance has similar problems because ROA measures how much profit a company earns for every dollar of its assets. Since long-term and short-term debts are not distinguished in the analysis, ROA may negatively bias the performance. In the case of ROIC, if the ROIC increases from the prior reporting period, it would suggest that the firm is more efficient in

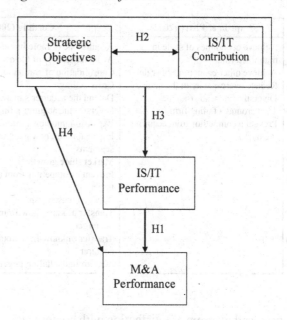

Figure 2. Research framework

managing its capital than it was during the prior reporting period. If the ROIC decreases from the prior reporting period, it would suggest that the firm is less efficient in managing its capital than it was during the prior reporting period. Hence, the performance of an M&A may be determined by taking the difference between the ROIC prior to the acquisition and the ROIC after the completion of the acquisition.

C Intervening Variable: IS/T Performance

We posit that IS/T performance is an important contributing factor for an effective M&A process. The literature in IS/T reveals a wide range of different measures of IS/T performance. In the context of M&A, this study examines user satisfaction. The importance of user satisfaction with the integrated system was noted by Robbins and Stylianou (1999) and Cossey (1991). Based on the more sophisticated measurement tools such as the End-User Computing Satisfaction instrument developed by Doll and Torkzadeh (1988), our proposed measure of IS/T performance is

Table 1. Examples of M&A objectives

Capron & Pistre (2002)	Cording (2004)	Feldman & Spratt (1999)
Achieve economies of scale in manufacturing Achieve other economies of scale Reduce overcapacity in the industry Diversify financial risk Turn around a failing firm Prevent a competitor from acquiring the target	Acquire one or more brands Avoid a takeover of the acquirer Consolidation of similar units Cross-selling Defend the acquirer's market position Diversify the acquirer's financial risk Expansion into new customer Expansion into new geographic market segments Market share growth Prevent a competitor from acquiring the target Reduce industry capacity Transfer of know-how from the acquirer to the target Transfer of know-how from the target to the acquirer Turn around a failing target	Access to additional management talent Access to additional technical talent Access to distribution channels Access to new brands Access to new markets Access to new products Access to new technologies Access to manufacturing capacity Access to manufacturing know-how Access to suppliers Enhanced reputation Entry to new industry Growth in market share Redirection of operating expenses Reduction in number of competitors Reduction in distribution costs Reduction in manufacturing costs

assessed in terms of satisfaction with content, accuracy, format, timeliness of information, and ease of use. While existing studies of M&A and IS/T have examined the performance of IS/T, none of them explored the potential relationship between the performance of M&A and the performance of IS/T. As already noted, it was found that past IS/T literature paid much attention to the performance of IS/T but offered limited discussion concerning the overall performance of the firm. However, it is possible that these two measures are related. One can argue that if the users of IS/T are satisfied, it implies that IS/T is contributing to the overall performance of the firm. In this case, if the users of IS/T are satisfied with its contribution to the M&A, the implication is that the M&A is performing well. This assumption leads to the following hypothesis.

Hypothesis 1: The IS/T performance will be positively associated with the M&A performance.

D Independent Variable: Strategic Objectives

According to Robbins and Stylianou (1999), firms engage in M&A for a variety of reasons. Their objectives range from enhancing the firms' competitive position to managing their financial performance to assimilating new technologies. Table 1 shows a compilation of various M&A objectives. Past studies (Capron & Pistre, 2000; Cording, 2004; Feldman & Spratt, 1999) identified a number of common strategic objectives that firms set when involved in an M&A. These objectives are frequently stated during an M&A announcement. This study adopted several specific objectives and used them to measure the M&A's association with the IS/T factor.

In this study, four types of M&A objectives were adopted for the proposed research model. Most of the strategic objectives listed in Table 1 can be classified as one of the three following scenarios derived from RBT: increase in efficiency, increase in new products, or increase in sales. Several objectives, such as reduction in number of competitors or transfer of know-how from the acquirer to the target, do not fit into the

Table 2. Strategic objectives from RBT perspective

Scenario/Strategic Goals	Related Specific Objectives
Case 1 - Increase Efficiency	• Access to supplier • Gaining market power • Opportunity to achieve higher economy of scale • Reduction in the number of employees • Reduction of duplicate and/or non-core operations • Turn around a failing target
Case 2 - New Products	• Allow entry into new industry • Create new services for the combined firm • Leverage skills/patents through integrating product development • Opportunity to achieve higher economy of scope
Case 3 - More Sales	• Access to distributor • Expand customer base to new market segment • Enhance product line • Market share growth in existing market segment • Opportunity to cross-sell products
Case 4 – Non-RBT Objectives	• Diversify financial risk • Opportunity to buy asset at a low price • Prevent competitor from acquiring target • Reduce industry capacity

RBT. Further, a few strategic objectives make sense for more than one scenario, for instance, access to new markets may apply to new products or to existing products. Thus, it is necessary to construct a set of objectives that actually test the individual scenarios as well as allow for frequently stated objectives. Hence, there are four categories of strategic objectives: (a) objectives that are related to the elimination of resources, (b) objectives that are related to the creation of new products or services, (c) objectives that are related to the potential increase in sales from existing products or services, and (d) all other frequently cited objectives that will be called Non-RBT objectives (Table 2).

E Independent Variable: IS/T Contribution

If a firm intends to achieve certain objectives, then it is expected to use its resources to reach such objectives. The importance of an objective can be determined by the priority assigned by the company. In an M&A, if a firm intends to become successful through increased efficiency, then ob-

jectives related to increased efficiency will have a higher priority. Further, if a firm intends to become successful through increased efficiency, then it is expected that IS/T will be used to achieve even higher efficiency. A similar argument can be made for increasing sales, introducing new products, and other non-RBT objectives. This observation leads to the following set of hypotheses that relate the strategic objectives to the role of IS/T.

Hypothesis 2a: The priority for efficiency improvement for an M&A will be positively associated with the contribution of IS/T on efficiency.

Hypothesis 2b: The priority for sales growth for an M&A will be positively associated with the contribution of IS/T on sales growth.

Hypothesis 2c: The priority for new products for an M&A will be positively associated with the contribution of IS/T on new products.

Hypothesis 2d: The priority for non-RBT objectives will be positively associated with the contribution of IS/T on these non-RBT objectives.

F Independent Variable: Alignment Between Priority of M&A Objectives and IS/T Contribution

Within the IS/T literature, alignment between corporate strategic objectives and IS/T contribution is an important indicator of the overall performance of the firm. *Alignment* has been defined by Reich and Benbasat (1996) as "the degree to which the IS/T mission, objectives, and plans support and are supported by the business mission, objectives, and plans." For this study, the alignment process focuses on how IS/T supports the strategic business objectives and plans for the M&A. The support of business missions, objectives, and plans for IS/T missions, objectives, and plans has little impact on the overall performance of the firm or the M&A activity.

Alignment between business strategy and IT strategy has been given significant attention in recent years and has been ranked among the top ten issues facing IT executives (Brancheau, Janz, & Wetherbe, 1996). Many authors have suggested that IT alignment with business strategy can result in competitive advantages for firms. In practice, many firms struggle to achieve alignment (Baets, 1992; Reich & Benbasat, 1996). However, Kearns and Lederer (2003) found that alignment between the IT plan and the business plan is significantly related to the use of IT for competitive advantage. Furthermore, Chan, Huff, Barclay, and Copeland (1997) found a positive relationship between IT alignment and firm performance in large companies, while Cragg and Hussin (2002) found a similar relationship between IT alignment and firm performance in small companies. Because it appears that alignment of IS/T strategy with corporate level objectives may influence the overall performance of the firm, we have an opportunity to test and possibly validate this proposition using the following argument: If the use of IS/T is aligned with the objectives of the M&A, then the IS/T would be used effectively in the eyes of senior executives. For this study, alignment between M&A objectives and IS/T is measured by the difference between the priority of strategic objectives and the IS/T contribution to those objectives. The smaller the absolute difference between the priority of the strategic objective and the IS/T contribution to the objective, the greater the alignment. A high IS/T alignment with the M&A objectives may result in a higher level of approval for IS/T from the senior executives because the IS/T would meet their needs in terms of accuracy, timeliness, report formats, or any other special needs they may have. Such performance would allow IS/T to achieve higher user satisfaction, which leads to the following hypothesis.

Hypothesis 3: The alignment of the role of IS/T with the firm's strategic objectives will be positively associated with the performance of IS/T.

The relationship between the role of IS/T to strategic objectives and the overall performance of the M&A can be argued as follows: If the role of IS/T is in alignment with the strategic objectives of the M&A, it is more likely that these strategic objectives will be realized because the firm's resources are being effectively used. If the acquirer is able to achieve all of its stated objectives, then the prediction made during the M&A announcement by the senior management team would result. Because the M&A announcement always provides a great outlook if the M&A is successful, achieving the predicted result would improve the performance of the firm, and the M&A should be considered a success. This argument leads to the next hypothesis.

Hypothesis 4: The alignment of the role of IS/T and the strategic objectives will be positively associated with the performance of the M&A.

IV METHODOLOGY

A Participants

To complete the objectives of the study, a mail survey was used to collect the data. The M&A sample was retrieved from the SDC Thompson Financial Database. All transactions since 1996 were collected to determine the experience of the acquirers. There were three criteria for the inclusion of a firm in the population:

1. The firm must have completed at least one M&A between March 2003 and January 2005. The purchase price and the percentage of ownership for the acquirer must have been disclosed. Additionally, the acquirer must own more than 50 percent of the target after the completion of the M&A.
2. The firm must be publicly traded so that financial reports and other accounting numbers were reported to various government agencies and could be easily retrieved.
3. The acquiring firm must be a U.S. company, thus eliminating differences in national cultures that might confound the performance of the M&A.

A total of 1,497 companies met all criteria specified above. Of those, 33 companies had a policy of not responding to surveys, and seven additional companies had undeliverable addresses, resulting in an effective number of 1,457 companies that could participate in this survey. These 1,457 companies were contacted, and 133 responded to the survey, for a response rate of 9.1%.

B Measures

The M&A performance in this study was based on the return on invested capital (ROIC). ROIC is deemed more robust than the stock price changes or ROA because ROIC is a much better indicator of how well a firm would do with additional

capital in the context of an M&A. For this study, the performance of an M&A was measured by assessing the difference between the ROIC prior to the M&A and the ROIC after the completion of the M&A.

IS/T performance is measured using Doll and Torkzadeh's (1988) instrument. Reasons for using Doll and Torkzadeh's instrument include it is shown to be valid in various studies (Gelderman, 1998; McHaneya, Hightower, & Pearson, 2002). Further, high internal consistency of these items was reported (Cronbach's $\alpha > 0.90$). In this study, IS/T performance was equated to user satisfaction. For this study, 12 questions in the instrument were used to measure five dimensions of user satisfaction: Satisfaction with content (4 items), accuracy (2 items), format (2 items), timeliness of information (2 items), and satisfaction with the system's ease of use (2 items). (See Table 3 for complete item descriptions.)

The M&A objectives in this study are primarily drawn from those related to the RBT; specifically, the 19 specific objectives included in this study's instrument were adopted directly from the work of Capron and Pistre (2002), Cording (2004), and Feldman and Spratt (1999). These strategic management researchers provided a comprehensive collection of M&A objectives that are frequently stated during an M&A announcement (see Table 2). Each of these objectives can be attributed to the four strategic goals that a company involved in an M&A may pursue. These four goals are (a) to increase efficiency, (b) to develop new products, (c) to generate more sales, and (d) to achieve non-RBT leverage through, for example, diversifying financial risks, reducing industry capacity, and so on.

C Instrument

A questionnaire was developed containing a list of strategic objectives and IS/T use and performance. Because there have been a number of previous survey studies on M&A, this study adopted prior

Table 3. IS/T user satisfaction scale (Doll & Torkzadeh, 1988)

Category	Item	Question
Content	C1	Does the system provide the precise information you need?
	C2	Does the information content meet your needs?
	C3	Does the system provide reports that seem to be just about exactly what you need?
	C4	Does the system provide sufficient information?
	C5	Do you find the output relevant?
Accuracy	A1	Is the system accurate?
	A2	Are you satisfied with the accuracy of the system?
	A3	Do you feel the output is reliable?
	A4	Do you find the system dependable?
Format	F1	Do you think the output is presented in a useful format?
	F2	Is the output information clear?
	F3	Are you happy with the layout of the output?
	F4	Is the output easy to understand?
Ease of Use	E1	Is the system user friendly?
	E2	Is the system easy to use?
	E3	Is the system efficient?
Timeliness	T1	Do you get the information you need in time?
	T2	Does the system provide up-to-date information?

measures when relevant and appropriate. For instance, the list of strategic objectives in the survey was drawn from studies of Capron and Pistre (2002), Cording (2004), Feldman and Spratt (1999), and Harzing (2002).

The questionnaire, along with a letter explaining the purpose of the study, was sent to individuals in charge of or involved in the M&A. The title of the respondents ranged from chief executive officer to vice president; more than 50% of the respondents were chief executive officers, presidents, or chief financial officers. The survey focused on the role of IS/T, and more than 10% of the respondents reported that they were the chief information officer for the firm. Among the respondents, 64.75% reported that they had responsibilities in the firm's strategic planning, 52.52% had responsibilities for business development, and 51.80% had responsibilities in general administration. As for the integration process of the IS/T after an M&A, 28.06% of the respondents had responsibility for operations, and 25.90% of the respondents had responsibility for IS/T.

The procedure to determine whether there was any bias in the responses was as follows:

1. Two demographic variables—target purchase price and acquisition experience—were used to determine whether the sample response was representative of the mailing list or not. These two variables provided the opportunity to conduct three tests as there were two factors in acquisition experience: three years acquisition experience and five years acquisition experience.

2. The target purchase price and acquisition experience were divided into different categories (see Table 4 and Table 5 for details), and the corresponding percentages for each category were determined.

3. The category for the three factors was determined for each survey response.

4. A goodness-of-fit test was used to determine whether there was any significant difference between the mailing population and the responses.

As shown in Tables 6, 7, and 8, there was no statistically significant difference between the mailing list population and the sample response. The p value for all three tests was greater than

Table 4. Target purchase price breakdown and corresponding percentages

Price (P) in Millions	Category Number	Percentages
$P < \$1$	1	0.0328
$\$1 <= P < \$5$	2	0.1226
$\$5 <= P < \$25$	3	0.2755
$\$25 <= P < \$100$	4	0.2661
$\$100 <= P < \$500$	5	0.2279
$\$500 <= P$	6	0.0751

Table 5. Acquisition experience breakdown and corresponding percentages

Three Years of Experience			Five Years of Experience		
Number of Acquisitions	Category Number	Percentages	Number of Acquisitions	Category Number	Percentages
1	1	0.4088	1	1	0.2989
2	2	0.1984	2	2	0.1575
3 to 5	3	0.2661	3 to 5	3	0.2949
6 to 10	4	0.0892	6 to 10	4	0.1515
more than 10	5	0.0375	10 to 20	5	0.0664
			more than 20	6	0.0308

Table 6. Goodness-of-Fit test on target purchase price

Category	Freq.	Percent (%)[1]	Test %[2]	Cumulative freq.	Cumulative %
1	2	1.50	3.28	2	1.50
2	21	15.79	12.26	23	17.29
3	37	27.82	27.55	60	45.11
4	37	27.82	26.61	97	72.93
5	29	21.80	22.79	126	94.74
6	7	5.26	7.51	133	100.00
Chi-Square Test for Specified Proportions					
Chi-Square df pr > ChiSq Sample Size =		3.6581 5 0.5996 133			

1. Results from the survey   2. Distribution from the mailing sample

Table 7. Goodness-of-Fit test on three years of acquisition experience

Category	Freq.	Percent (%)[1]	Test %[2]	Cumulative freq.	Cumulative %
1	61	45.86	40.88	61	45.86
2	25	18.80	19.84	86	64.66
3	35	26.32	26.61	121	90.98
4	8	6.02	8.92	129	96.99
5	4	3.01	3.75	133	100.00
Chi-Square Test for Specified Proportions					
Chi-Square *df* *pr* > ChiSq Sample Size = 1. Results from the survey			2.3394 4 0.6736 133 2. Distribution from the mailing sample		

Table 8. Goodness-of-Fit test on five years of acquisition experience

Category	Freq.	Percent (%)[1]	Test %[2]	Cumulative freq.	Cumulative %
1	50	37.59	29.89	50	37.59
2	23	17.29	15.75	73	54.89
3	34	25.56	29.49	107	80.45
4	12	9.02	15.15	119	89.47
5	9	6.77	6.63	128	96.24
6	5	3.76	3.08	133	100.00
Chi-Square Test for Specified Proportions					
Chi-Square *df* *pr* > ChiSq Sample Size = 1. Results from the survey			7.0358 5 0.2180 133 2. Distribution from the mailing sample		

20%, suggesting that the sample response was a good approximation of the entire population and was without bias, at least in the purchase price and M&A experience.

V DATA ANALYSIS: TESTING THE PROPOSED HYPOTHESES

This study examined the association of strategic objectives and IS/T use, the relationship between the IT performance and the alignment of strategic objectives and IS/T use, and the connection of all those and M&A performance. Correlation coef-

ficient analysis was used to determine whether a relationship existed or not.

A Result for Hypothesis #1

Hypothesis #1 – The IS/T performance will be positively associated with the M&A performance. The data analysis actually suggested that the IS/T performance was negatively correlated with the M&A performance (see Table 9 for details). Because the prediction that IS/T performance will have a positive impact on M&A performance is a one-tailed test, the result indicates that there is no support for this hypothesis. The overall per-

Table 9. Correlation coefficients between M&A performance and IS/T performance

M&A performance	IS/T performance		
	Performance of acquirer IS/T	Performance of target IS/T	Performance of overall IS/T
Revenue from target (survey)	$r = -0.11259$ $p = 0.2248$ $N = 118$	-0.06837 0.4862 106	-0.13248 0.1492 120
Revenue from acquirer (survey)	-0.17138 0.0624 119	-0.18279 0.0595 107	-0.23093 0.0105 122
Changes in ROIC (from COMPUSTAT)	-0.16371 0.0860 111	-0.13947 0.1708 98	-0.18592 0.0497 112

formance of IS/T correlated negatively with the objective measure of performance and changes in ROIC and was significant at the $p = 0.05$ level. Further analysis suggested that the negative performance came largely from the performance of the target IS/T. This result is counterintuitive in that it suggests an acquirer should not purchase a target with good IS/T capabilities because such action often results in lower performance. There are two possible explanations: First, if the target's IS/T capability is better than the acquirer's, then it appears that the acquirer tries to exploit the benefit of IS/T for the entire firm. However, trying to integrate or assimilate the target's IS/T may be too disruptive in the short run, which is the period this study measured, but it may result in greater value creation in the future. Second, if the acquirer ignores the target IS/T and imposes its own IS/T on the target, there may be less disruptions in the integration effort, but it may result in observable value destruction in the short-run. More investigation may be needed to assess the negative influence of IS/T performance on M&A performance.

B Results for Hypothesis #2

Hypothesis #2 – The priority for the strategic objective of an M&A will be positively associated with the contribution of IS/T to that strategic objective. Specifically, the priority for efficiency improvement, sales growth, new products, and non-RBT will be positively associated with the contribution of IS/T in efficiency improvement, sales growth, new products, and non-RBT objectives, respectively. The data analysis provides some support for this hypothesis. For the efficiency and non-RBT objectives (see Table 10) the test shows a highly significant p value ($p < 0.0001$); the correlation coefficient is the highest for both the type of strategic objective and the contribution from IS/T to the strategic objective. The correlation coefficients for new products and increased sales are highly significant ($p < 0.0001$ for new products and $p = 0.0003$ for increased sales), but the correlations are relatively low for both the type of strategic objective and the contribution from IS/T to the strategic objective. Hence, there is support for efficiency and non-RBT objectives, but no unqualified support for new product and increased sales objectives. Further studies are needed to more fully understand and explain what might have gone wrong in the implementation of new products and increased sales objectives in an M&A.

C Results for Hypothesis #3

Hypothesis #3 – The alignment of the role of IS/T with the firm's strategic objectives will be

Table 10. Correlation coefficients between priority of strategic objectives and IS/T contribution

IS/T contribution to	M&A objectives			
	Efficiency	New product	Increase sales	Non-RBT
Efficiency	$r = 0.64442$ $p < 0.0001$ $N = 134$	0.34476 p<0.0001 134	0.34233 0.0001 134	0.55271 <0.0001 133
New product	0.45691 <0.0001 134	0.39962 <0.0001 134	0.25235 0.0033 134	0.46195 <0.0001 133
Increase sales	0.37160 <0.0001 136	0.26358 0.0019 136	0.30383 0.0003 136	0.43927 <0.0001 135
Non-RBT	0.51762 <0.0001 133	0.28681 0.0008 133	0.33931 <0.0001 133	0.55776 <0.0001 133

Table 11. Correlation coefficients between alignment of strategic objectives with IS/T contribution and IS/T performance

IS/T performance	Alignment of strategic objectives with IS/T contribution			
	Efficiency	New product	Increase sales	Non-RBT
Performance of acquirer IS/T	$r = 0.19390$ $p = 0.0346$ $N = 119$	0.16283 0.0768 119	0.13255 0.1472 121	-0.03297 0.7219 119
Performance of target IS/T	0.09489 0.3309 107	0.06713 0.4921 107	0.02717 0.7802 108	-0.02804 0.7744 107
Performance of overall IS/T	0.18303 0.0454 120	0.16347 0.0744 120	0.13785 0.1300 122	-0.00544 0.9530 120

positively associated with the performance of IS/T. Support for this hypothesis came from the alignment of efficiency and new products objectives, where the correlation coefficients were significant at the 0.05 level for the efficiency objectives and the 0.10 level for the new product objectives (see Table 11 for details).

Further examination of the data revealed that the correlation with IS/T performance came predominantly from the capabilities of the acquirer. The correlation coefficient and the significance level of the acquirer's IS/T performance were similar to the performance of overall IS/T with the alignment of IS/T contribution and strategic goals.

While the data did not lend full support to the hypothesis that IS/T alignment is important to the organizational goal, the study did identify a scenario in which IS/T professionals or integration managers could focus their efforts on increasing efficiency goals or assisting the introduction of new products. Increasing efficiency and assisting in new product introduction may demand more IS/T resources than increasing sales. However, increasing sales may not need computerized IS/T because the sales force may use a hard copy of the new products that they are responsible to sell. Nevertheless, increasing efficiency and assisting in new product introduction would require, in addition to the function of information dissemination,

Table 12. Correlation coefficients between alignment of strategic objectives with IS/T contribution and M&A performance

M&A performance changes in ROIC (from COMPU-STAT)	Alignment of strategic objectives with IS/T contribution			
	Efficiency	New product	Increase sales	Non-RBT
	$r = 0.10585$ $p = 0.2479$ $N = 121$	0.01527 0.8680 121	-0.02921 0.7484 123	-0.03336 0.7152 122

information storage along with the capabilities of making quick updates to the most current status. These tasks would be time consuming if computerized IS/T were not available.

Future research should investigate whether the increase in efficiency is a result of eliminating duplicated IS/T resources or whether IS/T was helpful in identifying duplicated assets for the combined firm. This distinction is important because, in the first case, the senior management may have identified the duplicate IS/T resource and proceeded to dispose of the excess resource, which is a tactical use of IS/T. In the second case, IS/T may have assisted in the identification of waste, which is a strategic use of IS/T. If both are occurring, then it may be interesting to see whether there are any performance differences between the two different uses of IS/T.

D Results for Hypothesis #4

Hypothesis #4 – The alignment of the role of IS/T and the strategic objectives will be positively associated with the performance of the M&A. Data indicated that the performance of the acquirer, based on self-reported revenue, correlated with new products and increased sales; however, data analysis on the objective measure, return on capital, did not result in a significant correlation at the 0.10 level (see Table 12 for details). Therefore, data analysis did not provide support for this hypothesis.

This hypothesis addressed the important question of whether IS/T could contribute to the overall performance of the firm and, hence, be

considered a strategic tool. The data suggest that there was no relationship between IS/T contribution and M&A performance. There are at least two possible explanations for the observed result: First, the intervention of other variables is always of concern, but in this case there was no obvious variable to suspect. Second, IS/T may not be able to provide a performance improvement because it was not used at the strategic level. Thus, using IS/T at the tactical level may not provide opportunities for IS/T to contribute to the overall performance of the firm.

VI DISCUSSION AND CONCLUSION

The literature on the IS/T role and contribution in the success of M&A is scarce. While there have been past studies that examined IS/T capabilities and resources, most of these studies limited their scope to within an organization or across similar organizations. Very few examined the IS/T role and impact in the context of an M&A, where there is a transaction and a relationship between two different organizations. The reason for such scarcity is perhaps due to the complexity and difficulty involved in such a study. As a result, the relationship between the success of M&A and the contribution and performance of IS/T has not been well understood. The purpose of this study was to investigate this relationship empirically. Thus, this study is among the first empirical studies that have attempted to explore such a relationship from the resource-based theory perspective. This study contributes to the limited literature in this under-researched area by identifying IS/T as one important factor to be considered in an M&A transaction and by providing some empirical evidence to show a relationship between M&A performance and IS/T factors.

From the results of this study, it is interesting to observe that IS/T performance was negatively correlated with M&A performance. Because IS/T is of the utmost importance in the operation of modern businesses, an M&A may not succeed if IS/T planning is inappropriate (Alaranta, 2005). Furthermore, the negative correlation was un-expected because past resource-based literature seemed to suggest a positive relationship. The common assumption is that the resources and capabilities are expected to be vital in explaining an organization's performance (Barney, 1991; Dollinger, 1999; Wernerfelt, 1984; Wijerwarneda, De Zoysa, Fonseka, & Perera, 2004).

What might have contributed to the negative correlation? It is possible that disruptions were experienced as a result of combining different IS/T resources. In a complex transaction such as an M&A in which IS/T integration must occur, our findings suggest an effect of possible disruptions, especially when the IS/T resources and capabilities in the merging organizations were different. Furthermore, the impact of such reported disruptions might differ over time. Further studies are needed for deeper understanding of these disruptions.

According to the resource-based perspective, it is also suggested that sustained competitive advantage can be generated by the unique bundle of resources at the core of the firm. Resources have been found to be important antecedents to products and, ultimately, to performance (Wernerfelt, 1984). This study proposes that IS/T contribution and role and strategic objectives are among such antecedents with influence on the performance of IS/T and the success of the M&A. The findings from this study showed some correlation between the performance of IS/T and alignment between specific strategic objectives and IS/T capabilities of the acquirer. This result might suggest that the

alignment of specific strategic objectives between the parties in an M&A is more significant than the concern about the IS/T capabilities of the target organization. The implication is that some of the IS/T capabilities of the target organization, and even the combined IS/T capabilities, might have to be reduced as a result of duplicated function or to eliminate waste. Regarding the correlation between the IS/T contribution, the IS/T role, the strategic objectives, and the success of the M&A, the findings showed no relationship between IS/T contribution and M&A performance. This result is interesting because, while IS/T could be useful at the tactical level, its contribution at the strategic level, such as in an M&A performance, was not indicated in the analysis of this study.

The resource-based view describes how businesses build their competitive advantage from the resources and capabilities that they currently possess or can acquire (Dollinger, 1999). While this is generally true, in a complex transaction such as an M&A, only selective resources and capabilities are important. The implication is that the assets and resources integrated in an M&A transaction may lead to differences in the final M&A performance and outcome. Resources may be tangible or intangible and are shown as strengths or weaknesses through the process of M&A. As a result, competitive advantage is more likely to be derived when certain alignments at the strategic level between the parties in an M&A are identified and implemented.

Implications for Future Research

This study represents a first attempt to test the assumptions of RBT in an M&A context. Specifically, both Hypotheses 2 and 3 offered some support for the assumptions of the RBT that the firm would be more successful if it were able to use its resources more efficiently. However, the test concerning whether non-RBT objectives lower the performance of the M&A was inconclusive.

Additional analysis on how resources are used may indicate the need for future research.

Future research should focus on what type of improved efficiency should be made to the acquirer's integration plan to improve the combined firm's performance. Identifying which type of efficiency is easier to execute could help the M&A unit to decide whether increased efficiency through new product is worth the risk. Because this study was not able to suggest that, as a collective, the non-RBT objective should be avoided, additional studies could focus on whether there are any non-RBT M&A objectives to avoid.

Implications for the Practitioner

The results of the data analysis concerning the relationship between the performance of IS/T and the performance of the M&A would imply that well-executed IS/T integration may not improve the performance of an M&A. More data need to be collected to determine which resources IS/T must perform in order to improve the performance of an M&A. The implication for practitioners is that the acquirer should have a more sophisticated IS/T than the target company. If the target company has a better IS/T than the acquirer, the acquisition would be more likely to underperform as Mata et al. (1995) suggested.

Given this conclusion, it is important for senior IS/T executives of the acquirer to assess the capabilities of the target company. The assessment of the IS/T resource of the target company should be completed before the announcement of the acquisition so that the cost of the acquisition can accurately reflect the costs and benefits of IS/T integration. The assessment of the target should include the IS/T organization structure, the skill sets of the IS/T professionals, and a complete accounting of the hardware. A better understanding on the part of the acquirer's senior IS/T executives can help the M&A negotiation team be better informed of the possible costs and potential benefits of the integration of IS/T.

While there was no direct link between IS/T and the performance of the M&A, this study found that IS/T contributed in accordance with the priority of the M&A. However, that relationship or alignment, while significant, probably should be stronger. The findings suggest that IS/T is more useful in providing greater increases in efficiency and in new product introduction. These results are important because, for many IS/T professionals, the conclusion indicates that there may be some limits as to how IS/T can help in activities other than efficiency improvement or new product introduction in an M&A environment.

REFERENCES

Alaranta, M. (2005). Evaluating success in post-merger IS integration: A case study. *The Electronic Journal Information Systems Evaluation*, *8*, 143–150.

Amit, R., & Schoemaker, P. J. H. (1993). Strategic assets and organizational rent. *Strategic Management Journal*, *14*, 33–46. doi:10.1002/smj.4250140105

Baets, W. (1992). Aligning information systems with business strategy. *The Journal of Strategic Information Systems*, *1*, 205–214. doi:10.1016/0963-8687(92)90036-V

Baharadwaj, A. S. (2000). A resource-based perspective on information technology capability and firm performance: An empirical investigation. *Management Information Systems Quarterly*, *24*, 169–196. doi:10.2307/3250983

Barney, J. (1991). Firm resources and sustained competitive advantage. *Journal of Management*, *17*, 90–120. doi:10.1177/014920639101700108

Brancheau, J., Janz, B. D., & Wetherbe, J. C. (1996). Key issues in information system management: 1994–95 SIM delphi results. *Management Information Systems Quarterly, 20*, 225–242. doi:10.2307/249479

Buck-Lew, M., Wardle, C. E., & Pliskin, N. (1992). Accounting for information technology in corporate acquisitions. *Information & Management, 22*, 363–369. doi:10.1016/0378-7206(92)90031-A

Capron, L., & Pistre, N. (2002). When do acquirers earn abnormal returns? *Strategic Management Journal, 23*, 781–794. doi:10.1002/smj.262

Chan, Y. E., Huff, S. L., Barclay, D. W., & Copeland, D. G. (1997). Business strategic orientation, information systems strategic orientation and strategic alignment. *Information Systems Research, 8*(2), 125–150. doi:10.1287/isre.8.2.125

Chin, P. O., Brown, G. A., & Hu, Q. (2004). The impact of mergers and acquisitions on IT governance structures: A case study. *Journal of Global Information Management, 12*(4), 50–74.

Chu, H. W., & Hartman, J. B. (2008). Mergers and acquisitions: The argument for holistic, integrated measures of success. *Leadership & Organizational Management Journal, 2008*(4), 1-13.

Conner, K. R. (1991). A historical comparison of resource-based theory and five schools of thought within industrial organization economics: Do we have a new theory of the firm? *Journal of Management, 17*(1), 121–154. doi:10.1177/014920639101700109

Cook, C., & Spitzer, D. (2001). *World class transactions: Insights into creating shareholder value through mergers and acquisitions*. New York: KPMG.

Cording, M. P. (2004). *Organizational integrity and acquisition performance: The role of value in value creation*. Unpublished doctoral dissertation, University of Virginia, Charlottesville, VA.

Cossey, B. (1991). Systems assessment in acquired subsidiaries. *Accountancy, 107*(1169), 98–99.

Couturier, G. W., & Kumbat, T. A. (2000). Information technology costing methodology development after a corporate merger. *Industrial Management & Data Systems, 100*(1), 10–16. doi:10.1108/02635570010273009

Cragg, P., King, M., & Hussin, H. (2002). IT alignment and firm performance in small manufacturing firms. *The Journal of Strategic Information Systems, 11*, 109–132. doi:10.1016/S0963-8687(02)00007-0

Dierickx, I., & Cool, K. (1989). Asset stock accumulation and sustainability of competitive advantage. *Management Science, 35*, 1504–1513. doi:10.1287/mnsc.35.12.1504

Doll, W. J., & Torkzadeh, G. (1988). The measurement of end-user satisfaction. *Management Information Systems Quarterly, 12*, 259–274. doi:10.2307/248851

Dollinger, M. J. (1999). *Entrepreneurship strategies and resources*. Upper Saddle River, NJ: Prentice Hall.

Feldman, M. L., & Spratt, M. F. (1999). *Five frogs on a log: A CEO's field guide to accelerating the transition in mergers, acquisitions, and gut wrenching change*. New York: Harper Business Press.

Gelderman, M. (1998). The relation between user satisfaction, usage of information systems and performance. *Information & Management, 34*, 11–18. doi:10.1016/S0378-7206(98)00044-5

Giacomazzi, F., Panella, C., Pernici, B., & Sansoni, M. (1997). Information systems integration in mergers and acquisition: A normative model. *Information & Management, 32*, 289–302. doi:10.1016/S0378-7206(97)00031-1

Grant, R. M. (1991). The resource-based theory of competitive advantage: Implication for strategy formulation. *California Management Review, 33*(3), 114–135.

Grant, R. M. (1995). *Contemporary strategy analysis: Concepts, techniques, applications.* Cambridge, UK: Blackwell.

Harzing, A. (2002). Acquisitions versus greenfield investments: International strategy and management of entry modes. *Strategic Management Journal, 23,* 211–227. doi:10.1002/smj.218

Haspeslagh, P. C., & Jemison, D. B. (1991). *Managing acquisitions: Creating value through corporate renewal.* New York: Free Press.

Kearns, G. S., & Lederer, A. L. (2003). A resourced-based view of strategic IT alignment: How knowledge sharing creates competitive advantage. *Decision Sciences, 34*(1), 1–29. doi:10.1111/1540-5915.02289

Main, T. J., & Short, J. E. (1989). Managing the merger: Building partnership through IT planning at the new Baxter. *Management Information Systems Quarterly, 13,* 469–484. doi:10.2307/248735

Mata, F., Fuerst, W., & Barney, J. (1995). Information technology and sustainable competitive advantage: A resource-based analysis. *Management Information Systems Quarterly, 19,* 487–505. doi:10.2307/249630

McHaneya, R., Hightower, R., & Pearson, J. (2002). A validation of the end-user computing satisfaction instrument in Taiwan. *Information & Management, 39,* 503–511. doi:10.1016/S0378-7206(01)00119-7

McKiernan, P., & Merali, Y. (1995). Integrating IS after merger. *Long Range Planning, 28*(4), 54–62.

Mehta, M., & Hirschheim, R. (2007). Strategic alignment in mergers and acquisitions: Theorizing IS integration decision making. *Journal of the Association for Information Systems, 8*(3), 143–174.

Prahalad, C., & Hamel, G. (1990). The core competency of the company. *Harvard Business Review, 68*(3), 79–91.

Reich, B. H., & Benbasat, I. (1996). Measuring the linkage between business and information technology objectives. *Management Information Systems Quarterly, 20*(1), 55–81. doi:10.2307/249542

Robbins, S. S., & Stylianou, A. C. (1999). Post-merger systems integration: The impact on IS capabilities. *Information & Management, 36,* 205–212. doi:10.1016/S0378-7206(99)00018-X

Russo, M. V., & Fouts, P. A. (1997). A resource-based perspective on corporate environmental performance and profitability. *Academy of Management Journal, 40,* 534–560. doi:10.2307/257052

Schendel, D. (1994). Introduction to competitive organizational behavior: Toward an organizationally based theory of competitive advantage. *Strategic Management Journal, 15,* 1–4. doi:10.1002/smj.4250150901

Schulze, W. (1994). Two schools of thought in resource-based theory. In Shrivastiva, P., Huff, A., & Dutton, J. (Eds.), *Advances in strategic management* (pp. 127–151). New York: JAI Press.

Selden, L., & Colvin, G. (2003). M&A needn't be a loser's game. *Harvard Business Review, 81*(6), 70–79.

Shin, B., & Dick, K. (2005). Comparison of the business strategies of two telecommunication service providers. *Journal of Information Technology Case and Application Research, 7*(2), 19–30.

Stylianou, A. C., Jeffries, C. J., & Robbins, S. R. (1996). Corporate mergers and the problems of IS integration. *Information & Management, 31*(4), 203–213. doi:10.1016/S0378-7206(96)01082-8

Sumi, T., & Tsuruoka, M. (2002). Ramp new enterprise information systems in a merger & acquisition environment: A case study. *Journal of Engineering and Technology Management, 19*(1), 93–104. doi:10.1016/S0923-4748(01)00048-0

Weber, Y., & Pliskin, N. (1996). The effects of information systems integration and organizational culture on a firm's effectiveness. *Information & Management, 30,* 81–90. doi:10.1016/0378-7206(95)00046-1

Wernerfelt, B. (1984). A resource-based view of the firm. *Strategic Management Journal, 5,* 171–180. doi:10.1002/smj.4250050207

Wijerwarneda, H., De Zoysa, A., Fonseka, T., & Perera, B. (2004). The impact of planning and control sophistication on performance of small and medium-sized enterprises: Evidence from Sri Lanka. *Journal of Small Business Management, 42*(2), 209–217. doi:10.1111/j.1540-627X.2004.00106.x

Wilcox, H. D., Chang, K., & Grover, V. (2001). Valuation of mergers and acquisitions in the telecommunications industry: A study on diversification and firm size. *Information & Management, 38,* 459–471. doi:10.1016/S0378-7206(00)00082-3

This work was previously published in International Journal of Intelligent Information Technologies, Volume 6, Issue 2, edited by Vijayan Sugumaran, pp. 65-84, copyright 2010 by IGI Publishing (an imprint of IGI Global).

Chapter 9
Incremental Load in a Data Warehousing Environment

Nayem Rahman
Intel Corporation, USA

ABSTRACT

Incremental load is an important factor for successful data warehousing. Lack of standardized incremental refresh methodologies can lead to poor analytical results, which can be unacceptable to an organization's analytical community. Successful data warehouse implementation depends on consistent metadata as well as incremental data load techniques. If consistent load timestamps are maintained and efficient transformation algorithms are used, it is possible to refresh databases with complete accuracy and with little or no manual checking. This paper proposes an Extract-Transform-Load (ETL) metadata model that archives load observation timestamps and other useful load parameters. The author also recommends algorithms and techniques for incremental refreshes that enable table loading while ensuring data consistency, integrity, and improving load performance. In addition to significantly improving quality in incremental load techniques, these methods will save a substantial amount of data warehouse systems resources.

1. INTRODUCTION

The data in the warehouse is subject-oriented, integrated, identified by a timestamp, and non-volatile (Inmon, 2002). The primary goal of data warehousing is to provide access to information

that has high value for decision making (Brobst et al., 2008; Shin, 2003). It is designed to support strategic as well as tactical decisions, where each unit of data is relevant to some moment in time. Data warehouses get data from different heterogeneous sources. Because source and target tables reside in separate places a continuous flow of data

DOI: 10.4018/978-1-4666-0158-1.ch009

from source to target is critical to maintain data freshness in the data warehouse.

A variety of ETL tools (Kambayashi et al., 1999) and data warehouse utilities are currently used to get data from source and load it into a data warehouse. Source data is often placed in the staging area (Rahman, 2007) of a data warehouse. Upon loading operational data into the staging area the data is immediately loaded in the analytical subject areas of a data warehouse. Data can be loaded into the analytical tables using database specific transformation tools. Because data is already in staging area and needs to be moved to the analytical area of the same data warehouse, one efficient and convenient way is to load the analytical tables via database specific software, such as stored procedures. It is convenient for the database transformation engine to migrate data from source to the target because the database engine already knows the table structure, data semantics and other parameters.

An efficient, flexible, and scalable data warehousing architecture requires a number of technical advances (Widom, 1995). Incremental (a.k.a., delta) refresh technique is one such important technical advance. In this paper, we explore the possibility of using stored procedures as opposed to external transformation tools. Both full and incremental refreshes can be done by executing database specific stored procedures. Incremental refresh is very important for several reasons. Because data warehouse tables hold a large volume of data it is not practical to perform complete table re-loads at the expense of re-computing during each refresh cycle. Incremental maintenance is usually much cheaper than re-computation (Lee & Kim, 2005; Chan et al., 2000). During the last decade, organizations used to rebuild a data warehouse periodically (Santos & Bernardino, 2008) – monthly, weekly or daily usually in the overnight hours while business users were not online. As the data warehouse increases in complexity and the demand for more up to date data increases, the possibility of maintaining the data

warehouse in the same fashion becomes intractable (Bokun & Taglienti, 1998). With the advent of the Internet and increased global business operations by companies and business users located around the world, frequent data freshness has become more important than ever.

In order to increase the frequency of data freshness faster loading is essential. This frequent and faster loading requires availability of additional capacity of database systems. On the other hand, in order to have data warehouse reporting tools run efficiently, enough systems resources need to be reserved for these tools. While the amount of queries requesting up-to-date information is growing and the amount of data in the data warehouses has been increasing, the time window available to refresh data warehouse has been shrinking (Lee et al., 2001; Labio et al., 1999). All these factors demand that data warehouse loads need to be performed quickly, efficiently and without resource constraints. One technique that provides these is Incremental Refresh (Bokun & Taglienti, 1998). Incremental Refresh can help maintain a healthy and stable enterprise data warehousing environment.

The design and maintenance of data warehouses is a difficult task (Naggar et al., 2002) and involves many challenging issues in database research. The ETL transformation for performing incremental refresh is quite complex (Jörg & Deßloch, 2008). In a real world situation the author of this article observed that inefficient and nonstandard methods and logic for incremental refresh cause data consistency and integrity issues. Incorrect or missing data impacts strategic decision making. Ballou & Tayi (1999) argue that data availability is an attribute of data quality. Missing records can cause the need for a full refresh of a table and associated high resource cost due to re-computing. Data warehousing typically involves handling a large number of complex query processing (Sahama & Croll, 2007) that push database management technology to its resource limits in terms of CPU time and IO operation. An incremental refresh is crucial not only to minimize resource utilization but also to assure interactive response time to the On Line Analytical Processing (OLAP) users (Costa & Madeira, 2004; Lee et al., 2001; Norcott & Finnerty, 2008).

In this article, we propose methodologies to support incremental refreshes, stored procedure template for incremental load and a model to build a data warehouse environment. This will allow all ETL programmers to follow the same methodology and template and discourage them from using their individual logic or techniques. In a real world data warehouse environment, the author of this paper observed that programmers have a tendency to write code based on their individual approaches, inconsistent with other developers. In many cases this inconsistency causes data issues. In a large data warehouse where dozens of programmers write transformation logic there needs to be uniformity in coding practices of delta stored procedures in order to avoid data issues.

In section 2 we discuss related work. In section 3 we give a brief description of an ETL metadata model to facilitate incremental load. We also give an over view of an incremental load functionality. The main contribution of this work is presented in section 4. Here we describe our approach to perform incremental updates. We discuss loading facilities used to incrementally update an analytical subject area table with metadata information. In addition, we describe analytical subject area refresh techniques to detect and capture changes of interest in operational data sources. These techniques deliver the input for incremental load processes. We conclude in section 5 by summarizing the contribution made by this work, providing list of benefits and proposing the future works.

2. RELATED WORK

Most previous work on data warehousing focused on design issues, ETL tools, data maintenance strategies in connection with relational views

materialization and implementation issues (Cho & Garcia-Molina, 2000; Chaudhuri & Dayal, 1997; Sen & Jacob, 1998; Lujan-Mora & Palomar, 2001; Sen & Sinha, 2005; Kambayashi et al., 1999; Dey et al., 2006; Mumick et al., 1997; Ram & Do, 2000). In the literature, numerous proposals for the incremental maintenance of materialized views can be found (Griffin & Libkin, 1995; Cui & Widom, 2003; Zhuge et al., 1997; Labio at al., 2000; Yang & Widom, 2003; Bækgaard & Mark, 1995; Agrawal et al., 1997; Chao, 2004) and various methods have been proposed. Some of those proposals are based on the self maintenance of the views (Mohania & Kambayashi, 2000; García, 2006) and are commonly used in a data warehousing environment to support OLAP. Materialized views are generally defined over base relations. When base relations are changed materialized views also need to be updated. Materialized views are maintained by re-computation or incremental maintenance (Lee & Kim, 2005). Hwang & Kang (2005) investigated the materialization of XML views and their incremental refresh technique. In (Lee et al., 1998), an incremental view update issue for maintaining a mobile data warehouse is addressed. The work in (Griffin & Libkin, 1995) studies the challenge of efficient maintenance of materialized views that may contain duplicates. This issue is particularly important when queries against such views involve aggregate functions, which need duplicates to produce correct results. The work in (Zhuge et al., 1997) and (Kambayashi et al., 1999) study multiple view inconsistency issues and develop simple, scalable, algorithms for achieving multiple view consistency at a warehouse. Instead of computing everything from scratch again, Bækgaard & Mark (1995) proposes to use the intermediate database changes to modify the cached query results. García (2006) presented the self-maintainable strategy for the maintenance of data warehouse. The materialized views need to be updated when the base relations change since they typically require too much access to base relations, resulting in the performance degradation (Lee et al., 2001). Despite certain benefits of incremental view maintenance the maintenance of materialized views in a warehouse environment represents a difficult challenge (Quass et al., 1996; Zhuge et al., 1995).

The above research work talk about materialized view maintenance incrementally – loading data warehouse from analytical area to views. Our work concentrates on updating the data warehouse from staging area to analytical area. Data warehouse loading and maintenance of materialized views are related in the sense that both areas address incremental updates of physically integrated data (Jörg & Deßloch, 2008). In this article, we focus on how to improve performance of incremental loads. An incremental maintenance method for data warehouses allows improvements over the re-computation of views from scratch (Amo et al., 2004). We propose loading analytical tables with the help of global temporary tables and efficient indexes, to deal with performance issues.

Research work has been done on temporal data warehousing and lineage tracing (Patnaik et al., 1999; Bruckner & Tjoa, 2002; Moon et al., 2003; Rahman, 2008). In (Eder & Koncilia, 2001; Rahman, 2008), changes of dimension data in a temporal data warehouse is studied. The work in (Eder & Koncilia, 2001) proposes an extension of the multi-dimensional data model employed in data warehouses allowing for coping with changes in dimension data. A significant amount of work has been done on the ETL tool for updating data warehouses (Casati et al., 2007; Ou et al., 2008; Simitsis et al., 2005). During the last decade the market for ETL Software has steadily grown (Jörg & Deßloch, 2008). Numerous commercial ETL tools are available today (White, 2005) – however – they lack optimization tools (Simitsis et al., 2005). ETL tools rely on proprietary scripting languages or visual user interfaces (Jörg & Deßloch, 2008). Research in data streams has focused on issues relating to front-end, such as on-the-fly computation of queries (Casati et al., 2007). Our work is concerned with issues raised at the back-end of a data warehouse such as performance optimization of SQL inside the stored procedures for incremental load.

With incremental loading via a stored procedure, we are proposing database specific software to perform transformation and load data warehouse. The intent of proposing a stored procedure use is not to compete with existing ETL tools. The database specific software allows exploration on how a data warehouse system could be used to pull data from staging area tables, perform transformation, and load data in the actual analytic area of the same data warehouse system. We focus on utilizing the capabilities of current commercial database engines given their enormous power to do complex transformation and their scalability.

Our proposed stored procedure based incremental refresh is based on source tables in the staging area of the data warehouse. The staging area in ETL is a database where extracted data is staged to get it ready to be loaded into a data warehouse (Ejaz & Kenneth, 2004). It basically serves two purposes: as a landing area where extracted data lands, eliminating the need to repeat an extraction if anything goes wrong (extracting data may impact the operation of the source), and as a working area where data is checked and prepared for loading (Casati et al., 2007). It is convenient to transform staging data located in a data warehouse before loading in analytical tables of the same data warehouse because the database technology allows convenient lookup validation capabilities.

The basic idea behind this work is to perform data warehouse loading in support of an ETL metadata model. Another reason is to load data from a staging area into analytical subject area tables using database-specific stored procedures given both source and target tables reside in the same database and are managed by the same database system. In consequence, full information about changes to the source relation is available (Jörg & Deßloch, 2008). The stored procedures give huge opportunity to efficiently write transformation logic, use global temporary tables with appropriate index defined and influence the optimizer to choose a better execution plan. For an incremental refresh the changed data in multiple source tables could be isolated and stored in global temporary tables. During temporary table loads the tuples can be narrowed down by creating a table based on only those tuples that are needed to load the target table. The tuples could be limited to only those that are needed for target table load. This allows for achieving significant resource (CPU and IO) savings during target table load. We provide a stored procedure template for incremental load which could be used by ETL programmers.

3. THE DATA WAREHOUSE UPDATE FUNCTIONALITY

A truly general, efficient, flexible and scalable data warehousing architecture requires a number of technical advances (Widom, 1995). Data warehouse refresh is one of these technical advances. There is a close connection between incremental loading and successful data warehousing. Loading negatively impacts OLAP query performance if an inefficient loading technique is devised. In this article, we attempt to address issues encountered relating to incremental load.

In data warehouses, automated maintenance batch jobs should run periodically for efficiency reasons. In order to run thousands of jobs via batch cycles in different subject areas, the jobs need to be governed by an ETL metadata model to determine the load type, to capture different load metrics, errors and messages. In Figure 1 we describe a few metadata tables that are useful for incremental loading. The metadata model is based on metadata tables, wrapper stored procedure and utility stored procedures. The model introduces a new paradigm for batch processing by loading only those tables for which there are new records in the source tables. Inspection of the latest observation timestamp in a metadata data table for each of

the source tables referenced in the incremental load stored procedures detects the arrival of fresh data. The full and incremental load procedures are bypassed if source data has not changed.

The ETL metadata model allows for storing table level detailed metrics (timestamp, row count, and errors & messages for trouble shooting). By providing the source and the target table last load timestamp, row count, and load threshold information, the model allows accurate 'delta' Processing and enables a decision about a full or delta refresh.

Table 'target load parameters' holds one row of metadata for each target table in each subject area. After a job kicks off for the first time, a utility procedure checks if a metadata row exists for the table. If no row is found, a default row will be inserted on the fly with several parameters to do a full refresh. After a cycle refresh is completed, the column load_type_ind will be set to 'D' to perform delta load in the subsequent cycle refreshes.

Table 'source load log' holds a load timestamp for each source (staging) table. This timestamp indicates that a staging table is loaded up to a certain date and time. Table 'Target Load Log' stores an observation timestamp that is the dependent source table's last update timestamp. If a target table is loaded with data from multiple source tables, this table will store an observation timestamp for each of the source tables. An observation timestamp is the date and time at which the consistent set of triggered data was loaded into the target table. The trigger timestamp is always less-than-equal-to (<=) the observation timestamp.

Table 'load check option' stores job information (subj_area_nm, trgt_tbl_nm, load_enable_ind, load_type_cd). Per job, one entry is required to exist in this table. The entries are inserted into this table via a utility stored proc call from within the wrapper stored procedure. The load_type_cd field holds the value of 'Full' or 'Delta'. Based on this information a post load utility stored procedure will update the 'target load parameters' table to prepare it for the next refresh cycle. The column

Figure 1. Metadata model for incremental load

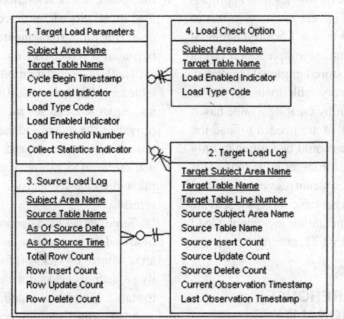

'load_enable_ind' holds the value of 'Y' or 'N'. Based on this information the post load stored proc will update the 'target load parameters' table to prepare it for the next cycle refresh behavior for individual tables.

A wrapper stored procedure is called by batch cycle jobs to load individual target tables. The wrapper procedure has intelligence to decide whether to Skip Refresh, Full Refresh, or Delta Refresh through a metadata driven approach. The "skip" is set if the model finds that the source observation timestamp has not changed. The full or delta refresh is set based on table level threshold values set for each target table load. If the new delta counts found in the source table are within the threshold percentage, the model runs a delta otherwise it turns on the full load procedure.

Figure 2 shows that the wrapper procedure checks the metadata table to see if the source load current observation timestamp is greater than the observation timestamp of the last time target table loaded. If the current source timestamp has not changed, the load is skipped. The next step of algorithm checks if the load type indicator is

full or delta. The default is delta load if no 'load type' value is provided.

4. INCREMENTAL REFRESH TECHNIQUES

The initial refresh of analytical tables is a full load. Subsequent refreshes are done using incremental load. During a full refresh, the existing data is truncated and the target table is reloaded with source data available in the staging area. An incremental refresh only loads the delta changes that occurred since last time the target table was loaded. In incremental refresh, only the delta or difference between target and source data is loaded at regular intervals. For incremental load the observation timestamp for the previous delta load is maintained in a metadata table. The data warehouse refresh may be performed via batch cycles so that the degree of information in the data warehouse is "predictable" (Chan et al., 2000). We propose periodic refreshes with predefined intervals such as eight, four, two or one hour.

Figure 2. High level architecture for full and delta load

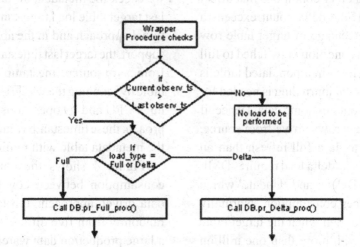

In a real world situation, the ETL programmers have a tendency to write delta stored procedures to run as stand-alone, most likely due to lack of an ETL metadata model. Here we propose a metadata model dedicated for incremental load purposes. We suggest the delta stored procedure design utilizing a metadata model. The assumption is that instead of using conventional ETL tool, the full and incremental loads could be done via database specific stored procedures and with the help of a metadata model.

From the data warehouse side, updating large tables and related structures (such as indexes, materialized views and other integrated components) presents issues executing OLAP query workloads simultaneously with continuous data integration (Santos & Bernardino, 2008). Our methodology minimizes the processing time and systems resources as stored procedures give ample opportunity to manipulate the load SQL and influence the optimizer to execute queries with parallel efficiency.

The ETL coding for incremental load is complex and a labor-intensive task because joins, aggregations and other complex transformation logic needs to be used. In most cases, non-standardized incremental load techniques cause data inconsistency or missing data which eventually causes a

full refresh at the expense of system resources. The author of this article noticed such cases in the real world. This paper presents a template to write delta stored procedures that could be used across the data warehouse.

4.1 Algorithm for Incremental Load Procedures

First we need to retrieve the latest source (staging) table load observation timestamp and new delta count information from the metadata table (Figure 1, Table 3) by executing a metadata utility stored procedure. Next we pull the target table load last observation timestamp and the row count from the metadata table (Figure 1, Table 2). Using both source and target table load timestamp information the wrapper procedure decides whether to perform a full or delta refresh. If the wrapper procedure decides to perform a delta load, it calls the delta stored procedure. The Delta stored procedure still checks if certain conditions are met to perform the refresh such as if the delta load threshold is exceeded or if the target table is empty, for some reason. A delta refresh is performed when small amount of new data (normally, less than 20% of the target rows) arrives in source table during each cycle refresh.

There are several other conditions that affect load decisions: (i) If the delta count exceeds a certain threshold percentage of target table row counts, then the load condition is switched to full refresh. The delta refresh in a populated table is slower because transient journaling is needed for a table that already contains some data. Hence, if a large number of new rows arrive from source, it is more efficient to do a full refresh than an incremental refresh. The delta load requires DML operations such as 'Delete' and 'Update' which causes more resources consumption. Normally a full refresh is performed when the target table needs to be loaded with more than one million rows. (ii) If for some reason the target table is found empty, a full refresh is needed and the delta stored procedure will call the full load stored procedure (iii) If the delta count is within a predetermined threshold percentage, then the delta load will be performed. Also delta refreshes are performed when full refreshes perform badly and can't be practically optimized any more.

Figure 3 provides a template consisting of the incremental load algorithm and transformation logic in sequence as well as dependency. First, we check metadata in the 'source load log' table to see if any rows were removed from source tables for business reasons. We do the same checking for all other source tables if data is merged from multiple source tables. In order to get that we run a utility procedure (e.g., pr_utl_chk_src_del_row()). Then we execute a delete operation against the target table by joining it to the source table. This is done only if any delete row counts were found in the metadata check. This helps avoid unnecessary delete operations in the case where data has not been removed from the source; thereby saving systems resources. Then we check the metadata in 'source load log' table to see if any new rows arrived in the source table (src_asof_dt and src_asof_tm). We execute a utility stored procedure (pr_utl_get_drv_info()) to complete this task. We do the same checking for all other tables if multiple source tables were used. Then

we check the metadata in 'target load log' to get last target table load timestamp. Under a conventional approach and in the absence of a metadata support, the target last timestamp is pulled directly from 'as of source timestamp' column of the target table by scanning the whole table at the expense of huge CPU and IO operations. Under the new approach, these timestamp values are retrieved from the metadata table with minimal resource usage.

Figure 4 shows the comparative resource consumption between conventional and metadata driven approach. Ten tables were selected randomly from five different subject areas from a large production data warehouse environment. The average CPU consumption for a table under new approach is 5.35 second compared to 112.9 second under conventional approach. The average IO for a table under the new approach is 3890.6 compared to 253,974.5 under a conventional approach. The new metadata driven approach seems very promising as it saves a significant amount of CPU and IO resources.

With source load and target table load observation timestamp information new delta rows are retrieved from the source tables. A global temporary table is loaded with delta rows from one or more source tables. Then we get load parameters from the metadata table, 'target load parameters.' This information is used to decide whether to do a full or delta refresh. If a large number of rows arrive from the source the decision is made to run full refresh. If a small amount of new or changed rows arrive we continue executing rest of delta refresh code for incremental refresh. In order to load incremental rows in the target table, first we remove any rows from it that conflict with changed rows (DML = U) in the source table. Then we insert the target table with new or changed rows (DML = U). Based on the new delta rows, we pull the latest date and time and capture that information in metadata table, 'target load log'. We update metadata with current load 'as of data and time.' This latest timestamp is used during the next incremental load to fetch data from source tables.

Figure 3. Stored procedure template for incremental load

```
REPLACE PROCEDURE appl_Asset_DRV_01.pr_Dasset_acum_yearly_value()
BEGIN
DECLARE subj_area VARCHAR(30) DEFAULT 'Asset_DRV' ;
DECLARE trgt_tbl, cycle_type VARCHAR(30) DEFAULT 'asset_acum_yearly_value';
DECLARE CRS_src_asof_dt, NBP_src_asof_dt DATE;
DECLARE CRS_src_asof_tm, NBP_src_asof_tm TIME(0) ;
DECLARE CRS_asof_src_ts, NBP_asof_src_ts TIMESTAMP(0) ;
DECLARE row_cnt_dlta,row_cnt_trgt,src_del_cnt,load_thrhld INTEGER DEFAULT 0;
** check metadata in 'source load log' table if any rows removed from source tables for biz reasons
** do the same checking for all other tables if multiple source tables used
CALL DWmgr_Xfrm_MET.pr_utl_chk_src_del_row(:subj_ara,:trgt_tbl,'Asset_CRS','asset_val', :CRS_src_asof_dt,
CRS_src_asof_tm,:src_del_cnt) ;
** execute delete operation only if any delete row count found in metadata check above
** this helps avoid unnecessary delete operation in case any data has not removed from source
IF src_del_cnt > 0 THEN
DELETE
FROM Asset_DRV_MET.v_asset_acum_yearly_value TrgtTbl
WHERE EXISTS (SELECT * FROM Asset.v_asset_val_CRS SrcTbl WHERE ...) ;
END IF ;
** check metadata in 'source load log' table if any new rows arrived in source table: CRS src_asof_dt and src_asof_tm
CALL DWmgr_.pr_DWm_get_drv_info(:subj_ara,:trgt_tbl, 'Asset_CRS', :CRS_src_asof_dt, :CRS_src_asof_tm) ;
** do the same checking for all other tables if multiple source tables used...

** populating temp table with DELTA rows from one or more source tables...
BEGIN REQUEST
INSERT INTO appl_Asset_DRV_01.gt_asset_acum_yearly_value
SELECT ... FROM Asset.v_asset_val_CRS
WHERE ((asof_src_dt = :CRS_src_asof_dt AND asof_src_tm > :CRS_src_asof_tm)  OR (asof_src_dt > :CRS_src_asof_dt ));
END REQUEST ;
IF row_cnt_ins = 0 THEN
** existing delta load since now row found in source
  LEAVE pr_Dasset_acum_yearly_value ;
END IF ;
SELECT :ACTIVITY_COUNT INTO :row_cnt_dlta ;
SELECT COALESCE(load_thrhld_nbr,0) INTO:load_thrhld
FROM DWmgr_Xfrm_MET.v_target_load_parameters WHERE subj_area_nm = :subj_ara AND trgt_tbl_nm = :trgt_tbl ;
-- *****************************************************************************************
IF row_cnt_dlta > row_cnt_trgt * load_thrhld / 100 THEN
SET cycle_type = 'F'; -- Delta count exceeds threshold - Switched to Full Refresh
ELSEIF row_cnt_trgt = 0 THEN
SET cycle_type = 'F'; -- Target Table was empty - Switched to Full Refresh
ELSE
SET cycle_type = 'D'; -- Delta count within threshold - Performed Delta Refresh
END IF;
-- *****************************************************************************************
IF cycle_type = 'F' THEN
CALL appl_Asset_ETL_01.pr_Fasset_acum_yearly_value() ; --Executing FULL procedure
            LEAVE pr_Dasset_acum_yearly_value()  -- Exiting Delta procedure
ELSE
**Continute executing rest of delta code for incremental refresh
** removing any rows from target that conflict with chnaged rows (DML = U) in source
DELETE FROM  Asset_DRV_DRV_MET.v_asset_acum_yearly_value WHERE ...
** inserting target table with new or chnaged rows (DML = U) in source
INSERT Asset_DRV_DRV_MET.v_asset_acum_yearly_value
SELECT ... FROM appl_Asset_DRV_01.gt_asset_acum_yearly_value ;

IF row_cnt_dlta > 0 THEN
SELECT  MAX(CASE WHEN src_sys_nm = 'SAP-CRS' THEN asof_src_ts END) AS CRS_asof_src_ts
,MAX(CASE WHEN src_sys_nm = 'SBI-NBP' THEN asof_src_ts END) AS NBP_asof_src_ts
INTO :CRS_asof_src_ts ,:NBP_asof_src_ts
FROM ( SELECT src_sys_nm ,CAST(MAX(asof_src_ts) AS CHAR(19)) AS asof_src_ts
  FROM appl_Asset_DRV_01.gt_asset_acum_yearly_value GROUP BY src_sys_nm )  ;
**updating metadata with current asof_src_ts ... to be used during the next DELTA load...
IF CRS_asof_src_ts IS NOT NULL THEN
UPDATE DWmgr_Xfrm_MET.v_load_config
SET config_txt = CRS_asof_src_ts
WHERE subj_area_nm = :subj_ara AND trgt_tbl_nm = :trgt_tbl AND obj_type = 'CRS_src_sys_nm' ;
END IF ;
...
END IF ;
END IF ;
END ;
```

Figure 4. Resource usage in conventional vs. new delta load

SL	SubjectArea	TableName	Conventional Approach: CPU	Conventional Approach: IO	New Approach: CPU	New Approach: IO
1	Asset_DRV	asset_acum_yearly_value	25	38858	4.66	4109
2	Asset_DRV	asset_ytd	39	54452	5.24	4142
3	Capital_DRV	fact_asset_depr_post	40	58478	3.8	4162
4	Capital_DRV	fact_captl_fin_doc_line	58	142367	5.5	4142
5	Capital_DRV	fact_ctrl_doc_captl_spnd	53	95870	5.5	4109
6	Capital_DRV	fact_depr_hist	32	73220	6.04	4203
7	Capital_DRV	fact_depr_hist_non_xfrm	72	108332	6.2	4203
8	Finance_Core_DRV	fin_doc_line	704	1823566	6.7	4142
9	Procurement_DRV	pmt_clr_supl_invc_assoc	53	51924	4.6	1552
10	Project_DRV	ctrl_doc_captl_spnd	53	92678	5.3	4142
11	**Average CPU and IO consumption**		**112.9**	**253974.5**	**5.35**	**3890.6**

4.2 Processing Changed Rows from Source Tables

In incremental load we use global temporary tables to process and stage new or changed rows. The changed rows are pulled from primary source tables and all dimension or secondary source tables and the target tables are loaded based on data in temporary tables. This allows eliminating the rows that are not used for the join operation. This makes join row numbers much smaller and helps in improving load performance. The use of a global temporary table also gives the opportunity to redefine indexes for better data row distribution. Another advantage of using global temporary tables is that we can narrow down tuples and rows while loading temp tables with source data. Global temporary tables are based on required columns which are used in projection and join operations. Global temporary tables holding only the required subset of rows and columns (which makes the table smaller) improve query performance significantly. Narrowing down of tuples and rows mean less IO and CPU time needed for read and write operations (Harizopoulos et al., 2006).

Processing new rows from multiple source tables to load a target table is a challenging task. The conventional incremental refresh is based on the join operation that directly uses source tables containing both historical and new/changed rows.

The downside of directly using source tables in the join is that the source can hold a large number of rows that are not required to process new or changed data for incremental refresh. For incremental load, it is imperative to avoid join operations between source and the target tables with a huge amount of data. In our approach, we separate out new or changed rows from the source tables by putting them into global temporary tables. A formula could be used to separate the new or changed rows.

First, let's get new or changed rows from the primary source table (also known as the driver source table), denoted as PS. Next, execute a delete operation against the target table to remove any rows that have a conflict with the PS (usually due to changed rows). Then commit inserts into the target table with new or changed rows from the PS. Second, to update the column values in the target table, the rows that need to be considered are the ones that just got loaded from PS. Also the new or changed rows from all dimension or secondary sources for a particular table load needs to be taken into consideration. Let the total rows from the secondary source table, SS = PS + SSNew. In one pass, the dimension or secondary source table needs to be interrogated by PS rows and staged into a global temporary table denoted as GT. In the second pass, the new or changed rows (i.e. SSNew) need to be pulled based on

Figure 5. Resource usage for DML: conventional vs. new delta load

SL	Subject Area	Table Name	Delta Rows	Conventional Approach: CPU usage for Delete and Update Operation	New Approach: CPU usage for Delete and Update Operation
1	Asset_DRV	asset_acum_yearly_value	2168	239	78
2	Asset_DRV	asset_post_trns	143	189	64
3	Capital_DRV	fact_captl_fin_doc_line	413	357	88
4	Capital_DRV	fact_ctrl_doc_captl_spnd	194	400	74
5	Capital_DRV	fact_depr_hist	1079619	1176	486
6	Project_DRV	ctrl_doc_captl_spnd	159	358	66
7	Project_DRV	fin_doc_tax	3145	340	97
8	Conventioanl vs New approach		1,085,841	3,059	953

the last target table load observation timestamp and loaded into GT. In this process, the new and changed data needs to be pulled from all dimension or secondary source tables to reflect new changes in the corresponding column values in the target table. This methodology has been successfully applied to four dozen incremental load stored procedures in a production data warehouse. This process not only resolved issues with missing or inconsistent data but also ensured accurate reflection of source dimension or secondary source data against corresponding columns of the target table.

The summary target table loads need a slightly different treatment. Because a delta summary is based on the changes that have occurred to a table, it is necessary to identify those changes after they have already occurred; various techniques may be used to identify the rows that are added to the base tables of a summary table after the most recent refresh operation (Norcott & Finnerty, 2008). To build a summary table with detailed rows in the source tables require special effort. To load the summarized table with new or changed rows in the source table two steps need to be followed. In the first pass, get summarized key column values, denoted as S1, based on new or changed rows from the primary source table and stage into a temporary table, called GT1. In the second pass, interrogate the primary source table again to pull all rows based on key values GT1 and stage into a global temporary table, called GT2. The second

pass not only pulls new or changed rows but, also pulls a complete set of rows from the source table consisting of new, changed and preexisting rows. This will ensure accurate summary of any amount values because complete set of rows is taken into account. The same procedure also needs to be followed in pulling the rows from the dimension or secondary source tables. The final pass is to insert the summary data from GT2 to the final target table.

With the proposed strategy the performance speed-up and scale-up obtained in the global temporary table use technique are not impaired by the presence of big dimensions. Large tables are often decomposed into smaller piece called partitions, in order to improve query performance and ease the data management (Chakkappen et al., 2008). Using global temporary tables helps significantly in achieving efficient load performance.

Figure 5 shows the comparative CPU and IO usage between conventional and metadata driven approach in performing delete and update operations against the target table to process delta rows. Seven tables were selected randomly from three different subject areas from a large production data warehouse environment. The average CPU consumption for a table under new approach is 953 to process 1,085,841 rows with seven delta stored procedures. On the other hand 3,059 CPU second used to process the same amount of rows under

Table 1. Comparison between row-limiting vs. non-limiting

Rank	Dimension	Dimension Rows	Duplicated Dimension Rows	Explain Step	Delta Dimension Rows	Duplicated Delta Dimension Rows
#1	v_dim_cur_rte	2,496,215	1,777,305,080	49-2	41	29,192
#2	v_dim_frcst_opr_hier	645,585	459,656,520	48-2	1,230	875,760
#3	v_dim_wbs	222,059	158,106,008	45-2	98	69,776
#4	v_dim_wrkr	191,878	136,617,136	44-2	95	67,640
#5	v_dim_cust	42,332	30,140,384	44-3	225	160,200
#6	v_dim_cost_centr	16,704	11,893,248	40	1,146	815,952
#7	v_dim_clndr	10,599	7,546,488	38	52	37,024
#8	v_dim_prft_centr_hier_curr	7,765	5,528,680	42-2	244	173,728
	Total:	3,633,137	2,586,793,544		3,131	2,239,952
						-99.91%

conventional approach. The new metadata driven approach shows a resource saving of 68.85%.

Before completing the incremental load process, performing a data quality check is essential. After an incremental refresh is done a simple query is run against the source table to get the total row count. The row count is compared against the row count in the target table. The 'target load log' holds the target table row count information. If any row count mismatch is found the full refresh stored procedure is turned on from inside the delta stored procedure. So, data quality is checked at the very moment of the delta load process. This is done during the load as opposed to checking via a conventional data quality monitoring cycle that runs after an actual load cycle runs. The data quality monitoring cycle reports the row count issue to the support team a bit late which increases data latency to fix the data issue. Our data quality checking is a new way of fixing the data issue during the analytical subject area refresh.

4.3. Limiting Row Processing in Dimension Tables

Normally a target table is loaded by fetching data from one or multiple source tables. In a delta

refresh the secondary source tables (also called dimension tables) could be rebuilt as global temporary tables to only include rows from the dimension tables that are referenced in the "delta" fact rows. This will allow a significant reduction of resource consumption in the batch cycles. One test result showed a 92% reduction in resource consumption for a delta insert into a one hundred million row table (drops from about 12,100 CPU seconds to 1,000 CPU seconds) when rows in the dimension tables are limited to those referenced in the incoming delta transactions in the fact table.

In order to populate the dimensional model in the target fact table the new transactions are then joined twice to several dimension tables (once for data since a particular year and once for data prior to a particular year). In a massively parallel DBMS the system typically duplicates the dimension tables to facilitate an efficient join across hundreds of Access Module Processors (AMP) in the system; hence each dimension row eliminated from consideration reduces processing in retrieve and join steps across all AMPs. The table below shows that about 99% (Table 1) of the data currently processed from the largest dimension tables can be eliminated by limiting dimension rows to those referenced in the incoming delta transactions.

The Table 1 shows the resource usage comparison in 'referenced dimension rows' (largest fact table dimensions). The left red column shows dimension rows get duplicated in the DBMS and the right hand green and red columns show that duplicating of rows in the DBMS gets reduced dramatically when dimension tables are built in global temporary tables with the required set of dimension rows needed for matching the primary source table fact delta rows.

This theory is experimented in a production environment by creating global temporary tables with the dimension rows that were referenced by the new incoming transactions in the fact table and then referencing views pointed to the global temporary tables in the Delta fact table insert. The amount of resources required in creating the global temporary tables and collecting statistics on the 3,131 rows in the reduced dimension tables was minimal.

Another approach is to consider incorporating a "recency indicator" into dimension tables that identifies dimension rows recently referenced by transactions in fact tables. This would allow for direct qualification of the desired rows from the dimension tables and eliminate the need for additional global temporary tables like those used for testing. The ultimate goal is to load the target table with minimum resource usage.

5. CONCLUSION

In this paper, we showed that by using an ETL metadata model and certain incremental refresh techniques loading could be made standardized, load behavior predictable, and efficient. The model helps identify those source tables that do not have new data. A wrapper stored procedure is utilized to decide full or delta refresh and execute accordingly. Performing a delta refresh through metadata driven approach enables saving resource in data warehouse. This also helps minimize cycle refresh times and stay within the Service Level Agreement with customers.

We presented an approach for generating incremental load processes for data warehouse refreshment based on ETL metadata model and separating out changed data from source table and staging them in global temporary tables. The use of global temporary table requires maintenance of additional table structures, but it pays off. Traditional incremental load processes, in contrast, directly use source tables with huge data that are not used in incremental load purposes. Our approach has clear performance benefits as it improves load performance in terms of response time and database systems resource consumption (CPU and IO). We further, demonstrated the standardization of algorithms and code blocks inside the delta stored procedures. We have presented a perfect stored procedure template for incremental load. This incremental load stored procedure template could be used by ETL programmers across the data warehouse.

By introducing an ETL metadata model, we are able to automate data warehouse batch cycle processes. We are confident that our work contributes to the improvement of ETL processes. By utilizing the staging area inside the data warehouse we are able to load analytical subject areas with data warehouse specific software such as stored procedures. Using the staging area, however, comes at the cost of additional IO operations (Jörg & Deßloch, 2008). Even so, this has lot of benefits. We can avoid maintenance of a dedicated ETL tool. We presented an efficient incremental load method for multiple joins that uses global temporary tables. We showed through experiment that the proposed incremental load method saves more resources such as CPU and IO. In a future endeavor, we intend to develop macros to generate automated full and delta stored procedure templates. The ETL programmers will generate full and delta stored procedures by running macros with subject area and table names as parameters.

ACKNOWLEDGMENT

The author wishes to thank his colleagues Peter W. Burkhardt and Scott W. Faulk who provided thoughtful review comments on earlier version of this paper and two anonymous referees for their useful comments which have led to this improved version of the paper.

REFERENCES

Agrawal, D., Abbadi, A., Singh, A., & Yurek, T. (1997). Efficient View Maintenance at Data Warehouse. *SIGMOD Record, 26*(2), 417–427. doi:10.1145/253262.253355

Amo, S. D., & Alves, M. H. F. (2004). Incremental Maintenance of Data Warehouses Based on Past Temporal Logic Operators. *Journal of Universal Computer Science, 10*(9).

Bækgaard, L., & Mark, L. (1995). Incremental Computation of Time-Varying Query Expressions. *IEEE Transactions on Knowledge and Data Engineering, 7*(4), 583–590. doi:10.1109/69.404031

Ballou, D. P., & Tayi, G. K. (1999). Enhancing Data Quality in Data Warehouse Environments. *Communications of the ACM, 42*(1). doi:10.1145/291469.291471

Bokun, M. & Taglienti, C. (1998). Incremental Data Warehouse Updates. *DM Review*, 1-5.

Brobst, S., McIntire, M., & Rado, E. (2008). Agile Data Warehousing with Integrated Sandboxing. *Business Intelligence Journal, 13*(1).

Bruckner, R. M., & Tjoa, A. M. (2002). Capturing Delays and Valid Times in Data Warehouses - Towards Timely Consistent Analyses. *Journal of Intelligent Information Systems, 19*(2), 169–190. doi:10.1023/A:1016555410197

Casati, F., Castellanos, M., Dayal, U., & Salazar, N. (2007, September 23-28). A Generic solution for Warehousing Business Process Data. In *Proceedings of the 33rd International Conference on Very Large Data Bases (VLDB '07)*, Vienna, Austria.

Chakkappen, S., Cruanes, T., Dageville, B., Jiang, L., Shaft, U., Su, H., & Zait, M. (2008, June 9-12). Efficient and Scalable Statistics Gathering for Large Databases in Oracle 11g. In *Proceedings of the 2008 ACM SIGMOD international conference on Management of data (SIGMOD '08)*, Vancouver, BC, Canada.

Chan, M., Leong, H. V., & Si, A. (2000, November). Incremental Update to Aggregated Information for Data Warehouses over Internet. In *Proceedings of the 3rd ACM International Workshop on Data Warehousing and OLAP (DOLAP '00)*, McLean, VA.

Chao, C. (2004). Incremental Maintenance of Object Oriented Data Warehouse. *Information Sciences, 1*(4), 91–110. doi:10.1016/j.ins.2003.07.014

Chaudhuri, S., & Dayal, U. (1997). An Overview of Data Warehousing and OLAP Technology. *SIGMOD Record, 26*(1). doi:10.1145/248603.248616

Cho, J., & Garcia-Molina, H. (2000). Synchronizing a Database to Improve Freshness. In *Proceedings of the 2000 ACM SIGMOD International Conference on Management of Data (SIGMOD '00)*, Dallas, TX.

Costa, M., & Madeira, H. (2004, November 12-13). Handling Big Dimensions in Distributed Data Warehouses using the DWS Technique. In *Proceedings of the 7th ACM international workshop on Data warehousing and OLAP (DOLAP '04)*, Washington, DC.

Cui, Y., & Widom, J. (2003). Lineage Tracing for General Data Warehouse Transformations. *The VLDB Journal, 12*, 41–58. doi:10.1007/s00778-002-0083-8

Dey, D., Zhang, Z., & De, P. (2006). Optimal Synchronization Policies for Data Warehouse. *Information Journal on Computing, 18*(2), 229–242.

Eder, J., & Koncilia, K. (2001, September 5-7). Changes of Dimension Data in Temporal Data Warehouses. In *Proceedings of the Third International Conference on Data Warehousing and Knowledge Discovery (DaWaK'01)*, Munich, Germany (pp. 284-293).

Ejaz, A., & Kenneth, R. (2004, December 16-18). Utilizing Staging Tables in Data Integration to Load Data into Materialized Views. In *Proceedings of the First International Symposium on Computational and Information Science (CIS'04)*, Shanghai, China (pp. 685-691).

García, C. (2006, March 10-12). Real Time Self-Maintainable Data Warehouse. In *Proceedings of the 44th Annual Southeast Regional Conference (ACM SE'06)*, Melbourne, FL.

Griffin, T., & Libkin, L. (1995). Incremental Maintenance of Views with Duplicates. In *Proceedings of the SIGMOD Record '95*, San Jose, CA.

Harizopoulos, H., Liang, V., Abadi, D. J., & Madden, S. (2006, September 12-15). Performance Tradeoffs in Read-Optimized Databases. In *Proceedings of the 32nd International Conference on Very Large Data Bases (VLDB'06)*, Seoul, Korea.

Hwang, D. H., & Kang, H. (2005). XML View Materialization with Deferred Incremental Refresh, the Case of a Restricted Class of Views. *Journal of Information Science and Engineering, 21*, 1083–1119.

Inmon, W. H. (2002). *Building the Data Warehouse* (3rd ed.). New York: John Wiley.

Jörg, T., & Deßloch, S. (2008, September 10-12). Towards Generating ETL Processes for Incremental Loading. In *Proceedings of the 2008 International Symposium on Database Engineering & Applications (IDEAS'08)*, Coimbra, Portugal.

Kambayashi, Y., Samtani, S., Mohania, M., & Kumar, V. (1999, November 19-20). Recent Advances and Research Problems in Data Warehousing. In Proceedings of Advances in Database Technologies: ER '98 (pp. 81–92). Singapore: Workshops on Data Warehousing and Data Mining, Mobile Data Access, and Collaborative Work Support and Spatio-Temporal Data Management.

Labio, W. J., Yang, J., Cui, Y., Garcia-Molina, H., & Widom, J. (2000). Performance Issues in Incremental Warehouse Maintenance. In *Proceedings of the 26th VLDB Conference*, Cairo, Egypt.

Labio, W. J., Yerneni, R., & Garcia-Molina, H. (1999). Shrinking the Warehouse Update Window. In *Proceedings of the 1999 ACM SIGMOD International Conference on Management of data (SIGMOD'99)*, Philadelphia, PA.

Lee, K. C. K., Si, A., & Leong, H. V. (1998). Incremental View Update for a Mobile Data Warehouse. In *Proceedings of the 1998 ACM symposium on Applied Computing (SAC'98)*.

Lee, K. Y., & Kim, M. H. (2005, November 4-5). Optimizing the Incremental Maintenance of Multiple Join Views. In *Proceedings of the 8th ACM International Workshop on Data Warehousing and OLAP (DOLAP'05)*, Bremen, Germany.

Lee, K. Y., Son, J. H., & Kim, M. H. (2001). Efficient Incremental View Maintenance in Data Warehouses. In *Proceedings of the Tenth International Conference on Information and Knowledge Management (CIKM'01)*, Atlanta, GA.

Lujan-Mora, S., & Palomar, M. (2001). Reducing Inconsistency in Integrating Data from Different Sources. In *Proceedings of the International Database Engineering & Applications Symposium (IDEAS '01)*.

Mohania, M., & Kambayashi, Y. (2000). Making Aggregate Views Self-Maintainable. *Journal of Data and Knowledge Engineering, 32*(1), 87–109. doi:10.1016/S0169-023X(99)00016-6

Moon, K. D., Park, J. S., Shin, Y. H., & Ryu, K. H. (2003). Incremental Condition Evaluation for Active Temporal Rules. In *Proceedings of Intelligent Data Engineering and Automated Learning* (pp. 816-820).

Mumick, I., Quass, D., & Mumick, B. (1997). Maintenance of Data Cubes and Summary Tables in a Warehouse. *SIGMOD Record, 26*(2), 100–111. doi:10.1145/253262.253277

Naggar, P., Pontieri, L., Pupo, M., Terracina, G., & Virardi, E. (2002, September 2-6). A Model and a Toolkit for Supporting Incremental Data Warehouse Construction. In *Proceedings of the 13th International Conference on Database and Expert Systems Applications (DEXA'02)*, Aix-en-Provence, France (pp. 123-132).

Norcott, W. D., & Finnerty, J. (2008). *Method and Apparatus for Incremental Refresh of Summary Tables in a Database System*. Retrieved December 17, 2008, from http://www.patentstorm.us/patents/6205451/description.html

Ou, J., Lee, C., & Chen, M. (2008). Efficient Algorithms for Incremental Web Log Mining with Dynamic Thresholds. *The VLDB Journal, 17*, 827–845. doi:10.1007/s00778-006-0043-9

Patnaik, S., Meier, M., Henderson, B., Hickman, J., & Panda, B. (1999, February). Improving the Performance of Lineage Tracing in Data Warehouse. In *Proceedings of the 1999 ACM Symposium on Applied Computing (SAC'99)*, San Antonio, TX.

Quass, D., Gupta, A., Mumick, I. S., & Widom, J. (1996). Making views self-maintainable for data warehousing. In *Proceedings of the 4th International Conference on Parallel and Distributed Information System*, Miami Beach, FL (pp. 158-169).

Rahman, N. (2007). Refreshing Data Warehouses with Near Real-Time Updates. *Journal of Computer Information Systems, 47*(3), 71–80.

Rahman, N. (2008, October 12-16). Refreshing Teradata Warehouse with Temporal Data. In *Proceedings of The 2008 Teradata Partners User Group Conference & Expo*, Las Vegas, NV.

Rahman, N. (2008, August 14-17). Updating Data Warehouses with Temporal Data. In *Proceedings of the 14th Americas Conference on Information Systems (AMCIS 2008)*, Toronto, ON, Canada.

Ram, P., & Do, L. (2000). Extracting Delta for Incremental Data Warehouse Maintenance. In *Proceedings of the 16th International Conference on Data Engineering (ICDE '00)*, San Diego, CA.

Sahama, T. R., & Croll, P. R. (2007). A Data Warehouse Architecture for Clinical Data Warehousing. In *Proceedings of the fifth Australasian symposium on ACSW Frontiers (ACSW'07)* (Vol. 68).

Santos, R. J., & Bernardino, J. (2008, September 10-12). Real-Time Data Warehouse Loading Methodology. In *Proceedings of the 2008 International Symposium on Database Engineering & Applications (IDEAS'08)*, Coimbra, Portugal.

Sen, A., & Jacob, V. S. (1998). Industrial-Strength Data Warehousing. *Communications of the ACM, 41*(9). doi:10.1145/285070.285076

Sen, A., & Sinha, A. P. (2005). A Comparison of Data Warehousing Methodologies. *Communications of the ACM, 48*(3). doi:10.1145/1047671.1047673

Shin, B. (2003). An Exploratory Investigation of System Success Factors in Data Warehousing. *Journal of the Association for Information Systems, 4*.

Simitsis, A., Vassiliadis, P., & Sellis, T. (2005, April 5-8). Optimizing ETL Processes in Data Warehouses. In *Proceedings of the 21st International Conference on Data Engineering (ICDE'05)*, Tokyo, Japan.

White, C. (2005). *Data Integration: Using ETL, EAI, and EII Tools to Create an Integrated Enterprise*. The Data Warehousing Institute.

Widom, J. (1995, November). Research Problems in Data Warehousing. In *Proceedings of the 4th International Conference on Information and Knowledge Management (CIKM'95)*, Baltimore, MD.

Yang, J., & Widom, J. (2003). Incremental Computation and Maintenance of Temporal Aggregates. *The VLDB Journal*, *12*, 262–283. doi:10.1007/s00778-003-0107-z

Zhuge, Y., García-Molina, H., Hammer, J., & Widom, J. (1995, June). View Maintenance in a Warehousing Environment. In *Proceedings of the 1995 ACM SIGMOD International Conference on Management of Data (SIGMOD'95)*, San Jose, CA.

Zhuge, Y., Wiener, J. L., & Garcia-Molina, H. (1997, April 7-11). Multiple View Consistency for Data Warehousing. In *Proceedings of the Thirteenth International Conference on Data Engineering*, Birmingham, UK.

This work was previously published in International Journal of Intelligent Information Technologies, Volume 6, Issue 3, edited by Vijayan Sugumaran, pp. 1-16, copyright 2010 by IGI Publishing (an imprint of IGI Global).

Chapter 10
A Fuzzy–Neural Approach with Collaboration Mechanisms for Semiconductor Yield Forecasting

Toly Chen
Feng Chia University, Taiwan

ABSTRACT

Yield forecasting is critical to a semiconductor manufacturing factory. To further enhance the effectiveness of semiconductor yield forecasting, a fuzzy-neural approach with collaboration mechanisms is proposed in this study. The proposed methodology is modified from Chen and Lin's approach by incorporating two collaboration mechanisms: favoring mechanism and disfavoring mechanism. The former helps to achieve the consensus among multiple experts to avoid the missing of actual yield, while the latter shrinks the search region to increase the probability of finding out actual yield. To evaluate the effectiveness of the proposed methodology, it was applied to some real cases. According to experimental results, the proposed methodology improved both precision and accuracy of semiconductor yield forecasting by 58% and 35%, respectively.

DOI: 10.4018/978-1-4666-0158-1.ch010

Figure 1. Effects of a favoring mechanism

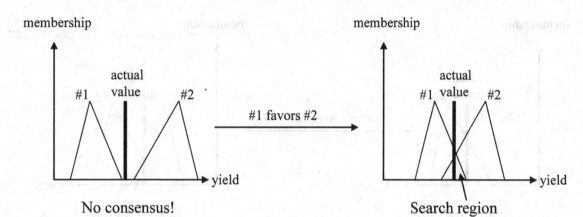

INTRODUCTION

The number one index of success in semiconductor manufacturing is yield. Although yield is not the only source of competitiveness, it does play a critical role in evaluating and improving the mid-term or long-term competitiveness (Chen & Wang, 2008).

Yield forecasting is very important to a semiconductor manufacturing factory. In capacity planning, the majority of capacity should be devoted to products with high yields and prices. Incorrectly releasing raw wafers to produce low-yield products will inevitably increase the average unit cost. Thus accurate yield forecasting is critical when making a production plan.

In order to further enhance the effectiveness of semiconductor yield forecasting, a fuzzy-neural approach with collaboration mechanisms is proposed in this study. The proposed methodology is modified from Chen and Lin's approach (Chen & Lin, 2008) by incorporating two collaboration mechanisms:

(1) Favoring mechanism: During collaborative semiconductor yield forecasting, some experts favor other experts' opinions, and modify their previous opinions to be as close as possible. For facilitating such actions, a

favoring mechanism is designed. A favoring mechanism helps to achieve the consensus among multiple experts, so as to avoid the missing of actual yield (see Figure 1).

(2) Disfavoring mechanism: Conversely, some experts disfavor other experts' opinions, and modify their opinions to be as far as possible. For facilitating such actions, a disfavoring mechanism is designed. If the consensus among experts is already high, then a disfavoring mechanism helps to shrink the region of searching for actual yield, so as to improve both precision and accuracy of forecasting (see Figure 2). First, the range of a fuzzy forecast narrows as search region shrinks, which increases precision. Second, the shrinkage in search region increases the probability of finding out actual yield, which enhances accuracy.

To prove the usefulness of the proposed methodology, some real cases containing the data collected from a random access memory manufacturing factory will be investigated.

The remainder of this paper is organized as follows. The second section reviews the related work. The fuzzy-neural approach with collaboration mechanisms is then introduced in the third section. To evaluate the effectiveness of the pro-

Figure 2. Effects of a disfavoring mechanism

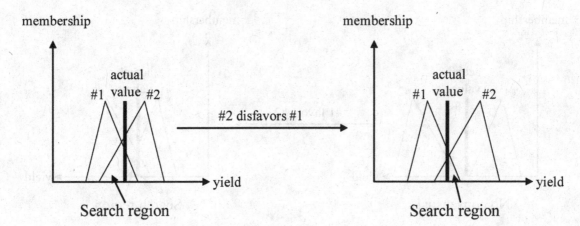

posed methodology, it was applied to some real cases in the fourth section. Finally, concluding remarks and directions for future research are given in the last section.

RELATED WORK

Approaches of semiconductor yield forecasting can be classified into two categories: micro yield modeling (MiYM) and macro yield modeling (MaYM). MiYM methods use critical device area, parametric sensitivity, redundancy effect, and other factors which rely on a detailed understanding of circuit design to estimate the effects of different classes of defects, process variability, and layout variation on yield. In this category, composite yield model and layered yield model are frequently applied (Hsieh et al., 2006). Recently, Shimada and Sakurai (2003) proposed an accurate analytical yield forecasting approach for system-large-scale-integration (LSI) embedded memories based on failure-related method to make it possible to treat both asymmetric repair and link set. Li et al. (2006) proposed a genetic programming (GP) approach that attempted to predict the yield of a wafer lot according to in-line inspection data. In a related field, Lin et al. (2006) constructed a grey forecasting model to forecast abnormal quality

characteristics in a silicon wafer slicing process. However, semiconductor yield forecasting is still a very difficult task from MiYM point of view. For instance, Hsieh and Tong (2006) mentioned even through defect count, defect size, and defect distribution are the same, the yield loss of a complicated manufactured product was less than that of a simple manufactured product. Besides, defect clustering increases as wafer size grows. As a result, conventional Poisson yield model tends to underestimate yield (Tong et al., 2007).

On the other hand, MaYM methods use die size, device density, and other large-scale a priori factors to predict yields for new designs. One common technique in MaYM is learning and transition analysis (LTA), in which a learning model is used to predict the future yield of a product and the transition of learning effects is investigated as well.

Gruber's general yield learning model is one of the most basic yield learning models (Gruber, 1984). However, the uncertainty and variation inherent in the learning process are difficult to work with. Studies incorporating uncertainty and/or stochasticity into learning phenomenon modeling include Spence (1981), Majd and Pindyck (1989), Mazzola and McCardle (1995), and others. Most of them assume parameter distributions are known in advance to a certain degree, and can be modified in a Bayesian manner after actual values are observed. In Watada et al. (1986), fuzzy set theory was applied to model learning uncertainty through fitting a possibility regression model. The concept is not to consider the difference between observed and estimated values as statistical error, but the result of system fuzziness. The necessity of specifying strict parameter distributions is relaxed, and fuzzy values are used to represent yield forecasts. In this way, parameter variation is contained in the range/support of a fuzzy forecast. Unlike the use of symmetric triangular fuzzy numbers (TFNs) in Watada et al.'s study, Chen and Wang (1999) proposed a fuzzy yield learning model with asymmetric parameters. However, human factors involved in the learning process often complicate matters. Expert opinions are valuable and effective in handling this situation. Chen and Wang therefore designed two correction functions to incorporate expert opinions – one for incorporating expert opinions on the asymptotic/final yield and the other for incorporating expert opinions on the learning constant/speed. However, competition in semiconductor industry is becoming increasingly fierce, which distorts yield learning process. For example, if the yield of a product could not reach a certain level before a given deadline, then its competitiveness will disappear and capacity will be re-allocated to other products. In this respect, a systematic procedure was proposed in Chen (2007b) to evaluate the mid-term competitiveness of a semiconductor product. To prevent the possibility of not reaching a required level by a certain deadline, some managerial actions, e.g., executing quality engineering (QE) projects, increasing the speed of mass production, etc., can be taken to accelerate yield learning. After these managerial actions, yield learning model has to be modified. Chen and Wang's fuzzy yield learning model was therefore modified to incorporate such managerial actions in Chen (2007a). Recently, Chen and Lin (2008) proposed a two-step approach for aggregating expert opinions so as to improve precision and accuracy of semiconductor yield forecasting. In

the two-step approach, multiple experts (usually experienced product engineers) construct their own fuzzy yield learning models from various viewpoints to predict product yield. The fuzzy yield forecasts made by these experts need to be aggregated. Each fuzzy yield learning model is modified from Chen and Wang (1999), and can be converted into an equivalent nonlinear programming problem to be solved. Expert opinions can also be considered as unequally important, and a two-step aggregation mechanism is applied for this purpose.

In short, existing approaches have the following problems:

(1) Even with advanced approaches, semiconductor yield forecasting remains a very difficult task (Hsieh et al., 2006; Dwivedi et al., 2008).

(2) At the same time, in addition to accuracy, precision is equally important from a managerial viewpoint. First, the possible maximal future yield has to be estimated in order to reserve enough production capacity in advance. Second, the possible minimal yield of that product must also be estimated. If it can not reach a certain level before a given deadline, then the product is not competitive and capacity will be re-allocated to other products.

(3) Most existing approaches use a single approach/model. However, a semiconductor manufacturing factory is a typical group-decision-making environment, and many experts will gather to predict product yields in a collaborative manner. There have been some information or knowledge integration approaches, e.g., Ashish and Maluf (2009), Campbell (2009).

(4) Chen and Lin's study had a few shortcomings. First, the two-step approach is too complicated to apply because it involves many operations of various types. Second, there are many human-machine/system in-

Figure 3. Procedure of the proposed methodology

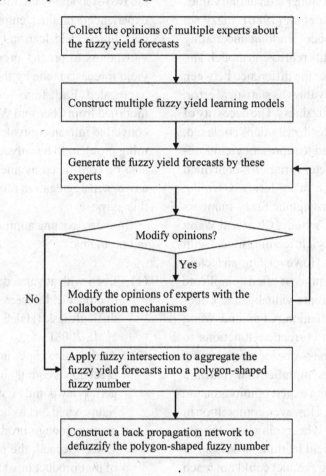

teractions that lack a convenient interface. Their approach is also impracticable if related operations are not automated (Russel & Yoon, 2009). To enhance the practicability, efficiency, and convenience of collaborative semiconductor yield forecasting, an online expert system can be constructed (Chen, 2008).

METHODOLOGY

Collect Multiple Experts' Opinions about Fuzzy Yield Forecasts

The procedure of the proposed methodology is shown in Figure 3. It consists of six steps which are described as follows. The first step is to collect expert opinions about fuzzy yield forecasts. In the proposed methodology, multiple experts (usually experienced product engineers) are asked to give their opinions about fuzzy yield forecasts. Their opinions are classified into four issues:

(1) Each expert's sensitivity to the uncertainty of a fuzzy yield forecast (o_k): A high sensitivity means the expert cares about even a very small value of forecasting error.

(2) Range of a fuzzy yield forecast desired by each expert (d_k): A narrower range is more precise. However, the probability that actual value falls outside the range is also higher.

(3) Required satisfaction level in fitting historical yield data (α_k). A higher satisfaction level

means historical data are more influential in forecasting the future yield.

(4) Relative importance of data outliers to each expert (m_k): An outlier is a yield higher or lower than expected. If an expert thinks that is normal, then s/he can choose a high relative importance for outliers.

To collect expert opinions, the following data or information are provided to each expert:

(1) Historical yield data of the product.
(2) Crisp yield learning curve.
(3) Four questions with different scales to collect expert opinions about the four issues.
(4) The instruction for answering each question.

Construct Multiple Fuzzy Yield Learning Models and Generate Fuzzy Yield Forecasts

The second step is to construct multiple fuzzy yield learning models. In the proposed methodology, experts construct fuzzy yield learning models to predict product yield. Fuzzy yield forecasts made by different experts need to be aggregated. Each fuzzy yield learning model is based on Chen and Wang's fuzzy yield learning model which is described as follows.

Unlike the use of symmetric TFNs in Watada et al. (1986), Chen and Wang used asymmetric parameters. Assume the asymptotic yield is $\tilde{Y}_0 = e^{(y_1, \ y_2, \ y_3)}$ (an asymmetric TFN after lognormalization) and learning constant is $\tilde{b} = (b_1, \ b_2, \ b_3)$ (an asymmetric TFN). Chen and Wang's fuzzy yield learning model is:

$$\tilde{Y}_t = \tilde{Y}_0 e^{-\frac{\tilde{b}}{t}+r(t)} = e^{(y_1-\frac{b_3}{t}, \ y_2-\frac{b_2}{t}, \ y_3-\frac{b_1}{t})+r(t)},$$

(1)

where $\tilde{Y}_t$ indicates the yield during period t; $r(t)$ is homoscedastic, serially non-correlated error term. The model is a fuzzy nonlinear equation, which can be transformed into the following fuzzy linear equation after lognormalization:

$$\ln \tilde{Y}_t = (y_1 - \frac{b_3}{t}, \quad y_2 - \frac{b_2}{t}, \quad y_3 - \frac{b_1}{t}) + r(t).$$

(2)

In Chen and Wang's study, for simplifying the calculation, fuzzy linear equation was fitted by solving a linear programming problem, according to Tanaka's fuzzy linear regression approach (Tanaka & Watada, 1988). There are other methods for converting fuzzy linear equation, e.g., Peters' fuzzy linear regression approach (Peters, 1994). For this reason, Chen and Lin (2008) adopted both conversion approaches, and constructed two non-linear programming models for the same purpose:

(Model I: Tanaka's viewpoint)

$$\text{Min } Z_1 = \sum_{t=1}^{T}(y_3 - \frac{b_1}{t} - y_1 + \frac{b_3}{t})^{o_k}$$

(3)

s.t.

$$\ln(Y_t) \geq y_1 - \frac{b_3}{t} + \alpha_k(y_2 - \frac{b_2}{t} - y_1 + \frac{b_3}{t}),$$

(4)

$$\ln(Y_t) \leq y_3 - \frac{b_1}{t} + \alpha_k(y_2 - \frac{b_2}{t} - y_3 + \frac{b_1}{t}),$$

(5)

$$0 \leq b_1 \leq b_2 \leq b_3,$$

(6)

$$y_1 \leq y_2 \leq y_3 \leq 0,$$

(7)

(Model II: Peters' viewpoint)

Table 1. Mapping between goals/constraints and the four issues

Issue	Inequality
Each expert's sensitivity to the uncertainty of a fuzzy yield forecast	(3) (9)
The range of a fuzzy yield forecast desired by each expert	(9)
The required satisfaction level in fitting the historical yield data	(4-5)(10-11) (12)(15)
The relative importance of the outliers of the data to each expert	(12)

$$\text{Max } Z_2 = \bar{\alpha} \tag{8}$$

s.t.

$$\sum_{t=1}^{T} (y_3 - \frac{b_1}{t} - y_1 + \frac{b_3}{t})^{o_k} \leq T \cdot d_k^{o_k}, \tag{9}$$

$$\ln(Y_t) \geq y_1 - \frac{b_3}{t} + \alpha_t (y_2 - \frac{b_2}{t} - y_1 + \frac{b_3}{t}), \tag{10}$$

$$\ln(Y_t) \leq y_3 - \frac{b_1}{t} + \alpha_t (y_2 - \frac{b_2}{t} - y_3 + \frac{b_1}{t}), \tag{11}$$

$$\bar{\alpha} = \sqrt[m_k]{\frac{\sum_{t=1}^{T} \alpha_t^{m_k}}{T}}, \tag{12}$$

$$0 \leq b_1 \leq b_2 \leq b_3, \tag{13}$$

$$y_1 \leq y_2 \leq y_3 \leq 0, \tag{14}$$

$$0 \leq \alpha_t \leq 1. \tag{15}$$

where o_k reflects the sensitivity of expert k to the uncertainty of fuzzy yield forecast; o_k ranges from 0 (not sensitive) to ∞ (extremely sensitive); α_k indicates the satisfaction level required by expert k; $0 \leq \alpha_k \leq 1$; d_k is the desired range of fuzzy

yield forecast by expert k; m_k represents the relative importance of outliers in fitting the yield model to expert k; $m_k \in R^+$. When $m_k = 1$, the relative importance of outliers is the highest and is equal to that of non-outliers; $k = 1 \sim n$ (the number of experts). Mapping between these goals/constraints and the four issues is shown in Table 1.

If there are n experts, then there will be at most $2n$ nonlinear programming problems to be solved. After solving all nonlinear programming problems, the optimal solution is used to construct a corresponding fuzzy yield learning model. Eventually, there will be at most $2n$ fuzzy yield learning models, each of which generates a fuzzy yield forecast at the third step.

Modify the Fuzzy Yield Learning Models with Collaboration Mechanisms

Forecasts by all experts, inconsistency among these forecasts, and the aggregation result will be gathered or calculated and then be provided to each expert for reference. After that, some experts modify their opinions. However, making direct and subjective changes to yield forecasts might violate the basic yield learning curve assumption. For this reason, in the proposed methodology the following collaboration mechanisms are provided:

Favoring mechanism: Assume the original opinions of two experts are denoted with (o_1, d_1, α_1, m_1, $Y_{0(1)}^*$, $\tilde{b}_{(1)}^*$) and (o_2, d_2, α_2, m_2, $Y_{0(2)}^*$, $\tilde{b}_{(2)}^*$), re-

Figure 4. The 5-point Likert scales for collaboration mechanisms

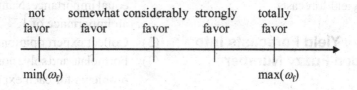

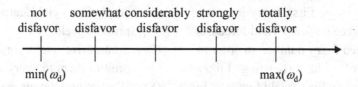

spectively. Expert #1 is favorable to expert #2's opinions. Then expert #1's opinions will be modified in the following way:

Expert #1's modified opinions = $(o_1 + \omega_f \cdot (o_2 - o_1), d_1 + \omega_f \cdot (d_2 - d_1), \alpha_1 + \omega_f \cdot (\alpha_2 - \alpha_1), m_1 + \omega_f \cdot (m_2 - m_1))$, (16)

$0 \leq \omega_f \leq 1$. According to the definitions of these parameters,

$$o_1 + \omega_f \cdot (o_2 - o_1) \geq 0, \quad (17)$$

$$d_1 + \omega_f \cdot (d_2 - d_1) \geq 0, \quad (18)$$

$$0 \leq \alpha_1 + \omega_f \cdot (\alpha_2 - \alpha_1) \leq 1, \quad (19)$$

$$m_1 + \omega_f \cdot (m_2 - m_1) \geq 0. \quad (20)$$

As a result,

$0 \leq \omega_f \leq \min(1, \text{if}(o_2 \leq o_1, -o_1 / (o_2 - o_1), \infty),$
$\text{if}(d_2 \leq d_1, -d_1 / (d_2 - d_1), \infty), \text{if}(\alpha_2 \geq \alpha_1, (1 - \alpha_1) / (\alpha_2 - \alpha_1), -\alpha_1 / (\alpha_2 - \alpha_1)), \text{if}(m_2 \leq m_1, -m_1 / (m_2 - m_1), \infty))$, (21)

where the function if(A, B, C) indicates "*If A is satisfied then the result is B; otherwise, the results is C*". Besides, a 5-point Likert scale with linguistic terms is provided for expert #1 to choose from (see Figure 4).

Disfavoring mechanism: Conversely, if expert #1 disfavors expert #2' opinions, then expert #1's opinions will be modified in the following way:

Expert #1's modified opinions = $(o_1 - \omega_d \cdot (o_2 - o_1), d_1 - \omega_d \cdot (d_2 - d_1), \alpha_1 - \omega_d \cdot (\alpha_2 - \alpha_1), m_1 - \omega_d \cdot (m_2 - m_1))$, (22)

$\omega_d \geq 0$. We can obtain the range of ω_d similarly:

$0 \leq \omega_f \leq \min(1, \text{if}(o_2 \geq o_1, o_1 / (o_2 - o_1), \infty), \text{if}(d_2 \geq d_1, d_1 / (d_2 - d_1), \infty), \text{if}(\alpha_2 \geq \alpha_1, -\alpha_1 / (\alpha_1 - \alpha_2), (1 - \alpha_1) / (\alpha_1 - \alpha_2)), \text{if}(m_2 \geq m_1, m_1 / (m_2 - m_1), \infty))$. (23)

Also, a 5-point Likert scale is provided for expert #1 with linguistic terms to choose from (see Figure 4).

Subsequently, fuzzy yield learning models are constructed again. Based on new fuzzy yield learning models, all fuzzy yield forecasts are re-generated. Then, a two-step mechanism is applied to aggregate fuzzy yield forecasts.

Aggregate Fuzzy Yield Forecasts into a Polygon-shaped Fuzzy Number

The fifth step is to apply fuzzy intersection to aggregatee fuzzy yield forecasts into a polygon-shaped fuzzy number. The aggregation mechanism is composed of two steps. First, fuzzy intersection is applied to aggregate fuzzy yield forecasts into a polygon-shaped fuzzy number, in order to improve precision of yield forecasting. Fuzzy intersection aggregates n fuzzy yield forecasts in the following manner:

$$\mu_{I(\tilde{A}_1, \ \tilde{A}_2, \ \dots, \ \tilde{A}_n)}(x) = \min(\mu_{\tilde{A}_1}(x), \quad \mu_{\tilde{A}_2}(x), \quad \dots, \quad \mu_{\tilde{A}_n}(x)), \tag{24}$$

where $I(\tilde{A}_1, \quad \tilde{A}_2, \quad \dots, \quad \tilde{A}_n)$ indicates the fuzzy intersection of n fuzzy yield forecasts $\tilde{A}_1 \sim \tilde{A}_n$. If fuzzy yield forecasts are approximated with TFNs, then their fuzzy intersection is a polygon-shaped fuzzy number. Fuzzy intersection used in this study is the minimum T-norm. An example is provided in Figure 5, which is the fuzzy intersection of three fuzzy yield forecasts and has the following corners:

$$\{(x_i, \mu_{x_i})\} = \{(0.60, 0), (0.62, 0.66), ((0.68, 0.81), (1.00, 0)\}.$$

After finding out the corners of a polygon-shaped fuzzy number, we evaluate the importance of each corner. The importance of a corner is decided by the fuzzy yield learning models from which the corner was derived. The importance of a fuzzy yield learning model is equal to the expert's importance which is determined by the following procedure:

(1) In the beginning, all expert opinions are of equal importance. Namely, every expert has an importance of 1.
(2) Collect expert opinions on the four issues.
(3) Formulate and solve nonlinear programming problems for each expert.
(4) Build fuzzy yield learning models based on optimization results.
(5) Correct fuzzy yield learning models.
(6) Apply fuzzy yield learning models to predict product yield.
(7) Summarize yield forecasting results and present them to every expert.
(8) If an expert favors another expert's yield forecasting results, then add 0.5 to the importance of the latter.

The output of this step is a polygon-shaped fuzzy number that specifies the range of yield forecast. However, in practical applications a crisp yield forecast is usually required. Therefore, a crisp yield forecast has to be generated from the polygon-shaped fuzzy number. To this purpose, a back propagation network is applied, because theoretically a well-trained back propagation network (without being stuck in a local minima) with a good selected topology can successfully map any complex distribution.

Defuzzify the Polygon-shaped Fuzzy Number

The final step is to construct a back propagation network to defuzzify the polygon-shaped fuzzy number. The configuration of the back propagation network is established as follows:

(1) Inputs: $2m+1$ parameters including the m corners of the polygon-shaped fuzzy number, membership function values of these corners, and period (see Figure 6). All input parameters have to be normalized.
(2) Single hidden layer: Generally speaking, one or two hidden layers are more beneficial for

Figure 5. Fuzzy intersection result

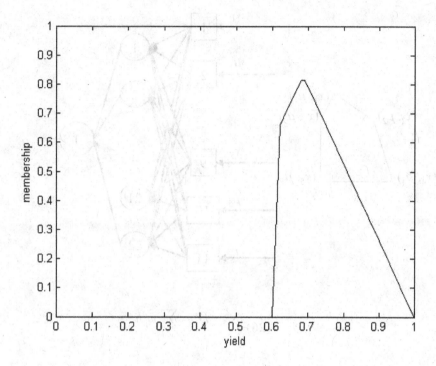

the convergence property of a back propagation network.

(3) Number of neurons in the hidden layer, which is chosen from 1~4m+2 according to a preliminary analysis, considering both effectiveness (forecasting accuracy) and efficiency (execution time).

(4) Output: crisp yield forecast.

(5) Network learning rule: Delta rule.

(6) Transformation function: Sigmoid function,

$$f(x) = \frac{1}{1 + e^{-x}}. \tag{25}$$

(7) Learning rate (η): 0.01~1.0.

(8) Batch learning.

(9) Number of epochs per replication: 60000.

(10) Number of initial conditions/replications: 1000. Because the performance of a back propagation network is sensitive to initial condition, training or testing will be repeated many times under different initial conditions that are randomly generated. Among the results, the best one is chosen for subsequent analyses.

(11) Training policy: The times of adopting the data of a corner in training are proportional to its importance.

Next we describe the procedure for determining parameter values. Every polygon-shaped fuzzy number fed into the back propagation network is called an example. The number of examples is decided by the number of time periods from which historical yield data were collected. A portion of examples is used as "training examples" into the back propagation network to determine parameter values. Two phases are involved in training. First, in the forward phase, inputs are multiplied with weights, summated, and transferred to the hidden layer.

Figure 6. Architecture of the back propagation network defuzzifier

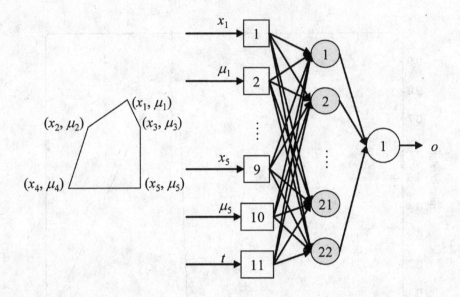

$$h_l = \frac{1}{1 + e^{-n_l^h}}, \tag{26}$$

where

$$n_l^h = I_l^h - \theta_l^h, \tag{27}$$

$$I_l^h = \sum_{\text{all } i} w_{il}^h x_i. \tag{28}$$

h_l's are also transferred to the output layer with the same procedure. Finally, the output of BPN is generated as:

$$o = \frac{1}{1 + e^{-n^o}}, \tag{29}$$

where

$$n^o = I^o - \theta^o, \tag{30}$$

$$I^o = \sum_{\text{all } l} w_l^o h_l. \tag{31}$$

Then the output o (i.e., the yield forecast F_i) is compared with actual yield A_i, for which RMSE is calculated:

$$\text{RMSE} = \sqrt{\frac{\sum_{i=1}^{n}(F_i - A_i)^2}{n}}. \tag{32}$$

Second, in the backward phase, the deviation between o and a is propagated backward, and the error terms of neurons in output and hidden layers can be calculated respectively as:

$$\delta^o = o(1-o)(a-o), \tag{33}$$

$$\delta_l^h = h_l(1-h_l)w_l^o\delta^o. \tag{34}$$

Based on this, adjustments that need to be made to connection weights and thresholds can be obtained as:

$$\Delta w_l^o = \eta \delta^o h_l, \tag{35}$$

$$\Delta w_{il}^h = \eta \delta_l^h x_i, \tag{36}$$

$$\Delta \theta^o = -\eta \delta^o, \tag{37}$$

$$\Delta \theta_l^h = -\eta \delta_l^h. \tag{38}$$

To accelerate convergence, a momentum can be added. For example,

$$\Delta w_l^o = \eta \delta^o h_l + \alpha(w_l^o(t) - w_l^o(t-1)). \tag{39}$$

Theoretically, network-learning stops when RMSE falls below a pre-specified level, or when improvement in RMSE becomes negligible with more epochs, or after a large number of epochs have been run. Then the remaining portion of examples in each category is used as "test examples" and fed into the back propagation network to once again evaluate the accuracy of network, which is also measured with RMSE. Finally, the back propagation network can be applied to defuzzify a polygon-shaped fuzzy number.

EXPERIMENTAL RESULTS AND DISCUSSION

To evaluate the advantages and/or disadvantages of the proposed methodology and to make comparison with some existing approaches – Gruber's general yield model (indicated with 'G'), Chen and Wang's fuzzy yield learning model (indicated with 'CW'), and Chen and Lin's approach (indicated with 'CL'), they were applied to the data of two practical cases of random access memory products in a real semiconductor manufacturing factory located in Hsinchu Science Park, Hsinchu, Taiwan, R.O.C. Collected yield data are sum-

Table 2. Collected yield data

	Product #1	Product #2
1	90%	80%
2	-	81%
3	88%	84%
4	88%	85%
5	81%	82%
6	85%	87%
7	85%	88%
8	83%	88%

marized in Table 2. Product specifications and details are not shown for confidentiality reasons.

Three experts were asked to submit their opinions on fuzzy yield forecasts. The results are shown in Table 3. These experts' opinions were considered unequally important. To determine the relative importance of each expert's opinions, the mutual assessment procedure established in Chen (2008) was applied. The results are also shown in Table 3. For either product there were six nonlinear programming problems to be solved. From the optimization result of each nonlinear programming problem, a corresponding fuzzy yield learning model was constructed. The parameters of all fuzzy yield learning models are summarized in Table 4. All six fuzzy yield learning models of a product were applied to forecast product yield, and then forecasting results were summarized and presented to all experts.

Subsequently, some experts applied the collaboration mechanisms to modify their original opinions. The process and results are summarized in Table 5. All fuzzy yield learning models were constructed again. Based on new fuzzy yield learning models, all fuzzy yield forecasts were re-generated (see Table 6).

After that, the fuzzy intersection of forecasting results is obtained, which was a polygon-shaped fuzzy number for each period. An example is given in Figure 7. We noticed that after applying collaboration mechanisms, the region of searching

Table 3. Three experts' opinions

Expert #	o_k	α_k	m_k	d_k	Importance
1	5	0.65	5	0.5	2
2	5	0.75	5	0.5	1
3	2	0.50	2	0.2	2

Table 4. Parameters in all fuzzy yield learning models

Product #	Model #	y_1	y_2	y_3	b_1	b_2	b_3
1	1I	-0.42	-0.10	-0.10	0.00	0.00	0.00
	1II	-0.52	-0.12	-0.02	0.00	0.00	0.00
	2I	-0.54	-0.10	-0.10	0.00	0.00	0.00
	2II	-0.52	-0.12	-0.02	0.00	0.00	0.00
	3I	-0.32	-0.10	-0.10	0.00	0.00	0.00
	3II	-0.28	-0.12	-0.08	0.00	0.00	0.00
2	1I	-0.28	-0.12	-0.11	0.10	0.10	0.10
	1II	-0.20	-0.20	-0.00	0.00	0.02	0.06
	2I	-0.35	-0.12	-0.11	0.10	0.10	0.10
	2II	-0.20	-0.20	-0.00	0.00	0.02	0.06
	3I	-0.23	-0.12	-0.11	0.10	0.10	0.10
	3II	-0.19	-0.19	-0.00	0.01	0.04	0.04

for actual yield did shrink, which was believed to be beneficial to forecasting accuracy and precision.

The data of the corners of all polygon-shaped fuzzy numbers, i.e. aggregated fuzzy yield forecasts of all periods, were used to train and test the back propagation network defuzzifier. An 8-fold cross-validation was adopted because of the limited sample size. This allows for more data (7/8 of the sample size) for training and less data (1/8 of the sample size) for testing the network. Finally, the back propagation network is applied to defuzzify a polygon-shaped fuzzy number input to the network to generate the representative value, i.e., crisp yield forecast.

In Chen and Wang's approach, the satisfaction level was given by the average of experts' values. The defuzzification approach applied in

Chen and Wang's approach was center-of-gravity (COG) (Liu, 2007).

Forecasting precision is measured with the average range of fuzzy yield forecasts, while forecasting accuracy is measured in terms of mean absolute percentage error (MAPE):

$$\text{MAPE} = \frac{\sum_{i=1}^{n} |F_i - A_i| / A_i}{n}, \qquad (40)$$

where F_i and A_i denote the i-th forecast and actual value, respectively; $i = 1 \sim n$. The performances achieved by applying different approaches were recorded and compared in Tables 7 and 8. Gruber's general yield learning model was adopted as the comparison basis in evaluating forecasting accuracy, while Chen and Wang's approach was compared in the precision respect. The percent-

Table 5. Application of collaboration mechanisms

Iteration #	1	2	3
Collaboration mechanism	Expert #3 somewhat disfavors expert #2	Expert #2 strongly favors expert #1	Expert #3 somewhat disfavors expert #1
Interval of ω_f or ω_d	[0, 0.67]	[0, 1]	[0, 0.43]
Chosen value of ω_f or ω_d	0.17	0.75	0.11
Updated opinions	$o_3 = 1.5$ $d_3 = 0.46$ $a_3 = 1.5$ $m_3 = 0.15$	$o_2 = 5$ $d_2 = 0.68$ $a_2 = 5$ $m_2 = 0.5$	$o_3 = 1.13$ $d_3 = 0.44$ $a_3 = 1.13$ $m_3 = 0.11$

Table 6. Parameters in modified fuzzy yield learning models

Product #	Model #	y_1	y_2	y_3	b_1	b_2	b_3
1	1I	-0.42	-0.10	-0.10	0.00	0.00	0.00
	1II	-0.52	-0.12	-0.02	0.00	0.00	0.00
	2I	-0.44	-0.10	-0.10	0.00	0.00	0.00
	2II	-0.60	-0.10	-0.10	0.00	0.00	0.00
	3I	-0.30	-0.10	-0.10	0.00	0.00	0.00
	3II	-0.21	-0.10	-0.10	0.00	0.00	0.00
2	1I	-0.28	-0.12	-0.11	0.10	0.10	0.10
	1II	-0.20	-0.20	-0.00	0.00	0.02	0.06
	2I	-0.29	-0.12	-0.11	0.10	0.10	0.10
	2II	-0.20	-0.20	-0.00	0.00	0.02	0.06
	3I	-0.22	-0.12	-0.11	0.10	0.10	0.10
	3II	-0.19	-0.19	-0.08	0.04	0.04	0.04

age of improvement over the comparison basis is enclosed in parentheses following the performance measure. Based on experimental results, we found:

(1) The forecasting accuracy (measured in terms of MAPE) of the proposed approach, was significantly better than those of the other approaches, achieving on average a 80% reduction in MAPE over the comparison basis – Gruber's approach. The average improvement over Chen and Wang's approach was 35%. Compared with Chen and Lin's approach, the superiority of the proposed methodology in accuracy was about 3%.

(2) At the same time, the forecasting precision (measured using the average range) of the proposed approach was also significantly better than those of the other fuzzy approaches, achieving an average of 58% reduction in the average range over the comparison basis – Chen and Wang's approach.

(3) The effects of collaboration mechanisms were most obviously revealed with the fact that the proposed methodology outperformed Chen and Lin's approach by 14% in precision.

(4) In order to consider both accuracy and precision, MAPEs and the average ranges by all approaches were compared simultaneously,

Figure 7. Shrinkage in search region

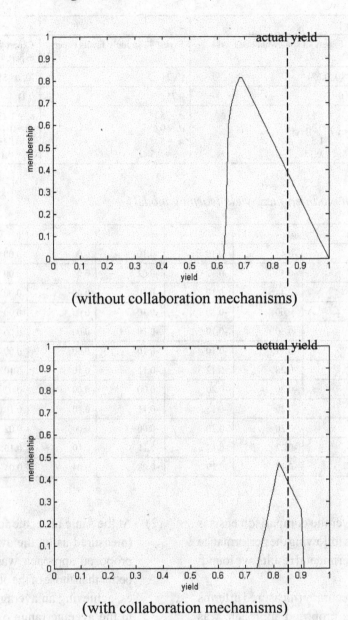

(without collaboration mechanisms)

(with collaboration mechanisms)

Table 7. Comparison of precision (the average ranges) of various approaches

Product #	G	CW	CL	The proposed methodology
1	-	0.21	0.15 (-29%)	0.09 (-57%)
2	-	0.12	0.05 (-58%)	0.05 (-58%)

Table 8. Comparison of accuracy (MAPEs) of various approaches

Product #	G	CW	CL	The proposed methodology
1	5.9%	3.0% (-49%)	2.0% (-66%)	1.9% (-68%)
2	4.3%	2.6% (-40%)	0.5% (-88%)	0.4% (-91%)

which supported the optimality of the proposed methodology because it dominated all other approaches.

CONCLUSION AND IMPLICATIONS FOR FUTURE RESEARCH

Yield forecasting is a very important task for a foundry. To further enhance the effectiveness of semiconductor yield forecasting, a fuzzy-neural approach with collaboration mechanisms is proposed in this study. The proposed methodology is modified from Chen and Lin's approach by incorporating two collaboration mechanisms: favoring mechanism and disfavoring mechanism. The former helps to achieve the consensus among multiple experts to avoid the missing of actual yield, while the latter shrinks the search region to increase the probability of finding out actual yield.

To prove the usefulness of the proposed methodology, some real cases were investigated. According to analysis results, both precision (measured with the average range) and accuracy (measured in terms of MAPE) of yield forecasting were improved significantly.

More sophisticated opinion aggregation mechanisms could be developed in future studies. At the same time, the proposed methodology should be applied to different cases to further evaluate its effectiveness. Finally, since the proposed methodology is a general approach, it can be easily applied to other fields.

REFERENCES

Ashish, N., & Maluf, D. A. (2009). Intelligent information integration: reclaiming the intelligence. *International Journal of Intelligent Information Technologies*, 5(3), 55–83.

Campbell, M. J. (2009). KStore: a dynamic meta-knowledge repository for intelligent BI. *International Journal of Intelligent Information Technologies*, 5(3), 68–80.

Chen, T. (2007a). A fuzzy logic approach for incorporating the effects of managerial actions on semiconductor yield learning. In *Proceedings of 2007 International Conference on Machine Learning and Cybernetics*.

Chen, T. (2007b). Evaluating the mid-term competitiveness of a product in a semiconductor fabrication factory with a systematic procedure. *Computers & Industrial Engineering*, 53, 499–513. doi:10.1016/j.cie.2007.05.008

Chen, T. (2008). An online collaborative semiconductor yield forecasting system. *Expert Systems with Applications*, 36(3), 5830–5843. doi:10.1016/j.eswa.2008.07.058

Chen, T., & Lin, Y.-C. (2008). A fuzzy-neural system incorporating unequally important expert opinions for semiconductor yield forecasting. *International Journal of Uncertainty, Fuzziness, and Knowledge-based Systems*, 16(1), 35–58. doi:10.1142/S0218488508005030

Chen, T., & Wang, M.-J. J. (1999). A fuzzy set approach for yield learning modeling in wafer manufacturing. *IEEE Transactions on Semiconductor Manufacturing, 12*(2), 252–258. doi:10.1109/66.762883

Chen, T., & Wang, Y. C. (2009). A fuzzy set approach for evaluating and enhancing the mid-term competitiveness of a semiconductor factory. *Fuzzy Sets and Systems, 160*, 569–585. doi:10.1016/j.fss.2008.06.006

Dwivedi, S., Huang, S. H., Shi, J., & VerDuin, W. H. (2008). Yield prediction for seamless tubing processes: a computational intelligence approach. *International Journal of Advanced Manufacturing Technology, 37*, 314–322. doi:10.1007/s00170-007-0964-5

Gruber, H. (1984). *Learning and Strategic Product Innovation: Theory and Evidence for the Semiconductor Industry*. Amsterdam: Elsevier.

Haller, M., Peikert, A., & Thoma, J. (2003). Cycle time management during production ramp-up. *Robotics and Computer-integrated Manufacturing, 19*, 183–188. doi:10.1016/S0736-5845(02)00078-9

Hsieh, K. L., & Tong, L. I. (2006). Manufacturing performance evaluation for IC products. *International Journal of Advanced Manufacturing Technology, 28*, 610–617. doi:10.1007/s00170-004-2382-2

Li, T.-S., Huang, C.-L., & Wu, Z.-Y. (2006). Data mining using genetic programming for construction of a semiconductor manufacturing yield rate prediction system. *International Journal of Advanced Manufacturing Technology, 17*, 355–361.

Lin, C. T., Chang, C. W., & Chen, C. B. (2006). Relative control philosophy – balance and continual change for forecasting abnormal quality characteristics in a silicon wafer slicing process. *International Journal of Advanced Manufacturing Technology, 26*, 1109–1114. doi:10.1007/s00170-004-2067-x

Liu, X. (2007). Parameterized defuzzification with maximum entropy weighting function - another view of the weighting function expectation method. *Mathematical and Computer Modelling, 45*, 177–188. doi:10.1016/j.mcm.2006.04.014

Majd, S., & Pindyck, R. S. (1989). The learning curve and optimal production under uncertainty. *The Rand Journal of Economics, 20*(3), 331–343. doi:10.2307/2555574

Mazzola, J. B., & McCardle, K. F. (1995). A Bayesian approach to managing learning-curve uncertainty. *Management Science, 42*(5), 680–692. doi:10.1287/mnsc.42.5.680

Peters, G. (1994). Fuzzy linear regression with fuzzy intervals. *Fuzzy Sets and Systems, 63*, 45–55. doi:10.1016/0165-0114(94)90144-9

Russell, S., & Yoon, V. Y. (2009). Agents, availability awareness, and decision making. *International Journal of Intelligent Information Technologies, 5*(4), 53–70.

Shimada, Y., & Sakurai, K. (2003). A new accurate yield prediction method for system-LSI embedded memories. *IEEE Transactions on Semiconductor Manufacturing, 16*(3), 436–445. doi:10.1109/TSM.2003.815636

Spence, A. M. (1981). The learning curve and competition. *The Bell Journal of Economics, 12*, 49–70. doi:10.2307/3003508

Tanaka, H., & Watada, J. (1988). Possibilistic linear systems and their application to the linear regression model. *Fuzzy Sets and Systems, 272,* 275–289. doi:10.1016/0165-0114(88)90054-1

Tong, L.-I., Wang, C. H., & Chen, D. L. (2007). Development of a new cluster index for wafer defects. *International Journal of Advanced Manufacturing Technology, 31,* 705–715. doi:10.1007/s00170-005-0240-5

Watada, J., Tanaka, H., & Shimomura, T. (1986). Identification of learning curve based on possibilistic concepts. In *Applications of Fuzzy Set Theory in Human Factors.* Amsterdam: Elsevier Science.

This work was previously published in International Journal of Intelligent Information Technologies, Volume 6, Issue 3, edited by Vijayan Sugumaran, pp. 17-33, copyright 2010 by IGI Publishing (an imprint of IGI Global).

Chapter 11
A Semantic-Enabled Middleware for Citizen-Centric E-Government Services

Ivo José Garcia dos Santos
UNICAMP, Brazil

Edmundo Roberto Mauro Madeira
UNICAMP, Brazil

ABSTRACT

Research efforts toward effective e-Government infrastructures have gained momentum, motivated mainly by increasing demands to improve citizen participation in public processes, promote social e-Inclusion, and reduce bureaucracy. One of the biggest challenges is providing effective techniques to handle the inherent heterogeneity of the systems and processes involved, making them interoperable. This paper presents a semantically enriched middleware for citizen-oriented e-Government services (CoGPlat), which facilitates the development and operation of new e-Government applications with higher levels of dynamism. It introduces the use of composition techniques based on semantic descriptions and ontologies. Requirements like autonomy, privacy and traceability are handled by applying policies that govern the interactions among services.

INTRODUCTION

The demands for the creation of mechanisms to increase the transparency of public administration processes have dramatically increased over the recent years (Watson & Mundy, 2001).

DOI: 10.4018/978-1-4666-0158-1.ch011

They represent a requirement for every government identified since the origins of the modern democracies: Thomas Jefferson once wrote that "whenever the people are well-informed, they can be trusted with their own government" (Jefferson, 1789). According to a UN (United Nations) recent report, the "strategic and meaningful application of Information and Communication Technologies for the purpose of improving the efficiency, transparency, accountability and accessibility of government is possible if the ultimate objective of e-government is to promote social inclusion" (Ahmed, 2006).

In order to fulfill these demands some important technical challenges must be handled. The first one is to promote interoperability, to face the heterogeneity of the information systems throughout the government entities and their partners. A higher level coordination mechanism to mediate and facilitate the interactions among the administrative processes may be required when providing composite inter-organizational citizen-centric services. Reusability, openness, compliance to the *de-facto* standards and scalability characteristics are also fundamental aspects that all e-Government platforms should seriously consider. If on one hand the adoption of SOA-based (Service-Oriented Architecture) approaches appears as a solution to the interoperability demands, on the other it introduces further challenges such as how to successfully describe the services, how to compose them as dynamically as possible and also how to mediate (or not) their interactions. Additional concerns include privacy, trust, autonomy and adequate identity management.

These challenges are similar – but go beyond – the ones found in the domain of enterprise applications, especially with respect to transparency, flexibility and interoperability requirements. According to Davies et al. (2007) these differences can be classified into the following categories: *regulatory aspects* such as privacy protection, eligibility, identity management, anonymity, accessibility, adoption of standards and fast reaction to changes in the legislation; and *organizational aspects* such as intra- and inter-government collaboration demands, administrative services similarities throughout different agencies (reuse is possible and desirable) and knowledge management (legal, financial etc.).

The specific research objectives of this paper are: a) discuss mechanisms to improve the qual-

ity, efficiency and reach of public administration services by promoting technical and semantic interoperability; b) propose techniques to increase the transparency and dynamism of the government administrative processes; c) facilitate citizen participation, through electronic means, on the government decision-making processes; and d) help shift the focus of the public services from the bureaucratic procedures to the citizen. Considering these goals the most important contribution of this paper is the proposal of a semantically enriched middleware for e-Government services called *CoGPlat* (**C**itizen-**o**riented e-**G**overnment **Plat**form), a middleware which provides a set of functionalities that simplify the development and operation of citizen-centric applications. This paper also defines new strategies to dynamically compose Semantic Web Services and techniques to increase the transparency of public administration processes. Another important contribution is the introduction of a set of policies to mediate service compositions, providing different levels of autonomy, privacy, traceability and identity management.

CONCEPTS, TECHNOLOGIES AND LITERATURE REVIEW

This section introduces related concepts and technologies, as well as the state of the art on e-government literature.

Interoperability and Services

Interoperability, defined as "*the ability of two or more systems or components to exchange information and to use the information that has been exchanged*" (IEEE, 1990), is a fundamental requirement in the context of distributed and dynamic applications. A solution adopted by many systems is to follow a Service-Oriented Architecture (SOA) approach, where services running over heterogeneous systems interact and are used as building blocks for the construction of applications (Papazoglou & Georgakopoulos, 2003). A composite service can be regarded as a combination of activities, which may be either atomic or also composite services, invoked in a predefined order and executed as a whole (Fluegge et al., 2006). Two different execution models for composite services are commonly defined: *orchestration* and *choreography*. In an *orchestration* all interactions that are part of the process are described and then executed by an engine, which has control of the overall composition. In contrast, *choreographies* are more collaborative and less centralized, with only the public message exchanges considered relevant (Peltz, 2003; Ross-Talbot & Bharti, 2005).

The specification, enactment and management of composite e-services are topics studied in the *eFlow* project (Casati & Shan, 2001). Both adaptative characteristics and also strategies on how to implement dynamic service process modifications are discussed and classified into two categories: *ad hoc changes*, when modifications are applied to a single running process instance; and *bulk changes*, when modifications are collectively applied to a subset (or to all) the running instances of a service process. A broker-based architecture (*QBroker*) is proposed in (Yu et al., 2007) to facilitate the selection of services based on Quality-of-Service (QoS) criteria. The approach uses both a combinatorial and a graph model defining multiple QoS criteria, taking global constraints into account. The *VieDAME* project (Moser et al., 2008) proposes an approach to monitor composite services (BPEL processes) according to QoS attributes. It also introduces partner service replacement strategies that can be applied automatically at runtime without interrupting the system. In (Schäfer et al., 2008) techniques to perform advanced compensations of web services transactions are introduced. The strategy is based on forward recovery principles and on contracts. It defines, like our work (see later), the concept of *abstract service*, but with a different perspective: they work as management

units that invoke concrete services, replace them with compatible ones in case of failures and also process externally triggered compensations. In (Fluegge et al., 2006) a discussion is held about the criteria that can be used to identify the levels of dynamism and automatization in service compositions. The authors propose a strategy using different techniques to compose services dynamically, considering a Model Driven Architecture.

The Semantic Web

It has been widely identified that both the Web and traditional Web Services lack support to describe the semantics of data. To overcome this weakness, the **Semantic Web** (Berners-Lee et al., 2001) proposes a scenario where data becomes meaningful to machines and can be automatically processed and understood. In it, ontologies play a fundamental role in the definition of concepts used to annotate data (Medjahed, 2004). An ontology can be defined as a *formal*, *explicit* specification of a *shared conceptualization* (Gruber, 1993; Borst, 1997), where *conceptualization* refers to an abstraction of a domain that identifies its relevant concepts, and *shared* implies that these concepts are equally defined and understood (consensus) by the participants of that domain.

The RDF (*Resource Description Framework*) and RDF-Schema specifications represented the first W3C (World Wide Web Consortium) initiatives to model metadata related to Web resources. A successful example of an RDFS compatible ontology is the YAGO project (Suchanek et al., 2007), which contains 1 million entities and 5 million facts automatically extracted from *Wikipedia* and *WordNet* (Miller, 1995) using a combination of rule-based and heuristic methods. An attempt to enrich and clarify the semantics of concepts in ontologies based on the notions of identity, rigidity, and dependency is discussed in (Tun & Tojo, 2008). The current W3C standard for specifying ontologies on the Web is the OWL (*Web Ontology Language*), which extended RDF by augmenting its vocabulary with the inclusion, for instance, of new class relationships.

The possibility of applying a similar strategy to describe services semantically, opening the road towards their automatic discovery, invocation and composition, motivated the proposal of different approaches for the definition of what was baptized as the **Semantic Web Services** (SWS). The OWL-S language (*Semantic Markup for Web Services*), adopted in our work, combines a set of inter-related OWL ontologies to define terms used in service-oriented applications. Two other proposals are also relevant: the WSMO (*Web Services Modeling Ontology*) and SAWSDL (*Semantic Annotations for WSDL and XML Schema*), recently adopted as a W3C recommendation.

The markup and automated reasoning technology to describe, simulate, test, and verify compositions of Web services are discussed in Narayanan and McIlraith (2002). The authors define the semantics for a relevant subset of OWL-S in terms of a first-order logical language (*Situation Calculus*). With the semantics in hand, service descriptions are encoded in a Petri Net formalism. The system is then able to read OWL-S service descriptions and perform simulations, enactment and analyses. The use of advanced workflow and activity concepts in the composition of Web services is the proposal of Fileto et al. (2003). This approach, called POESIA (*Processes for Open-Ended Systems for Information Analysis*), is an open environment for developing Web applications using metadata and ontologies to describe data processing patterns developed by domain experts. In Küster et al. (2007), a strategy to integrate the tasks of automated service discovery, matchmaking and composition is presented, focusing on services with multiple connected effects. A derivation mechanism that allows the (semi-)automatic annotation of operation parameters starting from already annotated ones within service compositions is discussed in Belhajjame et al. (2008). The mediation of SWS compositions involving heterogeneous data is

handled using context information in the strategy proposed in Mrissa et al. (2007). An end-to-end model-driven approach to design WSMO-based services is investigated in Brambilla et al. (2007). In D'Aubeterre et al. (2009) the authors propose an agent-based e-Marketplace that uses multi-criteria decision making techniques to rank matches. A conceptual framework to analyze user interactions based on mental representations described in OWL and SWRL (Semantic Web Rule Language) is introduced in Thomas et al. (2009). Quality of Service (QoS) and cognitive parameters build a hybrid selection model for the selection of services in the strategy presented by Kumar and Mishra (2008).

E-Government

The domain of **electronic Government** (e-Government) includes the "set of all processes which serve decision-making and services in politics, government and administration and which use information and communication technologies" (KBSt, 2006). A more modern approach to e-Government is gaining momentum: the *citizen-centric government*, where citizens and businesses are considered customers of the public administration, so that their needs come first, rather than bureaucracy or other imperatives inside the government machine (GOV3, 2006; Lee et al., 2005; Marchionini et al., 2003). In this context, usually a government-wide service-oriented architecture is applied to implement a unified access point to all government informational and transactional services. The requirements imposed to such a platform go beyond those found in the e-Business world, especially with respect to flexibility, transparency and interoperability demands. According to Davies et al. (2007), these requirements "reflect the collective needs and ambitions of our society, expressed through a combination of legislation and public opinion".

Several research efforts in the e-Government domain can be found in the literature. For instance, a system which automatically generates Web services customized to citizens' needs and also to government laws and regulations is presented in Medjahed and Bouguettaya (2005). It proposes three levels of service customization: the *citizen* level, the *service* level and the *user interface* level. Ontology to describe e-Government services and operations is also introduced. An approach for the semi-automated design of data flows between Web Services that are semantically described using different ontologies and data representations is introduced in Barnickel et al. (2006), including a rule-based mechanism for user-transparent mediation between ontologies spanning multiple application domains. The potential benefits of adopting Semantic Web Services in the e-Government domain are discussed in Gugliotta et al. (2008) by analyzing motivations, requirements and expected results and illustrated through a reusable framework based on the IRS-III broker (Cabral et al., 2006).

CoGPlat: THE CITIZEN-ORIENTED E-GOV PLATFORM

The contributions we present in this paper are related to the *CoGPlat* (Citizen-oriented e-Government **Plat**form) project (Santos et al., 2005). *CoGPlat* is a middleware that supports the interaction and collaboration of *entities* (governmental offices, private companies, non-governmental organizations and service providers) and *citizens* in different public administration scenarios, ranging from the electronic delivery of integrated services to the support for participation in government decisions. *CoGPlat* is a service-oriented middleware - not an end-user application - and provides a set of generic services and facilities that can be used by different e-government applications and tools.

Middleware Infrastructure

The *CoGPlat* middleware infrastructure is composed of the following elements (Figure 1):

- The **Service Bus**, an interface between the middleware and the applications. All services provided by the platform core facilities are exposed to the applications through this interface;
- Four **core** facilities:
  1. The **Transparent Services Center**, responsible for dynamically building the service compositions according to the application requests;
  2. The **Metamodel Management Center**, which offers services and tools to manage the models, metamodels and ontologies used in the description of services, compositions, processes and entities;
  3. The **E-Governance and E-Democracy Center**, which delivers generic services that aim to increase citizen participation in the public administration and to facilitate the decision-making processes;
  4. The **Traceability and Auditing Center**, which offers services and tools to monitor running processes and also to audit processes that have already been concluded.
- The Service **Discovery and Execution Layer**, responsible for selecting the services that will participate in the compositions and also for interacting with these services during execution time;
- A set of **Support Services** which provides security, persistence, reliable messaging and transaction support to the processes running over the platform.

Figure 1. CoGPlat - general infrastructure

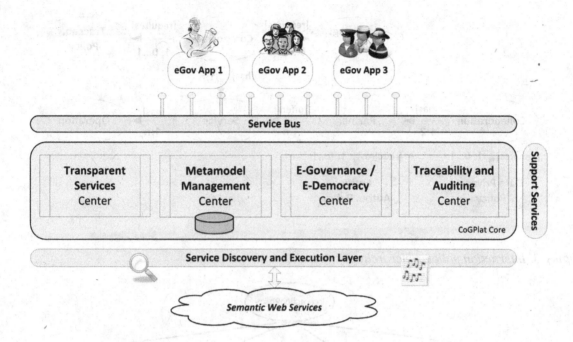

Collaborations Regulated through Interaction Policies

When composing e-Government services, the autonomy of the entities, the privacy and security of the data, the traceability of the processes and efficient identity management strategies are among the most important topics that need to be considered. In order to enable compositions that handle these topics, *CoGPlat* implements a set of *Interaction Policies*, first proposed and successfully applied in an e-Business scenario (Santos & Madeira, 2006) and now extended to match the e-Government application specificities.

The interaction policies are applied to regulate entity collaborations, where an *entity* is any governmental office, private company, nongovernmental organization or independent service provider which acts either as a service provider or consumer. We consider that two entities *collaborate* when both participate in the same composite service and there is at least one message

exchanged between them. The active policies are determinant in the dynamic construction of the composition flow and also during its execution. They are organized into the following categories:

- **Entity Autonomy Policies** (*CoGPlat x Entity*): determine the level of control the platform and the applications running over it may have over the internal operations of a composite service. The policies also impact the decision on which composition strategy to adopt. When one participant entity has control/supremacy over others, an orchestration approach can be applied. On the other hand when there is only collaboration among the entities (no administrative links or hierarchy and fully decentralized control), organizing a choreography might be more suitable;

- **Data Privacy Policies** (*Entity x Entity*): determine the trust levels on the interactions between two entities that participate

Figure 2. Compositions, services and policies in the ontology

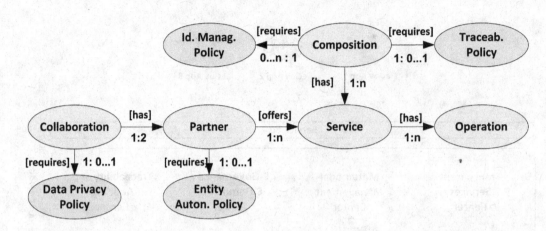

Figure 3. Interaction policies hierarchy

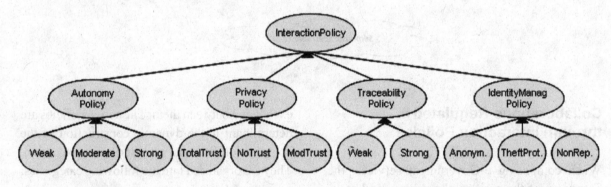

on the same composite service instance and also establish the privacy of information exchanged between these two entities;

- **Service Traceability Policies** (*CoGPlat x Service*): determine to what extent the internal operations of a service may/must be monitored/audited by the middleware. A straightforward example is a situation where a citizen wants to know details about the status of a given service he/she requested. In contrast, there are scenarios where a limitation on this ability is necessary and/or mandatory;

- **Identity Management Policies** (*Citizen/ Entity x CoGPlat*): establish where to provide mechanisms like anonymity, protection against identity theft and non-repudi-

ation for citizens and entities (when acting as service consumers).

Figure 2 presents an excerpt of *CoGPlat*'s ontology describing the relationships among policies, compositions and services. The Interaction Policies hierarchy is shown in Figure 3.

The Transparent Services Center

The **Transparent Services Center** (TSC) is the facility responsible for composing Web services as transparently and dynamically as possible. The service's client application needs no knowledge about the internals of a composite service - it knows only its semantic description. This introduces dynamism and a higher abstraction level when

Figure 4. The transparent services center infrastructure

Figure 4. The transparent services center infrastructure

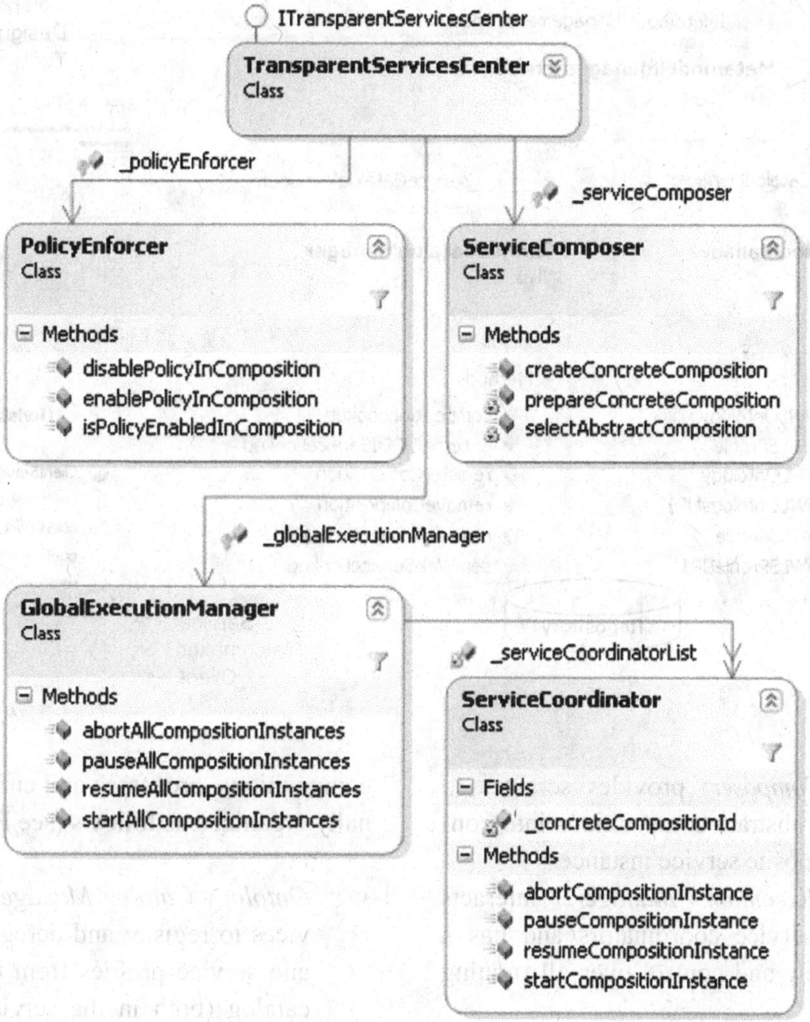

compared with what happens with the traditional Web services composition approach. Even though the application is not aware of the internal details of the composition, it should be also possible for it to transparently monitor the status of process execution.

Inside the middleware, the processes are created based on abstract compositions that were previously defined by a designer with the help of a domain expert. A composition is considered *abstract* when its activities are not bound to concrete services during design time. These activities represent service classes that are described using criteria such as **I**nputs, **O**utputs, **P**re-conditions and **E**ffects (*IOPE's*). The binding with concrete services is done at execution time, as we will show later in the paper.

The TSC is also responsible for managing the executions of processes, governed by the active interaction policies. Its internal infrastructure contains the following elements (see Figure 4 for the corresponding class diagram):

Figure 5. The Metamodel Management Center

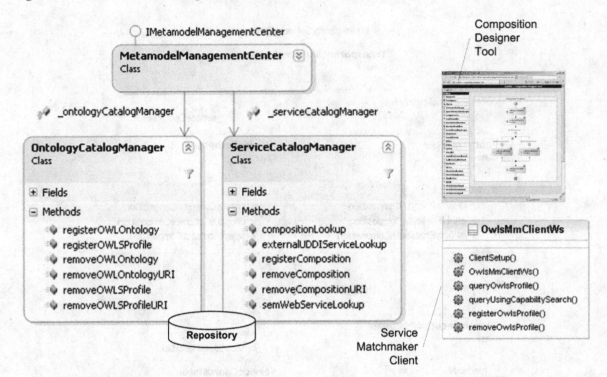

- *Service Composer*: provides services to transform abstract compositions into concrete composite service instances;
- *Global Execution Manager*: interacts with all service coordinators and has a global view and control over all running processes;
- *Service Coordinator*: controls the execution of one composite service instance;
- *Policy Enforcer*: verifies the correct application of the active interaction policies among the running composition instances and also offers a mechanism to enable or disable policies.

The Metamodel Management Center

The *Metamodel Management Center* (MMC) facilitates the management of models, metamodels and ontologies used in the description of services,

compositions, processes and entities. It is internally organized as follows (see Figure 5):

- *Ontology Catalog Manager*: provides services to register and deregister ontologies and service profiles from the middleware catalog (both in the service matchmaker knowledge base and in the repository);
- *Service Catalog Manager*: provides services to search, register and deregister compositions and services from the middleware catalog;
- *Composition Designer Tool*: web-based tool to create and edit abstract and concrete compositions that are stored in the middleware catalog and then delivered to the applications;
- *Service Matchmaker*: provides a semantic match between application service requests and the compositions and services registered in the middleware;

Figure 6. E-governance and e-democracy center

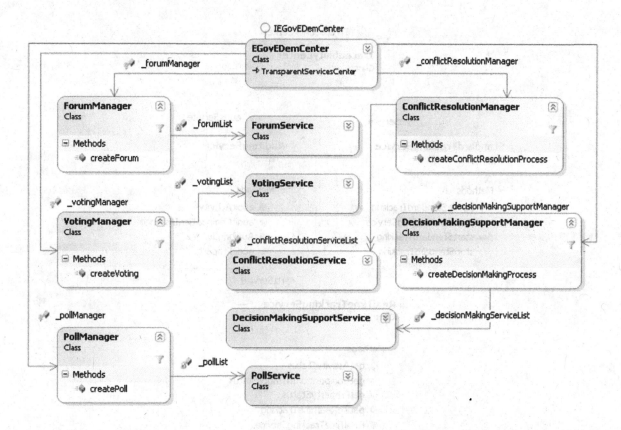

- *Repository*: provides persistence to the catalog (implemented using a traditional relational database).

The E-Governance and E-Democracy Center

The *E-Governance and E-Democracy Center* (EEC) provides generic services that can be used as part of the application compositions with the aim to increase citizen participation in the public administration and to facilitate and legitimate the decision-making processes. It provides the following service categories (see Figure 6 for the corresponding class diagram):

- *Forum*: service that allows citizen participation in a (mediated or free) discussion about some pre-defined topic;

- *Poll*: service to gather public opinion statistics;
- *Voting*: service that provides an abstract definition of an e-voting tool (must be further specialized according to the local legal requirements);
- *Decision Making Support*: service that, using some pre-defined criteria (e.g., poll results, legislation etc.), helps the public administrator in determining the political legitimacy of a decision;
- *Conflict Resolution*: service that tries to promote a friendly interaction between entity administrators when a conflict exists and needs to be solved before continuing the execution of a given process (e.g., interaction policy conflicts, legislation incompatibilities, conflicting poll results).

Figure 7. Traceability and auditing center

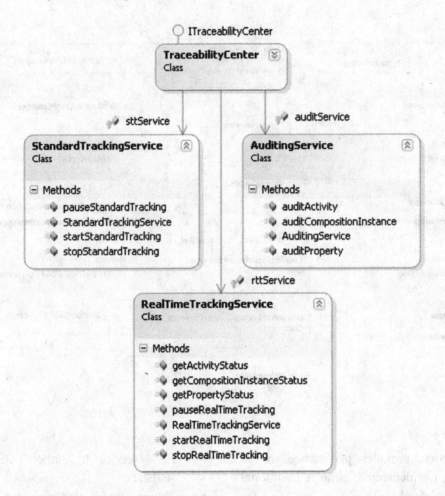

The Traceability and Auditing Center

Each of these services is defined as an abstract composition, using the same approach specified for the *Transparent Services* - note in the class diagram that the *EGovEDemCenter* class inherits from the *TransparentServicesCenter* class. When a request for a new service arrives, the concrete service is produced using the corresponding abstract definition (the strategy is discussed later in the paper). In order to support multiple service instances and to facilitate the coordination of these instances, each service category has an associated manager (*ForumManager*, *VotingManager*, *PollManager*, *ConflictResolutionManager* and *DecisionMakingSupportManager*).

The *Traceability and Auditing Center* (TAC) implements the necessary mechanisms to guarantee that the active traceability policies are respected during the execution of the composite services. Its internal infrastructure is composed of the following elements (see Figure 7 for the corresponding class diagram):

- The *Standard Tracking Service* collects all data from the generated tracking events, according to the active policy, and saves it into a repository;

Figure 8. Real-time status tracing

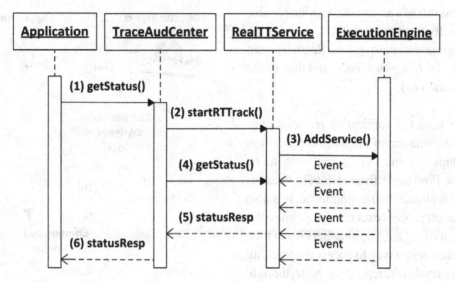

- The *Real-time Tracking Service* collects only representative data from the tracking events, also according to the active policy, but provides it in real-time to the platform client applications instead of saving it to a repository;
- The *Auditing Service* offers mechanisms to access tracking data of finished processes;
- The *Tracking Data Repository* stores the information generated by the tracking service events.

An abstract composition and individual abstract activities can be semantically annotated with the following *Service Traceability* policies:

- *Strong-traceability*: all events both at composition and at activity and service level are monitored. Customized traceability requirements can also be specified, for instance to monitor the behavior of an specific property or value throughout the instance execution;
- *Weak-traceability*: only composition level events are monitored. No customizations are allowed;

- *Zero-traceability*: There is no traceability at all. Indeed, if this policy is specified, there must be no trace (neither during nor after) of a given composition instance.

While a composition is running, it is possible monitor its status in real-time. This is achieved in the platform through the following steps (see Figure 8):

1. The Application calls the *getStatus()* operation from the Traceability and Auditing Center (*TraceAudCenter*) service;
2. The *TraceAudCenter* informs the Real Time Tracking Service (*RealTTService*) that a given composition instance should be tracked following a given policy;
3. The *RealTTService* subscribes to the tracking events generated by the WF Runtime Engine (*ExecutionEngine*) for the given instance. It uses a custom profile that implements the active traceability policy. From this moment, the events specified in the profile start to be delivered to the *RealTTService*;

4.   The *TraceAudCenter* asks the *RealTTService* for the status of a given composition (or also of an activity or property);

5.   The status response (*statusResp*) is sent back to the *TraceAudCenter* and then to the Application (6).

The next time the application requests real-time status information of the same composition instance, steps (2) and (3) do not need to be repeated (the flow starts from step (4)), because the instance is already being monitored. It is also possible to audit process execution any time after its conclusion using the Auditing Service, which provides a convenient way to access the tracking information stored in the repository. Note, though, that only information in accordance with the selected traceability policy will be persisted there.

Service Compositions in CoGPlat

Given the diversity and heterogeneity that can be found in public administration agencies, the integration of their services is a challenging task. The service composition process described next tries to shift to the middleware level the solution for the associated interoperability and integration problems. It includes two main processes: the definition of *abstract compositions* and the concrete creation of the *transparent services*. The abstract compositions describe the generic public processes that may run over the platform combining services from different agencies. No concrete binding is necessary at design time - actually only service classes, semantically annotated with IOPE's and Policies are included in the abstract composition flow.

The abstract compositions repository may be maintained/updated by a process designer/domain expert (or also by an application on their behalf) through special *CoGPlat* administrative services offered by the *Metamodel Management Center*. This process has the following steps (see Figure 9):

Figure 9. Defining a new abstract composition

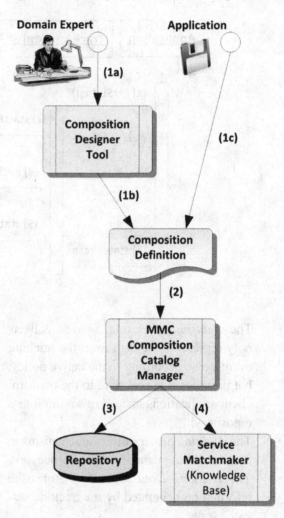

Figure 9. Defining a new abstract composition

1.   A domain expert uses the web-based composition designer tool to define the workflow associated with the abstract composition (1a). This tool exports the workflow definition as an XML-based document (using for instance the Windows Workflow Foundation XAML Format or WS-BPEL) (1b). Alternatively an application may provide the composition XML-based definition directly (1c);

2.   The abstract composition definition is received by the metamodel management center;

Figure 10. Composite service creation

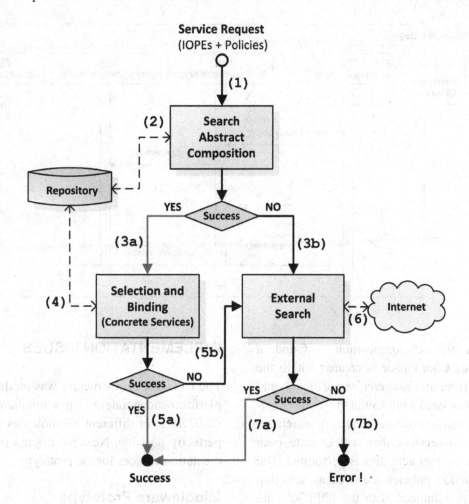

3. The metadata associated with the composition and the XAML abstract workflow description are stored in a repository (e.g. standard relational database);

4. The semantic service profile description (OWL-S), which includes the IOPE's of the service, is registered in the service matchmaker knowledge base.

The process to create concrete composite services based on the application requests has the following stages (see Figures 10 and 11):

*   An application sends a request (an OWL-S profile) to the *Transparent Services Center*

for a composite service (*TSC. ServiceComposer.createConcreteComposition()*). The request includes the IOPE's and the demanded interaction policies;

*   The *TSC Service Composer* uses the *Metamodel Management Center* to perform a search in the repository looking for an abstract composition that satisfies the application requirements (*MMC.ServiceCatalogManager.compositionLookup()*). The OWL-S matchmaker is queried to fulfill this task (*MMC.ServiceMatchmakerClient. queryOwlsProfile()*);

Figure 11. Composite service creation (UML sequence diagram)

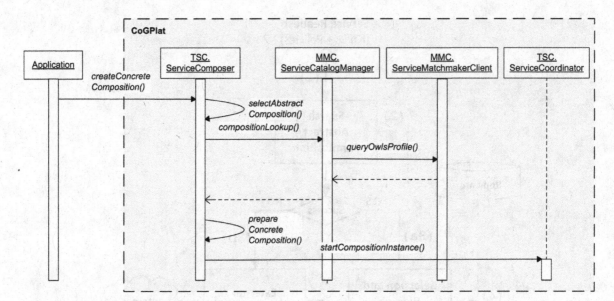

- If an abstract composition is found, a Service Coordinator is created within the TSC (*prepareConcreteComposition()*) and the associated workflow starts to run (*startCompositionInstance()* call). A search for concrete services that will execute each of its abstract activities is performed. The interaction policies are used as selection criteria combined with the IOPE's. If no services are found, a search for external services (not pre-registered in the platform) is tried;
- If a concrete composition was successfully built and executed, the results are returned to the calling application; if not, a search for an external service is tried within some trusted third party UDDI or semantic-enabled catalog.

The chances of success on the initial stages of the process of creation of a transparent composite service are directly related to the amount and diversity of abstract compositions registered in the platform.

IMPLEMENTATION ISSUES

The *CoGPlat* infrastructure was modeled to be platform-independent. An implementation of *CoGPlat* over different technologies would be perfectly possible. Next we discuss our implementation choices for the prototype.

Middleware Prototype

The *CoGPlat* middleware infrastructure was implemented with the support of the following technologies:

- The *Service Bus* exposes traditional Web Services (WSDL + SOAP/HTTP);
- The middleware core runs over the Microsoft .NET framework and is written in C\#;
- The matchmaker included in the *Metamodel Management Center* is based on OWLS-MX (Klusch et al., 2006), a JAVA/Jena based matchmaker that performs both semantic (OWL-S Profiles) and

syntactic matching between requisitions and services;

- The *Composition Designer Tool* is an extension of the *Atlas Workflow Designer* component (Flanders, 2006);
- The compositions are executed over the .NET 3.0 Windows Workflow Foundation (WF) runtime engine (Bukovics, 2007). The composite service definitions are based on the XML-based XAML format defined in the WF (WS-BPEL compositions are supported through the *BPEL for Windows Workflow Foundation* Microsoft add-on).

The WF offers native persistence mechanisms, facilitating the fault recovery process, and provides basic tracking services, used as a basis to implement the Traceability and Auditing Center functionalities. It also provides activities to call traditional Web Services, thus partially fulfilling *CoGPlat*'s composition process demands. To handle this WF limitation and considering that it supports dynamic updating (in execution time) of the execution plans through reflection mechanisms, new WF custom activities were implemented. They follow the service lookup strategy with support for semantic annotations (IOPE's and Policies) and dynamic web service binding and invocation.

The *InvokeTransparentService* activity presented in Figure 12 represents the basic building block in *CoGPlat*'s Compositions. It corresponds, for each individual concrete service, to the step (4) of the process previously described in Figure 10. Initially it receives as input annotations containing IOPE's and policy requirements and tries to find a suitable concrete service using the MMC semantic match services (*SemWServLookup* code activity) or a traditional UDDI lookup if not successful (*TraditionalWSUDDILookup* activity). Next, the compliance with the active interaction policies is checked (*VerifyPolicies/VerifyPolicies2*) and then the dynamic binding and invocation of the selected

concrete service is done through instances of the custom WF activities *DynamicWebServiceBind* and *DynamicWebServiceInvoke*.

CoGPlat Web Administrative Center

The *Web Administrative Center* is a web-based application that allows a domain administrator to interact with the middleware facilities and services. It offers the same services delivered to the middleware client applications, including the possibility of managing the repositories, requesting transparent services, monitoring and auditing processes, as well as designing new abstract compositions. Figure 13 presents a screenshot of this application.

Application Scenarios

We developed a prototypical application over *CoGPlat*, concerning *Civil Construction* processes, to evaluate its infrastructure. It implements the entire set of bureaucratic processes required to obtain an authorization to build houses, inspired in the Brazilian legislation. This scenario is considered dynamic because the selection of the concrete services that will be responsible for the actual activities is done at execution time according to IOPE's specified in the application request. Services may change, for instance, depending on the location of the building and also on the selected interaction policies. Two composite services are included in this example and accessed by the client application: the first is responsible for implementing the process to obtain an authorization to build the house and the second is responsible for the final authorization to move after the house is finished. The main steps of these interactions are (see Figure 14):

1. The application requests through the *CoGPlat Service Bus* the creation of a concrete composition that will handle the build

Figure 12. CoGPlat custom WF activity (InvokeTransparentService)

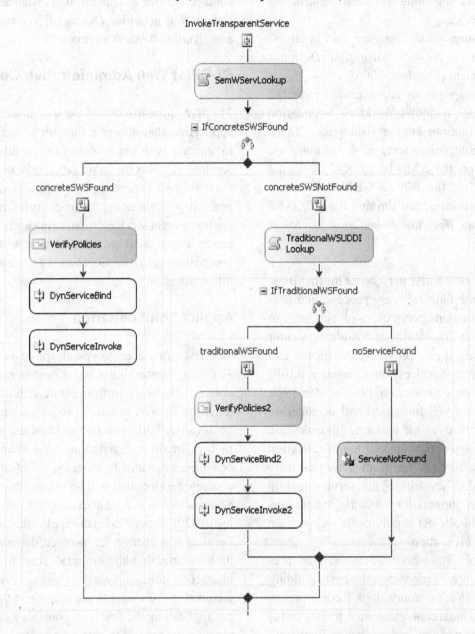

authorization process (using the *createConcreteComposition()* operation);

2. Internally (transparent to the application), *CoGPlat*'s facilities prepare the composite service following the overall strategy presented previously in the paper. As a result, the *BuildAuthorizationService* workflow is

selected and an instance thereof is created (shown in Figure 15);

3. The application, after receiving a notification that the composition is ready to run, calls the *startCompositionInstance()* operation to request its execution;

Figure 13. CoGPlat web administrative center screenshot

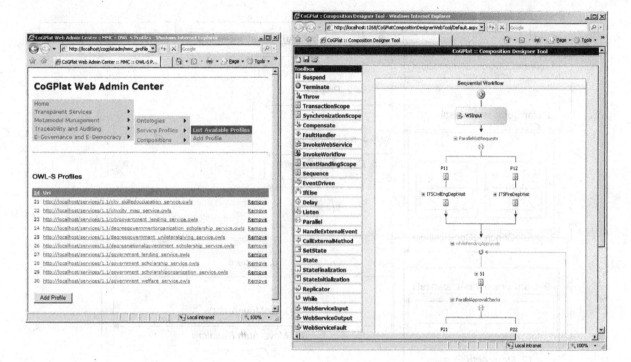

4. The composition execution is initiated through a call to the *reqBuildAuth()* operation exposed by the workflow;

5. The results are returned to the associated *ServiceCoordinator* and then back to the calling application (6);

7. The application now requests the creation of a concrete composition to handle the *move authorization* process. Note that this step will most likely happen a long time (months or even years) after the previous one. The result is an instance of the *MoveAuthorizationService* workflow (omitted for brevity). Steps (8-12) of Figure 14 show the interactions with the workflow.

It is important to note that the two abstract workflows were previously defined by a domain expert using the *Composition Designer Tool*. Next we illustrate the *BuildAuthorizationService* workflow, shown in Figure 15 using the WF notation. It performs the following activities:

- *WSInput*: input activity which defines that this workflow is accessed as a web service. Its input arguments are in conformance with the semantic descriptions defined in the associated OWL-S profile and registered in the MMC repository;

- *ITSProjectApprDept*: this is an instance of the *InvokeTransparentService* activity presented in Figure 12. It defines a call to a service provided by some project approval department. The service should be selected, according to the activity definition, at execution time based on the IOPE's;

- *checkRegionCategory (if-else)*: verifies whether the building address is part of a region regulated by some military organization (e.g., in Brazil, buildings close to the beach are under navy jurisdiction).

- *NonMilitaryRegion*: *ITSNeighbApproval Service*: if the region is not under military jurisdiction, a transparent service which manages a neighborhood approval

Figure 14. Application example

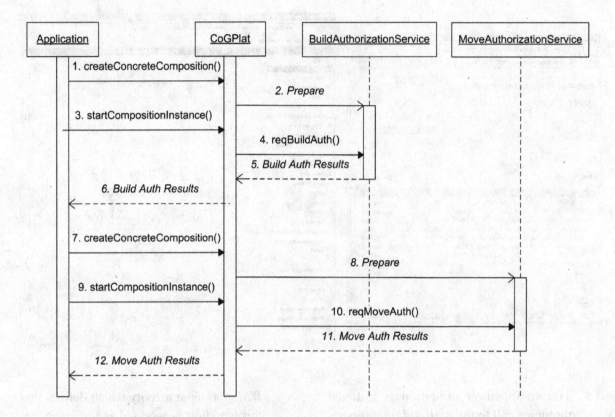

process is invoked (similar to what in the U.S. is called a *Public notice of action*), where comments or protests from the community concerning the proposed building plan may be collected and evaluated by a designated authority. One interesting alternative here is to select inside the transparent service activity another customized workflow (pre-defined by a domain expert) that relies on some of the services provided by *CoGPlat*'s *E-Governance and E-Democracy Center*;

- *MilitaryRegion*: *checkMilitaryRegion-Category (if-else)*: if the region is under military jurisdiction another check is performed to verify if it is under the army (e.g. close to an international border) or navy (e.g., close to the ocean) jurisdiction. Constructions in these areas are possible

with a special authorization from the corresponding entity and are subject to additional federal taxes;

- *BldgCloseToSecurityZone*: *ITSLocalArmy Authority / BldgCloseToOcean: ITSLocal NavyAuthority*: the corresponding local army or navy authority approval service is accessed (through an *InvokeTransparent Service* activity);

- *WSOutput*: activity associated with WSInput that exports the returning values.

Qualitative Evaluation

Based on the process to implement the civil construction scenario it was possible to observe that the application development efforts were mostly related with the user interaction mechanisms. The complexity usually associated with the definition

Figure 15. Abstract service example

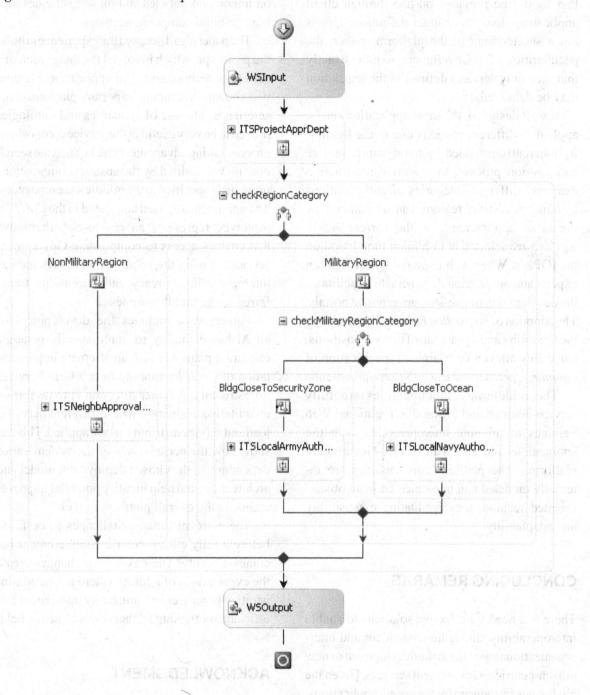

and execution of the composite public processes was transferred mostly to the middleware components.

Nevertheless, it is of utmost importance to remember that the success (or failure) of the dy-

namic composition processes is directly affected by the variety and coverage of the abstract compositions previously registered in the platform. The middleware administrators and the domain experts must guarantee that all public processes that should be provided on-line through client applications have an abstract definition. This is not a shortcoming of the platform; rather, the peculiarities of e-Government require exactly that, i.e., only services defined in the legislation may be delivered.

If well designed, the same application can be applied to different contexts due to the flexibility inherently provided by the dynamic service composition process. In the civil construction example, different categories of authorizations to build in distinct regions can be handled by the same application - as the corresponding services are selected at execution time based on the IOPE's. When well explored by the domain experts and application designers, this facilitates the development of one-stop government portals. The adoption of *Interaction Policies* also enhances the flexibility and dynamism of the compositions, since they allow a finer-grained specification of *autonomy*, *privacy* and *traceability* requirements.

The middleware functionalities are fully service-oriented and exposed as traditional Web Services to promote interoperability with the applications and also with other e-Government platforms. The platform core facilities are internally modeled and implemented in an object-oriented fashion, thus facilitating extensibility and adaptability.

CONCLUDING REMARKS

There is a need for effective solutions to enable interoperability among heterogeneous and inter-organizational systems in the development of new citizen-centric e-Government services. Given the challenges introduced by these new applications, we contribute in this paper proposing *CoGPlat* - a semantically-enriched and service-oriented middleware. Its main goal is to enable the collaboration among government entities, organizations and citizens in various public administration scenarios. We also contribute proposing a mechanism based on interaction policies and on semantic descriptions to build composite services.

The paper also discussed the experience to build the prototype, which involved the integration of a variety of technologies. An application example was shown, evidencing important platform characteristics. The use of semantics and ontologies proved to be very useful in the service composition process, taking advantage of the fact that the search domain was limited by the abstract compositions previously specified in the middleware repository. The approach proposed and tested in the *CoGPlat* prototype represents an end-to-end alternative that enables access to composite e-Government services, having the solutions for issues such as interoperability, privacy and traceability transferred to the middleware level.

Future work includes the development of an AI-based facility to automatically generate execution plans and also an alternate implementation of *CoGPlat* running over a Grid Services infrastructure. Another direction is to perform a quantitative evaluation where different network, load and service distributions are applied. This can show how the performance of the system varies depending on the chosen deployment model and architecture, and help identify potential improvements on the overall platform model.

There are still many challenges to be faced before a fully citizen-centric e-Government becomes a reality. The envisioned changes create the expectations of a future where public administration processes become really transparent and efficient, motivating further research in this field.

ACKNOWLEDGMENT

We would like to thank CAPES, CNPq and DAAD for financially supporting the project. Additional thanks to the Fraunhofer FOKUS Institute (Berlin, Germany).

REFERENCES

Ahmed, N. (2006). *An overview of e-participation models* (Tech. Rep.). United Nations: Department of Economic and Social Affairs.

Barnickel, N., Fluegge, M., & Schmidt, K.-U. (2006). Interoperability in egovernment through cross-ontology semantic web service composition. In *Proceedings of the Workshop Semantic Web for eGovernment / 3rd European Semantic Web Conference*, Budva, Montenegro.

Belhajjame, K., Embury, S. M., Paton, N. W., Stevens, R., & Goble, C. A. (2008). Automatic annotation of web services based on workflow definitions. *ACM Trans. Web*, *2*(2), 1–34. doi:10.1145/1346337.1346239

Berners-Lee, T., Hendler, J., & Lassila, O. (2001). The semantic web. *Scientific American*, *284*(5), 34–43. doi:10.1038/scientificamerican0501-34

Borst, W. N. (1997). *Construction of Engineering Ontologies*. Unpublished doctoral dissertation, University of Twente, Enschede, The Netherlands.

Brambilla, M., Ceri, S., Facca, F. M., Celino, I., Cerizza, D., & Valle, E. D. (2007). Model-driven design and development of semantic web service applications. *ACM Transactions on Internet Technology*, *8*(1), 3. doi:10.1145/1294148.1294151

Bukovics, B. (2007). *Pro WF: Windows Workflow in .NET 3.0*. New York: Apress.

Cabral, L., Domingue, J., Galizia, S., Gugliotta, A., Tanasescu, V., Pedrinaci, C., & Norton, B. (2006). Irs-iii: A broker for semantic web services based applications. In *5th International Semantic Web Conference (ISWC)* (LNCS 4273, pp. 201-214). Athens, GA: Springer.

Casati, F., & Shan, M. (2001). Dynamic and adaptive composition of e-services. *Information Systems*, *26*(3), 143–163. doi:10.1016/S0306-4379(01)00014-X

D'Aubeterre, F., Iyer, S., Ehrhardt, R., & Singh, R. (2009). Discovery Process in a B2B eMarketplace: A Semantic Matchmaking Approach. *International Journal of Intelligent Information Technologies*, *5*(4), 16–40.

Davies, J., Janowski, T., Ojo, A., & Shukla, A. (2007). Technological foundations of electronic governance. In *Proceedings of the ICEGOV '07: Proceedings of the 1st international conference on Theory and practice of electronic governance*, Macao, China (pp. 5-11). New York: ACM.

Fileto, R., Liu, L., Pu, C., Assad, E. D., & Medeiros, C. B. (2003). Poesia: An ontological workflow approach for composing web services in agriculture. *The VLDB Journal - The International Journal on Very Large Data Bases*, *12*(4), 352-367.

Flanders, J. (2006). *Atlas Workflow Designer*. http://www.masteringbiztalk.com/

Fluegge, M., Santos, I. J. G., Tizzo, N. P., & Madeira, E. R. M. (2006). Challenges and techniques on the road to dynamically compose web services. In *Proceedings of the ICWE '06: Proceedings of the 6th international conference on Web engineering*, Palo Alto, CA (pp. 40-47). New York: ACM Press.

GOV3. (2006). *Citizen Centric Government (White Paper)*. The GOV3 Foundation: Intel. Retrieved from www.intel.com/go/government.

Gruber, T. R. (1993). A translation approach to portable ontology specifications. *Knowledge Acquisition*, *5*, 199–220. doi:10.1006/knac.1993.1008

Gugliotta, A., Domingue, J., Cabral, L., Tanasescu, V., Galizia, S., & Davies, R. (2008). Deploying semantic web services-based applications in the e-government domain. *J. Data Semantics*, *10*, 96–132. doi:10.1007/978-3-540-77688-8_4

IEEE. (1990). *IEEE Standard Computer Dictionary: A Compilation of IEEE Standard Computer Glossaries*. Washington, DC: IEEE.

Jefferson, T. (1789). *Personal communication to R. Price.*

KBSt. (2006). *SAGA - Standards and Architectures for eGovernment Applications - Version 3.0.* Berlin: German Federal Ministry of Interior. Retrieved from www.kbst.bund.de/saga

Klusch, M., Fries, B., & Sycara, K. (2006). Automated semantic web service discovery with owls-mx. In *Proceedings of the 5th Intl. joint conference on Autonomous agents and multiagent systems (AAMAS)*, Hakodate, Japão (pp. 915-922). New York: ACM.

Kumar, S., & Mishra, R. B. (2008). A Hybrid Model for Service Selection in Semantic Web Service Composition. *International Journal of Intelligent Information Technologies, 4*(4), 55–69.

Küster, U., König-Ries, B., Stern, M., & Klein, M. (2007). Diane: an integrated approach to automated service discovery, matchmaking and composition. In *Proceedings of the 16th international conference on World Wide Web (WWW '07)*, Banff, Alberta, Canada (pp. 1033-1042). New York: ACM.

Lee, S. M., Tan, X., & Trimi, S. (2005). Current practices of leading e-government countries. *Communications of the ACM, 48*(10), 99–104. doi:10.1145/1089107.1089112

Marchionini, G., Samet, H., & Brandt, L. (2003). Digital government. *Communications of the ACM, 46*(1), 25–27.

Medjahed, B. (2004). *Semantic Web Enabled Composition of Web Services.* Unpublished doctoral dissertation, Virginia Polytechnic Institute and State University, Blacksburg, VA.

Medjahed, B., & Bouguettaya, A. (2005). Customized delivery of e-government web services. *IEEE Intelligent Systems, 20*(6), 77–84. doi:10.1109/MIS.2005.103

Miller, G. A. (1995). Wordnet: a lexical database for english. *Communications of the ACM, 38*(11), 39–41. doi:10.1145/219717.219748

Moser, O., Rosenberg, F., & Dustdar, S. (2008). Non-intrusive monitoring and service adaptation for ws-bpel. In *Proceeding of the 17th international conference on World Wide Web (WWW '08)*, Beijing, China (pp. 815-824). New York: ACM.

Mrissa, M., Ghedira, C., Benslimane, D., Maamar, Z., Rosenberg, F., & Dustdar, S. (2007). A context-based mediation approach to compose semantic web services. *ACM Transactions on Internet Technology, 8*(1), 4. doi:10.1145/1294148.1294152

Narayanan, S., & McIlraith, S. A. (2002). Simulation, verification and automated composition of web services. In *Proceedings of the 11th international conference on World Wide Web (WWW '02)*, Honolulu, HI (pp. 77-88). New York: ACM.

Papazoglou, M., & Georgakopoulos, D. (2003). Service-oriented computing. *Communications of the ACM, 46*(10), 25–28.

Peltz, C. (2003). Web services orchestration and choreography. *IEEE Computer, 36*(10), 46–52.

Ross-Talbot, S., & Bharti, N. (2005). *Dancing with Web Services: W3C chair talks choreography.* Retrieved from http://searchwebservices.techtarget.com/

Santos, I. J. G., & Madeira, E. R. M. (2006). Applying orchestration and choreography of web services on dynamic virtual marketplaces. *International Journal of Cooperative Information Systems, 15*(1), 57–85. doi:10.1142/S0218843006001281

Santos, I. J. G., Madeira, E. R. M., & Tschammer, V. (2005). Towards dynamic composition of e-government services - a policy-based approach. In *Proceedings of the 5th IFIP International Conference on e-Commerce, e-Business and e-Government (I3E)*, Poznan, Poland (Vol. 189, pp. 173-185). New York: Springer.

Schäfer, M., Dolog, P., & Nejdl, W. (2008). An environment for flexible advanced compensations of web service transactions. *ACM Trans. Web*, *2*(2), 1–36. doi:10.1145/1346337.1346242

Suchanek, F. M., Kasneci, G., & Weikum, G. (2007). Yago: a core of semantic knowledge. In *Proceedings of the 16th international conference on World Wide Web (WWW '07)*, Banff, Alberta, Canada (pp. 697-706). New York: ACM.

Thomas, M. A., Redmond, R. T., & Yoon, V. Y. (2009). Using Ontological Reasoning for an Adaptive E-Commerce Experience. *International Journal of Intelligent Information Technologies*, *5*(4), 41–52.

Tun, N. N., & Tojo, S. (2008). EnOntoModel: A Semantically-Enriched Model for Ontologies. *International Journal of Intelligent Information Technologies*, *4*(1), 1–30.

Watson, R. T., & Mundy, B. (2001). A strategic perspective of electronic democracy. *Communications of the ACM*, *44*(1), 27–30. doi:10.1145/357489.357499

Yu, T., Zhang, Y., & Lin, K.-J. (2007). Efficient algorithms for web services selection with end-to-end qos constraints. *ACM Trans. Web*, *1*(1), 6. doi:10.1145/1232722.1232728

This work was previously published in International Journal of Intelligent Information Technologies, Volume 6, Issue 3, edited by Vijayan Sugumaran, pp. 34-55, copyright 2010 by IGI Publishing (an imprint of IGI Global).

Chapter 12
Comparison of the Hybrid Credit Scoring Models Based on Various Classifiers

Fei-Long Chen
National Tsing Hua University, Taiwan

Feng-Chia Li
Jen-Teh Junior College and National Tsing Hua University, Taiwan

ABSTRACT

Credit scoring is an important topic for businesses and socio-economic establishments collecting huge amounts of data, with the intention of making the wrong decision obsolete. In this paper, the authors propose four approaches that combine four well-known classifiers, such as K-Nearest Neighbor (KNN), Support Vector Machine (SVM), Back-Propagation Network (BPN) and Extreme Learning Machine (ELM). These classifiers are used to find a suitable hybrid classifier combination featuring selection that retains sufficient information for classification purposes. In this regard, different credit scoring combinations are constructed by selecting features with four approaches and classifiers than would otherwise be chosen. Two credit data sets from the University of California, Irvine (UCI), are chosen to evaluate the accuracy of the various hybrid features selection models. In this paper, the procedures that are part of the proposed approaches are described and then evaluated for their performances.

DOI: 10.4018/978-1-4666-0158-1.ch012

INTRODUCTION

Credit scoring has been regarded as a critical topic, with its related departments striving to collect huge amounts of data to avoid making the wrong decision. Consumer credit prediction is a very important issue. Credit scoring models are developed to distinguish which customers belong to good or bad groups based on their related attributes, such as age, marriage status, and income, or on their past records. Credit scoring can be regarded as the binary classification problem of classifying an observation into pre-defined groups. Previous studies focused on increasing the accuracy rate of credit scoring models since even a little bit of improvement will result in significant cost savings. Modern data mining techniques have been adopted to build the credit scoring models (Huang, Chen, & Wang, 2007). Researchers have developed a variety of approaches, including linear discriminate approach (Bellotti & Crook, 2009; Lee & Chen, 2005; Thomas, 2000), decision tree approach (Huang & Wang, 2006), Rough sets theory approach (Caballero, Alvarez, Bel, & Garcia, 2007), F-score approach (Chen & Lin, 2005), Case-Based Reasoning (Osman, Taha, & Dhavalkumar, 2009), Association Analysis (Hashemi, Ray, & Le Blanc, 2009) and genetic programming approach (Ong, Huang, & Tzeng, 2005). Most credit scoring models have been widely developed to improve their accuracy in the past few years. Classic evaluation measures, such as accuracy, information, distance, and dependence, were used for removing irrelevant features. However, artificial intelligence and machine learning techniques have been used to solve some decision-making problems (Moisan & Sabine, 2010). Dash and Liu (1997) provided a detailed survey and overview of the existing methods for features selection and suggested a features selection process. Comparing the conclusions of previous studies, the results are often contradictory (Baesens et al., 2003). Recently, researchers have proposed the hybrid data mining approach

in the design of an effective credit scoring model. For example, Lee et al. (2002) integrated neural network with traditional discriminate analysis approach. Chou et al. (2006) applied machine learning techniques such as Back-Propagation Network (BPN), Decision Tree (DT), and Support Vector Machine (SVM) to solve credit scoring problems. According to previous studies, machine learning techniques are superior to traditional approaches in dealing with credit scoring problems, especially in nonlinear pattern classification (Wu, Huang, & Meng, 2008; Yu & Liu, 2004). For conventional statistical classification, an underlying probability model should be assumed. The more recently developed data mining techniques can perform the classification task without this limitation and achieve better performance than traditional statistical approaches (Huang et al., 2007). Features selection can be categorized as the filter and the wrapper approaches (Liu, 1998). The former approach selects important features and separates features from a classifier that is independent of any learning algorithm. It relies on various measures of the general characteristics of the training data, such as distance, information, dependency, and consistency. The wrapper approach usually uses the predictive accuracy of a pre-determined learning algorithm to determine the accomplishment of the selected subsets. Generally, filters are faster and can be used as a preprocessing step to reduce space dimensionality and over-fitting. On the other hand, the wrapper approach may perform better in finding useful subsets of relevant variables (Guyon & Elisseeff, 2003). However, the problem is known to be NP-hard (Amaldi & Kann, 1998) and the search becomes quickly computationally intractable. A large number of features are computationally expensive (John, Kohavi, & Pfleger., 1994). In this research, four classifiers are combined with four features selection approaches to perform a better classification. Also, parameters tuning is necessary before designing the hybrid features selection models. There are different parameters in the classifiers which need to be arranged to show the highest accuracy rate of credit scoring data sets.

This paper is organized as follows. The following section discusses the basic concepts of features selection approaches and the next section provides a description of the related classifiers. The subsequent section presents the architecture of combining the features selection approaches with the classifiers. The experimental results from the proposed approaches and four classifiers to classify two real-world data sets are provided in the next section. Finally, the last section provides some overall remarks and conclusions.

BASIC CONCEPTS OF FEATURES SELECTION APPROACHES

Linear Discriminate Analysis Approach

Linear discriminate analysis (LDA) is a well-known method originally proposed by Fisher as a classification technique (Fisher, 1936). LDA has been regarded as a data mining technique for handling classification problems by reducing the observed variables into a smaller number of dimensions that would result in decreasing the number of features for consideration by the classifiers. LDA can be expressed as:

$$ J(w(x_1, y_1, \ldots, x_n, y_n)) = \frac{(\mu_1 - \mu_0)^2}{\sigma_1^2 + \sigma_2^2} \qquad (1) $$

$y_i \in \{0,1\}$ for all i=1 to n where μ_y and σ_y^2 are group means and variances given by

$$ \mu_y = \frac{\sum_{i \in Ky} w \cdot x_i}{K_y}; \sigma_y^2 = \frac{\sum_{i \in Ky} (w \cdot x_i - \mu_y)^2}{K_y} \qquad (2) $$

where $K_y = \{i = 1, \ldots, n \mid y_i = y\}$.

LDA is a traditional statistical method and its credit scoring classification accuracy has been treated as the benchmark for other modern classification approaches. LDA was the first approach employed for features selection and had been proposed by Desai et al. (1996) for credit scoring. However, the covariance matrices of the good and bad credit classes may be unequal for the nature of the credit data. Researchers are investigating hybrid models to overcome the deficiencies of the LDA model. One of the efforts is combined with effective classifiers for credit scoring applications.

Rough Sets Theory Approach

Rough sets theory (RST) was first proposed by Pawlak (1984). It has been successfully used to discover data dependencies and reduce the number of attributes contained in a data set by purely structural methods. RST usually reduces the number of attributes in a decision table and deals with vagueness or uncertainty without any pre-assumptions or preliminary information about the data. RST has been successfully applied to real-world classification problems in a variety of areas, such as pattern recognition. Wang et al. (2007) proposed the new features selection approach based on rough sets and particle swarm optimization. Zhao et al. (2007) also conducted an empirical study for letter recognition to demonstrate the usefulness of the discussed relations and reducts. There are still other RST algorithms for features selections. The basic solution for finding minimal reducts is to generate all possible reducts and choose one with minimal cardinality, which can be done by constructing a kind of discernibility function from the data set and simplifying it. However, this is time-consuming and is therefore only practical for simple data sets. Finding minimal reducts or all reducts has been shown to be an NP-hard problem (Skowron, 1992).

Decision Tree Approach

The decision tree approach is able to represent knowledge in a flexible and easy form. Its popularity is the result of its interpretability and easy implementation. The first decision tree generating algorithm was introduced by Quinlan (1979). Selecting an attribute to place at the root node is the first step in constructing a decision tree and then one branch is made based on an attribute value test. This process is repeated recursively on each branch but only on those instances that actually reach the branch. Once all cases at a node have satisfied a certain criterion, we stop developing that part of the tree. Then we calculate the information gain for each attribute and choose the one that gained the most information to split on. The first measure that characterizes the purity of an arbitrary collection of instances is called entropy and is defined as:

$$Entropy(S) = -\sum_{i=1}^{c} p_i \log_2(p_i) \qquad (3)$$

where P_i is the proportion of S belongings to class i. The information gain, Gain (S, A) of an attribute A, the expected reduction in entropy caused by partitioning the examples according to this attribute relative to S, is defined as

$$Gain(S, A) = Entropy(S) - \sum_{value(A)} \frac{S_v}{S} * Entropy(S_v) \qquad (4)$$

where value (A) is the set of all possible values for attribute A, and S_v is the subset of S for which attribute A has value v. The decision tree model is a popular technique for classification and has been widely used in the data mining community. Classification trees are constructed in order to try and maximize their mean classification accuracy. The decision tree model is composed of three

basic elements: decision nodes corresponding to attributes, edges or branches corresponding to the different possible attributes, and leaves including objects that typically belong to the same class. Several algorithms for building decision trees have been developed such as ID3, C5.0 (Quinlan, 1979), and classification and regression trees (CART) (Breiman, Friedman, Olshen, & Stone, 1984). CART is a classification method that has been successfully used in many classification applications including cancer survival groups and credit scoring (West, 2000). Moreover, CART is a nonparametric statistical method via both categorical and continuous variables. When the dependent variable is categorical, CART produces a classification tree; when it is continuous, it will lead to a regression tree. CART algorithm considers all descriptors and split values. The split which gives the best reduction in impurity between father group (f_p) and son groups (f_L and f_R) is expressed as:

$$\Delta i(s, f_p) = i_p(f_p) - pLi(f_L) - pR_i(f_R) \qquad (5)$$

where i is the impurity, s is the candidate split value, and p_L and p_R are the fractions of the objects in the left and the right son group, respectively. The impurity i is usually defined as the total sum of squares of the deviations of the individual response from the mean response of the group in which the considered molecule is classified (Deconinck, Hancock, Coomans, Massart, & Heyden, 2005).

F-Score Approach

F-score is a simple technique which measures the discrimination of two sets of real numbers. Given training vectors x_k, k= 1, 2,...., m if the number of positive and negative instances are n+ and n-, respectively, then the F-score of the ith feature is defined as follows (Chen & Lin, 2005):

$$F(i) = \frac{(\bar{x}_i^{(+)} - \bar{x}_i)^2 + (\bar{x}_i^{(-)} - \bar{x}_i)^2}{\frac{1}{n_+ - 1}\sum_{k=1}^{n_+}(x_{k,i}^{(+)} - \bar{x}_i^{(+)})^2 + \frac{1}{n_- - 1}\sum_{k=1}^{n_-}(x_{k,i}^{(-)} - \bar{x}_i^{(-)})^2}$$

(6)

Where $\bar{x}_i$, $\bar{x}_i^{(+)}$, and $\bar{x}_i^{(-)}$ are the averages of the ith feature of the whole, positive, and negative data sets, respectively. The numerator indicates the discrimination between the positive and negative sets, and the denominator indicates the one within each of the two sets. The larger the F-score, the more likely this feature is more discriminative (Chen & Lin, 2005).

RELATED CLASSIFIERS DESCRIPTION

Support Vector Machine Classifier

Support vector machine (SVM) was first suggested by Vapnik (1995) and has emerged as a powerful tool for classification. Recently, it has also been applied to a number of real-world problems such as credit scoring (Huang et al., 2007; Martens, Baesens, Van Gestel, & Vanthienen, 2007; Schebesch & Stecking, 2005), handwritten characters and classification of disease diagnoses (Cho et al., 2008; Huang, Liao, & Chen, 2008; Su & Yang, 2008). SVM is based on the structured risk minimization (SRM) principles that seek to minimize an upper bound of the generalization error. A particular advantage of SVM is that it can be analyzed theoretically using concepts from computational learning theory and achieve good performance at the same time. Diversity data mining algorithms have been used on different classification applications. First, training

data need to be used to estimate a function for a classification problem. The function is described as follows

$f: R^N \rightarrow \{1, -1\}$, which are k N-dimensional patterns x_i and class labels y_i, where

$$(x_i, y_i), \ldots\ldots, (x_k, y_k) \in R^N x \{1, -1\}$$

(7)

According to the above equation, the SVM classifier should satisfy the following formulations:

$$w^T\phi(x_i) + b \geq +1 \text{ if } y_i = +1$$

(8)

$$w^T\phi(x_i) + b \leq -1 \text{ If } y_i = -1$$

(9)

which are equivalent to

$$y_i\left[w^T\phi(x_i) + b\right] \geq 1, \text{ i=1, 2 ...k}$$

(10)

The non-linear function ϕ will map the original space into a high-dimensional features space. The hyper plane will be constructed by the above mentioned inequalities and is defined as:

$$w^T\phi(x_i) + b = 0$$

(11)

Two classes will be discriminated by the optimal hyper plane, as shown in Figure 1.

Data preprocessing for scaling is necessary to avoid greater numeric ranges dominating those in smaller numeric ranges. It also avoids numerical difficulties during the calculation and helps increase accuracy. Each variable can be linearly scaled to the range [0, 1] by the normalized process using the formula (12), where v is original value, v^{new} is the scaled value, max^v is the upper bound of the feature value, and min^v is the lower bound of the feature value.

Figure 1. An example of a separable problem in a two-dimensional space

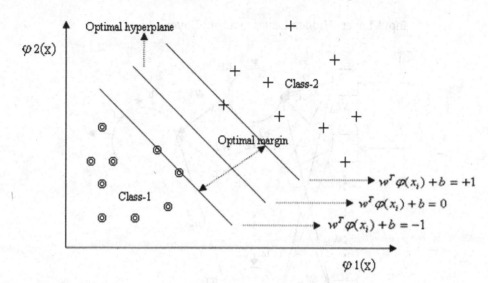

$$v^{new} = \frac{v - \min^{v}}{\max^{v} - \min^{v}} \qquad (12)$$

K Nearest Neighbor Classifier

K Nearest Neighbor (KNN) is a nonparametric classifier and has been applied in various classification problems (Michael, Travis, & Michael, 2005). The prediction for a new example y is given by the majority class label within a neighborhood of y in the training data. The class of a given input will be determined by the nearest neighbors among training data and the categories of the neighbors. The KNN classifier first produces the feature vectors and labels of the training instances, and then the same features will be computed for the test sample whose classes are not known. Distances between data points are computed and K nearest samples will be selected. The new data point is predicted to be a member of the most numerous group. Henley and Hand (Henley & Hand, 1997) use KNN for credit scoring and compare it with logistic regression and decision trees.

Back-Propagation Network (BPN) Classifier

Many types of artificial neural network (ANN) models have been suggested in the literature (Liao & Wen, 2007; Ul-Asar, Azzam, & Ullah, 2009) with the most popular one for classification being the back-propagation network (BPN). BPN techniques have long been applied to the classification field, but they started gaining wide acceptance in the 1990s (Razi & Athappilly, 2005). BPN requires desired outputs to learn like the human brain. The key element of BPN is the structure of the information processing system, which is composed of a large number of highly interconnected processing elements to solve specific problems (Hamdi & Mohamed Salah, 2008). BPN learns from examples and historical data so that the model can then be used to produce the output when the desired output is unknown. The goal of BPN is to create a model that correctly maps the input to the output. Figure 2 provides an example of BPN with one hidden layer and an output neuron.

Figure 2. BPN architecture

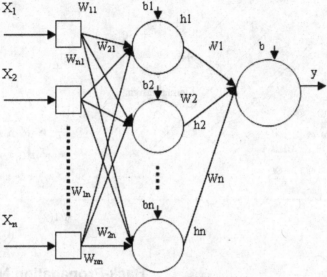

The output of the ith hidden neuron is then computed by processing the weighted inputs and its bias term b_i as follows:

$$h_i = f^h\left(b_i + \sum_{j=1}^{n} w_{ij}x_j\right) \qquad (13)$$

where w_{ij} represents the weight connecting input x_j to hidden unit h_i.

The output of the output layer is computed as follows:

$$y = f^{output}\left(b + \sum_{j=1}^{n} w_i x_j\right) \qquad (14)$$

with n being the number of hidden neurons and w_j representing the weight connecting hidden unit j to the output neuron. There are three parameters which need to be tested in the BPN classifier, namely, learning rate (η), momentum (β), and epoch (t). A transfer function is then ap-plied to map the network output y to a classification label. The transfer function allows the network to model nonlinear relationships in the data and does not require the number of hidden layer nodes to be the same as the number of input nodes.

Extreme Learning Machine (ELM) Classifier

Extreme learning machine (ELM) was proposed by Huang et al. (2006) for single-hidden layer feed forward neural networks (SLFNs) which randomly chooses hidden nodes and analytically determines the output weights of SLFNs by using the Moore Penrose (MP) generalized inverse. It is a faster tool for classification. Suppose that SLFNs with K hidden neurons are trained with an activation function vector $g(x)=(g_1(x),g_2(x),\ldots,g_K(x))$ to learn N distinct samples (X_i, T_i), where $X_i =[X_{i1}, X_{i2},\ldots,X_{in}]^T \in R_n$ and $t_i =[t_{i1}, t_{i2},\ldots,t_{in}]^T \in Rm$. If the SLFNs can approximate these N samples with a zero error for

$$\sum_{J=1}^{N} \| y_J - t_j \| = 0 \qquad (15)$$

where y is the actual output value of the SLFN. Besides, parameters β_i, w_i and b_i for

$$\sum_{i=1}^{k} \beta_i g_i(w_i \cdot x_j + b_i) = t_j, j = 1,.....N \qquad (16)$$

where $w_i = [w_{i1},...,w_m]^T$ is the weight vector connecting the ith hidden neuron and the input neurons, $\beta_i = [\beta_{i1},...,\beta_m]T$, $i = 1,...,K$ is the weight vector connecting the ith hidden neuron and the output neurons, and b_i is the threshold of the ith hidden neuron. The operation $W_i.X_j$ in the above equation denotes the inner product. The simple learning algorithm for SLFNs, called ELM, can have a learning speed that is thousands of times faster than traditional learning algorithm while obtaining better performance (Sun, Choi, Au, & Yu, 2008).

To clearly establish a hybrid features selection and parameter optimization system, the system architecture is shown in Figure 3. The following section discusses the two main steps or phases executed by the architecture and an empirical validation follows.

FEATURES SELECTION COMBINED WITH THE FOUR CLASSIFIERS

Features selection is an important issue in building classification systems. It is advantageous to limit the number of input features before entering a classifier and have a good predictive and less computationally intensive model. In this research, the two-phase hybrid classification architecture will be used in constructing the credit scoring models. There are 16 models under the hybrid combinations and 4 original classification models without features selection. The first phase emphasizes the importance of features selection.

Four approaches will be employed to keep the expected classification performance and avoid the risks of over-fitting or decreasing accuracy in the features selection stage. The purpose of this phase is to obtain the optimal features subset through accuracy, that is, by utilizing the training data as a criterion. The second phase then combines with four well-known classifiers that have been extensively used as a classification tool with a great deal of success in a variety of areas. The object of the final phase is to present these hybrid classifying approaches based on the techniques that are most effective in the designing of credit scoring models. These results will be compared using the Wilcoxon signed rank test to show if there is any significant difference between these hybrid models. The architecture of the two phases is represented in Figure 3.

Optimizing Features Subset Using Four Approaches

Before employing these classifiers, the four approaches should be used to obtain the optimal features subset. First, LDA is used to get the most remarkable features; the amount of which mainly depends on half the number of the original features. Coefficients of the LDA standardized canonical discriminate function indicate the effect on the discriminate function. The bigger the absolute value the greater the weight. There are 7 and 12 variables whose coefficients are greater than 0.13 in the real data set of Australian and German, respectively. Once the numbers of features have been decided, the other three approaches are followed on the basis of comparison. The data set is then randomly partitioned into training and independent testing sets via K fold cross validation. Each of the K subsets acts as an independent holdout test set for the model trained with the rest of the K-1 subsets. The influence of data dependency is minimized and the reliability of the results can be improved via cross-validation (Kudo & Sklansky, 2000). For each of the K subsets of the data set D, create a

Figure 3. Hybrid features selection architecture

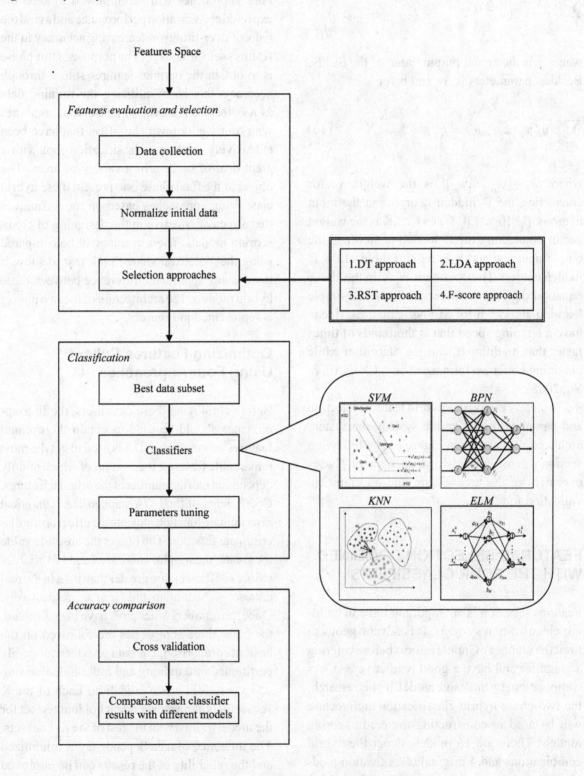

training set T = D-K, then run a cross-validation process (Chen & Lin, 2005; Hsu, Chang, & Lin, 2008). Overall accuracy is averaged across all K partitions. These K accuracy values also give an estimate of the accuracy variance of the algorithms. This study used K = 10, meaning all the data were divided into 10 parts, each of which took turns at being the testing data set. The other nine data parts served as the training data set for adjusting the model parameters. The primary process used is as follows:

Phase 1 - Selection from the Features Space

- Collect a set of observed data from UCI datasets.
- Normalize initial data and scale to the range [0, 1]
- Apply the selection approaches to calculate the optimal features subsets using four approaches to decide the initial input variables.

The first phase generates the optimal subsets according to the four approaches, namely, DT approach, LDA approach, RST approach, and F-score approach and then chooses the same number of features as the comparison base.

Classification Based on the Four Classifiers

Once the features selection is finished, the next phase is the application of the four classifiers. Each classifier has its own advantage in different data sets. No classifier is considered to have the best classification accuracy (Baesens et al., 2003; Wu et al., 2008). Hence, the issue of which classifier to use for credit scoring remains to be a very difficult and challenging problem. Phase 2 will focus on the parameters tuning to gain better accuracy. The second phase is composed of five steps as described below.

Phase 2 – Classification and Parameters Tuning

- Generating the best data subset and setting the reasonable ratio of training and testing data.
- Select various classifiers and combine with features selection approaches described in phase 1.
- Consider different parameters tuning. For KNN, BPN, SVM and ELM classifiers, the K value of the nearest neighbors taken from the training set, the three parameters of learning rate (η), momentum (β), and epoch (t), each hyper parameter pair (C, γ) in the grid search space and the number of hidden nodes should be adjusted, respectively.
- Choose appropriate parameters that lead to the lowest cross-validation error classification rate. Apply 10 fold cross validation and average the results to obtain the accuracy rate of these hybrid credit scoring models.
- Compare these hybrid models to the original models and obtain the best combination results for these classifiers.

Our implementation was carried out via the software Matlab 7.1 of MathWorks, using LIBSVM which was originally designed by Chang and Lin (Chang & Lin, 2008) and ELM Algorithm designed by Huang et al. (2006). The empirical evaluation was performed on an Intel Pentium 4 CPU running at 3.4 GHz and 1GB RAM.

EMPIRICAL ANALYSIS

Real Data Sets from the UCI Repository

Credit data sets in the real world include various attributes. Table 1 represents the two real-world

Table 1. Two adopted UCI repository data sets

Names	Total instances	Nominal features	Numeric features	Total features	Number of classes
German	1000	0	24	24	2
Australian	690	6	8	14	2

Table 2. Results of four classifiers before features selection (Australian data set)

The four classifier	Features selected	Accuracy rate Avg. (%)	Accuracy rate Std. (%)
KNN	14	89.10	11.98
ELM	14	87.70	6.15
BPN	14	84.78	5.37
SVM	14	84.34	5.69

data sets which were selected for this research, the Australian and German credit data sets. They were derived from the University of California, Irvine (UCI) Repository of Machine Learning Databases. The first accuracy evaluation data set is the German credit scoring data set, which is composed of 24 numeric features, including credit history, account balance, loan purpose, loan amount, employment status, personal information, age, housing, and job. Additionally, 700 cases are creditworthy while the rest of the other 300 applicants are not. The second data set from Australia consists of 307 "good" applicants and 383 "bad" ones. Each applicant contains 15 features, including six nominal, eight numeric attributes, and one class label (good or bad credit). These attributes' names have been changed to meaningless symbolic data for confidential reasons. The Australian data set is a good mixture of attributes—continuous, nominal with small numbers of values, and nominal with larger numbers of values.

Original Features Space in the Three Classifiers without Selection

Four approaches, namely, "LDA," "DT," "RST," and "F-score," and four classifiers, i.e., KNN, SVM, BPN and ELM, were used in this study.

There are 16 combinations consisting of the above items and four primitive models without selection. For the Australian and German data sets, there are 14 and 24 original attributes, respectively. Half of the original attributes were used as the benchmark for the same number of features. The results for the two data sets were obtained first without applying the four approaches for the following comparison, as summarized in Tables 2 and 3, respectively.

The highest accuracy rates of the four classifiers in the Australian and German data sets are KNN (89.10%) model and SVM model (75.40%), respectively. The ELM model is slightly inferior to the KNN model of Australian and SVM model of German in the average accuracy rate, but is superior in terms of the standard deviation. As proposed by Huang et al. (2006), ELM has better generalization performance than the gradient-based learning in most cases and less time on learning and training.

Experimental Results after Features Selection

The primitive 14 and 24 variables of the Australian and German data set without selection were input into the four classifiers, respectively. Half of the

Table 3. Results of four classifiers before features selection (German data set)

The four classifier	Features selected	Accuracy rate Avg. (%)	Accuracy rate Std. (%)
SVM	24	75.40	5.96
ELM	24	74.50	4.65
KNN	24	72.20	7.87
BPN	24	71.90	6.12

Table 4. Results of four classifiers after features selection (Australian data set)

Combined approaches	Features selected	Accuracy rate Avg. (%)	Accuracy rate Std. (%)	Difference after features selection
KNN	14	89.10	11.98	1.3
F-score + KNN	7	**90.40**	**10.36**	
SVM	14	84.34	5.69	2.18
LDA+ SVM	7	**86.52**	**5.45**	
BPN	14	84.78	5.37	**2.32**
DT+ BPN	7	**87.10**	**6.03**	
ELM	14	87.70	6.15	0.58
LDA+ ELM	7	**88.28**	**4.61**	

original features were used as the benchmark for the same numbers of variables. The improving results are summarized in Table 4. We have used a special notational convention where the higher accuracy rate in each classifier combined with the four approaches is underlined and denoted in bold face. The highest accuracy rate with respect to all classifiers is double underlined and also denoted in bold face. From Table 4, it is clear that the KNN classifier combined with the F-score approach achieves the best accuracy rate and each hybrid model is better than the original features space without selection. Table 4 also indicates that BPN classifier combined with DT approach will improve the accuracy rate (=2.32). In addition, the average accuracy rate of the KNN classifier combined with features selection approaches is better than the other three classifiers in the Australian data set.

Table 5 shows the results for the German data set after features selection. Half of the original

attributes were also used as the benchmark for the same number of features. The higher accuracy rates in each classifier combined with the four approaches are also underlined and denoted in bold face. In Table 5, the SVM classifier combined with the F-score approach achieves the highest accuracy rate and the hybrid models are better than the original features space without selection. F-score is a simple technique which measures the discrimination of two sets of real numbers (Chen & Lin, 2005). Our results demonstrate that F-score approach combined with classifiers can improve the classification accuracy significantly. Table 5 also indicates that KNN classifier combined with LDA approach will improve the accuracy rate (=2.30). In addition, the average accuracy rate of the SVM classifier combined with features selection approaches is better than the other three classifiers in the German data set.

Table 5. Results of four classifiers after features selection (German data set)

Combined approaches	Features selected	Accuracy rate Avg. (%)	Accuracy rate Std. (%)	Difference after selection
SVM	24	75.40	5.96	1.30
F-score +SVM	12	76.70	6.07	
KNN	24	72.20	7.87	2.30
LDA+ KNN	12	74.50	5.48	
BPN	24	71.90	6.12	1.44
F-score + BPN	12	73.34	5.33	
ELM	24	74.50	4.64	1.10
LDA+ ELM	12	75.60	3.84	

Comparison of Significance Testing

To compare the classificatory abilities of the four classifiers, nonparametric Wilcoxon signed rank tests were performed for the 10-fold testing set, as shown in Table 6. For the Australian data set, there is only one significant difference among the four classifiers (with α=0.05) before features selection approaches. The BPN classifier is slightly inferior to the ELM classifier. The result is similar to what was observed by Huang et al. (2006). The other classifiers achieved similar classification accuracies before features selection. For the German data set, the P-value (=0.01) is smaller than the reject region (with α=0.05) of SVM classifier and hence better than the BPN classifier before features selection approaches. Next, we compare the specific features selection approaches among the four classifiers. For the Australian data set, there is only one significant difference in the F-score approach (with P-value=0.03) between SVM and ELM classifiers. In other words, F-score as the first phase of features selection approach combined with ELM classifier is better than SVM classifier significantly. For German data set, the result is diverse. LDA approach as the preprocessing step of features selection causes the result of the four classifiers to be significantly different. LDA-BPN appears to be a worse combination for German credit data. This result is a little different from

that of Lee et al. (2002) whose research reported that the hybrid LDA-BPN model has the best credit scoring capability in terms of the average classification rate in comparison with LDA and BPN models on different data set. On the other hand, there are three models with statistical significance for the German data set in Table 6. The RST-SVM model is superior to the RST-BPN model, the DT-SVM model is superior to the DT-BPN model and the DT-ELM model is superior to the DT-BPN model. For German credit data, it seems that features selection approach combined with the BPN classifier is not suitable except for F-score approach.

Whether there is any significant difference between the four features selection approaches and original features space without selection among an identical classifier is another interesting issue. The results for this analysis are summarized in Table 7. For Australian data, LDA selection approach is significantly different from original feature without selection on SVM and BPN classifiers respectively. In addition, Table 7 reveals that LDA-ELM approach is significantly better than the RST-ELM approach (P-value=0.01). The LDA approach combined with effective classifiers for credit scoring applications is favorable as hybrid classification models. Different features selection approaches combined with specific classifiers certainly present significant differ-

Table 6. Wilcoxon signed rank test between two classifiers (with α =0.05)

Data sets	Approach	Classifier I	Classifier II	P-value
Australian	Original	BPN	ELM	0.05
	F-score	SVM	ELM	0.03
German	Original	BPN	SVM	0.01
	LDA	BPN	KNN	0.05
	LDA	BPN	SVM	0.005
	LDA	BPN	ELM	0.01
	RST	BPN	SVM	0.03
	DT	BPN	SVM	0.02
	DT	BPN	ELM	0.01

Table 7. Wilcoxon signed rank test between two approaches (with α =0.05)

Data sets	Classifier	Approach I	Approach II	P-value
Australian	SVM	Original	LDA	0.03
	BPN	Original	LDA	0.05
	ELM	RST	LDA	0.01
German	KNN	Original	LDA	0.04
	KNN	DT	LDA	0.02
	BPN	DT	F-score	0.01

ences. On the other hand, the German data from Table 7 shows that LDA approach combined with KNN classifier is significantly superior to original features without selection and the DT approach. BPN classifier significantly prefers F-score approach to DT approach (P-value=0.01). The result is interesting that the extreme value of the highest and smallest average accuracy rate of the features selection approaches do not have statistical significance in the KNN classifier of Australian data set and the SVM classifier of German data set respectively.

Comparison of All Combinations

As mentioned earlier, both the four features selection approaches and original features space without selection were used to combine with four classifiers that have 20 different combinations.

The top five accuracy rates of the two data sets are summarized in Table 8. For the Australian data set, the best hybrid classifier is the KNN classifier and the highest average accuracy rate is the F-score-KNN model (90.4%). In addition, the best hybrid classifier is the SVM classifier and the highest average accuracy rate is the F-score+ SVM model (76.7%) for the German data set.

Figures 4 and 5 show the top five accuracy rates in the 10 testing groups of the two data sets respectively. Group 11 represents the average accuracy rate of the 10 testing groups. The accuracy rates of groups 1 and 7 are significantly inferior to other groups shown in Figure 4; similarly, the groups 2 and 7 are the worst from Figure 5. In other words, these groups should be improved further to obtain better accuracy rates. This observation is similar to other research works (Baesens et al., 2003; Chen, Ma, & Ma, 2009; Kudo

Table 8. Top five accuracy rate of all combinations in the two data sets

Rank	Data sets	Approach	Classifier	Accuracy rate (%)
1	Australian	F-score	KNN	90.40
2		None	KNN	89.10
3		RST	KNN	88.54
4		DT	KNN	88.41
5		LDA	ELM	88.28
1	German	F-score	SVM	76.70
2		LDA	SVM	76.10
3		LDA	ELM	75.60
4		RST	SVM	75.60
5		None	SVM	75.40

Figure 4. Top five accuracy rate models of the Australian data set

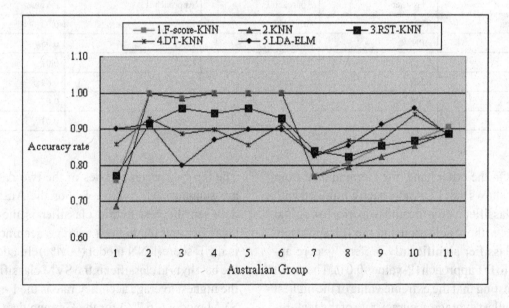

& Sklansky, 2000). Different classifiers perform well in comparison with other hybrid models but do not always give the best performance.

DISCUSSION

Hybrid data mining approach in the design of a better credit scoring model has been proposed by effective features selections approaches (Chen et al., 2009; Chen & Lin, 2005; Lee & Chen, 2005) and used to improve performance in this study. In order to investigate the existence of any prominent difference between the four classifiers after features selection approaches, the 10 fold testing data was used for statistical testing. After feature selection, four classifiers raise the accuracy rate by different degree for both the data sets. The DT approach and LDA approach especially help BPN classifier and KNN classifier, respectively, the most. A number of researchers are concerned about how to choose the optimal features input and

Figure 5. Top five accuracy rate models of the German data set

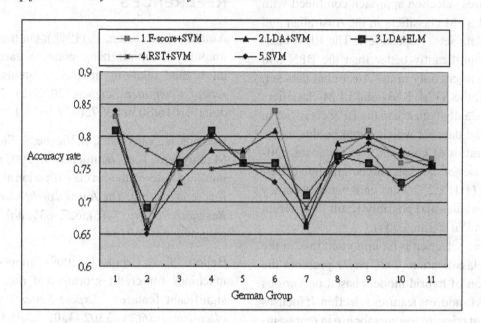

effective classifiers (Baesens et al., 2003; Huang et al., 2008; Li, Chen, & Wang, 2008). The findings of this study also specify that different combinations of hybrid classification models could be compared under the same number of features after selection. Overall, the ELM and SVM classifiers are better than BPN classifier by combining with other specific features selection approaches for the different ratio of good and bad instances of the data sets. Feature selection is advantageous to have a good predictive and less computationally intensive model (Zheng & Zhang, 2008). Although the differences between two classifiers or features selection approaches are not always significant from a statistical perspective, a little bit of improvement will result in significant cost savings in credit scoring (Schebesch & Stecking, 2005).

CONCLUSION

This study used four features selection approaches combined with four classifiers to construct the hybrid credit scoring models. The proposed hybrid models are demonstrated using data sets from the domain of credit scoring, yielding promising results. Features selection involves determining the highest classifier accuracy of a subset or seeking the acceptable accuracy of smallest features. This study compares the hybrid classification models by the same amount of features and original features space. A nonparametric test was also performed to show if there was any significant difference between classifiers or approaches. Application of the data dimensionality reduction preprocessing step is performed prior to the classification procedures, which greatly improves the overall classification performance. Four features selection approaches associated with effective classifiers illustrated a better combination in these hybrid models using half the number of original features. Fewer features mean that the credit department can concentrate on collecting relevant and essential variables. Loading of credit evaluation personnel can be reduced as they do not have to take into account a large number of features during the evaluation procedure, which will be less computationally intensive. In this research, F-score is deemed the best features selection approach combined with KNN and SVM classifiers in the Australian and German data sets, respectively. The ELM classifier is significantly better than the BPN and SVM classifiers only in the Australian data set. Moreover, the SVM, KNN and ELM classifiers are significantly better than the BPN classifier in the German data set which might be due to the different ratios of good and bad instances. Different classes of data sets can be split into different ratios (1:1, 1:2, 2:1) to gain better accuracy in future studies and possibly result in different inferences (Yu & Liu, 2004).

Features selection is an important task in the field of classification. This paper presents the comparison of hybrid models based on various classifiers to address features selection. It focuses on the most relevant features for use in representing data in order to delete those features considered as irrelevant. Specifically, it is concerned with not only reducing the number of variables but also eliminating noise features. The results of the study show that the hit rates of hybrid features selection models are mostly higher than those of individual methods, especially when the instances equal both parts (Australian data set). Additionally, the proposed approach selects the most relevant variables, but not necessarily the optimal ones, for the construction of a good model as the selected ones may be redundant. Although computationally expensive for a larger data set, the evolutionary wrapper approaches may perform better in finding useful subsets of relevant variables. Potential future work in this area includes developing a heuristic model for credit scoring. Many effective wrapper features selection approaches such as Genetic Algorithms (GA), Simulated Annealing (SA), Ant Colony Optimization (ACO), and Particle Swarm Optimization (PSO) have been developed and are worthy of further experimentation.

REFERENCES

Amaldi, E., & Kann, V. (1998). On the approximability of minimizing nonzero variables or unsatisfied relations in linear systems. *Theoretical Computer Science*, *209*(1-2), 237–260. doi:10.1016/S0304-3975(97)00115-1

Baesens, B., Van Gestel, T., Viaene, S., Stepanova, M., Suykens, J., & Vanthienen, J. (2003). Benchmarking state-of-the-art classification algorithms for credit scoring. *The Journal of the Operational Research Society*, *54*(6), 627–635. doi:10.1057/palgrave.jors.2601545

Bellotti, T., & Crook, J. (2009). Support vector machines for credit scoring and discovery of significant features. *Expert Systems with Applications*, *36*(2), 3302–3308. doi:10.1016/j.eswa.2008.01.005

Breiman, L., Friedman, J. H., Olshen, R. A., & Stone, C. J. (1984). *Classification and Regression Trees*. Monterey, CA: Wadsworth & Brooks.

Caballero, Y., Alvarez, D., Bel, R., & Garcia, M. M. (2007). Feature selection algorithms using Rough Set Theory. In L. D. Mourelle, N. Nedjah, J. Kacprzyk & A. Abraham (Eds.), *Proceedings of the 7th International Conference on Intelligent Systems Design and Applications* (pp. 407-411).

Chang, C.-C., & Lin, C.-J. (2008). *LIBSVM: a Library for Support Vector Machines*.

Chen, W., Ma, C., & Ma, L. (2009). Mining the customer credit using hybrid support vector machine technique. *Expert Systems with Applications*, *36*(4), 7611–7616. doi:10.1016/j.eswa.2008.09.054

Chen, Y.-W., & Lin, C.-J. (2005). *Combining SVMs with Various Feature Selection Strategies*.

Cho, B. H., Yu, H., Kim, K. W., Kim, T. H., Kim, I. Y., & Kim, S. I. (2008). Application of irregular and unbalanced data to predict diabetic nephropathy using visualization and feature selection methods. *Artificial Intelligence in Medicine*, *42*(1), 37–53. doi:10.1016/j.artmed.2007.09.005

Chou, C. H., Lin, C. C., Liu, Y. H., & Chang, F. (2006). A prototype classification method and its use in a hybrid solution for multiclass pattern recognition. *Pattern Recognition*, *39*(4), 624–634. doi:10.1016/j.patcog.2005.10.022

Dash, M., & Liu, H. (1997). Feature selection for classification. *Intelligent Data Analysis*, *1*, 131–156. doi:10.1016/S1088-467X(97)00008-5

Deconinck, E., Hancock, T., Coomans, D., Massart, D. L., & Heyden, Y. V. (2005). Classification of drugs in absorption classes using the classification and regression trees (CART) methodology. *Journal of Pharmaceutical and Biomedical Analysis*, *39*(1-2), 91–103. doi:10.1016/j.jpba.2005.03.008

Desai, V. S., Crook, J. N., & Overstreet, G. A. (1996). A comparison of neural networks and linear scoring models in the credit union environment. *European Journal of Operational Research*, *95*(1), 24–37. doi:10.1016/0377-2217(95)00246-4

Fisher, R. A. (1936). The Use of Multiple Measurements in Taxonomic Problems. *Annals of Eugenics*, *7*, 179–188.

Guyon, I., & Elisseeff, A. (2003). An introduction to variable and feature selection. *Journal of Machine Learning Research*, *3*, 1157–1182. doi:10.1162/153244303322753616

Hamdi, M. S. (2008). SOMSE: A Neural Network Based Approach to Web Search Optimization. *International Journal of Intelligent Information Technologies*, *4*(4), 31–54.

Hashemi, R., Le Blanc, L. A., Bahrami, A., Bahar, M., & Traywick, B. (2009). Association Analysis of Alumni Giving: A Formal Concept Analysis. *International Journal of Intelligent Information Technologies*, *5*(2), 17–32.

Henley, W. E., & Hand, D. J. (1997). *Construction of a k-nearest-neighbour credit-scoring system* (Vol. 8, pp. 305-321).

Hsu, C. W., Chang, C. C., & Lin, C. J. (2008). *A Practical Guide to Support Vector Classification*.

Huang, C. L., Chen, M. C., & Wang, C. J. (2007). Credit scoring with a data mining approach based on support vector machines. *Expert Systems with Applications*, *33*(4), 847–856. doi:10.1016/j.eswa.2006.07.007

Huang, C. L., Liao, H. C., & Chen, M. C. (2008). Prediction model building and feature selection with support vector machines in breast cancer diagnosis. *Expert Systems with Applications*, *34*(1), 578–587. doi:10.1016/j.eswa.2006.09.041

Huang, C. L., & Wang, C. J. (2006). A GA-based feature selection and parameters optimization for support vector machines. *Expert Systems with Applications*, *31*(2), 231–240. doi:10.1016/j.eswa.2005.09.024

Huang, G.-B., Zhu, Q.-Y., & Siew, C.-K. (2006). Extreme learning machine: Theory and applications. *Neurocomputing*, *70*(1-3), 489–501. doi:10.1016/j.neucom.2005.12.126

John, G. H., Kohavi, R., & Pfleger, K. (1994). *Irrelevant feature and the subset selection problem*. Paper presented at the Proceedings of the Eleventh International Conference on Machine Learning.

Kudo, M., & Sklansky, J. (2000). Comparison of algorithms that select features for pattern classifiers. *Pattern Recognition*, *33*(1), 25–41. doi:10.1016/S0031-3203(99)00041-2

Lee, T.-S., & Chen, I. F. (2005). A two-stage hybrid credit scoring model using artificial neural networks and multivariate adaptive regression splines. *Expert Systems with Applications, 28*(4), 743–752. doi:10.1016/j.eswa.2004.12.031

Lee, T.-S., Chiu, C.-C., Lu, C.-J., & Chen, I. F. (2002). Credit scoring using the hybrid neural discriminant technique. *Expert Systems with Applications, 23*(3), 245–254. doi:10.1016/S0957-4174(02)00044-1

Li, F. C., Chen, F. L., & Wang, G. E. (2008). *Proceedings of Comparison of feature selection approaches based on the SVM classification.* Piscataway, NJ.

Liao, S.-H., & Wen, C.-H. (2007). Artificial neural networks classification and clustering of methodologies and applications - literature analysis from 1995 to 2005. *Expert Systems with Applications, 32*(1), 1–11. doi:10.1016/j.eswa.2005.11.014

Liu, H. A. M. (1998). *Feature Selection for Knowledge Discovery and Data Mining.* Boston: Kluwer Academic Publishers.

Martens, D., Baesens, B., Van Gestel, T., & Vanthienen, J. (2007). Comprehensible credit scoring models using rule extraction from support vector machines. *European Journal of Operational Research, 183*(3), 1466–1476. doi:10.1016/j.ejor.2006.04.051

Michael, R. P., Travis, E. D., & Michael, L. R. (2005). *GA-facilitated classifier optimization with varying similarity measures.* Paper presented at the Proceedings of the 2005 conference on Genetic and evolutionary computation.

Moisan, S. (2010). Generating Knowledge-Based System Generators: A Software Engineering Approach. *International Journal of Intelligent Information Technologies, 6*(1), 1–17.

Ong, C.-S., Huang, J.-J., & Tzeng, G.-H. (2005). Building credit scoring models using genetic programming. *Expert Systems with Applications, 29*(1), 41–47. doi:10.1016/j.eswa.2005.01.003

Osman, T., Thakker, D., & Al-Dabass, D. (2009). Utilisation of Case-Based Reasoning for Semantic Web Services Composition. *International Journal of Intelligent Information Technologies, 5*(1), 24–42.

Pawlak. (1984). *Rough classification* (Vol. 20, pp. 469-483). Dordrecht, The Netherlands: Elsevier Academic Press Ltd.

Quinlan, J. R. (1979). Discovering rules from large collections of examples: a case study. *Expert Systems in the Micro-electronic Age,* 168-201.

Razi, M. A., & Athappilly, K. (2005). A comparative predictive analysis of neural networks (NNs), nonlinear regression and classification and regression tree (CART) models. *Expert Systems with Applications, 29*(1), 65–74. doi:10.1016/j.eswa.2005.01.006

Schebesch, K. B., & Stecking, R. (2005). Support vector machines for classifying and describing credit applicants: detecting typical and critical regions. *The Journal of the Operational Research Society, 56*(9), 1082–1088. doi:10.1057/palgrave.jors.2602023

Skowron, A., & Rauszer, C. (1992). The discernibility matrices and functions in information systems. In Slowinski, R. (Ed.), *Intelligent Decision Support--Handbook of Applications and Advances of the Rough Sets Theory* (pp. 311–362). New York: Kluwer.

Su, C. T., & Yang, C. H. (2008). Feature selection for the SVM: An application to hypertension diagnosis. *Expert Systems with Applications, 34*(1), 754–763. doi:10.1016/j.eswa.2006.10.010

Sun, Z.-L., Choi, T.-M., Au, K.-F., & Yu, Y. (2008). Sales forecasting using extreme learning machine with applications in fashion retailing. *Decision Support Systems, 46*(1), 411–419. doi:10.1016/j.dss.2008.07.009

Thomas, L. C. (2000). A survey of credit and behavioural scoring: forecasting financial risk of lending to consumers. *International Journal of Forecasting, 16*(2), 149–172. doi:10.1016/S0169-2070(00)00034-0

Ul-Asar, A., Ullah, M. S., Wyne, M. F., & Ahmed, J. A., ul-Hasnain, R. (2009). Traffic Responsive Signal Timing Plan Generation Based on Neural Network. *International Journal of Intelligent Information Technologies, 5*(3), 84–101.

Vapnik, V. N. (Ed.). (1995). *The nature of statistical learning theory*. New York: Springer Verlag.

Wang, X., Yang, J., Teng, X., Xia, W., & Jensen, R. (2007). Feature selection based on rough sets and particle swarm optimization. *Pattern Recognition Letters, 28*(4), 459–471. doi:10.1016/j.patrec.2006.09.003

West, D. (2000). Neural network credit scoring models. *Computers & Operations Research, 27*(11-12), 1131–1152. doi:10.1016/S0305-0548(99)00149-5

Wu, T.-K., Huang, S.-C., & Meng, Y.-R. (2008). Evaluation of ANN and SVM classifiers as predictors to the diagnosis of students with learning disabilities. *Expert Systems with Applications, 34*(3), 1846–1856. doi:10.1016/j.eswa.2007.02.026

Yu, L., & Liu, H. (2004). Efficient feature selection via analysis of relevance and redundancy. *Journal of Machine Learning Research, 5,* 1205–1224.

Zhao, Y., Yao, Y., & Luo, F. (2007). Data analysis based on discernibility and indiscernibility. *Information Sciences, 177*(22), 4959–4976. doi:10.1016/j.ins.2007.06.031

Zheng, H., & Zhang, Y. (2008). Feature selection for high-dimensional data in astronomy. *Advances in Space Research, 41*(12), 1960–1964. doi:10.1016/j.asr.2007.08.033

This work was previously published in International Journal of Intelligent Information Technologies, Volume 6, Issue 3, edited by Vijayan Sugumaran, pp. 56-74, copyright 2010 by IGI Publishing (an imprint of IGI Global).

Chapter 13

Facilitating Decision Making and Maintenance for Power Systems Operators through the Use of Agents and Distributed Embedded Systems

A. Carrasco
University of Seville, Spain

M. D. Hernández
University of Seville, Spain

M. C. Romero-Ternero
University of Seville, Spain

D. Oviedo
University of Seville, Spain

F. Sivianes
University of Seville, Spain

J. I. Escudero
University of Seville, Spain

ABSTRACT

This article examines the improvements provided when multimedia information in traditional SCADAS are included in electric facility management and maintenance. Telecontrol use in the electric sector, with the fundamental objective of providing increased and improved service to the operators who manage these systems, is also described. One of the most important contributions is the use of an agent network that is distributed around the electric facility. Through the use of multi-agent technology and its placement in embedded systems, to the authors design a system with a degree of intelligence and independence to optimize data collection and provide reaction proposals for the operator. The proposed agent-based architecture is also reviewed in this article, as are the design of an example agent and the results obtained in a pilot experience using the proposed hardware platform.

DOI: 10.4018/978-1-4666-0158-1.ch013

1. INTRODUCTION

Currently In modern times it is quite difficult to imagine a functioning domestic or industrial area that has no access to a reliable and continuous supply of electric energy. A good part of the comfort we enjoy in our homes, as well as a substantial part of industrial work output, are reliant on constant electric supply. As a result, it is absolutely necessary to guarantee a continuous and non-altering supply of electric energy at all times. In order for this supply to satisfy the needs of all who use it, the installation of a complex control and management device is required. Telecontrol allows this control and management to be carried out, therefore making it a very important mechanism which should be improved as much as possible. It will be possible to take advantage of the advances in new technology with these improvements, so that the decisions made in each moment are strongly supported by the most efficient telecontrol mechanisms. These telecontrol systems are managed by operators which execute commands and maneuvers. These operators have technical experience and are trained with specialization in handling these tools. They also have a vast knowledge of the electric distribution network they manage since the majority of them worked previously on the technical maintenance staff in these facilities.

Over the last few years the majority of the electrical companies have externalized these maintenance services, which has led to a lack of new operators which possess detailed network knowledge. On occasion there have been people who have never seen the facilities which they manage which greatly increases the complexity of certain actions.

In these cases SCADA systems become essential. The main aim of SCADA systems involves the supervision and remote control of devices, mainly sensors and actuators which are found in isolated and remote places (Boyer, 1999). The information being treated in these systems is usually processed in short frames which correspond to measurements and or specific states such as the state of the interrupters, tension levels, intensity, etc. As a result, technology that has been used traditionally is still adequate today for the management of the data of the device. This technology is so well-suited for the task that it will most likely continue to be used in the future.

The man-machine interface is used to make the management of the SCADA network operation simpler. This interaction normally indicates the current state of the information as a chain of text. It is however possible to see, in some cases, a symbol or color that signals the current state of the device as well. The inclusion of audio and video multimedia in these SCADA systems provides added value for the operators in charge of productively using the systems by making them more intuitive and eliminating the necessity of being physically familiar with the facilities as images are displayed from a distance whenever the operator wants (Escudero, 2005; Romero, 2004). Likewise, they facilitate the communication and follow up for the maintenance staff at the facilities in the execution of maneuvers.

The main aim of SCADA systems involves the supervision and remote control of devices, mainly sensors and actuators, which can be found in isolated and remote places. Information that these devices provide, for example the measurement of the intensity of an electric current on a power line, involves short information which is no longer than a few dozen bytes. As a result, technology that was traditionally used is still adequate today for the management of the device's data, and will probably continue to be used in the future.

Nevertheless, the transmissions and network technologies are among many fields that have spectacularly evolved over the last few years. Techniques involving information compression and the use of multimedia signals have also experienced notable advances in recent years. This has been brought about due to the modern day use of digital audio and video, which can be efficiently processed by PC systems at low cost. The digital audio and video is able to obtain good visual results of this information by using relatively low speeds to send the bits. Codecs such as MPEG-4 (ISO/IEC, 1991) make the compression of high resolution video signals at less than 1 Mbps possible.

In this article we will share our experience when multimedia signals in SCADA systems were included and treated. The new contribution consists of the use of multiagent and embedded systems for this objective, optimizing the information capture process in the field, and providing the system with a certain degree of intelligence which presents the operator with a proposal for action. With the use these technologies we have created a network of sensors which is used to accrue physical data about the system, including visible and thermal video and audio, and in addition gives the system a certain degree of autonomy. This information is compiled to be sent to a central node or base station where it is displayed, stored, treated, and sent to superior nodes in the remote management network.

2. IDOLO SYSTEM

Multimedia in SCADA systems

The focus of this section does not just explore the possibility of integrating multimedia data into SCADA systems, it takes the process one step further. The main idea of this section involves the possibility of integrating SCADA data into modern network systems. Typical transmission links and protocols used on SCADA networks do not fulfill the bandwidth requirements that multimedia data deployment impose. This is due to the fact that the data acquired from SCADA devices is usually transmitted over low-bandwidth links and also uses serial protocols.

Another important key factor is that temporal requirements regarding the reception of the acquired data are very tight on SCADA systems. It

Figure 1. Ethernet SCADA bridge

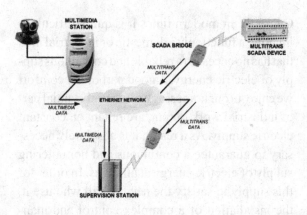

is determined that cycle time on SCADA buses generally ranges between 10 ms and 100 ms. Furthermore, transmission reliability is also very important in this context, due to the fact that loss of data could have a big impact on the integrity of the system.

We have successfully injected SCADA data into an Ethernet system, using a custom-built SCADA bridge (Figure 1). Data transmitted using the IEC870 (IEC, 1990) protocol from a Multitrans PLC device is injected into an Ethernet network using bidirectional serial-to-Ethernet converters. This feature gives data about the voltage and intensity of power lines, and also provides information about other relevant characteristics.

The converter we used is referred to as the IS-Server device. It takes serial data from the Multitrans device and then converts it into TCP packets. These packets are sent to a predefined IP network address. At times, control system needs to receive data in its original serial form. If this is the case, the inverse process may be applied using another IS-Server device.

In our tests, status data, which is periodically polled from a Multitrans device, travels between two Ethernet-based LANs connected via a 100Mbps fiber optic link. The outcome of this process is noted in the reception of the SCADA data in less than 10 ms. This holds true even when a raw multimedia stream, which tends to need nearly all the available bandwidth, is also sharing the fiber optic link at the same time.

As proven above, even with time constraints, it is possible to share the physical medium between SCADA and multimedia data in Ethernet networks, but transmission reliability must also be taken into consideration. Ethernet hub devices use CSMA-based medium sharing techniques (ISO/IEC, 1993), which can lead to packet loss in a high traffic scenario. This is due to the possibility of packet collision. Therefore, the focus of the starting point in the design of any multimedia SCADA system should be on the switches.

The possibility exists for Network management techniques such as Quality of Service (Arindam, 1999) to also be used to ensure that SCADA data always obtains the bandwidth it needs in any scenario. QoS allows for packet prioritization and bandwidth provision, which is based on one or more factors, such as the IP address of the sender.

Interface

The IDOLO interface has been built as a web-based software system, supported by a database system. This combination manages all needed system configuration, and allows operators to easily have access to all multimedia information of the SCADA system.

Being web-based allows for it to be independently run from an existing SCADA/HMI system, and at the same time makes it possible to be integrated into HMI systems supporting web navigation. HMI software supporting ActiveX technology can easily be integrated into the IDOLO software system. This is carried out by means of using an embedded ActiveX web browser.

Furthermore, there are some web browsers, such as Internet Explorer, which also support ActiveX components. As a result, software components specific to the IDOLO system have been developed as ActiveX controls.

The IDOLO navigation system has been developed by using two different languages: PHP programming language on the server side, and Javascript on the client side. PHP is used to control the content and layout of served HTML pages, and it also serves as the interface between the IDOLO system and a MySQL database server. The MySQL database server holds all system configurations, such as data about the cameras being used or the design of multimedia synoptics found at each station. Using Javascript permits interfacing with web-browser, which makes it possible for the IDOLO system to be informed of user input events (mouse clicks, for example), or control specific browser properties.

Camera Management

From a logical point of view, the IDOLO system is made up of 2 elements: stations and cameras. It is hierarchically organized so that stations own one or more cameras. Three types of cameras have been used. Each one has special features, which has led to the use of different approaches to manage each camera type.

Firstly, network cameras, which do not include internal storage systems, need an external system to store their video. The network camera chosen, the AXIS 230, uses MJPEG codec, which is no more than a sequence of JPEG images. MJPEG is not an efficient video codec, as it only performs spatial compression (based on Discrete Cosine Transformation), as opposed to MPEG-4 that performs both spatial and inter-frame compression. As it needs an external FTP server with enough storage space to stock the video, this can make for an excessive use of network bandwidth.

Webcams and analog cameras need PCs which are dedicated to performing the needed compression and streaming. We have chosen the Windows Media software platform to deal with these processes, which allows for full control over nearly all aspects regarding the previously mentioned procedures.

Figure 2. Screenshots comparing multimedia synoptics and classic synoptics

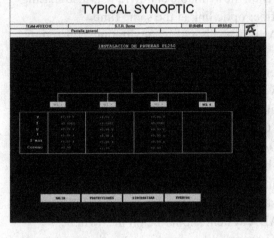

Windows Media Encoder is a software component that takes video and audio from USB cameras and frame grabbers and compresses them with Windows Media codecs, variants of MPEG-4 codec in the case of video and MP3 in the case of audio. It also allows for the immediate storage of compressed content in both local and remote storage. Although WME also allows for the use of streaming by using HTTP/TCP protocols, Windows Media Services is a specialized component that takes data compressed with WME and pushes it to the network using RTSP/UDP protocols. Apart from using more efficient network protocols for streaming, WMS is the necessary solution for allowing external stations to receive multimedia content from WME encoders, when the IP addresses of the encoder stations are inside the local scope.

Multimedia Synoptics

In typical circumstances, HMI systems use synoptics to show all the representative data about SCADA elements in a single screen. The IDOLO system takes this approach one step further and adapts it to the multimedia field (Figure 2) by the following process:

First, video and audio coming from cameras located at a given station are displayed.

Then, these displays provide graphics of all representative elements in a station. When these elements are clicked on, they are able to command the PTZ cameras to move to a preset position which allows them to focus on the specific element that has been previously selected.

When these steps are carried out, it permits the activation of manual control on PTZ cameras. It is possible to employ the manual control by using a mouse or even a joystick.

Multimedia synoptics also provide a solution to the inherent delay that can be noted by the use of the MPEG-family codecs. These can make the manual control of PTZ devices a bit confusing due to the fact that the images can run late in respect to camera movements.

3. CASE STUDY: IDOLO IMPLEMENTATION IN AN ELECTRIC FACILITY

The final goal of the IDOLO project involves the use and integration of our system into a real, working SCADA system (Escudero, 2004). For this reason, we have garnered the cooperation of the Medina Garvey electrical facility, a regional electrical provider located in the city of Seville, in southern Spain.

The existing facilities owned by Medina Garvey have been controlled and supervised using SCADA hardware and software developed by Team Arteche. A specific example of those SCADA components includes the Multitrans device which has been used in the integration tests.

In an effort to avoid compromising the integrity of existing system, it was decided that separate links for sending multimedia and SCADA information from remote stations to the supervision station would be used. The modern facilities in Medina Garvey were equipped with fiber optic links to provide communication with the supervision station, so spare fiber cabling was used for the creation of the separate link. These fiber optic links are more than adequate for the transmission of high-quality multimedia streams.

There are some older facilities that do not currently use the mentioned high-speed links. In such cases, serial radio links which do not have enough bandwidth to send multimedia information have been used for the transmission of SCADA status information. Additionally, these facilities were equipped with telephone lines, making it possible for ADSL technology to be used for sending out multimedia streams. However, using ADSL resulted in the limitation of the transmission to fewer, and lower-quality streams. We have tested the transmission of one 512 Kbps stream, and alternatively, two 256 Kbps streams, and the results were successful.

The SCADA/HMI system used by Medina Garvey, which is a SIPCON HMI system, is a private system, meaning it does not allow for the integration of external components. As a result, IDOLO software has been deployed separately, by using a PC with an Internet Information Services web-server, in order to provide web content to the intranet.

4. IMPROVING IDOLO WITH MULTI-AGENT AND EMBEDDED SYSTEMS TECHNOLOGIES

This section examines the different improvements discovered when the incorporation of embedded and multi-agent technologies took place. When this new system was installed in a real-life environment, we interviewed operators in order to get their reactions regarding their level of satisfaction. Those who were interviewed in turn provided ideas for a few additional improvements. One of the improvements that they proposed was to make IDOLO system function like a black box for them. This basically means that the system would be easy to maintain and configure, and in order to do so, the operator would only have to press a button. Experience with computers would not be required in order to operate this system. This led our project group to consider the possibility of developing the system by using embedded technology.

Embedded systems should not be considered to be PCs with general characteristics. It is, however, becoming more and more possible to replace them in some applications, mostly due to the recent development in the fields of microprocessing and microcontrolling.

Embedded systems could be considered as both hard and soft applications, which make them more interesting and resourceful as far as the immediate future of the Information and Communications Technology sector. The main idea is to use systems which are practically invisible and made up of microprocessors and software. These are in very small systems, and they allow us to obtain information and process it anywhere, in a quick and easy way (by means of ubiquitous computation). If we are able to create a network composed of these embedded systems, which are almost invisible, and we provide them with communication and action abilities, we can create a spatially distributed hardware structure. The result is that this structure is available at all times. This allows for the user to be able to anticipate things (by means of pervasive computation) (Marwedel, 2003; Sutter, 2002). It is possible to accomplish all of this in a more secure and reliable way. The maintenance is also quicker and easier, while the economic costs and electrical consumption are lower than those seen by the use of traditional PCs.

By introducing these systems in hierarchical schemes of "surveillance" as they are distributed into substations or to transformation centers, we can obtain automatic surveillance which specifically allows for preventive maintenance operations (Carrasco, 2009). By using this approach, we can anticipate possible anomalies that could produce blackouts. Blackouts are extremely problematic for the end users and, as a result, they can have significant negative economic impact on the electric utilities.

When talking about automatic surveillance in this article, we are referring to not only proactive surveillance, but reactive surveillance as well. The implication of this difference involves the fact that the elements which carry out the surveillance have human capacities and are able to make decisions and act by themselves. In certain capacities they are autonomous. This human behavior has to be programmed, and our current project involves achieving this by using multi-agent system (MAS) technology.

MAS are systems composed of multiple interacting computing elements, which are known as agents. Agents are computer systems that are equipped with two important capabilities (Wooldridge, 2002):

- They are capable of autonomous actions which allow them to decide by themselves.
- They are also capable of socially interacting with other agents, and able to co-operate, coordinate, and negotiate, among other abilities.

While keeping in mind these results, different interactions among the various kinds of agents are modeled. Each defined agent is responsible for the surveillance in a specific way, because each one has a fixed intelligence level. Some of them have less capacity to process, so they can only carry out a basic analysis of captured situations. Other defined agents, on the other hand, are endowed with more processing capacity, so they can accomplish an advanced analysis.

What kind of information is going to be analyzed by these defined agents? We are working with several types of sensors (in Figure 3) which are able to capture image (visible and infrared), smoke and volumetric measurements. The analysis is carried out in several different ways depending on the kind of data we are presented with. After modeling the interactions, the MAS is designed. The main objective is to be able to control the maximum amount of elements in the electrical facility environment (surveillance targets) by covering them with the minimum number of agents. This is done while keeping agents synchronized so they can co-operate and work together simultaneously. Autonomy and learning capacities are two MAS features that provide great advantages which are very important for our system

5. ARCHITECTURE AND TECHNOLOGY USED IN THE NEW SYSTEM

Two levels of surveillance are used in the architecture of the new system. In the lowest hierarchical level, a network composed by guard agents can be found. These guard agents don't need to have an excessive capacity for processing. These vigilant systems are always collecting information (through sensors) and they have to control their environment by generating alarms or with corrective actions (actuators) if deemed appropriate. They have to interact with their environment in a quick and easy way, and they must process in real time. They have certain mobility, but only within a limited area.

Figure 3. Scheme for the new system

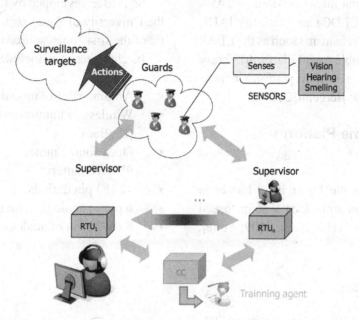

These reactive systems are in continuous interaction with the environment. Traditionally, they have always executed certain steps according to the environment in which they are placed, and have been classified as passive since they always waited for events to happen. When something would occur, they would carry out the process of operations by generating data and changing it to a new state. In this way, the capacity to anticipate is limited, due to the fact that it is restricted to a series of events generated from a series of known states. The process then leads the system to another waiting state.

However, if we change the system in order to make these guards interact, we can create a knowledge network that can be used among them. This network allows guards to request information as they are searching for the most adequate solution (Sasikumar, 2008). If it is not possible to find a solution, our system works by soliciting support from the highest level, where there is a supervisor with a higher computation capacity. At this point, the solution can be transmitted to the lower level, or additional information can be requested from other supervisors.

The high-level architecture is shown in Figure 3.

Description of the Environment Software Used

We based our project on a BDI (belief-desire-intention) architecture which was implemented under the development platform of multi-agent JADE (Java Agent Development Framework) systems (JADE, 2009; Zhang, 2005). This platform allows agent generation to take place as an independent process within a virtual Java (JVM) machine. It also permits the organization of this process by using "Containers" which are no more than independent virtual machines which can execute in a single host, or in various hosts. The communication among the agents and the platform meets the FIPA (Foundation for Intelligent Physical Agents) specifications, and the Drools tool was used for representation and knowledge management in the agents (FIPA, 2009; Proctor, 2007). A small expert system for each agent involved was implemented (Zhuangzhi, 2009). Lastly, it should be pointed out that hosts with moderate computing capacity and resources (such as embedded systems, mobile devices, etc.) in which micro versions of JAVA (specifically J2ME-CLDC) are used, the JADE platform provides mechanisms such as the LEAP (Lightweight Extensible Agent Platform) library which permits the start up of the platform in these systems (JESS, 2009; Bergenti, 2001).

Description of the Platform Hardware Used

The guard agent on the lower level has been implemented with an embedded system, based on SquidBee (Figure 4) (Libelium, 2009; Atmel, 2009).

SquidBee developed by Libelium (spin-off of the University of Zaragoza), has the characteristic of the first "open source mote" (Figure 5). Its characteristics include the following:

- Arduino control module.
- Wireless communication module, Xbee (ZigBee).
- Open source mote.
- 9V feed battery.
- 12 I/O pin digitals.
- 6 pin of analogical inputs.
- 5 PWM pin of analogical output.

Figure 4. SquidBee map

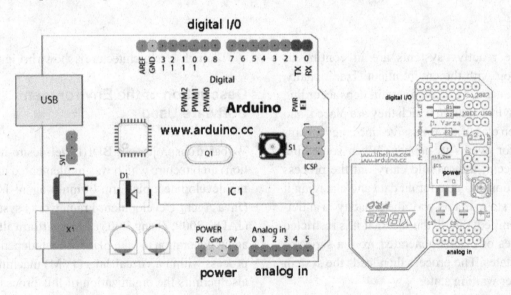

Figure 5. SquidBee mote

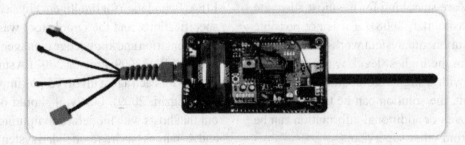

Figure 6. Meshlium card

- USB connection to PC (Windows, Linux and Mac compatible).
- Sensors of: Temperature, Humidity, Light levels and possibility of easily adding new sensors.
- Topology of Peer-to-peer, point-to-point, point-to-multipoint and mesh networks. Possibility of directing up to 65,000 motes.

Meshlium, an embedded system developed by Libelium, has been selected as the "supervisor" agent. Meshlium specifications are:

- 233 MHz AMD Geode SC1100 CPU (fast 486 core).
- 64 or 128 MB SDRAM.
- Operating system and application stored on Compact Flash card.
- About 3 to 5W at 12V DC.
- Three front panel LEDs, one push button switch, can be controlled through CPU GPIO pins. Console I/O redirected to serial port.

- LPC bus for adding serial ports, ISA style I/O, GPIO etc. I2C bus for user interface, software lock devices etc.
- 1 to 3 Ethernet channels (National DP83816), 2 or 1 mini PCI slots, 1 serial port (console)
- 1.2Kg weight (without the antennas).
- 1-2 minutes: time in which all services run

These Meshlium (Figure 6) teams are based on systems of building PC Engines which provide cost-effective added hardware value with SBC (Single Board Computer) to the processing and development network, including wireless routers, firewalls, VPN, industrial Ethernet devices, and other general networking devices.

Its CPU is 233 MHz, and it has an AMD Geode SC1100 CPU (fast 486 core) with 64 to 128 MB of SDRAM. The operative system and applications are stored in a Compact Flash card. It consumes around 3-5W to 12V DC (excluding the mini PCI cards which can be added). The feed can be supplied by a jack or through an Ethernet PoE (Power over Ethernet) cable. It accepts a

Figure 7. Meshlium architecture description

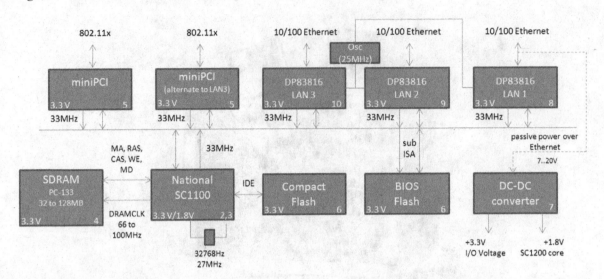

tension range between +7V y +18V DC. An LPD expansion bus is available to add series docks, GPIO and a I2C bus for user interfaces. Additionally, it includes a button and three leds which provide information on the current states. It features 1 to 3 ethernet channels (National DP83816), 2 or 1 slot mini PCI and a dock with a console.

The WRAP microcontrol panel includes the tiny BIOS PC Engines in the panel, in version 1.11. The operating system that it includes is a distribution of linux, supported in the 2.6 kernel, and based on WRAP specific distribution and voyage linux, which is based on Debian. Figure 7 features a diagram of system blocks.

6. PILOT EXPERIENCE

This chapter describes our experience during a pilot test carried out on the previously described platform hardware. The pilot test was based on the PC Engine panels.

This pilot test was done in collaboration with the Technology of Materials research group of the University of Cadiz (Spain). This group specializes in the application of multiagent systems in envi-ronments where automated production systems can be found. We proposed the execution of two different series of tests. The first one was with a group of agents we designed in a beta version; and the other was previously proven since it was productively used in different settings.

For the test using the consolidated agent, we took advantage of this group's concrete experience with agents in the production process and used an agent in the test which automatically managed the engineering project (Aguayo, 2007). This collaboration could be considered to be a kind of endorsement by a professional association. Initially it may seem that the topic was diverted (and directed towards electric facility control), yet we maintain that our true interest and focus involves the execution of an actual agent that is as refined as possible, and responds to all our demands for its use.

Description of the "Maintenance" Agents Designed

Four distinct kinds of agents have been defined (Romero, 2009):

- Preventive maintenance agent (PMA). This agent is responsible for supervising all preventive maintenance operations, which are defined by the electric facility.
- Corrective maintenance agent (CMA). This agent gives support to accomplish the corrective maintenance operations, guaranteeing less risk for the operators.
- Fire prevention agent (FPA). This agent is responsible for monitoring thermographic images and detecting any alarm regarded fire.
- Intrusion detection agent (IDA). This agent is responsible for detecting any intrusion to the interior.

Each of the four kinds of agents is explained in further detail:

A. Preventive maintenance

Utilities usually define specific maintenance ranges according to their installed equipment. Periodic revisions of maintenance (as a preventive measure) are set as fitness criteria for the good conservation state of the facilities and equipment. Low frequency range maintenance is carried out weekly, quarterly or yearly and its execution process includes activities involving a certain type of inspection: they can observe, notice, make notes and check, without the need to turn off the equipment. By analyzing the results of that inspection, the need of corrective intervention is evaluated, or the execution of a corresponding preventive range is initiated when the possible risks are considered.

These ranges are accomplished by the use of road maps and their results are controlled statistically. Although the utility of this kind of maintenance in the daily operation facilities has been proved statistically, the following should be considered:

- Requirements of corrective intervention are not uniform for all facilities, they de-

pend on several factors, and the characteristics of each facility.
- A high percentage of corrective actions taken from road maps don't call for immediate intervention when the risks are evaluated.

It is therefore suitable to reconsider the need to fix criteria which are different from the weekly set surveillance period of the facilities from the point of view of periodic maintenance.

When the revision period is reviewed, a maintenance cost reduction is obtained which may have a relevant effect on the budget. Nevertheless, it is necessary to set the limits and to know the risks of changing the frequency of inspections in the facilities. The factors which determine this change are:

- The pattern of productivity: importance inside the network, installed power and tension, necessity of transfer, urban or rural distribution, telecontrol, etc.
- The technological characteristics: age of the facility, type and technology of equipment, maneuver requests, etc.
- The detected incidences: recorded incidents in the facility, repetition and frequency of incidents, etc.
- Security: intrusion, geographic location, vandalism, etc.
- Productivity tasks: higher level facility maintenance, repairs or improvements of the facility, etc.

Within our system it is proposed that PMAs become responsible for continuous and automatic visual inspection with minimal operator interventions. In this way, both costs and risks are reduced. Also, when information about the installed equipment is included, PMAs are able to propose a road map based on updated statistical results and specific facility characteristics.

Figure 8. FSM for CMA

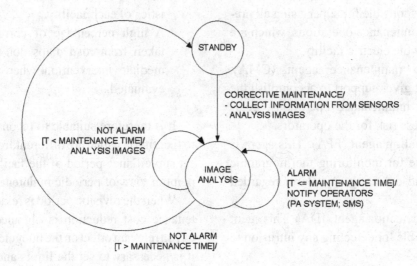

B. Corrective maintenance

In terms of corrective maintenance, our system helps to minimize the typical risks found during the execution of corrective operations which involve dangerous equipment for operators. CMA agents know the intervention procedures in corrective maintenance activities and they are responsible for monitoring the intervention and detecting anomalies in their execution. They immediately notify operators of possible health risk situations. Thus, the system has to be programmed with the different procedures, as well as the duration of each task (Figure 8).

C. Fire prevention and intrusion detection

Two important questions regarding facility maintenance involve supervision to prevent fires and to detect intruders in the substations. Both situations can cost the utilities a lot of money, so it is important to emphasize them. This is why we have incorporated agents which address both of these situations (FPA and IDA).

FPA agents use different types of sensors (smoke and humidity detectors, microphones and thermographic cameras), to examine information and determine if fire risk exists, both in the interior and exterior of the substations.

Fire risk depends on the operation temperature of equipment and environmental parameters which are continuously measured. IDA agents use volumetric sensors and locate possible intrusion alarms, by carrying out an image analysis and deciding if it is a false or real alarm, in which case the control center is notified (Figure 9).

Obtained Results

Keeping in mind that the main objective was to test the sturdiness and flexibility of the chosen support hardware, our research team thought it would be convenient to carry out this trial both in free use and in private environments. This was accomplished by executing one pilot test in a Microsoft (Windows XP SP3) platform and another by using the S.O. Linux (Ubuntu 9.04). The test involved installing and executing the agents in a machine that had limited resources, while simultaneously entering additional data to correctly verify the functioning actions.

In the case of the test which used the Microsoft platform, it was discovered that there was a high level of memory and capacity restriction,

Figure 9. FSM for IDA

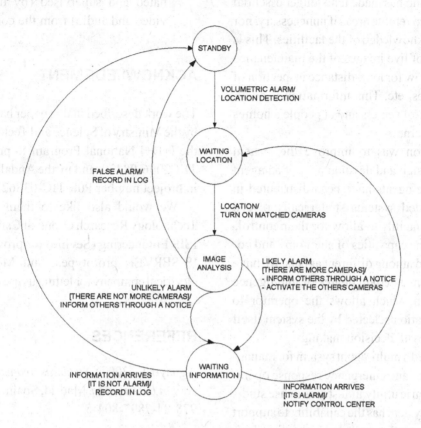

and therefore the S.O. load had to be decreased. This reduction was achieved by eliminating unnecessary S.O. applications, such as games, etc. Execution was completed, yet only after many failed library attempts. It has been ruled out that these failures were enough cause to use the hardware resources, since the original resources proved sufficient. After numerous tests, it was determined that the failures were due to an inappropriate .NET version. This was resolved by making the necessary adjustments. As a result, the correct .NET for this hardware platform was discovered and used in this context.

The experience in the Linux platform turned out to be more bearable. Keeping in mind the imposed hardware restrictions, the results are considered to be successful upon obtaining the execution of the agents of both platforms (although each platform encountered a different level of difficulty).

It can therefore be concluded that our research confirms the possibility of using embedded systems hardware with few resources. These embedded systems can be used for the field execution of specific tasks when agents are incorporated. For the final user, all stages of the task and the outcomes are transparent.

7. CONCLUSION

In this article we have described our IDOLO system which is dedicated to the incorporation of multimedia in SCADA for the telecontrol of electric networks. This system has been successfully tested at a real electric company allowing for the operators of this company to be provided with multi-media information from remote stations. This has provided faster and more complete system management, and has made it no longer essential for staff travel to remote areas if unnecessary, nor have previous knowledge of the facilities. This is due to the use of live images of the maintenance work which allow for long-distance inspection of remote facilities, etc. This information is available at the control centers and at people's homes through the internet.

Our intention was to improve the system through the design and development of an agent network. These agents have been distributed in certain embedded systems strategically placed by the electric facility to allow for their control.

Thanks to the capacities of autonomy and co-operation found among different agents, we have given the system a certain degree of intelligence and automation which allows the operator to receive information selected by the system itself and be helped with decision making.

We presented a multi-agent system for managing maintenance and emergency response operations in the electric utility industry as a case study. The proposed system has the capability to support maintenance operations and make planning decisions. While running on the proposed hardware platform, our system of agents was in production at real facilities for several months, where they obtained quite satisfactory results. We'd like to highlight the following results:

- Failure events are detected earlier, especially the ones related to surveillance, and the reaction time is reduced by 32%.
- There are important savings. A large portion of preventative maintenance can be automatically carried out by the system minimizing situations where the presence of a member of the maintenance staff is present.
- Quality of service is improved because fast reaction results in shorter cuts.
- Risk has been reduced as far as corrective maintenance and repair. Tasks carried out by the maintenance operators are coordi-

nated and supervised (by means of live video and audio) from the control center.

ACKNOWLEDGMENT

The work described in this paper has been funded by the Ministry of Science and Technology within the I+D+I National Program in project number TEC2006-08430, and by the Andalusian Council in project number P08-TIC-03862.

We would also like to thank the Material Technology Research Group of Cadiz University, ISIS Engineering (Seville) for providing us with IS-SERVER prototypes, and Medina-Garvey electrical company for letting us use their facilities.

REFERENCES

Aguayo, F. (2007). *Sistemas Avanzados de Fabricación Distribuida*. Madrid, Spain: Ra-Ma. ISBN 978-84-7897-804-5

Arindam, P. (1999). *QoS in Data Networks: Protocols and Standards*. Columbus, OH: The Ohio State University. Retrieved from http://www.cs.wustl.edu/~jain/cis7889/ftp/qos_protocols/index.html

Atmel. (2009). *Home*. Retrieved from http://www.atmel.com

Bergenti, F., Poggi, A., Burg, B., & Caire, G. (2001). Deploying FIPA-compliant systems on handheld devices. *IEEE Internet Computing*, 5(4), 20–25. doi:10.1109/4236.939446

Boyer, S. A. (1999). *SCADA: Supervisory Control And Data Acquisition* (2nd ed.). New York: ISA: The Instrumentation, Systems and Automation Society.

Carrasco, A., Hernández, M. D., Romero, M. C., Sivianes, F., & Escudero, J. I. (2009). Remote Controlling and Monitoring of Safety Devices Using Web-Interface Embedded Systems. In *Enterprise Information Systems* (Vol. 24, pp. 737-744). Berlin: Springer-Verlag. ISBN 978-3-642-013

Escudero, J. I., Rodriguez, J. A., Romero, M. C., & Diaz, S. (2005). Deployment of digital video and Audio Over electrical SCADA networks. *IEEE Transactions on Power Delivery, 20*(2), 691–695. doi:10.1109/TPWRD.2004.833906

Escudero, J. I., Rodriguez, J. A., Romero, M. C., & Luque, J. (2004). IDOLO: multimedia data deployment on SCADA systems. In *Proceedings of the IEEE Power Systems Conference and Exposition, 1*, 252–257.

FIPA. (2009). *Foundation for Intelligent Physical Agents*. Retrieved from http://www.fipa.org

IEC. (1990). Telecontrol and equipment systems - Part 5: Transmission protocols (IEC 60870-5).

ISO/IEC. (1993). Information technology – Local area networks – Part 3: Carrier sense multiple access with collision detection (ISO/IEC 8802-3).

ISO/IEC. (1999). Information technology – Coding of audio-visual objects – MPEG-4 (ISO/IEC 14496).

JADE. (2009). *Java Agent DEvelopment Framework.* Retrieved from http://jade.tilab.com

JESS. (2009). *Home.* Retrieved from http://www.jessrules.com

Libelium. (2009). *Home.* Retrieved from http://www.libelium.com

Liu, Z., Niu, D., Yang, X., & Sheng, W. (2009). Research on intelligent decision support system for power system. In *Proceedings of the ICIA: International Conference on Information and Automation* (pp. 412-417).

Marwedel, P. (2003). *Embedded System Design.* New York: Springer. ISBN 978-1-4020-7690-9

Proctor, M. (2007). Relational Declarative Programming with JBoss Drools. In *Proceedings of SYNASC: International Symposium on Symbolic and Numeric Algorithms for Scientific Computing* (pp. 26-29).

Romero, M. C., Díaz, S., Sánchez, G., & Escudero, J. I. (2004). SIP Application To Multimedia Telecontrol Of Power Systems. In *World Automation Congress Proceedings* (pp. 131-137).

Romero, M. C., Sivianes, F., Carrasco, A., Hernandez, M. D., & Escudero, J. I. (2009). Managing emergency response operations for electric utility maintenance. *IEEE Industrial Electronics Magazine, 3*(3), 15–18. doi:10.1109/MIE.2009.933883

Sasikumar, B., & Vasudevan, V. (2008). An agent based TCP/IP for Wireless Networks. *International Journal of Digital Content Technology and its Applications, 2*(3), 47-52.

Sutter, E. (2002). *Embedded System Firmware Demystified.* Berkeley, CA: Publishers Group West. ISBN 9781578200993

Wooldridge, M. (2002). *An Introduction to MultiAgent Systems.* New York: Wiley. ISBN 047149691

Zhang, H., & Huang, S.-Y. (2005). A parallel BDI agent architecture. In *Proceedings of the IEEE/WIC/ACM International Conference on Intelligent Agent Technology* (pp. 157-160).

This work was previously published in International Journal of Intelligent Information Technologies, Volume 6, Issue 4, edited by Vijayan Sugumaran, pp. 1-16, copyright 2010 by IGI Publishing (an imprint of IGI Global).

Chapter 14
Web 2.0 Based Intelligent Software Architecture for Photograph Sharing

Arzu Baloglu
Marmara University, Turkey

Mudasser F. Wyne
National University, USA

Yilmaz Bahcetepe
Marmara University, Turkey

ABSTRACT

With the development of Web 2.0 technologies, the sharing of photographs has increased. In this paper, the authors evaluate the art of photography, analyze how to develop intelligent photograph sharing system, and explaine the requirements of such systems. The authors present an architecture of an intelligent Web 2.0 based system and in future hope to add more modules for retention of users on the system. The system focuses on Web 2.0 usage, web mining for personalization service, and brings a different approach to collaborative filtering.

1. INTRODUCTION

Long ago the computer was introduced as a simple accounting and record keeping device but soon it motivated many other computer and IT related activities. Similarly, internet network that all over the world provides broad bandwidth to users, which allows users to transfer megabytes of data in seconds. Initially internet was more or less simply a social communication platform but now it is considered as one of the leading communication technology and one of the necessities of life. The extent to which business and research community as well as service sector utilizes web technology looks like, this technology and its associated services are going to expand even further. Therefore, in future, web technologies must be empowered by additional capabilities coupled with Semantic Web technologies to fulfill even broader and long term application promises.

DOI: 10.4018/978-1-4666-0158-1.ch014

In the past few decades the advancements in the field of IT has opened many more doors to various new kinds of internet applications. Social application is being one of them provide the environment for human social interaction and information sharing through web. This leads to the next phase in the Web's evolution namely, Web 2.0. It has received lots of attention from web users, business services and IT professionals. Web 2.0 is also sometimes referred to as the wisdom web, people centric web and read/write web (Murugesan, 2007). The cultural and social contribution brought by the Web 2.0 in the cyberspace is tremendous. It brings a new approach towards sharing information and interacting with other users over the internet in a collaborative manner thus providing opportunities for leveraging the web and engaging its users more effectively. This amalgamation of web technologies and social interactions has made Web 2.0 an important internet technology.

In this paper we concentrate on photograph sharing application and assume that internet users are willing to post and share their photographs and comments with other users. We describe a design of a photo sharing system using shared photo collections generated by multiple internet users. The system is based on a client-server architecture and focuses on new photographs sharing techniques and approaches.

2. DEVELOPMENT OF PHOTOGRAPHY

The traditional photographic process that has defined image reproduction for over 150 years and involves a long drawn series of chemical reactions. That begins with the capture of light on silver film and ends with transferring of the image onto paper or a transparency through the development processing. The final image is analog, which means it is composed of continuous gradients. There are number of issues related to traditional photography; the costs of films are high, there is no possibility to take an instant view of photographs taken on a screen, like digital cameras. In addition chemical processing of these films in darkroom is time consuming as well as not an easy process. Most importantly archiving these analog images in digital format is harder.

The traditional way to take a picture has not changed much with the advent of digital cameras (Merril, 2005) or has become a little easier, just point and press the button on a camera with automatic focus feature. Most digital images still start out from traditional media. However, digital photography offers more options for being creative with the end product, the images can be altered or digitally enhanced according to the photographer's context in different ways easily and more artistically using readily available softwares. In addition, digital images can be easily saved on a digital storage medium and add to personal collection, or share them with friends and family via email or with any of the available photo sharing websites. There are number of approaches presented in the literature for sharing digital photos. An approach that includes tabletop interface is described in (Balabanovic, Chu, & Wolff, 2000) although it is good for sharing photos but it lacks the portability. Leonard and Marsden (2007) present a mobile application allowing users to share their digital images with other users. The approach synchronizes the display on multiple mobile devices in asynchronous way and limited to only to maximum of four users at a time.

A photo sharing site is the one that provides the means for a user to upload their digital images (usually photos from a digital camera, but technically any file saved in a common image format such as JPEG, GIF or PNG) to a third party online server, where they are stored and hosted for public or private access and display. There are many commercially available photo sharing services such as Kodak Gallery, Picasa, and Flickr. These sites provide sharing experiences and communication among users. Among these Flickr is

Figure 1. Comparison of photo sharing sites (adapted from Desktop Publishing, 2009)

	Alexa	Ajax	Upload Client	Albums	Groups	Search	Tags	Print	Feeds	Widgets	API
Flickr	39	yes	yes	yes	yes	yes	yes	yes	yes	yes	yes
Photobucket	70	no	no*	yes	no	yes	no	yes	no	yes	yes
Kodakgallery	450	no	yes	yes	no	no	no	yes	no	no	no
MyPhotoAlbum	7000	no	yes	yes	no	no	no	yes	no	no	no
Pbase	600	no	yes	yes	no	yes	no	yes	no	no	no
Picasa	38500	no	yes	yes	no	yes	yes	yes	no	no	no
Picturetrail	3000	no	yes	yes	yes	no	no	yes	no	yes	no
Shutterfly	950	no	yes	yes	no	no	no	yes	no	no	no
Slide	2250	yes	no	yes	no	no	yes	no	no	yes	no
Smugmug	1400	yes	yes	yes	yes	yes	yes	yes	yes	no	yes
Snapfish	1060	no	yes	yes	no	no	no	yes	no	no	no
Webshots	160	yes	yes	yes	yes	yes	no	yes	yes	yes	yes
Zoomr	10482	yes	yes	yes	no	yes	yes	no	no	no	no
Zoto	17200	yes	yes	yes	yes	yes	yes	no	yes	yes	yes

one of the most popular photo sharing services. It also allows users to add labels or tags to the pictures by themselves as well as by others. These tags make retrieval of these pictures easy through proper organization. In addition, photographs can also be viewed over maps by using geotagged photographs. A collaborative guidance system for extracting information about the location of a user from a shared photo collection is proposed by Kadobayashi and Lim (2008). In this case tags attached to each photograph is associated to geographical information. However, Vronay and Davis (2006) argue that online photo sharing does not convey the emotion and feelings as in face-to-face setting. Other services that are also gaining popularity are photolog and moblog. A blog with photographs rather than text is called photolog where as mobilenabled blog is called moblog, allowing user to update their blogs through any mobile device. A person with camera phones can upload their photos on photo sharing services or blogs using services such as Pictavision and LocoBlog. These photologs, moblogs, and shared online photographs can be "Consumer-Generated Media" (CGM) (Blackshaw, 2009). An example of GCM mapcom is a site that allows users to post

and share their word-of-mouth information about sightseeing, restaurant, hotels, events, and so on.

However the overall leader in the photo sharing market in general, and with a good mix between mainstream and social web, is Photobucket. It has been able to add just enough social features, without getting too complex thus attracting lot of people from traditional photo sharing sites. Figure 1 shows a brief comparison between various sites based on the services that are provided and capabilities of these sites.

3. INTELLIGENT SHARING

Most Web structures are large and quite complex so users often miss the goal of their inquiry, or receive ambiguous results when they navigate through web site (Eirinaki & Vazirgiannis, 2003). Web personalization is defined as any action that adapts the information or services provided by a Web site to the needs of a particular user or a set of users, taking advantage of the knowledge gained from the users' navigational behavior and individual interests, in combination with the content and the structure of the Web site. The objective of a Web personalization system is to "provide users with the information they want or need, without expecting them to ask for it explicitly" (Mulvenna, Anand, & Buchner, 2000). Innovation allowed e-commerce companies to effectively set up and maintain web sites which address customers in personalized and pro-active ways (Abbattista, Degemmis, Licchelli, Lops, Semeraro, & Zambetta, 2002). Since user may not be able to find item that they are searching for on the web site. Specially, in case of photograph sharing websites, containing millions of photographs, thus using web personalization will give users the ability to efficiently find photograph that they are looking for and use system more effectively.

Most of existing photograph sharing sites on the internet provide users an environment where users can upload and share photographs, make comments and add labels or tags to the photographs. But, personalization of these photographers in terms of quality and nature of the photography is generally not the main purpose of these websites. There sole purpose is sharing the photographs among the users. Web personalization is being an important aspect leads us to develope a new photograph sharing system with web personalization as its prominent feature. In addition, the system also satisfies user requirements related to;

- Ability to suggest places and location to user for taking pictures.
- Provide users assistance by making statistical information available to them.
- Simplify the search for users.

4. OUR APPROACH

Internet users these days have access to incredible number of photographs on various websites with different categories and varying qualities. Users are mostly interested in the photographs which are relevant to their search criteria as well to their interest. However, they also expect to get the photographs which are not according to their interest. So, in millions of these photographs, how users can find what they like? Web mining can therefore be used to provide an automated solution to this problem. It should predict the photographs that user dislikes and therefore recommends only those photographs that user may like. Web mining is the application of data mining techniques to discover patterns from the Web. According to analysis targets, web mining can be divided into three different types, which are Web usage mining, Web content mining and Web structure mining (Wikipedia, 2009b).

Web 2.0 is a term describing the trend in the use of World Wide Web technology and web design that aims to enhance creativity, information sharing, and, most notably, collaboration among users (Wikipedia, 2009c). Therefore the design basis for the system that we propose in this paper is also Web 2.0. We provide information sharing through data mining that gives results based on cooperation of user data and modern visual design. Since our system design is based on personalization so we also focus on using web usage mining and brings a different approach to collaborative filtering. As mentioned earlier, most of the photographs sharing web sites do not provide statistical reports to users for their personal use. Our system therefore brings a good and new service to users. They are suggested new places for taking photograph that are in close proximity to their present location.

5. COLLABORATIVE FILTERING

Another approach called collaborative filtering is a successful recommender system technology. It works by matching user preferences to other users' preferences while making recommendations to user search criteria (Sarwar, Karypis, Konstan, & Riedl, 2000). Collaborative filtering systems especially make use of the user data; that is primarily the taste or preference data. Some of the leading websites that use collaborative filtering

Table 1. User and item rating matrix

	Item-1	Item-2	Item-3	Item-4	Item-5
User-1	4	2	4	5	5
User-2	1	1	5	3	4
User-3	2	4	3	5	3
User-4	4	3	4	5	?

are amazon.com, half.com, last.fm, and flickr. com. Collaborative filtering aims at finding the relationships among the new data values and the existing data in order to further determine the similarity and provide recommendations to the users (Chen & McLeod, 2006). Collaborating filtering systems are generally categorized as item-based and user-based collaborative filtering algorithms. Important issue in our case is, how to determine the similarity among the items or the users? For user-based approaches, the essential part is to get similarities among the users. Largely used method for user-based approach is nearest neighbor algorithm. The basic of nearest neighbor algorithm is to define the user who has similar preferences, according to the items they have ever preferred or searched. For example, assume an online music album selling website, there will be large group of users who purchased some albums. From this purchase data we would like to determine the users who have similar tastes among all the active users. Later using the data we would like to suggest the items that were liked by user from the same taste group.

As an example of a neighborhood based method, consider Table 1. The wish is to predict if User #4 will like the album Item-5. User #1 is User #4's best neighbor, since the two of them have agreed closely on all other albums (items). As a result, User #1's opinion of the album Item #5 will influence User #4's prediction the most. However, User #2 and User #3 are not as good neighbors because both of them have disagreed with User #4 on certain albums. As a result, their

influence on User #4's prediction is much lesser than User #1.

Correlation between users can be calculated via users' vectors that are set of items' ratings. Correlation coefficient is a statistical measure that indicates the strength and direction of a linear relationship of two random variables. One of the most popular methods is Pearson correlation coefficient for weighting user similarity. The Pearson correlation coefficient is a common measure of the correlation between two variables X and Y. Pearson's correlation reflects the degree of linear relationship between two variables. It ranges from +1 to -1. A correlation of +1 means is that there is a perfect positive linear relationship between variables. When one of the variables increases, other one increases too. A correlation of -1 means is that there is a perfect negative linear relationship between variables. When one of the variables increases then other one decreases. A correlation of 0 means there is no linear relationship between the two variables.

Personalization. The search history of users of our system is saved in order to keep track of the photographs that user have searched and looked. This stored information is then used to find users of similar interested of photographs using the Pearson correlation coefficient among the active and other users of the system. When all of the neighbors are determined, the photographs which some of the neighbors have looked at but have not been seen by the active user are recommended in the main page of our system. Since

Table 2. User and Category matrix

	Nature	Macro	Portrait	Journey	Fine Arts
Ahmet	120	270	40	30	270
Mehmet	220	150	450	2	18
Hasan	40	320	86	12	81
Hüseyin	270	60	20	39	14
Ali	285	54	18	47	33
Veli	41	33	2	5	3

this process is available to all users, so every user is provided with different main page that is personalized for that particular user.

For example, Table 3 shows users and categories of photographs, each cell represent the number of the photographs in a particular category that the related user liked.

Firstly, system translates these data values into proportional form. Therefore for user Ali, proportion of the *nature* photographs that he liked is 65%, percentage of photographs liked by Ali is important, not the number of photographs. After this operation, Pearson correlation coefficient is used for measuring the similarity weight between the users by using this table. According to results, the most similar users of the active user are determined. Then, the photographs which some of these similar users liked are recommended to active user in their main page. The records of data related to photographs liked and disliked by users are stored in another table.

Collaborative filtering techniques determine similarity between users based on similarity on huge amount of sparse data. However, measuring the similarity weight among the users by using the available taste data to gain better performance. The data is categorized according to categories of photographs. Because collaborative filtering has performance problems while it is dealing with large datasets. As it is shown in Table 2, to measure the similarity of two users, all items must be considered. It means that order of calculating

similarity is $O(m*n)$ for each user where m equals to number of users and n is number of items. When the number of users and number of items increases significantly, then the taste data space becomes sparse. Running prediction algorithms on this data ends up with performance loss. As seen in Table 3, the system uses photographs' categories instead of photographs for calculating similarities among users and it is really smaller than the tables that are used by the mentioned collaborative filtering techniques. Numbers of categories do not exceed nearly thirty (so, it is assumed constant), but number of photographs may even reach millions of photos. Therefore, order of this system is $O(m)$. After getting the similar profiles to any active user, system will select photographs in specified category which was liked by all users and never seen before active user.

Photographer development. The system provides users with the statistical information about personal development. The data presented is regarding the criticism made by other users during a certain time period. It gives opportunity to users for noticing their own deficiency regarding the criteria specified for photograph. The statistical information is presented in the form of a diagram presented by the system, accordingly to the votes given by other users. The system also suggests places to users where photograph can be taken. The system uses Google Map for these recommendations.

Table 3. User and category matrix in normalized form

	Nature	Macro	Portrait	Journey	Fine Arts
Ahmet	17%	37%	5%	4%	37%
Mehmet	26%	18%	54%	0%	2%
Hasan	8%	59%	16%	2%	15%
Hüseyin	67%	15%	5%	10%	3%
Ali	65%	12%	4%	11%	8%
Veli	49%	39%	2%	6%	4%

Search engine for photograph is significant property of the proposed system. The system allows users to search the photographs using tags or labels entered by owner of photograph.

6. SYSTEM ARCHITECTURE DESIGN

Three-tier architecture is the bases for the architecture for the system design presented in this paper. It is a is a client-server architecture in which the user interface, functional process logic ("business rules"), computer data storage and data access are developed and maintained as independent modules, most often on separate platforms (Eckerson, 1995). The 3-Tier architecture has the following three tiers: (Wikipedia, 2009a)

Presentation Tier. This is the top most layer of the application. It displays information related to services like, browsing, purchasing, and shopping cart contents. It communicates with other layers or tiers by transmitting results to the all other tiers in the network.

Application Tier (Business Logic/Logic Tier). The logic tier is drawn from the presentation tier. The function of this tier is to control an application's functionality; detailed processing is performed at this tier.

Data Tier. This tier consists of Database Servers. All of the information storage and retrieval operations are performed at this tier. However, data at this tier are kept neutral and independent from the above two tiers. This independence helps improve scalability and performance.

Java Platform had been chosen for developing this system. Thus, the system has JSP files, Servlets, POJO's, some classes for other operational purposes. Since JSP is used as front-end side of system, it is in Presentation Layer. Resource files like JavaScript, images, CSS files are also in Presentation Layer. Servlets, POJO's and some other operational classes like Pearson correlation coefficient calculator exist in Business Layer, since they provide the operational side of the system.

Hibernate is an open source project that presents powerful, high performance object/relational persistence as well as query service. It allows development of persistent classes following object-oriented idiom - including association, inheritance, polymorphism, composition, and collections (Hibernate, 2009). In addition Hibernate O/R mapping tools provides an ideal solution for enterprise application of any size. It handles all the logic to store and retrieve POJO objects (RoseIndia, 2009). Hibernate was chosen for making CRUD operations on database since it provides connection pooling, resource and transaction management options. Data Access Objects (DAO) is an important part of Hibernate. The codes about *select*, *insert* and *delete* operations are also part of them. Figure 2 shows the architecture of the proposed system. These three layers are physically located on same machine.

7. DATABASE AND GUI DESIGN

Basic objects in our system are photographs and the users. Database is designed for user information and photographs information. The link between different objects is established through relations. Since, the system is also supposed to provide statistical information data mining is also part of this activity. In presentation layer of the system, JSP was used. For advanced applications, and when more code is involved, it is important not to mix business logic with front-end presentation in the same file. Separating business logic from presentation, permits changes to either side without affecting the other (Sun Developer Network, 2009). So, as it is possible, it was avoided to use Java code inside of JSP file for preventing further code complexity. It was preferred to carry Java codes as much as possible to Servlets or other Java classes. Thus, presentation layer is mostly isolated from business layer.

Design of pages is critical for our system, since this system is related to users who are interested in photography, so their expectations about visual design are higher than normal users. Thus, it was paid attention to visual design of pages. Main colors, red, black and white, were selected to use all over the website to provide consistency among all pages in terms of used colors. CSS was used for stylizing the pages. JavaScript was used for client-side operations like validations. In general, servlets and other classes are designed according to the object oriented design approach. Hibernate classes were generated by using MyEclipse IDE. Object relational mapping are provided with hibernate classes and work flow of the system are made accordingly object relational mapping. On the other hand, some libraries were also used in the system, like JFreeChart. Besides, some pure algorithmic operations like minimizing photograph, calculating Pearson correlation coefficient were created in Java classes separately.

Figure 2. System architecture

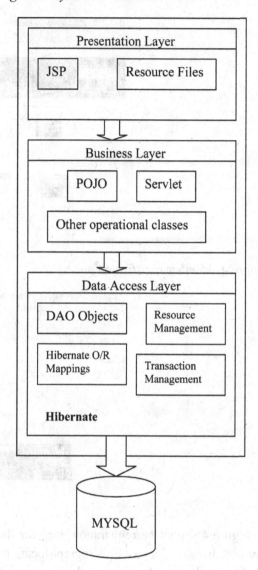

8. IMPLEMENTATION

The implementation of our proposed system is presented in this section. The actual implementation of the system is done in Turkish so a brief description of each screen shot is presented. Some of the screen shots are shown to share the the system outlook. Figure 3 shows the main page of the system. It also shows the photograph that has been voted as best picture of the week.

Figure 3. Main page

Figure 4. Member registration page

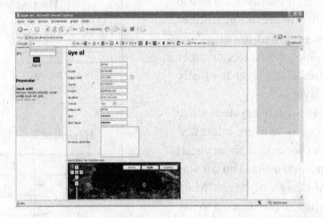

Figure 4 shows the registration page for the new user. It also indicates the photograph locations on the google map. In Figure 5 the photograph and the associated story is shown along with comments from other users. These comments are generally related to the quality of the photograph such as contrast ratio, aperture setting, esthetics, etc. The location of the photograph is displayed on the google map along with the information about the user who took the phograph.

Figure 6 shows the screen with different categories of the photographs that are available for user view. This categorization is done for user convenience incase they are interested only a specific category.

Figure 7 shows the photographs that are in queue to be rated by the users and Figures 8 and 9 show the statistics for the photograph that has been rated by the users. All the comments from the users related to this photograph can also be viewed.

9. CONCLUSION

After 2004 with Web 2.0, sharing of information and documents acquired great importance. The system we proposed presents new perspective on sharing of photograph as one application area for Web 2.0. This system in addition presents lots of

Figure 5. Picture story

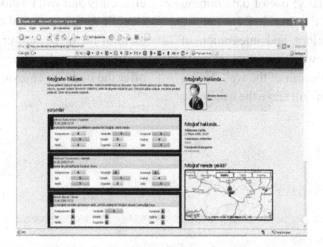

Figure 6. Photograph categories

Figure 7. Waiting photogrphs

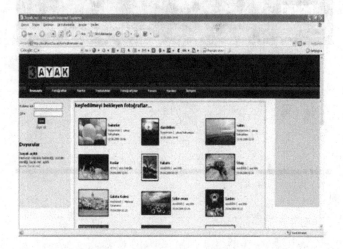

new approaches, especially; use of data mining is a new trend around the world. Data mining is new to web applications and integration of data mining techniques will make system more intelligent for personalization of the web. Using these techniques, system will serve the user more

efficiently and will be more specific to each user. Beneficial suggestion of the system and management of them. To sum up this system is pioneer in its own specific approach and will hopefully offer the users an enjoyable platform.

Figure 8. Photograph statistics

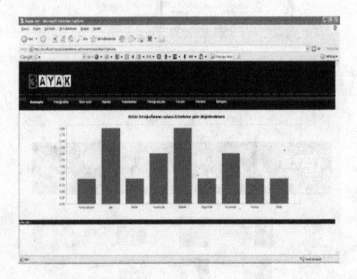

Figure 9. Photograph statistics

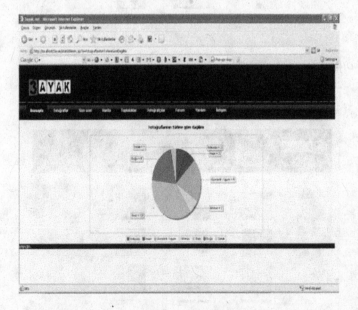

REFERENCES

Abbattista, F., Degemmis, M., Licchelli, O., Lops, P., Semeraro, G., & Zambetta, F. (2002, May 28). *Improving the usability of an e-commerce web site through personalization.* Paper presented at the Workshop on Recommendation and Personalization in eCommerce, Malaga, Spain.

Balabanovic, M., Chu, L., & Wolff, G. (2000, April 1-6). Storytelling with Digital Photographs. In T. Turner, G. Szwillus, M. Czerwinski, F. Peterno, & S. Pemberton (Eds.), ACM CHI 2000 Human Factors in Computing (pp. 564–571). Hague, The Netherlands.

Blackshaw, P. (2009). *The Pocket Guide t.* Retrieved June 10, 2009, from http://www.clickz.com/showPage.html?page=3515576

Chen, A., & McLeod, D. (2006). Collaborative Filtering for Information Recommendation Systems. In *Encyclopedia of E-Commerce.* E-Government, and Mobile Commerce.

Desktop Publishing. (2009). Retrieved June 15, 2009, from http://desktoppub.about.com/od/scanninggraphics/a/dig_trad_photos.htm

Eckerson, E. (1995). Three Tier Client/Server Architecture: Achieving Scalability, Performance, and Efficiency in Client Server Applications. *Open Information Systems, 10*(3), 1–20.

Eirinaki, M., & Vazirgiannis, M. (2003). Web mining for web personalization. *ACM Transactions on Internet Technology, 3*(1), 1–27. doi:10.1145/643477.643478

Hibernate. (2009). *Relational Persistence for Java and. NET.* Retrieved June 15, 2009, from http://www.hibernate.org

Kadobayashi, R., & Lim, A. (2008, January 14-16). Collaborative Guidance System using Multi-Gaze History and Shared Photography Collection. In *Proceedings of the Sixth International Conference on Creating, Connecting and Collaborating through Computing,* Poitiers, France (pp. 39-46). Washington, DC: IEEE Computer Society.

Leonard, M., & Marsden, G. (2007, September 9-12). Co-Present photo sharing on mobile devices. In *Proceedings of the 9th International Conference on Human Computer Interaction with Mobile Devices and Services,* Singapore (pp. 277-284).

Merril, D. (2005, September 10-11). *Ideas and Considerations for Digital Photograph Sharing.* Paper presented at the Workshop on Pervasive Image Capture and Sharing, Tokyo, Japan.

Mulvenna, M., Anand, S., & Buchner, A. (2000). Personalization on the Net using Web Mining. *Communications of the ACM, 43*(8), 123–125. doi:10.1145/345124.345165

Murugesan, S. (2007). Understanding Web 2.0. *IT Professional, 9*(4), 34–41. doi:10.1109/MITP.2007.78

Pata, K., & Laanpere, M. (2008, July 1-5). Supporting cross-institutional knowledge-building with Web 2.0 enhanced digital portfolios. In *Proceedings of the Eighth IEEE International Conference on Advanced Learning Technologies,* Santander, Spain (pp. 798-80).

RoseIndia. (2009). *Application Architecture.* Retrieved June 15, 2009, from http://www.roseindia.net/jsf/myfacesspring/application-architecture.shtml

Sarwar, B., Karypis, G., Konstan, J., & Riedl, J. (2000, August 20). Application of dimensionality reduction in recommender systems: A case study. In *Proceedings of ACM SIGKDD 2000, Workshop on Web Mining for E-Commerce: Challenges and Opportunities,* Boston (pp. 1-12).

Sun Developer Network. (2009). *Servlets and JSP Pages Best Practices*. Retrieved June 15, 2009, from http://java.sun.com/developer/technicalArticles/javaserverpages/servlets_jsp

Vronay, D., & Davis, S. (2006). *PhotoStory: Preserving emotion in digital photo sharing*. Virtual Worlds Group, Microsoft Research.

Wikipedia. (2009a). *Multitier Architecture*. Retrieved June 15, 2009, from http://en.wikipedia.org/wiki/Multitier_architecture

Wikipedia. (2009b). *Web mining*. Retrieved June 15, 2009, from http://www.en.wikipidia.org/wiki/Web_mining

Wikipedia. (2009c). *Web 2.0*. Retrieved June 15, 2009, from http://www.en.wikipidia.org/wiki/Web_2

This work was previously published in International Journal of Intelligent Information Technologies, Volume 6, Issue 4, edited by Vijayan Sugumaran, pp. 17-29, copyright 2010 by IGI Publishing (an imprint of IGI Global).

Chapter 15
Collusion–Free Privacy Preserving Data Mining

T. Purusothaman
Government College of Technology, India

M. Rajalakshmi
Coimbatore Institute of Technology, India

S. Pratheeba
Indian Institute of Science, India

ABSTRACT

Distributed association rule mining is an integral part of data mining that extracts useful information hidden in distributed data sources. As local frequent itemsets are globalized from data sources, sensitive information about individual data sources needs high protection. Different privacy preserving data mining approaches for distributed environment have been proposed but in the existing approaches, collusion among the participating sites reveal sensitive information about the other sites. In this paper, the authors propose a collusion-free algorithm for mining global frequent itemsets in a distributed environment with minimal communication among sites. This algorithm uses the techniques of splitting and sanitizing the itemsets and communicates to random sites in two different phases, thus making it difficult for the colluders to retrieve sensitive information. Results show that the consequence of collusion is reduced to a greater extent without affecting mining performance and confirms optimal communication among sites.

INTRODUCTION

Major technological developments and innovations in the field of information technology have made it easy for organizations to store a huge amount of data within its affordable limit. Data mining techniques come in handy to extract useful

information for strategic decision making from voluminous data which is either centralized or distributed (Agrawal & Srikant, 1994; Han & Kamber, 2001).

The term *data mining* refers to extracting or mining knowledge from a massive amount of data. Data mining functionalities like association rule mining, cluster analysis, classification, prediction etc. specify the different kinds of patterns mined.

DOI: 10.4018/978-1-4666-0158-1.ch015

Association Rule Mining (ARM) finds interesting association or correlation among a large set of data items. Finding association rules among huge amount of business transactions can help in making many business decisions such as catalog design, cross marketing, etc. A best example of ARM is market basket analysis. This is the process of analyzing the customer buying habits from the association between the different items which is available in the shopping baskets. This analysis can help retailers to develop marketing strategies. ARM involves two stages

i)   Finding frequent itemsets
ii) Generating strong association rules

Association Rule Mining: Basic Concepts

Let $I = \{i_1, i_2 \ldots i_m\}$ be a set of m distinct items. Let D denote a database of transactions where each transaction T is a set of items such that $T \subseteq I$. Each transaction has a unique identifier, called *TID*. A set of item is referred to as an *itemset*. An itemset that contains k items is a *k-itemset*. *Support* of an itemset is defined as the ratio of the number of occurrences of the itemset in the data source to the total number of transactions in the data source. Support shows the frequency of occurrence of an itemset. The itemset X is said to have a support s if $s\%$ of transactions contain X. The support of an association rule $X \rightarrow Y$ is given by

Support = (Number of transactions containing X U Y) / (Total number of Transactions)

where X is the antecedent and Y is the consequent

An itemset is said to be *frequent* when the number of occurrences of that particular itemset in the database is larger than a user-specified minimum support. *Confidence* shows the strength of the relation. The confidence of an association rule is given by,

Confidence = (Number of transactions containing X U Y) / (Total number of Transactions containing X)

An association rule is said to be *strong* when its confidence is larger than a user-specified minimum confidence. Association rules with support and confidence above the minimum support and minimum confidence alone are mined. Many algorithms have been proposed for frequent itemsets generation. They are Apriori, Pincer search, Frequent pattern tree, etc. (Agrawal & Srikant, 1994; Lin & Kedem, 2002; Han, Pei, Yin & Mao, 2004).

Distributed Data Mining

In the present situation, information is the key factor which drives and decides the success of any organization and it is essential to share information pertaining to an individual data source for mutual benefit. Thus, Distributed Data Mining (DDM) is considered as the right solution for many applications, as it reduces some practical problems like voluminous data transfers, massive storage unit requirement, security issues etc. Distributed Association Rule Mining (DARM) is a sub-area of DDM. DARM is used to find global frequent itemsets from different data sources distributed among several sites and interconnected using a communication network. The DARM scenario is illustrated in Figure 1.

In DARM, the local frequent itemsets for the given minimum support are generated at the individual sites by using data mining algorithms like Apriori, FP Growth tree, etc. (Agrawal et al., 1994; Han et al., 2001). Then, global frequent itemsets are generated by combining local frequent itemsets of all the participating sites with the help of distributed data mining algorithm (Cheung, Ng, Fu, & Fu, 1996; Ashrafi, Taniar, & Smith, 2004). The strong rules generated by distributed association rule mining algorithms satisfy both minimum global support and confidence threshold.

Figure 1. Distributed association rule mining

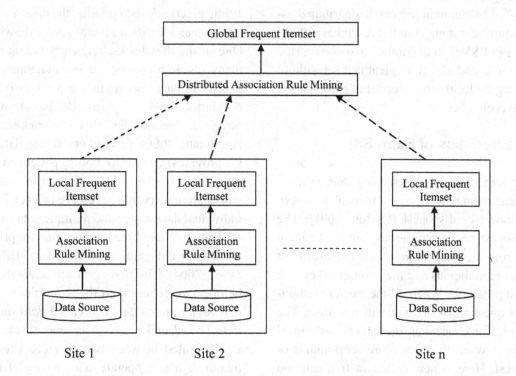

Let $D_1, D_2 ... D_n$ be the data sources which are geographically distributed. Let m be the number of items and $I = \{i_1, i_2 ... i_m\}$ be a set of items. *Global Support* of an itemset is defined as the ratio of the number of occurrences of the itemset in all the data sources to the total number of transactions in all the data sources. An itemset is said to be globally *frequent* when the number of occurrences of that particular itemset in all the data sources is larger than a user-specified minimum support.

Privacy

During global frequent itemset generation, local frequent itemsets of individual sites need to be shared. So, the participating sites learn the exact support count of all other participating sites. However, in many situations the participating sites

are not interested to disclose the support counts of some of their itemsets which are considered as *sensitive information*. Thus, it is essential to share information pertaining to an individual data source without revealing sensitive information (Vaidya & Clifton, 2004). This type of information sharing or allowing access to sensitive information of a data source is likely to cause some serious privacy issues in real time situations.

A typical example of a privacy-preserving data mining problem occurs in the field of medical research. Consider the case of a number of different hospitals that wish to jointly mine their patient data for the purpose of medical research. Further, assume that privacy policy and law prevents these hospitals from ever pooling their data or revealing it to each other, due to the confidentiality of patient records. In such cases, classical data mining solutions cannot be used. Hence, Secure Mutiparty Computational (SMC) solutions can be applied to maintain privacy in distributed association rule mining (Lindell & Pinkas, 2009). The goal of SMC in distributed association rule mining is to find global frequent itemset without revealing the local support count of participating sites to each other.

Characteristics of Each Site

In distributed privacy preserving data mining, the participating sites may be treated as honest, semi-honest or dishonest (Clifton, 2001). The semi-honest parties are honest but try to learn more from received information. The dishonest parties are malicious and they do not follow the defined protocols. When all the parties are honest the question of privacy will not arise. The real need for concealing the data of individual site arises when the parties are semi-honest or dishonest. Here, a new collusion free solution is proposed to find the global frequent itemsets among dishonest parties.

The main objectives of the proposed method are:

a) To find global frequent itemsets among dishonest multiple parties
b) To improve privacy amidst collusion
c) To reduce communication cost and time complexity

The subsequent sections of the paper are organized as follows. Firstly, related existing works are reviewed. Secondly, the proposed approach and its performance evaluation are discussed. Thirdly discussion and limitations are presented. Lastly, a suitable conclusion and future work for maintaining privacy is attempted.

RELATED WORK

While practicing data mining, the database community has identified several severe drawbacks. One of the drawbacks frequently mentioned in many research papers is about maintaining the privacy of data residing in a data source (Clifton & Marks, 1996; Verykios, Bertino, Provenza, Saygin & Theodoridis, 2004; Nedunchezhian & Anbumani, 2006). Privacy preserving data mining provides methods for finding patterns without revealing sensitive data. Numerous research works are underway to preserve privacy both in individual data source and multiple data sources.

There are two broad approaches for privacy-preserving data mining (Wang, Lee, Billis, & Jafari, 2004). The first approach alters the data before it is delivered to the data miner so that real values are hidden. It is called *data sanitization*. The second approach assumes that the data is distributed between two or more sites, and that these sites cooperate to learn the global data mining results without revealing the data at their individual sites. The second approach was named by Goldreich as *Secure Multiparty Computation (SMC)* (Goldreich, 1998, Lindell & Pinkas, 2009). Data mining on sanitized data results in loss of accuracy, while SMC protocols give accurate results with high computation or communication costs (Inan, Saygyn, Savas, Hintoglu, & Levi, 2006). Representative works from each of the approaches is discussed in the following sections.

Data Sanitization

Clifton and Marks (1996) have provided a well designed scenario which clearly reveals the importance of data sanitization. In this scenario, by providing the original unaltered database to an external party, some strategic association rules that are crucial to the data owner are disclosed with serious adverse effects. The sensitive association rule hiding problem is very common in a collaborative association rule mining project, in which one company may decide to disclose only part of knowledge contained in its data and hide strategic knowledge represented by sensitive rules. These sensitive rules must be protected before its data is shared. Also they suggest different measures to protect sensitive data such as limiting access, altering the data, eliminating unnecessary groupings, and augmenting the data in a single data source.

Atallah, Bertino, Elmagarmid, Ibrahim, and Verykios (1999) proposed the concept of *data sanitization* to resolve the association rule hiding problem. Its main idea is to select some transactions from original database and to modify them through some heuristics. They also proved that the optimal sanitization is an NP-hard problem. Moreover, data sanitization can produce a lot of I/O operations, which greatly increases the time cost, especially when the original database includes a large number of transactions.

The *sanitizing algorithm* explained in the paper (Stanley, Oliveira, & Zaıane, 2003) requires two scans of data source. The first scan is required to build the index for speeding up the sanitization process. The second scan is used to sanitize the original data source. This represents a more significant improvement compared to the other algorithms which require various scans depending on the number of association rules that are to be hidden.

Lee, Chang, and Chen (2004) define a sanitization matrix in their recent work. By multiplying the original transaction database and the sanitization matrix, a new database, which is sanitized for privacy concern is created. However, the construction of sanitization matrix for large data sources is a tedious process.

In order to hide sensitive rules, two fundamental approaches are presented in (Verykios, Elmagarmid, Bertino, Saygin, & Dasseni, 2004). The first approach prevents rules from being generated by hiding the frequent sets from which they are derived. The second approach reduces the importance of the rules by setting their confidence below a user-specified threshold. The approaches

used in the paper are moderately successful in hiding sensitive data, but they are computationally intensive and have side effects like generation of artifactual new rules and hiding the existing legitimate rules.

Wu, Chiang, and Chen (2007) have suggested a method for hiding sensitive rules with limited side effects. Templates are generated for sensitive rules to be hidden in order to minimize the side effects. But the cost involved in the template generation increases if the number of sensitive rules and the number of items in the individual sensitive rules are large.

The data sanitization approach is suitable for privacy preserving in case of a single data source, whereas multiple data sources requires the cooperation of sites to learn the global data mining results, yet this approach may fail and yield incorrect global mining results. Thus, secure multiparty computational techniques were proposed.

Secure Multiparty Computation (SMC)

The concept of Secure Multiparty Computation (SMC) was introduced in (Yao, 1986). In many applications the data is distributed between two or more sites, and for mutual benefit these sites cooperate to learn the global data mining results without revealing the data at their individual sites. The basic idea of SMC is that this computation is secure if at the end of the computation no party is unaware about the other participating sites except its input and the results.

The secure computation protocols are presented in the form of combinational circuit (Goldreich, Micali, & Wigderson, 1987). The idea is that the function F to be computed is first represented as a combinational circuit and then the parties run a short protocol to securely compute every gate in the circuit. Every participant gets corresponding shares of the input wires and the output wires for every gate. Here the size of the protocol depends on the size of the circuit, which depends on the size of the input. This is inefficient for large inputs as in data mining.

Vaidya and Clifton (2002) proposed a method for privacy preserving association rule mining in vertically partitioned data. Each site holds some of the attributes of each transaction. An efficient scalar product protocol was proposed to preserve the privacy among two parties. This protocol did not consider the collusion among the parties and was also limited to boolean association rule mining.

Kantarcioglu and Clifton (2004) proposed a work to preserve privacy among semi-honest parties in a distributed environment. It works in two phases assuming no collusion among the parties. But in some real life situations collusion is inevitable. The first phase identifies the global candidate itemsets using commutative encryption which is computationally intensive and the second phase determines the global frequent itemsets. This work only determines the global frequent itemsets but not their exact support counts. Whereas Ashrafi, Taniar, and Smith (2005) proposed privacy preserving algorithm for finding the exact support of global frequent itemsets among semi-honest parties. Here, each site generates local frequent one-length items. Randomization is applied to find the global one-length items in a secure manner. Then, higher length frequent itemsets are identified with the help of global one-length items. Through collusion and by closely watching the input and output of a particular site, details of local frequent itemsets of the site can be identified and the same can be used to estimate the supports of the higher length itemsets of the same site.

An algorithm using Clustering future (CF) tree and secure sum is proposed to preserve privacy of quantitative association rules over horizontally partitioned data (Luo, 2006) and fixing of proper threshold value for constructing the CF tree is not easy. The efficiency of the algorithm is unpredictable since it depends on the threshold value chosen to construct the CF tree. The present analysis proposes a novel, computationally simple

and secure multiparty computation algorithm for dishonest parties.

PROPOSED APPROACH

Let $S_1, S_2 ... S_n$ be the set of participating sites where $n > 2$. Let $D_1, D_2 ... D_n$ be the data sources of sites $S_1, S_2 ... S_n$ respectively which are geographically distributed and let $I = \{i_1, i_2 ... i_m\}$ be a set of items. Each transaction T in D_i such that $T \subseteq I$, where $i = 1$ to n. L_i be the local frequent itemset generated from a participating site S_i and G be the global frequent itemset. To generate the global frequent itemset G, each site needs to send its respective support counts of its local frequent itemsets to the other participating sites. The intended goal of this proposed approach is to discover the global frequent itemsets without revealing the sensitive information of all the participating sites, where the sites are assumed to be colluding.

A new approach is proposed in this paper to estimate the global frequent itemsets from multiple data sources while preserving the privacy of the participating sites amidst collusion. All sites in the mining process are assumed as dishonest. Any site can initiate the mining process. To protect sensitive information of each participating site, the proposed method works in two phases so as to withstand any kind of collusion among the parties.

Phase I

In *phase I* each site combines its actual local itemsets with some randomly generated spurious itemsets to form a set called *modified set*. The spurious itemsets are generated by the following two scenarios.

Scenario 1: Adding a false support to an existing itemset

Scenario 2: Including a new false itemset with some random support

Figure 2. Phase I of the proposed approach

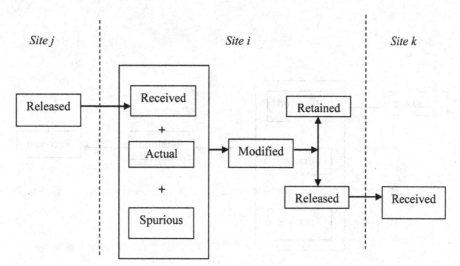

While generating spurious itemset for an individual site, either one or all of the above scenarios can be used. As this is known only to the individual sites, it makes it hard for the colluders to find the exact itemsets of any particular site.

Next, the *modified set* is divided into two sets called the *retained set* and the *released set*. The *retained set* is the set which is retained in the site itself and the *released set* is released to the randomly selected site. Thus, each participating site will send the sets in two rounds. When a site sends its data for the first time (*phase I*), the *retained set* is kept in the site itself and the *released set* is sent to the next randomly selected site. The destination site is randomly chosen excluding its immediate source site to send the *released set*. Every time the destination site is selected at random avoiding the immediate source. This helps in having different senders and receivers for a particular site at different stages of operations which in turn reduces the collusion problem. The immediate source may be considered for the sake of termination in certain unusual scenarios. The probability of unusual scenarios is very rare and even when it happens occasionally it is harmless. The *Phase I* is depicted in Figure 2.

In the figure, *site i* can be an originating site or an intermediate site. When a site is an originat-

ing site, it forms the so called *modified set* by adding some spurious itemsets with its local itemsets. In the case of intermediate site, *site i* collects the released set from a random *site j* and adds it to its local support to form the *modified set* as shown in Figure 2.

Phase II

When a site is selected for the second time then it is said to be in *phase II*. Thus in Figure 3, *site i* can be considered as a site which has already sent its released set in *phase I*. In its second turn, the received itemsets from another site are added with the retained itemsets and the spurious itemsets are removed which are included in the *phase I*. Then the rest is sent to a random site. The *Phase II* is depicted in Figure 3.

As the termination criterion, a list is maintained to keep track of the sites that have already sent their retained set. Once the list contains all the n-1 participating sites, excluding the current site, the spurious itemsets of the current site are eliminated and the remaining itemsets in it are considered as the globally frequent itemsets. The different steps of the proposed method are given as in algorithm in Figure 4.

Figure 3. Phase II of the proposed approach

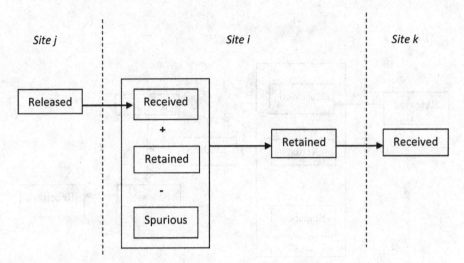

EXAMPLE

Assume that four sites namely *site 1, site 2, site 3* and *site 4* are taking part in the mining process. Table 1 shows the actual local frequent itemsets and spurious itemsets of the individual sites and Table 2 shows the communication sequence among the sites in the process of obtaining overall global frequent itemsets.

In this example, *site 1* is the initiator which initiates the mining process. As per *phase I*, it adds spurious itemsets with its actual itemsets and then it divides them into two sets namely the *retained set* and *the released set*. Here, while the *retained set* is kept in the site itself, the *released set* with its counts are sent to the *site 3*, which is randomly chosen. After the receipt of itemsets from *site 1*, *site 3* updates its contents and repeats the steps mentioned above for *site 1* as it is in *phase I*. Then *site 3* randomly chooses *site 2* for sending its released set. *Site 2* also repeats the same steps and selects *site 1* as its destination.

Site 1 enters into the second phase since it has already sent its released set. *Site 1* now updates its retained set by eliminating the already added

spurious itemsets and then it sends the modified set to a random *site 4*. Now the retained set of *site 1* is NULL. The same process is repeated until the retained set of all participating sites are NULL. Besides, a list is maintained to keep track of the sites that have already sent their retained set. Once the list contains all the n-1 participating sites excluding the current site, the modified itemsets in the current site are the global frequent itemsets. Thus the globally frequent itemsets in the above example are a:20, b:25 and ab:10.

PERFORMANCE EVALUATION

Distributed environment with four participating sites was simulated to evaluate the performance of the proposed algorithm. At each site, a P-IV, 2.8 GHz, 2 GB RAM machine is run on Windows operating system. The proposed method is implemented using Java and MS-Access. Three different data sources of size 10K, 50K, and 100K are synthetically generated to study the performance of the proposed work and Table 3 shows the characteristics of the data source. The local

Figure 4. Collusion free privacy preserving algorithm

Algorithm:
Description:
Given a distributed environment with a list of participating sites S, and each site having the list of Local Frequent Itemsets L, it is required to determine the Global Frequent Itemsets, GFS. The variables, Site and Next_site represent the active site and the destination site respectively. Two sub algorithms Random_Site_Select and Generate_spurious are used to randomly select the destination site and to generate the spurious itemsets with random support count.

Site level variables are represented using the structure SITE.
SITE [Actual: Original Local Frequent Itemsets with support count;
Spurious: False itemsets generated with random support count;
Received: List of Itemsets and support count received from the source site;
Retained: Portion of modified itemset retained in the site;
Released: Portion of modified itemset to be released to another site;
Modified: List used for intermediate processing;
Done_set: List that contains the sites that have completed processing
Source: Site from where the request is received]
Input: Local Frequent Itemsets of participating sites
List of participating sites, S
Output: Global Frequent Itemsets, GFS
Method:
Site_Processing (Source, Received, Done_set, Site)
{
Site.Recieved → Received;
Site.Source → Source;
Site.Done_set →Done_set;
// Phase I
If (Site.Retained is Empty and Site.Released is Empty) then
{   Site.Spurious → Generate_Spurious();
Site.Modified → Site.Actual + Site.Spurious;
If (Site.Recieved is not Empty) then
Site.Modified → Site.Modified + Site.Received;
Split Site.Modified into Site.Retained and Site.Released;
}
// Phase II
Else if (Site.Retained is not Empty) then
{
Site.Released → Site.Received+ Site.Retained – Site.Spurious;
Make an Entry in Done_set;
}
Next_Site → Random_Site_Select (Site.Source, Site.Done_set);
If (Next_Site is Not Empty) then
Site_Processing (Site, Site.Released , Site.Done_set, New_site);
Else if (Next_Site is Empty) then   // Termination Condition
Global Frequent Set,GFS → Site.Released;

Sub Algorithm:
Generate_spurious()
{
Return (False Itemsets with random support count)x;
}
Random_Site_Select (Source, Done_set)
{
Site_available_selection →Participating site list excluding Source and
Done_set entries;
Random_next_site = Select a Random site from the list site_available_selection
Return Random_next_site;
}

Table 1. Site wise Actual local frequent itemsets and Spurious itemsets

Site	Actual		Spurious	
	itemset	Local Support	itemset	Support
Site 1	a	5	a	10
	b	5	c	5
	ab	3		
Site 2	b	5	a	5
			ab	3
Site 3	a	10	d	5
	b	8	ab	4
	ab	4		
Site 4	a	5	a	3
	b	7		
	ab	3		

Table 2. Communication sequence among sites

Source Site	Phase	Received	Modified	Retained	Released	Destinat-ion site
1	I	Null	a:15,b:5, c:5, ab: 3	a:7,b:3, c:2, ab:2	a:8,b:2, c:3, ab:1	3
3	I	a:8,b:2,c:3, ab:1	a:18,b:10, c:3, d:5, ab:9	a:10,b:5,c:2, d:4, ab:5	a:8,b:5, c:1, d:1, ab:4	2
2	I	a:8,b:5, c:1, d:1, ab:4	a:13,b:10, c:1, d:1, ab:7	a:6,b:6, ab:4	a:7,b:4, c:1, d:1, ab:3	1
1	II	a:7,b:4, c:1, d:1, ab:3	a:4, b:7, c:-2, d:1, ab:5	Null	a:4, b:7, c:-2, d:1, ab:5	4
4	I	a:4, b:7, c:-2, d:1, ab:5	a:12,b:14, c:-2, d:1, ab:8	a:5,b:10, d:1, ab:4	a:7,b:4, c:-2, ab:4	2
2	II	a:7,b:4, c:-2, ab:4	a:8,b:10, c: -2, ab:5	Null	a:8,b:10, c: -2, ab:5	3
3	II	a:8,b:10, c: -2, ab:5	a:18,b:15,c:0, d:-1, ab:6	Null	a:18,b:15,c:0, d:-1, ab:6	4
4	II	a:18,b:15,c:0, d:-1, ab:6	a:20,b:25,c:0, d:0, ab:10	Null	a:20, b:25, ab:10	1

frequent itemsets of the participating sites which are the inputs for the algorithm is generated by using the Apriori algorithm for supports varying from 10% to 30%.

Ashrafi, Taniar, and Smith (2005) proposed a Privacy Preserving Distributed Association-Rule-Mining Algorithm (PPDAM) which follows secure multiparty computation. This is a well accepted approach and we compare the performance of the

proposed method against this benchmark. The performance of the proposed approach has extensively been studied to confirm its effectiveness.

Accuracy

Accuracy is one of the main objectives of secure multiparty computation. Table 4 shows the number of global frequent itemsets generated by both

Table 3. Data source characteristics

Data Set	Average Transaction Length (ATL)	No of Distinct Items |I|	No of Records |D|
10K	7	10	10000
50K	7	10	50000
100K	9	12	100000

Table 4. Accuracy

Data set	Support	No. of Sites	Total No. of Global Frequent Itemsets		Accuracy
			PPDAM	Proposed Work	
10K	0.10%	4	984	984	100%
	0.20%	4	385	385	100%
	0.30%	4	174	174	100%
50K	0.10%	4	1012	1012	100%
	0.20%	4	385	385	100%
	0.30%	4	175	175	100%
100K	0.10%	4	3301	3301	100%
	0.20%	4	1528	1528	100%
	0.30%	4	298	298	100%

PPDAM and proposed method. Global frequent itemsets generated by the proposed method has been found to be identical to the global frequent itemsets generated by PPDAM. Thus, accuracy of our proposed method is the same as PPDAM in all cases.

Communication Cost

Transfer of voluminous data over network might take extremely larger time and also requires an unbearable communication cost. Even a small quantity of data might create problems in wireless network environments with limited bandwidth. In the process of preserving privacy in distributed environment, existing methods face the problem of high communication cost. Figure 5 gives the communication costs of the proposed method compared with PPDAM. Communication cost here represents the number of communication among the sites.

Figure 5. Comparison of communication cost

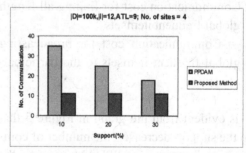

(a) Communication cost for 100K data source for different support (%)

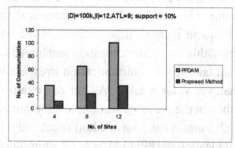

(b) Communication cost for 100 K data source for varying number of sites

Total communication cost (T_c) for finding global frequent itemset using PPDAM is

$$T_c = 2n + (n-1)*M_c - 1 + (n-1) * M_l \text{ -----------} \quad (1)$$

Where

n = Number of participating sites
M_c = Length of maximal candidate set
M_l = Length of maximal frequent itemset
$2n$ = Communication cost for finding 1-length itemset
$(n-1)*M_c - 1$ = Communication cost for broadcasting candidate itemsets to the initiator
$(n-1) * M_l$ = Communication cost for broadcasting frequent itemsets to all other participating sites

Total communication according to the proposed method is

$$T_c = 2n + (n-1) \text{ ---------} \quad (2)$$

$2n$ = Communication cost for finding all length global frequent itemsets
$(n-1)$ = Communication cost for broadcasting global frequent itemsets to the participating sites

It is evident from the graph in Figure 5 that when the support decreases, the number of communication increases for PPDAM because the number of local frequent itemsets generated is more. But in the proposed method, the number of communication remains the same because all the local frequent itemsets in an individual site will be sent within two communication and hence for n sites it takes *3n-1* communication irrespective of whatever value *n* takes. As per our example described in the previous section, to generate the 2-length itemset 'ab' our method takes only 11 communication and PPDAM takes 16 communica-

tion. Thus, the proposed method notably reduces the communication among the sites.

Collusion

In the PPDAM approach, the communication among sites happens in a sequential order. This gives the information about the sender and the receiver of a particular site. In such case, when the sender colludes with the receiver, the sensitive information of the individual site can be revealed. From the example illustrated in the previous section, if the existing approach is followed, all one length itemsets are communicated say in the sequence of Site1, Site2, Site3 and Site4. To know the one length itemset of Site 2, Site 1 and Site 3 can collude and the sum of actual itemset support and the random number added can be determined during obfuscation. During deobfuscation, the actual random number added to the itemset in Site 2 can be determined. Using both the information obtained during obfuscation and deobfuscation, the actual support count of the one length itemset of Site 2 can be determined by simple subtraction.

In the proposed method, the communication takes place in two different phases in a randomized order. Also, the destination site in each transaction is not known in prior and it is randomly selected. This random selection makes it difficult just for two sites to collude and requires all the *n-1* sites to collude to identify the sensitive information. Even when the sites collude, the information obtained at any time during the process will only be partial with some spurious itemsets as well as some portion of the information is retained in the site itself during *Phase I*. Thus, it makes it difficult for colluders to find sensitive information of a particular site, thereby the proposed method is more secure than the existing methods.

Time Complexity

Time complexity is another major criterion considered for performance evaluation. Figure

Figure 6. Comparison of Time complexity

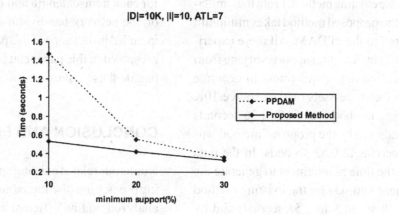

(a) Time complexity of 10K data source

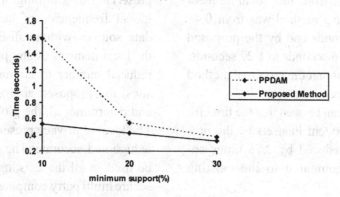

(b) Time complexity of 50K data source

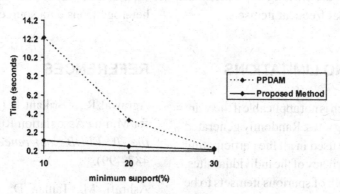

(c) Time complexity of 100K data source

6 compares the time complexity of the proposed method with the existing method. From the simulation results, the proposed method takes minimum time compared to the PPDAM. All these experiments are conducted for the supports varying from 30% to 10%. The time requirement to generate the global frequent itemsets on data source 10K by the existing method was from 0.36 seconds to 1.47 seconds and by the proposed method was from 0.33 seconds to 0.53 seconds. In the data source 50K, the time requirement to generate the global frequent itemsets by the existing method was from 0.38 seconds to 1.58 seconds and by the proposed method was from 0.33 seconds to 0.53 seconds. For the third data source 100K, the time requirement to generate the global frequent itemsets by the existing method was from 0.45 seconds to 12.34 seconds and by the proposed method was from 0.36 seconds to 1.27 seconds. From this, it is evident that the proposed method performs better on dense data sets.

From Figure 6, it can be seen that the time for generating global frequent itemsets by the proposed technique is reduced by 2.75 times approximately when compared to the existing method.

From the experimental results, it can be concluded that the proposed method has better accuracy, communication costs, privacy and time complexity than the existing approaches in determining the global frequent itemsets.

DISCUSSION AND LIMITATIONS

The proposed approach is not applicable if there are only two participating sites. Randomly generated spurious itemsets are used in all the participating sites to preserve the privacy of the individual sites. The number and length of spurious itemsets to be mixed with the actual itemsets in each individual site is not dealt in this paper. The message size may be large as all the itemsets of different lengths are communicated in just two rounds unlike the

existing approach which takes multiple rounds for each itemset length and it is highly dependent on the network bandwidth and this aspect is not included in the scope of this paper. Hence, the work presented in this paper can be further extended to handle these issues.

CONCLUSION AND FUTURE WORK

Numerous related existing approaches for preserving privacy in a distributed environment have been analyzed and an efficient algorithm for finding global frequent itemsets has been proposed and implemented. The new collusion free privacy preserving data mining approach estimates the global frequencies of itemsets from multiple data sources without disclosing the details of the local itemsets of any participating site. With reduced number of communication among the sites, the proposed approach securely collects and determines all the global frequent itemsets. The level of privacy preserved by this technique is high and accurate. The proposed method can be used in all the existing set ups wherein the secure multi party computation is used for global frequent itemset generation. Some of them include medical research, fraud detection, market basket analysis and supply chain management. This work can be extended to preserve privacy among heterogeneous data sources.

REFERENCES

Agrawal, R., & Srikant, R. (1994). Fast Algorithms for Mining Association Rules. In *Proceedings of the 20th VLDB Conference,* Santiago, Chile (pp. 487-499).

Ashrafi, M., Taniar, D., & Smith, K. (2004). ODAM: An Optimized Distributed Association Rule Mining Algorithm. *IEEE Distributed Systems Online, 5*(3).

Ashrafi, M., Taniar, D., & Smith, K. (2005). Privacy-Preserving Distributed Association Rule Mining Algorithm. *International Journal of Intelligent Information Technologies, 1*(1), 46–69.

Atallah, M., Bertino, E., Elmagarmid, A., Ibrahim, M., & Verykios, V. S. (1999). Disclosure limitation of sensitive rules. In *Proceedings of the IEEE Knowledge and Data Exchange Workshop (KDEX'99),* (pp. 45-52). Washington, DC: IEEE Computer Society.

Cheung, D., Ng, V., Fu, A., & Fu, Y. (1996). Efficient Mining of Association Rules in Distributed Databases. *IEEE Transactions on Knowledge and Data Engineering, 8*(6), 911–922. doi:10.1109/69.553158

Clifton, C. (2001). Secure Multiparty Computation Problems and Their Applications: A Review and Open Problems. In *Proceedings of the Workshop on New Security Paradigms,* Cloudcroft, NM.

Clifton, C., Kantarcioglu, M., & Vaidya, J. (2004). Defining privacy for data mining. In *Data Mining, Next generation challenges and future directions.*

Clifton, C., & Marks, D. (1996). Security and Privacy Implications of Data Mining. In *Proceedings of the ACM SIGMOD Workshop on Data Mining and Knowledge Discovery* (pp. 15-19).

Goldreich, O. (1998). *Secure Multiparty Computation.* Working Draft.

Goldreich, O., Micali, S., & Wigderson. (1987). How to play any mental game - a completeness theorem for protocols with honest majority. In *Proceedings of the 19th ACM Symposium on the Theory of Computing* (pp. 218-229).

Han, J., & Kamber, M. (2001). *Data Mining: Concepts and Technique.* San Fracisco: Morgan Kaufmann Publishers.

Han, J., Pei, J., Yin, Y., & Mao, R. (2004). Mining Frequent Patterns without Candidate Generation: A Frequent Pattern Approach. *IEEE Transactions on Data Mining and Knowledge Discovery, 8*(1), 53–87. doi:10.1023/B:DAMI.0000005258.31418.83

Inan, A., Saygyn, Y., Savas, E., Hintoglu, A. A., & Levi, A. (2006). Privacy preserving clustering on horizontally portioned data. In *Proceedings of the 22nd International Conference on Data Engineering Workshops (ICDEW'06).*

Kantarcioglu, M., & Clifton, C. (2004). Privacy-Preserving Distributed Mining of Association Rules on Horizontally Partitioned Data. *IEEE Transactions on Knowledge and Data Engineering, 16*(9). doi:10.1109/TKDE.2004.45

Lee, G., Chang, C., & Chen, A. L. P. (2004). Hiding sensitive patterns in association rules mining. In *Proceedings of the 28th Annual International Computer Software and Applications Conference.*

Lin, D., & Kedem, Z. M. (1998). Pincer-Search: A New Algorithm for Discovering the Maximum Frequent Set. In *Proceedings of the 6th International Conference on Extending Database Technology (EDBT)*, Valencia, Spain (pp. 105-119).

Lin, D., & Kedem, Z. M. (2002). Pincer-Search: An Efficient Algorithm for Discovering the Maximum Frequent Set. *IEEE Transactions on Knowledge and Data Engineering, 14*(3), 553–566. doi:10.1109/TKDE.2002.1000342

Lindell, Y., & Pinkas, B. (2009). Secure Multiparty Computation for Privacy-Preserving Data Mining. *Journal of Privacy and Confidentiality*, 59-98.

Luo, W. (2006). An Algorithm for Privacy-preserving Quantitative Association Rules Mining. In *Proceedings of the 2nd IEEE International Symposium.*

Nedunchezhian, R., & Anbumani, K. (2006). Rapid Privacy Preserving Algorithm for Large Databases. *International Journal of Intelligent Information Technologies, 2*(1), 68–81.

Saygin, Y., Verykios, S., & Elmagarmid, K. (2002). Privacy Preserving Association Rule Mining. In *Proceedings of the 12th International Workshop on Research Issues in Data Engineering: Engineering E-Commerce/E-Business Systems (RIDE'02)*, San Jose, CA (pp. 151-158).

Stanley, R., Oliveira, M., & Za"ıane, R. (2003). Algorithms for Balancing Privacy and Knowledge Discovery in Association Rule Mining. In *Proceedings of the Seventh International Database Engineering and Applications Symposium (IDEAS'03)*, Hong Kong, China (pp. 54-65).

Vaidya, J., & Clifton, C. (2002). Privacy Preserving Association Rule Mining in Vertically Partioned data. In *Proceedings of ACM SIGKDD '02.*

Vaidya, J., & Clifton, C. (2004). *Privacy-Preserving Data Mining: Why, How, and When*. IEEE Security and Privacy.

Verykios, S., Bertino, E., Provenza, I., Saygin, Y., & Theodoridis, Y. (2004). State- of- the -Art in Privacy Preserving Data Mining. *SIGMOD Record, 33*(1), 50–57. doi:10.1145/974121.974131

Verykios, S., Elmagarmid, K., Bertino, E., Saygin, Y., & Dasseni, E. (2004). Association Rule Hiding. *IEEE Transactions on Knowledge and Data Engineering, 16*(4), 434–447. doi:10.1109/TKDE.2004.1269668

Wang, S., Lee, Y., Billis, S., & Jafari, A. (2004). Hiding Sensitive Items in Privacy Preserving Association Rule Mining. In *Proceedings of the IEEE International Conference on Systems, Man and Cybernetics.*

Wu, Y., Chiang, C., & Chen, A. (2007). Hiding Sensitive Association Rules with Limited Side Effects. *IEEE Transactions on Knowledge and Data Engineering, 19*(1). doi:10.1109/TKDE.2007.250583

Yao, A. C. (1986). How to generate and exchange secret. In *Proceedings of the 27th IEEE Symposium on Foundations of Computer Science* (pp. 162-167).

This work was previously published in International Journal of Intelligent Information Technologies, Volume 6, Issue 4, edited by Vijayan Sugumaran, pp. 30-45, copyright 2010 by IGI Publishing (an imprint of IGI Global).

Chapter 16
Multi-Agent Negotiation in B2C E-Commerce Based on Data Mining Methods

Bireshwar Dass Mazumdar
Institute of Technology, Banaras Hindu University, India

R. B. Mishra
Institute of Technology, Banaras Hindu University, India

ABSTRACT

The Multi agent system (MAS) model has been extensively used in the different tasks of e-commerce like customer relation management (CRM), negotiation and brokering. For the success of CRM, it is important to target the most profitable customers of a company. This paper presents a multi-attribute negotiation approach for negotiation between buyer and seller agents. The communication model and the algorithms for various actions involved in the negotiation process is described. The paper also proposes a multi-attribute based utility model, based on price, response-time, and quality. In support of this approach, a prototype system providing negotiation between buyer agents and seller agents is presented.

INTRODUCTION

Various Multi-agent models have been developed. Chan, Cheng, and Hsu (2007) introduced an autonomous agent that represents the owner of an online store to bargain with customers. They consider that customers' behaviors are different, and the store should identify a customer's charac-

teristics and apply different tactics to make profits on customers. Various customer orientation based model are given in Park and Lee (2005). Ha, Bae, and Park (2002) proposed a survey based profitable customer segmentation system that conducts the customer satisfaction survey and those mining processes for the profitable customer segmentation.

Some issues of engineering agents that partially automate some of the activities of information brokering in e-commerce (Mong & Sim, 2000)

DOI: 10.4018/978-1-4666-0158-1.ch016

Figure 1. Interaction between buyer and seller agent

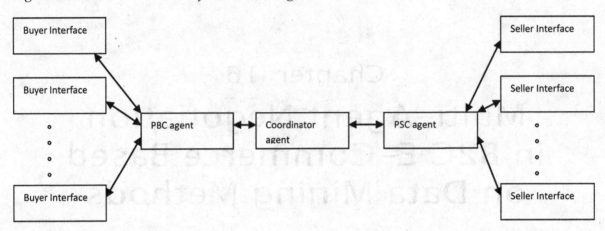

focus on addressing the problem of connecting buyers and sellers. The process of matching and connecting buyers and sellers is divided in four stages: selection, evaluation, filtering and assignment. Trading agent have been developed which can either take or reject recommendations made by the broker agent (Suwu, 2001). They can also provide feedback to the brokering test bed by indicating their satisfaction level. Empirical researches have shown that increasing overall satisfaction leads to greater repurchase intentions, as well as to actual repurchase behavior and companies with high customer satisfaction and retention can expect higher profits (Reichheld & Frederick, 1996).

For the success of CRM, it is important to target the most profitable customers of a company.

Customer orientation is a crucial component of an organizational culture and attention to information about customers' needs should be considered as a basic value of the firm. Many CRM researches have been performed to calculate customer profitability based on customer lifetime value and develop a comprehensive model of it. Intelligent computing models have been used in some of the problems of customer relationship management such as customer classification and customer supplier relationship. The interactive CRM model proposed by Hsien-Jung Wu provides

an agent-based approach of improving customer satisfaction as well as utilizing information technology to develop the knowledge management structure. They proposed CRM model which includes four management issues: customer relationship, customer requirement, customer interaction, and customer knowledge (Wu, 2005).

PROBLEM DESCRIPTION

From the perspective of customer orientation for customer relationship marketing (CRM), establishing and maintaining the best possible relationship with valuable buyer is a good way to survive in the competitive global market. The problem is firstly described by collecting information of 23 business and cognitive parameters of buyers and sellers agents.

The proposed model is orientation based profitable buyers and profitable seller categorization system based on data mining and agent technology that designs, executes (on-line, etc.) on business and cognitive parameters of buyers and sellers and conducts data mining process for the profitable buyers and sellers categorization. It has multi-agent based architecture and integration of data mining process into decision support system framework (Figure 1).

There are five types of intelligent agents within the architecture:

Coordinator agent: Coordinator agent with survey knowledge base that provides system co-ordination, facilitates (mined) knowledge communication, and takes the charge of design and execution of customer satisfaction survey. Coordinator agent acts as a mediator between buyer interface agent and seller interface agent and arrange priority order of the buyer and sellers agent according to categorization of out standing (OS), excellent (E), very good (VG), good (G), and average (A) and finally helps to negotiate between buyer and seller agents.

PBC agent: Profitable buyer categorization (PBC) agent that categorizes profitable buyers as out standing (OS), excellent (E), very good (VG), good (G), and average (A) among all the surveyed buyers through the mining of integrated data from the customer survey and accounting database. It also acts as a mediator agent between buyer assistant agent and coordinator agent.

Buyer assistant agent: Buyer assistant agent that acts as the intelligent interface agent between the user and the system.

PSC agent: Profitable seller categorization (PSC) agent that segments profitable sellers as out standing (OS), excellent (E), very good (VG), good (G), and average (A) among all the surveyed sellers through the mining of integrated data from the seller survey and accounting database. It also acts as a mediator agent between seller assistant agent and coordinator agent.

Seller assistant agent: Seller assistant agent that acts as the intelligent interface agent between the seller and the system.

A buyer agent looking for products may be supported by a broker agent that takes its buyer agent's queries and contacts other agents or looks at the web directly to find information on products with in the buyer agent's scope of interest. In the other hand it is important to target the most profitable buyer agent of a selected seller agent. From the perspective of customer orientation for CRM, establishing and maintaining the best possible relationship with valuable buyer is a good way to survive in the competitive global market. Our model addresses four stages: need identification, seller selection, valuable buyer selection and negotiation; where the seller selection stage is the integrated part of product brokering and merchant brokering and the valuable buyer selection applies the integrated concept of CRM.

PROPOSED APPROACH

The research architecture is as following (Figure 2):

Data Mining Approach

1. Collect information from data base provided by an agent mediated e-organization.
2. Obtain possible factors that affect business policies from literature and from business personnel involved in the business institute.
3. Screen, filter and delete some inappropriate and inconsistent data.
4. Produce training data sets and their related analytic variables after extracting and organizing the cleansed data.
5. Construct decision tree model using the obtained training data sets and variables of causes that affect the seller and buyer relation.

   Experiment: Use variables for analyzing factors that affect causes of seller and buyer relation as input of the decision trees to analyze the output outcomes.
6. Use the rules produced by test data through predictive model to determine final classification placement.

Figure 2. Research architecture

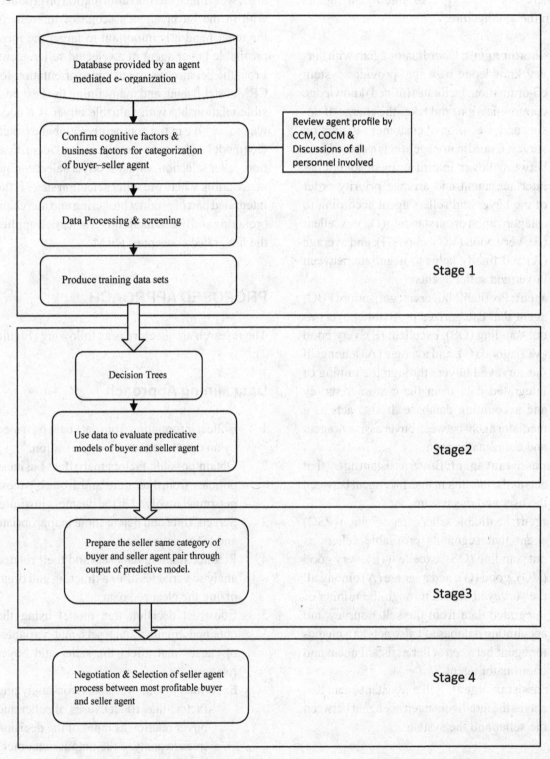

Figure 5. Tree structure

```
X21 in [ "L" ] [ Mode: G ] (33)
  X3 in [ "<=50" ] [ Mode: A ] (19)
      X6 <= 36 [ Mode: A ] => A (17; 0.882)
      X6 > 36 [ Mode: G ] => G (2; 1.0)
  X3 in [ ">50" ] [ Mode: G ] => G (14; 1.0)
X21 in [ "H" "M" ] [ Mode: VG ] (147)
  X12 in [ "L" ] [ Mode: G ] => G (6; 1.0)
  X12 in [ "H" "M" ] [ Mode: VG ] (141)
      X6 <= 36 [ Mode: VG ] (103)
  X14 in [ "L" ] [ Mode: G ] (25)
      X12 in [ "H" ] [ Mode: VG ] => VG (10; 0.8)
      X12 in [ "M" ] [ Mode: G ] => G (15; 0.867)
  X14 in [ "H" "M" ] [ Mode: VG ] => VG (78; 0.692)
      X6 > 36 [ Mode: VG ] (38)
  X11 in [ "H" ] [ Mode: E ] (11)
      X10 in [ "L" ] [ Mode: VG ] => VG (4; 0.75)
      X10 in [ "H" "M" ] [ Mode: E ] => E (7; 1.0)
  X11 in ["L" "M"] [Mode: VG] => VG (27; 1.0)
```

7. Based on the accuracy of experiment, analyze, compare the buyer and seller agent category.

Decision Tree (C&RT Algorithm)

There are nine cognitive parameters and fourteen business parameters. Data mining (DM) helps to extract and analyze the meaningful relationship between various cognitive and business parameters and it also provides the relative importance of various parameters based on 270 records. The cognitive parameters used are performance($X1$), belief ($X7$), desire($X8$), intention ($X9$), preference ($X10$), commitment($X11$), capability ($X12$), reputation($X13$), reliability($X14$). Apart from these parameters profit ($X2$), quality ($X3$), quantity ($X4$), brand ($X5$), serving time($X6$), start time ($X15$), payment mode ($X16$), payment type($X17$), loyalties($X18$), delivery time($X19$), address mode($X20$), support($X23$), self monitoring ($X21$), response to marketing stimuli ($X22$) are important business parameters which has been described in our proposed model In this model 180 dataset for training and 90 dataset for testing are deployed in decision tree algorithm to calculate the error rate report and obtain its tree-structure,

as shown in Figure 5. The rules in the Figure 6 have been generated by the program based upon the tree structure as shown in the Figure 5. There are 10 sets of rules each containing three lines for description in Figures 3 and 4.

The value given in form (a; b) in the right side of each rule represents the number of records to which the rules applies (a: instance) and the proportion of those records for which the rule is true (b: confidence). After obtaining the rules for category; the testing datasets is used to assess the accuracy of these rules. From the table it is found that there are one rule for excellent, one rule average, 4 rules for very good, 4 rules for good with different instance and confidence. 10 discriminate rules for five different types of category such as excellent (E), very good (VG), good (G) and average (A) are shown in Figure 4. According to the above-mentioned tables, the overall accuracy of the C&RT algorithm is 95.56%.

Extended Filtering Model Based on Predictive Model

PBC agent and PSC agent only categorize the buyer agent or seller agent using data mining technique according to their category from the predictive

Figure 6. Rule sets

```
Rules for A - contains 1 rule(s)
    Rule 1 for A (17; 0.882)
        if X21 in [ "L" ]
        and X3 in [ "<=50" ]
        and X6 <= 36
        then A
Rules for E - contains 1 rule(s)
    Rule 1 for E (7; 1.0)
        if X21 in [ "H" "M" ]
        and X12 in [ "H" "M" ]
        and X6 > 36
        and X11 in [ "H" ]
        and X10 in [ "H" "M" ]
        then E
Rules for G - contains 4 rule(s)
    Rule 1 for G (2; 1.0)
        if X21 in [ "L" ]
        and X3 in [ "<=50" ]
        and X6 > 36
        then G
    Rule 2 for G (14; 1.0)
        if X21 in [ "L" ]
        and X3 in [ ">50" ]
        then G
    Rule 3 for G (6; 1.0)
        if X21 in [ "H" "M" ]
        and X12 in [ "L" ]
        then G
    Rule 4 for G (15; 0.867)
        if X21 in [ "H" "M" ]
        and X12 in [ "H" "M" ]
        and X6 <= 36
        and X14 in [ "L" ]
        and X12 in [ "M" ]
        then G
Rules for VG - contains 4 rule(s)
    Rule 1 for VG (10; 0.8)
        if X21 in [ "H" "M" ]
        and X12 in [ "H" "M" ]
        and X6 <= 36
        and X14 in [ "L" ]
        and X12 in [ "H" ]
        then VG
    Rule 2 for VG (78; 0.692)
        if X21 in [ "H" "M" ]
        and X12 in [ "H" "M" ]
        and X6 <= 36
        and X14 in [ "H" "M" ]
        then VG
    Rule 3 for VG (4; 0.75)
        if X21 in [ "H" "M" ]
        and X12 in [ "H" "M" ]
        and X6 > 36
        and X11 in [ "H" ]
        and X10 in [ "L" ]
        then VG
    Rule 4 for VG (27; 1.0)
        if X21 in [ "H" "M" ]
        and X12 in [ "H" "M" ]
        and X6 > 36
        and X11 in [ "L" "M" ]
        then VG
Default: VG
```

model result (provided by R-Category) in such a way that each buyer agent can communicate for negotiation with all seller agents whose category is same as the buyer agent. As Figure 7 buyer agent B_m whose category is i can communicate with all seller agent $<S_p, S_q, ..., S_w>$ whose category are i.

Communication Model

In our system agent communication is implemented using FIFA ACL messages (see Figure 8). We have used the following messages: SUBSCRIBE, REQUEST, INFORM, FAILURE, PROPOSE, ACCEPT-PROPOSAL, REJECT-PROPOSAL, REFUSE. The SSUBSCRIBE messages are used by the buyer agent and selected seller agent to register with the broker agent for negotiate on a proposal. REQUEST messages are used by buyer agent to query the broker agent about specification of items (quality, time, and price) on the basis of initial proposal created by buyer. INFORM messages are used as responses to SUBSCRIBE or REQUEST messages. For example after subscribing the buyer agent to broker agent the buyer agent will get an INFORM message or after requesting the specification of items buyer agent gets an INFORM message that contain about the seller's name and ID. Now seller agent evaluate the proposal and build a proposal and INFORM to broker. Now broker agent INFORM to buyer agent. Now buyer agent reevaluated the proposal and INFORM to broker agent. Finally ACCEPT-PROPOSAL, REJECT-PROPOSAL, and REFUSE messages are being used by the negotiating agents.

Utility Computational Model

The utility of multi-agent negotiation depends upon the values of different attributes of the items. The presented utility function is dependent on the multiple attributes of items. We have considered three main attributes of a item i.e. price, quality,

Figure 3. Predictive analysis of seller agent [Table (27 fields, 90 records)]

	X1	X2	X3	X15	X4	X5	X6	X16	X17	X18	X19	X20	X21	X22	X23	X7	X8	X9	X10	X11	X12	X13	X14	CATEGORY	S-agent	SR-CATEGORY	SRC-CATEGORY
1	M	30-50	>50	>15	E	>=-6	27.000	D	FP	M	S	S	H	H	Y	L	H	M	L	H	H	M	H	OS	S1	VG	0.692
2	L	30-50	>50	>15	A	-6	42.000	CC	FP	L	A	A	H	H	Y	L	H	M	M	L	M	H	L	VG	S2	VG	1.000
3	M	30-50	-=50	-=15	G	-6	42.000	D	PP	M	G	G	H	H	N	L	H	M	M	M	M	H	M	VG	S3	VG	1.000
4	VL	30-50	>50	>15	G	>=-6	27.000	CQ	FP	VL	G	G	H	H	Y	L	H	M	M	H	H	H	H	VG	S4	VG	0.692
5	L	30-50	>50	>15	A	>=-6	30.000	CC	FP	L	A	A	H	H	Y	L	H	M	H	L	L	L	L	G	S5	G	1.000
6	M	30-50	>50	>15	E	>=-6	27.000	D	FP	M	S	S	H	H	Y	L	H	M	H	M	H	L	M	VG	S6	VG	0.692
7	L	30-50	-=50	-=15	E	>=-6	30.000	CC	PP	L	S	S	H	H	N	L	H	M	H	H	H	L	H	VG	S7	VG	0.692
8	M	30-50	-=50	-=15	A	>=-6	42.000	D	PP	M	A	A	M	M	N	L	M	H	L	M	M	M	L	VG	S8	VG	1.000
9	VL	51-75	-=50	-=15	G	-6	30.000	CQ	PP	VL	G	G	M	M	N	L	M	H	L	H	H	M	M	VG	S9	VG	0.692
10	L	51-75	>50	>15	G	-6	27.000	CC	FP	L	G	G	M	M	Y	L	M	H	M	L	M	M	H	VG	S10	VG	0.692
11	M	51-75	>50	>15	A	-6	30.000	D	FP	M	A	A	M	M	Y	L	M	H	M	M	M	H	L	E	S11	VG	0.800
12	L	51-75	>50	>15	E	-6	42.000	CC	FP	L	S	S	M	M	Y	L	M	H	M	H	H	H	M	E	S12	E	1.000

Figure 4. Predictive Analysis of Buyer Agent [Table (27 fields, 90 records)]

	X1	X2	X3	X15	X4	X5	X6	X16	X17	X18	X19	X20	X21	X22	X23	X7	X8	X9	X10	X11	X12	X13	X14	CATEGORY	B-agent	SR-CATEGORY	SRC-CATEGORY
1	M	30-50	>50	>15	E	>=-6	27.000	D	FP	M	S	S	H	H	Y	L	H	M	L	H	H	M	H	OS	B1	VG	0.663
2	L	30-50	>50	>15	A	-6	42.000	CC	FP	L	A	A	H	H	Y	L	H	M	M	L	M	H	L	VG	B2	VG	0.875
3	M	30-50	-=50	-=15	G	-6	42.000	D	PP	M	G	G	H	H	N	L	H	M	M	M	M	H	M	VG	B3	VG	0.875
4	VL	30-50	>50	>15	G	>=-6	27.000	CQ	FP	VL	G	G	H	H	Y	L	H	M	M	H	H	H	H	VG	B4	VG	0.663
5	L	30-50	>50	>15	A	>=-6	30.000	CC	FP	L	A	A	H	H	Y	L	H	M	H	L	L	L	L	G	B5	G	0.636
6	M	30-50	>50	>15	E	>=-6	27.000	D	FP	M	S	S	H	H	Y	L	H	M	H	M	H	L	M	VG	B6	VG	0.663
7	L	30-50	-=50	-=15	E	>=-6	30.000	CC	PP	L	S	S	H	H	N	L	H	M	H	H	H	L	H	VG	B7	VG	0.663
8	M	30-50	-=50	-=15	A	>=-6	42.000	D	PP	M	A	A	M	M	N	L	M	H	L	M	M	M	L	VG	B8	VG	0.875
9	VL	51-75	-=50	-=15	G	-6	30.000	CQ	PP	VL	G	G	M	M	N	L	M	H	L	H	H	M	M	VG	B9	VG	0.663
10	L	51-75	>50	>15	G	-6	27.000	CC	FP	L	G	G	M	M	Y	L	M	H	M	L	M	M	H	VG	B10	VG	0.663
11	M	51-75	>50	>15	A	-6	30.000	D	FP	M	A	A	M	M	Y	L	M	H	M	M	M	H	L	E	B11	VG	0.600
12	L	51-75	>50	>15	E	-6	42.000	CC	FP	L	S	S	M	M	Y	L	M	H	M	H	H	H	M	E	B12	E	0.667
13	M	76-100	>50	>15	E	>=-6	30.000	D	FP	M	S	S	M	M	Y	L	M	H	H	L	M	H	H	OS	B13	VG	0.663
14	L	30-50	-=50	-=15	A	>=-6	42.000	CC	PP	L	A	A	M	M	N	L	M	H	H	M	H	L	L	VG	B14	VG	0.875
15	L	76-100	-=50	-=15	G	-6	30.000	CC	PP	L	G	G	L	L	N	M	L	L	L	L	M	L	M	A	B15	A	0.727

Figure 7. Interaction between buyer and seller agent of same category

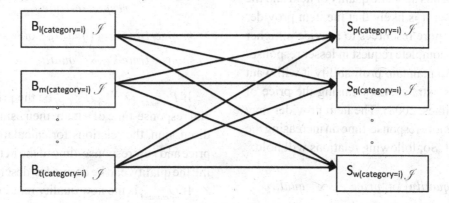

Figure 8. Communication model

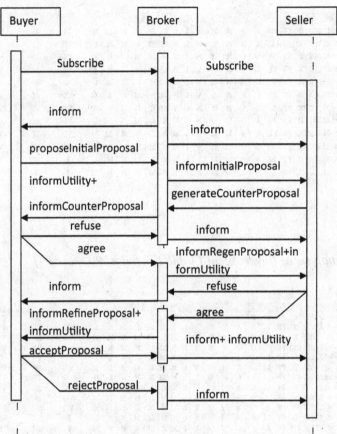

and time-period (response-time). So, utility can be expressed as a function of these attributes, *utility (price, quality, response-time)*. Further, the price of a item depends upon the quality of item and the response-time. It is likely that the item provider will expend more resources to provide a higher quality or to complete request in lesser response-time. Then, to maintain profitability it will want to recoup its extra costs by raising the price of the item (Wilkes, 2008). The item provider may also require more response-time on increasing the quality-level. So, following relations will hold:

$$price = f\big(quality\big) \text{ or } price \quad \propto \quad quality \tag{1}$$

$$price = f\left(\frac{1}{response\text{-}time}\right) \text{ or}$$

$$price \quad \propto \quad \frac{1}{response\text{-}time} \ldots \tag{2}$$

$$response\text{-}time = f\big(quality\big) \text{ or}$$

$$response\text{-}time \quad \propto \quad quality \ldots \tag{3}$$

If $P_{thresold}$, $Q_{thresold}$, $T_{thresold}$ be the price, quality, and response-time of a item, then using the above discussion, the relations for calculating the new price and new response-time of the item on changing the quality, can be derived as described below.

If $Q_{required}$ is the new quality required, then the percentage-change in quality can be represented as follows:

$$dQ = \frac{Q_{desired} - Q_{thresold}}{Q_{desired}} \times 100 \dots \quad (4)$$

Where, dQ is the percentage-change in quality and holds $0 \leq dQ \leq 100$.

Now, using relation (3), the percentage-change in response-time can be represented as below:

$$dT = w_{TQ} \times dQ \dots \quad (5)$$

Where, dT is the percentage-change in time due to quality-change and it holds $0 \leq dT \leq 100$. w_{TQ} is the constant holding relation, $0 \leq w_{TQ} \leq 1$. Its value is decided by the item provider. It represents the percentage of the percentage-change in quality (dQ) with which the response-time should be changed. It means that if the percentage-change in quality (dQ) is 80 and w_{TQ} is equal to 0.4, then the percentage-change in response-time (dT) will be 32. $w_{TQ} = 1$ implies that the response-time and quality have one-to-one ratio and response-time should be changed in the same ratio as change in quality. $w_{TQ} = 0$ implies that response-time is not dependent on the quality.

So, the new response-time should be:

$$T_{desired} = T_{thresold} + \left(\frac{T_{thresold} \times dT}{100} \right) \dots \quad (6)$$

In other form, the $T_{desired}$ can be represented as:

$$T_{desired} = T_{thresold} + \left(\frac{T_{thresold} \times w_{TQ} \times \left(\frac{Q_{desired} - Q_{thresold}}{Q_{thresold}} \times 100 \right)}{100} \right) \dots \quad (7)$$

Now, based on the relation (1), the percentage-change in price due to quality-change can be derived as follows:

$$dPq = w_{PQ} \times dQ \dots \quad (8)$$

Where, dPq is the percentage-change in price due to quality-change and it holds $0 \leq dPq \leq 100$. w_{PQ} is the constant holding relation, $0 \leq w_{PQ} \leq 1$. Its value is decided by the item provider. It represents the percentage of the percentage-change in quality (dQ) with which the price should be changed. It means that if the percentage change in quality (dQ) is 80 and w_{PQ} is equal to 0.7, then the percentage-change in price (dPq) will be 56. $w_{PQ} = 1$ implies that the price and quality have one-to-one ratio and price should be changed in the same ratio as change in quality. $w_{PQ} = 0$ implies that price is not dependent on the quality.

So, the new price after taking the quality-change into consideration will be:

$$Pq_{desired} = P_{thresold} + \left(\frac{P_{thresold} \times dPq}{100} \right) \dots \quad (9)$$

In other form, the $Pq_{desired}$ can be represented as:

$$Pq_{desired} = P_{thresold} + \left(\frac{P_{thresold} \times w_{PQ} \times \left(\frac{Q_{desired} - Q_{thresold}}{Q_{thresold}} \times 100 \right)}{100} \right) \dots \quad (10)$$

The equations (9) and (10) represent the new price after considering the effect of quality-change. On changing the quality, if the response-time has been changed according to the equation (7), then there should not be any change in price due to response-time change. But, if the change in response-time is not according to the equation (7), then this alteration of response-time from $T_{desired}$ will also affect the price. The percentage-change in price due to this alteration of response-time can be calculated as follows:

If actual new response-time is $T_{actualdesired}$, then the percentage-change in response-time from the required response-time $T_{desired}$ will be:

$$dT_{alteration} = \frac{T_{desired} - T_{actualdesired}}{T_{desired}} \times 100 \cdots$$

$$(11)$$

Where, $dT_{alteration}$ is the percentage-alteration of the response-time from the required response-time $T_{desired}$ and it holds $0 \leq dT_{alteration} \leq 100$.

Now, based on the relation (2), the percentage-change in price due to alteration in the required response-time can be calculated as follows:

$$dPt = w_{PT} \times dT_{alteration} \cdots$$

$$(12)$$

Where, dPt is the percentage-change in price due to alteration in response-time and it holds $0 \leq dPt \leq 100$. w_{PT} is the constant holding relation, $0 \leq w_{PT} \leq 1$. Its value is decided by the item provider. It represents the percentage of the percentage-change in response-time ($dT_{alteration}$) with which the price should be changed. It means that if the percentage-change in response-time ($dT_{alteration}$) is 30 and w_{PT} is equal to 0.3, then the percentage-change in price (dPt) will be 9. w_{PT} = 1 implies that the price and quality have one-to-one ratio and price should be changed in the same ration as alteration in response-time. w_{PT} = 0 implies that price is not dependent on the change in response-time.

To produce the results according to equation (2), the equation (11) has been designed in such a way that it produces negative value if $T_{actualdesired}$ is more than $T_{desired}$. It will further generate nega-

tive value from equation (12), which will cause decrease in price. Thus, with increase in response-time, the price is decreasing, which is in line with the equation (2).

So, the new price after taking the effect of change in required response-time will be:

$$Pt_{desired} = P_{thresold} + \left(\frac{P_{thresold} \times dPt}{100} \right) \cdots$$

$$(13)$$

In other form, $Pt_{desired}$ can be represented as:

$$Pt_{desired} = P_{thresold} + \left(\frac{P_{thresold} \times w_{PT} \times \left(\frac{T_{desired} - T_{actualdesired}}{T_{desired}} \times 100 \right)}{100} \right)$$

$$\cdots \qquad (14)$$

It can be inferred from equation (13) and (14) that if the actual response-time ($T_{actualdesired}$) is more than the required response-time ($T_{desired}$), then the price should be decreased, but if the actual response-time ($T_{actualdesired}$) is less than the required response-time ($T_{desired}$), then the price needs to be increased.

The new price, after considering the effect of change in quality as well as the effect of alternation of response-time, will be:

$$P_{desired} = P_{thresold} + \left(\frac{P_{thresold} \times w_{PQ} \times \left(\frac{Q_{desired} - Q_{thresold}}{Q_{thresold}} \times 100 \right)}{100} \right) + \left(\frac{P_{thresold} \times w_{PT} \times \left(\frac{T_{desired} - T_{actualdesired}}{T_{desired}} \times 100 \right)}{100} \right)$$

$$\cdots \qquad (15)$$

The above derived relations can be used for the calculation of utilities for Buyer Agent and Seller Agent. Consider that Buyer agent has some proposal $\langle P_{thresold}, Q_{thresold}, T_{thresold} \rangle$ and values of various constants w_{PT}, w_{PQ}, w_{TQ}, on which buyer agent agrees. These values can be maintained in the item profile of buyer agent. Let $\langle P_{offer}, Q_{offer}, T_{offer} \rangle$ be the proposal obtained by buyer agent from seller agent. The offered quality, Q_{offer}, can be treated as the new quality, $Q_{desired}$, and offered response-time, T_{offer}, as the actual response-time, $T_{actualdesired}$. Then, using equations (4) to (15) the value for required price $P_{desired}$ can be calculated, which is the value of price is considered appropriate by the buyer agent for the offered quality and response-time. This value of price, $P_{desired}$, which has been calculated by considering the effect of both quality-change and alternation in response-time, will represent the preferred-level of buyer agent or the level at which buyer agent is happy for the offered quality and response-time. Whereas, P_{offer} is the price offered for given quality and response-time. So, the ratio of $P_{desired}$ and P_{offer} will represent the happiness/preference level of buyer agent. On the other hand, the utility of (Buyer Agent)/ (Seller Agent) for a item also represents their respective happiness/preference (Wilkes, 2008). Hence, the utility of buyer agent can be represented as:

$$Utility_{BuyerAgent} = w_{pb}\left(\frac{P_{desired}}{P_{offer}}\right) + w_{qb}\left(\frac{Q_{desired}}{Q_{offer}}\right) + w_{tb}\left(\frac{T_{desired}}{T_{offer}}\right) \cdots \quad (16)$$

Where w_{pb}, w_{qb}, w_{tb} holding the relation, is constant representing the percentage value $0 \leq w_{pb} \leq 1$, $0 \leq w_{qb} \leq 1, 0 \leq w_{tb} \leq 1$. From the equation (16), it can be inferred that if the $P_{desired} < P_{offer}$ and $Q_{desired} > Q_{offer}$ and $T_{desired} < T_{offer}$ then the proposal will not be accepted. If $w_{pb} = 1$, $w_{qb} = 0$ and $w_{tb} = 0$ i.e. the offered-price is more than the required-price, then the utility of buyer agent will be less than one and the proposal will not be accepted. In the similar fashion, the utility

of seller agent can be calculated. The only difference is that in the case of seller agent, for the proposal to be acceptable, $P_{desired} < P_{offer}$ and $Q_{desired} > Q_{offer}$ and $T_{desired} < T_{offer}$. Hence, the utility of seller agent can be represented as:

$$Utility_{SellerAgent} = w_{ps}\left(\frac{P_{offer}}{P_{desired}}\right) + w_{qs}\left(\frac{Q_{offer}}{Q_{desired}}\right) + w_{ts}\left(\frac{T_{offer}}{T_{desired}}\right) \cdots \quad (17)$$

Where w_{ps}, w_{qs}, w_{ts} holding the relation, is constant representing the percentage value $0 \leq w_{ps} \leq 1$, $0 \leq w_{qs} \leq 1, 0 \leq w_{ts} \leq 1$. From the equation (17), it can be inferred that if $w_{ps} = 1$, $w_{qs} = 0$ and $w_{ts} = 0$ i.e. offered-price is less than the required-price, then the utility of seller agent will be less than one and the proposal will not be accepted.

The negotiation process and the utility model presented above can be extended by considering some other important parameters such as opportunity-cost, opportunity-gain, and negotiation-cost (Zhang et al., 2005). During the negotiation process, when the seller agent makes a commitment to perform a task, it looses the opportunity to perform some another incoming task of possibly higher utility. This loss occurring to the seller agent on committing a negotiation can be called as Opportunity-Cost. So, in the utility-calculation for the seller agent, not only the actual usage of resources should be considered, but the opportunity-cost should also be involved. Hence, the net utility of seller agent at a negotiation-step should be calculated by deducting the opportunity-cost from the utility-value (Zhang et al., 2005). The opportunity-cost of seller agent at a negotiation-step will depend on the utility gained by the seller agent at that step. So, the opportunity-cost can be represented as below:

$$Opportunity\text{-}Cost = w_{OC} \times Utility_{SellerAgent} \cdots \quad (18)$$

Where, w_{OC}, with value ranging between $0 \leq w_{OC} \leq 1$, is the constant representing the percentage-value.

Hence, the net utility of buyer at a negotiation-step should be calculated by adding the opportunity-gain with the utility-value (Zhang et al., 2005). The opportunity-gain of buyer agent at a negotiation-step will depend on the utility gained by the buyer agent at that step. So, the opportunity-gain can be represented as below:

$$Opportunity\text{-}Gain = w_{OG} \times Utility_{BuyerAgent} \cdots \tag{19}$$

Where, w_{OG}, with value ranging between $0 \leq w_{OG} \leq 1$, is the constant representing the percentage-value.

The negotiation process consumes resources such as time, computational capability, communication capacity etc. The negotiation process has an influence over the process and time of execution of task. This can also reduce the utility of process. These losses occurring due to the negotiation process can be termed as Negotiation-Cost or Negotiation-Effort. Negotiation-Effort can be measured by the number of negotiation steps and it increases with increase in the number of negotiation steps. To make the negotiation-effort and utility-gain comparable, the number of negotiation steps can be mapped into a certain percentage of initial utility without negotiation (Zhang et al., 2005). So, the negotiation-effort can be represented by the following relation:

$$Negotiation\text{-}Effort = w_{NC} \times N \times Utility_{thresold} \\ \cdots \tag{20}$$

Where, N has the value for number of negotiation-steps. $Utility_{thresold}$ is the initial utility of BUYER AGENT/SELLER AGENT if the task has been performed without negotiation. w_{NC} is the percentage-value, which can be chosen by

BUYER AGENT/SELLER AGENT. It decides how the negotiation-effort would affect the utility of BUYER AGENT/SELLER AGENT. The equation (20) implies that the each step of negotiation decreases the achieved utility by a value equal to the w_{NC} percentage of $Utility_{thresold}$.

Thus, on considering the opportunity-cost, opportunity-gain, and negotiation-effort the utility for buyer agent and seller agent can be given as below:

Net Utility for SELLER AGENT =
$$Utility_{SellerAgent} - Negotiation\text{-}Effort - Opportunity\text{-}Cost \tag{21}$$

Net Utility for BUYER AGENT =
$$Utility_{BuyerAgent} - Negotiation\text{-}Effort + Opportunity\text{-}Gain \tag{22}$$

Negotiation-Agreement Based Selection Model

Based upon the concepts described in the previous section on multi-attribute negotiation, two methods for selection of seller agent are possible:

1) Using the values of utility-factors of various candidates' seller agents.
2) Using the values of various attributes obtained after the successful negotiation with candidate seller agents.

In the first method, firstly the utility-theory based negotiation is performed with the various candidates seller agents. This results into the values of utility-factor for buyer agent for those candidates seller agents with which the negotiation results into successful agreement.

In the second selection method, firstly the negotiation is performed with the various candidates seller agents using any selected negotiation approach. Independent of the approach used for negotiation, it will result into some agreed-values of various involved attributes on successful negotiation. Using these values of various attributes, a selection index (SI) is calculated using the model described below and the seller agent with highest SI is selected. During the calculation of SI, the desired weights can be given to the various attributes.

Calculation of Index of Selection

After the successful negotiation of a buyer agent with a seller agent, a set of values of various involved attributes is resulted at which both buyer agent and seller agent agree. This set of values of attributes can be called as agreement-set of buyer agent with respect to seller agent. A buyer agent, before performing the negotiation, usually has some expectations about the values of various attributes of the item. As the agreement-set varies from one seller agent to another, so the selection of a seller agent will directly depends upon the gain obtained by buyer agent from the agreement-set of corresponding seller agent. Hence, the SI (selection index) of a buyer agent with respect to a seller agent will satisfy the following relation:

$$SI \propto Gain(AgreementSet) \ldots \quad (23)$$

Where, $Gain(AgreementSet)$ is the overall-gain of a buyer agent with respect to the reference seller agent.

So, the SI of a buyer agent for a seller agent can be defined as the weighted mean of the individual gains of the buyer agent for the various attributes involved in the negotiation between buyer agent and the corresponding seller agent. Hence, SI can be calculated as follows:

Let $a_1, a_2 \ldots a_n$ be the various attributes used for reaching the agreement in the negotiation process between buyer agent and a reference seller agent. So, if $Gain(a_i)$ be the gain of buyer agent with respect to the reference seller agent

for the attribute a_i and w_i be the weight-age given to the $Gain(a_i)$ in the calculation of SI, then SI can be represented by the following equation:

$$SI = \frac{w_1 \times Gain(a_1) + w_2 \times Gain(a_2) + \ldots + w_n \times Gain(a_n)}{w_1 + w_2 + \ldots + w_n}$$

$$\ldots \quad (24)$$

OR

$$SI = \frac{\sum_{i=1}^{n} w_i \times Gain(a_i)}{\sum_{i=1}^{n} w_i} \ldots \quad (25)$$

Now, the calculation for $Gain(a_i)$ can be done as follows:

Various attributes of a item can have user-tendency of either 'lower the better' or 'higher the better'. For example, for the attribute such as price, lower the value of this attribute more favorable this will be to the requester, so it has user-tendency of 'lower the better', while for the attribute such as quality, higher the value of this attribute more favorable this will be to the requester, so it has user-tendency of 'higher the better'. Let, out of the n number of attributes, $a_1, a_2 \ldots a_t, a_{t+1} \ldots a_n$, of a item, the t number of attributes, $a_1, a_2 \ldots a_t$, have the user-tendency of 'lower the better' and the remaining $(n - t)$ number of attributes, $a_{t+1}, a_{t+2} \ldots a_n$, have the user-tendency of 'higher the better'. Further consider that for the attribute set $(a_1, a_2 \ldots a_t, a_{t+1} \ldots a_n)$, the negotiation between the buyer agent and the reference seller agent results into the actual agreement-set $(vact_1, vact_2 \ldots vact_t, vact_{t+1} \ldots vact_n)$ and the desire-set of buyer agent is $(vdes_1, vdes_2 \ldots vdes_t, vdes_{t+1} \ldots vdes_n)$. Then, the gain of buyer agent with reference to an individual attribute a_k for reference seller agent can be defined as:

For $k = 1, 2 \ldots t$, the gain of buyer agent with reference to the attribute a_k can be defined by the value the agreed attribute-value, $vact_k$, is lower than the expected attribute-value, $vdes_k$, and hence is represented by the equation (26). Similarly for $k = t+1, t+2 \ldots n$, the gain of buyer agent with reference to the attribute a_k can be defined by the value the agreed attribute-value, $vact_k$, is higher than the desire attribute-value, $vdes_k$, and hence is represented by the equation (27).

For $k = 1, 2 \ldots t$
$$Gain(a_k) = \frac{vdes_k - vact_k}{vdes_k} \ldots \tag{26}$$

For $k = t+1, t+2 \ldots n$
$$Gain(a_k) = \frac{vact_k - vdes_k}{vact_k} \ldots \tag{27}$$

We can see that different attributes have different value-ranges, value-types, and measurements. As was discussed, the user may have different tendencies towards different attributes. In addition, the attribute may have higher weight in calculation of IoS, but its impact may be lowered by its smaller value than other attributes. The above model solves these problems by presenting the normalization of attributes. Equations (26) and (27) provide the normalization using the denominators $vdes_k$ and $vact_k$ such that gain-values of all the attributes lie between 0 and 1. The numerators in equations (26) and (27) generate the attribute-values such that all gain-values have the user-tendency of 'higher the better'.

Thus, the equation (25) can be given the following form:

$$SI = \frac{\sum_{i=1}^{t} W_i \times Gain(a_i) + \sum_{i=t+1}^{n} W_i \times Gain(a_i)}{\sum_{i=1}^{n} W_i}$$

IMPLEMENTATION

C&RT generates decision tree and rules based upon business and cognitive factors. So buyers and sellers agent are classified according to their category.

The java based extended filtering model based on predictive results, performs negotiation in between same category of buyer and seller agent using algorithm 1, 2 and 3 and hence select the best seller agent on the basis of gain. The algorithm 1 is for generation of new proposal by seller agent. The algorithm 2 is for generation of new proposal by buyer agent and 3 & 4 are for checking proposals and 5 for checking termination condition for negotiation process (Figure 9).

RESULT AND DISCUSSION

In C&RT based DM model datasets for training and datasets for testing are deployed in decision tree algorithm to calculate the error rate report and obtain its tree-structure. After obtaining the rules for the testing datasets are used to assess the accuracy of these rules. According to the tables, the overall accuracy of the C&RT algorithm is 95.56%.

Result from the experiment has been shown in the tabular form in Figure 3 and Figure 4. From the Figure 3 and Figure 4 lists the seller agents and buyer agents after applying the business parameters and cognitive parameters based filtering through DM respectively. As Table 2 buyer agent B1whose category is very good (VG) negotiates with various seller agents whose category is VG. The intermediate stapes of the negotiation are

Figure 9. Algorithms 1 through 5

```
Algorithm 1: Generation of New Proposal by Seller Agent
ideal proposal: idea_p (ideal price), idea_q (ideal quality), idea_t (ideal time-period)
current proposal: current_p (current_proposed_price), current_q (current_proposed_quality),
current_t (current_proposed_time-period)
previous proposal : pre_p (previous price), pre_q (previous quality), pre_t (previous time-period)
delt_p: a short price-value
delt_q: a short quality-value
delt_t: a short period of time
price_increase_ratio: a small number used to increase the ideal-price
quality_decrease_ratio: a small number used to decrease the ideal-quality
time_increase_ratio: a small number used to increase the ideal time-period
begin
  if (first proposal)
              //set values for the first proposal from Seller Agent
              current_p ? price_increase_ratio * idea_p;
              current_q ? quality_decrease_ratio * idea_q;
              current_t ? time_increase_ratio * idea_t;
  else
              //set values for other new proposals from Seller Agent  in due course of negotiation
              if (pre_p > idea_p)
                          current_p ? pre_p − delt_p;
                          current_q ? pre_q;
                          current_t ? pre_t;
              else
                          if (pre_t > idea_t)
                                      current_p ? pre_p;
                                      current_q ? pre_q;
                                      current_t ? pre_t − delt_t;
                          else
                                      if (pre_q < idea_q)
                                                  current_p ? pre_p;
                                                  current_q ? pre_q + delt_q;
                                                  current_t ? pre_t;
                                      end-if
                          end-if
              end-if
  end
```

```
Algorithm 2: Generation of New Proposal by Buyer Agent
ideal proposal: idea_p (ideal price), idea_q (ideal quality), idea_t (ideal time-period)
current proposal: current_p (current_proposed_price), current_q
(current_proposed_quality), current_t (current_proposed_time-period)
previous proposal : pre_p (previous price), pre_q (previous quality), pre_t (previous time-period)
delt_p: a short price-value
delt_q: a short quality-value
delt_t: a short period of time
price_decrease_ratio: a small number used to decrease the ideal-price
quality_increase_ratio: a small number used to increase the ideal-quality
time_decrease_ratio: a small number used to decrease the ideal time-period
begin
  if (first proposal)
              //set values for the first proposal from Buyer Agent
              current_p ? price_decrease_ratio * idea_p;
              current_q ? quality_increase_ratio * idea_q;
              current_t ? time_decrease_ratio * idea_t;
  else
              //set values for other new proposals from Buyer Agent  in due course of
negotiation
              if (pre_p < idea_p)
                          current_p ? pre_p + delt_p;
                          current_q ? pre_q;
                          current_t ? pre_t;
              else
                          if (pre_t < idea_t)
                                      current_p ? pre_p;
current_q ? pre_q;
current_t ? pre_t + delt_t;
                          else
                                      if (pre_q > idea_q)
                                                  current_q ? pre_q;
current_q ? pre_q − delt_q;
                                                  current_t ? pre_t;
                          end-if
              end-if
  end
```

```
Algorithm3: Checking Proposal for buyer agent
received proposal: rec_p (price in received proposal), rec_q (quality in received proposal),
rec_t (time-period in received proposal)
utility_v: variable to store utility value
desired sent proposal: desired_p (price in desired sent proposal), desired_q (quality in
desired sent proposal), desired_t (time-period in  desired sent proposal)
begin
          utility_v ? calculate_utility(rec_p, rec_q, rec_t);
  // The formulation for calculate_utility() is different for Seller Agent  and Buyer Agent
          if (rec_p<= desired_p & & rec_q>= desired_q & & rec_t <= desired_t)
                      received proposal is acceptable;
          else
                      received proposal is not acceptable;
          end-if
  end
```

```
Algorithm4: Checking Proposal for Seller agent
received proposal: rec_p (price in received proposal), rec_q (quality in received proposal),
rec_t (time-period in  received proposal)
utility_v: variable to store utility value
offer proposal: offer_p (offer price), offer_q (offer quality), offer_t (offer time-period)
begin
          utility_v ? calculate_utility(rec_p, rec_q, rec_t);
  // The formulation for calculate_utility() is different for Seller Agent  and Buyer Agent
          if (rec_p<= offer_p & & rec_q>= offer_q & & rec_t <= offer_t)
                      received proposal is acceptable;
          else
                      received proposal is not acceptable;
          end-if
  end
```

```
Algorithm 5: Checking Termination Condition for Negotiation Process
utility_v: utility-value for the received proposal
ideal proposal: idea_p (ideal price), idea_q (ideal quality), idea_t (ideal time-period)
latest sent proposal: last_p (price in latest sent proposal), last_q (quality in latest sent
proposal), last_t (time-period in  latest sent proposal)
begin
  if (utility_v >= 1)
  // utility more than or equal to 1 implies that the received proposal is acceptable
  //to accept the proposal and terminate negotiation process with agreement

              terminate negotiation
  end-if
  if (last_p = idea_p & & last_q = idea_q & & last_t = idea_t)
  // negotiation-steps exceed the maximum threshold limit.
  // the number of steps in threshold limit is decided by the values of delt_p, delt_q, delt_t
  // ratio_p, ratio_q, and ratio_t as defined in the algorithm for generating new proposal

              terminate negotiation
  end-if
  end
```

shown in Figures 10 and 11. For a seller agent S1 negotiation at step 3 is successful because achieve utility 1.0136 which is greater than one. So for an agent, if the negotiation is successful at step3 then they are filtered for calculation of IS for the buyer agent B1 using negotiation agreement based selection model. The second, third, and fourth column in the table show the values of gain in price, quality, and response-time calculated using the equations (26), (27), and (26) respectively. Using these values, the final SI is calculated for the seller agent using equation (28), which is shown in the last column of the table. It can be seen from the table that the seller agent 'S1' has highest SI and hence it get selected as the seller agent for a set of items. 'S1' can effectively satisfy the buyer agent B1 needs.

The strategies of the model presented here can be used to predict the mental, cognitive and business features of seller and buyer agent through broker. Another important issue discussed in this paper is semi cooperative negotiation. The proposed method supports the importance of the following factors in our model for B2C process: selection of seller agent and profitable buyer agent on the basis of DM model, semi cooperative negotiation, consumer satisfaction, profit, minimal financial margin (profit). The limitation of our work is not providing a learning module which keeps for further work.

EMPIRICAL VALIDATIONS AND EVALUATION

In the experiment values were chosen such that they provide both stable behavior of the system and assure a termination property i.e. in most instances lead the conclusion of the selection of a seller agent and profitable buyer agent for negotiation on the basis SI and also lead to the conclusion of the negotiation in a relatively small number of negotiation steps in semi cooperative negotiation session.

Figure 10. Negotiation-Agreement between buyer and seller

NameOfAgent	Offerd_Price	Offerd_Quality	Offerd_Time	Achived_Price	Achived_Qua...	Achived_Time	Utility
S1	300	15	2.3	-	-	-	0.9231
B1	200	12.5	1.7	-	-	-	1.0136
S1	-	-	-	200	12.5	1.7	-
S2	406.25	7.5	5	-	-	-	0.1191
B1	200	12.5	1.9	-	-	-	0.3160
S2	-	-	-	200	12.5	1.9	-
S3	391.25	7.5	5	-	-	-	0.1191
B1	200	11.3	1.9	-	-	-	0.3261
S3	-	-	-	200	11.3	1.9	-

Figure 11. Selection of seller agent on the basis of negotiation agreement

NameOfAgent	Price_Gain	Quality_Gain	Time_Gain	SI
S1	0	0.2	0.15	0.12
S2	0	0.2	0.05	0.09
S3	0	0.118	0.047	0.06
S4	0	0.115	0.05	0.06
S9	0	0.191	0.046	0.09

To intelligently segment profitable customers of a company in terms of their profitability, we present an easy and efficient alternative approach based on the deterministic computational instead of using a complicated customer profitability model.

RELATED WORK

In the proposed work we determine the preferences of the customer as well as determine the potential of the customer (capability) of the customer using deterministic method which is helpful to determine the customer orientation value before negotiating. Chan, Cheng and Hsu formulation use statistical method. Various customer orientation based model are found in Park and Lee (2005). Ha, Bae, and Park (2002) proposed a survey based profitable customer segmentation system that conducts the customer satisfaction survey and those mining processes for the profitable customer segmenta-

tion. Their survey is based on customer satisfaction data, socio-demographic data and accounting data but in their research there is no direct concept of historical evaluation, need, fit, capability, preference and other cognitive features of buyer agents for ordering of buyer agents queue.

Cooperative one to one multi-criteria negotiation model (Jonker, Robu, & Treur, 2007) is proposed agent based system using the historical data of agent that predicts the preferences of the agents. In our model broker agent helps to select a seller agent by BDI and mental state characteristics of seller agent and also ordering the buyer agent queue for selected seller agent by cognitive parameters, matching the business policies of seller agent and buyer agent and competitive negotiation. Then cooperative negotiation mechanism is introduced. With the help of this mechanism broker stabilize a deal between buyer and seller by maximize the CUI which satisfy both parties in multiple round of negotiations.

Various negotiation models are proposed (Gutman & Maes, 1998; Faratin, Sierra, & Jennings, 2003; Fatima, Wooldridge, & Jennings, 2003) but in their approach there is no view available for combined approach of competitive and cooperative negotiation. In their research there is no direct concept of mental and cognitive features which help in the selection of a seller agent and profitable buyer agent in B2C e-commerce. In our approach it is possible to specify both type of competitive as well as cooperative negotiation which satisfies both parties.

In research (Kwang, 2000) also proposed algorithms for selection, evaluation and filtering using broker but they did not consider about cognitive values and mental states of an agent.

In conclusion, we can say that we have been successful in meeting our stated research

goal, which is to improve the efficiency of negotiations using combined negotiation model in electronic environments for B2C process integrated with concept of cognitive, mental and customer orientation computational model which is clear from the comparative table (Table 1).

The proposed negotiation approach mainly focuses on the computation of utility-factor, communication model, and an extension of traditional negotiation approach by using concepts of opportunity-cost, opportunity-gain, and negotiation-effort. Multi-attribute negotiation presents a utility based multi-attribute negotiation.

The evaluation of proposed work by comparing it with existing similar works is presented next. Jonker et al. (2007) have presented the utility based multi-attribute negotiation for multi-agent systems. They have presented the concept of financial utility and ease utility in the negotiation process. But, the presented utility-calculation neither considers the interdependence of different attributes such as effect of quality-change over the price and response-time, nor it gives any consideration to opportunity-cost, opportunity-gain, and the cost of negotiation. Similarly, the work by Zhang et al. (2005) has presented the multi-dimensional,

multi-step, multi-attribute negotiation from multi-agent perspectives only. They have presented the utility-calculation for cooperative negotiation between agents, but their utility-calculation also does not consider the interdependence of different attributes. However, their work has discussed the concept of the negotiation-cost in detail, but only a brief discussion on the opportunity-cost and opportunity-gain has been provided without any formalization for their computation. Xiaolong et al. (2006) have presented a multi-attribute negotiation framework based on multi-agent systems for large-scale construction projects supply chain coordination. Their model can be helpful in the utility determination, but does not seem to provide concrete results for the target utility.

Zhang et al. (2005) have also provided the formulation for calculation of quality-gain, cost-gain, and duration-gain. Like our proposed model, this work also properly handles the user-tendency and generates the gain-values with user-tendency of 'higher the better' irrespective of the user-tendency of attribute. But, our formulation is better in the sense that it is more near to the human intuition. The gain-values calculated by Zhang et al. (2005) always lies between 0 and 1, so it will always indicate that the buyer agent has some gain irrespective that the corresponding seller agent has agreed on value lower than the expected value or higher than the expected value. For example, if the expected quality is 30 and the agreed quality is 20, then actually it is loosing, but the formulation by Zhang et al. (2005) will show the gain-value of 0.667 i.e. positive gains. On the other hand, our formulation will generate the negative gain-value of -0.5 indicating that the buyer agent is losing. This fact can be easily verified by the following calculation:

For this purpose, we have borrowed the test data from an example described in (Zhang et al., 2005). They have used the following values of different parameters: required threshold for quality, cost, and duration is 50, 50, and 55 respectively and the achieved values for an intermediate proposal

Table 1. Comparison Table

Feature	(Jonker et al., proposed method)	(Zhang et al., proposed method)	(Makedon et al., proposed method)	(Hsien-Jung Wu proposed method)	(Xiaolong et al., proposed method)	(Stamoulis et al., proposed method)	(Lai et al., proposed method)	(Lai and Sycara, proposed method)	(Pau-robally et al., proposed method)	(C.C. Henry Chan Chi-Bin Cheng Chih-Hsiung Hsu proposed method)	(Olmedilla et al., proposed method)	(Gutman, Maes proposed method)	(Lee, Park proposed method)	(Nejdl et al., proposed method)	Our Proposed Approach
Communication model and negotiation environment	Yes	Yes	No	No	Yes	No	No	No	No	No	No	No	No	No	Yes
Cognitive and mental features in customer orientation value for customer relation in e-commerce	Only preferences are predict on the basis of history. Nothing about customer relationship.	No	No	Accumulate customer knowledge without specific cognitive analysis. Generating customer relationship based upon data analysis.	No	No	No	No	No	No	No	Nô	Survey based profitable customer segmentation system Cognitive parameters are not used for customer analysis.	No	Consider the mental and cognitive features through deterministic computational model. Generating customer relationship.

Continued on following page

Table 1. Continued

Feature														
Business features for customer relation in e-commerce	No	No	No	No	No	Yes	No	No	No	No	No	Yes	No	No
Computation model for decision-making during negotiation process such as utility model	Yes	Yes	Yes	Not Specify	Yes, but the model does not seems to provide the concrete result for utility, as it represents the utility in the form of other type of utility-values	Yes, but the model does not seems to provide the concrete result for utility, as it represents the utility in the form of other type of utility-values	Yes, but the model does not seems to provide the concrete result for utility, as it represents the utility in the form of other type of utility-values	No	Negotiation, and this transforms the fully competitive price bargaining to a cooperative atmosphere.	No	Yes, but no view to provide the concrete utility result	No	Without formulated accounting data used	No	Yes, Semi-cooperative
Consider interdependence of attributes by considering effect of quality-change over change in price etc.	No	No	No	No	No	No	No	No	No	No	No	No	No	Yes

Continued on following page

Table 1. Continued

Generating concrete value for utility by representing utility in the form of basic attributes such as price, quality etc.	Yes	Yes	Yes	No	No	No	No	No	No	No	No	No	Yes
Consider opportunity-cost, opportunity-gain and negotiation-effort	No	Only negotiation-effort has been formulated, but others are only given a brief discussion	No	No	No	No	No	No	No	No	No	No	Yes
Role of broker agent for seller and buyer	Not specify	Not specify	Not specify	No	Not specify	Not specify	Not specify	Not specify	No	Not specify	No	Not specify	Act as an advisor or manager (coordinator) for seller agent and buyer agent
DM Method	No	No	No	No	No	No	No	Yes	No	Yes	No	No	Yes

is 30, 30, and 27 for quality, cost, and duration respectively. Out of these parameters, quality has the user-tendency of 'higher the better' and the rest of two have user-tendency of 'lower the better'. So, it can be observed from general human intuition that the buyer agent is losing in the case of quality by value 20 i.e. gain of -20, and is gaining in the cases of cost and duration by values 20 and 28 respectively. The quality-gain, cost-gain, and duration-gain calculated using the formulation by Zhang et al. (2005) result into values 0.6, 0.4, and 0.51 respectively. On the other hand, using equation (27) of our proposed model, for calculation of quality-gain and using equation (26) for calculation of cost-gain and duration-gain result into values -0.67, 0.4, and 0.51 for quality-gain, cost-gain, and duration-gain respectively. It can observed from these values that the gain-values calculated using our proposed model is clearly indicating that the buyer agent is losing in the case of quality, which is consistent with the actual situation. It can also be seen from the Figure 12 (a,b,c) that the nature of curve corresponding to the gain-values calculated using our proposed model is more similar to the curve generated using actual gain-values than the curve generated by values calculated using formulation from Zhang et al. (2005). Hence, the proposed selection model will result into more reliable results.

CONCLUSION

We have shown the application of B2C process integrated with concept of DM integrated with cognitive, mental and customer orientation for the purchase domain in a semi-cooperative system. The buyer agent has set of requirements of items for which it needs some seller agents. To perform this, the seller agent can choose from several alternatives that produce different qualities and consume different resources. This context requires a negotiation that leads to a satisfying solution with increasing utility. Our approach identifies and

Figure 12. Gain - Values

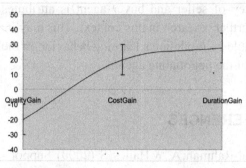

(a). Actual Gain-Values

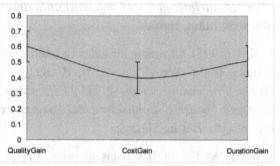

(b): Gain-Values calculated using model from Zhang et al. (2005)

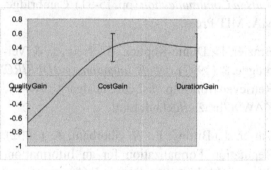

(c): Gain-Values calculated using our proposed model

ordering profitable buyer and seller agents queue and apply semi-cooperative negotiation strategies to most profitable buyer agent and most profitable seller agent according to predictive analysis model. This mechanism helps to evaluate a good solution for fulfilling the requirements. After carefully analyzing the trace of the negotiation mechanism, for further work, this part of research is still ongoing to develop an algorithm for better way to evaluate the difficulty of a specific negotiation problem in the agents' negotiation. Prevention from cheating, and maintaining the privacy of seller and buyer agent is attributes for further research in this context. This may be possible by modeling a learning behavior on the part of the negotiating agents.

REFERENCES

Abdul-Rahman, A., & Hailes, S. (2000). Supporting Trust in Virtual Communities. In *Proceedings of the Hawaii International Conference on Systems Sciences,* Maui, Hawaii.

Bell, J. (1995). Changing attitudes In Intelligent Agents. In M. Wooldridge & N. R. Jennings (Eds.), *Proceedings of the ECAI-94 Workshop on Agent Theories, Architecture and Languages* (pp. 40-50). Berlin: Springer.

Bratman, M. E. (1990). What is intention? In P. R. Cohen, J., Morgan, M. E. Pollack (Eds.), *Intentions in Communication* (pp. 15-31). Cambridge, MA: MIT Press.

Brazier, F., Dunin-Keplicz, B., Treur, J., & Verbrugge, R. (1997). *Beliefs, Intentions and DESIRE*. Retrieved from http://ksi.cpsc.ucalgary.ca/KAW/KAW96/brazier/default.html

Carter, J., Bitting, E., & Ghorbani, A. (2002). Reputation Formalization for an Information-Sharing Multi-Agent Sytem. *Computational Intelligence, 18*(2), 515–534. doi:10.1111/1467-8640.t01-1-00201

Castelfranchi, C., & Falcone, R. (1998). Principles of Trust for MAS: Cognitive Anatomy, Social Importance and Quantification. In *Proceedings of the International Conference on Multi-Agent Systems (ICMAS'98),* Paris (pp. 72-79).

Chan, H. C., Cheng, C. B., & Hsu, C. H. (2007). Bargaining strategy formulation with CRM for an e-commerce agent. *Electronic Commerce Research and Applications, 6,* 490–498. doi:10.1016/j.elerap.2007.02.011

Chee, C. N. (2004). *Three Critical Steps to Customer-centric Business Orientation.* Retrieved from http://www.metacore-asia.biz

Esfandiari, B., & Chandrasekharan, S. (2001). On How Agents Make friends: Mechanisms for Trust Acquisition. In *Proceedings of the Fourth Workshop on Deception, Fraud and Trust in Agent Societies,* Montreal, Canada (pp. 27-34).

Faratin, P., Sierra, C., & Jennings, N. (2003). Using Similarity Criteria to Make Issue Trade-offs in Automated Negotiations. *Journal of Artificial Intelligence, 142*(2), 205–237. doi:10.1016/S0004-3702(02)00290-4

Fatima, S. S., Wooldridge, M., & Jennings, N. R. (2003, July). Optimal Agendas for Multi-Issue Negotiation. In *Proceedings of the Second International Conference on Autonomous Agents and Multiagent Systems (AAMAS-03),* Melbourne, Australia (pp. 129-136).

Gutman, R., & Maes, P. (1998). Cooperative vs. Competitive Multi-Agent Negotiation in Retail Electronic Commerce. In *Proceedings of the Second International Workshop on Cooperative Information Agents (CIA'98),* Paris.

Ha, S. H., Bae, S. M., & Park, S. C. (2002). Customer's time-variant purchase behavior and corresponding marketing strategies: an online retailer's case. *Computers & Industrial Engineering, 43,* 801–820. doi:10.1016/S0360-8352(02)00141-9

Jonker, C. M., Robu, V., & Treur, J. (2007). An Agent Architecture for Multi-Attribute Negotiation Using Incomplete Preference Information. *Autonomous Agents and Multi-Agent Systems, 15*(2), 221–252. doi:10.1007/s10458-006-9009-y

Kang, N., & Han, S. (2002). Agent-based e-marketplace system for more fair and efficient transaction. *Decision Support Systems, 34*, 157–165. doi:10.1016/S0167-9236(02)00078-7

Kraus, S., Sycara, K., & Evenchil, A. (1998). Reaching agreements through argumentation: A logical model and implementation. *Artificial Intelligence, 104*, 1–69. doi:10.1016/S0004-3702(98)00078-2

Krulwich, B. (1996). The Bargainfinder Agent: Comparison Price Shopping on the Internet. In Williams, J. (Ed.), *Bots and Other Internet Beasties* (pp. 257–263). New York: Macmillan Computer Publishing.

Lee, J. H., & Park, S. C. (2005). Intelligent profitable customers segmentation system based on business intelligence tools. *Expert Systems with Applications, 29*, 145–152. doi:10.1016/j.eswa.2005.01.013

Mazumdar, B. D., & Mishra, R. B. (2009). Multiagent Paradigm for the Agent Selection and Negotiation in a B2c Process. *International Journal of Intelligent Information Technologies, 5*(1), 61–82.

Mishra, R. B. (2009). Rule Based and ANN model for the evaluation of Customer Orientation in CRM. *Institution of Engineers, 20*, 28–33.

Panzarasa, P., Jennings, N. R., & Norman, T. J. (2002)... *Formalizing Collaborative Decision-making and Practical Reasoning in Multi-agent System, 12*(1), 55–117.

Reichheld, F. F. (1996). *The Loyalty Effect*. Cambridge, MA: Harvard Business School Press.

Sabater, J., & Sierra, C. (2005). Review on Computational Trust and Reputation Models. *Artificial Intelligence Review, 24*, 33–60. doi:10.1007/s10462-004-0041-5

Sandholm, T. W. (1999). Distributed rational decision making. In *Multiagent System*.

Shoham, Y. (1993). Agent Oriented Programming. *Artificial Intelligence, 60*(1), 51–92. doi:10.1016/0004-3702(93)90034-9

Sim, K. M., & Chan, R. (2000). A Brokering Protocol for Agent-Based E-Commerce. *IEEE Transactions on Systems, Man and Cybernetics. Part C, Applications and Reviews, 30*(4).

Suwu, W., & Das, A. (2001). An Agent System Architecture for E-Commerce. In *Proceedings of the 12th International Workshop on Database and Expert Systems Applications* (pp. 715-719).

Tang, T. Y., Winoto, P., & Niu, X. (2003). *Investigating Trust between Users and Agents in A Multi Agent Portfolio Management System: a Preliminary Report*.

Von Wright, G. H. (1980). *Freedom and Determination*. Amsterdam, The Netherlands: North Holland Publishing Co.

Wilkes, J. (2008). *Utility Functions, Prices, and Negotiation* (Tech. Rep. HPL-2008-81). Retrieved from http://www. Hpl.hp.com/techreports/2008/HPL-2008-81.pdf.2008

Winer, R. S. (2001). *Customer Relationship Management: A Framework*. Research Directions, and the Future.

Wu, H. J. (2005). An Agent-Based CRM Model for Multiple Projects management. In *Proceedings of the IEEE Engineering Management Conference* (pp. 851-855).

Wu, W., Ekaette, E., & Far, B. H. (2003). Uncertainty Management Framework for Multi-Agent System. In *Proceedings of ATS* (pp. 122-131).

Xu, Z. (2008). *Factors which affect the dynamics of privately-owned Chinese firms: an interdisciplinary empirical evaluation*. Unpublished PhD thesis.

Yu, B., & Singh, M. P. (2001). Towards a Probabilistic Model of Distributed Reputation Management. In *Proceedings of the Fourth Workshop on Deception, Fraud and Trust in Agent Societies,* Montreal, Canada (pp. 125-137).

Zacharia, G. (1999). *Collaborative Reputation Mechanisms for Online Communities.* Unpublished master's thesis, Massachusetts Institute of Technology.

Zhao, X., Wu, C., Zhang, R., Zhao, C., & Lin, Z. A. (2004). *Multi-Agent System for E-Business Processes Monitoring in a Web-Based Environment.* Beijing, China: TCL Group Corporation, Department of Information Science, Peking University.

This work was previously published in International Journal of Intelligent Information Technologies, Volume 6, Issue 4, edited by Vijayan Sugumaran, pp. 46-70, copyright 2010 by IGI Publishing (an imprint of IGI Global).

Compilation of References

Abbattista, F., Degemmis, M., Licchelli, O., Lops, P., Semeraro, G., & Zambetta, F. (2002, May 28). *Improving the usability of an e-commerce web site through personalization.* Paper presented at the Workshop on Recommendation and Personalization in eCommerce, Malaga, Spain.

Abdullah, M. S., Paige, R., Kimble, C., & Benest, I. (2007, August). A UML profile for knowledge-based systems modelling. In *Proceedings of the 5th ACIS International Conference on Software Engineering Research, Management & Applications (Sera'07)*, Busan, Korea (pp. 871-878). Washington DC: IEEE Computer Society.

Abdul-Rahman, A., & Hailes, S. (2000). Supporting Trust in Virtual Communities. In *Proceedings of the Hawaii International Conference on Systems Sciences*, Maui, Hawaii.

About.com. (n.d.). Retrieved February 12, 2009, from http://www.about.com

Agrawal, R., & Srikant, R. (1994). Fast Algorithms for Mining Association Rules. In *Proceedings of the 20th VLDB Conference*, Santiago, Chile (pp. 487-499).

Agrawal, D., Abbadi, A., Singh, A., & Yurek, T. (1997). Efficient View Maintenance at Data Warehouse. *SIGMOD Record, 26*(2), 417–427. doi:10.1145/253262.253355

Aguayo, F. (2007). *Sistemas Avanzados de Fabricación Distribuida.* Madrid, Spain: Ra-Ma. ISBN 978-84-7897-804-5

Ahmed, N. (2006). *An overview of e-participation models* (Tech. Rep.). United Nations: Department of Economic and Social Affairs.

Akkermans, H. (2001). Emergent supply networks: System dynamics simulation of adaptive supply agents. In *Proceedings of the 34th Hawaii International Conference on System Sciences*.

Alaranta, M. (2005). Evaluating success in post-merger IS integration: A case study. *The Electronic Journal Information Systems Evaluation, 8*, 143–150.

Allwood, J., & Lee, J. (2005). The design of an agent for modelling supply chain network dynamics. *International Journal of Production Research, 43*(22), 4875–4898. doi:10.1080/00207540500168295

Amaldi, E., & Kann, V. (1998). On the approximability of minimizing nonzero variables or unsatisfied relations in linear systems. *Theoretical Computer Science, 209*(1-2), 237–260. doi:10.1016/S0304-3975(97)00115-1

Amit, R., & Schoemaker, P. J. H. (1993). Strategic assets and organizational rent. *Strategic Management Journal, 14*, 33–46. doi:10.1002/smj.4250140105

Amo, S. D., & Alves, M. H. F. (2004). Incremental Maintenance of Data Warehouses Based on Past Temporal Logic Operators. *Journal of Universal Computer Science, 10*(9).

Arindam, P. (1999). *QoS in Data Networks: Protocols and Standards.* Columbus, OH: The Ohio State University. Retrieved from http://www.cs.wustl.edu/~jain/cis7889/ftp/qos_protocols/index.html

Ashish, N., & Maluf, D. A. (2009). Intelligent information integration: reclaiming the intelligence. *International Journal of Intelligent Information Technologies, 5*(3), 55–83.

Ashrafi, M., Taniar, D., & Smith, K. (2004). ODAM: An Optimized Distributed Association Rule Mining Algorithm. *IEEE Distributed Systems Online, 5*(3).

Ashrafi, M., Taniar, D., & Smith, K. (2005). Privacy-Preserving Distributed Association Rule Mining Algorithm. *International Journal of Intelligent Information Technologies, 1*(1), 46–69.

Atallah, M., Bertino, E., Elmagarmid, A., Ibrahim, M., & Verykios, V. S. (1999). Disclosure limitation of sensitive rules. In *Proceedings of the IEEE Knowledge and Data Exchange Workshop (KDEX'99),* (pp. 45-52). Washington, DC: IEEE Computer Society.

Atmel. (2009). *Home*. Retrieved from http://www.atmel.com

Aviv, Y. (2001). The effect of collaborative forecasting on supply chain performance. *Management Science, 47*(10), 1326–1343. doi:10.1287/mnsc.47.10.1326.10260

Axtell, R. (2000). *Why agents? On the varied motivations for agent computating in the social sciences*. Retrieved from http://docs.google.com/viewer?a=v&q=cache:o0vtAsiH7S8J:citeseerx.ist.psu.edu/viewdoc/download%3Fdoi%3D10.1.1.90.9253%26rep%3Drep1%26type%3Dpdf+Axtell,+R.+(2000).+Why+agents%3F+On+the+varied+motivations+for+agent+computating+in+the+social+sciences.&hl=en&gl=us&pid=bl&srcid=ADGEESgml7tFbcHv4zCeHuD4BBbDtXOBfJLX2uL9ffMgyiA15V8wyXZY0SvhRrFcdjKzJ27uy3qEg920fa0TF5DSeGUnPgZ9KyU3k0T4LVY_2rhVXiSD9eQW7sGjfgdrkoSSmAO70uiK&sig=AHIEtbQx5cug6U2FKBNOGHB9HxxvwndWVQ

Azzedin, F., & Maheswaran, M. (2002). Towards trust-aware resource management in grid computing systems. In *Proceedings of the International Symposium on Cluster Computing and the Grid (CCGRID-2002),* Berlin, Germany (pp. 452).

Babenyshev, S., & Rybakov, V. (2008). Logic of plausibility for discovery in multi-agent environment—deciding algorithms. In *Knowledge-based intelligent information and engineering system* (LNAI 5179, pp. 210-217).

Bækgaard, L., & Mark, L. (1995). Incremental Computation of Time-Varying Query Expressions. *IEEE Transactions on Knowledge and Data Engineering, 7*(4), 583–590. doi:10.1109/69.404031

Baesens, B., Van Gestel, T., Viaene, S., Stepanova, M., Suykens, J., & Vanthienen, J. (2003). Benchmarking state-of-the-art classification algorithms for credit scoring. *The Journal of the Operational Research Society, 54*(6), 627–635. doi:10.1057/palgrave.jors.2601545

Baets, W. (1992). Aligning information systems with business strategy. *The Journal of Strategic Information Systems, 1,* 205–214. doi:10.1016/0963-8687(92)90036-V

Baffo, I., Confessore, G., & Rismondo, S. (2007). *Uno strumento di modellazione e simulazione della dinamica di una rete di attori operanti in un territorio*. Paper presented at the XXVIII Italian Conference of Regional Science.

Baffo, I., Dedonno, L., Confessore, G., & Rismondo, S. (2006). *Descrizione ex-post di una rete relazionale territoriale e realizzazione di uno strumento per la simulazione dinamica ex-ante*. Paper presented at the XXVII Italian Conference of Regional Science.

Baharadwaj, A. S. (2000). A resource-based perspective on information technology capability and firm performance: An empirical investigation. *Management Information Systems Quarterly, 24,* 169–196. doi:10.2307/3250983

Baker Ryan, S. J. D. (2007, April 28-May 3). Modeling and understanding students' off-task behavior in intelligent tutoring systems. In *Proceedings of CHI 2007: Learning & Education,* San Jose, CA (pp. 1059-1068). ACM Publishing.

Balabanovic, M., Chu, L., & Wolff, G. (2000, April 1-6). Storytelling with Digital Photographs. In T. Turner, G. Szwillus, M. Czerwinski, F. Peterno, & S. Pemberton (Eds.), ACM CHI 2000 Human Factors in Computing (pp. 564–571). Hague, The Netherlands.

Ballou, D. P., & Tayi, G. K. (1999). Enhancing Data Quality in Data Warehouse Environments. *Communications of the ACM, 42*(1). doi:10.1145/291469.291471

Barney, J. (1991). Firm resources and sustained competitive advantage. *Journal of Management, 17,* 90–120. doi:10.1177/014920639101700108

Barnickel, N., Fluegge, M., & Schmidt, K.-U. (2006). Interoperability in egovernment through cross-ontology semantic web service composition. In *Proceedings of the Workshop Semantic Web for eGovernment / 3rd European Semantic Web Conference,* Budva, Montenegro.

Barringer, H., Fisher, M., Gabbay, D., & Gough, G. (1999). *Advances in temporal logic*. Dordrecht, The Netherlands: Kluwer Academic Publishers.

Belhajjame, K., Embury, S. M., Paton, N. W., Stevens, R., & Goble, C. A. (2008). Automatic annotation of web services based on workflow definitions. *ACM Trans. Web*, *2*(2), 1–34. doi:10.1145/1346337.1346239

Bell, J. (1995). Changing attitudes In Intelligent Agents. In M. Wooldridge & N. R. Jennings (Eds.), *Proceedings of the ECAI-94 Workshop on Agent Theories, Architecture and Languages* (pp. 40-50). Berlin: Springer.

Bellotti, T., & Crook, J. (2009). Support vector machines for credit scoring and discovery of significant features. *Expert Systems with Applications*, *36*(2), 3302–3308. doi:10.1016/j.eswa.2008.01.005

Bergenti, F., Poggi, A., Burg, B., & Caire, G. (2001). Deploying FIPA-compliant systems on handheld devices. *IEEE Internet Computing*, *5*(4), 20–25. doi:10.1109/4236.939446

Berners-Lee, T., Hendler, J., & Lassila, O. (2001). The semantic web. *Scientific American*, *284*(5), 34–43. doi:10.1038/scientificamerican0501-34

Berstel, B., & Bonnard, P. (2007). Reactive Rules on the Web. In *Proceedings of Summer School Reasoning Web 2007* (LNCS 4636, pp.183-239).

Blackburn, P., & Marx, M. (2003). Constructive interpolation in hybrid logic. *Journal of Symbolic Logic*, *68*(2), 463–480. doi:10.2178/jsl/1052669059

Blackshaw, P. (2009). *The Pocket Guide t.* Retrieved June 10, 2009, from http://www.clickz.com/showPage.html?page=3515576

Bodoff, S., Armstrong, E., Ball, J., & Carson, D. B. (2004). *The J2E tutorial* (2nd ed.). Boston: Addison-Wesley Longman.

Bokun, M. & Taglienti, C. (1998). Incremental Data Warehouse Updates. *DM Review*, 1-5.

Bordini, R. H., Fisher, M., Visser, W., & Wooldridge, M. (2004). Model checking rational agents. *IEEE Intelligent Systems*, *19*(5), 46–52. doi:10.1109/MIS.2004.47

Borst, W. N. (1997). *Construction of Engineering Ontologies*. Unpublished doctoral dissertation, University of Twente, Enschede, The Netherlands.

Boyer, S. A. (1999). *SCADA: Supervisory Control And Data Acquisition* (2nd ed.). New York: ISA: The Instrumentation, Systems and Automation Society.

Bradshaw, J. M. (1997). An Introduction to Software Agents. In Bradshaw, J. M. (Ed.), *Software Agents* (pp. 3–46). Cambridge, MA: AAAI Press/MIT Press.

Brambilla, M., Ceri, S., Facca, F. M., Celino, I., Cerizza, D., & Valle, E. D. (2007). Model-driven design and development of semantic web service applications. *ACM Transactions on Internet Technology*, *8*(1), 3. doi:10.1145/1294148.1294151

Brancheau, J., Janz, B. D., & Wetherbe, J. C. (1996). Key issues in information system management: 1994–95 SIM delphi results. *Management Information Systems Quarterly*, *20*, 225–242. doi:10.2307/249479

Bratman, M. E. (1990). What is intention? In P. R. Cohen & M. J. Pollack (Eds.), *Intentions in communication* (pp. 15-31). Cambridge, MA: MIT Press.

Brazier, F., Dunin-Keplicz, B., Treur, J., & Verbrugge, R. (1997). *Beliefs, Intentions and DESIRE*. Retrieved from http://ksi.cpsc.ucalgary.ca/KAW/KAW96/brazier/default.html

Breiman, L., Friedman, J. H., Olshen, R. A., & Stone, C. J. (1984). *Classification and Regression Trees*. Monterey, CA: Wadsworth & Brooks.

Breuker, J. (1995, November). Problems, tasks and problem solving methods: Constructing the common KADS. In *Proceedings of First International Workshop on Knowledge-Based Systems for the (Re) Use of Program Libraries (KBUP '95)*, Sophia Antipolis, France. INRIA.

Briot, J.-P., Charpentier, S., Marin, O., & Sens, P. (2002, July). A fault-tolerant multi-agent framework. In *International Joint Conference on Autonomous Agents and Multiagent Systems*, Bologna, Italy (pp. 672-673). ACM Publishing.

Brobst, S., McIntire, M., & Rado, E. (2008). Agile Data Warehousing with Integrated Sandboxing. *Business Intelligence Journal*, *13*(1).

Brooks, R. A. (1986). A Robust Layered Control System for a mobile robot. *Journal of Robotics and Automation, 2*(1), 349–355.

Bruckner, R. M., & Tjoa, A. M. (2002). Capturing Delays and Valid Times in Data Warehouses - Towards Timely Consistent Analyses. *Journal of Intelligent Information Systems, 19*(2), 169–190. doi:10.1023/A:1016555410197

Buck-Lew, M., Wardle, C. E., & Pliskin, N. (1992). Accounting for information technology in corporate acquisitions. *Information & Management, 22*, 363–369. doi:10.1016/0378-7206(92)90031-A

Bukovics, B. (2007). *Pro WF: Windows Workflow in NET 3.0*. New York: Apress.

Caballero, Y., Alvarez, D., Bel, R., & Garcia, M. M. (2007). Feature selection algorithms using Rough Set Theory. In L. D. Mourelle, N. Nedjah, J. Kacprzyk & A. Abraham (Eds.), *Proceedings of the 7th International Conference on Intelligent Systems Design and Applications* (pp. 407-411).

Cabral, L., Domingue, J., Galizia, S., Gugliotta, A., Tanasescu, V., Pedrinaci, C., & Norton, B. (2006). Irs-iii: A broker for semantic web services based applications. In *5th International Semantic Web Conference (ISWC)* (LNCS 4273, pp. 201-214). Athens, GA: Springer.

Cachon, G. P., & Fisher, M. (2000). Supply chain inventory management and the value of shared information. *Management Science, 46*(8), 1032–1048. doi:10.1287/mnsc.46.8.1032.12029

Camarinha-Matos, L. M., & Afsarmanesh, H. (2004). Towards next business models. In L. Camarinha-Matos & L. M. Afsarmanesh (Eds.), *Collaborative networked organizations: A research agenda for emerging business models* (pp. 3-6). Boston: Springer.

Camarinha-Matos, L. M., & Afsarmanesh, H. (2006). A modelling framework for collaborative networked organizations. In L. Camarinha-Matos, L. M. Afsarmanesh, & H. M. Ollus (Eds.), *Network-centric collaboration and supporting frameworks* (Vol. 224, pp. 3-14). Boston: Springer.

Campbell, M. J. (2009). KStore: a dynamic meta-knowledge repository for intelligent BI. *International Journal of Intelligent Information Technologies, 5*(3), 68–80.

Capron, L., & Pistre, N. (2002). When do acquirers earn abnormal returns? *Strategic Management Journal, 23*, 781–794. doi:10.1002/smj.262

Caridi, M., Cigolini, R., & Marco, D. (2005). Improving supply-chain collaboration by linking intelligent agents to cpfr. *International Journal of Production Research, 43*(20), 4191–4218. doi:10.1080/00207540500142134

Carrasco, A., Hernández, M. D., Romero, M. C., Sivianes, F., & Escudero, J. I. (2009). Remote Controlling and Monitoring of Safety Devices Using Web-Interface Embedded Systems. In *Enterprise Information Systems* (Vol. 24, pp. 737-744). Berlin: Springer-Verlag. ISBN 978-3-642-013

Carter, J., Bitting, E., & Ghorbani, A. (2002). Reputation Formalization for an Information- Sharing Multi-Agent Sytem. *Computational Intelligence, 18*(2), 515–534. doi:10.1111/1467-8640.t01-1-00201

Casati, F., Castellanos, M., Dayal, U., & Salazar, N. (2007, September 23-28). A Generic solution for Warehousing Business Process Data. In *Proceedings of the 33rd International Conference on Very Large Data Bases (VLDB'07)*, Vienna, Austria.

Casati, F., & Shan, M. (2001). Dynamic and adaptive composition of e-services. *Information Systems, 26*(3), 143–163. doi:10.1016/S0306-4379(01)00014-X

Castelfranchi, C., & Falcone, R. (1998). Principles of Trust for MAS: Cognitive Anatomy, Social Importance and Quantification. In *Proceedings of the International Conference on Multi-Agent Systems (ICMAS'98)*, Paris (pp. 72-79).

Cavalieri, S., Cesarotti, V., & Introna, V. (2003). A multiagent model for coordinated distribution chain planning. *Journal of Organizational Computing and Electronic Commerce, 13*(3/4), 267–287. doi:10.1207/S15327744JOCE133&4_07

Chakkappen, S., Cruanes, T., Dageville, B., Jiang, L., Shaft, U., Su, H., & Zait, M. (2008, June 9-12). Efficient and Scalable Statistics Gathering for Large Databases in Oracle 11g. In *Proceedings of the 2008 ACM SIGMOD international conference on Management of data (SIGMOD'08)*, Vancouver, BC, Canada.

Chan, M., Leong, H. V., & Si, A. (2000, November). Incremental Update to Aggregated Information for Data Warehouses over Internet. In *Proceedings of the 3rd ACM International Workshop on Data Warehousing and OLAP (DOLAP '00)*, McLean, VA.

Chang, C.-C., & Lin, C.-J. (2008). *LIBSVM: a Library for Support Vector Machines.*

Chan, H. C., Cheng, C. B., & Hsu, C. H. (2007). Bargaining strategy formulation with CRM for an e-commerce agent. *Electronic Commerce Research and Applications, 6*, 490–498. doi:10.1016/j.elerap.2007.02.011

Chan, Y. E., Huff, S. L., Barclay, D. W., & Copeland, D. G. (1997). Business strategic orientation, information systems strategic orientation and strategic alignment. *Information Systems Research, 8*(2), 125–150. doi:10.1287/isre.8.2.125

Chao, C. (2004). Incremental Maintenance of Object Oriented Data Warehouse. *Information Sciences, 1*(4), 91–110. doi:10.1016/j.ins.2003.07.014

Chaudhuri, S., & Dayal, U. (1997). An Overview of Data Warehousing and OLAP Technology. *SIGMOD Record, 26*(1). doi:10.1145/248603.248616

Chee, C. N. (2004). *Three Critical Steps to Customer-centric Business Orientation.* Retrieved from http://www.metacore-asia.biz

Chen, T. (2007a). A fuzzy logic approach for incorporating the effects of managerial actions on semiconductor yield learning. In *Proceedings of 2007 International Conference on Machine Learning and Cybernetics.*

Chen, Y.-W., & Lin, C.-J. (2005). *Combining SVMs with Various Feature Selection Strategies.*

Chen, A., & McLeod, D. (2006). Collaborative Filtering for Information Recommendation Systems. In *Encyclopedia of E-Commerce*. E-Government, and Mobile Commerce.

Chen, C. (2008). Intelligent web-based learning system with personalized learning path guidance. *Computers & Education, 51*, 787–814. doi:10.1016/j.compedu.2007.08.004

Chen, C. M., Lee, H. M., & Chen, Y. H. (2005). Personalized e-learning system using item response theory. *Computers & Education, 44*(3), 237–255. doi:10.1016/j.compedu.2004.01.006

Chen, C. M., Liu, C. Y., & Chang, M. H. (2006). Personalized curriculum sequencing using modified item response theory for web-based instruction. *Expert Systems with Applications, 30*(2), 378–396. doi:10.1016/j.eswa.2005.07.029

Chen, F. (1998). Echelon reorder points, installation reorder points, and the value of centralized demand information. *Management Science, 44*(12), 221–234. doi:10.1287/mnsc.44.12.S221

Chen, F. (1999). Decentralized supply chains subject to information delays. *Management Science, 45*(8), 1076–1090. doi:10.1287/mnsc.45.8.1076

Chen, F., Ryan, J. K., & Simchi-Levi, D. (2000). The impact of exponential smoothing forecasts on the bullwhip effect. *Naval Research Logistics, 47*, 269–286. doi:10.1002/(SICI)1520-6750(200006)47:4<269::AID-NAV1>3.0.CO;2-Q

Chen, F., & Zheng, Y. (1994). Evaluating echelon stock (r, nq) policies in serial production/inventory systems with stochastic demand. *Management Science, 40*, 1426–1443. doi:10.1287/mnsc.40.11.1426

Chen, T. (2007b). Evaluating the mid-term competitiveness of a product in a semiconductor fabrication factory with a systematic procedure. *Computers & Industrial Engineering, 53*, 499–513. doi:10.1016/j.cie.2007.05.008

Chen, T. (2008). An online collaborative semiconductor yield forecasting system. *Expert Systems with Applications, 36*(3), 5830–5843. doi:10.1016/j.eswa.2008.07.058

Chen, T., & Lin, Y.-C. (2008). A fuzzy-neural system incorporating unequally important expert opinions for semiconductor yield forecasting. *International Journal of Uncertainty, Fuzziness, and Knowledge-based Systems, 16*(1), 35–58. doi:10.1142/S0218488508005030

Chen, T., & Wang, M.-J. J. (1999). A fuzzy set approach for yield learning modeling in wafer manufacturing. *IEEE Transactions on Semiconductor Manufacturing, 12*(2), 252–258. doi:10.1109/66.762883

Chen, T., & Wang, Y. C. (2009). A fuzzy set approach for evaluating and enhancing the mid-term competitiveness of a semiconductor factory. *Fuzzy Sets and Systems, 160*, 569–585. doi:10.1016/j.fss.2008.06.006

Chen, W., Ma, C., & Ma, L. (2009). Mining the customer credit using hybrid support vector machine technique. *Expert Systems with Applications, 36*(4), 7611–7616. doi:10.1016/j.eswa.2008.09.054

Cheung, D., Ng, V., Fu, A., & Fu, Y. (1996). Efficient Mining of Association Rules in Distributed Databases. *IEEE Transactions on Knowledge and Data Engineering, 8*(6), 911–922. doi:10.1109/69.553158

Cheung, K., & Lee, H. (2002). The inventory benefit of shipment coordination and stock rebalancing in a supply chain. *Management Science, 48*(2), 300–306. doi:10.1287/mnsc.48.2.300.251

Chew, T. Y., Henz, M., & Ng, K. B. (2000). A toolkit for constraint-based inference engines. In E. Pontelli & V. S. Costa (Eds.), *Practical aspects of declarative languages, Second International Workshop PADL'00* (pp. 185-199). Springer-Verlag.

Chin, P. O., Brown, G. A., & Hu, Q. (2004). The impact of mergers and acquisitions on IT governance structures: A case study. *Journal of Global Information Management, 12*(4), 50–74.

Chithralekha, T., & Kuppuswami, S. (2008). A Generic Internal State Paradigm for the Language Faculty of Agents for Task Delegation. *International Journal of Intelligent Information Technologies, 4*(3), 58–78.

Cho, J., & Garcia-Molina, H. (2000). Synchronizing a Database to Improve Freshness. In *Proceedings of the 2000 ACM SIGMOD International Conference on Management of Data (SIGMOD'00),* Dallas, TX.

Cho, B. H., Yu, H., Kim, K. W., Kim, T. H., Kim, I. Y., & Kim, S. I. (2008). Application of irregular and unbalanced data to predict diabetic nephropathy using visualization and feature selection methods. *Artificial Intelligence in Medicine, 42*(1), 37–53. doi:10.1016/j.artmed.2007.09.005

Chou, C. H., Lin, C. C., Liu, Y. H., & Chang, F. (2006). A prototype classification method and its use in a hybrid solution for multiclass pattern recognition. *Pattern Recognition, 39*(4), 624–634. doi:10.1016/j.patcog.2005.10.022

Chu, H. W., & Hartman, J. B. (2008). Mergers and acquisitions: The argument for holistic, integrated measures of success. *Leadership & Organizational Management Journal, 2008*(4), 1-13.

Chu, W. H. J., & Lee, C. C. (2006). Strategic information sharing in a supply chain. *European Journal of Operational Research, 174*(3), 1567–1579. doi:10.1016/j.ejor.2005.02.053

Clarke, E., Grumberg, O., & Hamaguchi, K. P. (1997). Another look at LTL model checking. *Formal Methods in System Design, 10*(1), 47–71. doi:10.1023/A:1008615614281

Clerckx, T., Vandervelpen, C., Luyten, K., & Coninx, K. (2006). A Task-Driven User Interface Architecture for Ambient Intelligent Environments. In *Proceedings of Intelligent User Interfaces 2006,* Sydney, Australia (pp. 309-311).

Clifton, C. (2001). Secure Multiparty Computation Problems and Their Applications: A Review and Open Problems. In *Proceedings of the Workshop on New Security Paradigms,* Cloudcroft, NM.

Clifton, C., & Marks, D. (1996). Security and Privacy Implications of Data Mining. In *Proceedings of the ACM SIGMOD Workshop on Data Mining and Knowledge Discovery* (pp. 15-19).

Clifton, C., Kantarcioglu, M., & Vaidya, J. (2004). Defining privacy for data mining. In *Data Mining, Next generation challenges and future directions.*

Confessore, G., Liotta, G., & Rismondo, S. (2006). A new model for achieving value added goals in a collaborative industrial scenario. In L. Camarinha-Matos, L. M. Afsarmanesh, & H. M. Ollus (Eds.), *Network-centric collaboration and supporting frameworks* (Vol. 224, pp. 121-128). Boston: Springer.

Connell, T. A. O. (2000). A Simplistic Approach to Internationalization: Design Considerations for an Autonomous Intelligent Agent. In *Proceedings of the Sixth ERCIM Workshop on User Interfaces for All*, Florence, Italy.

Conner, K. R. (1991). A historical comparison of resource-based theory and five schools of thought within industrial organization economics: Do we have a new theory of the firm? *Journal of Management, 17*(1), 121–154. doi:10.1177/014920639101700109

Constantinides, E. (2002). The 4S Web-Marketing Mix Model. *Electronic Commerce Research and Applications, 1*(1), 57–76. doi:10.1016/S1567-4223(02)00006-6

Cook, C., & Spitzer, D. (2001). *World class transactions: Insights into creating shareholder value through mergers and acquisitions.* New York: KPMG.

Cording, M. P. (2004). *Organizational integrity and acquisition performance: The role of value in value creation.* Unpublished doctoral dissertation, University of Virginia, Charlottesville, VA.

Cossey, B. (1991). Systems assessment in acquired subsidiaries. *Accountancy, 107*(1169), 98–99.

Costa, M., & Madeira, H. (2004, November 12-13). Handling Big Dimensions in Distributed Data Warehouses using the DWS Technique. In *Proceedings of the 7th ACM international workshop on Data warehousing and OLAP (DOLAP'04),* Washington, DC.

Couturier, G. W., & Kumbat, T. A. (2000). Information technology costing methodology development after a corporate merger. *Industrial Management & Data Systems, 100*(1), 10–16. doi:10.1108/02635570010273009

Cragg, P., King, M., & Hussin, H. (2002). IT alignment and firm performance in small manufacturing firms. *The Journal of Strategic Information Systems, 11*, 109–132. doi:10.1016/S0963-8687(02)00007-0

Crestani, F., & Lalmas, M. (2001). Logic and uncertainty in information retrieval. In *Lectures on information retrieval* (LNCS 1980, pp. 179-206).

Crocker, M. W., Pickering, M., & Clifton, C. (1999). *Architecture and Mechanisms for Language Processing.* Cambridge, UK: Cambridge University Press. doi:10.1017/CBO9780511527210

Crubézy, M., Aubry, F., Moisan, S., Chameroy, V., Thonnat, M., & di Paola, R. (1997). *Managing complex processing of medical image sequences by program supervision techniques.* Paper presented at SPIE International Symposiuon Medical Imaging, Newport Beach, CA.

Cui, Y., & Widom, J. (2003). Lineage Tracing for General Data Warehouse Transformations. *The VLDB Journal, 12*, 41–58. doi:10.1007/s00778-002-0083-8

D'Aubeterre, F., Iyer, S., Ehrhardt, R., & Singh, R. (2009). Discovery Process in a B2B eMarketplace: A Semantic Matchmaking Approach. *International Journal of Intelligent Information Technologies, 5*(4), 16–40.

Daniele, M., Giunchiglia, F., & Vardi, M. (1999). *Improved automata generation for linear temporal logic.* Paper presented at CAV'99: International Conference on Computer-Aided Verification, Trento, Italy.

Dash, M., & Liu, H. (1997). Feature selection for classification. *Intelligent Data Analysis, 1*, 131–156. doi:10.1016/S1088-467X(97)00008-5

Datta, P., Christopher, M., & Allen, P. (2007). Agent-based modelling of complex production/distribution systems to improve resilience. *International Journal of Logistics: Research and Applications, 10*(3), 187–203. doi:10.1080/13675560701467144

Davies, J., Janowski, T., Ojo, A., & Shukla, A. (2007). Technological foundations of electronic governance. In *Proceedings of the ICEGOV '07: Proceedings of the 1st international conference on Theory and practice of electronic governance,* Macao, China (pp. 5-11). New York: ACM.

Day, G. S., Fein, A. J., & Ruppersberger, G. (2003). Shakeouts in digital markets: Lessons from b2b exchanges. *California Management Review, 45*(2), 131–150.

De Bodt, M., & Graves, S. (1985). Continous review policies for a multi-echelon inventory problem with stochastic demand. *Management Science, 31*, 1286–1295. doi:10.1287/mnsc.31.10.1286

de Nunes Barros, L., Hendler, J., & Benjamins, V. (1997, August). Par-KAP: A knowledge acquisition tool for building practical planning systems. In M. E. Pollack (Ed.), *15ᵗʰ International Joint Conference on Artificial Intelligence (IJCAI'97),* Nagoya, Japan (p. 1246-1251).

Deconinck, E., Hancock, T., Coomans, D., Massart, D. L., & Heyden, Y. V. (2005). Classification of drugs in absorption classes using the classification and regression trees (CART) methodology. *Journal of Pharmaceutical and Biomedical Analysis*, *39*(1-2), 91–103. doi:10.1016/j.jpba.2005.03.008

Desai, V. S., Crook, J. N., & Overstreet, G. A. (1996). A comparison of neural networks and linear scoring models in the credit union environment. *European Journal of Operational Research*, *95*(1), 24–37. doi:10.1016/0377-2217(95)00246-4

Desktop Publishing. (2009). Retrieved June 15, 2009, from http://desktoppub.about.com/od/scanninggraphics/a/dig_trad_photos.htm

Dey, D., Zhang, Z., & De, P. (2006). Optimal Synchronization Policies for Data Warehouse. *Information Journal on Computing*, *18*(2), 229–242.

Dierickx, I., & Cool, K. (1989). Asset stock accumulation and sustainability of competitive advantage. *Management Science*, *35*, 1504–1513. doi:10.1287/mnsc.35.12.1504

Dix, J., Fisher, M., Levesque, H., & Sterling, L. (2004). Special issue on logic-based agent implementation. Editorial. *Annals of Mathematics and Artificial Intelligence*, *41*(2-4): 131--133.

Dollinger, M. J. (1999). *Entrepreneurship strategies and resources*. Upper Saddle River, NJ: Prentice Hall.

Doll, W. J., & Torkzadeh, G. (1988). The measurement of end-user satisfaction. *Management Information Systems Quarterly*, *12*, 259–274. doi:10.2307/248851

Dwivedi, S., Huang, S. H., Shi, J., & VerDuin, W. H. (2008). Yield prediction for seamless tubing processes: a computational intelligence approach. *International Journal of Advanced Manufacturing Technology*, *37*, 314–322. doi:10.1007/s00170-007-0964-5

Eckerson, E. (1995). Three Tier Client/Server Architecture: Achieving Scalability, Performance, and Efficiency in Client Server Applications. *Open Information Systems*, *10*(3), 1–20.

Eder, J., & Koncilia, K. (2001, September 5-7). Changes of Dimension Data in Temporal Data Warehouses. In *Proceedings of the Third International Conference on Data Warehousing and Knowledge Discovery (DaWaK'01)*, Munich, Germany (pp. 284-293).

Eirinaki, M., & Vazirgiannis, M. (2003). Web mining for web personalization. *ACM Transactions on Internet Technology*, *3*(1), 1–27. doi:10.1145/643477.643478

Ejaz, A., & Kenneth, R. (2004, December 16-18). Utilizing Staging Tables in Data Integration to Load Data into Materialized Views. In *Proceedings of the First International Symposium on Computational and Information Science (CIS'04)*, Shanghai, China (pp. 685-691).

Elvang-Goransson, M., Krausel, P., & Fox, J. (2006). Acceptability of arguments as 'logical uncertainty'. In *Proceedings of the European Conference on Symbolic and Quantitative Approaches to Reasoning and Uncertainty* (LNCS 747, pp. 85-90).

Eng, T. (2004). The role of e-marketplaces in supply chain management. *Industrial Marketing Management*, *33*, 97–105. doi:10.1016/S0019-8501(03)00032-4

Eriksson, H. (2004). *JessTab Manual: Integration of Protégé and Jess*. Linkoping, Sweden: Linkoping University.

Escudero, J. I., Rodriguez, J. A., Romero, M. C., & Diaz, S. (2005). Deployment of digital video and Audio Over electrical SCADA networks. *IEEE Transactions on Power Delivery*, *20*(2), 691–695. doi:10.1109/TPWRD.2004.833906

Escudero, J. I., Rodriguez, J. A., Romero, M. C., & Luque, J. (2004). IDOLO: multimedia data deployment on SCADA systems. In. *Proceedings of the IEEE Power Systems Conference and Exposition*, *1*, 252–257.

Esfandiari, B., & Chandrasekharan, S. (2001). On How Agents Make friends: Mechanisms for Trust Acquisition. In *Proceedings of the Fourth Workshop on Deception, Fraud and Trust in Agent Societies*, Montreal, Canada (pp. 27-34).

Fagin, R., Geanakoplos, P., Halpern, J., & Vardi, M. (1999). The hierarchical approach to modelling knowledge and common knowledge. *International Journal of Game Theory*, *28*(3), 331–365. doi:10.1007/s001820050114

Fagin, R., Halpern, J., Moses, Y., & Vardi, M. (1995). *Reasoning about knowledge*. Boston: MIT Press.

Faratin, P., Sierra, C., & Jennings, N. (2003). Using Similarity Criteria to Make Issue Trade-offs in Automated Negotiations. *Journal of Artificial Intelligence, 142*(2), 205–237. doi:10.1016/S0004-3702(02)00290-4

Farlex. (n.d.). *Commitment*. Retrieved September 5, 2008, from http://www.thefreedictionary.com/commitment

Fatima, S. S., Wooldridge, M., & Jennings, N. R. (2003, July). Optimal Agendas for Multi-Issue Negotiation. In *Proceedings of the Second International Conference on Autonomous Agents and Multiagent Systems (AAMAS-03)*, Melbourne, Australia (pp. 129-136).

Feldman, M. L., & Spratt, M. F. (1999). *Five frogs on a log: A CEO's field guide to accelerating the transition in mergers, acquisitions, and gut wrenching change*. New York: Harper Business Press.

Fensel, D., Horrocks, I., van Harmelen, F., Decker, S., Erdmann, M., & Klein, M. (2000, October). OIL in a nutshell. In R. Dieng & O. Corby (Ed.), *12th International Conference on Knowledge Engineering and Knowledge Management (EKAW'2000)*, Juan les Pins, France. Springer-Verlag.

Fensel, D., Motta, E., van Harmelen, F., Benjamins, R., Crubezy, M., & Decker, S. (2003). The unified problem-solving method development language UPML. *Knowledge and Information Systems, 5*(1), 83–131. doi:10.1007/s10115-002-0074-5

Fileto, R., Liu, L., Pu, C., Assad, E. D., & Medeiros, C. B. (2003). Poesia: An ontological workflow approach for composing web services in agriculture. *The VLDB Journal - The International Journal on Very Large Data Bases, 12*(4), 352-367.

FIPA. (2009). *Foundation for Intelligent Physical Agents*. Retrieved from http://www.fipa.org

Fisher, M. (2005). Temporal development methods for agent-based systems. *Journal of Autonomous Agents and Multi-Agent Systems, 10*(1), 41–66. doi:10.1007/s10458-004-3140-4

Fisher, R. A. (1936). The Use of Multiple Measurements in Taxonomic Problems. *Annals of Eugenics, 7*, 179–188.

Flanders, J. (2006). *Atlas Workflow Designer*. http://www.masteringbiztalk.com/

Fluegge, M., Santos, I. J. G., Tizzo, N. P., & Madeira, E. R. M. (2006). Challenges and techniques on the road to dynamically compose web services. In *Proceedings of the ICWE '06: Proceedings of the 6th international conference on Web engineering*, Palo Alto, CA (pp. 40-47). New York: ACM Press.

Fridman-Hill, E. (2002). *Jess in action: Java rule-based systems (In Action series)*. Greenwich, CT: Manning Publications.

Friedman-Hill, E. J. (2006). *Jess - The Rule Engine for the Java Platform*. Albuquerque, NM: Sandia National Laboratories.

Gabbay, D., & Hodkinson, I. (1990). An axiomatisation of the temporal logic with until and since over the real numbers. *Journal of Logic and Computation, 1*, 229–260. doi:10.1093/logcom/1.2.229

García, C. (2006, March 10-12). Real Time Self-Maintainable Data Warehouse. In *Proceedings of the 44th Annual Southeast Regional Conference (ACM SE'06)*, Melbourne, FL.

Gavirneni, S. (2001). Benefits of co-operation in a production distribution environment. *European Journal of Operational Research, 130*, 612–622. doi:10.1016/S0377-2217(99)00423-3

Gavirneni, S. (2002). Information flows in capacitated supply chains with fixed ordering costs. *Management Science, 48*(5), 644–651. doi:10.1287/mnsc.48.5.644.7806

Gavirneni, S. (2006). Price fluctuations, information sharing, and supply chain performance. *European Journal of Operational Research, 174*(3), 1651. doi:10.1016/j.ejor.2005.04.037

Gelderman, M. (1998). The relation between user satisfaction, usage of information systems and performance. *Information & Management, 34*, 11–18. doi:10.1016/S0378-7206(98)00044-5

Genesereth, M., & Fikes, R. (1992). *Knowledge interchange format version 3.0 reference manual* (Tech. Rep. No. 94305). Palo Alto, CA: Computer Science Department, Stanford University.

Gennari, J., Musen, M., Fergerson, R., Grosso, W., Crubezy, M., & Eriksson, H. (2003). The evolution of Protégé: An environment for knowledge-based systems development. *International Journal of Human-Computer Studies*, *58*, 89–123. doi:10.1016/S1071-5819(02)00127-1

Georgeff, M., Pell, B., Pollack, M., Tambe, M., & Wooldridge, M. (1999). The belief-desire-intention model of agency. In *Proceedings of the International Workshop on Intelligent Agents V: Agent Theories, Architectures, and Languages,* Paris (Vol 5, pp. 1-10). Springer Verlag.

Giacomazzi, F., Panella, C., Pernici, B., & Sansoni, M. (1997). Information systems integration in mergers and acquisition: A normative model. *Information & Management*, *32*, 289–302. doi:10.1016/S0378-7206(97)00031-1

Gjerdrum, J., Shah, N., & Parageorgiou, L. (2001). A combined optimization and agent-based approach to supply chain modelling and performance assessment. *Production Planning and Control*, *12*(1), 81–88. doi:10.1080/09537280150204013

Glasserman, P., & Tayur, S. (1994). The stability of a capacitated, multi-echelon production-inventory system under a base-stock policy. *Operations Research*, *42*(5), 913–925. doi:10.1287/opre.42.5.913

Goldberg, D. (1989). *Genetic algorithms in search, optimization, and machine learning.* Reading, MA: Addison-Wesley.

Goldblatt, R. (1992). *Logics of time and computation* (CSLI lecture notes, No. 7). Palo Alto, CA: Stanford.

Goldblatt, R. (2003). Mathematical modal logic: A view of its Evolution. *Journal of Applied Logic*, *1*(5-6), 309–392. doi:10.1016/S1570-8683(03)00008-9

Goldreich, O., Micali, S., & Wigderson. (1987). How to play any mental game - a completeness theorem for protocols with honest majority. In *Proceedings of the 19th ACM Symposium on the Theory of Computing* (pp. 218-229).

Goldreich, O. (1998). *Secure Multiparty Computation.* Working Draft.

GOV3. (2006). *Citizen Centric Government (White Paper).* The GOV3 Foundation: Intel. Retrieved from www.intel.com/go/government.

Grandison, T., & Sloman, M. (2000). A survey of trust in internet applications. *IEEE Communications Surveys and Tutorials*, *4*(4), 2–16.

Grant, R. M. (1991). The resource-based theory of competitive advantage: Implication for strategy formulation. *California Management Review*, *33*(3), 114–135.

Grant, R. M. (1995). *Contemporary strategy analysis: Concepts, techniques, applications.* Cambridge, UK: Blackwell.

Grey, W., Olavson, T., & Shi, D. (2005). The role of e-marketplaces in relationship-based supply chains: A survey. *IBM Systems Journal*, *44*(1).

Griffin, T., & Libkin, L. (1995). Incremental Maintenance of Views with Duplicates. In *Proceedings of the SIGMOD Record '95,* San Jose, CA.

Gronback, R. C. (2009). *Eclipse modeling project: A domain-specific language (DSL) toolkit.* Reading, MA: Addison-Wesley.

Gruber, H. (1984). *Learning and Strategic Product Innovation: Theory and Evidence for the Semiconductor Industry.* Amsterdam: Elsevier.

Gruber, T. R. (1993). A translation approach to portable ontology specifications. *Knowledge Acquisition*, *5*, 199–220. doi:10.1006/knac.1993.1008

Gugliotta, A., Domingue, J., Cabral, L., Tanasescu, V., Galizia, S., & Davies, R. (2008). Deploying semantic web services-based applications in the e-government domain. *J. Data Semantics*, *10*, 96–132. doi:10.1007/978-3-540-77688-8_4

Guo, Z., Fang, F., & Whinston, A. B. (2006). Supply chain information sharing in a macro prediction market. *Decision Support Systems*, *42*(3), 1944–1958. doi:10.1016/j.dss.2006.05.003

Gutman, R., & Maes, P. (1998). Cooperative vs. Competitive Multi-Agent Negotiation in Retail Electronic Commerce. In *Proceedings of the Second International Workshop on Cooperative Information Agents (CIA'98),* Paris.

Guyon, I., & Elisseeff, A. (2003). An introduction to variable and feature selection. *Journal of Machine Learning Research*, *3*, 1157–1182. doi:10.1162/153244303322753616

Haller, M., Peikert, A., & Thoma, J. (2003). Cycle time management during production ramp-up. *Robotics and Computer-integrated Manufacturing, 19,* 183–188. doi:10.1016/S0736-5845(02)00078-9

Halpern, J., & Shore, R. (2004). Reasoning about common knowledge with infinitely many agents. *Information and Computation, 191*(1), 1–40. doi:10.1016/j.ic.2004.01.003

Hamdi, M. S. (2008). SOMSE: A Neural Network Based Approach to Web Search Optimization. *International Journal of Intelligent Information Technologies, 4*(4), 31–54.

Hammami, A., Burlat, P., & Champagne, J. P. (2003). Evaluating orders allocation within networks of firms. *International Journal of Production Economics, 86,* 233–249. doi:10.1016/S0925-5273(03)00066-5

Han, J., & Kamber, M. (2001). *Data Mining: Concepts and Technique.* San Fracisco: Morgan Kaufmann Publishers.

Han, J., Pei, J., Yin, Y., & Mao, R. (2004). Mining Frequent Patterns without Candidate Generation: A Frequent Pattern Approach. *IEEE Transactions on Data Mining and Knowledge Discovery, 8*(1), 53–87. doi:10.1023/B:DAMI.0000005258.31418.83

Harizopoulos, H., Liang, V., Abadi, D. J., & Madden, S. (2006, September 12-15). Performance Tradeoffs in Read-Optimized Databases. In *Proceedings of the 32nd International Conference on Very Large Data Bases (VLDB'06),* Seoul, Korea.

Harmelen, F., Lifschitz, V., & Porter, B. (2007). *Handbook of Knowledge Representation (Foundations of Artificial Intelligence).* Maryland Heights, MO: Elsevier Science Publishers.

Harzing, A. (2002). Acquisitions versus greenfield investments: International strategy and management of entry modes. *Strategic Management Journal, 23,* 211–227. doi:10.1002/smj.218

Ha, S. H., Bae, S. M., & Park, S. C. (2002). Customer's time-variant purchase behavior and corresponding marketing strategies: an online retailer's case. *Computers & Industrial Engineering, 43,* 801–820. doi:10.1016/S0360-8352(02)00141-9

Hashemi, R., Le Blanc, L. A., Bahrami, A., Bahar, M., & Traywick, B. (2009). Association Analysis of Alumni Giving: A Formal Concept Analysis. *International Journal of Intelligent Information Technologies, 5*(2), 17–32.

Haspeslagh, P. C., & Jemison, D. B. (1991). *Managing acquisitions: Creating value through corporate renewal.* New York: Free Press.

Hefley, W. E., & Murray, D. (1993). Intelligent User Interfaces. In *Proceedings of the First International Conference on Intelligent User Interfaces* (pp. 3-10). Orlando, FL.

He, M., Jennings, N. R., & Leung, H. (2003). On agent-mediated electronic commerce. *IEEE Transactions on Knowledge and Data Engineering, 15*(4), 985–1003. doi:10.1109/TKDE.2003.1209014

Hendler, J. (2001). Agents and the semantic web. *IEEE Intelligent Systems, 16*(2), 30–37. doi:10.1109/5254.920597

Henley, W. E., & Hand, D. J. (1997). *Construction of a k-nearest-neighbour credit-scoring system* (Vol. 8, pp. 305-321).

Hibernate. (2009). *Relational Persistence for Java and. NET.* Retrieved June 15, 2009, from http://www.hibernate.org

Hodkinson, I. (2000). Temporal logic and automata. In Gabbay, D. M., Reynolds, M. A., & Finger, M. (Eds.), *Temporal logic: mathematical foundations and computational aspects* (Vol. 2, pp. 30–72). Oxford, UK: Clarendon Press.

Hoffman, D. L., & Novak, T. P. (1997). A New Marketing Paradigm for Electronic Commerce. *The Information Society. Special Issue for Electronic Commerce, 13*(1), 43–54.

Hoffman, D. L., Novak, T. P., & Peralta, M. A. (1999). Information Privacy in the Marketspace: Implications for the Commercial Uses of Anonymity on the Web. *The Information Society, 15,* 129–139. doi:10.1080/019722499128583

Hong, S., Nag, B. N., & Yao, D.-Q. (2007). Modeling agent auctions in a supply chain environment. *International Journal of Intelligent Information Technologies, 3*(1), 14–36.

Hosoda, T., Naim, M. M., Disney, S. M., & Potter, A. (2008). Is there a benefit to sharing market sales information? Linking theory and practice. *Computers & Industrial Engineering, 54*(2), 315. doi:10.1016/j.cie.2007.07.014

Hou, J. W., & Cesar, R. (2002). *Internet Marketing: An Overview*. Oxford, MS: University of Mississippi, School of Business Administration.

Hsieh, K. L., & Tong, L. I. (2006). Manufacturing performance evaluation for IC products. *International Journal of Advanced Manufacturing Technology, 28*, 610–617. doi:10.1007/s00170-004-2382-2

Hsu, C. W., Chang, C. C., & Lin, C. J. (2008). *A Practical Guide to Support Vector Classification*.

Hu, X. R., & Atwell, E. (2005). *A survey of Machine Learning Approaches to Analysis of large Corpora*. Retrieved from http://www.bultreebank.org/SProLaC/paper05.pdf

Huang, E., Haft, R., & Hsu, J. (2000). *Developing a Roadmap for Software Internationalization*. Retrieved from http://www.symbio-group.com/ knowledge_center.html

Huang, C. L., Chen, M. C., & Wang, C. J. (2007). Credit scoring with a data mining approach based on support vector machines. *Expert Systems with Applications, 33*(4), 847–856. doi:10.1016/j.eswa.2006.07.007

Huang, C. L., Liao, H. C., & Chen, M. C. (2008). Prediction model building and feature selection with support vector machines in breast cancer diagnosis. *Expert Systems with Applications, 34*(1), 578–587. doi:10.1016/j.eswa.2006.09.041

Huang, C. L., & Wang, C. J. (2006). A GA-based feature selection and parameters optimization for support vector machines. *Expert Systems with Applications, 31*(2), 231–240. doi:10.1016/j.eswa.2005.09.024

Huang, G.-B., Zhu, Q.-Y., & Siew, C.-K. (2006). Extreme learning machine: Theory and applications. *Neurocomputing, 70*(1-3), 489–501. doi:10.1016/j.neucom.2005.12.126

Hwang, D. H., & Kang, H. (2005). XML View Materialization with Deferred Incremental Refresh, the Case of a Restricted Class of Views. *Journal of Information Science and Engineering, 21*, 1083–1119.

IEC. (1990). Telecontrol and equipment systems - Part 5: Transmission protocols (IEC 60870-5).

IEEE. (1990). *IEEE Standard Computer Dictionary: A Compilation of IEEE Standard Computer Glossaries*. Washington, DC: IEEE.

Inan, A., Saygyn, Y., Savas, E., Hintoglu, A. A., & Levi, A. (2006). Privacy preserving clustering on horizontally portioned data. In *Proceedings of the 22nd International Conference on Data Engineering Workshops (ICDEW '06)*.

Inmon, W. H. (2002). *Building the Data Warehouse* (3rd ed.). New York: John Wiley.

IPD. (n.d.). *What is performance*. Retrieved September 5, 2008, from http://www.ipdoccupiers.com/Advisors/Whatisperformance/tabid/1384/Default.aspx

ISO/IEC. (1993). Information technology – Local area networks – Part 3: Carrier sense multiple access with collision detection (ISO/IEC 8802-3).

ISO/IEC. (1999). Information technology – Coding of audio-visual objects – MPEG-4 (ISO/IEC 14496).

Ito, T., & Abadi, S. M. (2002). Agent-based material handling and inventory planning in warehouse. *Journal of Intelligent Manufacturing, 13*, 201–210. doi:10.1023/A:1015786822825

JADE. (2009). *Java Agent DEvelopment Framework*. Retrieved from http://jade.tilab.com

James, M. L. (2001, March). An autonomous diagnostic and prognostic monitoring system for NASA's deep space network. In *Proceedings of the IEEE Aerospace Conference*, Big Sky, MT (pp. 403-414). Washington DC: IEEE Computer Society.

Jaques, P. A., & Vicari, R. M. (2007). A BDI approach to infer student's emotions in an intelligent learning environment. *Computers & Education, 49*, 360–384. doi:10.1016/j.compedu.2005.09.002

Jefferson, T. (1789). *Personal communication to R. Price*.

Jennings, N. R., & Wooldridge, M. (1995). Applying agent technology. *Applied Artificial Intelligence, 9*, 357–369. doi:10.1080/08839519508945480

Jeremic, Z., & Devedži, V. (2004). *Design pattern ITS: Student model implementation*. Paper presented at the IEEE International Conference on Advanced Learning Technologies (ICALT'04).

JESS. (2009). *Home*. Retrieved from http://www.jess-rules.com

John, G. H., Kohavi, R., & Pfleger, K. (1994). *Irrelevant feature and the subset selection problem.* Paper presented at the Proceedings of the Eleventh International Conference on Machine Learning.

Johnson, R. E. (1997). Frameworks = (Components + Patterns). *CACM, 10*(40), 39–42.

Jonker, C. M., Robu, V., & Treur, J. (2007). An Agent Architecture for Multi-Attribute Negotiation Using Incomplete Preference Information. *Autonomous Agents and Multi-Agent Systems, 15*(2), 221–252. doi:10.1007/s10458-006-9009-y

Jörg, T., & Deßloch, S. (2008, September 10-12). Towards Generating ETL Processes for Incremental Loading. In *Proceedings of the 2008 International Symposium on Database Engineering & Applications (IDEAS'08),* Coimbra, Portugal.

Joshua, D. (2003). *Rich Internet Applications, sponsored by Macromedia and Intel.* Framingham, MA: IDC.

Kacprzak, M. (2003). Undecidability of a multi-agent logic. *Fundamenta Informaticae, 45*(2-3), 213–220.

Kadobayashi, R., & Lim, A. (2008, January 14-16). Collaborative Guidance System using Multi-Gaze History and Shared Photography Collection. In *Proceedings of the Sixth International Conference on Creating, Connecting and Collaborating through Computing,* Poitiers, France (pp. 39-46). Washington, DC: IEEE Computer Society.

Kaelbling, L. P., Cassandra, A. R., & Kurien, J. A. (1996). Acting under uncertainty: Discrete Bayesian models for mobile-robot navigation, In *IEEE/RSJ International Conference on Intelligent Robots and Systems (IROS'96)* (pp. 963-972). Washington, DC: IEEE Computer Society.

Kalu, T. C. U. (1999). Capital budgeting under uncertainty. *International Journal of Production Economics, 58,* 235–251. doi:10.1016/S0925-5273(98)00121-2

Kalyanam, K., & McIntyre, S. (2002). The Marketing Mix: A Contribution of the E-Tailing Wars. *Journal of the Academy of Marketing Science, 30*(4), 483–495. doi:10.1177/009207002236924

Kambayashi, Y., Samtani, S., Mohania, M., & Kumar, V. (1999, November 19-20). Recent Advances and Research Problems in Data Warehousing. In Proceedings of Advances in Database Technologies: ER '98 (pp. 81–92). Singapore: Workshops on Data Warehousing and Data Mining, Mobile Data Access, and Collaborative Work Support and Spatio-Temporal Data Management.

Kang, N., & Han, S. (2002). Agent-based e-marketplace system for more fair and efficient transaction. *Decision Support Systems, 34,* 157–165. doi:10.1016/S0167-9236(02)00078-7

Kantarcioglu, M., & Clifton, C. (2004). Privacy-Preserving Distributed Mining of Association Rules on Horizontally Partitioned Data. *IEEE Transactions on Knowledge and Data Engineering, 16*(9). doi:10.1109/TKDE.2004.45

Kaplan, S., & Sawhney, M. (2000). E-hubs: The new b2b marketplaces. *Harvard Business Review,* (May-June): 97–103.

Karabati, S., & Sayin, S. (2008). Single-supplier/multiple-buyer supply chain coordination: Incorporating buyers' expectations under vertical information sharing. *European Journal of Operational Research, 187*(3), 746–764. doi:10.1016/j.ejor.2006.05.046

Kathawala, Y., Abdou, K., & Franck, C. (2002). Supply chain/electronic hubs: A comparative analysis. *Benchmarking: An International Journal, 9*(5), 450–470. doi:10.1108/14635770210451460

KBSt. (2006). *SAGA - Standards and Architectures for eGovernment Applications - Version 3.0.* Berlin: German Federal Ministry of Interior. Retrieved from www.kbst.bund.de/saga

Kearns, G. S., & Lederer, A. L. (2003). A resourced-based view of strategic IT alignment: How knowledge sharing creates competitive advantage. *Decision Sciences, 34*(1), 1–29. doi:10.1111/1540-5915.02289

Ketzenberg, M. E., Rosenzweig, E. D., Marucheck, A. E., & Metters, R. D. (2007). A framework for the value of information in inventory replenishment. *European Journal of Operational Research, 182*(3), 1230. doi:10.1016/j.ejor.2006.09.044

Kleindorfer, P. R., & Wu, D. J. (2003). Integrating long- and short-term contracting via business-to-business exchanges for capital-intensive industries. *Management Science, 49*(11), 1597–1615. doi:10.1287/mnsc.49.11.1597.20583

Klusch, M., Fries, B., & Sycara, K. (2006). Automated semantic web service discovery with owls-mx. In *Proceedings of the 5th Intl. joint conference on Autonomous agents and multiagent systems (AAMAS)*, Hakodate, Japão (pp. 915-922). New York: ACM.

Kohavi, R., John, G., Long, R., Manley, D., & Pfleger, K. (1994). *MLC++: A machine learning library in C++.* In *Proceedings of the 6th International Conference on Tools with Artificial Intelligence,* New Orleans, LA (pp. 740-743). Washington DC: IEEE Computer Society.

Kramer, J., & Magee, J. (2007). Self-Managed Systems: an Architectural Challenge. In *Proceedings of the International Conference on Future of Software Engineering (FOSE'07)*. Washington, DC: IEEE Computer Society Press.

Kraus, S., Sycara, K., & Evenchil, A. (1998). Reaching agreements through argumentation: A logical model and implementation. *Artificial Intelligence, 104*, 1–69. doi:10.1016/S0004-3702(98)00078-2

Krokhmal, P. A., & Pardalos, P. M. (2009). Random assignment problems. *European Journal of Operational Research, 194*, 1–17. doi:10.1016/j.ejor.2007.11.062

Krulwich, B. (1996). The Bargainfinder Agent: Comparison Price Shopping on the Internet. In Williams, J. (Ed.), *Bots and Other Internet Beasties* (pp. 257–263). New York: Macmillan Computer Publishing.

Kudo, M., & Sklansky, J. (2000). Comparison of algorithms that select features for pattern classifiers. *Pattern Recognition, 33*(1), 25–41. doi:10.1016/S0031-3203(99)00041-2

Kuhlmann, T., Lamping, R., & Massow, C. (1998). Intelligent decision support. *Journal of Materials Processing Technology, 76*, 257–20. doi:10.1016/S0924-0136(97)00357-9

Kumar, S., & Mishra, R. B. (2008). A hybrid model for service selection in semantic web service composition. *International Journal of Intelligent Information Technologies, 4*(4), 55–69.

Küster, U., König-Ries, B., Stern, M., & Klein, M. (2007). Diane: an integrated approach to automated service discovery, matchmaking and composition. In *Proceedings of the 16th international conference on World Wide Web (WWW '07)*, Banff, Alberta, Canada (pp. 1033-1042). New York: ACM.

Labio, W. J., Yang, J., Cui, Y., Garcia-Molina, H., & Widom, J. (2000). Performance Issues in Incremental Warehouse Maintenance. In *Proceedings of the 26th VLDB Conference*, Cairo, Egypt.

Labio, W. J., Yerneni, R., & Garcia-Molina, H. (1999). Shrinking the Warehouse Update Window. In *Proceedings of the 1999 ACM SIGMOD International Conference on Management of data (SIGMOD '99)*, Philadelphia, PA.

Lancastre, A., & Lages, L. F. (2006). The relationship between buyer and a b2b e-marketplace: Cooperation determinants in an electronic market context. *Industrial Marketing Management, 35*, 774–789. doi:10.1016/j.indmarman.2005.03.011

Langdon, C. S. (2005). Agent-based modeling for simulation of complex business systems: Research design and validation strategies. *International Journal of Intelligent Information Technologies, 1*(3), 1–13.

Langdon, C. S., & Sikora, R. T. (2006). Conceptualizing co-ordination and competition in supply chains as complex adaptive system. *Information Systems and E-Business Management, 4*, 71–81. doi:10.1007/s10257-005-0005-6

Lang, J. (2000). Possibilistic logic: complexity and algorithms. In *Handbook of defeasible reasoning and uncertainty management systems* (pp. 179–220). New York: Springer.

Lauterborn, B. (1990). New Marketing Litany: Four P's Passe: C-Words Take Over. *Advertising Age, 61*(41).

Lavrac, N., & Mozetic, I. (1989). Second Generation Knowledge Acquisition Methods and their refinement. *Second Generation Expert System, ACM SIGART Bulletin, Special Issue on Knowledge Acquisition,* 108.

Lee, G., Chang, C., & Chen, A. L. P. (2004). Hiding sensitive patterns in association rules mining. In *Proceedings of the 28th Annual International Computer Software and Applications Conference.*

Lee, K. C. K., Si, A., & Leong, H. V. (1998). Incremental View Update for a Mobile Data Warehouse. In *Proceedings of the 1998 ACM symposium on Applied Computing (SAC'98)*.

Lee, K. Y., & Kim, M. H. (2005, November 4-5). Optimizing the Incremental Maintenance of Multiple Join Views. In *Proceedings of the 8th ACM International Workshop on Data Warehousing and OLAP (DOLAP'05)*, Bremen, Germany.

Lee, K. Y., Son, J. H., & Kim, M. H. (2001). Efficient Incremental View Maintenance in Data Warehouses. In *Proceedings of the Tenth International Conference on Information and Knowledge Management (CIKM'01)*, Atlanta, GA.

Lee, J. H., & Park, S. C. (2005). Intelligent profitable customers segmentation system based on business intelligence tools. *Expert Systems with Applications, 29*, 145–152. doi:10.1016/j.eswa.2005.01.013

Lee, L. H., Lee, C., & Bao, J. (2006). Inventory control in the presense of an electronic marketplace. *European Journal of Operational Research, 174*, 797–815. doi:10.1016/j.ejor.2005.03.018

Lee, M. G. (2001). Profiling students' adaptation styles in web-based learning. *Computers & Education, 36*, 121–132. doi:10.1016/S0360-1315(00)00046-4

Lee, S. M., Tan, X., & Trimi, S. (2005). Current practices of leading e-government countries. *Communications of the ACM, 48*(10), 99–104. doi:10.1145/1089107.1089112

Lee, T.-S., & Chen, I. F. (2005). A two-stage hybrid credit scoring model using artificial neural networks and multivariate adaptive regression splines. *Expert Systems with Applications, 28*(4), 743–752. doi:10.1016/j.eswa.2004.12.031

Lee, T.-S., Chiu, C.-C., Lu, C.-J., & Chen, I. F. (2002). Credit scoring using the hybrid neural discriminant technique. *Expert Systems with Applications, 23*(3), 245–254. doi:10.1016/S0957-4174(02)00044-1

Lejouad-Chaari, W., Moisan, S., Sevestre-Ghalila, S., & Rigault, J.-P. (2007, August). Distributed intelligent medical assistant for osteoporosis detection. In Proceedings of the *29th International Conference of the IEEE Engineering in Medicine and Biology Society*, Lyon, France (pp. 4347-4350). Washington DC: IEEE Computer Society.

Leonard, M., & Marsden, G. (2007, September 9-12). Co-Present photo sharing on mobile devices. In *Proceedings of the 9th International Conference on Human Computer Interaction with Mobile Devices and Services*, Singapore (pp. 277-284).

Leung, E. W. C., & Li, Q. (2007). An experimental study of a personalized learning environment through open-source software tools. *IEEE Transactions on Education, 50*(4). doi:10.1109/TE.2007.904571

Liao, S.-H., & Wen, C.-H. (2007). Artificial neural networks classification and clustering of methodologies and applications - literature analysis from 1995 to 2005. *Expert Systems with Applications, 32*(1), 1–11. doi:10.1016/j.eswa.2005.11.014

Libelium. (2009). *Home*. Retrieved from http://www.libelium.com

Li, F. C., Chen, F. L., & Wang, G. E. (2008). *Proceedings of Comparison of feature selection approaches based on the SVM classification*. Piscataway, NJ.

Li, J., Sikora, R., Shaw, M. J., & Woo Tan, G. (2006). A strategic analysis of inter organizational information sharing. *Decision Support Systems, 42*(1), 251. doi:10.1016/j.dss.2004.12.003

Li, L. (2002). Information sharing in a supply chain with horizontal competition. *Management Science, 48*(9), 1196–1212. doi:10.1287/mnsc.48.9.1196.177

Lin, D., & Kedem, Z. M. (1998). Pincer-Search: A New Algorithm for Discovering the Maximum Frequent Set. In *Proceedings of the 6th International Conference on Extending Database Technology (EDBT)*, Valencia, Spain (pp. 105-119).

Lin, C. T., Chang, C. W., & Chen, C. B. (2006). Relative control philosophy – balance and continual change for forecasting abnormal quality characteristics in a silicon wafer slicing process. *International Journal of Advanced Manufacturing Technology, 26,* 1109–1114. doi:10.1007/s00170-004-2067-x

Lin, D., & Kedem, Z. M. (2002). Pincer-Search: An Efficient Algorithm for Discovering the Maximum Frequent Set. *IEEE Transactions on Knowledge and Data Engineering, 14*(3), 553–566. doi:10.1109/TKDE.2002.1000342

Lindell, Y., & Pinkas, B. (2009). Secure Multiparty Computation for Privacy-Preserving Data Mining. *Journal of Privacy and Confidentiality,* 59-98.

Lin, F., Strader, T., & Shaw, M. (2000). Using swarm for simulating the order fulfillment process in divergent assembly supply chains. In Luna, F., & Stefansson, B. (Eds.), *Economic simulations in swarm: Agent-based modeling and object oriented programming* (pp. 225–249). Boston: Kluwer Academic Publishers.

Lin, F., Sung, Y., & Lo, Y. (2005). Effects of trust mechanisms on supply-chain performance: A multi-agent simulation study. *International Journal of Electronic Commerce, 9*(4), 91–112.

Lin, F., Tan, G., & Shaw, M. (1999). Multiagent enterprise modeling. *Journal of Organizational Computing and Electronic Commerce, 9*(1), 7–32. doi:10.1207/s15327744joce0901_2

Li, S., & Lin, B. (2006). Accessing information sharing and information quality in supply chain management. *Decision Support Systems, 42*(3), 1641–1656. doi:10.1016/j.dss.2006.02.011

Li, T.-S., Huang, C.-L., & Wu, Z.-Y. (2006). Data mining using genetic programming for construction of a semiconductor manufacturing yield rate prediction system. *International Journal of Advanced Manufacturing Technology, 17,* 355–361.

Liu, Z., Niu, D., Yang, X., & Sheng, W. (2009). Research on intelligent decision support system for power system. In *Proceedings of the ICIA: International Conference on Information and Automation* (pp. 412-417).

Liu, H. A. M. (1998). *Feature Selection for Knowledge Discovery and Data Mining.* Boston: Kluwer Academic Publishers.

Liu, X. (2007). Parameterized defuzzification with maximum entropy weighting function - another view of the weighting function expectation method. *Mathematical and Computer Modelling, 45,* 177–188. doi:10.1016/j.mcm.2006.04.014

Lu, D., & Antony, F. (2003). Implications of b2b marketplace to supply chain development. *The TQM Magazine, 15*(3), 173–179. doi:10.1108/09544780310469271

Lujan-Mora, S., & Palomar, M. (2001). Reducing Inconsistency in Integrating Data from Different Sources. In *Proceedings of the International Database Engineering & Applications Symposium (IDEAS '01).*

Luo, W. (2006). An Algorithm for Privacy-preserving Quantitative Association Rules Mining. In *Proceedings of the 2nd IEEE International Symposium.*

Main, T. J., & Short, J. E. (1989). Managing the merger: Building partnership through IT planning at the new Baxter. *Management Information Systems Quarterly, 13,* 469–484. doi:10.2307/248735

Majd, S., & Pindyck, R. S. (1989). The learning curve and optimal production under uncertainty. *The Rand Journal of Economics, 20*(3), 331–343. doi:10.2307/2555574

Maksimova, L. (2003). Complexity of some problems in positive and related calculi. *Theoretical Computer Science, 1*(303), 171–185. doi:10.1016/S0304-3975(02)00450-4

Maksimova, L. (2006). Definability and interpolation in non-classical logics. *Studia Logica, 82*(2), 271–291. doi:10.1007/s11225-006-7203-1

Malone, T., Yates, J., & Benjamin, R. (1987). Electronic markets and electronic hierarchies: Effects of information technology on market structure and corporate strategies. *Communications of the ACM, 30*(6), 484–497. doi:10.1145/214762.214766

Manna, Z., & Pnueli, A. (1992). *The temporal logic of reactive and concurrent systems: Specification.* Berlin, Germany: Springer-Verlag. doi:10.1007/978-1-4612-0931-7

Manna, Z., & Pnueli, A. (1995). *Temporal verification of reactive systems: Safety.* Berlin, Germany: Springer-Verlag. doi:10.1007/978-1-4612-4222-2

Marchionini, G., Samet, H., & Brandt, L. (2003). Digital government. *Communications of the ACM, 46*(1), 25–27.

Martens, D., Baesens, B., Van Gestel, T., & Vanthienen, J. (2007). Comprehensible credit scoring models using rule extraction from support vector machines. *European Journal of Operational Research, 183*(3), 1466–1476. doi:10.1016/j.ejor.2006.04.051

Marwedel, P. (2003). *Embedded System Design.* New York: Springer. ISBN 978-1-4020-7690-9

Mata, F., Fuerst, W., & Barney, J. (1995). Information technology and sustainable competitive advantage: A resource-based analysis. *Management Information Systems Quarterly, 19,* 487–505. doi:10.2307/249630

Mazumdar, B. D., & Mishra, R. B. (2009). Multiagent paradigm for the agent slection and negotiation in a B2C process. *International Journal of Intelligent Information Technologies, 5*(1), 61–83.

Mazzola, J. B., & McCardle, K. F. (1995). A Bayesian approach to managing learning-curve uncertainty. *Management Science, 42*(5), 680–692. doi:10.1287/mnsc.42.5.680

McHaneya, R., Hightower, R., & Pearson, J. (2002). A validation of the end-user computing satisfaction instrument in Taiwan. *Information & Management, 39,* 503–511. doi:10.1016/S0378-7206(01)00119-7

McKiernan, P., & Merali, Y. (1995). Integrating IS after merger. *Long Range Planning, 28*(4), 54–62.

Medjahed, B. (2004). *Semantic Web Enabled Composition of Web Services.* Unpublished doctoral dissertation, Virginia Polytechnic Institute and State University, Blacksburg, VA.

Medjahed, B., & Bouguettaya, A. (2005). Customized delivery of e-government web services. *IEEE Intelligent Systems, 20*(6), 77–84. doi:10.1109/MIS.2005.103

Mehta, M., & Hirschheim, R. (2007). Strategic alignment in mergers and acquisitions: Theorizing IS integration decision making. *Journal of the Association for Information Systems, 8*(3), 143–174.

Merril, D. (2005, September 10-11). *Ideas and Considerations for Digital Photograph Sharing.* Paper presented at the Workshop on Pervasive Image Capture and Sharing, Tokyo, Japan.

Meuter, M. L., Amy, L. O., Robert, I. R., & Mary, J. B. (2000). Self-Service Technologies: Understanding Customer Satisfaction With Technology – Based Service Encounters. *Journal of Marketing, 64*(3), 50–64. doi:10.1509/jmkg.64.3.50.18024

Michael, R. P., Travis, E. D., & Michael, L. R. (2005). *GA-facilitated classifier optimization with varying similarity measures.* Paper presented at the Proceedings of the 2005 conference on Genetic and evolutionary computation.

Miller, G. A. (1995). Wordnet: a lexical database for english. *Communications of the ACM, 38*(11), 39–41. doi:10.1145/219717.219748

Mishra, R. B. (2009). Rule Based and ANN model for the evaluation of Customer Orientation in CRM. *Institution of Engineers, 20,* 28–33.

Mohania, M., & Kambayashi, Y. (2000). Making Aggregate Views Self-Maintainable. *Journal of Data and Knowledge Engineering, 32*(1), 87–109. doi:10.1016/S0169-023X(99)00016-6

Moinzadeh, K. (2002). A multi-echelon inventory system with information exchange. *Management Science, 48*(3), 414–426. doi:10.1287/mnsc.48.3.414.7730

Moisan, S. (2003). *Program supervision: Yakl and Pegase+ reference manual* (Tech. Rep. No. 5066). Sophia Antipolis, France: INRIA.

Moisan, S., Ressouche, A., & Rigault, J.-P. (2003, September). Behavioral substitutability in component frameworks: A formal approach. In *Proceedings of the Specification and Verification of Component-Based Systems (SAVCBS'2003) Workshop at ESEC/FSE 2003,* Helsinki, Finland (pp. 22-28).

Moisan, S., Ressouche, A., & Rigault, J.-P. (2004). Towards formalizing behavorial dubstitutability in component frameworks. In *Proceedings of the 2nd International Conference on Software Engineering and Formal Methods* Beijing, China (p. 122-131). Washington, DC: IEEE Computer Society Press.

Moisan, S. (2010). Generating Knowledge-Based System Generators: A Software Engineering Approach. *International Journal of Intelligent Information Technologies*, 6(1), 1–17.

Moisan, S., Ressouche, A., & Rigault, J.-P. (2001). Blocks, a component framework with checking facilities for knowledge-based Systems. *Informatica. Special Issue on Component Based Software Development*, 25(4), 501–507.

Molina-Morales, F. X. (2001). European industrial district: Influence of geographic concentration on performance of the firm. *Journal of International Management*, 7, 277–294. doi:10.1016/S1075-4253(01)00048-5

Molkentin, D. (2007). *The book of Qt 4: The art of building Qt applications*. Munich, Germany: Open Source Press.

Moon, K. D., Park, J. S., Shin, Y. H., & Ryu, K. H. (2003). Incremental Condition Evaluation for Active Temporal Rules. In *Proceedings of Intelligent Data Engineering and Automated Learning* (pp. 816-820).

Moser, O., Rosenberg, F., & Dustdar, S. (2008). Non-intrusive monitoring and service adaptation for ws-bpel. In *Proceeding of the 17th international conference on World Wide Web (WWW '08)*, Beijing, China (pp. 815-824). New York: ACM.

Mrissa, M., Ghedira, C., Benslimane, D., Maamar, Z., Rosenberg, F., & Dustdar, S. (2007). A context-based mediation approach to compose semantic web services. *ACM Transactions on Internet Technology*, 8(1), 4. doi:10.1145/1294148.1294152

Mui, L., Mohtashemi, M., & Halberstadt, A. (2002). A computational model of trust and reputation. In *Proceedings of the 35th International Conference on System Science* (pp. 280-287).

Mukhopadhyay, S. K., Yao, D.-Q., & Yue, X. (in press). Information sharing of value-adding retailer in a mixed channel hi-tech supply chain. *Journal of Business Research*.

Muller, J. P., & Pischel, M. (1994). Modeling Interacting Agents in Dynamic environments. In *Proceedings of the Eleventh European Conference on Artificial Intelligence (ECAI 94)* (pp. 709-713).

Muller, J. P., Pischel, M., & Thiel, M. (1995). Modelling reactive behavior in vertically layered agent architectures. In Wooldridge, M., & Jennings, N. R. (Eds.), *Intelligent Agents: Theories, Architectures, and Languages* (pp. 261–276). Berlin, Germany: Springer Verlag.

Mulvenna, M., Anand, S., & Buchner, A. (2000). Personalization on the Net using Web Mining. *Communications of the ACM*, 43(8), 123–125. doi:10.1145/345124.345165

Mumick, I., Quass, D., & Mumick, B. (1997). Maintenance of Data Cubes and Summary Tables in a Warehouse. *SIGMOD Record*, 26(2), 100–111. doi:10.1145/253262.253277

Mundici, D. (2000). Foreword: Logics of uncertainty. *Journal of Logic Language and Information*, 9, 1–3. doi:10.1023/A:1008374211520

Murugesan, S. (2007). Understanding Web 2.0. *IT Professional*, 9(4), 34–41. doi:10.1109/MITP.2007.78

Naggar, P., Pontieri, L., Pupo, M., Terracina, G., & Virardi, E. (2002, September 2-6). A Model and a Toolkit for Supporting Incremental Data Warehouse Construction. In *Proceedings of the 13th International Conference on Database and Expert Systems Applications (DEXA'02)*, Aix-en-Provence, France (pp. 123-132).

Narayanan, S., & McIlraith, S. A. (2002). Simulation, verification and automated composition of web services. In *Proceedings of the 11th international conference on World Wide Web (WWW '02)*, Honolulu, HI (pp. 77-88). New York: ACM.

Nedunchezhian, R., & Anbumani, K. (2006). Rapid Privacy Preserving Algorithm for Large Databases. *International Journal of Intelligent Information Technologies*, 2(1), 68–81.

Norcott, W. D., & Finnerty, J. (2008). *Method and Apparatus for Incremental Refresh of Summary Tables in a Database System*. Retrieved December 17, 2008, from http://www.patentstorm.us/patents/6205451/description.html

Noy, N. F., & McGuinness, D. L. (2001). *Ontology Development 101: A Guide to Creating Your First Ontology*. Palo Alto, CA: Stanford University.

Olmedilla, D., Rana, O., Matthews, B., & Nejdl, W. (2005). Security and trust issues in semantic grids. In *Proceedings of the Dagsthul Seminar, Semantic Grid: The Convergence of Technologies* (Vol. 05271).

Ong, C.-S., Huang, J.-J., & Tzeng, G.-H. (2005). Building credit scoring models using genetic programming. *Expert Systems with Applications, 29*(1), 41–47. doi:10.1016/j.eswa.2005.01.003

Osman, T., Thakker, D., & Al-Dabass, D. (2009). Utilisation of Case-Based Reasoning for Semantic Web Services Composition. *International Journal of Intelligent Information Technologies, 5*(1), 24–42.

Ou, J., Lee, C., & Chen, M. (2008). Efficient Algorithms for Incremental Web Log Mining with Dynamic Thresholds. *The VLDB Journal, 17*, 827–845. doi:10.1007/s00778-006-0043-9

Oussalah, M. (2003). Reuse in KBS: A component approach. *Expert Systems with Applications, 24*(2), 173–181. doi:10.1016/S0957-4174(02)00140-9

Owan, H., & Nickerson, J. A. (2002). *A theory of B2B exchange formation*. Retrieved from http://ssrn.com/abstract=315121

Page, M., Gensel, J., Capponi, C., Bruley, C., Genoud, P., Ziebelin, D., et al. (2001). A new approach in object-based knowledge representation: the AROM System. Paper presented at IEA/AIE'2001, Budapest, Hungary.

Panzarasa, P., Jennings, N. R., & Norman, T. J. (2002)... *Formalizing Collaborative Decision-making and Practical Reasoning in Multi-agent System, 12*(1), 55–117.

Papanikolaou, K. A., Grigoriadou, M., Magoulasb, G. D., & Kornilakisa, H. (2002). Towards new forms of knowledge communication: The adaptive dimension of a web based learning environment. *Computers & Education, 39*, 333–360. doi:10.1016/S0360-1315(02)00067-2

Papazoglou, M., & Georgakopoulos, D. (2003). Service-oriented computing. *Communications of the ACM, 46*(10), 25–28.

Parunak, H. V. D., Savit, R., Riolo, R. L., & Clark, S. J. (1999). *Dasch: Dynamic analysis of supply chains*. Ann Arbor, MI: Center for Electronic Commerce, ERIM, Inc.

Pata, K., & Laanpere, M. (2008, July 1-5). Supporting cross-institutional knowledge-building with Web 2.0 enhanced digital portfolios. In *Proceedings of the Eighth IEEE International Conference on Advanced Learning Technologies*, Santander, Spain (pp. 798-80).

Patnaik, S., Meier, M., Henderson, B., Hickman, J., & Panda, B. (1999, February). Improving the Performance of Lineage Tracing in Data Warehouse. In *Proceedings of the 1999 ACM Symposium on Applied Computing (SAC'99)*, San Antonio, TX.

Pawlak. (1984). *Rough classification* (Vol. 20, pp. 469-483). Dordrecht, The Netherlands: Elsevier Academic Press Ltd.

Pazienza, M. T., Stellato, A., Henriksen, L., Paggio, P., & Zanzotto, F. M. (2005). Ontology mapping to support multilingual ontology-based question answering. In *Proceedings of the Fourth International Semantic Web Conference (ISWC)*, Galway, Ireland.

Peltz, C. (2003). Web services orchestration and choreography. *IEEE Computer, 36*(10), 46–52.

Peters, G. (1994). Fuzzy linear regression with fuzzy intervals. *Fuzzy Sets and Systems, 63*, 45–55. doi:10.1016/0165-0114(94)90144-9

Pnueli, A. (1977). The temporal logic of programs. In *Proceedings of the 18th Annual Symposium on Foundations of Computer Science* (pp. 46-57).

Pnueli, A., & Kesten, Y. (2002). A deductive proof system for CTL*. In *Proceedings of the 13th Conference on Concurrency Theory* (LNCS 2421, pp. 24-40).

Powell, A. (2001). *The role of b2b exchanges and implications for the future*. New York: The Conference Board, Inc.

Prahalad, C., & Hamel, G. (1990). The core competency of the company. *Harvard Business Review, 68*(3), 79–91.

Prism, Ltd. (n.d.). *Commitment*. Retrieved September 5, 2008, from http://www.prismltd.com/commit.htm

Proctor, M. (2007). Relational Declarative Programming with JBoss Drools. In *Proceedings of SYNASC: International Symposium on Symbolic and Numeric Algorithms for Scientific Computing* (pp. 26-29).

Quass, D., Gupta, A., Mumick, I. S., & Widom, J. (1996). Making views self-maintainable for data warehousing. In *Proceedings of the 4th International Conference on Parallel and Distributed Information System,* Miami Beach, FL (pp. 158-169).

Quinlan, J. R. (1979). Discovering rules from large collections of examples: a case study. *Expert Systems in the Micro-electronic Age,* 168-201.

Rahman, N. (2008, August 14-17). Updating Data Warehouses with Temporal Data. In *Proceedings of the 14th Americas Conference on Information Systems (AMCIS 2008),* Toronto, ON, Canada.

Rahman, N. (2008, October 12-16). Refreshing Teradata Warehouse with Temporal Data. In *Proceedings of The 2008 Teradata Partners User Group Conference & Expo,* Las Vegas, NV.

Rahman, N. (2007). Refreshing Data Warehouses with Near Real-Time Updates. *Journal of Computer Information Systems, 47*(3), 71–80.

Ram, P., & Do, L. (2000). Extracting Delta for Incremental Data Warehouse Maintenance. In *Proceedings of the 16th International Conference on Data Engineering (ICDE '00),* San Diego, CA.

Ram, S., & Liu, J. (2005). An agent-based approach for sourcing business rules in supply chain management. *International Journal of Intelligent Information Technologies, 1*(1), 1–16.

Rao, A. S., & Georgeff, M. P. (1991). Modeling rational agents within a BDI architecture. In Fikes, R., & Sandewall, E. (Eds.), *Proceedings of Knowledge Representation and Reasoning (KR&R).* San Mateo, CA: Morgan Kaufmann Publishers.

Razi, M. A., & Athappilly, K. (2005). A comparative predictive analysis of neural networks (NNs), nonlinear regression and classification and regression tree (CART) models. *Expert Systems with Applications, 29*(1), 65–74. doi:10.1016/j.eswa.2005.01.006

Reich, B. H., & Benbasat, I. (1996). Measuring the linkage between business and information technology objectives. *Management Information Systems Quarterly, 20*(1), 55–81. doi:10.2307/249542

Reichheld, F. F. (1996). *The Loyalty Effect.* Cambridge, MA: Harvard Business School Press.

Reid, D., & Newhouse, C. P. (2004, December 5-8). But that didn't happen last semester: Explanations of the mediated environmental factors that affect online tutor capabilities. In R. Atkinson, C. McBeath, D. Jonas-Dwyer, & R. Phillips (Eds.), *Beyond the comfort zone: Proceedings of the 21st ASCILITE Conference,* Perth (pp. 791-797). Retrieved from http://www.ascilite.org.au/conferences/perth04/procs/reid.html

Ren, F., & Shi, H. (2000). A General Ontology Based Multilingual Multi-Function Multi-Media Intelligent System. In *Proceedings of the IEEE International Conference on Systems, Cybernetics,* Nashville, TN (pp. 2362-2368).

Ritter, M., Meier, U., Yang, J., & Waibel, A. (1999). A Multimodal Translation Agent. In *Proceedings of Auditory Visual Speech Processing.* Face Translation.

Robbins, S. S., & Stylianou, A. C. (1999). Post-merger systems integration: The impact on IS capabilities. *Information & Management, 36,* 205–212. doi:10.1016/S0378-7206(99)00018-X

Robinson, W., & Elofson, G. (2001). Electronic broker impacts on the value of postponement in a global supply chain. *Journal of Global Information Management, 9*(4), 29–43.

Romero, M. C., Díaz, S., Sánchez, G., & Escudero, J. I. (2004). SIP Application To Multimedia Telecontrol Of Power Systems. In *World Automation Congress Proceedings* (pp. 131-137).

Romero, M. C., Sivianes, F., Carrasco, A., Hernandez, M. D., & Escudero, J. I. (2009). Managing emergency response operations for electric utility maintenance. *IEEE Industrial Electronics Magazine, 3*(3), 15–18. doi:10.1109/MIE.2009.933883

RoseIndia. (2009). *Application Architecture.* Retrieved June 15, 2009, from http://www.roseindia.net/jsf/myfacesspring/application-architecture.shtml

Ross-Talbot, S., & Bharti, N. (2005). *Dancing with Web Services: W3C chair talks choreography.* Retrieved from http://searchwebservices.techtarget.com/

L

Russell, S., & Yoon, V. Y. (2009). Agents, availability awareness, and decision making. *International Journal of Intelligent Information Technologies, 5*(4), 53–70.

Russel, S., & Norvig, P. (1995). *Artificial Intelligence: A Modern Approach*. New York: Prentice Hall.

Russo, M. V., & Fouts, P. A. (1997). A resource-based perspective on corporate environmental performance and profitability. *Academy of Management Journal, 40*, 534–560. doi:10.2307/257052

Rybakov, V. V. (2005a). Logical consecutions in intransitive temporal linear logic of finite intervals. *Journal of Logic Computation, (Oxford Press), 15*(5), 633- -657.

Rybakov, V. V. (2006). Linear temporal logic with until and before on integer numbers, deciding algorithms. In D. Grigoriev, J. Harrison, E. A. Hirsch (Eds.), *Computer science – theory and applications* (LNCS 3967, pp. 322-334).

Rybakov, V. V. (2007a). Until-since temporal logic based on parallel time with common past. In S. N. Artemov & A. Nerode (Eds.) *Logical Foundations of Computer Science* (LNCS 4514, pp. 486-497).

Rybakov, V. V. (2007b). Logic of discovery in uncertain situations – deciding algorithms. In *Proceedings of Knowledge Based Intelligent Systems: KES 2007*, Verti sul Mare, (LNAI 4693, pp. 950-958).

Rybakov, V. V. (2008). Logic with interacting agents based at linear temporal logic, deciding algorithms. In *Artificial Intelligence and Soft Computing – ICAISC 2008* (LNAI 5097, pp. 1243-1253).

Rybakov, V. V. (1984). A criterion for admissibility of rules in the modal system *S*4 and the intuitionistic logic. *Algebra and Logic, 23*(5), 369–384. doi:10.1007/BF01982031

Rybakov, V. V. (1992). Rules of inference with parameters for intuitionistic logic. *Journal of Symbolic Logic, 57*(3), 912–923. doi:10.2307/2275439

Rybakov, V. V. (1995). Hereditarily structurally complete modal logics. *Journal of Symbolic Logic, 60*(1), 266–288. doi:10.2307/2275521

Rybakov, V. V. (1997). Admissible logical inference rules. In *Studies in logic and the foundations of mathematics*. New York: Elsevier.

Rybakov, V. V. (2001). Construction of an explicit basis for rules admissible in modal system S4. *Mathematical Logic Quarterly, 47*(4), 441–451. doi:10.1002/1521-3870(200111)47:4<441::AID-MALQ441>3.0.CO;2-J

Rybakov, V. V. (2005b). Logical consecutions in discrete linear temporal logic. *Journal of Symbolic Logic, 70*(4), 1137–1149. doi:10.2178/jsl/1129642119

Rybakov, V. V., Kiyatkin, V. R., & Oner, T. (1999). On finite model property for admissible rules. *Mathematical Logic Quarterly, 45*(4), 505–520. doi:10.1002/malq.19990450409

Saaty, T. L. (1980). *The analytic hierarchy process: planning, priority setting, resource allocation*. New York: McGraw Hill.

Saaty, T. L. (2008). Relative measurement and its generalization in decision making: Why pairwise comparisons are central in mathematics for the measurement of intangible factors - the analytic hierarchy/network process. *RACSAM (Review of the Royal Spanish Academy of Sciences, Series A, Mathematics), 102*(2), 251-318.

Sabater, J., & Sierra, C. (2005). Review on Computational Trust and Reputation Models. *Artificial Intelligence Review, 24*, 33–60. doi:10.1007/s10462-004-0041-5

Sadeh, N. M., Hildum, D. W., & Kjenstad, D. (2003). Agent-based e-supply chain decision support. *Journal of Organizational Computing and Electronic Commerce, 13*(3/4), 225–241. doi:10.1207/S15327744JOCE133&4_05

Sadeh, N. M., Hildum, D. W., Kjenstad, D., & Tseng, A. (2001). Mascot: An agent-based architecture for dynamic supply chain creation and coordination in the internet economy. *Production Planning and Control, 12*(3), 212–223. doi:10.1080/095372801300107680

Sahama, T. R., & Croll, P. R. (2007). A Data Warehouse Architecture for Clinical Data Warehousing. In *Proceedings of the fifth Australasian symposium on ACSW Frontiers (ACSW'07)* (Vol. 68).

Sam, K. M., & Chatwin, C. R. (2005a). Multi-product Generalizability of a Scale for Profiling International Internet Consumers' Decision Making styles in E-Commerce. In *Proceedings Conference on Information Management in Modern Enterprise* (pp. 132-138).

Sam, K. M., & Chatwin, C. R. (2005b). The Mapping Between Business E-Marketing Mix and Internet Consumers' Decision-Making Styles in E-Commerce. In *Proceedings of the Fifth International Conference on Electronic Business (ICEB 2005)*.

Samaddar, S., Nargundkar, S., & Daley, M. (2006). Inter-organizational information sharing: The role of supply network configuration and partner goal congruence. *European Journal of Operational Research, 174*(2), 744. doi:10.1016/j.ejor.2005.01.059

Sandholm, T. W. (1999). Distributed rational decision making. In *Multiagent System*.

Santos, I. J. G., Madeira, E. R. M., & Tschammer, V. (2005). Towards dynamic composition of e-government services - a policy-based approach. In *Proceedings of the 5th IFIP International Conference on e-Commerce, e-Business and e-Government (I3E)*, Poznan, Poland (Vol. 189, pp. 173-185). New York: Springer.

Santos, R. J., & Bernardino, J. (2008, September 10-12). Real-Time Data Warehouse Loading Methodology. In *Proceedings of the 2008 International Symposium on Database Engineering & Applications (IDEAS'08)*, Coimbra, Portugal.

Santos, I. J. G., & Madeira, E. R. M. (2006). Applying orchestration and choreography of web services on dynamic virtual marketplaces. [IJCIS]. *International Journal of Cooperative Information Systems, 15*(1), 57–85. doi:10.1142/S0218843006001281

Sarwar, B., Karypis, G., Konstan, J., & Riedl, J. (2000, August 20). Application of dimensionality reduction in recommender systems: A case study. In *Proceedings of ACM SIGKDD 2000, Workshop on Web Mining for E-Commerce: Challenges and Opportunities*, Boston (pp. 1-12).

Sasikumar, B., & Vasudevan, V. (2008). An agent based TCP/IP for Wireless Networks. *International Journal of Digital Content Technology and its Applications, 2*(3), 47-52.

Sassano, A. (2004), *Modelli e algoritmi della ricerca operativa*. Venice, Italy: Franco Angeli.

Saygin, Y., Verykios, S., & Elmagarmid, K. (2002). Privacy Preserving Association Rule Mining. In *Proceedings of the 12th International Workshop on Research Issues in Data Engineering: Engineering E-Commerce/E-Business Systems (RIDE'02)*, San Jose, CA (pp. 151-158).

Schäfer, M., Dolog, P., & Nejdl, W. (2008). An environment for flexible advanced compensations of web service transactions. *ACM Trans. Web, 2*(2), 1–36. doi:10.1145/1346337.1346242

Schebesch, K. B., & Stecking, R. (2005). Support vector machines for classifying and describing credit applicants: detecting typical and critical regions. *The Journal of the Operational Research Society, 56*(9), 1082–1088. doi:10.1057/palgrave.jors.2602023

Schendel, D. (1994). Introduction to competitive organizational behavior: Toward an organizationally based theory of competitive advantage. *Strategic Management Journal, 15*, 1–4. doi:10.1002/smj.4250150901

Schiaffino, S., Garcia, P., & Amandi, A. (2008). eTeacher: Providing personalized assistance to e-learning students. *Computers & Education, 51*, 1744–1754. doi:10.1016/j.compedu.2008.05.008

Schlueter-Langdon, C., Bruhn, P., & Shaw, M. J. (2000). Online supply chain modeling and simulation. In Luna, F., & Stefansson, B. (Eds.), *Economic simulations in swarm: Agent-based modeling and object oriented programming* (pp. 251–272). Boston: Kluwer Academic Publishers.

Schreiber, G., Wielinga, B., & Breuker, J. (1999). *KADS: A principled approach to knowledge-based system development*. London: Academic Press.

Schulze, W. (1994). Two schools of thought in resource-based theory. In Shrivastiva, P., Huff, A., & Dutton, J. (Eds.), *Advances in strategic management* (pp. 127–151). New York: JAI Press.

Selden, L., & Colvin, G. (2003). M&A needn't be a loser's game. *Harvard Business Review, 81*(6), 70–79.

Sen, A., & Jacob, V. S. (1998). Industrial-Strength Data Warehousing. *Communications of the ACM, 41*(9). doi:10.1145/285070.285076

Sen, A., & Sinha, A. P. (2005). A Comparison of Data Warehousing Methodologies. *Communications of the ACM, 48*(3). doi:10.1145/1047671.1047673

Serugendo, G. D. M., Fitzgerald, J., Romanovsky, A., & Guelfi, N. (2006). *Dependable Self-Organizing Software Architectures – An approach for Self-Managing Systems* (Tech. Rep. No. BBKCS-06-05). London, UK: Birkbeck College, School of Computer Science and Information Systems.

Shekhar, C., Burlina, P., & Moisan, S. (1997). Design of self-tuning IU systems. In *Proceedings of the DARPA Image Understanding Workshop,* New Orleans, LA (Vol. 1, pp. 529-536).

Shevchenko, A. A., & Shevchenko, O. O. (2005). B2b e-hubs in emerging landscape of knowledge based economy. *Electronic Commerce Research and Applications, 4*(2), 113. doi:10.1016/j.elerap.2004.10.001

Shimada, Y., & Sakurai, K. (2003). A new accurate yield prediction method for system-LSI embedded memories. *IEEE Transactions on Semiconductor Manufacturing, 16*(3), 436–445. doi:10.1109/TSM.2003.815636

Shin, B. (2003). An Exploratory Investigation of System Success Factors in Data Warehousing. *Journal of the Association for Information Systems, 4.*

Shin, B., & Dick, K. (2005). Comparison of the business strategies of two telecommunication service providers. *Journal of Information Technology Case and Application Research, 7*(2), 19–30.

Shkapenyuk, V., & Suel, T. (2002). Design and implementation of a high-performance distributed web crawler. In *Proceedings of the IEEE International Conference on Data Engineering (ICDE)* (pp. 357-368).

Shoham, Y. (1993). Agent Oriented Programming. *Artificial Intelligence, 60*(1), 51–92. doi:10.1016/0004-3702(93)90034-9

Signorile, R. (2002). Simulation of a multiagent system for retail inventory control: A case study. *Simulation, 78*(5), 304–311. doi:10.1177/0037549702078005552

Sikora, R., & Shaw, M. J. (1998). A multi-agent framework for the coordination and integration of information systems. *Management Science, 44*(11), 65–78. doi:10.1287/mnsc.44.11.S65

Simitsis, A., Vassiliadis, P., & Sellis, T. (2005, April 5-8). Optimizing ETL Processes in Data Warehouses. In *Proceedings of the 21st International Conference on Data Engineering (ICDE'05),* Tokyo, Japan.

Sim, K. M., & Chan, R. (2000). A Brokering Protocol for Agent-Based E-Commerce. *IEEE Transactions on Systems, Man and Cybernetics. Part C, Applications and Reviews, 30*(4).

Skowron, A., & Rauszer, C. (1992). The discernibility matrices and functions in information systems. In Slowinski, R. (Ed.), *Intelligent Decision Support--Handbook of Applications and Advances of the Rough Sets Theory* (pp. 311–362). New York: Kluwer.

Soshnikov, D. (2000). Software toolkit for building embedded and distributed knowledge-based systems. In *Proceedings of the 2nd International Workshop on Computer Science and Information Technologies* (pp. 103-111).

Spence, A. M. (1981). The learning curve and competition. *The Bell Journal of Economics, 12,* 49–70. doi:10.2307/3003508

Sproles, G. B. (1985). *From Perfectionism to Fadism: Measuring Consumers' Decision-Making Styles* (pp. 79–85). Proceedings, American Council on Consumer Interests.

Sproles, G. B., & Kendall, E. L. (1986). A Methodology for Profiling Consumers' Decision-Making Styles. *The Journal of Consumer Affairs, 20*(4), 267–279.

Stanley, R., Oliveira, M., & Za"ıane, R. (2003). Algorithms for Balancing Privacy and Knowledge Discovery in Association Rule Mining. In *Proceedings of the Seventh International Database Engineering and Applications Symposium (IDEAS'03),* Hong Kong, China (pp. 54-65).

Stephanidis, C., Karagiannidis, C., & Koumpis, A. (1997). Decision Making in Intelligent User Interfaces. In *Proceedings of the Second International Conference on Intelligent User Interfaces* (pp. 195-202).

Stylianou, A. C., Jeffries, C. J., & Robbins, S. R. (1996). Corporate mergers and the problems of IS integration. *Information & Management, 31*(4), 203–213. doi:10.1016/S0378-7206(96)01082-8

Su, C. T., & Yang, C. H. (2008). Feature selection for the SVM: An application to hypertension diagnosis. *Expert Systems with Applications, 34*(1), 754–763. doi:10.1016/j.eswa.2006.10.010

Suchanek, F. M., Kasneci, G., & Weikum, G. (2007). Yago: a core of semantic knowledge. In *Proceedings of the 16th international conference on World Wide Web (WWW '07)*, Banff, Alberta, Canada (pp. 697-706). New York: ACM.

Sumi, T., & Tsuruoka, M. (2002). Ramp new enterprise information systems in a merger & acquisition environment: A case study. *Journal of Engineering and Technology Management, 19*(1), 93–104. doi:10.1016/S0923-4748(01)00048-0

Sun Developer Network. (2009). *Servlets and JSP Pages Best Practices*. Retrieved June 15, 2009, from http://java.sun.com/developer/technicalArticles/javaserverpages/servlets_jsp

Sun, Z.-L., Choi, T.-M., Au, K.-F., & Yu, Y. (2008). Sales forecasting using extreme learning machine with applications in fashion retailing. *Decision Support Systems, 46*(1), 411–419. doi:10.1016/j.dss.2008.07.009

Surana, A., Kumara, S., Greaves, M., & Raghavan, U. N. (2005). Supply-chain networks: A complex adaptive systems perspective. *International Journal of Production Research, 43*(20), 4235–4265. doi:10.1080/00207540500142274

Suraweera, P., & Mitrovic, A. (2004). An intelligent tutoring system for entity relationship modeling. *International Journal of Artificial Intelligence in Education, 14*(3-4), 375-417. ISSN:1560-4292

Sutter, E. (2002). *Embedded System Firmware Demystified*. Berkeley, CA: Publishers Group West. ISBN 9781578200993

Suwu, W., & Das, A. (2001). An Agent System Architecture for E-Commerce. In *Proceedings of the 12th International Workshop on Database and Expert Systems Applications* (pp. 715-719).

Swaminathan, J. M. (1997). *Effect of sharing supplier capacity information*. Retrieved from http://citeseerx.ist.psu.edu/viewdoc/summary?doi=10.1.1.46.3933

Tah, J. H. M. (2005). Towards an agent-based construction supply network modelling and simulation platform. *Automation in Construction, 14*, 353–359. doi:10.1016/j.autcon.2004.08.003

Talon, X., & Pierret-Golbreich, C. (1996). *TASK: From the specification to the implementation*. Paper presented at the 8th International Conference on Tools with Artificial Intelligence (ICTAI).

Tanaka, H., & Watada, J. (1988). Possibilistic linear systems and their application to the linear regression model. *Fuzzy Sets and Systems, 272*, 275–289. doi:10.1016/0165-0114(88)90054-1

Tang, T. Y., & Mccalla, G. (2003, July 20-24). Smart recommendation for evolving e-learning system. In *Proceedings of the 11th International Conference on Artificial Intelligence in Education, Workshop on Technologies for Electronic Documents for Supporting Learning*, Sydney, Australia (pp. 699-710).

Tang, T. Y., Winoto, P., & Niu, X. (2003). *Investigating Trust between Users and Agents in A Multi Agent Portfolio Management System: a Preliminary Report*.

Thomas, L. C. (2000). A survey of credit and behavioural scoring: forecasting financial risk of lending to consumers. *International Journal of Forecasting, 16*(2), 149–172. doi:10.1016/S0169-2070(00)00034-0

Thomas, M. A., Redmond, R. T., & Yoon, V. Y. (2009). Using Ontological Reasoning for an Adaptive E-Commerce Experience. *International Journal of Intelligent Information Technologies, 5*(4), 41–52.

Thomason, S. K. (1972). Semantic snalysis of tense logic. *Journal of Symbolic Logic, 37*(1).

Thonnat, M., Clément, V., & Ossola, J. C. (1995). Automatic galaxy description. *Astrophysical Letters and Communication, 31*(1-6), 65-72.

Tomic, B., Jovanovic, J., & Devedzic, V. (2006). JavaDON: An open-source expert system shell. *International Journal of Expert Systems with Applications, 31*(3), 595–606. doi:10.1016/j.eswa.2005.09.085

Tong, L.-I., Wang, C. H., & Chen, D. L. (2007). Development of a new cluster index for wafer defects. *International Journal of Advanced Manufacturing Technology, 31*, 705–715. doi:10.1007/s00170-005-0240-5

Trichet, F., & Tchounikine, P. (1999). DSTM: A framework to operationalize and refine a problem-solving method modeled in terms of tasks and methods. *International Journal of Expert Systems with Applications, 16*(2), 105–120. doi:10.1016/S0957-4174(98)00065-7

Tun, N. N., & Tojo, S. (2008). EnOntoModel: A Semantically-Enriched Model for Ontologies. *International Journal of Intelligent Information Technologies, 4*(1), 1–30.

Turunen, M., & Hakulinen, J. (2000). *Jaspis – A Framework for Multilingual Adaptive Speech Applications.* Paper presented at the Sixth International Conference of Spoken Language Processing, Beijing, China.

Ul-Asar, A., Ullah, M. S., Wyne, M. F., & Ahmed, J. A., ul-Hasnain, R. (2009). Traffic Responsive Signal Timing Plan Generation Based on Neural Network. *International Journal of Intelligent Information Technologies, 5*(3), 84–101.

Unitime Systems Literature. (2006). *The Unitime Version 8 Smart Client Advantage.* Boulder, CO: Unitime Systems.

Vaidya, J., & Clifton, C. (2002). Privacy Preserving Association Rule Mining in Vertically Partioned data. In *Proceedings of ACM SIGKDD '02.*

Vaidya, J., & Clifton, C. (2004). *Privacy-Preserving Data Mining: Why, How, and When.* IEEE Security and Privacy.

van Benthem, J. (1983). *The logic of time.* Dordrecht, The Netherlands: Synthese Library.

van Benthem, J., & Bergstra, J. A. (1994). Logic of transition systems. *Journal of Logic Language and Information, 3*(4), 247–283. doi:10.1007/BF01160018

van den Elst, J. (1996). *Modélisation de connaissances pour le pilotage de programmes de traitement d'images.* Unpublished doctoral dissertation, Université de Nice.

van der Hoek, W., & Wooldridge, M. (2003). Towards a logic of rational agency. *Logic Journal of the IGPL, 11*(2), 133–157. doi:10.1093/jigpal/11.2.133

van der Meyden, R., & Shilov, N. V. (1999). Model checking knowledge and time in systems with perfect recall. In *Proceedings of the 19th Conference on Foundations of Software Technology and Theoretical Computer Science* (LNCS 1738, pp. 432-445).

van Rijsbergen, C. J. (2000). Another look at the logical uncertainty principle. *Information Retrieval, 2*(1), 17–26. doi:10.1023/A:1009969229281

Vapnik, V. N. (Ed.). (1995). *The nature of statistical learning theory.* New York: Springer Verlag.

Vardi, M. (1994). *An automata-theoretic approach to linear temporal logic.* Paper presented at the Banff Workshop on Knowledge Acquisition (Banff'94).

Vardi, M. (1998). Reasoning about the past with two-way automata. In *Automata, Languages and Programming* (LNCS 1443, pp. 628-641).

Venderhaeghen, D., & Loos, P. (2007). Distributed model management platform for cross-enterprise business process management in virtual enterprise networks. *Journal of Intelligent Manufacturing, 18*, 553–559. doi:10.1007/s10845-007-0060-6

Verykios, S., Bertino, E., Provenza, I., Saygin, Y., & Theodoridis, Y. (2004). State- of- the -Art in Privacy Preserving Data Mining. *SIGMOD Record, 33*(1), 50–57. doi:10.1145/974121.974131

Verykios, S., Elmagarmid, K., Bertino, E., Saygin, Y., & Dasseni, E. (2004). Association Rule Hiding. *IEEE Transactions on Knowledge and Data Engineering, 16*(4), 434–447. doi:10.1109/TKDE.2004.1269668

Vidal, J.-P., Moisan, S., Faure, J.-B., & Dartus, D. (2005). Towards a reasoned 1-D river model calibration. *Journal of Hydroinformatics, 7*(2), 79–90.

Von Wright, G. H. (1980). *Freedom and Determination.* Amsterdam, The Netherlands: North Holland Publishing Co.

Von, W. G. H. (1980). *Freedom and determination.* Amsterdam, The Netherlands: North Holland Publishing.

Vronay, D., & Davis, S. (2006). *PhotoStory: Preserving emotion in digital photo sharing.* Virtual Worlds Group, Microsoft Research.

Wang, S., Lee, Y., Billis, S., & Jafari, A. (2004). Hiding Sensitive Items in Privacy Preserving Association Rule Mining. In *Proceedings of the IEEE International Conference on Systems, Man and Cybernetics.*

Wang, X., Yang, J., Teng, X., Xia, W., & Jensen, R. (2007). Feature selection based on rough sets and particle swarm optimization. *Pattern Recognition Letters, 28*(4), 459–471. doi:10.1016/j.patrec.2006.09.003

Watada, J., Tanaka, H., & Shimomura, T. (1986). Identification of learning curve based on possibilistic concepts. In *Applications of Fuzzy Set Theory in Human Factors*. Amsterdam: Elsevier Science.

Watson, R. T., & Mundy, B. (2001). A strategic perspective of electronic democracy. *Communications of the ACM, 44*(1), 27–30. doi:10.1145/357489.357499

Weber, Y., & Pliskin, N. (1996). The effects of information systems integration and organizational culture on a firm's effectiveness. *Information & Management, 30*, 81–90. doi:10.1016/0378-7206(95)00046-1

Wernerfelt, B. (1984). A resource-based view of the firm. *Strategic Management Journal, 5*, 171–180. doi:10.1002/smj.4250050207

Westbrook, R. A., & Black, W. C. (1985). A Motivation-Based Shopper Typology. *Journal of Retailing, 61*(1), 78–103.

West, D. (2000). Neural network credit scoring models. *Computers & Operations Research, 27*(11-12), 1131–1152. doi:10.1016/S0305-0548(99)00149-5

White, A., Daniel, E. M., & Mohdzain, M. (2005). The role of emergent information technologies and systems in enabling supply chain agility. *International Journal of Information Management, 25*, 396–410. doi:10.1016/j.ijinfomgt.2005.06.009

White, A., Daniel, E., Ward, J., & Wilson, H. (2007). The adoption of consortium b2b e-marketplaces: An exploratory study. *The Journal of Strategic Information Systems, 16*, 71–103. doi:10.1016/j.jsis.2007.01.004

White, C. (2005). *Data Integration: Using ETL, EAI, and EII Tools to Create an Integrated Enterprise*. The Data Warehousing Institute.

Widom, J. (1995, November). Research Problems in Data Warehousing. In *Proceedings of the 4th International Conference on Information and Knowledge Management (CIKM'95)*, Baltimore, MD.

Wijerwarneda, H., De Zoysa, A., Fonseka, T., & Perera, B. (2004). The impact of planning and control sophistication on performance of small and medium-sized enterprises: Evidence from Sri Lanka. *Journal of Small Business Management, 42*(2), 209–217. doi:10.1111/j.1540-627X.2004.00106.x

Wikipedia. (2009a). *Multitier Architecture*. Retrieved June 15, 2009, from http://en.wikipedia.org/wiki/Multitier_architecture

Wikipedia. (2009b). *Web mining*. Retrieved June 15, 2009, from http://www.en.wikipidia.org/wiki/Web_mining

Wikipedia. (2009c). *Web 2.0*. Retrieved June 15, 2009, from http://www.en.wikipidia.org/wiki/Web_2

Wikner, J., Towill, D. R., & Naim, M. (1991). Smoothing supply chain dynamics. *International Journal of Production Economics, 22*, 231–248. doi:10.1016/0925-5273(91)90099-F

Wilcox, H. D., Chang, K., & Grover, V. (2001). Valuation of mergers and acquisitions in the telecommunications industry: A study on diversification and firm size. *Information & Management, 38*, 459–471. doi:10.1016/S0378-7206(00)00082-3

Wilkes, J. (2008). *Utility Functions, Prices, and Negotiation* (Tech. Rep. HPL-2008-81). Retrieved from http://www. Hpl.hp.com/techreports/2008/HPL-2008-81.pdf.2008

Winer, R. S. (2001). *Customer Relationship Management: A Framework*. Research Directions, and the Future.

Wissinger, J., Ristroph, R., Diemunsch, J., Severson, W., & Freudenthal, E. (1999). MSTAR extensible search engine and model-based inference toolkit. *SPIE, 372*, 554–570. doi:10.1117/12.357671

Witten, I., Frank, E., Trigg, L., Hall, M., Holmes, G., & Cunningham, S. (1999). Weka: Practical machine learning tools and techniques with Java implementations. In *Proceedings of the ICONIP/ANZIIS/ANNES'99 International Workshop: Emerging Knowledge Engineering and Connectionist-Based Info. Systems* (pp. 192-196).

Wooldridge, M. (2002). *An Introduction to MultiAgent Systems*. New York: Wiley. ISBN 047149691

Wooldridge, M. (2000). *Reasoning about rational agents*. Cambridge, MA: MIT Press.

Wooldridge, M. J. (1999). Intelligent Agents. In Weiss, G. (Ed.), *Multiagent systems – A modern approach to Distributed Artificial Intelligence* (pp. 27–78). Cambridge, MA: MIT Press.

Wu, H. J. (2005). An Agent-Based CRM Model for Multiple Projects management. In *Proceedings of the IEEE Engineering Management Conference* (pp. 851-855).

Wu, W., Ekaette, E., & Far, B. H. (2003). Uncertainty Management Framework for Multi-Agent System. In *Proceedings of ATS* (pp. 122-131).

Wu, T.-K., Huang, S.-C., & Meng, Y.-R. (2008). Evaluation of ANN and SVM classifiers as predictors to the diagnosis of students with learning disabilities. *Expert Systems with Applications, 34*(3), 1846–1856. doi:10.1016/j.eswa.2007.02.026

Wu, Y., Chiang, C., & Chen, A. (2007). Hiding Sensitive Association Rules with Limited Side Effects. *IEEE Transactions on Knowledge and Data Engineering, 19*(1). doi:10.1109/TKDE.2007.250583

Xie, M., & Chen, J. (2004). Studies on horizontal competition among homogenous retailers through agent-based simulation. *Journal of Systems Science and Systems Engineering, 13*(4), 490–505. doi:10.1007/s11518-006-0178-7

Xu, Z. (2008). *Factors which affect the dynamics of privately-owned Chinese firms: an interdisciplinary empirical evaluation*. Unpublished PhD thesis.

Xu, K., Dong, Y., & Evers, P. (2001). Towards better coordination of the supply chain. *Transportation Research Part E, Logistics and Transportation Review, 37*, 35–54. doi:10.1016/S1366-5545(00)00010-7

Yadav, M., & Varadarajan, R. R. (2005). Understanding product migration to the electronic marketplace: A conceptual framework. *Journal of Retailing, 81*(2), 125–140. doi:10.1016/j.jretai.2005.03.006

Yang, J., & Widom, J. (2003). Incremental Computation and Maintenance of Temporal Aggregates. *The VLDB Journal, 12*, 262–283. doi:10.1007/s00778-003-0107-z

Yao, A. C. (1986). How to generate and exchange secret. In *Proceedings of the 27th IEEE Symposium on Foundations of Computer Science* (pp. 162-167).

Yu, B., & Singh, M. P. (2001). Towards a Probabilistic Model of Distributed Reputation Management. In *Proceedings of the Fourth Workshop on Deception, Fraud and Trust in Agent Societies*, Montreal, Canada (pp. 125-137).

Yue, X., & Liu, J. (2006). Demand forecast sharing in a dual-channel supply chain. *European Journal of Operational Research, 174*, 646–667. doi:10.1016/j.ejor.2004.12.020

Yu, L., & Liu, H. (2004). Efficient feature selection via analysis of relevance and redundancy. *Journal of Machine Learning Research, 5*, 1205–1224.

Yu, T., Zhang, Y., & Lin, K.-J. (2007). Efficient algorithms for web services selection with end-to-end qos constraints. *ACM Trans. Web, 1*(1), 6. doi:10.1145/1232722.1232728

Zacharia, G. (1999). *Collaborative Reputation Mechanisms for Online Communities*. Unpublished master's thesis, Massachusetts Institute of Technology.

Zhang, H., & Huang, S.-Y. (2005). A parallel BDI agent architecture. In *Proceedings of the IEEE/WIC/ACM International Conference on Intelligent Agent Technology* (pp. 157-160).

Zhang, C., Tan, G.-W., Robb, D. J., & Zheng, X. (2006). Sharing shipment quantity information in the supply chain. *Omega, 34*, 427–438. doi:10.1016/j.omega.2004.12.005

Zhao, X., Wu, C., Zhang, R., Zhao, C., & Lin, Z. A. (2004). *Multi-Agent System for E-Business Processes Monitoring in a Web-Based Environment*. Beijing, China: TCL Group Corporation, Department of Information Science, Peking University.

Zhao, Y., Yao, Y., & Luo, F. (2007). Data analysis based on discernibility and indiscernibility. *Information Sciences, 177*(22), 4959–4976. doi:10.1016/j.ins.2007.06.031

Zheng, H., & Zhang, Y. (2008). Feature selection for high-dimensional data in astronomy. *Advances in Space Research, 41*(12), 1960–1964. doi:10.1016/j.asr.2007.08.033

Zheng, Y.-S., & Federgruen, A. (1991). Finding optimal (s, s) policies is about as simple as evaluating a single policy. *Operations Research*, *39*(4), 654–665. doi:10.1287/opre.39.4.654

Zhou, H., & Benton, W. C. Jr. (2007). Supply chain practice and information sharing. *Journal of Operations Management*, *25*(6), 1348–1365. doi:10.1016/j.jom.2007.01.009

Zhuge, Y., García-Molina, H., Hammer, J., & Widom, J. (1995, June). View Maintenance in a Warehousing Environment. In *Proceedings of the 1995 ACM SIGMOD International Conference on Management of Data (SIGMOD '95),* San Jose, CA.

Zhuge, Y., Wiener, J. L., & Garcia-Molina, H. (1997, April 7-11). Multiple View Consistency for Data Warehousing. In *Proceedings of the Thirteenth International Conference on Data Engineering,* Birmingham, UK.

Zhu, K. (2002). Information transparency in electronic marketplaces: Why data transparency may hinder the adoption of b2b exchanges. *Electronic Markets*, *12*(2), 92–99. doi:10.1080/10196780252844535

About the Contributors

Vijayan Sugumaran is Professor of Management Information Systems in the department of Decision and Information Sciences at Oakland University, Rochester, Michigan, USA. He is also WCU Professor of Service Systems Management and Engineering at Sogang University, Seoul, South Korea. He received his PhD in Information Technology from George Mason University, Fairfax, VA. His research interests are in the areas of service science, ontologies and Semantic Web, intelligent agent and multi-agent systems, component based software development, and knowledge-based systems. His most recent publications have appeared in *Information systems Research, ACM Transactions on Database Systems, IEEE Transactions on Education, IEEE Transactions on Engineering Management, Communications of the ACM, Healthcare Management Science,* and *Data and Knowledge Engineering.* He has published over 150 peer-reviewed articles in journals, conferences, and books. He has edited ten books and two journal special issues. He is the editor-in-chief of the *International Journal of Intelligent Information Technologies* and also serves on the editorial board of seven other journals. He was the program co-chair for the 13th International Conference on Applications of Natural Language to Information Systems (NLDB 2008). In addition, he has served as the chair of the Intelligent Agent and Multi-Agent Systems mini-track for Americas Conference on Information Systems (AMCIS 1999 - 2012) and Intelligent Information Systems track for the Information Resources Management Association International Conference (IRMA 2001, 2002, 2005 - 2007). He served as Chair of the E-Commerce track for Decision Science Institute's Annual Conference, 2004. He was the Information Technology Coordinator for the Decision Sciences Institute (2007-2009). He also regularly serves as a program committee member for numerous national and international conferences.

* * *

Arzu Baloglu completed her undergraduate from Technical University of Istanbul, her MBA in production management and her PhD in Information Technology from University of Istanbul. has experience of 15 years in production and technology management working for various manufacturing, service and consulting companies. Dr. Baloglu has also worked in SAP Business for a long time and managed various SAP/ERP projects in Turkey and other countries. She has given numerous presentations at conferences and company training sessions. Dr. Baloglu has more than 15 professional and academic papers, published in various technology magazines and books. She is currently working as an Associate Professor for Department of Business Administration Marmara University.

Ilaria Baffo, born in 1981, is graduated in Management Engineering from the University of Rome "Tor Vergata" in 2005 and she will receive the PhD in Production and Management Engineering from the above mentioned University in this Dicember. Since 2006 she is working with The Institute of Industrial Technologies and Automation (ITIA) of the Italian National Research Council. Her main area of interests are: supply chain and operation management, multi agent system, collaborative networks. She realized in these last years many papers published on international conference proceedings and actually she is working to her PhD Thesis.

Yılmaz Bahçetepe graduated from Marmara University from Computer Science Engineering department. He is currently involved in various software development and system development project. Hospital management system, banking application, call center application are some of his successful projects. Mr. Bachcetepe considers Software engineering in general as his main area of interest. In this context, he generally focuses on Java platform, web technologies, open source and database systems.

Siddhartha Bhattacharyya is an Associate Professor of Information and Decision Sciences in the College of Business, University of Illinois, Chicago. His research interests are in the areas of intelligent decision support, data mining, and computational modeling. His papers appear in journals like *Complex Systems, Decision Support Systems, European Journal of Operational Research, Evolutionary Computation, IEEE Transactions, Journal of Economic Dynamics and Control, Information Technology and Management, International Journal of Electronic Business*, and in various conferences.

C. R. Chatwin holds the Chair of Engineering, University of Sussex, UK; where, *inter alia*, he is Research Director of the "iims Research Centre." and the Laser and Photonics Systems Engineering Group. At Sussex he is a member of the University: Senate, Council and Court. He has published two research monographs: one on numerical methods, the other on hybrid optical/digital computing - and more than two hundred international papers. Professor Chatwin is on the editorial board of the *International Journal "Lasers in Engineering"*. He is also a member of: the Institution of Electrical and Electronic Engineers; the British Computer Society; the Association of Industrial Laser Users. He is a Chartered Engineer, Euro-Engineer, International Professional Engineer, Chartered Physicist, Chartered Scientist and a Fellow of: The Institution of Electrical Engineers, The Institution of Mechanical Engineers, The Institute of Physics and The Royal Society for Arts, Manufacture and Commerce.

Fei-Long Chen is Professor of Industrial Engineering and Engineering Management at National Tsing-Hua University (NTHU), Hsinchu, Taiwan. He received his B.S. degree in Industrial Engineering from National Tsing Hua University, Taiwan, in 1982, and his M.S. and Ph.D. degrees in Industrial Engineering from Auburn University, USA, in 1988 and 1991, respectively. He has been with the Department of Industrial Engineering, National Tsing Hua University since 1992. Dr. Chen currently serves as the Editor for Journal of the Chinese Institute of Industrial Engineers (JCIIE) and the International Journal of E-Business Management (IJEBM). His current research interests include enterprise integration, enterprise resource planning, global logistics management; computer integrated manufacturing, total quality management, and engineering data analysis.

Toly Chen: Dr. Chen received the B. S. degree, the M S. degree, and the Ph. D. degree in industrial engineering from National Tsin Hua University. He is now an Associate Professor in the Department of Industrial Engineering and Systems Management of Feng Chia University, an IEEE member, and an IIE senior member. Dr. Chen received IEA/AIE Best Paper Award from Internation Society of Applied Intelligence in 2009. He has publications in journals such as Computers and Industrial Engineering, Fuzzy Sets and Systems, International Journal of Advanced Manufacturing Technology, European Journal of Operational Research, Journal of Intelligent Manufacturing, Neurocomputing, Intelligent Data Analysis, International Journal of Innovative Computing, Information and Control, and Applied Soft Computing. He is also on the editorial boards of Open Operational Research Journal, Open Artificial Intelligence Journal, and Open Statistics and Probability Journal.

T. Chithralekha is a Reader in the Dept. of Banking Technology, Pondicherry University. She completed her PhD, MTech., and BTech in Computer Science and Engineering from Pondicherry University. Her research interests are in the areas of Agent Technology, Distributed Systems and Information Security. She has carried out many project works in Agent Technology research and also application of Software Agents and Multi-Agent Systems in the domains of Multilingual Computing, Context Aware Computing, Semantic Web Services and E-learning. She has fourteen years of teaching and research experience.

Hung W. Chu is an Assistant Professor of Management for the School of Business at Manhattan College. Dr. Chu holds a BE degree from Cooper Union, ME degree from City College of New York, MBA degree from Baruch College, and PhD degree from City University of New York. His teaching expertise are in the area of operation management as well as strategic management. His current research interests are in the areas of information resource management, information system implementation strategies, mergers and acquisitions integration, supply chain management, application of resource based theory, and behavior of Chinese enterprises. He had programming experience with government, not-for-profit, and for profit institutions.

Giuseppe Confessore, born in Rome-Italy in 1967, is graduated in Electronic Engineering from the University of Rome "La Sapienza" in 1992 and he has received the PhD in Production and Management Engineering from the University of Rome "Tor Vergata" in 1998. Since 1999 was researcher at Institute of Industrial Technologies and Automation (ITIA) of the Italian National Research Council, and since 2001 is senior researcher at the same Institute. Since 2002 is the coordinator of the Rome Division of the ITIA involved in research activities and research projects in production and logistics fields by using operations research and management science methodologies. Since 2002 he belongs to the Board of Experts of the Italian Educational, University and Research Ministry to evaluate industrial research projects financed by public funds. Author of over 20 papers published on international journals and international conference proceedings, his main research interests are in areas of resource management, transportations, discrete optimization.

Graziano Galiano, born in Salerno-Italy in 1976, is graduated in Computer Science from the University of Salerno in 2002 and he has received the PhD in Computer Science from the University of Salerno in 2008. Since 2003 he is a contract researcher at the Institute of Industrial Technologies and Automation (ITIA) - Italian Council of Research (CNR) and he carries out several activities as consultant for small and medium enterprices. During the last years he collects more than 10 papers published on international journals and international conference proceedings on supply chain management and optimization process. His research interests are in modeling of complex systems, development and implementation of optimization systems of technological platforms for business use in manufacturing and logistics, development of heuristics and meta-heuristics techniques applied to logistics and production process management and to process simulation systems.

Minh Q. Huynh is an Associate Professor of MIS at Southeastern Louisiana University. He received his PhD from State University of New York at Binghamton. His teaching expertise are in the areas of E-commerce, database management, decision support systems, and emerging technology. Research interests include IS outsourcing, IS integration, enterprise systems, open source software, IS in small-medium enterprises, and E-learning. His publications appear in such journals as the Communications of ACM, Journal of AIS, Communications of AIS, European Journal of IS, Journal of Electronic Commerce in Organizations, International Journal of E-Business Research. Prior to his academic career, he had worked in the areas related to computer programming, systems management, technical support, and network security.

S. Kuppuswami is currently the Principal of Kongu Engineering College, Perundurai, Tamilnadu, India. He has completed his B.E. and MSc Engg from the University of Madras and Dr. Ing. from the University of Rennes I, France. He has 32 years of academic èxperience. He has worked as faculty of Computer Science at Anna University and University of Rennes I, France. He has been the Professor and Head of the Department of Computer Science at Pondicherry Engineering College and Pondicherry University. He has served in different capacities in various administrative, academic, technical, bodies of the University, Central and State Governments and National Commissions. He has published more than 60 research papers. His research interests are in the areas of Parallel Processing Systems, Multilingual Computing, Software Engineering, Agent Technology and Genetic Algorithms.

Feng-Chia Li is a PhD student at the Department of Industrial Engineering, National Tsinghua University, Taiwan. He received his masters degree in Information Management in 1997 from the Da-Yeh University, Taiwan. Mr. Li currently serves as the chairman of Information department, Jente Junior College, Taiwan. His research interests are Data Mining and application of Data Mining to business. Mr. Li has been actively involved in several cross-discipline research projects in the domains of data mining, intelligent technologies, and E-business in which he applies his expertise in solving classification problems with domain experts. His most recent work has been submitted to Journal of Industry Engineering, Journal of the Chinese Institute of Industrial Engineers and accepted in Journal of Expert System with Application.

E.R.M. Madeira is an Associate Professor at the Institute of Computing of University of Campinas – UNICAMP, Brazil. He received his PhD in Electrical Engineering from UNICAMP in 1991. He has published over 120 papers in national and international conferences and journals. He has also supervised more than 40 Master and PhD students. His research interests include grid computing, middleware design and development, and network and service management.

Bireshwar Dass Mazumdar obtained MCA degree from UP Technical University, Lucknow, India in the year of 2005.He has 2 years experience of teaching in the field of computer science and engineering. Presently he is a fulltime research scholar in Department of Computer Engineering, Institute of Technology, B.H.U; Varanasi India. His research interest is Multiagent system and its application in e-commerce, e-governance, and biomedical.

Sam Kin Meng got his PhD degree at the University of Sussex in 2008 and is now an assistant professor at the Department of Accounting and Information Management at the University of Macau. He has published a few conference and journal papers regarding to Internet consumers' decision-making styles, e-marketing mix and ontology. He is now a member inside the Graduate Studies Committee and Academic Council Committee in the University of Macau.

Kiran Mishra is full time research scholar in department of computer engineering, Institute of Technology, Banaras Hindu University, Varanasi, India. She got B.E. in 2002 from Choudhary Charan Singh university, Meerut. She has 4½ years experience of teaching in the field of computer science at B.Tech. and MCA level. Her main research fields include Artificial Intelligence and Intelligent Tutoring System.

R.B. Mishra (BSc. Engg. M.Tech. PhD) is a professor with department of computer engineering, Institute of Technology, Banaras Hindu University, Varanasi, India. He has 30 years of teaching experience. He has published over 100 research papers in journals and conferences. He has visited West Virginia University USA (Oct-Dec 1990) and University of Bath, UK (April-June 1997). He has supervised 23 M.Tech. dissertations and five PhD theses. His research areas are: Artificial Intelligence and Multiagent system and their applications in medical computing, Semantic Web and Intelligent Tutoring System.

Sabine Moisan has been a Research Scientist at INRIA Sophia Antipolis since 1983. She graduated as a Computer Science Engineer from ENSEEIHT (Toulouse, France). She received her PhD in Computer Science from the University of Toulouse and her HDR (*Habilitation à diriger les recherches*) from the University of Nice-Sophia Antipolis. Her research interests cover Artificial Intelligence and Software Engineering, more specifically knowledge-based system design through software techniques such as reusable components and modeling. She has been involved in the development of a commercialized knowledge-based system generator, SMECI, dedicated to design in engineering. She is currently interested in model-driven engineering applied to video-surveillance systems. She has published more than 50 papers in journals and international conferences and she was part of several conferences organizing committee, including ECOOP 2000 in Cannes. She has also been teaching UML modeling and meta-programming for about 10 years.

S. Pratheeba, received her B.E (CSE) degree from Government College of Technology, Coimbatore. Currently she is pursuing her M.S degree at Indian Institute of Science, Bangalore. Her areas of interest include Data mining, Soft computing and Database Management Systems.

T. Purusothaman, received his BE degree in 1988 from Madras University and completed his ME (CSE) degree at Government College of Technology, Coimbatore in 2002. He received his Ph.D. from Anna University in 2006. He has 21 years of teaching experience. He is currently working as Assistant

Professor in the Department of Computer science and Engineering at Government College of Technology, Coimbatore. His research areas include Network Security and cryptography, Distributed operating systems, Mobile computing, Advanced Genetic Algorithm and Grid Computing. He has published ten Research articles in reputed Indian and International Journals and fifty Research articles in national and international conferences. He is currently supervising 20 Ph.D., Research Scholars. He is a life member of ISTE. He served as member of Inspection committee representing DOTE, Tamil Nadu for inspecting Polytechnic colleges. He also served as a member of Academic council of various Universities. He has guided many B.E., M.E. and M.C.A Projects. He is the co-investigator of the project titled "Optimization of search time for evaluation of ciphers using Genetic Algorithm based cryptanalysis" sponsored by Ministry of Communications & Information Technology, New Delhi. He has presented a paper in an international conference and attended a Faculty Development Program at Canada.

Nayem Rahman is a Senior Application Developer in Enterprise Data Warehouse Engineering (EDWE) - ETL, Intel Corp. He has implemented several large projects using data warehousing technology for Intel's Mission critical Enterprise DSS platforms and solutions. He holds an MBA degree in Management Information Systems (MIS), Project Management, and Marketing from Wright State University, Ohio, USA. He is a Teradata Certified Master. He is also an Oracle Certified Developer and DBA. His most recent publications on Data Warehousing appeared in proceedings of the 14th Americas Conference on Information Systems (AMCIS 2008) and the Journal of Computer Information Systems. His principal research areas are Active Data Warehousing, Changed Data Capture and Management in Temporal Data Warehouses, Change Management and Process Improvement for Data Warehousing projects, Decision Support System, Data Mining for Business Analysts, and Sustainability of Information Technology.

M. Rajalakshmi, received her B.E (CSE) degree from Bharathiar University and M.E (CSE) degree from PSG college of Technology, Coimbatore affiliated to Anna university. Currently she is pursuing Ph.D. at Anna University. She is working as a Senior grade Lecturer in the Department of Computer Science and Engineering & Information Technology at Coimbatore Institute of Technology, Coimbatore. She has 16 years of teaching experience. Her areas of interest include Data mining, Distributed Computing, Data structures and Algorithms and Database Management Systems. She is a life member of ISTE. She has guided many B.E and M.E projects.

Vladimir Rybakov is professor of logic in the Department of Computing and Mathematics at Manchester Metropolitan University, Manchester, UK. His research interests are in the areas of Non-Classical Mathematical Logic (Modal, Temporal, Intuitionistic logics, Hybrid Logics, Multi-Agent Logics) and its applications to AI, Knowledge Representation, Data Analysis. He has published over 120 peer-reviewed articles in Journals, Conferences, and Books. He has edited several books, conference proceedings, and served on the Editorial Boards of international journals. His most recent publications have appeared in Journal of Logic and Computation (Oxford Press), Annals of Pure and Applied Logic, Theoretical Computer Systems, Fudamenta Informatica, and Journal of Symbolic Logic.

Ivo J. G. dos Santos is a Researcher and Software Design Engineer at the European Microsoft Innovation Center in Aachen, Germany. He received his PhD in Computer Science from the University of Campinas (Brazil) in 2008, has worked as a guest researcher at the Fraunhofer-FOKUS institute

(Germany) and at Microsoft Research (USA). He is an expert in distributed information systems, service oriented architectures, semantic computing, complex event processing and e-applications. His current research focuses on middleware and tools for distributed information systems.

Mudasser F. Wyne is currently serving as a Professor of Computer Science at, School of Engineering and Technology, Technology and Health Sciences Center of National University, USA. He is Co-Lead for MSc in Computer Science programs. Dr. Wyne has a Ph.D. in Computer Science, M.Sc. in Engineering and B.Sc., in Electrical Engineering. He has been in academics for 20+ years and with the Accreditation Board of Engineering and Technology (ABET), USA for more than 8 years. He is serving as a commissioner with Computing Accreditation Commission (CAC) of ABET. In addition, he is a guest editor and associate editor for a journal, and serving on editorial boards for four international journals. He has also served as Chair and Co-Chair of numerous conferences, workshops, tracks and panels, in addition to serving on the program committee for numerous international conferences. Dr. Wyne has published number of articles in peer reviewed international journals and peer reviewed international conferences.

Yifeng Zhang is an assistant professor at University of Illinois at Springfield. He received his PhD degree in Management Information Systems from University of Illinois at Chicago. His research interests include agent-based modeling, business-to-business e-commerce, supply chain management, and data mining. Using agent-based modeling, Dr. Zhang has studied various supply network and B2B e-commerce issues, such as e-marketplace and inventory management, and vendor selection strategy on e-marketplaces. He also studied effectiveness of machine learning techniques for calibrating agent-based models. Dr. Zhang's latest research interests include business implications of online social networking. Dr. Zhang's research works have been published in various journals, such as *Information Sciences* and *Information Systems* and *E-Business Management*.

Index